The JavaScript Sourcebook Web site provides up-to-date information on JavaScript, plus scores of free examples and other goodies. You'll also find additions and corrections for this book, to ensure that it is the most up-to-date source on JavaScript available. Visit us at:

    http://gmccomb.com/sourcebook/

About This Book

This book is about JavaScript, the built-in HTML scripting language supported by Netscape 2.0 and 3.0, Microsoft Internet Explorer 3.0, and other Internet products. This book is designed for all levels of programming experience, from the "newbie" to the seasoned pro. In it you'll find full details about JavaScript and how to use its many features.

Chapters lead you from the basics though a reference of JavaScript commands, then on to real-world use of JavaScript. And, for the adventurous, this book provides plenty of hard-core, roll-up-your-shirtsleeves advanced material that you can use to make your Web pages come alive. And of course, you'll find lots of tips, tricks, and great ideas that will help you become a JavaScript expert.

Reminder! This book is not about Java, an object-oriented Internet programming language. See Chapter 1 if you're unsure of the difference between JavaScript and Java.

Who Should Read This Book

This book is for you if:

- You are intrigued by the notion of "programming for the Web," but don't have the skills to write "applets" and "plug-ins" using esoteric languages such as Java or C++.

- You want to improve the appearance of your Web pages and make them more "user friendly."

- You've read Netscape's documentation for JavaScript, and you want to learn more.

- You'd like to add nifty stuff like forms, hit counters, clocks, sound, animation, and other exciting media to your Web pages.
- You want to make your pages dynamic—changing day-to-day or even hour-to-hour!—all on their own.

Where Do I Start?

This book is designed with a "tiered" approach so that anyone, regardless of programming and JavaScript experience, can benefit from it. Feel free to read it cover-to-cover, or begin at the chapter that's best for your knowledge level.

I am...	Begin here
New to JavaScript, new to programming	Chapter 1
New to JavaScript, some programming experience	Chapter 3
Somewhat familiar with JavaScript, some programming experience	Chapter 4
Very familiar with JavaScript, any programming experience	Chapter 11
Familiar with JavaScript/programming; interested in new ideas	Chapter 12
Brand new to the Internet	Internet basics book
Familiar with the Internet, brand new to HTML	HTML authoring book

JavaScript™ Sourcebook

Create Interactive JavaScript Programs for the World Wide Web

Gordon McComb

WILEY COMPUTER PUBLISHING

John Wiley & Sons, Inc.

New York • Chichester • Brisbane • Toronto • Singapore

To Mercedes Noell and Marshall Lee (Max) McComb.

Publisher: Katherine Schowalter
Editor: Philip Sutherland
Assistant Editor: Kathryn A. Malm
Managing Editor: Sue Curtin
Text Design & Composition: Benchmark Productions, Inc.

Designations used by companies to distinguish their products are often claimed as trademarks. In all instances where John Wiley & Sons, Inc., is aware of a claim, the product names appear in initial capital or ALL CAPITAL LETTERS. Readers, however, should contact the appropriate companies for more complete information regarding trademarks and registration.

This text is printed on acid-free paper.

This publication is designed to provide accurate and authoritative information in regard to the subject matter covered. It is sold with the understanding that the publisher is not engaged in rendering legal, accounting, or other professional service. If legal advice or other expert assistance is required, the services of a competent professional person should be sought.

Library of Congress Cataloging-in-Publication Data:

McComb, Gordon.
    JavaScript sourcebook : create interactive JavaScript programs for the World Wide Web / Gordon McComb.
        p.   cm.
    Includes index.
    ISBN 0-471-16185-3 (pbk : alk. paper)
    1. JavaScript (Computer program language) 2. World Wide Web (Information retrieval system) I. Title.
QA76.73.J38M353   1996
005.2--dc20   96-2977
                                                            CIP

Printed in the United States of America
10 9 8 7 6 5 4 3 2 1

CONTENTS

v

Table of JavaScript Commands

Function List

INTRODUCTION

In the 1970s, the acceptance of the personal computer came slowly. Most people of the era never heard of the concept of a "personal computer," preferring instead to imagine all computers the size of a Buick, and about as smart.

More than a decade passed with little significant change in the personal computer. Oh, since the late 1970s there have been several shifts in the operating system used to power a PC. And computers have been endowed with greater thinking power over time. But all in all, the general notion of the personal computer—and how it's used—hasn't changed much in all these years.

Until now.

Since you're reading the introduction to this book, you surely know the cause of this massive change: the Internet. What started as a rather simplistic electronic mail system has become a sophisticated global interconnection of tens of millions of users.

An integral part of this ongoing change in computing is Netscape Navigator, now used by more than 70 percent of all those who surf the Internet's World Wide Web. The newest release of Netscape—now up to version 3.0—offers a unique blend of features that make it almost infinitely extensible. These features include plug-ins, Java applets, and JavaScript programs. These features turn Netscape or any JavaScript-compatible browser into just about anything a programmer can imagine.

JavaScript: The Great Liberator

It is the last feature in the previous list, JavaScript, that is of interest to us and that is the subject of this book. Why is JavaScript so important?

- JavaScript is an authoring language for the typical Web page designer—perhaps someone like you—who is more interested in designing great Web documents, not thinking up a new computer algorithm for an opening chess gambit.

- Unlike plug-ins and Java, which require you to have extensive programming experience to use, JavaScript is a means for most anyone to extend the features of Netscape.

- JavaScript is fast becoming an industry standard, with a number of companies supporting it, including Microsoft.

- With JavaScript, you can forget having to learn about objected-oriented programming design, object classes, inheritance, constructors, destructors, C syntax, and other esoterica that can consume six months or more of your life, because the language is based on a far simpler structure.

- With JavaScript, you can forget having to buy or download "software developer's kits" in order to write just one line of a program because everything you need to make and enjoy JavaScript programs is already in the Netscape browser. You merely add the JavaScript program to your HTML document, and then load the document into the browser.

What's Inside
JavaScript Sourcebook

JavaScript is a language designed for Web page authors using the HTML markup language. JavaScript is simple enough that you need not be a confirmed programming geek to use it. This doesn't mean JavaScript is for amateurs and hacks. On the contrary, to do anything extraordinary with JavaScript, you have to be *very good* at it. That's the key focus of this book. In it, you'll find everything you need for becoming a JavaScript expert, including:

- Basic stuff, like what JavaScript is and how it's used
- Reference material on all of JavaScript's "commands" (more properly referred to as statements, expressions, objects, and properties, but we'll get to that)
- Lots and lots and lots of examples that help you learn by doing
- Nitty-gritty information, such as how to use JavaScript to improve HTML forms, and how to get JavaScript to work with CGI
- Great ideas, like integrating sound and animation using JavaScript
- Neat tips, tricks, and secrets that can jazz up your Web pages

"Plug-and-play" routines that you can add to your own JavaScript programs, saving your hours—maybe days—in writing these functions yourself. Just copy and paste and you're done!

Here's a broad overview of what you'll find in this book:

Part 1—Introducing JavaScript

This part tells you what JavaScript is, and what it's good for. It also provides a handy introduction to programming concepts, all of which are used in later chapters, so be sure to read this part if you're relatively new to the programming game.

Part 2—Core JavaScript

Read these chapters to learn all about what makes up JavaScript: its objects, properties, methods, functions, and events. Also read here for the lowdown on how to construct expressions and variables for use with JavaScript.

Part 3—JavaScript in the Real World

Parts 1 and 2 are "JavaScript in the Lab." The title of this part says it all. Here you'll find all sorts of interesting examples of using JavaScript, including many complete and working JavaScript applications. Be sure to read Chapter 12, "How Do I?," for dozens of commonly asked questions about implementing JavaScript.

Part 4—Extending JavaScript

Want to do something special with JavaScript, like GIF animation, counters, and CGI? This part addresses these and other advanced JavaScript and HTML topics. You'll also find useful background chapters here on the HTML markup language, and additional sources on the Web for JavaScripting.

Is This Book for Me?

JavaScript Sourcebook is written for the person already somewhat familiar with the Internet, as well as with the general process of electronic publishing of HTML documents on the World Wide Web. But no other special skill or knowledge is assumed. This book can be used by those with little or no programming experience. Of course, the more programming experience you have, the faster you'll be able to learn and use JavaScript.

Here are some specifics:

- I don't assume you already know about programming topics such as arrays, so I explain these concepts when they are first introduced. Skip these pages if you know this stuff already.

- The chapters of this book are organized so that if you already know programming fundamentals, you can go straight to learning about JavaScript.

- This book is not for the Internet newbie. If you don't know what the Web is, and if you've never seen a document in HTML format, let alone created one, this book isn't for you. Pick up some good introductory books on the Internet and the Web. Then come back to this one.

You Mean This Book *Isn't* about Java?

Java and JavaScript are not the same, although they have similar names.

Java is a full-featured programming language designed to add greater flexibility and functionality to pages on the World Wide Web. Java is a complex language, requiring knowledge of C++ programming, classes, and other aspects of object-oriented software design. It also requires a software development kit and special compiler.

This book concentrates on JavaScript, a lower-level *scripting* language in which the "program" is included as part of the HTML document retrieved by the browser. JavaScript programs don't need to be developed using a software development kit, and there's no need to compile JavaScript code before you can use it in a browser. JavaScript language was intentionally kept simple so that Web authors with limited programming experience can adequately harness its power.

If you're looking for a book on Java, put this one down, and keep scanning the shelves. The publisher would like to recommend the following:

- *The Java Sourcebook*, by Ed Anuff
- *Java for C/C++ Programmers*, by Mike Daconta

These books are published by Wiley Computer Books, and are probably just a foot or two away from where you found this one.

Copyright Information

By its nature, the Internet is a sharing medium. It's always been that way, and likely will remain so. This book continues in that spirit. You are welcome to incorporate all or parts of JavaScript code you find in this book in your Web pages, for whatever purpose—private or commercial—under the following conditions:

- If you use a JavaScript program from this book in its entirety, please include the following copyright notice within JavaScript code (this helps to prevent my work from falling into the public domain):

```
// (c) Copyright 1996, by Gordon McComb. All Rights Reserved.
// From "JavaScript Sourcebook," published by Wiley Computer Books.
```

- You may use portions of JavaScript programs, and make revisions to the code in any way you wish, without including the above copyright notice. However, a notation of where the portions came from would be appreciated. Word of mouth is important in this business.

- Redistribution of the original JavaScript programs in this book is prohibited unless you first get written permission from the publisher and author. So, don't post projects from this book on your Web or FTP site, include them in your book, or stuff them away on your BBS unless you check with us first.

Links Gratefully Accepted

Though certainly not a requirement for using the examples in this book, feel free to provide a link on your page to my Web page at *http://gmccomb.com/sourcebook/*.

Included at my site is a submission form for "JavaScript Site of the Week." Let me know what JavaScript magic you've done, and how you've used this wonderful new language! I'll showcase the most interesting and innovative JavaScript applications.

Stuff You Can Probably Skip

Book introductions are notorious for overstating the obvious, and I've probably done that enough already. But it's a good place to put all the "housekeeping chores" necessary when presenting a book. If you're itching to start learning JavaScript, then by all means stop reading now, and proceed directly to Chapter 1. Otherwise, for the interminably curious, here's some semi-useful information you may want to know about.

Conventions Used in This Book

JavaScript example code is displayed in a special type style, like this:

```
var CurrentRoom = 0;
var TextFrame = parent.frames["text"];
var ResultFrame = parent.frames["result"];
var CtrlFrame=parent.frames["ctrl"];
var Doc = ResultFrame.document;
```

```
var RoomVisited = new Array(5);
```

CD-ROM

fakename.html

Most code examples are short, and you can readily type them yourself if you want to test them. Longer JavaScript programs are included on the CD-ROM; references to these program files are shown with a CD-ROM icon, like that shown in the margin. The name of the file is provided for you. Refer to the master *filelog.txt* file in the root directory of the CD-ROM to locate the file in the disc's directory structure.

Text of a special nature—like a note, tip, or caution—is set off in special shaded boxes. The first three chapters provide a special "FAQ section"—FAQ stands for *frequently asked questions*. The FAQ sections are primarily used for beginner-oriented questions and answers.

A Note about the CD-ROM

This book comes with a CD-ROM. It contains all the sample JavaScript files and applications detailed in *JavaScript Sourcebook*, as well as a number of useful Internet tools and utilities, many of them exclusive to this book. See Appendix A for full details on using the CD-ROM.

Software Compatibility

This book was written for all platforms of Netscape Navigator 2.0 and later. JavaScript is not supported on earlier versions of Netscape Navigator, such as 1.0 or 1.22.

JavaScript is an evolving language, and its implementation is still somewhat incomplete. Therefore, there may be some changes in behavior of JavaScript if you're using a later version of Netscape Navigator, or are using a different browser than Netscape. What I describe in this book is up-to-date for Netscape 2.0 and beta [tk] of version 3.0, as well as beta versions of Microsoft Internet Explorer 3.0, but all bets are off for other versions.

JavaScript behaves somewhat differently between the four platforms supported by Netscape: Windows 3.1, Windows 95/NT, Macintosh, and X-Windows. This means that a JavaScript program that works fine on one platform may not operate properly on another platform.

I've tried to take these quirks and differences into account as much as possible, but there's no guarantee that every script and example will work with every combination of Netscape 2.0 or 3.0. When possible, I try to warn you if there are any known cross-platform problems.

And Now a Word about JavaScript Bugs

While Netscape is a good, solid product, there are many JavaScript-related bugs that you'll have to contend with as you learn and use the language. Some are minor and relatively innocuous. But others are downright menacing, with a potential of completely crashing Netscape. Here's one killer you'll find in version 2.0:

```
<HTML>
<HEAD>
<SCRIPT = "JavaScript">
        document.write ("this is a test");
        document.close();
</SCRIPT>
</HEAD>
<BODY>
Hello, there!
</BODY>
</HEAD>
```

Later in the book, you'll find out why this causes a crash; but for now, just know that improperly-constructed JavaScript can cause the Netscape browser to fail. So program with caution, and test, test, test!

Netscape is known for making free updates of its products, and the most damaging of bugs are regularly fixed in these updates. For this reason, always use the latest version you can.

Finally, I'd like to thank you for buying my book—or at least thumbing though it at the bookstore. An unread book is a sad thing indeed.

May, 1996

San Diego, California

ACKNOWLEDGMENTS

How time flies when you're working fourteen hours a day!

I'm sure this book would have taken much longer had it not been for the following generous souls who helped me along the way. I'm especially indebted to Brendan Eich of Netscape Communications; Brendan was the lead developer in charge of JavaScript. Not only did he do a bang-up job with the language, but he still managed to be available for lots of questions. Kudos also go to Netscapians Frank Hecker, Gregor Fisher, Richard Yaker, and Rand McKinney, who fielded tons of questions.

A number of people active on the Netscape developer's newsgroups, as well as other newsgroups and Internet mailing lists, helped tremendously with the "information base" that I was able to draw from during the preparation of this book. At the top of the list are Bill Dorch of hIdaho Design, and Achille Hui, a graduate student at Stanford University. Many thanks also go to Andrew Augustine, Stephen Raab, Stephan Koch, David N. Smith, Olaf Walkowiak, John Ray, Brian Stoler. and the rest of the gang.

JavaScript community is by-in-large a giving one. Other authors of JavaScript books banded together whenever possible to help each other out. My thanks and good wishes to my old friend Danny Goodman, as well as to newfound JavaScript friends and fellow authors Wes Tatters and Andrew Woolridge. May all of our books sell a million copies!

A tip of JavaScripter's hat to Rush Walsh for letting me borrow his most-excellent bitmap images for inclusion in this book, and to the many other folks who gave me permission to include their efforts on the CD-ROM.

On the business side, an avalanche of huzzahs for my agent Matt Wagner, for going out of his way to get the best deal possible, and for Phil Sutherland and Katherine Schowalter, of Wiley Computer Books, for being so enthusiastic and supportive of this project.

Finally, had my family—wife Jennifer and children Mercie and Max—not been so understanding, there is no way I could work 'till two A.M., then sleep until seven! I love you all!

INTRODUCING

JAVASCRIPT

WHAT JAVASCRIPT

IS ALL ABOUT

The HTML language used to create pages for the World Wide Web was originally
designed to produce plain and static documents, stuff like engineering notes and
long-winded arguments by scientist types. When the Web first started, the only brows-
ing software available for it was text-based, so "plain and static" was acceptable.

The Web took a major step with the release of Mosaic, the first graphical Web
browser. Suddenly, it was obvious that "plain and static" wasn't enough. Users
cried out for more creative control over the pages they published on the Web, and
they were rewarded with features such as in-line images, tables, and frames.

JavaScript continues the tradition of enhancing the Web by making HTML "come
alive." JavaScript is a scripting language for HTML and the Netscape Navigator
browser, version 2.0 and later. JavaScript "scripts" are small programs that interact with Netscape and the HTML content of a page. You can create a JavaScript
program to add sound or simple animation, pre-validate a form before the user's
response is sent to your company's server, search through a small database, set
options based on user preferences, and much more.

JavaScript performs the same function as a *macro* in a word processor or electronic spreadsheet program. A macro is small program designed solely to run inside a program, automating some task or enhancing a feature of the program. The difference here is that instead of a word processor or electronic spreadsheet application, JavaScript is designed for use with Netscape and surfing on the World Wide Web.

The Birth of JavaScript

JavaScript started life as "LiveScript." The concept of LiveScript began at Netscape, as the company planned the features of the Netscape Navigator 2.0 product, released in January 1996. LiveScript was designed from the start to augment HTML pages, and Netscape planners saw it as a tool for the average Web page designer.

At first, interest in LiveScript was mild, due mostly to the frenzy surrounding a more robust Internet programming language, named Java. Java was developed over a three-year period at Sun Microsystems, a company long entrenched in the Internet. Programmers flocked to Java because of its potential, at first leaving LiveScript in the cold.

When Netscape announced its intention to support Java in the Netscape 2.0 product, it also announced a collaboration with Sun to re-engineer LiveScript, now named JavaScript. Suddenly, interest in the "little scripting language that could" blossomed. Whereas Java requires in-depth programming knowledge and a software development kit, JavaScript programs can be written by most HTML page designers. No software development kit is needed.

As of this writing, JavaScript is used in Netscape 2.0 and later versions, as well as in Microsoft Internet Explorer 3.0 and later versions. As the co-developers of JavaScript, Netscape has wanted to make JavaScript an "open standard," meaning that other companies can use and implement JavaScript in their own Internet products. When JavaScript was first announced in December of 1995, over two dozen companies jumped on the bandwagon, promising to support it in future products. Those products–from companies such as Microsoft, America Online, Borland, IBM, Symantec, and many others–are just now coming out, or will be released shortly.

Why JavaScript Is So Important (and Why Should I Care?)

JavaScript is poised to do for Web publishing what Visual Basic did for Windows programming.

- JavaScript offers a scripting language accessible to "mere mortals," allowing almost anyone to use it in their Web pages. JavaScript closely follows the Web principle of bringing electronic publishing to the general public. You don't need lots of money or technology to publish on the Web; likewise with JavaScript, you don't need a programming degree to take advantage of the language.

- Both Java and JavaScript are already becoming de facto standards for Web page programming. As a developer, this means you can assume that the technology you invest in today will not disappear tomorrow. Already there are thousands of Web sites that use JavaScript to some degree. Because Netscape has captured a healthy percentage of the browser market, potential users of your site are in the millions.

- All major on-line services, including CompuServe and America Online, are now offering Web document space to their customers. This means a lot of people are just now getting the taste of Web publishing, and are looking for ways to improve their work. Many are turning to JavaScript to add value and spice.

Uses for JavaScript

If you've spent much time on the Web, you've probably encountered a few JavaScript examples. Probably the most popular use of JavaScript is as a calculator, you know, the kind you can buy at Wal-Mart for $3.97. This application by no means indicates the full breadth and scope of JavaScript! Rather, JavaScript calculators spread because they are relatively easy to write. And Netscape's first JavaScript examples were calculators, so this is what pioneer JavaScripters emulated.

Feel free to write as many JavaScript calculators as you like, but don't limit JavaScript to just this application. As with many new things, it can be hard to imagine practical uses for JavaScript. Here are some ideas that can get you started in thinking about what JavaScript can do for you.

Tailor Pages for the User

Imagine a Web page with JavaScript that responds to the user's choice of preferences, such as asking if the reader wants to view simple low-resolution thumbnail images for an entire page, or wait a little while longer for larger, high-resolution images. Offering these and other custom interface choices helps you tailor your pages to a user's needs and preferences. All readers no longer view the same page.

Make Interactive Pages

You can use JavaScript's built-in commands to add interactively to your Web pages. For instance, a JavaScript page can determine what time it is on the user's computer, and display the current time on the screen (see Figure 1.1). It can even select one of several images to display an appropriate graphic or background for the time of day—a sunrise for morning, full sun for the day, a sunset for late afternoon, and the moon for evening.

Another great use of JavaScript for interactivity is conditionally displaying text and hypertext links, depending on the user's response to a query. Suppose, for example,

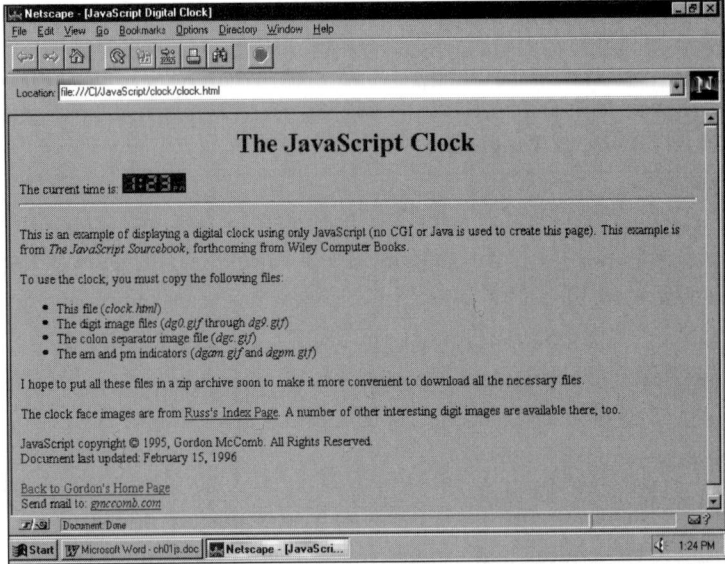

■■■■■■■ **Figure 1.1** Interactivity is easy to do using JavaScript. A few simple lines of code can "personalize" your pages for users.

your page contains descriptions of products for your company. Your company makes lots of diverse products in various product lines. Rather than display text and hyper-text links for products the user may not want—and run the risk of confusing or bor-ing the reader–you can use JavaScript to display only text and links that relate to the user's field of interest. This streamlines the content of Web pages.

Provide Computer–Aided Instruction

You can easily use JavaScript for computer–aided instruction. A JavaScript page can be "smart"—it can determine if the reader provides proper answers to questions, and can tally up the score. It can even keep track of how long it takes for a reader to answer questions. If your test has a time-limit, you can use JavaScript to automatically end the test when the limit is up.

Process Forms

JavaScript is also ideal for use with form-processing programs located on an Internet server. (For the uninitiated, a form is a collection of text boxes and buttons that pro-vide for user feedback, much like a Windows or Macintosh dialog box provides for user feedback.) The traditional way to use forms on a Web page is to send all the user's entries to a "script" or program running on the computer, typically using a technique called common gateway interface, or CGI. The primary task of most CGI programs is to verify that the user entered valid data. Entry validation, such as that shown in Figure 1.2, is something JavaScript can do, and it can do it very easily, thus making CGI programs much easier to write and implement.

Oh, Yes—And Special Effects, Too!

An oft-cited use of JavaScript is for special effects. With JavaScript, you can easily add sound—even background or repeating sound—to your page. Click a button, and a voice might ring out. In addition, you can do a great deal with animation and color effects, even "fading" a page slowly from black to white, as in a movie.

JavaScript gives you greater control over the graphical elements of your page. For instance, you can use JavaScript to intelligently resize an image. This is useful if you have a solid-color GIF. You can use JavaScript to expand or contract the size of the

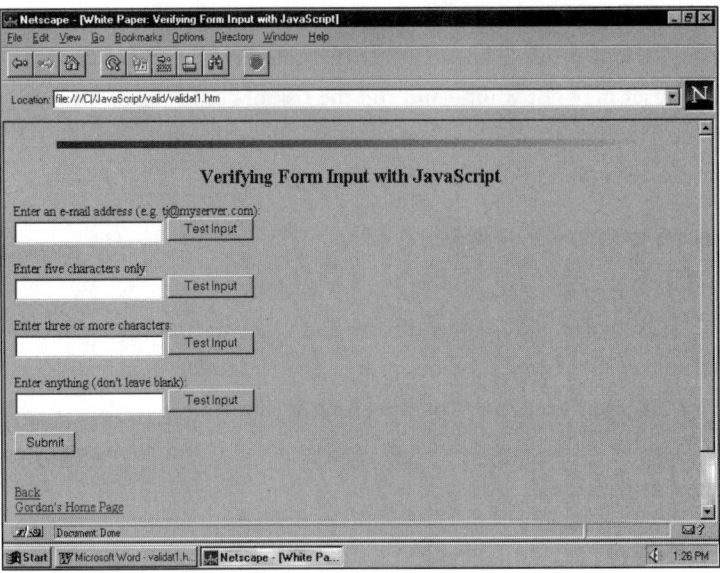

■■■■■■■■ **Figure 1.2** Form validation is a favorite application for JavaScript. The form can be pre-validating, before it is sent to a server for processing.

GIF, as it appears in Netscape. Possible uses include bar charts, colored divider lines (no more plain <HR> horizontal rules!), and more.

Using JavaScript in an HTML Document

A JavaScript program consists of one or more *instructions* (also referred to as *code* or *commands*) included with the *HTML markup tags* that form your Web documents. When Netscape encounters a JavaScript instruction, it stops to process it. For example, the instruction might tell Netscape to format and display text and graphics on the page. Unlike a program written in Java, JavaScript programs are not in separate files (though this is an option using Netscape 3.0 and later). Instead, the JavaScript instructions are mixed together with familiar HTML markup tags such as <H1>, <P>, and <IMG>.

Consider the very basic HTML document shown here. It renders a heading and some text on the page. Figure 1.3 shows how the page looks when viewed in Netscape.

```
<HTML>
```

```
<HEAD>
<TITLE>This Is a Basic Document</TITLE>
</HEAD>
<BODY>
<H1>This Is a Basic Document</H1>
<P>This is a pretty basic document.  It doesn't have much of anything in it.
Just a heading, and this text.</P>
</BODY>
</HTML>
```

Though there is no rational reason for doing so, you can use JavaScript to insert the text you see above. Here's how to use JavaScript to insert the heading.

```
<HTML>
<HEAD>
<TITLE>This Is a Basic Document</TITLE>
</HEAD>
<BODY>
<SCRIPT>
```

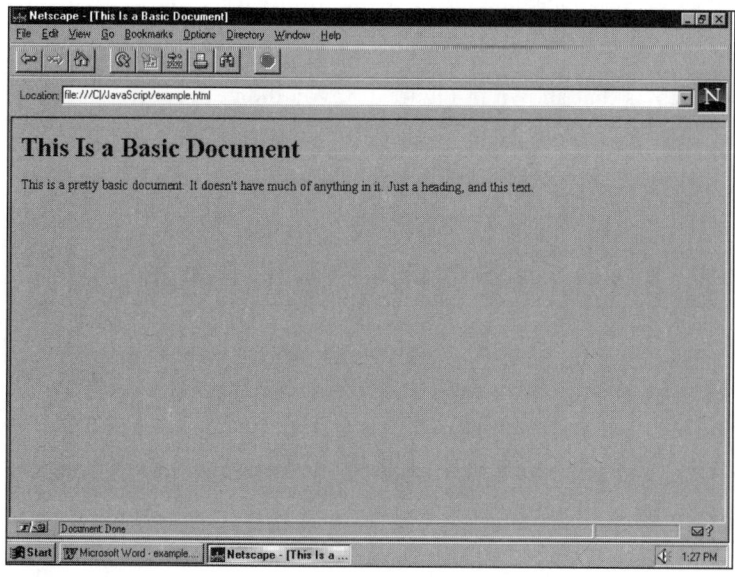

Figure 1.3 A basic HTML document, as rendered in Netscape.

```
document.write ("<H1>This Is a Basic Document</H1>");
</SCRIPT>
<P>This is a pretty basic document.  It doesn't have much of anything in it.
Just a heading, this text, and a graphic of some line.</P>
</BODY>
</HTML>
```

Trying the Script Yourself

Because JavaScript is embedded in HTML documents, you can use any text editor or Web page editor to write your JavaScript programs. The only requirement is that the editor must allow direct input. Web page programs that only let you insert a given set of HTML markup tags cannot be used because they don't allow you to insert the JavaScript code.

You can try the example from the previous section to see how JavaScript works. Retype the example exactly as you see it. When done, save the document as *samáple.htm*. Close the file (if necessary), and start Netscape. Choose File, Open, locate the file, and choose Open. The file should look at least something like that shown in Figure 1.4. Review your version if the document appears very different.

If you see an error box such as that shown in Figure 1.5, you didn't properly type the text between the <SCRIPT> and </SCRIPT> tags. Carefully review your work and try again.

The Role of the <SCRIPT> Tag

Netscape needs to be told that you're giving it JavaScript instructions, and these instructions are enclosed between <SCRIPT> tags. Within the script tag you can have only valid JavaScript instructions. You can't put HTML tags for Netscape to render inside the <SCRIPT> tags, and you can't put JavaScript instructions outside the <SCRIPT> tags. The following is allowed:

```
<HTML>
<BODY>
```

```
<SCRIPT>

<H1>Here's JavaScript-generated text!</H1>

document.write ("Hello there!");

</SCRIPT>

</BODY>

</HTML>
```

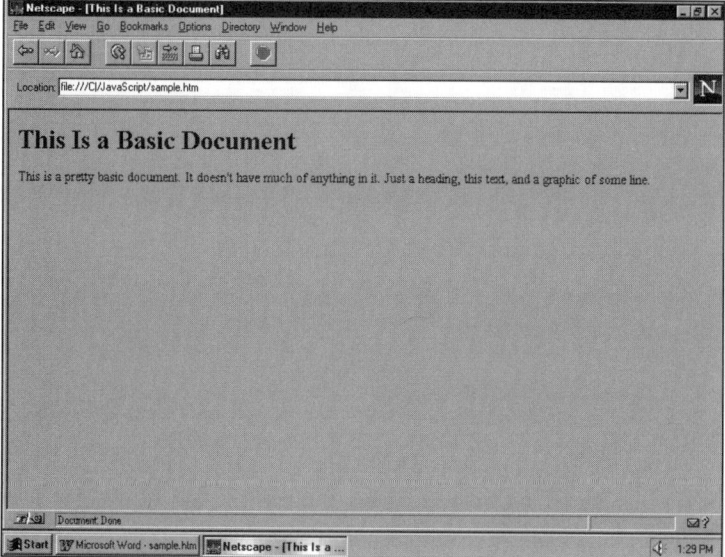

Figure 1.4 The output results of the sample.htm document.

Figure 1.5 JavaScript displays an error message if it detects a problem in the code.

But these are not allowed:

```
<--No script tags around the JavaScript instruction-->
<HTML>
<BODY>
<H1>Here's JavaScript-generated text!</H1>
document.write ("Hello there!");
</BODY>
</HTML>


<--HTML markup tags inside the script tags-->
<HTML>
<BODY>
<H1>Here's JavaScript-generated text!</H1>
<SCRIPT>
<H1>Here's JavaScript-generated text!</H1>
document.write ("Hello there!");
<P>
</SCRIPT>
</BODY>
</HTML>
```

■■■■■■ **NOTE**

There may be other HTML scripting languages in the future, and the
<SCRIPT> tag is designed to allow for differentiation in the language used.
So, from here on in this book, the first instance of the <SCRIPT> tag in
complete JavaScript programs in a document will also include the LAN-
GUAGE="JavaScript" attribute. Here is an example:

```
<SCRIPT LANGUAGE="JavaScript">
```

Strictly speaking, this attribute is optional in current versions 2.0 and 3.0 of
Netscape, but it is included for the sake of completeness.

■■■■■■

A Realistic Use of JavaScript

Obviously, you don't use JavaScript to insert the text that HTML can otherwise do all by itself. The example above was used because it's simple and demonstrates the basic JavaScript concept of embedded scripts in an HTML page.

JavaScript is ideal for making your Web pages "smart." Here's an example. Suppose you want to change a graphic depending on whether it's day or night. JavaScript has a rich selection of date-oriented functions, one of which returns the current hour, as set by the user's computer. Here's how that basic document uses JavaScript instructions to programmatically select the right GIF for the time of day:

```
<HTML>
<HEAD>
<TITLE>This Is a Basic Document</TITLE>
</HEAD>
<BODY>
<H1>This Is a Basic Document</H1>
<P>This is a pretty basic document.  It doesn't have much of anything in it.
Just a heading, this text, and a graphic of some line.</P>
<SCRIPT>
now = new Date();
if ((now.getHours() > 5) && (now.getHours()<18))
        document.write ("<IMG SRC='http://mydoamin.com/day.gif'>");
else
        document.write ("<IMG SRC='http://mydomain.com/night.gif'>");
</SCRIPT>
</BODY>
</HTML>
```

This example uses a JavaScript *if* statement to determine the time of day. The if statement takes one action if the *expression* is true, or takes another if the expression is false. If the hour is later than 5 A.M., but earlier than 6 P.M., it's daylight (see Figure 1.6). JavaScript inserts an image (<IMG>) tag using the DAY.GIF image. If the current time is not between these hours, it is nighttime and JavaScript inserts the NIGHT.GIF image.

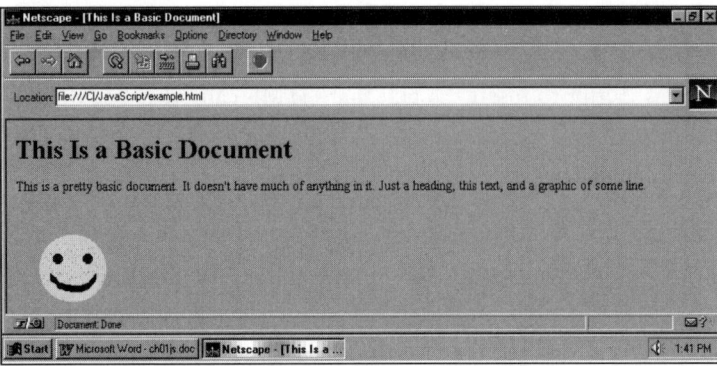

■■■■■■■ **Figure 1.6** Use JavaScript to conditionally display an image depending on the time of day.

HTML alone lacks decision-making capability, so this example is a perfect job for JavaScript. The page contains the basic HTML tags to render the document, along with JavaScript for any tasks that require "thinking."

Viewing JavaScript "Objectively"

You've probably heard of *object-oriented programming*. In this style of programming, software is created using self-contained modules. Each module is designed to take a certain type of data and do something with it. The term "object-oriented" comes from how the data is viewed: as an object. While object-oriented programming is more difficult than the traditional "procedural" programming (such as using Basic or C), the end result is usually easier to maintain and fix. Almost all major software products released today are written using object-oriented techniques.

JavaScript uses *objects*, but it is not an object-oriented programming language. Objects are used in JavaScript to represent "things." The document as viewed in the Netscape browser is a "thing." The fill-in form that you see on the browser page is a "thing." The hypertext link you click on to go to another URL is a "thing."

These things, er, objects, are best viewed as a total entity to make programming easier. Objects have *properties*, which are characteristics of that object. As in real life, not all objects have the same properties. Imagine a window. That's an object. Now imagine that window having a property for open/closed (the one property can represent both states).

Now imagine the lamp by your desk. It's an object too, but it doesn't have an open/closed property. Instead, it has an on/off property.

A good example of a JavaScript object is the document that you view in the Netscape window. The document has many properties, including the background color, the text color, and the title. When you work with JavaScript, you uniquely identify the properties you want as belonging to a certain object. You don't just say "change the color of the background to green"; JavaScript won't have the slightest idea what you're talking about. *What* background? Rather, to change the background of the document, you must specify the document object.

JavaScript uses a special syntax for the object-property relationship. You use the object name (in this case, document), a period, and the property name, which is bgColor. Put them together and you have:

```
document.bgColor
```

This is enough to tell JavaScript what object you want to work with, and what property of that object you want to change or test. For example, assume that you want to change the background of a document. That's easy. The following instruction changes the background color to black:

```
document.bgColor - "black",
```

Test this for yourself Here's a short script that sets the background according to the time of day. It uses document.bgColor to set the background color, and fgColor to set the foreground (text) color. The page is rendered black-on-white for the daytime, and white-on-black for the nighttime. This example uses the color names rather than the #nnnnnn color triplet values you may generally use. Both are valid with Netscape.

bgsetter.html

```
<HTML>
<HEAD>
<TITLE>This Is a Basic Document</TITLE>
<SCRIPT LANGUAGE="JavaScript">
```

```
now = new Date();
if ((now.getHours() > 5) && (now.getHours()<18)) {
        document.bgColor = "white";
        document.fgColor = "black";
} else {
        document.bgColor = "black";
        document.fgColor = "white";
}
</SCRIPT>
</HEAD>
<BODY>
<H1>This Is a Basic Document</H1>
<P>This is a pretty basic document.  It doesn't have much of anything in it.
Just a heading, this text, and a graphic of some line.</P>
</BODY>
</HTML>
```

■■■■■■ NOTE

Placement of the <SCRIPT> tags can make a difference. You can change the background property of the document at any time, even after the page has been rendered in the browser (this applies to the Windows platforms only when you are using Netscape 2.0; bugs in the Macintosh and X-Windows platforms cause the text to be obliterated when the background changes).

However, the same doesn't apply to the foreground (text) property. You can change the property, but only before the text is rendered in the browser. Therefore, putting the <SCRIPT> tag after the text will not yield proper results. Keep this in mind when writing your JavaScript programs.

■■■■■■

When you retype this, be very sure to check all of your work. Don't forget the { and } brace characters for the if statement. Netscape displays an error message if these are missing. (For the curious, the braces are needed in this example because more than one line of code follows the if statement.)

A Method to Its Madness

Closely related to objects are *methods*. A method is something you can do with an object. Like properties, methods are contextually tied to "belong" to objects, and not all objects have the same methods. Think of a method as an action that causes the object to change or respond in some way. Consider that window and desk lamp again. A valid method for the window is to open and close it. A valid method for the lamp is to turn it off and on.

You've already seen a JavaScript method at work: document.write. Write is a method of the document object. This method causes JavaScript to send HTML output to the document. Whenever you want to insert text or tags in the document, use *document.write*. Similarly, there are methods for the document property to open a new document, to close a document, and much more.

Methods cause something to happen to an object. There are dozens of methods, each one contextually related to the object it serves. Adding to this canopy of choices are a very small sprinkling of JavaScript *functions*. Unlike methods, however, functions are not related to an object. For example, a commonly used JavaScript function is parseInt, used in converting number formats.

Statements Tie It All Together

Statements are programming commands. You've already been introduced to the if statement. There are others, including return, var, while, and for. Statements are used to construct the thinking and doing portion of your JavaScript programs.

JavaScript currently supports few statements—about a dozen—but more will come as the language matures. With new statements come additional capabilities. This doesn't mean JavaScript is anemic when it comes to programming prowess. On the contrary, with a bit of ingenuity and imagination, you can construct very complex programs, even with as limited a selection of statements as JavaScript currently offers.

JavaScript FAQ

Following are frequently asked questions about the JavaScript and Web published topics addressed in this chapter.

What Is HTML?

HTML stands for hypertext markup language, a method of representing text and formatting for a document delivered via the Internet's World Wide Web. HTML documents consist only of readable text. Graphics, sounds, movies, and other elements are stored in special files. Hypertext links within the HTML document invoke these files so that they can be loaded into the user's computer. The result is a homogenized text/graphics/sound multimedia presentation. Graphics are shown interspersed with text contained in the HTML document. "Helper programs" or add-in modules are used to render other media files, such as sound and movies.

What Is a Tag?

A tag is the way formatting is expressed in an HTML document. All HTML tags take the form <TAG>, where TAG describes the name of the tag. The greater than and less than symbols enclose the tag name, so that browser software can distinguish the tag from the rest of the text in the document. Some tags are simple. For example, the <B> tag turns on bolding, and the </B> tag turns it off.

Other tags, such as the <IMG> (image) tag, also contain a variety of options, called *attributes*. These attributes tell the browser the special things that need to be done with that tag. For example, for the <IMG> tag you must specify the filename of the image to display. Other optional attributes, also provided within the tag, include the alignment of the image, alternate text to show if the browser cannot render images, and several others. A typical fully implemented <IMG> tag looks like this:

```
<IMG SRC="http://www.anywhere.com" ALT="Our home page" ALIGN="top">
```

What Is Object-Oriented Programming?

Object-oriented programming is a methodology for writing computer software. The term comes from the use of *objects*, which are discrete and highly formalized containers for data. This data can be numbers, text, graphics, sounds, or just about anything else. Objects permit modularized programming, which is considered good because software can be written and tested piece by piece.

The framework of an object-oriented program is the *class*. A class is a description of how the data of an object is supposed to be handled. The class is the template; the object is the result. The classic way of thinking of the relationship of classes and objects is to imagine the class as a cookie cutter, and the object as the cookies.

The concept of object-oriented programming differs from traditionally *procedural* programming in other ways. For example, in a typical procedural program, the flow of the code starts at the beginning and goes through the various commands to the end. Object-oriented programs are designed around the *event*, such as when the user clicks a button. When an event occurs, control is handed to a part of the program that is specifically designed to understand that event. This makes programming easier and more straightforward.

What Is an Object?

An object is merely a means to represent data. For example, a valid object is a program window, such as one that you see in Windows or in the Netscape Navigator browser program. Elements of a window are part of that object. These elements can include a menu bar at the top, a scrollbar, various buttons, and a window for the contents of the Web page.

Each of these elements has a particular behavior: the scrollbar doesn't look or act like the menu bar, and the menu bar doesn't look or act like the scrollbar. This is an important part of understanding objects: elements (called *properties*) of an object can't process data they weren't designed to process. While this may sound restrictive, it's actually "a good thing."

Does a JavaScript Program Run on My Computer or the Server?

Both. But let's consider traditional JavaScript first. JavaScript is typically contained in the HTML document fetched from a server computer on the Web. The JavaScript program is executed by the browser in your computer, either as the document is loading or after it has been loaded. For this type of JavaScript, called client-side, the Web server is not involved in the execution of a JavaScript program on your computer.

JavaScript can also run on a Web server. This is known as server-side. Such JavaScript programs typically act as control software. For example, the program might process a form submitted by the user and search through a very large database contained on the server. Server-side JavaScript requires the Netscape LiveWire software, which runs on a Netscape server.

■■■■■■ **NOTE**

This book does not address server-side JavaScript. However, many of the techniques and language elements apply to both server-side and client-side JavaScript.

■■■■■■

What Tools Do I Need to Write a JavaScript Program?

You don't need anything special to write a JavaScript program. Any text editor and most any well-designed Web page editor will do. One good choice is Netscape Navigator Gold 2.0, which combines a browser and an editor in one package. Microsoft Word or WordPerfect word processors are good choices because these programs let you use templates and macros to make the page creation process easier. In fact, many of these templates and macros have been included in the CD-ROM that accompanies this book.

Is JavaScript Supported in Browsers Other Than Netscape?

As of this writing, JavaScript support is limited to Netscape 2.0 and later versions, as well as Microsoft Internet Explorer 3.0 and later. However, a number of other companies have pledged support for JavaScript and plan Internet-related products for it. Look for JavaScript in browsers distributed by America Online and Spyglass. And look for JavaScript tools, utilities, and assistants from such companies as Borland, Apple, Computer Associates, and AT&T.

Who Developed the JavaScript Language?

Netscape is primarily responsible for developing the JavaScript language. It was, however, developed in cooperation with Sun Microsystems, the original developer of Java, if for no other reason than because JavaScript shares Java's name (the two are very different languages, however). At Netscape, the original implementation of JavaScript is due mostly to Brendan Eich, a member of the Netscape Navigator team. He and Bill Joy (of Sun Microsystems) are also primarily responsible for the JavaScript language specification, which is still ongoing as of this writing. This specification details how the JavaScript language is used and implemented, and it can be used by other companies wishing to add JavaScript support to their Internet products.

2

STUFF YOU SHOULD

KNOW: BASIC

PROGRAMMING

JavaScript is a rich and full-featured programming language. As included in Netscape—as well as in Microsoft Internet Explorer and other products—it has a fairly narrow application: to enhance HTML documents you view on the Web. With just a little bit of ingenuity, however, you can create JavaScript code that can generate, from scratch, specialized pages customized for each person visiting your Web site, games, calculators, reminder calendars, a self-testing and scoring quiz game, and much, much more. In short, there is almost no limit to what you can do with JavaScript.

If you're new to programming or need a refresher course, be sure to read this chapter. It details some of the key concepts you will need on your way to becoming a JavaScript expert. This chapter explains the basic concepts of programming, such as flow control, conditional testing, variables, expressions, and other topics.

Thinking Like a Nerd...,er...,Programmer

Although you don't need any previous training or experience at computer programming to master JavaScript, you will find that it does help. At the very least, you should learn how to "think like a programmer" or at least think in terms of programming and problem solving. Of course, this does not mean that you must *become* a programmer. You can master JavaScript and not take up programming as a new career. If you already consider yourself a programmer, then JavaScript will be a fun learning experience for you.

It is not the intent of this book to teach programming principles; that would require far too many pages. However, you can gain a good grasp of programming fundamentals by concentrating on the 11 main areas of JavaScript program design:

- Objects
- Flow
- Routines
- Variables
- Expressions
- Strings
- Numeric values
- Conditional statements
- Looping
- Entering data
- Outputting data

The Object *Is* the Game

As with many modern computer languages these days, JavaScript is designed around the *object*, which is sort of like a virtual "black box" machine. You can think of an object as a Creepy Crawlers Machine for computer programs. You gather raw ingredients (the "creepy"), put them in the machine, and out comes the finished crawler. The idea here is that such machines as the Creepy Crawlers are designed to accept only certain kinds of ingredients and output certain kinds of items. One machine in your house may be designed to pump out rubber toys, another may be made to produce the perfect waffle, and a third might be only good for making julienne fries.

JavaScript objects are designed with specific tasks in mind. One object might represent the current document, another the entire window, and yet another a form within that document. Objects impose a strict compliance; you can't manipulate an object in any way you like. This is a departure from many older programming languages, such as C or Basic, in which you have complete freedom to manipulate the data in your programs. This freedom, however, also comes with a price: it's rather easy to shoot yourself in the foot by making a relatively minor programming error. Objects are supposed to make programming safer and more streamlined.

With few exceptions, everything you do in JavaScript revolves around the object. Because of this, JavaScript uses its own object-related jargon. Here are the most important terms to learn:

- *Method*. This is something you can do with (or to) an object.
- *Property*. This is a value you can fetch from an object.
- *Event*. This is a condition that the object reacts to and will signal you when it occurs.

Read more about objects in these chapters:

- Chapter 3, "Overview of JavaScript Programming"
- Chapter 4, "Objects"
- Chapter 11, "Defining Functions, Objects, and Methods"

Going with the Flow

The *flow* is the order of events your program takes to complete its task. That flow can be dictated by a strict progression from start to finish that never varies between uses. Or it can deviate depending on user input or some other condition. Flow is something you have to visualize or your programs may become hopelessly confusing to you. You'll lose track of what they are supposed to do, and when.

Simple, one-function scripts can be created without a blueprint or flow chart, but you should still give extra thought and consideration to what your program is supposed to do. As you gain experience writing JavaScript programs, you'll do this subconsciously. But at first you'll have to force yourself to think in terms of progression.

You will particularly want to consider flow if a program is complex. You may find it helpful to draw a programming *flow chart* that includes the basic steps of the script, such as that in Figure 2.1. Each box contains a complete step; arrows connect the boxes to indicate the progress of steps through the script.

Flow charts are particularly handy when you are creating scripts that involve other scripts as part of a complex interaction using frames. For example, the JavaScript in one frame can control what happens in another frame. By making a "map" of the JavaScript program and how it interacts with everything, you can better visualize the requirements and design principles involved.

Read more about flow control in these chapters:

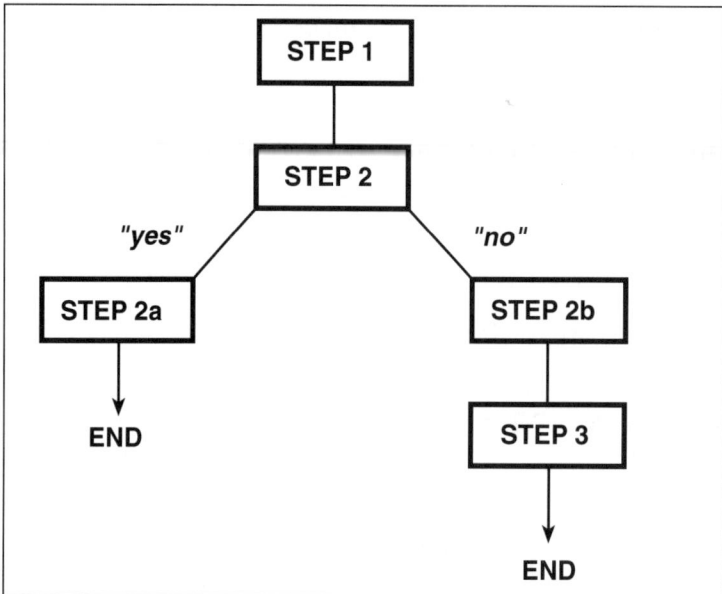

Figure 2.1 A flow chart helps you to visualize the construction of your JavaScript program.

- Chapter 3, "Overview of JavaScript Programming"
- Chapter 7, "Expressions"
- Chapter 8, "Statements"

The Benefit of Routines

One of the first things a programmer does when he or she starts on a project is to map out the individual segments, or *routines*, that make up the software. Even the longest, most complex program—and this includes JavaScript programs—consists of little more than bite-size routines. The script progresses from one routine to the next in an orderly and logical fashion.

What is a routine? A routine is any self-contained segment of code that performs a basic action. In the context of a JavaScript program, a routine can be a single command or character of text, or it can take up the bulk of a mammoth 200K HTML document (though this is obviously an extreme). Suppose your script formats text and graphics on a page, and also displays a list from which the user makes a selection. Once a selection is made, the script clears the screen and displays the result. The script can be divided into three distinct routines:

- *Routine 1:* Format the document with text, graphics, and list box
- *Routine 2:* Determine the user's choice from the list
- *Routine 3:* Clear the screen and display the choice

While there's no need to physically separate these routines within a script, it does help to think of the script as being composed of distinct parts. If the script doesn't work properly, you can analyze the problem more easily if you can identify a specific segment of the code that is causing the problem. For example, if the script is not responding to the user's choice in the list, but is formatting the screen with the proper text and graphics, then you can reasonably narrow the problem to routine 2.

Many scripts simply start at the beginning and advance one step at a time to the end, taking each instruction in turn and acting on it. This is the approach taken by the sample script just cited. Better program design calls for segmenting the routines into something called functions. That way, the functions can be used in any order, and even repeated. For example, your script could easily be revised to repeat routine 1 (formatting the document), after the user has successfully picked an item from the list and the response is shown on the screen.

> Here's another benefit of working with discrete routines. Because the code for a particular task is all contained in a routine, it can more easily be transported to other scripts. This lets you share code so you don't have to write everything from scratch.
>
> This is the technique used in Chapter 13, "Plug-and-Play Routines." This chapter contains dozens of ready-to-use routines that you can drop into your JavaScript programs.

JavaScript doesn't use line numbers, as found in some other programming languages, such as old versions of Basic. Rather, you identify routines by function name. You merely provide the name of the function (routine) you want JavaScript to execute, and it executes that routine. This makes it extremely easy to revise your program because you don't need to worry about changing line numbers as you add and remove contents.

Read more about routines in these chapters:

- Chapter 3, "Overview of JavaScript Programming"
- Chapter 8, "Statements"
- Chapter 11, "Defining Functions, Objects, and Methods"
- Chapter 13, "Plug-and-Play Routines"

Variables

A *variable* is a special holding area for information. A variable "remembers" a piece a information for use later in the program. JavaScript uses named variables, and the names can be almost any length. You make up the name of the variable as you write the script. The contents of the variable are specified by one of the following:

- You, when you write the script

- The browser, when the script is run
- The server, which houses your Web page, when the page is sent to you
- The user, who enters some data or makes a selection

The information in the variable is kept so that it can be used elsewhere in the script (see Figure 2.2). This information can take many forms, including numbers and text. When the page is unloaded from the browser, the variable is lost.

JavaScript follows a variable paradigm known as "loose typing." This means that the contents of variables are not tightly controlled. Unlike many other languages, such as C and the older versions of Basic, you can put a text value into a variable, then replace it with a number value. JavaScript will cope by automatically figuring out what kind of data is being stored and adjust its internal memory-handling requirements to suit. In JavaScript, you do not need to "declare" a variable type, such as

```
int MyInteger;
```

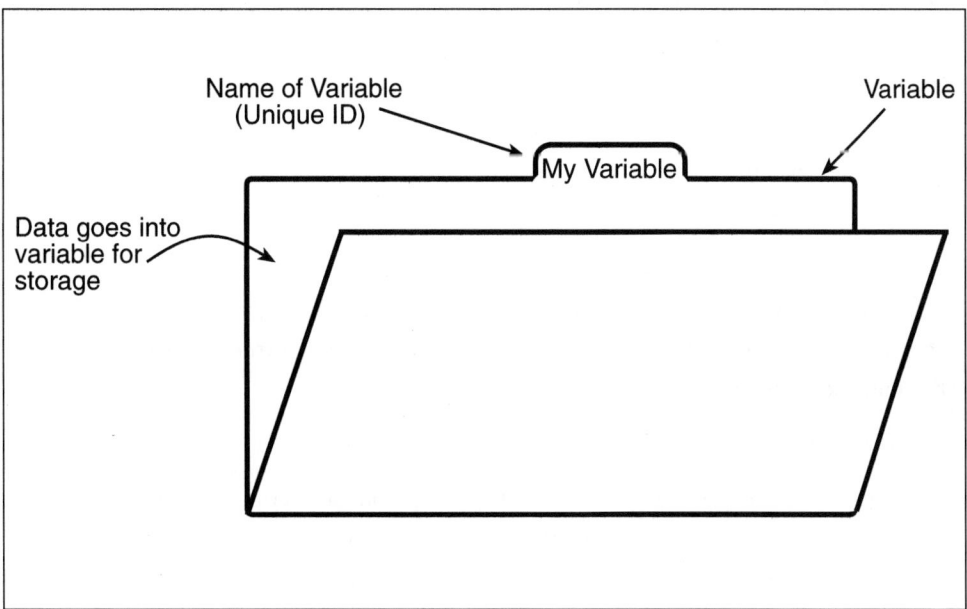

∎∎∎∎ **Figure 2.2** Variables store information for later retrieval in a JavaScript program.

to define a variable named MyInteger that will contain an integer (whole number) value. In addition, you can often mix and match numbers and text without bothering to convert them to the proper data format first. This makes programming in JavaScript much easier and cuts down on potential mistakes.

Read more about variables in these chapters:

- Chapter 3, "Overview of JavaScript Programming"
- Chapter 7, "Expressions"
- Chapter 8, "Variables"

Expressions

An expression is a list of steps a JavaScript program must follow to complete a task you've given it. Sometimes the expression is a simple math problem: "Take the contents of this variable and apply it to that value." Oftentimes, the expression is a little more complex, such as "Take this number from this variable, add 15 to it, and compare it to the value in this other variable."

When you ask a JavaScript program to perform some type of calculation or thinking process, you're asking it to *evaluate an expression*. For example, if the expression reads "1+1," then the script must first evaluate that expression (add 1 and 1 to make 2) before proceeding.

Some more advanced JavaScript expressions may appear exotic, but you'll have plenty of chance to use them. One of the most common expressions evaluates whether a statement is *true* or *false*. Here's a good example of a *true/false* expression that must be evaluated by a script:

```
if Number equals 10, then alert ("the number is ten");
```

If you evaluate the expression (which is not in acceptable JavaScript notation, but it's close), you see that it says "if the contents of the Number variable are equal to 10, then display a message." Before proceeding with the remainder of the program, JavaScript must pause, examine the Number variable, and apply the results to the logical expression. If the result is *true*, then the script displays a message that reads, "the number is 10." If it's *false* (the Number variable contains a number other than 10), then something else happens.

Read more about expressions in these chapters:

- Chapter 3, "Overview of JavaScript Programming"
- Chapter 7, "Expressions"

Strings

A common term in programming circles is the *string*. A string is simply a sequence of alphabetic or numeric characters, as shown in Figure 2.3. These characters are stored within the computer's memory one right after the other, like beads on a string. Therein lies the root of the word *string*.

In the context of JavaScript and other programming languages, strings are typically used in variables. Once stored in a variable, a string can be acted upon by the program. For example, if the string is text, you can compare it with another string to see if the two are the same. The concept of comparing strings comes in handy when you are designing interactive scripts. The advanced scripts throughout this book rely heavily on string comparisons.

Strings are also used to display messages to the user and display text in the browser. For example, you use a string to display a paragraph of text generated by JavaScript. Strings are especially important in JavaScript because an HTML document is nothing but text. Images, sounds, Java applets, plug-ins, and more—all of these elements are stored in an HTML document as textual tags.

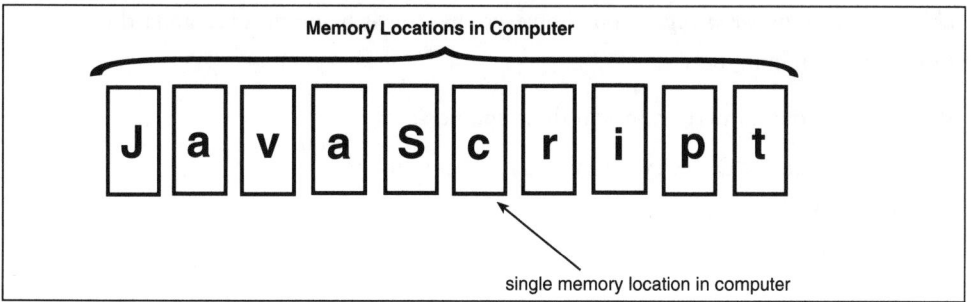

Figure 2.3 Strings are composed of one or more characters—which can be letters, numbers, or symbols—strung one after the other.

Read more about strings in these chapters:

- Chapter 3, "Overview of JavaScript Programming"
- Chapter 4, "Objects"
- Chapter 5, "Properties"
- Chapter 7, "Expressions"

Numeric Values

Computers are designed from the ground up to work with *numeric values* (numbers). The size of the number is inconsequential and is entirely up to the application running on the computer. In fact, JavaScript programs can deal with numbers as large as 1e+308—that's 1 with over 300 zeros after it! Unless you're having an argument with Carl Sagan over the number of stars in the known universe, you'll probably never have a reason to use a number that large. (However, such numbers are handy when dealing with high-precision decimal values. JavaScript can work with numbers with an accuracy of up to 15 digits to the right of the decimal point.) As with strings (see above), numerical values are most often used in variables.

Numbers differ from strings in one important area: the computer can perform math calculations on two numbers and provide you with the result. Calculations are not possible with strings because you can't multiply or divide strings.

Note that JavaScript programs can store digits as numbers or as strings. It can sometimes be difficult to tell when a "number" (such as 1 or 263) is a numeric value and when it's a string. For the sake of clarity, numbers stored as digits in the computer's memory are referred to in this book as *numeric values* and numbers stored as text characters as *number strings*. Note, however, that this is by no means standard notation in programming books.

Read more about numeric values in these chapters:

- Chapter 3, "Overview of JavaScript Programming"
- Chapter 7, "Expressions"
- Chapter 9, "Variables"

Conditional Statements

Scripts can be constructed so that they perform certain routines in one instance, and other routines in another. The script responds to specific conditions, set by the user, by the browser, by information from the server, or by some other source.

A *conditional statement* is a fork in the road with a choice of two directions to take, depending on the response to a simple true/false question. JavaScript programs provide many ways to create conditional statements, but they all have the same purpose: to activate a certain routine (or group of routines) depending on external data.

Here's an example of a conditional statement. "If it's cold outside, I'll wear my jacket. Otherwise, I'll leave the jacket at home." The statement can be broken down into three segments:

- The condition to be met (if it's cold)
- The result if the condition is *true* (wear the jacket)
- The result if the condition is *false* (leave the jacket at home)

This isn't the kind of conditional statement you'll write with JavaScript. But you can design a conditional statement, for example, that loads one document depending on one type of user input, or another document depending on other types of user input.

All conditional statements have a condition that must be met, and a specified action if the condition is *true* or *false*—there is no other possible outcome. Not all conditional statements specify an action for both a *true* and a *false* outcome, but most do.

Spend some time learning all the ropes of conditional statements because this is the element of programming that gives JavaScript true intelligence. While your JavaScript programs may never have a life of their own—though you may sometimes think they do!—conditional statements endow them with limited smarts to perform the actions you want.

Read more about conditional statements in these chapters:

- Chapter 3, "Overview of JavaScript Programming"
- Chapter 7, "Expressions"
- Chapter 8, "Statements"

Looping

A *loop* is a command or routine that repeats two or more times. A typical loop used in some programming languages is a "keyboard scan" in which the program checks the keys you press. If you press the key for which the loop routine is looking, the program breaks out of the loop (usually just momentarily) and continues on with some other routines. If the key isn't the one for which the loop is looking, the routine is restarted again.

Keyboard scans are not possible with JavaScript, as JavaScript is engineered to interact with the browser, not the computer running it. In the realm of JavaScript, you might construct a routine that insists the user respond to a prompt by providing valid data. The loop is repeated until valid data is entered.

In many ways loops are really specialized versions of conditional statements. Instead of stopping to provide a choice of two directions, the script is designed to continue the loop until a certain condition, which may be internal or external, is met. JavaScript programs contain many sophisticated ways to construct loops, including the for loop and the while loop—both of which will be familiar to you if you've done any programming. You'll find loops helpful in tackling the most demanding JavaScript assignments.

Read more about looping in these chapters:

- Chapter 3, "Overview of JavaScript Programming"
- Chapter 7, "Expressions"
- Chapter 8, "Statements"
- Chapter 9, "Variables"

Entering Data

The basic JavaScript program is merely a series of commands. But you can also program scripts to stop and wait for *user input*. After the user has entered the data, the script uses the information—be it text, a number, a some other value—to complete its task.

For example, you might have your script prompt the user for her real name or e-mail name, or some other variable information. Your script may then use that information to create a personalized page. Input data can be entered directly into the document or can be temporarily stored in a variable. The script can then extract the contents of the variable and use that information in a conditional statement, a branch, or a loop—or even save it for use later on.

JavaScript user input takes two forms: via an HTML form, through which you enter text or make a selection, or via a response to one of JavaScript's pop-up message boxes. There's a box for a "confirmation" message as well as for a "prompt" message that asks for text input. The latter is shown in Figure 2.4. For security reasons, JavaScript does not allow you any other data input access.

Read more about inputting date in these chapters:

- Chapter 3, "Overview of JavaScript Programming"
- Chapter 4, "Objects"
- Chapter 5, "Properties"
- Chapter 6, "Methods and Functions"
- Chapter 16, "Using JavaScript in Forms"

Outputting Data

For reasons of security, JavaScript is restricted to displaying text and graphics in the browser's main window and also in messages boxes (in addition, JavaScript can be used to store certain kinds of restricted information in a special file on the user's computer). This display is how JavaScript *outputs data* for the user.

■■■■ **Figure 2.4** Message boxes prompt for user input.

If you're used to other programming environments such as C or Basic, you'll find this somewhat restrictive because you can't always make the text and graphics appear the way you want. While this can be viewed as a limitation, it's also a challenge: you must think in terms of presenting data that is compatible with the "host operating system"—which in this case is not Windows, the Macintosh, or Unix, but Netscape.

The appearance of this data is completely up to your unique JavaScript program. You can display plain text or add special formatting and imaging, as desired. Any Web document you can create using HTML commands you can duplicate with JavaScript.

Read more about outputting data in these chapters:

- Chapter 3, "Overview of JavaScript Programming"
- Chapter 4, "Objects"
- Chapter 5, "Properties"
- Chapter 6, "Methods and Functions"
- Chapter 16, "Using JavaScript in Forms"

Other JavaScript Topics of Interest

You've learned about the main tools in the programmer's toolbox. There are a few additional buzzwords and topics that will help you as you explore the JavaScript programming language. These are:

- Syntax
- Parameters
- Arguments
- Comments

Syntax

Syntax is the way a programming language is written. Computers are relatively stupid, and you can't as yet type program in English or some other human language and expect the computer to understand what you want. Rather, you must instruct the computer using code words and format those code words in a specific way that it can sift through the program and determine what exactly you want to do. If you fail to format your program using the proper syntax, JavaScript displays an error message. This error message will remain until the syntax is correct and JavaScript can understand your intentions.

JavaScript has a fairly simple syntax, modeled after the syntax used in the C programming language. While the syntax is simple, it's not always obvious. JavaScript uses parentheses, braces (the { and } characters), commas, semicolons, periods, and other symbols to mean special things. You must study the use of these symbols and how they are used in order to master JavaScript's syntax.

Syntax is discussed in-depth in Chapter 3, "Overview of JavaScript Programming."

Parameters and Arguments

A parameter is data you supply to a JavaScript object, method, or function.. Think of parameters as digits in a phone number. In order to connect with anyone, you must provide at least seven numbers (for a phone number in the United States). Leave out a number and the call isn't complete. Parameters in JavaScript are much the same. The parameters tell JavaScript what you want to do with the object, method, or function. Not all objects, methods, and functions use parameters, but many do.

Closely aligned with the parameter is the argument. In fact, some programmers consider parameters and arguments to be the same thing. This book makes a distinction for the sake of simplicity:

- A parameter is data that's needed to carry out a given task. The parameter might be "any valid seven-digit phone number."

- An argument is the actual data you provide. The argument might be a specific phone number, such as "555-1212."

Entities and Instructions

Because of JavaScript's use of objects, talking about the language can become redundant. For completeness, you may make statements such as "A parameter is data you supply to a JavaScript object, method, or function." Repeating "object, method, or function" each time you mention a parameter can become tiresome. Instead, the word *entities* is used (in this book at least) to generically refer to JavaScript objects, methods, properties, functions, and events.

An *instruction* is a generic term for one or more commands given to JavaScript to execute. In other programming languages, instructions are sometimes called "commands" or "command lines."

Comments

JavaScript programs are designed to be read by a machine—or more accurately, Netscape (or other browser) running on a machine. What these programs do isn't always obvious, so most programmers add *comments* to their work for the benefit of themselves as well as others. The comments explain—usually briefly—what a given JavaScript instruction does. The comment is marked off using special syntax: the // (double-slash characters) is the most commonly used. Comments can also be used to include copyright and distribution in the script.

The HTML markup language also supports comments, but the syntax is different from that used in JavaScript. As used in Netscape, a comment in HTML markup begins with the character sequence <!-- and ends with the sequence -->.

JavaScript FAQ

Following are frequently asked questions about the JavaScript and Web published topics addressed in this chapter.

Where Can I Learn More about Computer Programming?

It all depends on your personal preference. Some people like to learn on their own, and books on programming are an ideal method for learning programming. You can visit your local neighborhood library or book store for the latest titles. Here are some books published by Wiley Computer Books (the publisher of the book you're reading now, naturally), to get you started:

- *Joy of C*, Third Edition, by Lawrence Miller and Alex Quilici
- *Mastering C++*, Second Edition, by Cay Horstmann
- *Understanding Programming Languages*, by Monti Ben-Ari
- *Visual Basic for Windows 95 Insider*, by Peter G. Aitken

The resources on the Internet are vast and constantly changing. A number of sites provide introductory and intermediate tutorials on all kinds of programming topics. Some of the better-known sites are listed in sources.htm, found on the CD-ROM accompaning this book." But you should also check with the several Web site databases available. Four of the most popular databases are:

- http://www.yahoo.com/
- http://www.altavista.com/digital/
- http://www.webcrawler.com/
- http://www.lycos.com/

With each you can type in a search string, such as *C programming*, and you're given a list of all the sites that match your search criteria. You'll find that a topic such as C programming may return a lot of "hits," so plan to spend some time looking through the list. You may even want to narrow the search with something like *C programming begin*, which will find all sites with the words C, programming, and begin.

Classes in computer programming are available at most high schools, colleges, and university extensions. Check with the local schools in your area to see what's available. Most public colleges and universities also offer continuing adult education classes, and many are geared to beginner-level courseware.

Should I Learn C or Java Before I Learn JavaScript?

There's really no need to learn a higher-level language, such as C or Java, just to master JavaScript. However, the more you learn about programming in general, the better you'll be able to solve problems in JavaScript. A knowledge of C and/or Java command and syntax is helpful in learning JavaScript, but not necessary.

If, after reading through the material in this book, you still feel JavaScript is too advanced for your programming skills, you may wish to bone up on more of the bare basics using a programming language such as Basic. Basic is available for all computer platforms, and the language has been around for so long that there are scores of books and training materials available. Look in the local library or used book stores for bargains.

If you use an Intel-based PC, the MS-DOS operating system since version 5.0 has included a run-time version of a Basic interpreter, called QBasic. This is a relatively advanced version of Basic that lets you write programs without line numbers. While QBasic is still ancient technology compared to JavaScript, and some of the programming techniques and syntax are completely different, experimenting with QBasic will enhance your general programming skills and help you to become a better JavaScript programmer.

If you don't have an Intel-based PC, there are freeware, shareware, and commercial versions of the Basic interpreter available from a variety of sources. As usual, check the Internet first, starting with the Web site databases, such as Yahoo and Webcrawler, mentioned above.

Can I Learn Programming by Studying Other People's Work?

Yes. In fact, this is the *best* way to learn computer programming.

3

OVERVIEW OF

JAVASCRIPT

PROGRAMMING

As you read in Chapters 1 and 2, JavaScript uses an almost bewildering array of things called objects, methods, properties, statements, and events to perform its magic. Together, these make up the "programming entities" of JavaScript. These entities are the nuts and bolts with which you build your JavaScript programs.

If you are familiar with so-called object-oriented programming—such as C++, Java, or Visual Basic 4.0—you will probably be acquainted with these terms. For the programming newbie, the entities can be confusing at first because there doesn't seem to be much rhyme or reason for their design and use. But as you become more familiar with JavaScript, you will come to appreciate the use of specific entities rather than lumping everything together as a "command."

JavaScript supports six types of entities that act as programming instructions. This chapter reviews these entities and briefly discusses what each one does. The chapters in Part 2 of this book go into minute detail concerning each entity type. Here's a list of JavaScript's entities, along with the chapter in Part 2 devoted to explaining it.

- *Objects* (Chapter 4)—Strictly designed elements of the browser, and the HTML documents displayed in the browser
- *Properties* (Chapter 5)—Behaviors of objects, such as an object name or its contents
- *Methods* (Chapter 6)—Unique tasks that can be performed on certain JavaScript objects
- *Functions* (Chapter 6)—Special-purpose methods that can be applied irrespective of most objects
- *Statements* (Chapter 8)—Programming instructions that tell JavaScript how to process the script
- *Events* (Chapter 10)—Actions evoked by the user that can trigger a response in JavaScript

An Overview of JavaScript Objects

Ninety-nine percent of what JavaScript does, it does with objects. As far as JavaScript is concerned, an object is a specific element of the browser, or of the page rendered in the browser. For example, there's an object for the current document. This object—like real-world objects—has certain characteristics. In a programming language like JavaScript, these characteristics are more accurately called properties (this subject is discussed in the next section). By tying properties to objects, you can more easily manipulate the individual components of the browser (such as Netscape) or its documents.

JavaScript supports the objects shown in Figure 3.1. These objects are depicted in hierarchical order, so you can get a sense of how they interact. Notice that it is entirely possible for one object to belong to another object. Think of the chimney in your house; a chimney is an object, and so is your house. The house is considered a "top-level" object because it is not dependent on any other object (at least for the sake of this discussion). The chimney, however, is entirely dependent on the house. Without the house, the chimney can't stand.

This object-to-object hierarchy is very important in JavaScript, and it can make JavaScript a bit bewildering at first. The reason is that, up the hierarchical ladder, an object can be both an object and a property of an object. For example, as you can see

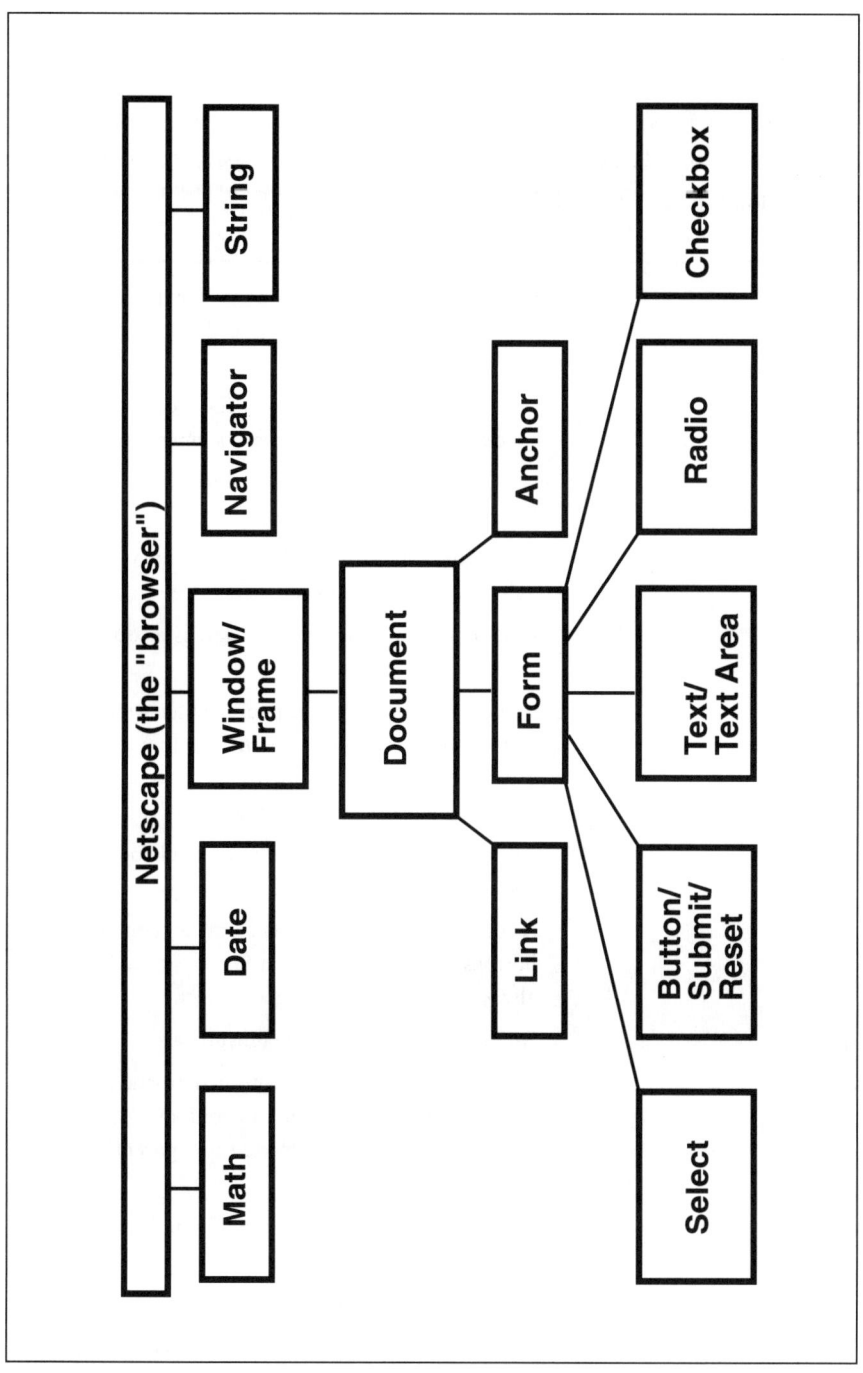

Figure 3.1 JavaScript supports numerous objects.

from the illustration, *document* belongs to the window object (it is said to be a "property of the window object"), and *document* is an object in its own right.

Here are JavaScript's objects, briefly described, in alphabetical order. "The browser" is Netscape—or any other browser that happens to support JavaScript. Top-level objects do not belong to any other object.

Object	Description
anchor	A target (that is, destination) for a hypertext link. Anchors always belong to the document object.
anchors[]	An array (list of variables sharing a common function) of the anchors in a document.
button	A push button in a form. Buttons always belong to the form object.
checkbox	A checkbox in a form. Checkboxes always belong to the form object.
Date	Gets or sets the date or time. Date is a top-level object.
document	The document as viewed in a browser window, or in a specific frame when the window is separated into frames. Documents can belong to a window object or a frame object.
elements[]	An array of all the items in a form. Elements always belong to the form object.
form	A form in a document. The form can contain buttons, text boxes, and list boxes. Forms always belong to a document object.
forms[]	An array of forms in a document.
frame	A window that is divided into many panes, called frames. Each frame can contain a different document. Frames belong to a "parent" window object.
frames[]	An array of frames in a "parent" window.
hidden	A hidden (nonvisible) text box in a form. Hidden boxes always belong to the form object.
history	A list of pages the browser has visited. History always belongs to the document object.

Object	Description
link	A hypertext link. Links always belong to the document object.
links[]	An array of links in a page.
location	The URL of the current document. Location always belongs to the document object.
Math	Performs math with numbers. Math is a top-level object.
navigator	Information about the browser, including its name and version. Navigator is a top-level object.
options[]	An array of all the items in a selection list (see select).
password	A password text box in a form. Password boxes always belong to the form object.
radio	A radio button in a form. Radio buttons always belong to the form object.
reset	A reset button in a form. Reset buttons always belong to the form object.
select	A selection list in a form. Select lists always belong to the form object.
string	A series of text. Strings belong to the document that created them.
submit	A submit button in a form. Submit buttons always belong to the form object.
text	A text box in a form. Text boxes always belong to the form object.
textarea	A text area (multiple-line) box in a form. Text areas always belong to a form object.
window	A browser window. Window is a top-level object.

An Overview of JavaScript Properties

Properties are behaviors of objects. There are actually two kinds of properties, shown graphically in Figure 3.2:

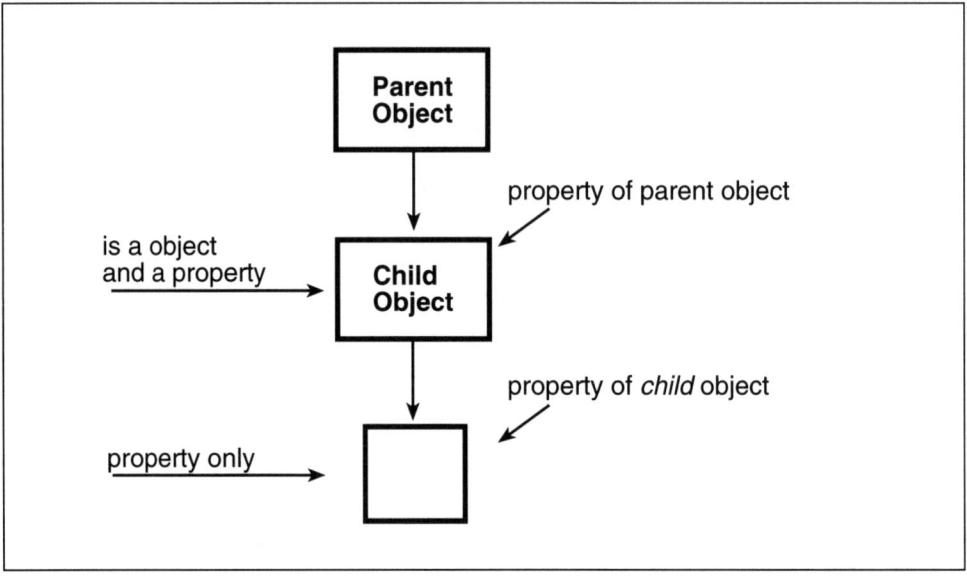

Figure 3.2 Properties can contain values (strings, numbers, and so forth) or other objects.

- *Some properties are themselves objects.* These are properties of a parent object, but also act as an object to their own child properties. For example, a form is a property of the document object. Form is also an object.

- *Some properties are "single-ended," containing a specific value.* Single-ended properties do not themselves support objects of their own. For example, the bgColor property represents the background color of the document object.

The rest of this section lists JavaScript's properties by group. Many properties can be both retrieved and set using JavaScript; that is, you can use the property to determine the current state of an object, and you can change the value of the property to make the object change. But other properties are read-only, meaning that you can read the value contained in them, but you can't directly change them. Note that Nestcape 3.0 supports additional object properties. See Chapter 22 for a list of these properties.

Browser Info Properties

The browser information properties return settings in the navigator object.

Property	What It Does
appCodeName	"Code name" for the current browser
appName	Application name for the current browser

Property	What It Does
appVersion	Version number of the current browser
userAgent	The user agent string sent from the browser to the server

Document Info and Appearance Properties

The properties for document appearance return and change the look of the document. Additional properties for document information return current information about the document.

Property	What It Does
alinkColor	The color for active links in the document
anchors[]	List of all anchors in the document
bgColor	Background color of the document
cookie	Semi-permanent storage of textual information
defaultStatus	Default text of status bar
fgColor	Text color of the document
forms[]	List of forms in the document
lastModified	The date the document was last modified
linkColor	The color of unvisited links in the document
links[]	A list of links in the document
location	The complete URL of the document
referrer	The URL of the referring (linked from) document
status	The current text of the status bar
title	The title of the document
vlinkColor	The color of visited links in a document

Forms Properties

The forms properties return (and some change) form elements, including the form itself and all controls (also called "widgets") in the form.

Property	What It Does
action	Destination URL for a form

Property	What It Does
defaultChecked	Default selection state of a check box or radio button
defaultSelected	Default selection of an option list
defaultValue	Default value of text box or text area
checked	State of a check box or radio button in form
elements[]	List of form elements in the document
encoding	MIME encoding format for a form
form	Parent form object
index	A specific option in a selection list within a form
length	The number of items in the list
method	Posting method for a form (get or post)
name	The name of a form object
options[]	A list of options in a selection list within a form
selected	Current state of a check box or radio button
selectedIndex	The selected option in a selection list within a form
target	The name of the targeted form
text	The text of an option in a selection list within a form
value	The text of a text box or text area

Link and Anchor Properties

The links and anchors properties return and change aspects of links (<A HREF=...>) and anchors (<NAME=...>).

Property	What It Does
hash	Text following the hash (#) symbol in a URL
host	The hostname:port portion of a URL
hostname	The host and domain (or IP address) of a URL
href	An entire URL
length	The number of anchors or links
pathname	The path portion of a URL
port	The port portion of a URL

Property	What It Does
protocol	The protocol portion of a URL
search	The search portion of a URL
target	The name of the targeted link

Math Properties

The math properties provide standard values used in math equations.

Property	What It Does
E	Euler's constant and the base of natural logarithms (About 2.118)
LN2	The natural logarithm of 2
LN10	The natural logarithm of 10
LOG2E	The base 2 logarithm of e
LOG10E	The base 10 logarithm of e
PI	The numeric equivalent of PI, rounded to 3.14
SQRT1_2	The square root of one-half
SQRT2	The square root of 2

Strings

The string object has one property, which is length (the content of the string is not a true property).

Property	What It Does
length	The length of a string

Window URL Properties

The URL property returns or changes the current document URL.

Property	What It Does
hash	Text following the hash (#) symbol in a URL
host	The hostname:port portion of a URL
hostname	The host and domain (or IP address) of a URL
href	An entire URL
pathname	The path portion of a URL

Property	What It Does
port	The port portion of a URL
protocol	The protocol portion of a URL
referrer	The URL of the referring (linked from) document
search	The search portion of a URL

Window and Frame

The window and frame properties turn and change aspects of the browser windows, and the frames within the windows. All window and frame properties are typically used as read-only.

Property	What It Does
frames[]	Array (list) of frames in the window
length	The number of frames in a window
name	The name of a window object
parent	The parent window or frame
self	The current window or frame
top	The top browser window
window	Current window or frame

An Overview of JavaScript Methods and Functions

Methods are actions you can take with JavaScript objects. A method is analogous to a standard command in a programming language that is not object-based. Methods are always associated with an object, and JavaScript displays an error (or does nothing) if you attempt to use a method with an object that doesn't support that method. For example, consider the open method. This method applies only to the document and window objects. If you try to use open with another object, such as a form, JavaScript displays an error.

JavaScript also supports something called a function. A function is similar to a method, except that functions aren't tied to objects. All of the current JavaScript functions support converting numbers.

The rest of this section lists JavaScript methods and functions separated by category. Unless specifically indicated, every entry in the tables is a method. Note that Netscape 3.0 provides additional object methods and functions. See Chapter 22.

Date Methods

The date methods are used with the built-in Date object. The majority get or set different parts of the time or date.

Method/Function	What It Does
getDate	Returns the day of month of a specified date
getDay	Returns the day of week of a specified date
getHours	Returns the hour of a specified date
getMinutes	Returns the minutes of a specified date
getMonth	Returns the month of a specified date
getSeconds	Returns the seconds of a specified date
getTime	Returns the number of seconds between January 1, 1970, and specified date
getTimeZoneoffset	Returns the time zone offset in minutes for the current locale
getYear	Returns the year of specified date
parse	Returns the number of milliseconds in a date since January 1, 1970, 00:00:00
setDate	Sets the date
setHours	Sets the hours of a specified date
setMinutes	Sets the minutes of a specified date
setMonth	Sets the month of a specified date
setSeconds	Sets the seconds of a specified date
setTime	Sets the time of a specified date
setYear	Sets the year of a specified date
toGMTString	Converts a date to a string using GMT conventions
toLocaleString	Converts a date to a string using locale conventions
toString	Converts the value of a date object or current location object to a string

Method/Function	What It Does
UTC	Converts a comma-delimited date to the number of seconds since January 1, 1970

Document Methods

The document write methods let you open, close, and write to a document window.

Method/Function	What It Does
clear	Clears the window
close	For a document, closes the output stream; for a window, closes the window
open	Opens a document or a window
write	Writes text to a document or window
writeln	Writes text to a document or window with the new line character appended

Form Methods

Form methods allow you to interact with form objects. These objects include text boxes, radio buttons, and checkboxes. (In Netscape 2.0, many of these methods are broken, depending on the platform.)

Method/Function	What It Does
blur	Removes focus from a text, text area, and password form control
click	Simulates a click on a form button (push button, radio button, checkbox)
focus	Sets focus to a text, text area, and password form control
select	Selects the text inside a text, text area, and password form control
submit	Submits a form to a server

History Methods

The history methods let you change the URL of a window or frame using previously visited URLs.

Method/Function	What It Does
back	Loads to the previous URL from the history list
forward	Loads the next URL from the history list
go	Loads a URL from the history list

JavaScript Functions

JavaScript functions are built into the core language, and they do not "belong" to any given object. They are therefore considered functions rather than methods.

Method/Function	What It Does
escape	Returns the encoded ASCII value (%xx) of a character in the ISO Latin-1 character set
eval	Evaluates an expression
isNAN	Tests a number to determine if it's "not a number"
parseFloat	Converts a number string to a floating-point value
parseInt	Converts a number string to an integer value
toString	Converts an object to a string
unescape	Returns the ASCII character for a specified value

Math Methods

The math functions apply to the built-in math object and give you extra arithmetic and computational capabilities, such as square roots and rounding. A number of trigonometry functions, such as acos and tan, are thrown in for good measure.

Method/Function	What It Does
abs	Returns the absolute value of a number
acos	Returns the arc cosine of a number
asin	Returns the arc sine of a number
atan	Returns the arc tangent of a number
ceil	Returns the least integer greater than or equal to a number
cos	Returns the cosine of a number
eval	Evaluates the contents of a string expression (for example, "2+2"); eval is a function

Method/Function	What It Does
exp	Returns e (Euler's constant) to the power of a number
floor	Returns the greatest integer less than or equal to its argument
isNAN	Determines if a value is a number (or "not a number")
log	Returns the natural logarithm (base e) of a number
max	Returns the greater of two values
min	Returns the lesser of two values
pow	Returns the value of a number times a specified power
random	Returns a random number (X-platforms only)
round	Returns a number rounded to the nearest whole value
sin	Returns the sine of a number
sqrt	Returns the square root of a number
tan	Returns the tangent of a number

String Methods

String methods are used with text strings. The write and writeln methods listed here really belong to the document object, but they are always used to print a string of characters to the document, so they are included in this category, too.

Method/Function	What It Does
anchor	Creates a named anchor (hypertext target)
big	Sets text to big
blink	Sets text to blinking
bold	Sets text to bold
charAt	Returns the character at a specified position
fixed	Sets text in fixed-pitch font
fontcolor	Sets the font color

Method/Function	What It Does
fontsize	Sets font size
indexOf	Returns the first occurrence of character x starting from position y
italics	Sets text to italics
lastIndexOf	Returns the last occurrence of character x starting from position y
link	Creates a hyperlink
small	Sets text to small
strike	Sets text to strikeout
sub	Sets text to subscript
substring	Returns a portion of a string
sup	Sets text to superscript
toLowerString	Converts a string to lowercase
toUpperString	Converts a string to uppercase
write	Writes text to a document or window
writeln	Writes text to a document or window with new line character appended

User Interface Methods

User interface methods let you interact with the user with a variety of message boxes (additional user interface methods are available under the Form category).

Method/Function	What It Does
alert	Displays a message box with OK button
confirm	Displays a message box with Yes and No buttons
prompt	Displays a message box prompting the user for text entry

Window Methods

Use the window control methods when you need to interact with the browser window—typically to change the URL of the current window, or move back and forth in the history list.

Method/Function	What It Does
clear	Clears the window
clearTimeout	Clears a previous set timer (using setTimeout)
close	For a document, closes the output stream; for a window closes the window
open	Opens a document or a window
setTimeout	Sets a timer

An Overview of JavaScript Statements

Statements are programming control commands. As such, they are used to control the flow and action of the entities (objects, properties, and so forth) within the JavaScript program. There are relatively few JavaScript programs; they are listed below in alphabetical order.

Statement	What It Does
break	Breaks out of a while or for loop
comment (//)	Inserts a comment that is not interpreted by JavaScript as a command
continue	Starts a new pass in a for or while loop, skipping any commands following
for	Repeats a series of instructions one or more times
for...in	Iterates through the properties of an object (one pass through the loop for each property of the object)
function	Defines a user-created function or object
if...else	Tests if an expression is true or false
return	Returns execution from a function
var	Declares a variable
while	Repeats a series of instructions until an expression proves false
with	Associates an object with properties and methods

An Overview of JavaScript Event Handlers

The last JavaScript entity is the event handler. An event is a condition generated by the browser when some action takes place—usually the result of something the user did. For example, when the user clicks a button in a form, it generates a "click event." JavaScript picks up this event and will tell you about it, if you wish.

You can always tell an event handler by its name: all start with the word "on." There are relatively few event handlers, and even fewer still are used to any degree. The most common are onClick, onLoad, and onMouseOver. The majority of the event handlers are used in conjunction with forms.

Note that several of the event handlers deal with "focus." Focus is when the flashing insertion point is placed in a form control, such as a text box, text area, or selection list.

Event Handler	What It Does
onBlur	Trigger when focus leaves a text box, text area, or selection list
onChange	Trigger when text changes in a text box, text area, or selection list, and focus leaves the control
onClick	Trigger when a form button or hypertext link is clicked
onFocus	Trigger when focus is set in a text box, text area, or selection list
onLoad	Trigger when a document has been completely loaded
onMouseOver	Trigger when the mouse passes over a hypertext link
onSelect	Trigger when text is selected in a text box or text area
onSubmit	Trigger when a form has been submitted to a server
onUnload	Trigger when a document is about to be unloaded

Authoring Programs in JavaScript

Like all computer programming languages, JavaScript insists you format things in a specific way. Otherwise, JavaScript cannot interpret what you want to do and displays an error. This section covers some programming fundamentals you'll want to keep in mind as you learn and use JavaScript.

Saving in Text Format

JavaScript is contained in the same document as the HTML used to define a Web page. As such, all JavaScript programs are in text-only format. You can use most word processor, text editing, or HTML editing programs to write JavaScript programs, as long as the program saves in text-only format.

Always Put JavaScript Code Between <SCRIPT> Tags

The JavaScript interpreter built into the browser is designed to ignore any text unless it is placed within <SCRIPT> tags. Material within the <SCRIPT> tags is considered for JavaScript's use only. Do not place any HTML markup tags within these tags.

To start the tag, you insert:

```
<SCRIPT LANGUAGE="JavaScript">
```

The LANGUAGE attribute is optional, but it's a good idea to include it for future compatibility. To end the tag you insert:

```
</SCRIPT>
```

Here is an example:

```
<SCRIPT LANGUAGE="JavaScript">
alert ("Welcome to JavaScript!!");
</SCRIPT>
```

This short script is executed as the browser loads the page.

Using Quotation Marks

Quotation marks are always used to define strings of text. Without the marks, JavaScript will mistake the text for something else, such as the name of a variable or object. JavaScript understands two kinds of quotation marks: the single quotation mark (') and the double quotation mark ("). You can use either type of quotation mark, but you must remember to use the same one to start and end a string. Here is an example:

Allowed	Not Allowed	Why It's Not Allowed
"Hello"	Hello	No quotation marks at all
"Hello"	"Hello	No ending quotation mark
'Hello'	"Hello'	Mismatched quotation marks

You can also use the two types of quotation marks to embed quotation marks in a string. Suppose you want to display the word *don't*. As you can see, the word has an apostrophe in it—and an apostrophe is another use for a single quotation mark. Ordinarily, this would result in an error, because JavaScript always insists on using quotation marks in pairs. But JavaScript allows you to use both quotation mark types so that you can embed a quotation mark in a string.

In addition, JavaScript lets you include quotation characters by "escaping" them with the \ backslash character. The escape method lets you sneak in a quotation mark when JavaScript might otherwise return an error. Here are three examples, with the results shown in Figure 3.3:

"Don't do that."

'"Do not do that," she said.'

'"Don\'t wear that again around me!," she yelled."'

Inserting a Comment in a JavaScript Program

Comments are notes designed for readers. JavaScript ignores comments because they do not include instructions for it. You might use a comment to remind you of how a new feature works or to document a procedure for someone else trying to use your script.

There are two types of comments used within JavaScript: the single-line comment and the multiple-line comment.

▬▬▬▬ **Figure 3.3** The ' and " quotation characters can be inserted into text using the \ "escape" character.

- The single-line comment is created using the // characters. All text up to the next hard return is treated as a comment.
- The multiple-line comment is created using the /* and */ characters. All text between these characters is treated as a comment.

Here are some examples of comments:

```
// This is a comment all on one line alert ("Welcome to JavaScript!")
// This is a comment after an executed instruction
/*This is the start
of a multiple-line comment*/
```

Hiding JavaScript Code from Non-JavaScript Browsers

Not all Web browsers understand JavaScript. This can be a problem if you need your Web documents to be viewable with non-JavaScript browsers. The natural tendency of a browser is to ignore an HTML tag it doesn't understand. Any text outside the tag is rendered, and is visible, in the browser screen.

To prevent non-JavaScript browsers from printing your JavaScript code, enclose it in HTML comments. The HTML comment tag begins with <!— and ends with —> (although many browsers, especially non-Netscape browsers, consider just the > character as the end of the comment). Here is an example:

```
<H1>Here's JavaScript-generated text!</H1>
```

```
<SCRIPT>
<--Hide this code from "old" browsers
document.write ("Hello there!")
// stop hiding-->
</SCRIPT>
```

Notice the double slash (//) characters on the line with the end comment tag. JavaScript treats double-slashes as its own comment and ignores anything on that line. If you forget the // characters, JavaScript tries to interpret the —> characters, and that will result in the error you see in Figure 3.4.

Programming Considerations

Here are some semi-random thoughts regarding programming in JavaScript. Feel free to skip these topics if they have no interest for you. This is not critical, "gotta know" stuff here.

JavaScript Syntax: A Lot Like C

The syntax of JavaScript was intentionally modeled after Java, which was itself modeled after the C++ language. And, the basic syntax of C++ was modeled after C. So it can be rightfully said that the syntax of JavaScript is a lot like C.

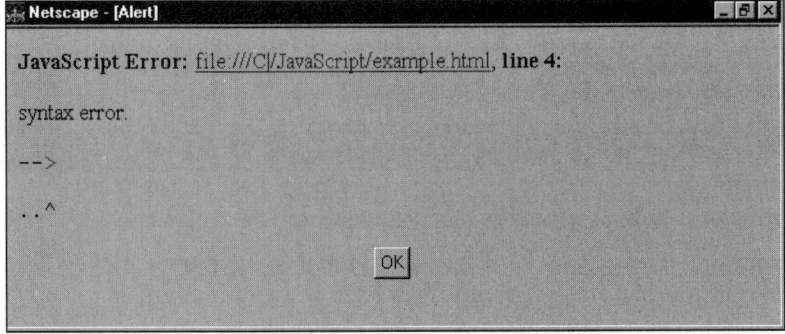

▉▉▉▉▉ **Figure 3.4** The syntax error message complains when you forget to add the // comment characters to force JavaScript to ignore the —> end tag of an HTML comment.

If you're familiar with C, then you'll be instantly familiar with JavaScript. They both use similar syntax and structure, and they share many of the same statements. In fact, some C code can actually be plugged into a JavaScript with little or no change. If you're not familiar with C—perhaps you've worked with Basic or Cobol or Pascal—the syntax will look odd and perhaps a bit like Sanskrit. Unlike Basic and especially Pascal, C is not known for being a "readable" language; that is, you can't easily read over a C program and instantly grasp the whole process. The C language was designed this way for speed in writing and compiling. The syntax of the language is rather threadbare, thus making it easier for the compiler to turn the code into a form the computer can understand. As a result, though, C is harder to learn and use.

C is a "dot every i" kind of language, in which a special character misplaced here or there will cause the whole program to stop in its tracks. That said, JavaScript is generally quite lenient regarding the code it expects in its programs. Keep the following few points in mind and you'll do well:

- JavaScript uses semicolons at the end of command lines. This is a C tradition. But unlike C, the use of semicolons in JavaScript is optional. Many programmers use them for consistency, but you have a choice.

- JavaScript is a *case-sensitive* language. Names of objects, methods, properties, and other elements must use the proper capitalization, or the program will not work.

- JavaScript uses the { and } brace characters to form what's known as "statement blocks." There are rules (covered in later chapters) about the proper use of these characters. Forget one, and your script will fail.

- Like C, JavaScript is a minimalist language. A lot is inferred because of context. For example, unlike languages such as Basic and Pascal, there are no end if commands to mark the end of an if statement. Instead, the "end if" is inferred or is marked using the { and } statement block characters.

- When defining text, enclose it in ' (single) or " (double) quotation marks. This tells JavaScript that the text should be treated as an assemblage of characters and not as a command name or some other element.

- To test for equality in an expression (such as that used in an if statement), use two equals signs, as in ==. JavaScript throws a tantrum if you use just one equals. This is one of the most common problems that beset new JavaScripters.

Using Other Web Page Features That Complement JavaScript

While JavaScript gives the Web page author incredible new flexibility, it's not an end-all. You should consider JavaScript as just another—albeit powerful—component of a well-designed Web page. As you develop solutions with JavaScript, you will undoubtedly tap into other Web page design techniques. These might include:

- More advanced HTML tags, such as text and graphics manipulation, client pull, backgrounds, frames, and tables.

- Embedded Java programs that run with or instead of a JavaScript program.

- Optional plug-ins, which are programs specifically designed to work with a given Web browser program, are another option.

- CGI scripts and programs, located on the server that the user connects with. Like JavaScript, these programs can control what the user sees and does in your Web page.

- Additional JavaScript programming *located on the server* that takes the place of a more complex CGI script or program.

Because these elements are key to using JavaScript successfully, you will learn more about each of them in this book. Do keep in mind that this book is primarily about JavaScript, however. A full discussion of these other topics is outside the scope of this book, and there are sources available that detail these subjects.

JavaScript and Computer Security

In the late 1980s, personal computers began to be "infected" by computer viruses—rogue programs that appeared to multiply from one program on the computer to the next. Once a virus infects a computer, it can taint any program that is subsequently run. Not all computer viruses destroy data, but all are nuisances.

Protection against computer viruses has become a major issue for computing in the 1990s. Many companies have strict policies against running any program—and even inserting diskettes—not previously vetted by an approved "anti-virus" program. This helps to minimize the effects of a virus breakout.

The Internet is ideal for spreading computer viruses. Data can be freely distributed across the net, and many companies have inadequate tools for testing against malevolent programs and documents obtained through the Internet. Fortunately, the design of Web pages, as well as the browser programs that fetch and view them, makes distributing a virus very difficult, if not downright impossible. Most security pundits consider it highly unlikely for a virus to be transmitted via a regular Web page, as documents formatted with HTML tags have no way to infect other programs or files.

Things are a little different with JavaScript. An HTML-only page is a relatively "dumb" document, with little or no decision-making capabilities. JavaScript, however, endows a Web document with smarts, so it stands to reason that with those smarts come the potential for catching a virus through the Web.

While the potential may exist, it is highly unlikely a virus will be passed. JavaScript programs absolutely cannot access memory locations in your computer. And, except for a very narrow and strict set of methods, a JavaScript program cannot store and retrieve data on your computer's hard drive. You do not have to worry that a rogue JavaScript page will somehow erase all the files on your company's server computer, because a JavaScript program simply lacks the means to do this.

Some might view JavaScript's inability to manipulate memory and files in a client computer as a shortcoming, and as a limitation to writing more sophisticated JavaScript applications. However, the restrictions placed on JavaScript are intentional, precisely to limit the possibility of spreading a virus via a Web page.

JavaScript and Computer Privacy

Spreading a virus via the Internet is only one of the issues of security. Another is the privacy of the data stored on your computer. The concern has been voiced that a Web page might contain the ability to covertly examine the contents of your computer's hard disk drive, looking for valuable data such as passwords and credit card numbers.

While this kind of scenario is somewhat plausible if you use browser enhancements such as plug-ins or Java, it is considered impossible or at least highly improbable with JavaScript. Again, the reason is a lack of commands that access memory locations in your computer and files on your hard drive.

Furthermore, JavaScript employs a data protection mechanism that constantly ensures that a program on the other end of the Internet connection does not attempt to access sensitive information. This mechanism was added when it was discovered—in an early beta of Netscape Navigator 2.0—that it was possible for a program running on an Internet server to obtain a list of previous sites you visited during the current on-line session. These lists can contain sensitive information such as passwords and database query statements. This security hole was quickly plugged in later beta versions of Netscape.

■■■■■■ **NOTE**

The initial release of Netscape 2.0 contained a flaw making it relatively easy for someone to "steal" e-mail names just by having a person visit a Web site. Since Netscape 2.01, JavaScript will not allow automatic and unassisted transmission of e-mail.

■■■■■

Differences between Java and JavaScript

Tables 3.1 through 3.6 give some specifics about the similarities and differences between Java and JavaScript. Bear in mind that these aren't the only differences, just the most salient ones.

■■■■■■ **Table 3.1** Command Structure

Java
_____

All computer languages use a group of programming commands to control execution. Many of these commands, such as *if*, are used identically across a broad number of languages. Java borrows the structure of its programming commands from the C and C++ languages. Like C (and its more complex brother, C++), Java uses a highly structured syntax that can take some time to learn. Despite popular belief, Java is not based on either C or C++. Rather, Java is a brand-new language that happens to use C/C++ command syntax.

JavaScript
_____

JavaScript's command syntax is also modeled after C and C++ (but mostly C). The designers of JavaScript intentionally made the JavaScript language syntax similar to Java so that you could learn JavaScript programming, then advance to Java programming if you wish. The Java/JavaScript compliance is mostly a nonissue, except for the case sensitivity of programming commands. Like C and C++, the command names in Java and JavaScript are case-sensitive. This is a common "gotcha" for programmers familiar with case-insensitive languages such as Basic.

■■■■■

■■■■■ **Table 3.2** Object Orientation

Java
___

Java is based on the design constructs of the C++ programming language. As mentioned above, Java's command structure is similar to C++, and it also uses the object-oriented design principles espoused in C++. Java requires very strict adherence to object-oriented design principles. You must be well versed in object-oriented program design and fully understand how to create and use classes and objects, how to hide or expose methods, and how to create and use all the data types used in a given Java program.

JavaScript
___

Conversely, while JavaScript uses C/C++-like commands, it is not based on object-oriented design principles. Because you do not need to create and use classes, JavaScript is considerably easier to use. While JavaScript isn't objected oriented, it does use the notion of rudimentary "objects" to simplify programming. Even if you've never encountered objects in a programming language before, you'll find their application in JavaScript relatively easy to comprehend.

■■■■■

■■■■■ **Table 3.3** Data Types

Java
___

Programs store and use a variety of data types, including numeric integers and "strings" of text characters. Like C and C++ programs, Java programs are built with strict adherence to data types. Before you create data such as a text string, you must first declare its type. You cannot later mix it with another data type. Professional programmers tend to prefer this method, even with its restrictions, because it helps to build more reliable programs.

JavaScript
___

In contrast to Java, JavaScript uses what's known as *loose data typing*. You do not need to define the type of data you want before you can use it. For example, if you want to store an integer value, you only need to tell JavaScript what number to use. You do not need to tell it that the number is an integer; JavaScript figures out the data type itself. In addition, you can readily mix and match data types. While this freedom does mean you have to be careful—otherwise your programs will not behave predictably—you will find that it's generally easier to write programs this way.

■■■■■

▰▰▰▰ **Table 3.4** References to Objects

Java
_____

As you've read, Java is based on object-oriented programming techniques, and one of these techniques is the ability to use and reference objects. In a Java program, references to objects are carefully checked to make sure the programmer hasn't made any serious mistakes. For instance, if the programmer has referenced an object that doesn't exist—the name of the object has been misspelled, for example—the compiler flags the error so that it can be repaired. This leads to more stable software, but it can be difficult and time-consuming as well.

JavaScript
_____

JavaScript also references objects (the design of the objects in JavaScript is much simpler than the design used in Java). Unlike Java, however, the names of objects aren't checked until the JavaScript program is run. Mistakes, if any, are encountered as "run-time errors," and the JavaScript program prematurely ends. Because of this, JavaScript programs can and do fail unexpectedly. Careful attention to detail, and thorough testing of the finished JavaScript program, helps to avoid many of these problems.

▰▰▰▰

▰▰▰▰ **Table 3.5** Source Code and Compilation

Java
_____

Java programs are written with a text editor or a Java editing program, then compiled using a special compiler written just for Java. The compiler produces a class file that is then referenced in your Web page, using the <APPLET> HTML tag. When a reader visits your Web page, the browser downloads the compiled applet file, and the Java program is then executed. Readers who visit your page can retain the class file on their computer for later (such as off-line) use. Because Java programs are compiled, the programming contained within them cannot be viewed. Those peeking at a Java class file see gibberish instead of recognizable programming code.

JavaScript
_____

JavaScript programs are entirely contained within Web documents and are not compiled. The programming commands are part of the Web page and are executed depending on the use of any of several HTML tags. Because JavaScript programs do not require a compilation step, they are naturally easier to write and implement. You place all the JavaScript commands within a set of <SCRIPT> and

■■■■ **Table 3.5** *Continued*

JavaScript
_____

</SCRIPT> tags in the document, and the user's Web browser takes care of the rest. Because a JavaScript program is not compiled, its contents can be easily viewed. If you wish to protect the programming you develop for your Web pages, Java—or some other technique, such as the add-in mechanism provided by Netscape—is more suitable.

■■■■

■■■■ **Table 3.6** Graphics Applications

Java
_____

Java is based on a predefined set of routines that you can use in your own programs. Among these routines are methods to display graphics within the browser window. Such graphics aren't limited to static GIF or JPEG images. Rather, Java graphics can be completely animated and produced on-the-fly. For example, a typical Java application displays an animated image of a football rotating in the air. Or, a Java application can create a wireframe model of a three-dimensional object and allow the reader to control the perspective of the object.

JavaScript
_____

JavaScript has no built-in graphics or animation features. JavaScript is limited to the same image display techniques already provided in Web documents—namely, the HTML <IMG> tag. You can use JavaScript to display GIF and JPEG images, but you have very little real control over what those images do, where they are located, and how they appear, beyond what is given to you with the <IMG> tag. Still, it's possible to create pseudo-animations with JavaScript. For example, you can load four or five images to create a little repeating cartoon. Another example is to use JavaScript to create graphics-enhanced games, such as the old memory game using pictures. Click on a square, and JavaScript can display the image hidden underneath. Click on another square to see if you've found a match of the same image.

■■■■

JavaScript FAQ

Following are frequently asked questions about the JavaScript and Web published topics addressed in this chapter.

What Is a Data Type?

First, let's define data. Data is information your computer stores or processes. The number 2 is data. It's called an integer data type because it's a whole number. Likewise, the number 3.14 is data, but it's called a floating-point number because it contains a decimal point.

The text "This is a test" is data. It's called a string because it is composed of a string of characters. Finally, the abstract values true and false are data. These values are called Boolean because they represent the two possible logic states—true and false.

Different data types are used to represent different forms of data. The more accurate the representation is, the better the output from the program. You cannot accurately represent a floating-point value such as 3.14 using an integer data type because integers can represent only whole numbers. Likewise, you cannot accurately represent a string as a number, especially if the string contains non-numeric digits (0 through 9).

Can I Use C Code with JavaScript?

Depends. The basic structure of JavaScript is very similar to C, using the same syntax for the following statements:

- /" and "/ comments (as well as the // C++ style of comments)
- if
- for
- while
- return

JavaScript also generally uses the same method of variable assignment and expression. That means a statement block (for example, if) can be constructed the same way:

```
if (name == "gordon") {
      // name equals "gordon"
} else {
      // name doesn't equal "gordon"
}
```

Very simple C programs can often be used as the basis of writing JavaScript code, but you should expect some hand-tweaking. It helps to be familiar with C syntax, so you know what all the language elements do. If you don't know C, you should not try to convert C to JavaScript. Learn C first, then tackle the job of rewriting it into JavaScript.

Here are the biggest areas of departure between C and JavaScript. Because C is a more robust language, it's easier to approach this from the standpoint of what JavaScript does not currently offer. This list isn't exhaustive, but points up the major differences.

- No data types (data types are determined by JavaScript when the script runs)
- No need (or way) to declare a variable type (no *int myvar*)
- No var[]={...} type implicit arrays
- No switch statement
- No file input or output library (for example, printf or sprintf)
- No console input library (such as scanf); input to the script is through objects such as form controls and hypertext links
- No support for strings as arrays of type char (in JavaScript, a string is just a collection of text in a special object)
- No pointers
- No structures or unions, though JavaScript does support structure- and union-like capabilities with array objects

In addition, JavaScript's variable scoping rules are slightly different than C's. Here are the rules:

- In JavaScript, a variable defined outside of a function is visible anywhere in the same document, including inside other functions, as long as the script is loaded. This is equivalent to a global variable declared outside of a function in C, except that in JavaScript the variable remains in memory even after the script has ended (in C, the variable vanishes when the program stops).
- In JavaScript, a variable defined in a function is also global, in the same manner as above, *unless* you precede it with the var statement. This is unlike C, in which variables declared inside a function are visible only within that function.

What Are the Main Differences between Java and JavaScript?

Java is a sophisticated and advanced programming language designed to create self-contained programs, as well as "applets" for use with software such as a World Wide

Web browser. Java is based on the C++ programming language and deeply embraces object-oriented programming precepts. Java programs must be compiled to a binary form before a browser such as Netscape 2.0 can use them. This compiling requires a software development kit, which is available free from Sun Microsystems, Java's creators, as well as from several third-party language development companies, such as Borland and Symantec.

JavaScript is a user-level scripting language. The JavaScript "program" is included as part of the HTML document retrieved by the browser program, and it does not need to be compiled before use. JavaScript programs don't need to be developed using a software development kit.

The JavaScript language was intentionally kept simple so that Web authors with limited programming experience could adequately harness its power. Because of this, JavaScript does not have the same power and capabilities as Java. Java allows for specific control of screen objects, files, and data. With it you can program complete computer applications, including a World Wide Web browser (such as HotJava, published by Sun).

Conversely, JavaScript limits access to the computer, prohibiting programmers from manipulating the screen or opening and saving data files. Many of these limitations in JavaScript also help to make it a "safer" programming language for the Internet. Lacking the ability to read, write, or erase files on your disk drive makes JavaScript an unlikely candidate for a damaging computer virus.

What about Compatibility with Browsers That Don't Support JavaScript?

One of the attractions of the Web is that most Web pages use the same standardized HTML tags. This makes it possible to view pages using a variety of browser programs. It also means that such pages are written for the lowest common denominator and tend to have a dry and static look. If you've visited a really "hot" (some describe them as "cool"!) Web page, no doubt it uses HTML tags that are not part of the accepted international standards. Such Web sites typically carry a disclaimer or notice that the page is best suited for a particular browser. This browser is often Netscape Navigator 2.0 or later, or Microsoft Internet Explorer 3.0 or later.

Like the added HTML tags in advanced browsers such as Netscape and Internet Explorer, JavaScript is not an Internet standard—at least not as of this writing—and not all browsers support it. Those browsers that lack JavaScript support cannot run the JavaScript programs embedded in the page. This limitation can have a major or minor impact, depending on how the page was designed.

On one end of the scale, if the contents of a page are built using JavaScript rather than standard HTML tags, then a non-JavaScript browser will display nothing. Generally, these kinds of pages are not recommended unless you are sure that your readership is equipped with JavaScript-compatible browsers. For example, if you're creating a Web page for exclusive use within your company, and you know all readers are equipped with a JavaScript-compatible browser, then you can be sure your pages will be properly rendered.

On the other end of the scale, if just the enhancements or accessories of a page require JavaScript, most visitors to your page will still be able to access its content (assuming the content is formatted using regular HTML tags). These readers may miss out on the advantages JavaScript provides, but they can nonetheless enjoy the other aspects of the page. This kind of page design is well suited for a Web site that might be visited by anyone, using any browser.

Is JavaScript the Best Tool for Every Job?

No. JavaScript is nifty–make no mistake about that. But it can be overused, too. Be careful of giving jobs to JavaScript that could be more easily handled using some other HTML technique. For example, suppose you want to reload the contents of a frame from the server every 30 seconds. While you could write a JavaScript for this purpose, the META tag as used in Netscape offers a far simpler approach. All you need is the following:

```
<META HTTP-EQUIV="Refresh" CONTENT=30>
```

Is JavaScript Cross-Platform?

Yes. JavaScript is not limited to any specific platform. In its current implementation in Netscape 2.0 and 3.0, JavaScript is supported under Windows 3.1 and 95/NT, Macintosh, and Unix X-Windows. JavaScript is openly and freely licensed and can be incorporated into any Internet application.

CORE JAVASCRIPT

4

OBJECTS

JavaScript is object crazy. You can't escape JavaScript's objects, no matter how hard you try. So, you might as well get to know them. You might even like them when you're through! In this chapter you'll find basic documentation on JavaScript's objects. Additional specific details on using the properties, methods, and events of these objects can be found in the following chapters:

- Chapter 5, "Properties"
- Chapter 6, "Methods and Functions"
- Chapter 10, "Events"

Also, consult the chapters in parts 3 and 4 of this book to discover practical, hands-on uses for these objects. Be sure to read these chapters for a more complete discussion on JavaScript objects:

- Chapter 11, "Defining Functions, Objects, and Methods," discusses creating user-defined objects.
- Chapter 15, "Using JavaScript and Frames," provides a full discourse on using JavaScript with the frames feature.

- Chapter 16, "Using JavaScript in Forms," and Chapter 18, "Using CGI with JavaScript," detail the combination of forms, CGI programs, and JavaScript.
- Chapter 21, "All About HTML," provides an overview of the structure of the most common HTML elements. Read this chapter as a review of HTML authoring.

Note that Netscape 3.0 supports additional objects, as described in Chapter 22.

Anchor Object

Properties	Methods	Events
None	None	None

The anchor object represents text used in the target of a hyperlink.

Property Of

document object

Syntax

Anchor objects are defined in a document using the <A> tag, as follows:

```
<A NAME=TargetName>Optional Text</A>
```

TargetName is the name of the anchor; *OptionalText* is optional text you wish to display with the target.

More Information

You may also create an anchor using the anchor method of the string object. See also anchors[] array, below.

Anchors[] Array

Properties	Methods	Events
length	None	None

The anchors[] array is an array variable listing all of the anchors in the document. In Netscape 2.0 and 3.0 the elements of the array are actually empty; the only possibly valuable information is provided by the length property.

Property Of

document object

Syntax

```
document.anchors.length
```

More Information

The following example demonstrates how to use the anchors[] array to determine the number of anchors in a document:

```
Ret = document.anchors.length;
alert ("Number of anchors in this document: " + Ret);
```

This array is somewhat useful, assuming that you name or number the anchors in the document in a consistent manner. For example, you can use the length information to determine the last anchor in a document. Your JavaScript program can then go to the last anchor:

```
Ret = document.anchors.length;
location = "#" + Ret;
```

The anchors in the document are named in this way:

```
<A NAME="1"></A>
...
<A NAME="2"></A>
...
```

Button Object

Properties	Methods	Events
form	click	onClick
name		
value		

Property Of

form object

Syntax

Buttons are created using the <INPUT> tag within a form:

```
<INPUT TYPE="button" NAME="myButton" VALUE="Click">
```

More Information

Buttons are most useful as "triggers" in JavaScript programs when used with the onClick event. Use buttons to activate some portion of your JavaScript. Here's a basic example:

```
<SCRIPT>
function testMe (button) {
        alert ("The text of the button you clicked is: " + button.value);
}
</SCRIPT>
<FORM>
<INPUT TYPE="button" NAME="button" VALUE="Click Me" onClick="testMe(this)">
</FORM>
```

■■■■■■ **NOTE**

The click method yields unpredictable results under Netscape 2.0. Avoid using it.

■■■■■■

Checkbox Object

Properties	Methods	Events
checked	click	onClick
defaultChecked		
form		
name		
value		

The checkbox object represents checkbox controls in forms.

Property Of

form object

Syntax

Check boxes are created using the <INPUT> tag within a form:

```
<INPUT TYPE="checkbox" NAME="myBox">This is a checkbox
```

More Information

Check boxes are used to turn options on and off. When off, the box is empty; when on, the box contains a check. Use the checked property (*not* the value property) of the checkbox to determine the current state. The value of the checked property is true if the box is checked and false if it is not. Here's a basic example:

```
<SCRIPT>
function testMe (form) {
        Ret = form.box.checked;
        alert ("The check box is: " + Ret);
}
</SCRIPT>
<FORM>
<INPUT TYPE="checkbox" NAME="box">This is a checkbox<P>
<INPUT TYPE="button" NAME="button" VALUE="Click Me"
onClick="testMe(this.form)">
</FORM>
```

▪▪▪▪▪▪▪ **NOTE**

The click method yields unpredictable results under Netscape 2.0. Avoid using it.

▪▪▪▪▪▪▪

Date Object

Properties	Methods	Events
None	getDate	None
	getDay	
	getHours	
	getMinutes	
	getMonth	

Properties	Methods	Events
	getSeconds	
	getTime	
	getTimeZoneoffset	
	getYear	
	parse	
	setDate	
	setHours	
	setMinutes	
	setMonth	
	setSeconds	
	setTime	
	setYear	
	toGMTString	
	toLocaleString	
	toString	
	UTC	

The Date object is used to return the current date and to perform date-related calculations.

Property Of

None (built-in object)

Syntax

Use the new construction operator every time you wish to work with a Date object:

```
date_obj = new Date(date/time);
```

date_obj is the name of the new date object you are creating; *date/time* is the optional date and time you wish to use for the date object. Omitting this parameter returns the current date and time. Once the new date object has been created, you may use one of the Date methods to extract useful information from the object.

More Information

Following are some examples of using the Date object:

```
// myDate object contains current date/time
```

```
myDate = new Date();
// myDate object contains date of last day in 1999
myDate = new Date(99, 11, 31);
// myDate object contains date of last day in 1999
myDate = new Date("December 21, 1999");
```

The date/time parameter for the Date object takes several formats: string and value.

The string method is "month day, year hours:minutes:seconds." The hours:minutes:seconds is optional if you don't care about the time.

The value method is "year, month, day, hours, minutes, seconds." The hours, minutes, and seconds parameters are optional if you don't care about the time.

- The month is zero-based, so January is 0.
- The year should be in the form *xx* (such as *97*) for years before 2000, and 1*xx* (such as *101*) for years 2000 and beyond.

▰▰▰▰ **NOTE**

A bug in Netscape 2.0 prevents you from using dates prior to January 1, 1970. Another bug prevents you from using the string method to create Date objects beyond 1999. Use the value method, described above, when creating Date objects for the years 2000 and over.

▰▰▰▰

After a Date object is created, use any of several properties. For example, the getHours property extracts the hours portion from the date object:

```
now = new Date();
Ret = now.getHours();
alert ("The hour is: " + Ret);
```

For the above, the hours are in 24-hour format, with *0* being midnight, *12* being noon; and *23* being 11 P.M.

Document Object

Properties	Methods	Events
alinkColor	clear	None
anchors[]	close	

Properties	Methods	Events
bgColor	open	
cookie	write	
fgColor	writeln	
forms[]		
lastModified		
linkColor		
links[]		
location		
referrer		
title		
vlinkColor		

The document object contains information about the current document, such as its title, when it was last modified, and the color of the background.

Property Of

window (or frame) object

Syntax

```
document.propertyname
```

or

```
document.method
```

propertyname is the name of a property you wish to see or set; *method* is the name of a document method you wish to use.

More Information

The document object is typically used the most in JavaScript programs because most objects you work with are themselves properties of the document object. For example, when referring to a control on a form, you use:

```
document.formname.controlname
```

where *formname* is the name of the form and *controlname* is the name of the control. If you don't specify the document object, JavaScript will not know how to refer to *formname*.

Elements[] Array

Properties	Methods	Events
Length	None	None

The elements[] array is an array variable listing all of the controls in the form.

Property Of

form

Syntax

```
document.formname.elements[x].propertyname
```

or

```
document.formname.elements.length
```

x is the number of the element as it appears in the form, starting with 0 for the first element, 1 for the second, and so forth. *Propertyname* is the property of the link you wish to get or set. *Formname* is the name of the form.

Frame Object

Properties	Methods	Events
frames[]	clearTimeout	onLoad
name	setTimeout	onUnload
length		
parent		
*self		
window		

*self is a synonym for the current frame

Frames are a special form of window object. To JavaScript, each frame is considered a separate window, which in turn has a "parent" window. This parent window is typically the frameset document, the document that includes the <FRAMESET> tags that define the frames. However, Netscape and other frames-compatible browsers support nested frames, so frames can be objects of other frames. For the sake of simplicity, this book assumes non-nested frame sets, which are by far the more common.

Property Of

window (or another frame)

Syntax

Frames are defined in the <FRAMESET> tag following this basic procedure:

```
<FRAMESET COLS="50%, 50%">
        <FRAME SRC="doc1.html" NAME="frame1">
        <FRAME SRC="doc2.html" NAME="frame2">
</FRAMESET>
```

The above creates two frames formatted in equal columns. The filenames *doc1.html* and *doc2.html* are used for the content. Frames are named to make them easier to use with JavaScript. Of course the above is just one of hundreds of possible permutations of frame arrangements.

More Information

To refer to a frame object, use "parent" to denote the parent frameset document, then the name of the frame:

```
parent.framename
```

where *framename* is the name of the frame to which you wish to refer. For example, if the name of the frame is myFrame, then you'd refer to it as:

```
parent.myFrame
```

You typically use frame references when testing or changing properties of the frame, or a document contained within a frame. For instance, suppose you wish to determine the URL of the frame. Continuing with the myFrame example, you'd use:

```
Ret = parent.myFrame.location;
alert (Ret);
```

Or, to determine the background color of the document used in myFrame, use:

```
Ret = parent.myFrame.document.bgColor;
alert ("The background color is: " + Ret);
```

An alternative method to referring to frame objects is using the frames[] array, detailed in the next section.

Frames[] Array

Properties	Methods	Events
length	None	None

The frames[] array is an array variable listing all of the frames in the frameset.

Property Of

window

Syntax

```
parent.frames[x]
```

x is the number of the frame you wish to use; start at 0 for the first frame defined in the frameset.

More Information

The frames[] array provides an alternative method to using frame objects. You can use numbers instead of names to refer to a frame. For example, if you wish to refer to the first frame of the frameset, use:

```
parent.frames[0]
```

Another handy use of the frames[] array, in conjunction with the length property, is to determine the number of frames in a frameset. If the number is 0, you know the window contains no frames. This can be useful information if you want to design a page that works with and without frames:

```
if (parent.frames.length == 0)
        // no frames used
else
        // frames used
```

Form Object

Properties	Methods	Events
action	submit	onSubmit
elements[]		
encoding		
length		
method		
name		
target		

The form object contains all the controls ("widgets") used in a given form of the document. Forms allow users to provide information, such as their name and e-mail address, and select options from lists, radio buttons, and checkboxes. Forms can be used with a CGI program on a server computer, or they can be used with JavaScript alone.

Property Of

document

Syntax

```
document.formname
```

formname is the name of the form.

More Info

Use the form object whenever you wish to interact with controls in a form. Because there can be more than one form in a document, the form object provides a way for JavaScript to differentiate between multiple forms. The form object to use can be referred to by name. The name of the form is defined in the <FORM> as follows:

```
<FORM NAME="formname">
```

Here's an example of retrieving the value of a text box in a form named myform, and displaying the value in an alert box:

```
<SCRIPT>
function testMe () {
        Ret = document.myform.box.value;
        alert ("The value of the text box is: " + Ret);
```

```
}
</SCRIPT>
<FORM NAME="myform">
Type something here<INPUT TYPE="text" NAME="box"><P>
<INPUT TYPE="button" NAME="button" VALUE="Click Me" onClick="testMe()">
</FORM>
```

You can also pass the current form object to a function using this keyword, as shown below. In this case, a variable named form (not to be confused with the generic name of the form object) passed to the testMe function serves to identify the form object to use.

```
<SCRIPT>
function testMe (form) {
        Ret = form.box.value;
        alert ("The value of the text box is: " + Ret);
}
</SCRIPT>
<FORM>
Type something here<INPUT TYPE="text" NAME="box"><P>
<INPUT TYPE="button" NAME="button" VALUE="Click Me" onClick="testMe(this.form)">
</FORM>
```

Forms[] Array

Properties	Methods	Events
length	None	None

The forms[] array is an array variable listing all of the forms in the document.

Property Of

document

Syntax

```
document.forms[x]
```

x is the number of the form you wish to use; start at 0 for the first form defined in the document.

More Information

The forms[] array provides an alternative method to using form objects. You can use numbers instead of names to refer to a form. For example, if you wish to refer to the first form of the document, use:

```
document.forms[0]
```

Hidden Object

Properties	Methods	Events
defaultValue	None	None
form		
name		
value		

The hidden object represents a form control defined using the TYPE="hidden" attribute. Hidden objects are text boxes that are not displayed in the document. They can be used for temporary storage of data that the user does not see.

Property Of

form

Syntax

```
formname.hiddenname
```

formname is the name of the form; *hiddenname* is the name of the hidden control.

More Information

Hidden objects are created using the following syntax:

```
<INPUT TYPE="hidden" NAME="hiddenbox" VALUE="initial">
```

You can provide your own NAME (hiddenbox has been used here). The VALUE attribute defines the initial value when the document is loaded or reset. You may omit this attribute if you don't wish to define an initial value.

Hidden objects store textual information within a form that the user doesn't see. Hidden text boxes are typically used with CGI scripts to pass special data from the browser to the server, and back again.

▬▬▬▬ **NOTE**

The value of hidden boxes is reset when the document is reloaded. This is contrary to the value of most other form elements, such as text boxes or checkboxes.

▬▬▬▬

To read a value from a hidden box, use the syntax:

```
Ret = formname.hiddenname.value
```

where *Ret* is a variable, *formname* is the name of the form, and *hiddenname* is the name of the hidden text box. Here is an example:

```
Ret = myform.hiddenbox.value;
```

To set a value in a hidden box, use the syntax:

```
formname.hiddenname.value = val
```

where *val* is the value to set, *formname* is the name of the form, and *hiddenname* is the name of the hidden text box. Here is an example:

```
myform.hiddenbox.value = "1000";
```

History Object

Properties	Methods	Events
length	back	None
	forward	
	go	

Use the history object to view a list of the URLs the user has visited. You can use the history object to go forward or back through the history list. In Netscape 2.0, the history object is intentionally crippled so that the content of the history list is not visible to JavaScript. As a result, a script is not allowed to report the URLs that a user has visited.

Property Of

window

Syntax

```
window.location
```

More Information

The back and forward methods replicate the functionality of the Back and Forward buttons of the browser. Use them with the history object to navigate one URL at a time through the history list. For example, you can use:

```
history.back() // go back one URL in the history list
history.forward() // go forward one URL in the history list
```

The go method goes to a specific URL in the history list; provide the "offset" of the URL that you want to go to relative to the current URL in the history list. For example, if the URL you want is three back in the history list, use:

```
history.go(-3);
```

Link Object

Properties	Methods	Events
hash		onClick
host		onMouseOver
hostname		
href		
pathname		
port		
protocol		
search		
target		

The link object represents text used in a hyperlink.

Property Of

document object

Syntax

Link objects are defined in a document using the <A> tag, as follows:

```
<A LINK=URL>Text_or_Image</A>
```

Url is the URL you want to link to, *Text_or_Image* is the text and/or <IMG> image you wish to display as the link (or "click") text.

More Information

The link object serves to provide information about each link in a document. This information includes the URL of the link. The link object is also used with the onClick and onMouseOver event handlers to specify how JavaScript should act when the link is clicked, and when the mouse is passed over the link, respectively.

Each link object in a document is uniquely identified using the links[] array, detailed below. You may also create a link using the link method of the string object.

links[] array

Properties	Methods	Events
length	None	None

The links[] array is an array variable listing all of the links in the document. The links[] array can be used to set or get the properties of a specific link in the document.

Property Of

document object

Syntax

```
document.links[x].propertyname
```

or

```
document.links.length
```

x is the number of the links as they appear in the document, starting with 0 for the first link in the document, 1 for the second, and so forth. *Propertyname* is the property of the link you wish to get or set.

More Information

The following example demonstrates how to use the links[] array to determine the HREF of the first link in the document.

```
Ret = document.links[0].href;
alert ("The href of the first link is: " + Ret);
```

Use the length property of the links[] array to determine the number of links in a document. A length of 0 means there are no links. The following quick test enumerates all of the links and displays the HREF for each one (if there are no links, the alert box never appears):

```
<A HREF="test1.html">Click 1</A>
<A HREF="test2.html">Click 2</A>
<A HREF="test3.html">Click 3</A>
<SCRIPT>
for (Count = 0; Count < document.links.length; Count++) {
        Ret = document.links[Count].href;
        alert ("The HREF for link #" + Count + " is " + Ret);
}
</SCRIPT>
```

Location Object

Properties	Methods	Events
hash		None
host		
hostname		
href		
pathname		
port		
post		
protocol		
search		
target		

Use the location object to get or set the URL of a window or frame.

Property Of

window

Syntax

window.location

The window object is optional if you are referring to the location of the current window.

More Information

The location object has two uses:

- It returns the URL (or parts of the URL) of the window.
- It sets the URL of the window.

To return the URL of the window, use the location object and one of its properties, such as href or host:

```
Ret = location.href;    // URL of window
Ret = location.host     // host portion of URL of window
```

To set the URL of the window, specify the URL for the location object. JavaScript lets you specify a property to change just one aspect of the URL, but changing the entire URL is generally safer, using one of the following approaches:

```
location = "newurl.html";
location.href = "newurl.html";
```

In both cases, newurl.html is the URL you want to use for the window.

You are not limited to setting the URL of just the main window. You can use the URL of individual frames, providing that you specify the full path to the frame object. For best results, provide a fully qualified absolute URL, rather than just a relative URL. Here is an example:

```
parent.frame1.location = "http://domain.com/new_location.html"
```

Math Object

Properties	Methods	Events
E	abs	None
LN2	acos	

Properties	Methods	Events
LN10	asin	
LOG2E	atan	
LOG10E	ceil	
PI	cos	
SQRT1_2	exp	
SQRT2	floor	
	log	
	max	
	min	
	pow	
	random	
	round	
	sin	
	sqrt	
	tan	

The Math object provides a number of built-in advanced math functions.

Property Of

None (built-in object)

Syntax

```
Math.propertyname
```

or

```
with (Math) {

        propertyname

    }
```

propertyname is one of the Math object properties.

More Information

All of the properties of the Math object are read-only and are used to provide additional math capabilities. For example, the round property rounds a number. Here's an example:

```
Ret = Math.round (123.456);
alert (Ret);    // displays 123
```

Navigator Object

Properties	Methods	Events
appName	None	None
appVersion		
appCodeName		
userAgent		

The navigator object provides useful information about the browser, including its name, its version, and the platform under which it is running.

Property Of

None (navigator is considered a built-in object of Netscape)

Syntax

```
navigator.propertyname
```

propertyname is one of the navigator object properties.

More Information

Use the navigator object when you need to know the version or platform of Netscape being used. For example, the following displays the version of Netscape, as well as platform information:

```
Ret = navigator.appVersion;
alert ("This version of Netscape is " + Ret);
```

Options[] Array

Properties	Methods	Events
options[].defaultSelected	None	None
options[].index		
options[].length		
options[].name		
options[].selected		
options[].selectedIndex		
options[].text		
options[].value		

The options[] array is an array variable listing all of the options in a form selection list. The primary use of the options[] array is to determine which options the user has chosen.

Property Of

select object

Syntax

```
document.formname.selectname.options[x]
```

formname is the name of the form in the document, *selectname* is the name of the select list, and *x* is the number of the option in the list (counting starts at 0).

More Information

Use the options[] array to test the selected option in a selection list. Here's an example:

```
<SCRIPT>
function testMe (form) {
        Ret = form.selection.selectedIndex;
        Item = form.selection.options[Ret].text
        alert ("Item number is " + Ret + "\nItem text is " + Item)

}
</SCRIPT>

<FORM>
<SELECT NAME="selection">
<OPTION>Item 1
<OPTION>Item 2
<OPTION>Item 3
<OPTION>Item 4
</SELECT><P>
<INPUT TYPE="button" NAME="button" VALUE="Click" onClick="testMe(this.form)">
</FORM>
```

The testMe function first determines the selected option using the selectedIndex property of the select object (named selection). It then determines the text of the selected option using the text property of the options[] array. This information is then displayed in an alert box.

Password Object

Properties	Methods	Events
defaultValue	focus	None
form	blur	
name	select	
value		

The password object represents a form control defined using the TYPE="password" attribute. Password objects are text boxes that display asterisks when the user types into them. They are useful for sending passwords to CGI programs running on a server.

Property Of

form

Syntax

```
formname.passwordname
```

formname is the name of the form; *passwordname* is the name of the password control.

More Information

Password objects are created using the following syntax:

```
<INPUT TYPE="password" NAME="passwordbox">
```

You can provide your own NAME (passwordbox was used here). Unlike text boxes and hidden boxes, the VALUE attribute is not defined with password boxes.

▬▬▬ NOTE

Because of security reasons, the value of password boxes cannot be read using JavaScript. The value property is always blank.

Radio Object

Properties	Methods	Events
checked	click	onClick
defaultChecked		
form		
length		
name		
value		

The radio object represents radio button controls in forms.

Property Of

form object

Syntax

Radio buttons are created using the <INPUT> tag within a form:

```
<INPUT TYPE="radio" NAME="groupName">This is a radio button
```

More Information

Radio buttons are used in groups of two or more; only one button in the group can be selected at time. When off (unselected), the radio button is empty; when on, the button is filled. Use the checked property (*not* the value property) of the radio button to determine the current state. The value of the checked property is true if the button is checked, false if it is not. Radio buttons are referenced as an array, using the name of the radio button group as the array name. Here's a basic example:

```
<SCRIPT>
function testMe (form) {
        Ret = form.rad[0].checked;
        alert ("Radio button 1 is: " + Ret);
}
</SCRIPT>
<FORM>
<INPUT TYPE="radio" NAME="rad" onClick=0>This is radio button 1<P>
<INPUT TYPE="radio" NAME="rad" onClick=0>This is radio button 2<P>
```

```
<INPUT TYPE="radio" NAME="rad" onClick=0>This is radio button 3<P>
<INPUT TYPE="button" NAME="button" VALUE="Click Me" onClick="testMe(this.form)">
</FORM>
```

■■■■■ NOTE

The click method yields unpredictable results under Netscape 2.0. Avoid using it.

■■■■■

Reset Object

Properties	Methods	Events
form	click	onClick
name		
value		

The reset object is the "Reset" button in a form. This button is typically used to reset the content of a form that is used with a CGI program running on a server.

Property Of

form object

Syntax

```
form.resetname
```

resetname is the name of the reset button.

More Information

The Reset button is typically not used with JavaScript. In fact, clicking the Reset button resets the form even when you have specified an onClick event handler with the Reset button or an onSubmit event for the form.

■■■■■ NOTE

JavaScript under Netscape 2.0 lacks a reset method to easily reset the contents of forms. However, you can accomplish the same thing with the following:

```
location = location;
```

This simply causes Netscape to reload the entire page, including the form. The form controls are reset to blank, or their default values.

■■■■

Select Object

Properties	Methods	Events
form	None	onBlur
length		onChange
name		onFocus
options[]		
selectedIndex		

The select object represents selection lists in forms.

Property Of

form object

Syntax

```
document.formname.selectname
```

formname is the name of the form, and *selectname* is the name of the select list.

Select lists are creating using the following basic syntax:

```
<SELECT NAME="name">
<OPTION>This is option 1
<OPTION>This is option 2
<OPTION>This is option 3
</SELECT>
```

More Information

The following example demonstrates how to use JavaScript to determine the number of the option that is currently selected in the list. (If there is no selection, the value is −1.)

```
<HTML>
<HEAD>
```

```
<TITLE>List Box Test</TITLE>
<SCRIPT LANGUAGE="JavaScript">
function testSelect(form) {
        alert (form.list.selectedIndex);
}
</SCRIPT>
</HEAD>
<BODY>
<FORM NAME="myform" ACTION="" METHOD="GET">
<INPUT TYPE="button" NAME="button" Value="Test" onClick="testSelect(this.form)">
<SELECT NAME="list" SIZE="3">
<OPTION>This is item 1
<OPTION>This is item 2
<OPTION>This is item 3
</SELECT>
</FORM>
</BODY>
</HTML>
```

String Object

Properties	Methods	Events
length	anchor	None
	big	
	blink	
	bold	
	charAt	
	fixed	
	fontcolor	
	fontsize	
	indexOf	
	italics	
	lastindexOf	
	link	
	small	

Properties	Methods	Events
	strike	
	sub	
	substring	
	sup	
	toLowerCase	
	toUpperCase	

The string object is implicit; whenever you define a new variable containing a string, JavaScript creates a string object for it. You don't reference the string object itself, but rather the resulting variable.

Property Of

None (string objects are considered built into the browser)

Syntax

```
stringname = "value"
```

stringname is the name of the string variable; *value* is the content you want to store in the variable. The *stringname* variable can then be referenced elsewhere in the script.

Submit Object

Properties	Methods	Eventt
form	click	onClick
name		
value		

The submit object is the Submit Query button on a form. This button is typically used to submit the content of a form that is used with a CGI program running on a server.

Property Of

form object

Syntax

```
form.submitname
```

submitname is the name of the submit button.

More Information

You may use either a submit button or a user-defined button to submit a form to a CGI program using JavaScript. The submit button is handy if the form will be used by non-JavaScript browsers. Those with a JavaScript-enabled browser can enjoy the extra benefits your JavaScript code provides; those without a JavaScript-enabled browser will still be able to submit forms to a CGI program.

For example, those with a JavaScript browser will be prompted if they wish to submit the form. The user can respond by choosing OK or Cancel. The form is submitted without prompt for those without JavaScript.

```
<SCRIPT>
function submitMe (form) {
        if (confirm ("Are you sure you submit this form?"))
                return (true);
        else
                return (false);
}
</SCRIPT>

<FORM onSubmit="return submitMe(this)">
<INPUT TYPE="text" NAME="box" VALUE="">
<INPUT TYPE="submit">
</FORM>
```

Text Object

Properties	Methods	Events
defaultValue	focus	onBlur
form	blur	onChange
name	select	onFocus
value		onSelect

The text object represents a form control defined using the TYPE="text" attribute. Text objects are text boxes that the user can type into.

Property Of

form object

Syntax

```
formname.textname
```

formname is the name of the form; *textname* is the name of the text control.

More Information

Text objects are created using the following syntax:

```
<INPUT TYPE="text" NAME="textbox" VALUE="initial">
```

You can provide your own NAME (textbox was used here). The VALUE attribute defines the initial value when the document is loaded or reset. You may omit this attribute if you don't wish to define an initial value.

To read a value from a text box, use the syntax:

```
Ret = formname.textname.value
```

where *Ret* is a variable, *formname* is the name of the form, and *textname* is the name of the text box. Here is an example:

```
Ret = myform.textbox.value;
```

To set a value in a text box, use the syntax:

```
formname.textname.value = val
```

where *val* is the value to set, *formname* is the name of the form, and *textname* is the name of the text box. Here is an example:

```
myform.textbox.value = "1000";
```

Textarea Object

Properties	Methods	Events
defaultValue	focus	onBlur
form	blur	onChange
name	select	onFocus

Properties	Methods	Events
value		onSelect

The textarea object represents a form control defined using the <TEXTAREA> tag. Textarea objects are multi-line text boxes that the user can type into.

Property Of

form object

Syntax

```
formname.textareaname
```

formname is the name of the form; *textareaname* is the name of the text control.

More Information

Textarea objects are created using the following syntax:

```
<TEXTAREA NAME="textareabox" COLS="20" ROWS="5">
</TEXTAREA>
```

You can provide your own NAME (textareabox was used here). The COLS and ROWS attributes are optional, but recommended as the default size of the text area is generally too small to use. The example above creates a text area that's 20 character columns wide, by 5 lines (rows) high.

To read a value from a textarea box, use the syntax:

```
Ret = formname.textareaname.value
```

where *Ret* is a variable, *formname* is the name of the form, and *textareaname* is the name of the text box. Here is an example:

```
Ret = myform.textareebox.value;
```

To set a value in a textarea box, use the syntax:

```
formname.textareaname.value = val
```

where *val* is the value to set, *formname* is the name of the form, and *textareaname* is the name of the textarea box. Here is an example:

```
myform.textareabox.value = "1000";
```

Window Object

Properties	Methods	Events
defaultStatus	alert	onLoad
frames[]	close	onUnload
length	clearTimeout	
name	confirm	
parent	open	
self*	prompt	
status	setTimeout	
top		
window		

*self is a synonym for the current window

The window object represents the content of an entire browser window. Each window opened by the browser has a separate identity and a separate history list. Windows can further be divided into frames. Documents are opened into the whole window, or each pane if using frames.

Property Of

none (the window object is considered to belong to the browser)

Syntax

```
window.propertyname
```

or

```
window.methodname
```

propertyname is the name of a property; *methodname* is the name of a method.

■■■ NOTE

The window object is usually inferred, and therefore reference to it is omitted. For example, the following do the same thing:

```
window.location = "myurl.html";
location = "myurl.html";
```

The window object can also be referred to using any of several synonyms, depending on the context. Assuming a single window (no frames), all of the following have the same meaning:

```
window.location = "myurl.html";
parent.location = "myurl.html";
top.location = "myurl.html";
self.location = "myurl.html";
location = "myurl.html";
```

The synonyms come in handy when you use frames and need to differentiate between window objects (each frame is considered a window object, "owned" by a parent window object).

▮▮▮▮▮▮

More Information

New window objects can be opened using JavaScript, with the window.open method. This method lets you open new, blank windows, or new windows containing content from an HTML document. Here is the basic syntax for both approaches:

```
// open a new, blank window
win = window.open ("", "newwin");
// open a new window, and fill it with the specified document
win = window.open ("mydoc.html", "newwin");
```

▮▮▮▮▮▮ **NOTE**

The Macintosh and X-Windows platforms of Netscape 2.0 suffers a bug whereby you must call the window.open method twice in order to open a new window and fill it with a document. For example:

```
win = window.open ("mydoc.html", "newwin");
win = window.open ("mydoc.html", "newwin");
```

This does not adversely affect Netscape under other platforms, so it is safe to include this code for all versions.

Another work-around for this bug is to call the window.open method once, then explicitly set the URL of the new window using the location object:

```
win = window.open ("mydoc.html", "newwin");
win.location = "mydoc.html";
```

■■■■

Netscape names all windows you open with window.open, as long as you provide a name as the second parameter for window.open. This name is considered a target name and behaves as any other Netscape target name; targets are typically used to load URLs into window using links. For example, the following link also opens a new window and loads the specified document into it. If a window with the specified target name is already open, then Netscape keeps the same window and opens the specified document into it.

```
<A HREF"mydoc.html" TARGET="newwin">Click Me!</A>
```

Because the window name is a target, it must follow target naming standards: specifically, no spaces or other punctuation characters. You may use the _ (underscore) character, except as the first character in the name. You can use upper- and lowercase letters, but standard practice is to use all lowercase.

PROPERTIES

Properties are behaviors of objects. A behavior is something that describes a particular aspect of an object. In the real world, a window has an obvious behavior: it's either opened or closed. A TV has a number of behaviors: whether it's on or off, what channel it is showing, its volume, and so forth.

In the world of JavaScript, properties are used to "reflect" a certain state of the browser or the document being viewed. For instance, one property for the document object is bgColor. The bgColor property reflects the current background color of the document.

This chapter is a reference guide to JavaScript's object properties. The properties are listed by group so that you can see how they interact.

Note that Netscape 3.0 offers additional object properties. Refer to Chapter 22 for more information.

Browser Properties

The browser properties reflect settings in the navigator object. All browser properties are read-only.

Property	Description
appCodeName	"Code name" for the current browser
appName	Application name for the current browser
appVersion	Version number of the current browser
userAgent	The user agent string sent from the browser to the server

Syntax

The syntax for all navigator properties is:

```
navigator.property;
```

where *property* is the property you wish to use, such as:

```
navigator.userAgent;
```

Example

The following example displays the application name of the browser (Netscape in this case).

```
Ret = navigator.appName;
alert (Ret);
```

More Information

This table displays some typical values returned from the navigator properties:

Property	Typical Value
appCodeName	Mozilla
appName	Netscape
appVersion	2.0 (Win95; I)
userAgent	Mozilla/2.0 (Win95; I)

userAgent is one of the more useful navigator properties because it provides all the information you need to determine the name, version, and platform of the user's browser. The general format is:

Name/Version (*Platform*; *OtherInfo*)

- *Name* is the code name or real name of the browser. In the case of Netscape, this name is Mozilla.

- *Version* is the version of the browser, such as 2.0, 2.01, or 3.0.

- *Platform* is the platform the user is running under, such as Win95, Win16, X11 (Unix), or Macintosh.

- *OtherInfo* provides additional information about the browser, such as I for International version or U for the domestic (US) version for the Windows versions. Macintosh versions provide the processor (68K or PCC) for *OtherInfo*.

▬▬▬ **NOTE**

None of the navigator properties is guaranteed to return the same kind of information in all cases for all platforms. If you wish to test for the existence of a given string in the userAgent return value, use the indexOf method to locate the string anywhere within the value. Do not depend on the absolute position of characters in the string, as this will vary depending on platform, version, and other variables.

▬▬▬

Document Information and Appearance Properties

The properties for document appearance return and control the look of the document. Additional properties for document information return current information about the document. Document information properties (marked with an asterisk) are read-only.

Property	Description
alinkColor	The color for active links in the document*
anchors[]	List of all anchors in the document*
bgColor	Background color of the document
cookie	Semi-permanent storage of textual information
defaultStatus	Default text of status bar
fgColor	Text color of the document*

Property	Description
forms[]	List of forms in the document*
lastModified	The date the document was last modified
linkColor	The color of unvisited links in the document*
links[]	A list of links in the document*
location	The complete URL of the document
referrer	The URL of the referring (linked from) document
status	The current text of the status bar
title	The title of the document*
vlinkColor	The color of visited links in a document*

Syntax

Use this basic syntax for all the document properties:

```
document.property;
```

property is the property you wish to use.

Examples

To read a property:

```
Ret = document.title;   // returns the title
alert (Ret);
```

To set a property (assuming it is not read-only):

```
document.status = "This is new status text";
```

More Information

Here are typical values returned from document properties. Values shown in <> brackets are array objects; each element of the array contains data about a specific item in that object.

Property	Typical Value
alinkColor	#ff0000
anchors	<array of anchors in document, if any>
bgColor	#c0c0c0
cookie	(text string of "cookies" for this document, if any)

Property	Typical Value
defaultStatus	This is a specified default status
fgColor	#000000
forms	<array of forms in document, if any>
lastModified	Tue Mar 12 13:35:50 1996
linkColor	#0000ee
location	http://thisdoc.html
referrer	http://somedoc.html
status	This is a specified status
title	This is a Document
vlinkColor	#551a8b

████████ **NOTE**

In Netscape 2.0 the xxColor properties are generally considered read-only. However, under the Windows platforms of Netscape 2.0, you can set the background color using bgColor. Setting the bgColor property immediately changes the background color, but only for the Windows platforms. On other platforms the color does not change—or it does change, but any text displayed in the document is obliterated.

████████

Form and Form Control Properties

The forms properties return and control form elements, including the form itself, and all controls ("widgets") in the form.

Property	Description
action	Destination URL for a form
defaultChecked	Default selection state of a check box or radio button
defaultSelected	Default selection of an option list
defaultValue	Default value of text box or text area
checked	State of a check box or radio button in form
elements[]	List of form elements in the document

Property	Description
encoding	MIME encoding format for a form
form	Parent form object
index	A specific option in a selection list within a form
length	The number of items in a form object
method	Posting method for a form (get or post)
name	The name of a form object
options[]	A list of options in a selection list within a form
selected	Current state of a check box or radio button
selectedIndex	The selected option in a selection list within a form
target	The name of the targeted form
text	The text of an option in a selection list within a form
value	The text of a text box or text area

Syntax

The following properties return text or number values:

- action
- defaultChecked
- defaultSelected
- defaultValue
- checked
- encoding
- index
- length
- method
- name
- selected
- selectedIndex
- target

- text
- value

These properties are used with the syntax:

document.*formname.controlname.property*

formname is the name of the form in the document, *controlname* is the name of the control; and *property* is the property you wish to use.

(Instead of *formname,* you can use forms[x], where x represents the number of the form in the document. Numbering starts at 0 for the first form in the document, such as *document.forms[0].* This alternative method applies to all of the references to *formname* throughout this section.)

The following properties are arrays; each element of the array contains additional properties of the form.

- elements[] (all form elements)
- options[] (all options in a selection list)

The syntax for the elements[] property is:

document.*formname.controlname*.elements[x]

formname is the name of the form in the document, *controlname* is the name of the control; x is the index of the form element (such as push button or text box) you want to reference.

The syntax for the options[] property is:

document.*formname.listname*.options[x]

formname is the name of the form in the document, *listname* is the name of the selection list in the form; x is the index of the option you want to reference.

Examples

Here are examples of using the form and form control properties. The examples use the following test form:

```
<FORM NAME="myform" ACTION="http://mydomain.com/test.html" METHOD=get>
```

```
<INPUT TYPE="text" NAME="textbox" VALUE="Original value"><BR>
<INPUT TYPE="radio" NAME="rad" VALUE=0 CHECKED onClick=0><BR>
<INPUT TYPE="radio" NAME="rad" VALUE=0 onClick=0><BR>
<INPUT TYPE="radio" NAME="rad" VALUE=0 onClick=0><BR>
<INPUT TYPE="checkbox" NAME="chk" VALUE=1 CHECKED><BR>
<INPUT TYPE="button" NAME="button" VALUE="Click Me" onClick="test()"><BR>
<SELECT NAME="selectlist">
<OPTION SELECTED>This is item 1
<OPTION>This is item 2
<OPTION>This is item 3
</SELECT><BR>
</FORM>
```

Examples Property	Examples Return Value
document.myform.textbox.value	Returns/sets the text in the textbox
document.myform.rad[1].checked	Returns/sets selection state of the second radio button
document.myform.rad[0].defaultChecked	Returns "true"
document.myform.rad[1].defaultChecked	Returns "false"
document.myform.chk.checked	Returns/sets selection state of the checkbox
document.myform.selectlist.selectedIndex	Returns the number of the selected option in the list box
document.myform.selectlist[0].defaultSelected	Returns "true"
document.myform.selectlist[2].defaultSelected	Returns "false"
document.myform.action	Returns "http://mydomain.com/test.html"
document.myform.method	Returns "get"
document.myform.length	Returns "7"
document.myform.name	Returns "<undefined>"
document.myform.textbox.name	Returns "textbox"

Content of text boxes, and the selection state of radio buttons and checkboxes, can be read as well as set using JavaScript. The following code displays this text in the text box, then changes it.

```
alert (document.myform.textbox.value);
document.myform.textbox.value = "New value";
```

This displays the current selection state of the checkbox, then sets it in the opposite state (note the ! not operator used on the second line):

```
alert (document.myform.chk.checked);
document.myform.chk.checked = !document.myform.chk.checked;
```

More Information

Not all properties apply to each form control. The following lists provide the categories.

Properties for the form object include:

- action–action (URL) for form
- elements[]—array of controls in form
- encoding—encoding of form
- length—number of controls in form
- method—action (get, post) for form
- target—target for form

Properties for text boxes, password boxes, hidden text boxes, and text areas include:

- defaultValue—default content of box or text area
- form—name of parent form
- value—current content of box or text area

Properties for radio buttons include:

- defaultChecked—default checked state
- checked—current checked state
- form—name of parent form
- length—number of radio buttons in group
- name—name of button control group
- value—value of button (VALUE=...)

Properties for checkboxes include:

- defaultChecked -0- default checked state
- checked—current checked state

- form—name of parent form
- name—name of checkbox
- value—value of button (VALUE=...)

Properties for buttons (button, submit, reset) include:

- form—name of parent form
- name—name of button
- value—text of button

Properties for selection lists include:

- form—name of parent form
- length—number of items in selection
- name—name of selection list
- options[]—array of options (text items) in list
- selectedIndex—index value of selected option (starts at 0)
- options[x].defaultSelected—default setting for x option
- options[x].index—index of x option
- options[x].selected—selection state of x option
- options[x].text—text of x option
- options[x].value—value of x option (set dynamically and passed to server)

The JavaScript/form combination is a somewhat complex and detailed science. Be sure to read Chapter 16, "Using JavaScript in Forms," to learn how these properties interact with one another and how you can use them to read and/or change form content.

Link Properties

The link properties return and control aspects of links (except for anchors.length, the anchors[] array returns only null). Link properties are read/write, but it is safest to use them as read-only.

Property	Description
hash	Text following the hash (#) symbol in a URL
host	The hostname:port portion of a URL

Property	Description
hostname	The host and domain (or IP address) of a URL
href	An entire URL
length	The number of anchors or links
pathname	The path portion of a URL
port	The port portion of a URL
protocol	The protocol portion of a URL
search	The search portion of a URL
target	The name of the targeted link

Syntax

The syntax for all link properties is:

```
document.links[x].property;
```

x is the index of the link you wish to use (numbering starts at 0 for the first link); *property* is the property you wish to use.

Example

This example retrieves the href of the first link in the document and displays it:

```
Ret = document.links[0].href;
alert (Ret);
```

More Information

Given the URL:

```
http://mydomain.com:80/javascript/index.html#contents
```

here's how the different document URL properties divvy up the returned string. If a property doesn't belong to the string (there is no hash value, for example), then the property is blank.

Property	Resulting String
hash	#contents
host	mydomain.com:80
hostname	mydomain.com:80

Property	Resulting String
href	http://mydomain.com:80/javascript/index.html#contents
pathname	/mydomain.com:80/javascript/index.html
port	:80
protocol	http:
search	N/A; see below

The location.search property is special case. It contains the "search" portion of a URL; this is the portion of the URL following the ? character.

Math Properties

These properties provide standard values used in math equations. The Math properties are read-only. (The property names are capitalized here following a programming convention whereby *constants*—values constant that cannot be changed—are indicated by using all uppercase.)

Property	Description
E	Euler's constant and the base of natural logarithms (About 2.118)
LN2	The natural logarithm of 2
LN10	The natural logarithm of 10
LOG2E	The base 2 logarithm of e
LOG10E	The base 10 logarithm of e
PI	The numeric equivalent of PI, or approximately 3.14
SQRT1_2	The square root of one-half
SQRT2	The square root of 2

Syntax

All of the Math properties use the same basic syntax:

```
Math.property
```

property is the property you wish to use, such as

Math.E

Math.PI

Example

The following example returns pi, or 3.14159....

```
Ret = Math.PI;
alert (Ret);
```

String Properties

The string object has one property, which is length (the content of the string is not a traditional property of the string object).

Property	Description
length	The length of a string

Syntax

```
string.length
```

string is the string you wish to use.

NOTE

In JavaScript some things that look like strings aren't. For example, the return value of

```
Ret = window.location;
```

is actually an object, though if you were to view the object using the alert method you'd see a string value. These objects-as-strings must be converted to a true string before you can use the length property. Here's one method:

```
Temp = window.location.toString();
Ret = Temp.length;
alert (Ret);
```

Window URL Properties

The window URL properties return or control the current window URL. Except for the base URL itself, URL properties are considered read-only. JavaScript generally allows you to change one property of the URL without changing the entire URL, but this can lead to unexpected results.

Property	Description
hash	Text following the hash (#) symbol in a URL
host	The hostname:port portion of a URL
hostname	The host and domain (or IP address) of a URL
href	An entire URL
pathname	The path portion of a URL
port	The port portion of a URL
protocol	The protocol portion of a URL
referrer	The URL of the referring (linked from) document
search	The search portion of a URL

Syntax

The syntax for all window properties is:

location.*property*;

property is the property you wish to use.

■■■■■ **NOTE**

There are two "locations" in JavaScript: a location object under the window object, and a location property under the document object. *The properties in this section are not used with document.location.*

■■■■■

Example

The following example displays the URL of the current window:

```
Ret = location.href;
alert (Ret);
```

More Information

To change the URL of the window, specify the new URL using just the location object, as in:

```
location = "newurl.html";
```

The href property, described in this section, is not needed.

The location object defaults to the current window. Using location alone is the same as the following, assuming you're at a top-level window:

```
window.location;
self.location;
top.location;
```

To read or set the location of another window, specify the window object you want to use. For example, the following first displays the URL of a frame named frame1, then changes the name to "newurl.html":

```
alert (parent.frame1.location);
parent.frame1.location = "http://mydomain.com/newurl.html";
```

Given the URL:

```
http://mydomain.com:80/javascript/index.html#contents
```

here's how the different document URL properties divvy up the returned string. If a property doesn't belong to the string (there is no hash value, for example), then the property is blank.

Property	Resulting String
hash	#contents
host	mydomain.com:80
hostname	mydomain.com:80
href	http://mydomain.com:80/javascript/index.html#contents
pathname	/mydomain.com:80/javascript/index.html
port	:80
protocol	http:

Property	Resulting String
referrer	N/A; see below
search	N/A; see below

The location.referrer and location.search properties are special cases:

- *location.referrer* contains the URL for the page that was linked from, using a hypertext link <A HREF=...>. If no referrer exists—the user typed in the URL for the current page from the Location box—location.referrer returns an empty string.

- *location.search* contains the "search" portion of a URL; this is the portion of the URL following the ? character.

Window and Frame Properties

The window and frame properties return and control aspects of the browser windows, and the frames within the windows. All window and frame properties are typically used as read-only.

Property	Description
frames[]	Array (list) of frames in the window
length	The number of frames in the frameset window
name	The name of a window object
parent	The parent window or frame
self	The current window or frame
top	The top browser window
window	Current window or frame

Syntax

The syntax for the frames, length, and name properties is:

window.*property*

property is the property you wish to use.

Example

The following example displays the number of frames in a frameset window.

```
Ret = parent.frames.length;
alert (Ret);
```

More Information

The window properties can become confusing because some are true properties of a window. Others are aliases for other window objects. The Netscape JavaScript documentation refers to them as properties of the top-level window. This object is never directly referenced and is always assumed.

Property	How It's Used
window.frames[x]	Array object containing the list of frames in a parent window
window.name	Name of the current window, if any
window.length	Number of frames in that window, if any

The window, parent, top, and self properties all refer to window objects. Here's how they are typically used.

Property/Object	How It's Used
window	Current window
self	Current window
top	Top-most browser window
parent	Frameset of a window with frames

Keep the following in mind when using window properties:

- The *top* browser window, as well as any window opened with the File, New Browser command, does not have a name. The window.name property returns an empty string when used with these windows.

- When used with a single browser window, *window* and *self* are synonymous. The self property allows you to differentiate between the current window name and a form or form element of the same name, if such a form/form element exists (generally, avoiding such duplication of names is a good idea).

- When used with frames, *top* and *parent* are synonymous.

- The *window* object/property refers to the current window. "Current" is the window containing the JavaScript used to access the window. This applies whether the window is a standalone or in a frame.

See Figure 5.1 for a graphic depiction of the hierarchy of windows and frames.

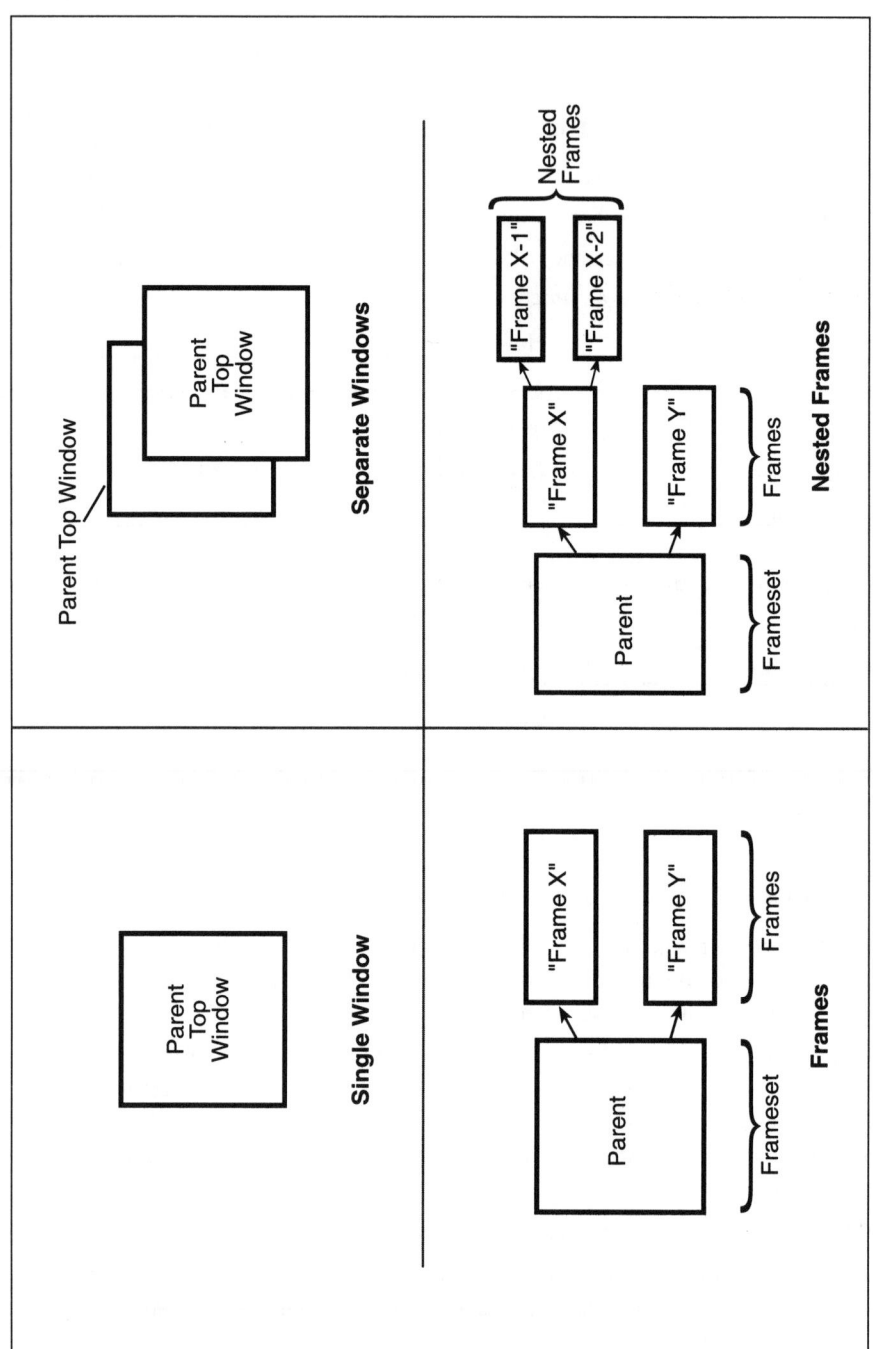

Figure 5.1 Frames are subordinate wincows to a parent, or frameset, window.

METHODS AND FUNCTIONS

This chapter details JavaScript's methods and functions. Methods are "commands" that act upon a given object (functions are not associated with objects). The methods and functions in this chapter are separated by category for greater ease. The categories are:

- Date methods
- Document methods
- Form methods
- History methods
- JavaScript functions
- Math methods
- String methods
- Text methods
- User Interface methods
- Window methods

Note that Netscape 3.0 offers additional object methods and functions. Refer to Chapter 22 for more details.

Date Methods

The Date methods use the Date object, which is a built-in object of JavaScript. To use this object, you must create a new "instance" of it using the following syntax:

date_obj = new Date();

date_obj is a new date object.

The above syntax creates a new Date object for now, the current date and time. You can create a Date object for any date and time since January 1, 1970, 00:00:00 by including that information as the Date object parameter. There are two methods for doing so:

- A string in the format "Jan 1, 1999 hour:min:sec"
- A comma-delimited list of values, in the format year, month, day, hour, min, sec

In both instances, the time values (hour, minute, second) are optional. Here are some examples:

```
now = new Date();              // date object for now
xmas = new Date("Dec 25,1997"); // date object for Christmas, 1997
decade = new Date (99, 11, 31, 23, 59, 59)     // End of 1900s
```

■■■■■■■ **NOTE**

- When using the limited number list, the month is 0-based, with January=0.
- The hours are based on a 24-hour clock.
- Do not use date values before January 1, 1970, as such values may cause Netscape to crash.
- Do not use the string format for dates after December 31, 1999, as such values may cause Netscape to crash.

■■■■■■■

After the Date object has been created, it can be used with any of the following Date methods. Be sure to read Chapter 4, "Objects," for more information on the Date object.

get (date) Methods

The get date methods (getDate, getDay, and so forth) retrieve the date and time from a Date object. This object can contain the current date and time, or it can contain some other specified date and time. All of the get date methods are used in the same way. The basic syntax is:

```
date_obj.getMethod();
```

date_obj is the date object, and *getMethod* is the date method you wish to use.

For example, the following returns the current hours:

```
now = new Date();
Ret = now.getHours();
Alert (Ret);
```

Method	What It Returns
getDate	Day of week (0=Sunday)
getDay	Day of month
getHours	Hours (0 to 23)
getMinutes	Minutes (0 to 59)
getMonth	Month of year (0=January)
getSeconds	Seconds (0 to 59)
getTime	Milliseconds since Jan 1, 1990 00:00:00
getTimezoneOffset	Offset in minutes from GMT
getYear	Year—70 to 99 for 1900s, 100 onward for 2000 beyond

parse Method

The parse method returns the number of milliseconds since January 1, 1970, 00:00:00, local time (the UTC method does the same thing, but for GMT time).

Syntax

parse.UTC (*datestring*)

datestring is a valid JavaScript date string, in the form *Mon, 25 Dec 1995 00:00:00 GMT*.

Further Information

- The time value is optional.

- The day of the week is optional.

- Local time is assumed if you omit the "GMT."

- If you wish to use GMT, but also want the time to reflect local time, use the format GMT+xx:xx, where xx:xx is the number of hours and minutes of the timezone offset, such as GMT+8, or GMT+12:30 (you may also use GMT-xx:xx).

Example

The following example returns a string object containing the number of seconds since January 1, 1970, until April 1, 1999:

```
Ret = Date.parse ("Apr 1, 1999 GMT");
alert (Ret);
```

The return value is 922982400000, which is the number of milliseconds since January 1, 1970, GMT.

set (date) Methods

The set date methods (setDate, setDay, and so forth) set the date and time in a Date object. All of the set date methods are used in the same way. The basic syntax is:

date_obj.getMethod(val);

date_obj is the Date object, *getMethod* is the Date method you wish to use, and *val* is the new value you wish to set.

For example, the following code gets and sets the current hours:

```
now = new Date();
Ret = now.getHours();
Alert ("Original time: " + Ret);
now.setHours(3);
Ret = now.getHours();
Alert ("New time: " + Ret);
```

Method	What It Sets
setDate	Day of week (0=Sunday)
setHours	Hours (0-23)

Method	What It Sets
setMinutes	Minutes (0 to 59)
setMonth	Month of year
setSeconds	Seconds (0 to 59)
setTime	Milliseconds since Jan 1, 1990 00:00:00
setYear	Year

toGMTString Method

GMT stands for Greenwich Mean Time, the international timezone standard for setting clocks (the timezone bisects the United Kingdom). The toGMTString method converts a Date object to a string, using GMT conventions.

Syntax

date_obj.toGMTString();

date_obj is a date object, created using *new Date()*;

Example

This example converts the current time to GMT string format (you must be using a computer where the time zone setting is known to be accurate).

```
now = new Date();
Ret = now.toGMTString();
alert (Ret);
```

The result is a string in the format: Tue, 12 Mar 1996 05:24:46 GMT.

toLocaleString method

The toLocaleString method formats the date and time using the string conventions on the local computer (such as US, UK, French, or German). The idea of toLocaleString is that it presents the date and time in a style familiar to the person viewing your page, no matter what that person's location.

Syntax

date_obj.toLocaleString();

date_obj is a Date object, created using *new Date()*;

Example

This example converts the current time to local string format (this format depends on the locale settings of the computer's operating system):

```
now = new Date();
Ret = now.toLocaleString();
alert (Ret);
```

The result is a string dependent on locale. In the United States, one possible result would be:

03/11/96 21:29:45

where the standard format is month/day/year hour:minutes:seconds.

UTC Method

The UTC method returns the number of milliseconds since January 1, 1970, 00:00:00, Universal Coordinated Time (even though the acronym would suggest the name was "Universal Time Coordinated"!). In JavaScript, UTC is the same as GMT, which stands for Greenwich Mean Time.

Syntax

Date.UTC (*year, month, day, hour, minute, second*)

The date and time are provided as whole numbers. The time values (hour, minute, second) are optional.

Further Information

- The year is in shorthand notation (70 to 99 for 1970 to 1999, 100+ for 2000 and beyond).
- The month is zero-based: 0 is January.
- The hour is defined with a 24-hour clock, with 0 being midnight, 12 being noon, 23 being 11 P.M.

Example

The following example returns a string object containing the time for April 1, 1999:

```
Ret = Date.UTC (99, 3, 1);
alert (Ret);
```

The return string is in the format 922982400000, which is the number of milliseconds since January 1, 1970.

Document Methods

The document methods interact with the document. The most commonly used document method is document.write, which writes text to the browser window.

The document object is itself a property of the window object. JavaScript assumes you mean the current window when you use the syntax:

```
document.method();
```

However, if you need to specify a different document (in another window or in another frame), you must specify the window. For a window, this is the name of the window object, as in:

```
win = window.open ("loadme.html", "newwin");
win.document.write ("This is in a new document");
```

For a frame, this is the target name of the frame. You must include the "full path" to the frame, starting from the parent or top-level frameset document:

```
parent.framename.document.write ("This goes into a frame");
```

clear Method

The clear method is supposed to clear the contents of the window. *In Netscape 2.0 the clear method does nothing*.

Syntax

document.clear()

Example

Use the clear method to empty the contents of a window. This example opens a new window, writes some text into it, then clears and closes it:

```
temp = open("");
temp.document.write ("This is a test");
temp.document.clear();
temp.document.close();
```

Because the clear method doesn't function in Netscape 2.0, an alternative approach is needed. Here's how to simulate the clear method to empty the contents of a document. This example opens a new window for output, writes to it, then clears it:

```
temp = open("");
temp.document.write ("This is also a test");
temp.document.close();
temp.document.open();
temp.document.write ("");
temp.document.close();
```

The clear method clears the document so you can start from a fresh canvas. As such, the clear method really isn't necessary. To clear the document stream, close it (using document.close), then reopen it (using document.open). Anything you write to the document—using document.write—writes over the old contents.

■■■■■■■ **NOTE**

> Use a separate window or frame when writing script that clears, opens, and writes to documents. In Netscape 2.0 the underlying JavaScript program is flushed from memory after a document is rewritten—even if it is rewritten dynamically with JavaScript.

■■■■■■■

close Method (as used with document object)

When used with a document object, the close method closes the output stream—the stream is the text and images you send to the document using JavaScript code. The output stream is closed so that text and images written to the document will be displayed. (You can also force display of text and images, without using the close method, by sending any HTML tag that produces a new line, such as <P>, <BR>, or <H1>, as well as using font layout tags, such as <BIG> and <CENTER>.)

When a document is closed, the browser indicates that the document is done. In Netscape this state is indicated by the message "Document:Done" in the status bar. In addition, the meteor shower stops in the Netscape icon in the upper-right corner.

■■■■■ **CAUTION**

> The close method may cause a *fatal error* in Netscape if it is used improperly. Do not place the close method in script where it will close the output stream before Netscape has a chance to completely load the document.

■■■■■

Syntax

document.close();

Example

The following example opens a new document output stream (but not a new window), writes some text, and closes the stream:

```
document.open();
document.write ("This is a test");
document.close ();
```

If you wish to test this code, insert it in a function that is called when a button is clicked in a form, such as:

```
<SCRIPT>
function test()  {
        document.open();
        document.write ("This is a test");
        document.close();
}
</SCRIPT>
<FORM>
<INPUT TYPE="button" NAME="button1" VALUE="Click" onClick="test()">
</FORM>
```

■■■■■ **NOTE**

> Once run, this script will overwrite the previous document contents. Reload the script to try it again.

■■■■■

More Information

You use the document.close method when you want to write text and/or images to the document. Without the close method, any text and images that do not end with an HTML tag that creates a new line will not appear. For example, this JavaScript code alone will not display anything on the screen:

```
document.write ("Nothing appears here");
```

One way to make the text appear is to enclose it in <P> and </P> tags, as shown here. This automatically starts a new paragraph after the text. You can continue appending text and images to the screen in this fashion:

```
document.write ("<P>Now something appears here</P>");
```

open Method as used with document object

Used with the document object, the open method opens an output stream in the window. As the document.write and document.writeln methods automatically open a new output stream if one is not available, the open method is actually optional. However, it can be used to explicitly open an output stream of a given MIME type. Valid MIME types are those supported by Netscape (and most other browsers that support JavaScript) and include those listed in the following table.

MIME Type	Description
text/html	Text document with HTML markup
text/plain	Text document with plain ASCII characters (no markup)
image/gif	Text document with encoded bytes for a GIF header and data
image/jpeg	Text document with encoded bytes for a JPEG header and data
image/x-bitmap	Text document with encoded bytes for a bitmap image
application/*xyz*	Loads the specified plug-in and uses the plug-in for the destination write/writelin methods; xyz is the unique identifier for the plug-in, such as application/x-director for Shockwave

Syntax

document.open (*MIMEType*)

MIMEType is one of the MIMETypes above, or any other supported by the browser. This parameter is optional.

Example

This example opens a new data output stream using the default MIME type and writes to the document:

```
document.open();
document.write("Text goes here<P>");
```

More Information

The output stream is the stream of data provided by an HTML document or from JavaScript. The browser transforms that data to text and shows the result in the window. For an HTML document, the browser opens a new output stream when it receives a document and closes the stream when the document has been completely loaded.

The document.open method has no effect if the output stream is already open. That is, if the document has not finished loading, using document.open has no effect. This rule applies even if the document.open method specifies a different MIME type than the document that is currently open.

write and writeln Methods

The write and writeln methods insert text into the document. The two methods are identical, except that writeln appends a new line character to the end of the string. This character is ordinarily ignored in HTML, except in <PRE> and <TEXTAREA> tags. For the most part, you will use the document.write method exclusively.

Syntax

document.write(*text*)

document.writeln(*text*)

text is the text you wish to insert

Example

The following inserts text in the current document:

```
document.write ("This is text");
```

More Information

The document.write and document.writeln methods are JavaScript's sole method of creating any document. You can use these methods in place of hard-coded HTML, as they can create HTML markup and not just text. For example, to display a level 1 heading, you could use this line:

```
document.write ("<H1>This is a level 1 heading</H1>");
```

For the most part, you will have little reason to use the document.writeln method, except when you want to insert a hard return (new line) in a <PRE> or <TEXTAREA> structure. The document.writeln method appends a new line character at the end of the string, and it appears in the <PRE> or <TEXTAREA> structure as a separate line. Here are some examples (see Figure 6.1):

```
// No new line
document.write("<TEXTAREA>This is new text");
document.write("This is more text</TEXTAREA>");

// New line added
document.writeln("<TEXTAREA>This is new text");
document.writeln("This is more text</TEXTAREA>");
```

Form Methods

The form methods act upon forms and the controls in forms. Many of these methods are not functioning in Netscape 2.0.

blur Method

The blur method removes the focus from the currently active password, text, selection list, or text area control in a form. The control with the focus is the one that contains the flashing insertion point.

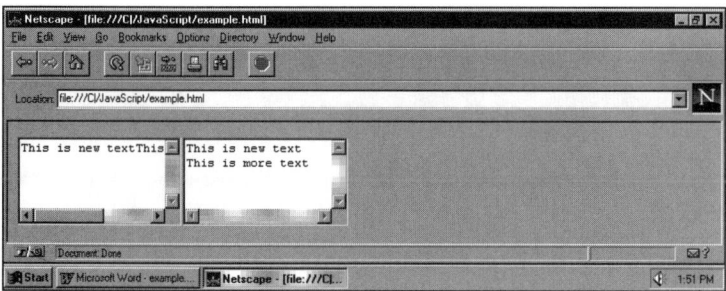

Figure 6.1 Use the document.writeln method to insert text with newline characters.

In Netscape 2.0 the blur method may yield inconsistent results and should be avoided.

Syntax

document.*formname.control*.blur()

control is the name of the form control you want to "de-focus" (push button, radio button, or checkbox); *formname* is the name of the form that contains the control.

Application

The method applies to text, textarea, password, and select objects.

Example

The following example removes the focus from a text box named "box1" in the form named "myform":

```
document.myform.box1.blur();
```

More Information

Use the blur method to remove focus from text, a textarea, and password objects so that the insertion point no longer blinks inside them. When blurred, no object in the form has focus.

■■■■■ NOTE

Because only one form object can have focus, you can use this method to remove the focus from one object and give it to another.

■■■■■

click Method

The click method simulates a mouse click on a form button. A form button can be a push button, a radio button, or a checkbox.

■■■■■ NOTE

In Netscape 2.0 the click method may yield inconsistent results and should be avoided.

■■■■■

Syntax

document.*formname.control*.click();

control is the name of the form button control (push button, radio button, or checkbox); *formname* is the name of the form that contains the control.

Application

The method applies to push buttons, radio buttons, or checkbox objects.

Example

These examples show how to simulate a click on a checkbox control. In both instances, the checkbox is named MyCheckBox using HTML markup:

```
<INPUT TYPE=checkbox" NAME="MyCheckBox">
// checkbox in form referenced by array value
document.forms[0].MyCheckBox.click();

// checkbox in form referenced by name MyForm
document.MyForm.MyCheckBox.click();
```

More Information

The click method really has very little practical use because its effects can be duplicated using other methods.

- When used with a push button, the click method simulates clicking on that button. Instead, just call the same onClick function defined for the push button.
- When used with a radio button or checkbox, the click method simulates clicking on that button, selecting or unselecting the option. Instead, just specify the selected property of the control, as in:

  ```
  document.form.checkbox.checked = !document.form.checkbox.checked;
  ```

The above example shows how to toggle the setting of the button—checked becomes unchecked, and unchecked becomes checked. Following is a threadbare example you can try to verify this approach:

```
<SCRIPT>
function test() {
        document.form.checkbox.checked = !document.form.checkbox.checked
}
</SCRIPT>
<FORM NAME="form">
<INPUT TYPE="button" NAME="button" VALUE="Click" onClick="test()">
<INPUT TYPE="checkbox" NAME="checkbox">This is a checkbox
</FORM>
```

focus Method

The focus method sets the focus (insertion point) in the specified form object. Valid form objects that can accept focus are text boxes (both standard and password) and a textarea.

 NOTE

In Netscape 2.0 the focus method may yield inconsistent results and should be avoided.

Syntax

document.*formname*.*control*.focus()

control is the form control (text, password, textarea, or selection list) you wish to set focus to; *formname* is the name of the form that contains the control.

Application

The method applies to text, textarea, password, and select objects.

Example

The following example gives focus to a text box named "box1" in the form named "myform":

```
document.myform.box1.focus();
```

More Information

Use the focus method to set focus in text, a textarea, password, and selection list objects so that the insertion point blinks inside them. Because only one form object can have focus, you can also remove the focus from an object and give it to another by using this method.

The focus method is buggy on most platforms of Netscape 2.0. You can work around the majority of these bugs by calling the focus method, then the select method, as follows:

```
document.myform.box1.focus();
document.myform.box1.select();
```

This approach will set the focus in box1 and select the text as well.

select Method

The select method selects the text in the specified form object. Valid form objects that can accept focus are text boxes (both standard and password) and textareas.

■■■■

In Netscape 2.0 the select method may yield inconsistent results and should be avoided.

■■■■

Syntax

document.*formname*.*control*.select()

control is the form control (text, password, textarea, or selection list) you wish to select; *formname* is the name of the form that contains the control.

Application

The method applies to text, textarea, and password.

Example

The following example gives selects to a text box named "box1" in the form named "myform":

```
document.myform.box1.select();
```

More Information

The select method is buggy on most platforms of Netscape 2.0. You can work around the majority of these bugs by calling the focus method, then the select method, as follows:

```
document.myform.box1.focus();
document.myform.box1.select();
```

submit Method

The submit method submits a form. The most common use of submit is to provide a button on the form that includes an onClick event handler. When the button is clicked, the event handler calls the submit method or a user-defined function that includes the submit method.

Syntax

document.*formname*.submit()

formname is the name of the form.

Application

The method applies to form.

Example

The following example submits a form when a button is clicked:

```
<INPUT TYPE="button" VALUE="Click" onClick="this.form.submit()">
```

More Information

The submit method is particularly handy when you want JavaScript to temporarily intervene in the form-submitting process. For example, you can test the contents of one or more text boxes to ensure that they contain valid data. See Chapter 16, "Using JavaScript in Forms," for a complete discussion of validating forms with JavaScript.

History Methods

The history methods let you change the URL of a window or frame using previously visited URLs. These URLs are stored in the browser's history list. Bear in mind that the history list is specific to each window; if you have multiple windows open, or multiple frames, each one has its own history list.

back Method

The back method loads the previous URL from the history list. Consider this example. If you load the URL:

```
http://www.anywhere.com/first.html
```

and then load:

```
http://www.anywhere.com/second.html
```

the back method returns you to http://www.anywhere.com/first.html.

Syntax

history.back()

Example

This example included here returns the browser to the previously loaded URL, if there is one. If there is no previous URL in the history list the method has no effect.

```
history.back();
```

More Information

The back method is used to step back one URL in the browser's history list. You can use it to return the user to the previous page. However, do exercise caution because the back method steps back one URL, which may not necessarily be the page you want. Still, the back method can be useful if you want to control navigation within a series of pages, but don't want to do so using specific URLs.

The back method is used to move to the next URL in the history list for a given window. Each window can have a separate history list; therefore, the history list applies to a given window. The same rule applies to frames. Using history.back defaults to the current window or frame. You can specify the name or identifier of a window if you want to move to the previous URL in the history list for another window.

Instruction	What It Does
history.back()	Moves back in current window
self.history.back()	Moves back in current window
winname.history.back()	Moves back in winname window
parent.frame1.history.back()	Moves back in frame1 window

The back method is functionally identical to history.go(−1).

forward Method

The forward method loads the next URL from the history list. Here is an example. If you load the URL:

```
http://www.anywhere.com/first.html
```

and then load:

```
http://www.anywhere.com/second.html
```

and go back to the first page, the forward method returns you to the second page.

Syntax

history.forward()

Example

This example included here changes to the next URL in the history list for the current window. If there is no next URL in the history list, the method has no effect.

```
history.forward();
```

More Information

The forward method is used to step forward one URL in the browser's history list. Use it with caution because the forward method steps forward one URL, which may not necessary be the page you want. The forward method can be useful if you want to control navigation within a series of pages, but don't want to use specific URLs.

The forward method is used to move to the next URL in the history list for a given window. Each window can have a separate history list; therefore, the history list applies to a given window. The same rule applies to frames. Using history.forward defaults to the current window or frame. You can specify the name or identifier of a window if you want to move to the next URL in the history list for another window.

Instruction	What It Does
history.forward()	Moves forward in current window
self.history.forward()	Moves forward in current window
winname.history.forward()	Moves forward in winname window
parent.frame1.history.forward()	Moves forward in frame1 window

The forward method is functionally identical to history.go(1).

go Method

The go method moves forward or backward in the user's history list. You can specify how many URLs to move forward or backward. For example, history.go(-5) moves the user back five URLs in the history list (if the history goes back that far). Similarly, history.go(3) moves forward three URLs in the history list.

Syntax

history.go(*position*)

position is a positive or negative value representing the URL to which you want to move. A value of 0 means the current page.

Example

The following example moves forward one URL in the history list for the current window:

history.go(1);

More Information

The go method is most often used as a substitute for the history.back and history.forward methods. The go method is more flexible in that it allows you to move a specified number of URLs through the history list. You can also force a reload of the current page or frame by using history.go(0).

Each window has its own history list. Using history.go() defaults to the current window or frame. You can specify the name or identifier of a window if you want to move to the next URL in the history list for another window.

Instruction	What It Does
history.go(x)	Moves forward/back in current window
self.history.go(x)	Moves forward/back in current window
winname.history.go(x)	Moves forward/back in winname window
parent.frame1.history.go(x)	Moves forward/back in frame1 window

JavaScript Functions

JavaScript functions are built into the core language; they do not "belong" to any given object. These functions work with number variables, and number variables are not objects. Because these are functions and not object methods, you never have to declare a parent object to use them, as you do with methods such as document.write.

escape Function

The escape function (it is not a method) returns the hexadecimal (base-16) ASCII value of a character (using the ISO Latin-1 character set). It also appends the % symbol, which is regularly used on the Internet for encoding ASCII characters as numeric values.

Syntax

escape(*string*)

string is one or more characters you want to convert.

Example

You use the escape function to translate text characters to ASCII encoding. For example, the following example displays %20 as 20 is the hexadecimal ASCII equivalent of a space. Only those characters that require URL encoding are converted.

```
Ret = escape (" "); // space
alert (Ret);
```

More Information

The escape function is handy if you need to parse a string in URL encoded fashion. This is necessary, for example, when storing data in the Netscape cookie file (which permits persistent data storage). URL encoding is also used to strip invalid characters from URL strings. These include spaces and colons.

You are not limited to encoding just one character at a time, although this is typically how the escape function is used. The string "this is a test" comes out as "this%20is%20a%20test" when converted by the escape function.

Use the unescape function to convert URL encoded characters back to their ISO Latin-1 characters.

Eval Function

The eval function evaluates an expression. The expression can be in string format, which is beneficial when constructing expressions "on the fly."

■■■■■■ CAUTION

The eval function can cause an immediate crash when used with the Windows 3.1 version of Netscape 2.0. Therefore, you should not use the eval function if users of the Windows 3.1 version have access to your JavaScript documents. However, this problem is fixed in Netscape 2.01 and later.

■■■■

Syntax

eval(*expression*)

expression is the expression you wish to evaluate. It can be enclosed in quotation marks.

Example

This function evaluates an expression that contains numbers, operators, and strings. For example, the following example results in 4. Note the unusual construction of the eval expression: the entire expression is a string.

```
Val = 2;
Ret = eval ("2 + Val");
alert (Ret);
```

isNaN function

The isNaN function tests a number to determine if it's "not a number" (hence the name of the function!). It is used to provide easier comparisons of number and string types, and to ensure that your code doesn't erroneously attempt to perform math on alphabetical character strings. By using isNaN first, you can determine if a value contains a valid number. You can also use it in conjunction with the parseInt and parseFloat functions, as these return the string "NaN" when the argument is not a number. (Windows platforms for Netscape 2.0 are an exception; see parseInt and parseFloat for more details.)

▰▰▰▰▰ **NOTE**

The isNaN function is available only on the Unix platform of Netscape 2.0.

▰▰▰▰▰

Syntax

isNaN(*value*)

value is the value you wish to test.

Example

The following example displays "Is a number" or "Is not a number," depending on the value provided in the prompt box.

```
Ret = prompt ("Enter something");
if (!isNaN(Ret))
        alert ("Is a number");
else
        alert ("Is not a number");
```

More Information

The isNaN function provides a quick and easy method of determining if a value contains only a number, or a string of numeric characters. If the value is a number, the function returns *true*; if the value is not a number, the function returns *false*. You can use isNaN as a method to determine proper entry in a prompt box or form text box. In the following example, the while loop continues until the user provides a number-only response. (This demonstration works only for the Unix version of Netscape 2.0.)

```
LoopCtrl=true;
while (LoopCtrl) {
        Ret = prompt ("Enter a number only");
        Ret = parseInt(Ret);
        if (!isNaN(Ret)
                LoopCtrl=false;
}
```

parseFloat Function

This function converts (and parses) a string argument, returning a floating-point number.

The parseFloat function (it is not a method) converts strings into numeric value equivalents. If the function encounters a character other than a sign (+ or -), numeral (0-9), a decimal point, or an exponent, it returns the value up to that point and ignores everything else. If the first character cannot be converted to a number, parseFloat returns one of the following values:

- 0 on Windows platforms.
- "NaN" on any other platform

Syntax

parseFloat(*string*)

string is a string that represents the value you want to "parse."

Example

The following example returns 123.456:

```
Ret = parseFloat ("123.456");
alert (Ret);
```

More Information

Use the parseFloat function when you must convert a string into a numeric value—for example, to perform arithmetic functions on it. In the lines of code below, the first example results in "123.4561," while the second results in 124.456, which is the desired value.

```
Val = "123.456";
Val = Val + 1;
```

```
alert (Val);


Val = "123.456";
Val = parseFloat(Val) + 1;
alert (Val);
```

parseInt Function

This function converts (and parses) a string argument, returning an integer value. The parseInt function (it is not a method) converts strings into numeric value equivalents. An optional parameter lets you convert numbers from another base (hexadecimal, octal) into decimal. If the function encounters a character other than a sign (+ or -), numeral (0-9), a decimal point, or an exponent, it returns the value up to that point and ignores everything else. If the first character cannot be converted to a number, parseInt returns one of the following values:

- 0 on Windows platforms
- "NaN" on any other platform

Syntax

parseInt(*string*, *radix*)

string is a string that represents the value you want to convert; *radix* is an integer that represents the radix of the return value.

Example

The following example converts a string to its numeric value equivalent:

```
Ret = "123";
Ret = parseInt (Ret);
alert (Ret);
```

More Information

Use the parseInt function when you must convert a string into a numeric value—for example, when you want to perform arithmetic functions on it. The first of the following lines of code results in "1231," while the second results in 124, which is the desired value.

```
Val = "123";
Val = Val + 1;
```

```
alert (Val);

Val = "123";
Val = parseInt(Val) + 1;
alert (Val);
```

The radix parameter lets you convert numbers from one base to decimal (the parseInt function, however, does not do the reverse, which would be decimal to some other number base). Here are some examples:

```
Ret = parseInt ("ff", 16)      // hexadecimal conversion, returns 255
Ret = parseInt ("0xff", 16)    // hexadecimal conversion, returns 255
Ret = parseInt ("1111", 2)     // decimal conversion, returns 15
Ret = parseInt ("765", 8)      // octal conversion, returns 501
```

Number	Base
2	Binary
8	Octal
10	Decimal
16	Hexadecimal

When the radix parameter is omitted, JavaScript assumes the value is in decimal format, unless the number is formatted as noted in the following table.

Parameter	Assumes Format
0x*nnn*	Hexadecimal
0*nnn*	Octal

The function returns 0 (or NaN on Unix platforms) if a conversion cannot be made.

toString Function

The toString function converts the string-like output from an object to a real string. For example, the location object provides the URL of the current window. You can see this URL with:

```
Ret = location;
alert (Ret);
```

What you're seeing, however, is not a true string. If you were to attempt to manipulate the value returned from the location object, using the substring or indexOf methods, for example, JavaScript would complain with an error. The string methods fail because only the string object supports them; other objects like location do not support these methods.

One way around this limitation is to use a property of the object that returns a true string, if available. In the case of the location object, you can use the href property:

```
Ret = location.href.substring (0, 5);   // get first five characters
alert (Ret);
```

Some objects don't have properties that return true strings. For these, you can use the toString function. It converts the value returned from an object to a string. The converted value can be manipulated using the string methods.

Syntax

object_name.toString();

Example

This example converts the value returned from location object to a string, then fetches the filename only from the result:

```
Ret = location.toString();
Ret = Ret.substring (Ret.lastIndexOf("/") +1, Ret.length)
alert (Ret)
```

unescape Function

The unescape function (it is not a method) translates one or more URL-encoded characters of the form %nn to their ISO Latin-1 characters.

Syntax

unescape(*string*)

string is one or more encoded characters you want to convert.

Example

Use the unescape function to translate text characters that have been previously encoded using the escape function. For example, the escape sequence %20 is converted to a space.

```
Ret = unescape ("%20"); // space
alert (Ret);
```

More Information

See the escape function for more information on the practical use of encoded strings.

Math Methods

The Math methods let you work with special math functions within JavaScript. These go beyond simple arithmetic and include trigonometric functions, rounding functions, and comparison functions. There are two ways to use the Math methods:

```
Math.method (val)
```

or

```
with (Math) {
method(val)
}
```

- *method* is the Math method you wish to use.
- *val* is the value you wish to use (some Math methods require multiple values).

The with structure lets you use a series of Math methods without having to append the Math.object to them each time.

abs Method

The abs method returns the absolute value of a number. Absolute means the value is positive only. Apply a negative number to the abs method and it returns a positive number. Try this example and you get back 576 (note the lack of the minus sign). The RetVal variable contains the value returned from the abs method.

```
RetVal=Math.abs(-576);
alert (RetVal);
```

acos Method

The acos method returns the arc cosine (in radians) of a value. Here is an example:

```
Ret = Math.acos(0.12);
```

asin Method

The asin method returns the arc sine (in radians) of a value. Here is an example:

```
Ret = Math.acos(0.12);
```

atan Method

The atan method returns the arc sine (in radians) of a value. Here is an example:

```
Ret = Math.atan(0.12);
```

ceil Method

The ceil method returns an integer greater than or equal to a number. The result is similar to rounding a number, except that the rounding logic is as follows:

- If the number is a positive value such as 23.45, the result is 24.
- If the number is a negative value such as -23.45, the result is -23.

The following example shows how ceil returns integers from both positive and negative values:

```
Ret = Math.ceil(101.25);        // returns 102
alert ("Ceiling of 101.25 is: " + Ret);
Ret = Math.ceil(-101.25); // returns 101
alert ("Ceil of -101.25 is: " + Ret);
```

cos Method

The cos method returns the cosine (in radians) of a number. Here is an example:

```
Ret = Math.acos(0.12);
```

exp Method

The exp method returns e(number), where *number* is a numeric value, and *e* is Euler's constant, the base of natural logarithms. Here is an example:

```
Ret = Math.exp(0.0009);
```

floor Method

The floor method returns an integer less than or equal to a number. The result is similar to rounding a number, except that the rounding logic is as follows:

- If the number is a positive value such as 23.45, the result is 23.

- If the number is a negative value such as −23.45, the result is −24.

The following example shows how floor returns integers from both positive and negative values:

```
Ret = Math.floor(101.25);       // returns 102
alert ("Floor of 101.25 is: " + Ret);
Ret = Math.floor(-101.25); // returns 101
alert ("Floor of -101.25 is: " + Ret);
```

log Method

This method returns the natural logarithm (base)e of a number. Here is an example:

```
Ret = Math.log(1.1);
```

max Method

This method returns the greater of two numbers. For example, the following displays "10":

```
Ret = max (5, 10);
alert (Ret);
```

min Method

This method returns the lesser of two numbers. For example, the following code displays "5":

```
Ret = Math.min(5, 10);
alert (Ret);
```

pow Method

This method returns base to the exponent power; for example: 2 raised to the 10th power is 1024. The pow method takes two arguments:

pow (*base*, *exponent*)

This example displays 1048576

```
Ret = Math.pow (2, 20);
alert (Ret);
```

random Method

This method returns a random number from 0 to 1, though the form is predominantly 0.*xxxxxxxxxxxxxxx*. The first 15 digits to the right of the decimal point are valid. The random method is available on the Unix platform only for Netscape 2.0. The random number is "seeded" by the computer's clock. The following example displays a random number:

```
alert (Math.random);
```

round Method

This method returns a value rounded up or down. The value is rounded up if the significant digit to the right of the decimal is 5 or higher; it is rounded down if the digit is 0 to 4. Here are two examples:

```
alert (Math.round(123.456)     // rounded to 123
alert (Math.round (234.567)    // rounded to 235
```

sin Method

This method returns the sine of a number, in radians. Here is an example:

```
Ret = Math.sin(1.5);
```

sqrt Method

This method returns the square root of a number. The following example returns 1331 (this one is for the "Original Star Trek" Trekkies out there):

```
Ret = Math.sqrt (1771561);
alert (Ret)
```

tan Method

This method returns the tangent of a number, in radians. Here is an example:

```
Ret = Math.tan(1.5);
```

String Methods

The string methods let you manipulate strings. You can work on a literal string or a string in a variable. Here are some examples:

```
"This is a literal string".method();
```

or

```
InString = "This is a string in a variable";
InString.method;
```

■■■■■ **NOTE**

> Many of JavaScript's objects seem to return string values, but these objects themselves do not support the string methods. The window.location object is a case in point. The following example displays the URL of the current document in the browser:
>
> ```
> alert (window.location);
> ```
>
> What you're seeing is indeed a string, but the value cannot be manipulated as a string. JavaScript raises an error if you attempt to determine the length of the string:
>
> ```
> alert (window.location.length);
> ```
>
> To work around this problem, you must find a method of the object that returns a string, if any, or convert the object's "string-like" value to a true string. You can then use the string methods that follow on the resulting string. Here is an example:
>
> ```
> Ret = window.location.toString();
> alert (Ret.length);
> ```

■■■■■

anchor Method

The anchor method makes an anchor out of a string. In other words, if you give the anchor method a string such as "Table of Contents," JavaScript creates the following equivalent HTML code:

```
<A NAME="contents">Table of Contents</A>
```

Syntax

string.anchor(*name*)

string is the string that appears between the <A> and </A> tags; *name* is the name of the anchor.

Example

Here's a demonstration of how the anchor method is used:

```
AnchorString="Top of the Page";
Ret = AnchorString.anchor("top");
document.write (Ret);
```

Another option is this:

```
Ret = "Top of the page".anchor("top");
document.write (Ret);
```

This example creates a target (sometimes called a bookmark) anchor named "top" and displays the text "Top of the Page". The equivalent HTML tag structure is as follows:

```
<A NAME="top">Top of the Page</A>
```

You can now use a link elsewhere in the document to link to this target. Such a link would have the following HTML syntax:

```
<A HREF="#top">Go back to the top of the page</A>
```

More Information

Use the anchor method whenever you want a quick and easy way to create a target anchor. The anchor can then be referenced by a link elsewhere in the document. Another, less direct method of creating a named anchor using JavaScript is:

```
Ret = '<A NAME="top">Top of the Page</A>';
document.write (Ret);
```

big Method

The big method displays text with the "big" attribute, which is a larger-than-normal font. The big method is equivalent to using the following HTML tags:

```
<BIG>This is sure a big font!</BIG>
```

Syntax

string.big()

string is the string you want to display in a big font.

Example

The following examples show how to use the big method:

```
MyString="This is sure is a big font!";
Ret = MyString.big();
document.write (Ret);
```

or

```
Ret = "This sure is a big font!".big();
document.write (Ret);
```

More Information

The following code produces the same result as the big method:

```
Ret='<BIG>This is some big text!</BIG>';
document.write (Ret);
```

blink Method

You use the blink method to creating blinking text. The blinking is relatively slow and, when used sparingly and with small portions of text, isn't too objectionable. However, some users find it annoying, especially when used to blink large areas of heading text.

Syntax

string.blink()

string is the string you want to blink.

Example

The following examples show how to use the blink method with various parts of text.

```
Result="This text will blink";
Ret = Result.blink();
document.write (Ret);
```

or

```
Ret = "This text will blink".blink();
document.write (Ret);
```

or

```
LinkText='This is a link that blinks";
LinkURL="http:/www.anywhere.com";
Ret = LinkText.blink().link(LinkURL);
document.write (Ret);
```

More Information

You can also create blinking with:

```
Result ='<BLINK>This blinking text sure is annoying!</BLINK>';
document.write(Result);
```

■■■■■■ **NOTE**

For a fun insight into how Netscape views the blinking text controversy, in Netscape type about:mozilla in the Location box.

bold Method

The bold method makes text stand out. The bolded text appears thicker and heavier in relation to the other text in the document; use the method when you want to draw attention to a word or phrase. Note that bolding has no effect on text, such as a heading, that is already bold.

Syntax

string.bold()

string is the string you want to make bold.

Example

The following examples show how to use the bold method with various parts of text.

```
Ret = "This text is in bold".bold();
document.write (Ret);
```

or

```
Result = "This text is in bold";
Ret = Result.bold();
```

```
document.write (Ret);
```

More Information

You can also created bolded text with:

```
Result='<B>This blinking text sure is annoying!</B>';
document.write(Result);
```

charAt Method

The charAt method returns the character at a given position in a string. For example, if the string is "JavaScript" and the position is 5, the character returned by charAt is "a." Character positions start at 0 and are counted left to right.

Syntax

string.charAt (*index*)

- *string* is the string you want to search through.
- *index* is the position of the character you want to return.

Example

This example prints each letter of the text "JavaScript" on a separate line:

```
TestString ="JavaScript";
for (Count = 0; Count < TestString.length; Count++) {
        document.write (TestString.charAt(Count) + "<BR>")
}
```

More Information

Use the charAt method whenever you want to pick out a character from a string. Most often, you will know the contents of the string and, therefore, will know which character to get. One possible use is converting the numbers 1 through 26 to letters. The following displays "k" because it's the eleventh letter in the alphabet:

```
var GetChar = 11;
Alphabet = "abcdefghijklmnopqrstuvwxyz";
alert (Alphabet.charAt(GetChar-1));
```

fixed Method

You use the fixed method to format text in fixed (monospace) font.

Syntax

string.fixed()

string is the string you want to format as fixed.

Example

The following examples show how to use the fixed method with various parts of text.

```
Ret = "This text is in monospace".fixed();
document.write (Ret);
```

or

```
Result = "This text is in monospace";
Ret = Result.fixed();
document.write (Ret);
```

More Information

You can also create monospace text with:

```
Result='<TT>This is monospace text</TT>';
document.write(Result);
```

fontcolor Method

Use the fontcolor method to color specified text (use the TEXT attribute or the fgColor property to change the color of all text in a document).

Syntax

string.fontcolor(*color*)

string is the string you want to color; *color* is the color you want to use.

Example

The following examples show how to use the font method with various parts of text. You can use hexadecimal triplet values or color names. See "Deciphering RGB Triplet Values" in Chapter 21 for a list of valid color names.

```
document.write ("This text is colored red".fontcolor("red"));
```

or

```
Result = "This text is colored red";
```

```
document.write (Result.fontcolor ("#ff0000"));
```

More Information

You can also create colored text with:

```
Result = '<FONT COLOR="blue">This text is blue</FONT COLOR>';
document.write(Result);
```

fontsize Method

Use the fontsize method to change the size of specified text.

Syntax

string.fontsize(*size*)

string is the string you want to change; *size* is the size of the font, which can be either an absolute value or a relative value.

Example

The following examples show how to use the fontsize method with various parts of text. Valid font size values are from 1 to 7. Using a + or - with the size specifies a sizing relative to the current size of the body text.

```
document.write ("This text is really big ".fontsize(7));
```

or

```
Result = "This text is bigger than normal text";
document.write (Result.fontsize (+2));
```

More Information

You can also change font size with:

```
Result = '<FONT SIZE=6>This is font size 6</FONT SIZE>';
document.write(Result);
```

indexOf Method

The indexOf method returns the position of a character within a string. A typical use of indexOf is to determine if a string contains a given character. If it does not, the charAt method returns −1. If the character is contained in the string, the value is 0 or greater, with 0 being the position of the first character in the string, 1 being the position of the second character, and so forth. If the character is contained in the string more than once, then the indexOf method returns the position of the first character it finds.

Syntax

string.indexOf (*character*)

string is the string you want to search in; *character* is the character for which you want to look.

Example

This example returns 5: the letter "s" is first found at position 5 in the string (remember string positions start at 0).

```
TestString.indexOf("s");
Ret = TestString = "This is a test";
Alert(Ret);
```

More Information

You already know about using indexOf to determine if a character is found within a string. What are some practical uses of this capability? One is to determine if a character is a number or a letter.

```
TestChar = "5";
RefString = "0123456789";
if (RefString.indexOf(TestChar) == -1);
        alert ("not a number character")
else
        alert ("is a number character")
```

You are not limited to searching for a single character. The indexOf method can also look for groups of characters. This ability comes in handy when you are converting three-letter month abbreviations to their respective numbers. The following returns 3:

```
ThisMonth = "Mar";
RefMonth = JanFebMarAprMayJunJulAugSepOctNovDec";
MonthNumber = (RefMonth.charAt(ThisMonth)+1) / 3 +1;
```

italics Method

Use the italics method to make text stand out.

Syntax

string.italics()

string is the string you want to italicize.

Example

The following examples show how to use the italics method with various parts of text.

```
ret = "This text is in italics".italics();
document.write (Ret);
```

or

```
Result = "This text is in italics";
Ret = Result.italics();
document.write (Ret);
```

More Information

You can also create italicized text with:

```
Result = '<I>This blinking text sure is annoying!</I>';
document.write(Result);
```

lastIndexOf Method

The lastIndexOf method returns the last position of a given character within a string. A typical use of lastIndexOf is to return the position of a slash character in a string, for use with URLs. This last slash indicates the beginning of the filename. If the character is in the string, the lastIndexOf method returns its position within the string (starting from 0 for the first character). If the character is not in the string, the method returns -1. You can specify an offset value, and the lastIndexOf method will start looking at that point in the string.

Syntax

string.lastIndexOf (*character, offset*)

string is the string you want to search in; *character* is the character for which you want to look; offset is the position in the string where you wish to start searching.

Example

The following example locates the last instance of the letter "e" in the test string. The result is 11 (remember, strings are 0 based).

```
TestString = "This is a test";
Ret = TestString.lastIndexOf("e");
alert (Ret);
```

More Information

The lastIndexOf method is particularly handy when parsing out strings, such as URLs. This example returns just the filename of the current URL, chopping off the host and path portion:

```
URL = location.href;
LastSlash = URL.lastIndexOf("/") + 1;
FilenameOnly = URL.substring(LastSlash, URL.length-1);
alert (FilenameOnly);
```

You are not limited to searching for a single character. The lastIndexOf method can also look for groups of characters as well.

link Method

The link method creates a clickable link on the page.

Syntax

string.link(*href*)

string is the "click text" of the link, such as "Click here"; *href* is the HREF of the link.

Example

This example creates a link with the click text "Table of Contents" and an HREF of #TOC. Clicking on the resulting link takes you to the TOC anchor elsewhere on the page.

```
Ret = "Table of Contents".link("#TOC");
document.write (Ret);
```

More Information

You can also create a link with:

```
Result = '<A HREF="linked.html">Click me now!</A>';
document.write(Result);
```

small Method

The small method displays text with the "small" attribute, which is a smaller-than-normal font. Applying the small method is equivalent to using the following HTML tags:

```
<SMALL>This is small text</SMALL>
```

Syntax

string.small()

string is the string you want to display in a small font.

Example

The following examples show how to use the small method:

```
MyString = "This is small text";
Ret = MyString.small();
document.write(Ret);
```

or

```
Ret = "This is small text".small();
document.write(Ret);
```

The following code produces the same result as using the small method.

```
Result = '<SMALL>This is some big text!</SMALL>';
document.write(Result);
```

strike Method

Use the strike method to create strikeout text, which is text that is displayed with a line through it. Strikeout text is useful when you are proposing changes to text.

Syntax

string.strike()

string is the string you want to format.

Example

The following examples show how to use the strike method with various parts of text.

```
Result = "This text is struck out";
Ret = Result.strike();
document.write(Ret);
```

or

```
Ret = "This text is struck out".strike();
document.write(Ret);
```

More Information

Strikeout text can also be created with:

```
Result='<STRIKE>This is text that I want you to remove</STRIKE>';
document.write(Result);
```

sub Method

Use the sub method to create text in subscript. The text is displayed in a smaller-than-normal font and is aligned slightly below the baseline of the regular text.

Syntax

string.sub()

string is the string you want to format.

Example

The following examples show how to use the sub method with various parts of text.

```
Result = "th";
Ret = Result.sub();
document.write("Today is Friday the 13" + Ret);
```

or

```
"th".sub();
document.write("Today is Friday the 13" + Ret);
```

More Information

Subscripted text can also be created with:

```
Result = '<SUB>This is subscripted text</SUB>';
document.write(Result);
```

substring Method

The substring method returns a portion of a string. You specify the beginning and ending of the portion you want to "extract" by indicating the position of the start and stop point in the string. JavaScript strings are zero-based, so the first character is 0. The last character is string.length-1—that is, one less than the length of the string.

Syntax

string.substring (*start*, *stop*)

string is the string from which you want to get text; *start* is the starting position of the extracted text; *stop* is the ending position of the extracted text.

■■■■■■ NOTE

Unlike some programming languages, you do not provide the number of characters you want to extract for the stop parameter.

■■■■■■

Example

The following example extracts the first four characters from a string:

```
InString = "This is a test";
Ret = InString.substring(0, 4);
alert (Ret);
```

More Information

Use different values for the start and stop arguments to extract whatever text you want from the string, "I like JavaScript a whole lot."

```
InString = "I like JavaScript a whole lot."
Ret = InString.substring(0, 11)   // returns first 11 characters, or "I like Java"
Ret = InString.substring(7, 17) // returns "JavaScript"
```

```
Ret = InString.substring(1, 0)  // returns nothing
Ret = InString.substring(0, InString.length)          // returns all of string
Ret = InString.substring(0, InString.length-1)  // returns all of string
Ret = InString.substring(InString.indexOf("J"), InString.indexOf("J")+10)
//returns "JavaScript"
```

sup Method

Use the sup method to create text in superscript. The text is displayed in a smaller-than-normal font and is aligned slightly above regular text. You use the sup method, for example, to display footnote or endnote references or for scientific notation.

Syntax

string.sup()

string is the string you want to format.

Example

The following examples show how to use the sup method with various parts of text.

```
Result="30";
Ret = Result.sup();
document.write(Ret);
```

or

```
"30".sup();
document.write(Ret);
```

More Information

Superscripted text can also be created with:

```
Result = '<SUP>This is superscripted text</SUP>';
document.write(Result);
```

toLowerCase Method

The toLowerCase() method converts a string to all lowercase.

Syntax

string.toLowerCase()

string is the string you want to convert.

Example

Both of these examples display "this is a test" in the alert box.

```
//Example 1
Ret = "This Is A Test".toLowerCase();
alert (Ret);


//Example 2
CvtString = "This Is A Test";
Ret =CvtString.toLowerCase();
alert (Ret);
```

toUpperCase Method

The toUpperCase method converts a string to all uppercase.

Syntax

string.toUpperCase()

string is the string you want to convert.

Example

Both of these examples display "THIS IS A TEST" in the alert box.

```
//Example 1
Ret = "This Is A Test".toUpperCase();
alert (Ret);


//Example 2
CvtString = "This Is A Test";
Ret =CvtString.toUpperCase();
alert (Ret);
```

User Interface Methods

The user interface methods are special methods of the window object. They are categorized here because they all display a dialog box asking for user input.

JavaScript assumes the current window when you use a user interface method by itself. That is,

```
alert ("Hello JavaScripters!");
```

is the same as:

```
window.alert ("Hello JavaScripters!");
```

If necessary, you can "attach" the user interface method to a specific window, so that the dialog box appears over that window. For instance,

```
win = window.open ("loadme.html", "newwin");
win.alert ("This is over the new window");
alert ("This is over the old window");
```

alert Method

Use the alert method whenever you wish to display a message. The message is displayed in a dialog box; the user reads the message and chooses OK to dismiss the dialog box.

Syntax

alert (*value*)

value is the string you want to display in the alert box.

Example

This example displays the message "Hello JavaScripters!" in an alert box:

```
alert ("Hello JavaScripters!");
```

More Information

The alert method can display any kind of value—numeric, string, Boolean, even the identity of an object. JavaScript automatically converts numeric and most object values to a string type, relieving you of having to do so. The following examples show various ways to use the alert method.

```
alert ("Read this message");        // display string
alert (12);                         // display number 12
alert (Count);                      // display contents of Count variable
```

```
alert ("The value is "+Count);          // display string and contents of COUNT
alert(true)                             // display "true"
```

Here's another example. The alert method is used to remind the user to provide a valid entry in response to a prompt dialog:

```
Ctrl=true;
while (Ctrl)   {
        RetVal=prompt("Enter your name");
        if (RetVal!="")
                alert("Please type your name!");
        else
                Ctrl=false;
}
```

The alert method is the primary means to communicate directly with the user. The message requires the user to respond to the message (by choosing OK or pressing the Enter key).

Use the alert method for warnings and status message. You can also use alert to display a test value when you're writing a script. This can be handy if you need to check the value of a variable. As used in Navigator JavaScript lacks debugging tools, and the alert method is one of the best ways to determine current values of variables and objects.

> If you need the user to respond to a yes or no question, use the confirm method instead.

confirm Method

The confirm method displays a dialog box with a prompt and OK/Cancel buttons. When the user clicks a button, the dialog box is dismissed from the screen, and JavaScript returns a value indicating which button was pressed. A value of 1 means that the OK button was pressed; a value of 0 means the Cancel button was pressed.

Syntax

confirm(*message*)

message is the message you want to display in the confirm dialog box.

Example

The following example displays a confirm message, then displays the response in an alert box (*true* for OK, *false* for Cancel).

```
Ret = confirm ("Press OK or Cancel");
alert (Ret);
```

More Information

The confirm method provides a method to ask the user a question and tests for the response. Here's an example of using the confirm method to close Netscape:

```
Ret = confirm ("Are you sure you want to exit Netscape?");
if (Ret)
        window.close();
```

Use the confirm method whenever you want to prompt the user for an OK/Cancel response. You can specify the message, but you cannot remove the "JavaScript Confirm" prompt. You also cannot replace the text of the OK and Cancel buttons. One practical use of the confirm method is in combination with an anchor that links to a very big file.

```
<SCRIPT>
function test (filename) {
        if (confirm ("Are you sure?  It's a really big file!"))
                location = filename;
        else
                alert ("Chicken!")
}
</SCRIPT>
<A HREF="#1" NAME="1" onClick="test('bigfile.gif')">
        Download full image (1.2 gigabytes)</A>
```

prompt Method

The prompt method displays a dialog with a single-line text entry box. Users type something into the entry box and click OK (or press Enter). The user's response is returned and can be stored in a variable or used in an expression. The prompt box also provides a Cancel button that can be used to cancel the box. When canceled, the prompt method returns the value of null.

Syntax

prompt (*message, default_text*)

message is the text you wish to display in the prompt box; *default_text* is the default text you wish to display in the text entry field (omitting this parameter causes the prompt box to display an ugly "<undefined>" value in the text field).

Example

The following example displays a prompt, then displays what you typed in an alert box.

```
Ret = prompt ("Type something", "");
alert (Ret);
```

More Information

The value returned from the prompt box can take any of three forms:

- *String*: User typed in text, then pressed OK.
- *Empty string*: User typed in nothing or cleared text in text box, then pressed OK.
- *Null*: User pressed Cancel.

You will probably want to test each of these values, as shown in the code below, to determine the course of action your script should take.

```
Ret = prompt ("Type something");
if (Ret == "<undefined>");
        alert ("You left '<undefined>' in the box");
else if (Ret == null)
        alert ("You cancelled");
else if (Ret == "")
        alert ("You typed nothing ");
else
        alert ("You typed: " + Ret);
```

Window Methods

The window methods act upon windows. To JavaScript, a window is a browser window or a frame.

clearTimeout Method

The clearTimeout method cancels a timer that was previously created with the setTimeout method.

Syntax

clearTimeout (*timerid*)

timerid is the "identification handle" of the timer created with the setTimeout method.

Example

See setTimeout for more information on using the clearTimeout method.

close Method (used with window object)

The close method used with a window object closes that window. Ordinarily you use the close method with the window object to close some previously opened browser window. You can also use the close method with the main browser window to exit the browser. Moral: use this method with care.

Syntax

window.close() or *windowname*.close()

windowname is a specific name for the window you want to close. When it is used with the *window* object, JavaScript assumes the current window.

Example

The following example displays a window that contains a push button. Click the push button and the window closes.

```
temp=window.open("", "TempWindow");
Result = '<FORM>';
```

```
Result +='<INPUT TYPE="button" VALUE="Close" onClick="window.close()">';
Result +='</FORM>';
temp.document.write(Result);
```

More Information

The close method (when used with the window object) is most often used to close a new browser window that you have created using the window.open method. JavaScript allows you to open complete, fully functional browser windows. You can also open windows that lack the traditional Netscape elements, such as a menu bar, scrollbars, navigation bar, and so forth. You can specify a size, in pixels, for the window. See window.open for more details.

One practical example of the window.close method, used in conjunction with window.open, is to display a help or "hint" box. The box appears with a Close button so that the user can easily close it (alternatively, the user can close the box using the window closing controls that the graphical operating system offers). Here is an example of a window that displays a message in a small window:

```
var HintText = "<H3>Hint!</H3>"
HintText += "This is an example of a hint<P>"
hint=window.open("", "TempWindow",
"toolbar=no,location=no,directories=0,status=no," + "menubar=no,width=200,
        height=140");
var Result = HintText;
Result +='<CENTER><FORM>';
Result +='<INPUT TYPE="button" VALUE="OK" onClick="window.close()">';
Result +='</FORM></CENTER>';
hint.document.write(Result);
```

open Method

The window.open method opens a new browser window (note that only a browser window is opened, not a second "instance" of Netscape). You can open a new, blank window, or a window containing a specified document. The window.open method also allows you to define attributes for the window. Those attributes are detailed below.

Syntax

- *winname* = window.open (*URL*, *name*, *options*)
- *winname* is a variable that contains a reference to the new window object. You can use this variable when referring to a window.
- *URL* specifies the URL to open in the new window.
- *name* is the window name to use in the TARGET attribute of a <FORM> or <A> tag. The name can contain only alphanumeric or underscore (_) characters.
- *options* is a comma-separated list of any of the options and values displayed in the following table.

Window Option	Choice	What It Does
toolbar	=yes/no, =1/0	Toolbar access buttons
location	=yes/no, =1/0	Location box
directories	=yes/no, =1/0	Directory buttons
status	=yes/no, =1/0	Status bar at bottom of window
menubar	=yes/no, =1/0	Menu bar for commands
scrollbars	=yes/no, =1/0	Horizontal and vertical scroll bars
resizable	=yes/no, =1/0	User can resize window
width	=pixels	Width of window
height	=pixels	Height of window

The window object variable and all parameters are optional.

■■■■■■ **NOTE**

A bug in the Netscape 2.0 Unix platform requires that you enumerate all of the window options to ensure that the window style you want appears.

Another bug, which afflicts the Macintosh and Unix platforms in Netscape 2.0, requires that you call the window.open method twice when opening an existing document into a new window. You can merely repeat the window.open instruction a second time (this will have no effect when used under the Windows platforms):

```
window.open("openme.html")        // Display openme.html in new window
window.open("openme.html")        // Call again for Unix/Mac bug
```

■■■■■

Example

The following example opens a new, blank window.

```
window.open();
```

More Information

Such a window opened as in the example above is effectively useless. In most cases, you will either want to open a new window and specify the URL of a document to display in it, or you will define a variable with a window object variable and/or a name so that the window can be referenced later with other JavaScript code.

```
window.open("openme.html")            // Display openme.html in new window
win = window.open();                  // new window object identified as win
win = window.open("", "newwin")       // Specify "new win as target of window
win = window.open ("file.html", "new") // Open file.htm, specify target name
```

Each item is separated by a comma, and no spaces are allowed. JavaScript defaults to 0 (or false) for all items when not specified; for height and width, JavaScript defaults to full-screen resolution when not specified. Some examples that work:

```
// No toolbar, height=200 pixels, width=100 pixels
window.open ("", "new", "toolbar=0,height=200,width=100")


//Toolbar, no scrollbar, status bar
window.open ("", "new", "toolbar=1,scrollbar=0,status=yes")


//Toolbar, height=100 pixels, width=512
window.open ("", "new", "toolbar=1,height=100,width=512")


//Plain window, full size
window.open ("", "new", "")


// "Fully-equipped" window, full size
window.open ("", "new", "")
```

Some examples that don't work:

```
//space in options list
window.open ("", "new", "toolbar=1,height=100, width=512")


//Must include both height and width
window.open ("", "new", "toolbar=1,height=100")
```

◼◼◼◼◼◼ **NOTE**

In Netscape 2.0 there is no way to determine the location of the window on the screen, and there is no way to make the window "modal" or force it to stay on top. With a modal window, you cannot switch to another browser window without first closing it.

For consistent results on all platforms, specify all items that you do not want as item=0.

◼◼◼◼◼

setTimeout Method

The setTimeout method creates a timer, which executes a function after some specified interval.

Syntax

TimerId = setTimeout (*"function"*, *delay*)

- *TimerId* is a variable that contains a "handle" that identifies this specific timer (there can be more than one timer specified at a time). TimerId is optional.

- *function* is an instruction you want carried out after the specified delay. The instruction is always enclosed in quotation marks.

- *delay* is the time delay until the function is executed, specified in milliseconds (thousands of the second). In Netscape 2.0 the delay can be set from 0 on up, but time resolutions below 333 milliseconds are ignored.

Example

The following example creates a timer with a delay of one second and displays an alert box at the end of the interval.

```
setTimeout = "alert('Hello JavaScripters!')", 1000);
```

More Information

Clocks and scrolling marquee banners are among the most common uses of setTimeout. See Chapter 12, "How Do I?...," among other chapters, for more information on using timers in JavaScript.

7

EXPRESSIONS

An *expression* tells JavaScript what to do with the data you provide. For example, an expression can be used in an if statement to test for a certain condition. If the user's name is Fred, for example, the script displays a personalized message just for him. Everyone else receives a standardized greeting.

Expressions are also used to perform basic math functions using JavaScript (additional math functionality is provided with the JavaScript Math object, detailed in Chapter 4, "Objects"). For example, a typical expression adds a value to another value stored in a variable. In this way, JavaScript can keep track of its environment, storing important information it might need later.

This chapter describes how to use expressions in JavaScript, including how to use expressions to create variables, to build conditional statements (such as if statements), and to calculate math.

Creating Expressions

An expression tells JavaScript what you want to do with information given to it. An expression consists of two parts:

- One or more values, called *operands*
- An *operator* that tells JavaScript what you want to do with these values

Sounds complex at first, but all we're really talking about is 2+2.

In JavaScript programs, you use expressions such as this one to define the contents of variables. Here are some other examples:

```
Test1 = 1+1;
Test2 = (15*2)+1;
Test3 = "This is" + " a test";
```

JavaScript processes the expression and places the result in the variable.

Expressions can also be part of a more elaborate scheme using other JavaScript constructs. Used in this way, expressions provide a way for your scripts to think on their own (although they may seem to act on their own more than you'd like them to!). Expressions are most commonly used with the for, if, and while JavaScript statements.

The following sections describe the operators used to construct expressions. Most of these operators work with numbers only, but some can also be used with strings. The discussion is divided into three parts:

- *Assignment* operators, which assign values to variables
- *Math* operators, which apply to number values only, with one exception
- *Relational* operators, which apply to both numbers, and some of which apply to strings

Assignment Operators

These operators assign values to variables. You are likely to use only the = assignment operator for the bulk of your JavaScript programs, but others are available in case you need them. If you're new to the concept of variables, be sure to read Chapter 9, "Variables."

Operator	Function
=	Assigns value to variable—for example, Var=1
+=	Adds value to value already in variable—for example, Var+=1
-=	Subtracts value to value already in variable—for example, Var−=1
*=	Multiplies value with value already in variable—for example, Var*=1
/=	Divides value with value already in variable—for example, Var/=1
%=	Divides value with value already in variable; returns remainder—for example, Var%=1

▰▰▰ **NOTE**

Additional assignment operators are provided for bitwise operations. These are detailed separately in "Using the Bitwise Operators," later in this chapter.

▰▰▰

Using the = (Equals)Assignment Operator

Use the = (equals sign) assignment operator whenever you wish to assign a new value to variable. If the variable previously contained a value, that value is replaced. Here are some examples:

```
MyStringVar = "This is a string"      // assign text to variable
MyNumverVar = 100                     // assign number to variable
MyObjectVar = document.form[0]        // assign document.form[0] object to
                                         variable
```

Using the Shorthand Assignment Operators

The shorthand assignment operators let you add, subtract, multiply, and divide values to values already in a variable. The most commonly used shorthand assignment is +=.

- If the value in the variable and the value to append are *numbers*, += adds the values.
- If the value in the variable and the value to append are *strings*, += combines them into one long string.

Here is a number example:

```
Var = 1;
Var += 5;
// Var now contains 6
```

Another way you could write the above code is as follows:

```
Var = 1;
Var = Var + 5;
```

A text string example is as follows:

```
Var = "Java";
Var += "Script";
// Var now contains "JavaScript
```

Another way you could write this example is as:

```
Var = "Java";
Var = Var + "Script";
```

The remaining shorthand operators let you subtract, multiply, and divide values:

- x = val for subtracting x times val. Equivalent to x = x − val.
- x *= val for multiplying x times val. Equivalent to x = x * val.
- x /= val for dividing x into val. Equivalent to x = x / val.
- x %= val for dividing x into val, leading the remainder (modulus). Equivalent to x = x % val.

In these examples, the variable Val contains 5 in each case:

```
Val -= 3          // result: 2
Val *= 3          // result: 15
Val /= 3          // result: 1.666 (etc.)
Val %= 3          // result: 2
```

Math Operators

These operators perform math calculations with one or more numbers. *V1* and *V2* represent numeric values.

Operator	Function
– *value*	Treats the *value* as a negative number.
v1 + *v2*	Adds values *v1* and *v2* together. Can also be used to connect (concatenate) two or more strings together.
v1 - *v2*	Subtracts value *v2* from *v1*
v1 * *v2*	Multiplies values *v1* and *v2*
v1 / *v2*	Divides value *v1* by *v2*
v1 % *v2*	Divides value *v1* by *v2*; the result is the floating-point remainder of the division
v1++	Adds 1 to *v1*
v1--	Subtracts 1 from *v1*

NOTE

The + operator is dual use. When used with numbers, the + operator adds them together. When used with strings, the + operator connects the strings (called concatenation) and makes them one.

The ++ and–operators (borrowed from C, C++, and Java) can be used in a number of ways. The most common is v1++, whereby you increment the value already in *v1* by 1. (Similarly, the instruction v1– decrements the value already in v1 by 1.) You can actually use the ++ and–increment/decrement operators before or after the value.

- When the operators are used after the value (*postfix*), JavaScript returns the original value, *then* increments—for example, Var++ or Var--.
- When the operators are used before the value (*prefix*), JavaScript increments the value and returns the incremented result—for example, ++Var or --Var.

Suppose the Var variable contains the number 10. In each of the following lines of code, Var is incremented by 1. But the RetVal variable will contain different values because of the order JavaScript uses in incrementing and returning the value.

```
RetVal = Var++  // returns 10
RetVal = ++Var  // returns 11
```

A similar postfix/prefix technique works with the –decrement operator:

```
RetVal = Var–   // returns 10
RetVal = –Var   // returns 9
```

Relational Operators

Relational operators compare two values to see if they are equal, not equal, greater than, or less than (and sometimes a combination of these). *V1* and *V2* represent numeric values.

Operator	Function
v1 == v2	Tests that *v1* and *v2* are equal (note the two equal signs).
v1 <> v2	Tests that *v1* and *v2* are not equal.
v1 > v2	Tests that *v1* is greater than *v2*.
v1 >= v2	Tests that *v1* is greater than or equal to *v2*.
v1 < v2	Tests that *v1* is less than *v2*.
v1 <= v2	Tests that *v1* is less than or equal to *v2*.
! *value*	Evaluates the logical NOT of *value*. The logical NOT is the inverse of an expression: *true* becomes *false*, and vice versa.
v1 && v2	Evaluates the logical AND of *v1* and *v2*.
v1 || v2	Evaluates the logical OR of *v1* and *v2*.

Relational operators are also known as Boolean or *true/false* operators. Whatever they test, the answer is either yes (*true*) or no (*false*). For example, the expression 2==2 would be *true*, but the expression "2==3" would be *false*.

How to Use the && (AND) and || (OR) Relational Operators

The && and || (AND and OR) operators work with numbers and expressions that result in a *true/false* condition. They are not used with strings, unless the strings are a part of a *true/false* expression. JavaScript balks if you try to use the operators with a string alone. For example, the following examples are not allowed:

```
This = "Java";
That = "Script";
Result = This && That;
```

Any of these lines of code results in an error. Instead of combining the *This* and *That* variables into *Result*, JavaScript responds with an error message. As you've read earlier in this chapter, the correct way to combine the two strings is to use the + operator, as in *This+That*.

- Use the && (AND) operator to determine if *both* values in an expression are *true*. If both A AND B are *true*, then the result is *true*. But if A or B is *false*, then the result of the AND is *false*.

- Use the || (OR) operator to determine if *either* value in an expression is *true*. If at least one of them is *true*, then the result is *true*. Only when both values are *false* is the result of the OR expression *false*.

Using a "truth table" to view the action of the AND and OR operators is helpful. The table shows all the possible outcomes given to values in an expression. Truth values are shown for Boolean *true* and *false*, and also for the numeric digits 0 and 1. JavaScript's Boolean operators work the same with either kind of value. (Note: In JavaScript, *true/false* values are distinct from 1/0.)

AND Truth Table

Val1	Val2	Result
false (0)	false (0)	false (0)
false (0)	true (1)	false (0)
true (1)	false (0)	false (0)
true (1)	true (1)	true (1)

OR Truth Table

Val1	Val2	Result
false (0)	false (0)	false (0)
false (0)	true (1)	true (1)
true (1)	false (0)	true (1)
true (1)	true (1)	true (1)

Using the AND and OR Operators in More Complex if Expressions

A common use of the && (AND) and || (OR) relational operators is in if expressions (and also in expressions using the while statement). These expressions are sometimes built to test for one of several conditions, or a number of conditions together.

When at least one of the conditions is *true*, that portion of the script is complete and JavaScript proceeds to the next. Here is an example:

```
if (Var1 == 100) {
        isTrue();
} else if (Var1 == 200) {
        isTrue();
} else if (Var1 == 300) {
        isTrue();
} else {
        isFalse();
}
```

The structure of the routine is referred to as *OR logic*. If Var1 is equal to 100 *OR* 200 *OR* 300, the script executes the *isTrue* function. Any other condition causes the script to execute the *isFalse* function. Many of the scripts in this book revolve around OR logic for if expressions.

What if you want to build expressions that execute the *isTrue* function only if *ALL* of the conditions are met? This structure is more commonly called *AND logic*, and you can easily use this type of logic in scripts by moving the instructions around a bit.

Following are four test scripts that you can use to experiment with the operation of AND and OR logic. The examples show how to create AND and OR logic by using multiple if statements, as well as by using the && (AND) and || (OR) operators. You will find that, in general, using the AND and OR operators is the easier method. You can practice with all four examples by including them in the following script:

```
<HTML><HEAD>
<TITLE>And/Or test</TITLE>
<SCRIPT>
function doTest() {


        // insert AND/OR script segment here


}


function isTrue() {
        alert ("It is true")
}


function isfalse() {
        alert ("It is false")
}
</SCRIPT>
</HEAD>
<BODY>
<FORM>
<INPUT TYPE="button" VALUE="Test" onClick="doTest()">
</FORM>
</BODY></HTML>
```

AND—Separate if Statements

```
var Var1=1, Var2=1;
if (Var1 == 1) {
        if (Var2 == 1)
                isTrue();
        else
                isFalse();
```

```
} else
        isFalse();
```

OR—Separate if Statements

```
var Var1=1, Var2=1;
if (Var1 == 1) {
        isTrue();
} else if (Var2 == 1)
        isTrue();
else
        isFalse();
```

AND—Single if Statement

```
var Var1=1, Var2=1;
if ((Var1 == 1) && (Var2 == 1))
        isTrue();
else
        isFalse();
```

OR—Single if Statement

```
 var Var1=1, Var2=1;
if ((Var1 == 1) || (Var2 == 1))
        isTrue();
else
        isFalse();
```

■■■■■ **NOTE**

Important! Be sure to format the expression with parentheses and brace characters (the { and } characters) as shown; otherwise JavaScript might have trouble parsing it into a meaningful function.

■■■■■

Here's an example of a real-world application of OR/AND in testing the response from the user:

```
RetVal=prompt("Go again (Y/N)?", "Y")
if ((RetVal == "Y") || (RetVal == "y"))
        alert ("You pressed Y or y")
```

The && (AND) and || (OR(operators are not limited to if expressions. Here is an example of how to use the AND operator in a while loop. The example ensures that the value entered at the prompt dialog box is between 100 and 200.

```
CtrlLoop=true;
Value=0;
while (CtrlLoop) {
        Value=prompt ("Enter a value between 100 and 200", Value);
        if ((Value>=100) && (Value<=200))
                CtrlLoop=false;
}
alert (Value)
```

The ! (NOT) Operator

The ! (NOT) operator is used whenever you want to negate a *true* or *false* expression. The statement !true becomes *false*, and !false becomes *true*.

Ordinarily, you use this operator to reverse the outcome of an expression that results in a true/false answer. You might want to test if a certain condition is NOT met, so you can write a more efficient if statement (you can also apply the ! (NOT) operator in for and while loops for additional flexibility).

Let's try an example of the ! (NOT) operator. Suppose you want to ask the user to respond to a prompt. You do not want them to respond with a blank entry, so you write the following code to allow your JavaScript to redisplay the prompt dialog if the entry blank is blank. Notice also the extra if statement that determines if the user chooses the Cancel button. This returns a null value, and the loop ends with a break statement.

```
CtrlLoop=true;
Value="";
while (CtrlLoop) {
```

```
Value=prompt ("Type something", Value);
if (Value == null)
        break;
if (Value != "") {
        CtrlLoop=false;
        alert (Value)
}
}
```

Using the ? Conditional Expression Statement

JavaScript supports an alternative method to creating conditional expressions. It is a "shorthand" method used in C and some other languages, and it is useful if you want to construct a quick and simple test. The syntax is:

(condition) ? *istrue* : *isfalse*

condition is the expression you want to test, *istrue* is what happens if the condition is *true,* and *isfalse* is what happens if the condition is *false.*

You must include statements for both the true and false outcomes and include the colon character.

For example, the following example displays an alert box depending on what you type in response to the prompt box:

```
Ret = prompt ("Type something or click Cancel", "");
(Ret == null) ? alert ("You clicked cancel") : alert ("You typed:"+Ret);
```

■■■■■■ NOTE

While the conditional expression can aid as a shortcut, I personally feel it hard-to-read code. The logic of the if statement, though a bit more "bulky," is generally easier to decipher, especially when you are reading other people's scripts. Of course, adopt or ignore the JavaScript conditional expression as you choose.

The Bitwise Operators

JavaScript supports unique operators that work with numbers only. These are the *bitwise* operators, because they deal with the individual bits that make up each number. The bitwise operators have only occasional use in JavaScript programs. If you have a programming background, these operators may be of use to you in creating more complex scripts. The bitwise operators are listed in the following table.

Operator	Name	Function
&	Bitwise AND	Performs AND test on each bit in a number
|	Bitwise OR	Performs OR test on each bit in a number
^	Bitwise XOR	Performs XOR test on each bit in a number
<<	Shift left	Shifts the values of the bits 1 or more bits to the left
>>	Shift right	Shifts the values of the bits 1 or more bits to the right
>>>	Shift right, zero fill	Same as Shift right, but also fills the digits to the left with zeros.

For example, the following code displays 8, which is the value of 2 when shifted to the left four bits (binary 10 to binary 1000):

```
Temp = 2;
Temp = Temp << 2;
alert (Temp);
```

Using the Bitwise Operators

Bitwise operators manipulate numbers one bit at a time. Suppose you put a *9* into variable *This* and *14* in variable *That*. Use the bitwise AND operator with them and you get *8* as a result. In the following discussion, the words AND, OR, and XOR are used to represent the bitwise operators, rather than their symbols (&, |, and ^), which you would use in a script.

Refer to the tables earlier in this chapter for the AND and OR truth tables. Notice what happens when you use AND with two binary digits in an expression (recall that a binary digit is a 0 or a 1). When both digits are 1, the result is 1. In all other instances, the result is 0. This relationship is the reason for the name AND: "If A AND B...."

With the logical OR expression, the output is 0 when both input digits are 0. In all other instances, the output is 1. Finally, with the logical XOR (which means eXclusive OR) expression, the output is 1 if one digit is 1 and the other is 0. If both digits are the same (either 1 or 0), then the output is 0.

To visualize how JavaScript returns a result of 8 when the numbers 9 and 14 are joined together with the AND operator, you have to reduce those numbers to their binary equivalents. These equivalents are shown in the following table.

Decimal Number	Binary Equivalent
9	1001
14	1110

Using the truth table, you can manually compute the result of joining these two numbers together with AND.

$$1001 = 9$$
$$1110 = 14$$

AND _____

$$1000 = 8$$

Binary 1000 is equivalent to decimal 8. Using the same numbers, perform an OR computation:

$$1001 = 9$$
$$1110 = 14$$

OR _____

$$1111 = 15$$

For your reference, the following table lists the binary equivalents of the first 16 numbers (counting 0 as the first digit and ending with 15). You can count higher by adding an extra 1 or 0 digit on the left. The extra digit increases the count by a power of two–31, 63, 127, 255, 511, 1023, and so forth.

Decimal Number	Binary Equivalent
0	0000
1	0001
2	0010
3	0011
4	0100
5	0101
6	0110
7	0111
8	1000
9	1001
10	1010
11	1011
12	1100
13	1101
14	1110
15	1111

How can bitwise operations be used in a JavaScript program? One way is to combine more than one numeric value in a single variable, and then use the AND bitwise operator ($\&$) to determine the numbers in the variable. This process uses "powers of two" numbers–that is, 1, 2, 4, 8, 16, 32, 64, and so forth. Each of these numbers contains a single 1 bit; the other bits are 0.

Consider, for example, the numbers 2, 8, and 16. The following table displays the binary representations of these numbers:

Number	Binary Equivalent
2	00010
8	01000
16	10000

Add these numbers together, and you get 26 (2+8+16). The binary equivalent of 26 is 11010. Notice that there's a 1 in the binary equivalent for every 1 in the numbers that were summed.

Now comes the task of finding out what powers-of-two numbers are contained in 26. You do this by ANDing the number with 26. Let's take each powers-of-two number in turn and look at the result. If the answer is 0, then the powers-of-two number used in the expression is *not* part of the value 26.

$$00001 = 1$$
$$11010 = 26$$

AND   _____

$$00000 = 0 \qquad \text{–no match}$$

$$00010 = 2$$
$$11010 = 26$$

AND   _____

$$00010 = 2 \qquad \text{–a match!}$$

$$00100 = 4$$
$$11010 = 26$$

AND   _____

$$00000 = 0 \qquad \text{–no match}$$

$$01000 = 8$$
$$11010 = 26$$

AND   _____

$$01000 = 8 \qquad \text{–a match!}$$

$$10000 = 16$$
$$11010 = 26$$

AND   _____

$$10000 = 16 \qquad \text{–a match!}$$

As you can see from the above tests, the answer is 0 for the values that are *not* contained (1 and 4) within the number 26. The other tests result in the same number used as the testing value.

Now for a practical use. Suppose you want to pass a single variable to a user-defined procedure you have created. This function displays any of a combination of four messages in a JavaScript alert box dialog box. You specify which message you want to appear by using the values 1, 2, 4, and/or 8. You can use these values or add them together if you want to show multiple messages.

```
function test ()  {
        Ret=showMessage (15);
        alert (Ret);
}


function showMessage (MessageVal) {
        OutputString = "\n";
        if (MessageVal & 1)
                OutputString += "You've just won a million dollars!\n";
        if (MessageVal & 2)
                OutputString += "Payment will begin next Monday!\n";
        if (MessageVal & 4)
                OutputString += "We'll pay you in cash!\n";
        if (MessageVal & 8)
                OutputString += "You will be audited by the IRS!\n";
        return (OutputString);
}
```

Some sample single-message results are as follows:

MessageVal	String
0	Nothing
1	You've just won a million dollars!
2	Payment will begin next Monday!
4	We'll pay you in cash!
8	You will be audited by the IRS!

Some sample multiple-message results are shown in the following table:

MessageVal	Strings
3	You've just one a million dollars!
	Payment will begin next Monday!

MessageVal	Strings
10	Payment will begin next Monday!
	You will be audited by the IRS!

Note that a MessageVal of 15 displays all four messages.

Operators and Strings

Recall that in a JavaScript program, a string is any assortment of text characters. You can't perform math calculations with text, but you can compare one string of text against another.

With the exception of && (AND) and || (OR), the relational operators can be used with strings for the purpose of comparing them. For instance, you may want to see if two strings are the same, as in:

```
if ("MyString" == "StringMy");
```

This statement results in *false* because the strings are not the same. In a working script, you would probably construct the string comparison to work with variables, as in:

```
if (StringVar1 == StringVar2);
```

JavaScript compares the *contents* of the two variables and reports *true* or *false*, accordingly.

JavaScript considers the case of the characters when you compare strings. The strings must match exactly, including the case of the string. Some examples are displayed in the following table.

String 1	String 2	Result
hello	hello	Match
Hello	hello	No Match
HELLO	hello	No Match

While the == (equals) operator is used extensively in comparing strings, you can use !<, !>, <, >, <=, and >= as well. The != (not equals) operator is an obvious choice: you can use it to check if one string is not equal to another. But why the others? Don't they check if one value is greater or lesser than the other? How can one string have "less" or "more" value than the other?

The < and > operators do indeed test for greater than and less than; and while they will work with strings, they don't work in exactly the way you may think. Strings–whether they are composed of one character or many–have a numeric value in JavaScript.

- If there is one character in the string, the value is the ASCII equivalent of the character. For example, the ASCII equivalent of the letter "A" is 65.

- If there is more than one character in the string, the value is a composite of the ASCII equivalents of all the characters.

String comparisons using the < and > operators are not often used, except when performing certain special operations such as sorting. See Chapter 13, "Plug and Play Routines," for a sort routine that uses comparisons to put strings in alphabetical order.

Multiple Operators

JavaScript can handle more than one operator in an expression. This allows you to string three or more numbers, strings, or variables together to make complex expressions, such as 5+10/2*7.

With this feature of multiple operators comes a penalty: You must be careful of the *order of precedence*, which is the order in which JavaScript evaluates an expression. Like many programming languages and electronic spreadsheet programs, JavaScript doesn't merely start at the left side of the expression and calculate to the other side. Rather, it calculates multiplication and division first, then addition and subtraction, and so forth, following a general left-to-right progression..

The following table displays the order in which JavaScript evaluates an expression, from highest to lowest.

Order	Operator
1	-(unary minus), +(unary plus), ~(bitwise not), !(logical not), ++, --
2	*(multiply), /(divide), %, /
3	+(add), –(subtract)
4	<<(shift left) >>(shift right), >>>(shift right, zero-fill)
5	<(less than), <=(less than or equal to), >(greater than), >=(greater than or equal to), !>(not equal), ==(equal)

Order	Operator
6	&(bitwise and)
7	^(bitwise xor)
8	|(bitwise or)
9	AND(logical and)
10	XOR(logical xor)
11	OR(logical or)
12	?:(conditional)
13	assignment
14	, (comma)

JavaScript doesn't distinguish between operators on the same level or precedence. If it encounters a + for addition and a - for subtraction, it will evaluate the expression by using the first operator it encounters, going from left to right. You have to be careful, though, and discern the difference between subtraction and a number that you have identified as negative.

As you can see, you can get some wild results if you let the "natural" order or precedence JavaScript uses take control. You can specify another calculation order by using parentheses. Values and operators inside the parentheses are evaluated first. You can write complex expressions using parentheses inside other parentheses. JavaScript always starts at the innermost parentheses and works outward, such as in this expression:

```
Ret=2*((45+2)/10)
```

This expression is evaluated as follows (the answer is 9.4, with rounding):

1. Add 45 plus 2.
2. Divide the result obtained in step 1 by 10.
3. Multiply the result obtained in step two by 2.

Logical (*true/false*) expressions also use parentheses to control the order of evaluation. Controlling the order of evaluation is particularly important in logical expressions, because leaving out parentheses or using them incorrectly, can cause JavaScript to evaluate a *true* expression as *false*, and vice versa. The general syntax is:

((*true/false* test1) && (*true/false* test2))

Note the parentheses around the two *true/false* tests, and a third set around everything.

> JavaScript doesn't mind if you put extra spaces between the parentheses of your expressions. An expression using ((is just as valid as one using ((. The spaces can help you visualize the structure of the expression. Use whatever method is the most comfortable for you.

Here is the basic rule of thumb for setting the order of precedence for logical expressions: Each complete logical expression should be enclosed in its own parentheses. You can then apply additional logical operators. The entire expression is then enclosed in parentheses for the script state (if, while, for, and so forth). Here are some examples:

```
// If MyVar equals 10, AND YourVar equals 30, then true
if ((MyVar == 10)&& (YourVar == 30))


// If either Path or MyPath is "http://domain.com", then true
if ((Path == "http://domain.com") || (MyPath == "http://domain.com"))


// If Name is either "Fred" or "John," then true
if ((Name == "Fred") || (Name == "John"))
```

CHAPTER

8

STATEMENTS

JavaScript uses the term *statements* for its programming commands. These are commands that are designed to work independently of any JavaScript object. There only 11 statements in the Netscape Navigator 2.0 implementation of JavaScript; more are on the way and will help to enrich the capabilities of JavaScript. The currently available statements are:

// comment

break

continue

for

for...in

function

if...else

new

```
return

var

while
```

In this chapter you'll learn what the statements are and how to use them. Short examples are given so you can see how the statements work in context.

// (Comment)

The // characters tell JavaScript that you want to include explanatory comments in your program. The comment ends at the first hard return that is encountered. JavaScript places no limit on the length of the comment, as long as there is no hard return before the comment ends. JavaScript assumes text after the hard return is valid code.

```
// This is a simple comment

// This is another comment that spans more than one line. Though the
   comment wraps to the second line, the first line ends with a "soft return"
   in the text editing program. No hard return character is inserted.
```

You can place the // comment characters anywhere on the line. JavaScript will treat *all* the text on that after the // as a comment.

```
MyVariable="This is a test"      // assigns text variable MyVariable
```

Comments are ignored when the script is played, so they do not greatly affect the speed of execution. However, lots of comments increase the file size of scripts and take longer to transmit to the user's computer over a dial-up Internet connection. For best results, limit comments in JavaScript programs to brief single lines.

When writing long comments it's better to use the alternate commenting characters /* and */ Text between these characters is treated as a comment. Alternatively you can start each line with the // comment characters.

```
// This section checks to see if the Enter key is pressed,
// then continues on
```

or

```
/* This section checks to see if the Enter key is pressed,
   then continues on */
```

■■■■ **NOTE**

The /* and */ comment markup is ideal for copyright and version notices, like this:

```
/*_____

JavaScript Magic!, Version 1.0

(c) Copyright 2001, by John P. Doe.

All Rights reserved.

Copy this and die!!

_____*/
```

■■■■

break

The break statement tells JavaScript to exit a "controlled structure," and resume execution at a point after the structure. The break statement is used with structures built using the following commands:

- for
- for...in
- while

The most common use of the break statement is to prematurely end a for loop. For example:

```
for (Count=1; Count<=10; Count++) {
        if (Count == 6)
                break;
    document.write ("<P>Loop: " + Count + "</P>");

}
```

This example shows a for loop that counts from 1 to 10 and prints the number at each iteration of the loop (see Figure 8.1). An if statement inside the for loop is used to test if the value in the Count variable is equal to 6. If Count equals 6,

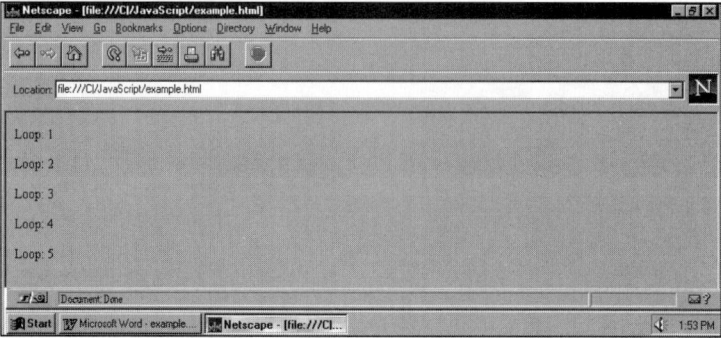

Figure 8.1 For loops are used to repeat a series of steps, like writing repetitive text to the browser window.

the break statement is executed, and the script leaves the for loop. As used in this simple example, the script will count from 1 to 6, then stop. It exits the for loop before it can count up to 10.

continue

The continue statement tells JavaScript to skip any instructions that may follow in a for, for...in, or while loop, and proceed with the next iteration. The most common use of the continue statement is to conditionally skip instructions in the loop, but not exit the loop (as the break statement does). For example:

```
for (Count=1; Count<=10; Count++) {
        if (Count == 6)
                continue;
document.write ("<P>Loop: " + Count + "</P>");
}
```

This example shows a for loop that counts from 1 to 10 and prints the number at each iteration of the loop. An if statement inside the for loop is used to test if the value in the Count variable is equal to 6. If Count equals 6, the continue statement is executed, and the script skips the document.write instruction on the next line. But, the loop doesn't end. Instead, it continues, and prints lines for the remaining numbers. As used in this simple example, the script will count from 1 to 5, skip 6, then print 7 through 10.

Also see the JavaScript break statement for another way to control the iterations in for, for...in, and while loops.

for

The for statement repeats a block of instructions one or more times. The number of iterations is controlled by values supplied as arguments. The syntax of the for statement is:

```
for (InitVal; Test; Increment)
```

- *InitVal* is the starting value of the for loop, and is often 0 or 1. But it can be any number. *InitVal* is an expression that establishes the initial value and assigns that value to a variable. For example, *Count=0* or *i=1*.

- *Test* is the expression used by the for statement to control the number of iterations of the loop. As long as the *Test* expression is *true*, the loop continues. When the *Test* expression proves *false*, the loop ends. Example: Count<10 is *true* as long as the value in the Count variable is less than 10.

- *Increment* indicates how you want the for loop to count, by 1s, 2s, 5s, 10s, etc. This is also an expression and usually takes the form of *CountVar++*, where *CountVar* is the name of the variable first assigned in the *InitVal* expression. Example: Count++ increases the value in the Count variably by 1 for each iteration.

▬▬▬▬ **NOTE**

Unlike all of the other constructs in JavaScript, the for statement uses semi-colons to separate its arguments, rather than commas. This is in keeping with the syntax used in C, C++, and Java.

▬▬▬▬

Here's an example of a for loop that counts from 1 to 10, stepping one digit at a time. At each iteration the script inserts some text and begins a new line. The JavaScript you wish to repeat is enclosed in { and } characters following the for statement—this forms the *for statement block*. You can provide one line or many within the { and } characters.

```
for (Count=1; Count<=10; Count++) {
        document.write ("Iteration: "+Count+"<BR>");
}
```

Count is the variable name used to store the for loop counter. The for loop starts out with 1 and proceeds to 10. The test expression is Count<=10 which reads:

Count is less than or equal to 10

As long as this expression is *true*, the for loop continues. Do note that the *Increment* argument is also an expression and in the example uses the Count variable to increment the for loop by 1 for each iteration. There's no law that says you must increment the for loop by 1s. Here's just one of the many alternatives:

```
for (Count=1; Count<101; Count+=10) {
        document.write ("Iteration: "+Count+"<BR>");
}
```

This example counts by 10s, from 10 to 100.

for...in

The for...in statement is a special version of the for statement, described in the previous section. For...in is used to display the property names and and/or property contents of objects. It is mostly handy as a debugging and testing tool: if a portion of your JavaScript code isn't working properly, and you suspect it may be the fault of a JavaScript object you are trying to use, you can examine all of the properties for that object with the for...in statement.

Unlike the for statement, for...in doesn't use incrementing tests or other expressions. You provide the name of a holding variable (the name of the variable is up to you), and the object you want to use.

The basic syntax for the for...in statement is

for (*var* in *object*) {

   statements }

- *var* is the name of a variable
- *object* is the object you wish to example

- *statements* are one or more JavaScript instructions you wish to execute for each property returned by the for...in loop.

Here's an example. Suppose you want to determine the properties of the navigator object (this object contains details about the Netscape Navigator or other browser you are using). The following code displays each property name in an alert box. Click OK to proceed to the next property names. The loop automatically ends when there are no more properties in the object.

```
for (temp in navigator) {
        alert (temp);
}
```

A variation of this example is shown below. It not only displays the property names, but the contents of each property (some properties are empty, and therefore no contents are shown for them). The contents of the properties is displayed by using the syntax *object[var]*, or in this case navigator[temp].

```
for (temp in navigator) {
        alert (temp + ": " + navigator[temp]);
}
```

The for..in loop can be used for all object types. You can use it to iterate through all the properties for a form in a document, for example, or through the properties of a user-defined object (an object you've defined). For example, to cycle through all the properties of a form, you'd use the for...in loop like this (assume the form name is "myform"):

```
<SCRIPT>
function test() {
for (temp in document.myform) {
        alert (temp);
}
}
</SCRIPT>
<FORM NAME="myform">
<INPUT TYPE="text" NAME="box1">
<INPUT TYPE="text" NAME="box2">
<INPUT TYPE="text" NAME="box3">
```

```
<INPUT TYPE="button" VALUE="Click" onClick="test()">
</FORM>
```

function

The function statement lets you create your own user-defined functions (as well as user-defined objects and methods for those objects). Functions are self-contained routines that can be "called" elsewhere within your JavaScript code. For example, if you have a function named writeMyName, which displays your name in headline text, you can activate it merely by referring to the name writeMyName someplace within your JavaScript code. Here's a short test that shows how this might work:

```
<HTML>
<HEAD>
<TITLE>Function Test</TITLE>
<SCRIPT LANGUAGE="JavaScript">
function writeMyName () {
        MyName="John Doe"
alert (MyName)
}
</SCRIPT>
</HEAD>
<BODY>
<FORM>
<INPUT TYPE="button" NAME="button1" VALUE="Click Me!"
onClick="writeMyName()"><P>
</FORM>
</BODY>
</HTML>
```

The writeMyName function is defined within <SCRIPT>...</SCRIPT> tags. It is activated (otherwise known as *called*) when the form button is pushed. This calling action is accomplished using the onClick event handler, defined in the <INPUT> tag for the form button.

> Functions can also be used to create your own methods, which can inter-act with JavaScript objects, either ones built into JavaScript or ones you create yourself.
>
> User-defined functions represent a huge portion of what you'll do in JavaScript. So I've devoted an entire chapter on this topic. See Chapter 11, "Defining Functions, Objects, and Methods," for more information.

if...else

The if—along with its optional else—statement is used to build an "if condi-tional" expression. It is called a *conditional* expression because it tests for a spe-cific condition.

- If the expression is *true*, the script performs the instructions following the if statement.
- If the expression is *false*, the script jumps to the instructions that follow the else statement. If there is no else statement, the script jumps past the if statement entirely and continues from there.

The syntax for if is:

```
if (expression)
```

The result of the if expression is always either *true* or *false*. The following syntax is acceptable when there's only one instruction following the if and else statements.

```
if (ExampleVar == 10)
        Start();
else
        Stop();
```

Should there be more than one instruction that follows the if or else statement, the { and } characters must be used to define an *if statement block*. With the { and } char-acters in place, JavaScript knows to execute all of the instructions within the block.

```
if (ExampleVar == 10) {
        Count = 1;
        Start();
} else {
        Count = 0;
        Stop();
}
```

■■■■■ **NOTE**

There's no rule that says you can't always use the { and } brackets for if statements. The following is perfectly acceptable:

```
if (ExampleVar == 10) {
        Start();
} else {
        Stop();
}
```

In fact, this approach is probably the safest method to use because you're always assured the if statement will work as you expect. Your script will behave erratically—or you will receive an error message—if you forget the { and } characters, and which to execute more than one instruction.

For example, the following code executes the alert method regardless of whether the if statement is true or false. The reason: As there are no { and } characters to define a statement block, JavaScript assumes the alert method is not part of the if statement.

```
if (ExampleVar == 10)
        Start();
else
        Stop();
        alert ("You chose stop");
```

■■■■■

Expressions in if statements are not limited to the == equality operator. You can test if values are not equal to one another, greater than, less than, and more. See Chapter 7, "Expressions," for more information on creating JavaScript expressions using if statements.

new

The new statement (actually considered an operator, but is grouped here for consistency) creates a new copy of an object. It is used in either of two ways:

- To define a new Date object (Date is a built-in JavaScript object)
- To define a new user-defined object

The syntax is the same with either use:

objectname = new *objectName*(*params*);

- *varname* is the name of the new object. Acceptable names are the same as for JavaScript variables. In fact, you can consider the created object as a JavaScript variable.
- *objectName* is the name of the object. When using the built-in Date object, you use the word Date (note the capitalization—this is mandatory). When using a user-defined object function, you provide the name of the object function.
- *params* are one or more parameters that you pass to the object function, if needed.

■■■■■■■ **NOTE**

New is actually considered a "constructor operator" in object-oriented programming lingo. I include it with the list of statements for convenience.

■■■■■■■

Here's an example of using the new statement to create an copy—otherwise known as an "instance"—of the Date object:

```
now = new Date();
```

The now object, which can be considered a JavaScript variable, has all the properties and methods of the JavaScript Date object. For example, you use the now object to determine the current hour of the day:

```
now = new Date();
HourNow = now.getHours();
```

Here's an example of using the new statement to create an instance of a user defined object. The object function—the thing that defines the object—is also shown. This simplistic object assigns the string passed to it to a name property. That property is displayed in an alert box, using the syntax *alert (newObj.name)*.

```
newObj = new myObject ("Gordon");
alert (newObj.name);
function myObject (Param1) {
        this.name = Param1;
}
```

■■■■■■ **NOTE**

You cannot use the new statement to create other JavaScript object types, such as document or window. These objects are defined implicitly when a new document or window is created in the browser. If you try you'll get a *"xxx* is not a constructor" error message, where *xxx* is the JavaScript object you tried to use.

■■■■■

return

The return statement is used to mark the end of a function. When JavaScript encounters the return statement, it "returns" to that spot immediately after the call to the function. The return statement can be used with and without a return value.

- If a value is included with the return statement, then the function returns that value.

- If value is included with the return statement, then the function returns a null (nothing).

The return statement may not be used outside of a function. JavaScript reports an error if you attempt to use return outside a function.

Here's are two examples of return, with and without a value:

```
function myFunc() {
        var OutString = "This is a test";
        return (OutString);
}
function myFunc() {
        OutString = "This is a test";
        return;
}
```

Common JavaScript practice is to omit the parentheses surrounding the return value. I use the parentheses in deference to traditional C programming practice. Feel free to drop the parentheses if you choose.

████████

When using return in more than one statement in a function, be sure to use it in the same way each time. Otherwise, JavaScript will display a warning message. For instance, suppose your function tests if a value passed to it is less than 5. You want the function to return differently depending on whether this value is less than or more than 5. Here's the wrong way to do it. Note that only one return statement returns a value.

```
function testMe (Val) {
        if (Val < 5)
                return (true);
        else
                return;
}
```

Now the right way:

```
function testMe (Val) {
        if (Val < 5)
                return (true);
        else
                return (false);
}
```

this

The this keyword (it's not really a statement) refers to the current object and is short-hand for using the formal name of the object. It is typically used in one of three ways:

- To refer to the current form or control in an event handler (such as onClick or onSubmit)
- To define a new property in a user-defined object.

The syntax for this is:

```
this
```

or

```
this.object
```

The object name helps to *disambiguate* what "this" means. For instance, suppose you want to return the whole form with an onClick event handler. You'd do it this way, to tell JavaScript you want the entire form object:

```
<INPUT TYPE="button" NAME="button" VALUE="Click" onClick="test(this.form)">
```

Using just the this keyword, the onClick event handler passes only the button.

```
<INPUT TYPE="button" NAME="button" VALUE="Click" onClick="test(this)">
```

The this keyword is also often used to define a new property in a user-defined object:

```
newObj = new myObject ("Gordon", "McComb);
alert (newObj.name);
function myObject (First, Last) {
        this.firstname = First;
        this.lastname = Last;
}
```

And, the this keyword can be used to refer to any other object, including JavaScript objects, but this application isn't used as much because there are other ways to accomplish the same thing (it's usually better just to refer to the object directly by name). Here are some examples of this last technique. Note that in all cases the this keyword must be used inside a function. An error will occur if you attempt to use it outside a function.

```
// this used alone defaults to window object
function test () {
for (temp in this)
        alert (temp + ": " + this[temp])
}
// this used with document refers to document property of the window object
function test () {
for (temp in this.document)
        alert (temp + ": " + this.document[temp])
}
```

var

Use the var statement to explicitly declare a variable. You may also define a value for the variable at the same time as you declare it, but this is not necessary. The var statement also sets the "scope" of a variable when the variable is defined inside a function. More about this in a bit.

The basic syntax is:

```
var VariableName;
```

or

```
var VariableName = value;
```

- *VariableName* is the name of the variable you wish to use.
- *value* is the value you want to assign to the variable.

In the first example, the variable VariableName is declared (allocated in memory), but its contents remain empty. In the second example, the VariableName variable is declared and a value assigned to it at the same time.

Used outside of a user-defined function, both of these do exactly the same thing:

```
var VariableName = "value";
VariableName = "value";
```

Both create a *global* variable (the variable is considered "global in scope"); that is a variable that can be accessed from any function in any window or frame that is currently loaded. For example, the following works, because MyVar is declared outside the function and is therefore global (again, the var statement is optional here):

```
var MyVar = 5;
// or MyVar = 5;
function testVariable () {
        alert (MyVar);
}
```

Conversely, this will result in an error because the MyVar variable is assigned in another function with the var statement, making it *local* to that function. The variable is considered "local in scope."

```
function defineVariable() {
        var MyVar = 5;
}
function testVariable () {
        alert (MyVar);
}
```

■■■■■■ **NOTE**

JavaScript also lets you fudge by making a global variable inside a function simply by leaving off the var statement. This works but is considered substandard programming because MyVar is not explicitly defined as global by placing the variable assignment expression outside of a function:

```
function defineVariable() {
        MyVar = 5;
}
function testVariable () {
        alert (MyVar);
}
```

■■■■■

You also use var statement if you've defined a global variable (see above) and want to use a separate, local, variable of the same name in a function. In this example,

MyVar is declared globally outside the testVariable() function. It is again defined inside the testVariable() function, this time with the var keyword to make it local. When this test is run JavaScript displays 10 in the first alert box in the testVariable() function, and 5 in the anotherTest() function.

```
var MyVar = 5;
function testVariable () {
        var MyVar = 10
        alert ("testVariable function: " + MyVar);
        anotherTest();
}
function anotherTest() {
        alert ("anotherTest function: " + MyVar);
```

while

The while statement sets up a unique repeating loop that causes the script to repeat a given set of instructions. The looping continues as long as the expression in the while statement is *true*. When the while statement proves false, the loop is broken and the script continues. Any JavaScript code inside the *while statement block*—defined by using the { and } characters—is considered part of the loop and is repeated.

The syntax of the while statement is:

while (*Expression*) {

// stuff to repeat

}

In the following example the while loop is repeated for a total of ten times. With each iteration of the loop JavaScript prints text to the screen.

```
Count=0;
while (Count <10) {
        document.write ("Iteration: "+Count+"<BR>")
        Count++;
}
```

Here's how the this example works. First, the Count variable is set to 0. This is the initial value that will be compared in the while expression, which is Count <10. Count starts at 0. With each iteration of the loop, text is printed to the screen, and the Count variable is increased by 1.

The first 10 times the loop is repeated Count <10 is true, so the loop continues. After the tenth trip, the Count variable contains the number 10, and the while expression proves false. The loop is broken, and JavaScript skips to the end of the while statement block (that portion after the } character).

The while loop is what is known as an *entry* loop. The test expression appears at the beginning of the loop structure. The contents of a while loop may never be executed, depending on the outcome of the test expression

Take the following code (please!):

```
Response = prompt ("Please enter a number greater than 1");
Count = 1;
while (Count <= Response) {
        document.write ("Count: "+ Count + "<BR>");
        Count++;
}
```

In this JavaScript example, a prompt method asks you to enter a number greater than 1. This number is then used to control the iterations of a while loop. If you type 5, for example, then the loop will repeat five times. The loop continues as long as the while expression—*Count<=Response*—remains *true*.

Notice that the *Count* variable starts at 1. In this way, if you enter a 0 in response to the prompt, the while loop fails, and the instructions inside the while loop block are never executed (because 1<=0 is *false*).

While loops are particularly handy for insisting that the user enters valid data. Here's a simplified version of a data validator:

```
Response = "";
while ((Response == "") || (Response == "<undefined>")){
        Response=prompt ("Please enter your name");
}
```

```
if (Response != null)
        alert ("Hello, " + Response);
```

The first step is to assign an empty string to the Response variable. Since Response is empty, the while expression evaluated to true, and the prompt dialog appears, asking for the user's name. Since the Response string is empty, the prompt dialog appears with <undefined> in the text box. The script will not allow you to proceed unless you either click the Cancel button or type some text.

Notice the if test. Should the user click on Cancel, the value returned from the prompt dialog is null. Should the value be other than null, the script assumes it's a valid name, and an alert box, greeting the user, is displayed.

with

The with statement is designed as a time and space saver. You use it to help you cut down on extraneous keystrokes when writing a JavaScript program. The with statement is typically used with the built-in Math object, as it requires you to specify the object name when accessing any of its properties, such as:

```
alert (Math.PI);
alert (Math.round(1234.5678));
```

The syntax for with is:

```
with (object) {
        statements
}
```

- *object* is the object you want to use.
- *statements* are one or more statement you want to execute using the object as the default.

By using the with statement, you can cut out the references to the Math object, as they become implied to JavaScript. Be sure to enclose all the property constructions you wish to associate with the with statement inside { and } characters. These characters define the *with statement block* and are mandatory.

```
with (Math) {
        alert (PI);
        alert (round(1234.5678));
}
```

You are not limited to using the with statement with just Math. You can use it with most any object, even objects you define yourself (this topic is addressed in more detail in Chapter 11, "Defining Functions, Objects, and Methods"). For example, suppose you want to perform several actions on the document.forms[0].textbox object—a textbox control in the first form of the document. There's no need to define this long and drawn out object name; you can use the with statement instead.

```
function test () {
        with (document.forms[0].textbox1) {
                alert (name);
                alert (value);
        }
}
```

Because you've used the name and value properties in a with statement block, JavaScript automatically assumes they refer to the object specified in the with expression, in this case document.forms[0].textbox1.

Another way to save space when referring to objects is to assign the object name to a variable, such as obj. Then use the obj variable to refer to the full object.

```
function test () {
        obj = document.forms[0].textbox1;
        alert (obj.name);
        alert (obj.value);

}
```

VARIABLES

Variables let you can store information that the script, the user, or some other source provides. You can then use that information later in your script. For example, a variable might be used to store a person's name so it can be used at some point in the script.

This chapter details the use of variables in a JavaScript program. It covers how to assign variables and how to use the values contained within variables. Both "regular" variables and array variables are covered.

Understanding Variables

Variables are temporary holders of information. A variable can hold numeric values ("numbers"), character strings, *true/false* values, or an object (JavaScript variables can hold a few other kinds of data, but these are by far the most common types).

- *Numeric values* are numbers that can be added together. Here is an example: 2+2 =4.

- *Character strings* are a collection of text, such as "JavaScript" or "My name is Mudd." Strings can contain number characters, but they are not treated as numbers. Adding 2+2 when the numbers are strings results in "22."
- *True/false values* are the Boolean *true* and *false*.
- *Objects* are JavaScript or user-defined objects.

Placing a value in a variable is referred to as *assigning* or *assigning a value to a variable*. When you see a phrase such as, "Assign the value of 10 to variable *Num*," you know that it means to store the number 10 in a variable referred to as *Num*.

JavaScript variables "belong" to the script document that created them. The variables are lost when the document is unloaded. In addition, the contents of a variable are erased when you reassign them with a new value.

Though a variable created in one document script is not usually seen by another document script, JavaScript does provide ways to share variables between them. You do this by referencing the name of the document along with the name of the variable. This technique is described later in this chapter in "Referencing Variables in Other Loaded Documents."

Several JavaScript instructions create and store variables, but the basic way to accomplish this manually is with the equals (=) assignment operator. The basic syntax is:

VariableName = value

- *The first argument is the name of the variable.* Variable names can be very long, but you are restricted in the characters you can use. See "Variable Naming Conventions," later in this chapter, for more information on valid variable names.
- *The second argument is the contents of the variable.* Variable values can include many different types of information, such as numbers, strings, and math expressions (such as 2+2).

If you're a Pascal user, you may be tempted to construct the variable assignment using:=. This syntax is not supported in JavaScript.

▰▰▰▰▰▰ **NOTE**

> JavaScript allows you to store an almost unlimited number of variables. The maximum number of variables you can create and use in a program depends on what kind of information the variable contains and the amount of available memory in your computer. Most of your scripts will create a dozen or two variables; even if all of these are filled with fairly long strings, you will not be in any particular danger of running out of memory.

▰▰▰▰▰

The rest of this section provides further detail, including examples, concerning the four most common types of contents for JavaScript variables.

Numbers in Variables

A number is one or more digits stored in the computer in such a way that JavaScript can perform math calculations with them. JavaScript can store extraordinarily large numbers, from 1.7×10^{-308} to $1.7 \times 10^{+308}$. Spreadsheet users may know this span of numbers as "scientific" values with 15-digit precision. That is, the numbers are precise up to 15 digits to the right of the decimal point. Programmers familiar with other computer languages may know this span of numbers as "double precision floating point" numbers.

To place a number in a variable, just provide the variable name, the equals sign—this is the variable assignment operator—and the value you want to use. For example, to place the number 10 in a variable named MyVar, use this code:

```
MyVar = 10;
```

Strings in Variables

A string is one or more text characters arranged in memory in single file. Strings can contain numbers (digits), letters, punctuation, or a combination of these. Math calculations cannot be performed on strings. Strings are assigned to JavaScript variables by enclosing them in a set of single or double quotation marks, like this:

"I am a string" or 'I am a string'

Why are the quotation marks necessary? Without the marks, JavaScript mistakes each word in *I am a string* as the name of a function or variable. When you try to play the program, JavaScript responds with an error message. This line of code works as a means of placing a string into a variable:

```
MyVar = "This is JavaScript";
```

Boolean Values in Variables

There are two Boolean values: *true* and *false*. Some programming languages don't have a separate set of Boolean values, and instead use 0 for *false* and 1 or -1 (or any other non-zero value) for *true*. JavaScript can also use these numbers to represent *true* and *false*, but in addition reserves the words "true" and "false" to mean Boolean *true* and *false*. You can think of the Boolean *true* and *false* values as being equivalent to on/off or yes/no.

To assign a Boolean value to a variable, provide just the word true or false, without quotation marks. Here is an example:

```
MyVar = true;
```

Objects in Variables

Variables can contain objects, including JavaScript objects. There are really two kinds of object variables:

- With the exception of the Date and Array objects, variables that contain built-in JavaScript objects—window, document, navigator, and so forth— are really *references* to the original object. They are like copies, but the copies change if the original changes. In some cases, making a change to the object in the variable affects the original JavaScript object.
- Variables that contain user-defined objects represent the actual object. Make a change to the object in the variable, and you change only that object.

To assign a JavaScript object to a variable, provide the name of the object, as in:

```
MyVar = navigator;
```

To assign a new copy of a user-defined object to a variable, use the new statement and provide the name of the object function (don't worry if you are not familiar with these steps; this topic is discussed more fully in Chapter 11, " Defining Functions, Objects, and Methods"):

```
MyVar = new myObject();
```

Other Variable Values

You have some other useful options for variable assignments. Some of them are outlined here.

Strings That Look Like Numbers

These are numbers you want JavaScript to treat as a string of text, not as a numeric value. Examples include your phone number or your Zip code:

```
Phone = "555-1212";
Zip = "09876";
```

Contents of Other Variables

You can also assign the innards of one variable to the innards of another. Here is an example (both contain the same string, "This is a test"):

```
OriginalVar = "This is a test";
CopyCatVar = OriginalVar;
```

Expressions

An expression is some formula you want JavaScript to calculate for you. The "formula" is usually a math expression of some type. Expressions are used quite heavily in assigning variables:

```
Result=2+2                    // Add 2+2; value stored in variable is 4;
Count=Count+1                 // Add 1 to value in Count; store it back
                                 in Count;
MyName=FirstName+LastName     // Add contents of these variables
                                 to MyName;
```

Object Properties

You already know variables can contain any JavaScript object, either objects you define or objects that are a part of JavaScript. You can manipulate an object contained in a variable exactly as you would manipulate the object itself. You can also assign a property of an object to a variable:

```
obj = document.forms[0].textbox        // textbox object;
Val = document.forms[0].textbox.value  // value from textbox object;
```

Look at the capitalization scheme used in the above examples and throughout this book. Variables that hold values are given names with initial caps. Variables that hold objects are given names that start with initial lowercase. This is not a widespread rule, of course, but merely one approach to a consistent naming scheme. With a consistent scheme, you can glance at a variable and determine what it contains.

Variable Naming Conventions

JavaScript provides a great deal of latitude when it comes to the names you can give variables. JavaScript variables can be almost unlimited in length, though for practical reasons you'll probably keep your variable names under 10 or 15 characters. Shorter variable names help JavaScript execute the program faster.

Keep the following principles in mind when naming your variables:

- Variable names should consist of letters only, without spaces. You can use numbers, as long as the name doesn't start with a digit. For example, MyVar1 is acceptable, but 1MyVar is not.
- Don't use punctuation characters in variable names. The under_score character is the exception. That is, the variable My_Var is acceptable, but My*Var is not. Variables can begin with the underscore character.
- *Variable names are case sensitive*! The variable MyVar is a distinctly different variable from myVar, myvar, or other variations.

The following examples are valid JavaScript variable names:

MyVar

myvar

MyVar1

My_Var

_MyVar

These are not valid JavaScript variables (all of these will result in an error):

1MyVar

MyVar:

My*Var

Understanding JavaScript's "Loose" Variable Data Types

Unlike some other programming languages such as Java or C, there is no need to explicitly define the type of variable you want to create in JavaScript. This behavior of JavaScript is called *loose data typing*, in contrast to the *strict data typing* required by languages such as C++ or Java.

In addition, you do not need to differentiate variable types by appending special characters to the end of the variable name, such as MyVar$ for a string variable. JavaScript internally decodes the variable type based on its contents. In fact, using a symbol such as the dollar sign in a variable name results in an error.

There are, however, occasions when you want to ensure that a variable specifically contains a string or a number. JavaScript provides for the simple conversion of string and number data types. This subject is covered in Chapter 7, "Expressions."

Using the var Statement to Assign a Variable

JavaScript supports a var statement that can be used to explicitly define a variable. The syntax is merely the statement *var*, a space, and the same variable assignment expression detailed above.

Here is an example:

```
var MyVar = "This is a variable";
```

You can also use the var statement with the variable name to declare the variable, but not define a value for it. This form is also acceptable:

```
var MyVar;
```

In this case, you've defined MyVar in memory, but have yet to assign a value to it. This technique is often used when setting up what's known as *global variables*—variables that can be freely shared anywhere in your script. See "Understanding the Scope of Variables," later in this chapter, for more information about global variables.

The Rules and Regulations of Assigning Variables

By this point, you know the ways to assign values to script variables as well as what kinds of data variables can contain. As a review, this list highlights some points you'll want to keep in mind.

- When assigning a numeric value, just enter the number.

- When assigning the contents of another variable, use the name of that variable. This variable must already have been assigned in the script. If not, you'll get an error when the script is run.

- When assigning a string, enclose it in single or double quotation marks.

- When assigning math expressions, include just the math expression. Don't use quotation marks.

- When assigning an object, use the same syntax as you normally would when referring to that object. For example, if the object is referred to as *document.myform*, that's the syntax you should use when defining the variable as well.

Here are some examples:

Variable Type	Example
Number	NumVar=65363;
Another variable	OtherVar=ImAnotherVariable;
String	StrVar="This is a string";

JavaScript is not too particular when it comes to spaces in assigning variables. These two lines of code have the same effect:

```
StrVar = "This is the neat way"
StrVar = "This is the sloppy way"
```

In fact, some JavaScript writers like to use extra spaces, and even tabs, to separate the elements of a variable assignment. For example, these are all perfectly legitimate:

```
MyVar = "contents"            // Space either side
MyVar = "contents"            // Tab either side
MyVar= "contents"             // Contents separated from rest of assignment
```

String Length Limitations and Combining String Variables

JavaScript imposes a limit of 254 characters for each string variable assignment in your program. If you go over the 254-character limit, JavaScript responds with an "Unterminated string literal" error message (other error messages can occur as well).

You can, however, create longer strings by "piecing" them together, as long as each piece is 254 characters or less. After assigning a string to each variable, you combine them using the + character. This is called "concatenation." The following example shows how concatenation works:

```
MyVar = "This is the start " + of how you " + " can build strings";
```

Each individual string segment–defined by text within the quotes–can be up to 254 characters. To make a string longer than 254 characters, merely add more segments.

Another approach is to build strings using the += assignment operator, as shown here:

```
MyVar = "This is the start "
MyVar += "of how you "
MyVar + = can build strings "
```

You can continue to concatenate strings this way as long as your computer has the necessary memory. JavaScript can hold larger strings than those allowed by other programming languages (such as Basic, which limits you to 64K). Creating huge string variables, however, can severely degrade the performance of the system.

Number or String in a Variable: When Does It Make a Difference?

As noted earlier in this chapter, JavaScript variables can contain numbers of two different types: numeric values and numbers that are strings. Differentiating between the two is helpful because you can do math calculations with numbers, but not with strings. For example, this line of code returns the expected value (17):

```
MyVar = 15+2;
```

But this line of code doesn't do what you might expect:

```
MyVar = "Text"+2;
```

Instead of *MyVar* holding something like TextText (which you might read as "Text plus 2"), it holds Text2. When you stop to think about it, all of this is fairly obvious.

Notice that JavaScript is smart enough to automatically convert the number 2 into a string so it can add the "2" to the "Text". In many other programming languages, writing this line of code would be verboten, but not in JavaScript. JavaScript knows you can't add a number value to a string, so it just assumes you meant the 2 to be a string character, and not a numeric value.

Again as noted earlier, you can assign string variables by putting quotation marks around the text, as in:

```
MyVar = "This is a test";
```

You can do the same for numbers_and in fact there are a few times when you will wish to do so:

```
MyVar = "12345";
```

The technique of placing quotation marks around numbers comes in handy if you need to work with phone numbers, Social Security numbers, and Zip codes and so forth. JavaScript can misinterpret these kinds of numbers as math expressions. Take the phone number 555-1212, for example. Here's what happens to it when it's assigned as a numeric value and as a string:

Variable Assignment	Result
MyVar=555-1212	−657
MyVar="555-1212"	555-1212

As you can see, the quotation marks tell JavaScript that you want to store the numbers as a string—without evaluating the numbers as a math expression.

Recall that you can combine a text string and a numeric value; JavaScript automatically converts the numeric value to a string and adds the numeric value as if it were a text character. It's a nice feature to have and saves you a lot of time. But the feature can get you into trouble if you're not careful. JavaScript does not do the reverse when you want to add a numeric string value and a number value. Consider this line:

```
MyVar = 2 + "12345";
```

The result is 212345. You can add these two sets of numbers—even though one is technically a string—but JavaScript elected not to do so automatically. Instead, it merely appended the 2 to the second number and came up with 212345. The same principle applies when you put the numeric value after or try to add two numeric strings together. These all result in a return of 11, rather than of 2:

```
MyVar = 1 + "1";
MyVar = "1" + 1;
MyVar = "1" + "1";
```

If you specifically want to sum the numbers, use the parseInt function to change the numeric string value to a numeric value. The following line results in 2, rather than 11:

```
MyVar = 1 + parseInt("1");
```

If both numbers are strings, you must use the parseInt function for both of them:

```
MyVar = parseInt("1") + parseInt("1");
```

Conversely, you may wish to change a numeric value into a string, specifically because you do not wish JavaScript to perform math calculations with it. In this case, merely append a set of empty quotation marks in front of the number. This approach forces JavaScript to treat the value as a string, rather than as a number:

```
MyVar = ""+1;
```

Understanding the Scope of Variables

The "scope of a variable" has nothing to do with optics or mouthwash, but rather with the extent to which a variable is visible to other parts of a JavaScript program.

Unless you provide explicit instructions to tell JavaScript otherwise, the scope of its variables is managed as follows:

- Variables defined outside of a function are available to any function within the script, as long as the script is in the same document. These are referred to as *global variables*.

- Variables defined inside of a function are also global, assuming the var statement is not used when first declaring that variable (*MyVar = "hello"*).

- Variables defined inside of a function with the var statement are local to that function only. These are referred to as *local variables*.

- Global variables remain in memory even after a script has stopped execution. The variable remains in memory until the document is unloaded.

Local variables are treated as if they don't exist outside of the function where they are defined. As a result, you can use a variable inside a function, and that variable won't "collide" with a variable with the same name elsewhere in the script.

Following is an example that demonstrates this principle. When you click the button, the script displays three alert boxes and JavaScript:

- Calls firstFunction, which assigns the value of 1 to a local variable named MyVar. The contents of MyVar are displayed.

- Calls secondFunction, which assigns the value of 2 to a local variable, also called MyVar. The contents of MyVar are displayed.

- Returns to firstFunction, where the contents of MyVar are again displayed. The result is 1, which is the value of MyVar *local* to firstFunction.

testscope.html

CD-ROM

```
<HTML>
<HEAD>
<TITLE>This is a test</TITLE>
<SCRIPT LANGUAGE="JavaScript">
function firstFunction () {
        var MyVar = 1;
        alert ("firstFunction: " + MyVar);
        secondFunction();
        alert ("firstFunction: " + MyVar);
```

```
      }

      function secondFunction () {
            var MyVar = 2;
            alert ("secondFunction: " + MyVar);
      }
</SCRIPT>
</HEAD>
<BODY>
<FORM NAME="testform">
<INPUT TYPE="button" NAME="button1" VALUE="Start" onClick="firstFunction()"><P>
</FORM>
</BODY>
</HTML>
```

Referencing Variables in Other Loaded Documents

Sharing variables across documents is often necessary when you are using frames. A frame can contain a variable needed by one or more other frames. By their nature, variables (even global ones) are not visible outside of the document that created them. So, when you want to reference a variable in another document_and assuming that document is loaded into the browser_you need to explicitly reference that variable by adding the window name in front of the variable name. The syntax goes like this:

winname.varname

winname is the name of the document, and *varname* is the name of the variable.

You can assign and reference variables using this technique. For example, this line sets the MyVar variable in the mydoc window to 1:

```
mydoc.MyVar = 1;
```

And this line assigns the value of a local MyVar variable in the mydoc window:

```
VarInThisDoc = mydoc.MyVar;
```

You may be wondering about the source of the names for the windows. The answer depends on how the windows are used.

To use a variable in the main browser window from a window that you've created, first provide a "link" to the parent window object, using this method:

```
newwindow = window.open ("","NewWindow");  //repeat this for Mac/X Netscape 2.0
newwindow.creator = self;
```

Then, in this new window you can refer to any variable in the main window using the syntax:

```
creator.MyVar;
```

See the section "Sharing Variables Across Windows" later in this chapter for additional information on this topic.

To use a variable in a window you've

created, refer to it using the object name you've provided when you created the window. For instance, you'd use *newwindow* for a window created with the following line:

```
newwindow = window.open ("","NewWindow");
```

Now refer to that variable using the syntax:

```
newwindow.MyVar;
```

To use a variable defined in the

frameset—that is, the document containing <FRAMESET> tag—refer to it as *parent*. Here is an example:

```
parent.MyVar;
```

To use a variable in another frame document,

refer to it using the frame name you've provided in the <FRAME> tag. For instance, you'd use:

```
parent.frame1.MyVar;
```

for a frame created with the following line:

```
<FRAME SRC="framedoc.html" NAME="frame1">
```

This is such an important issue for frames that the subject is covered in a special section in Chapter 15, "Using JavaScript with Frames."

Sharing Variables across Windows

The best way to explain how to share variables across windows is to provide a good example. The lines of code that follow create a new window, write a variable to it, and then access the variable.

CD-ROM

crossvar.html

```
<HTML>
<HEAD>
<TITLE>Cross-Variable Test</TITLE>
<SCRIPT LANGUAGE="JavaScript">
function testVariable() {
        newWindow = window.open ("", "MyNewWindow"); // repeat for Mac/
                                                        X Netscape 2.0
        Temp = "\<SCRIPT\>WindowVar = 5\</SCRIPT\>";
        newWindow.document.write (Temp);
        newWindow.document.write (newWindow.WindowVar+"<P>");
        alert (newWindow.WindowVar);
}

</SCRIPT>
</HEAD>
<BODY>
<FORM NAME="testform">
<INPUT TYPE="button" NAME="button1" VALUE="Click Me!" onClick="testVariable()">
</FORM>
</BODY>
</HTML>
```

Experiment with JavaScript's ability to fetch a variable from another window by changing the line:

```
alert (newWindow.WindowVar);
```

to:

```
alert (WindowVar);
```

You will find that JavaScript reports an error—the variable is undefined. This is because JavaScript is looking for the variable in the current document, the document that contains the above script, rather than in the newly created document window.

Understanding When Variables Are Lost

JavaScript variables don't hang around forever. In Netscape 2.0 a variable is lost when one of the following events happens:

- The document where the variable was assigned is unloaded (you load another document to take its place, for example).
- You reload the document or frameset.
- You resize the browser window (this causes the document to be reloaded).
- You use the document.write method to write to a window or frame where the variable was assigned.

Losing variables when a document is reloaded or resized is one of the most aggravating behaviors of JavaScript. Each time a document is reloaded or resized, you effectively start over. The same is true of frames. If the user resizes a frame (by dragging the frame border), this causes the browser to reload the page, thus losing all the previous contents of the variable.

Most of the time, however, whether the page is reloaded or resized is immaterial, because your JavaScript code behaves as if the page were just accessed. But the behavior can be a problem if you need to set and keep variables as the user works through some process you've provided on your page. You need to consider workarounds if losing the variable will corrupt your script. There are several methods to accomplish this.

One method is used in the slide show presenter, shown in Figure 9.1. This script (detailed more fully in Chapter 17, "Using JavaScript with Advanced HTML") uses a variable to keep track of the current slide number. If the page is reloaded or resized, the slide shown in the top frame doesn't change, but the variable containing the slide number is lost. The script gets around this problem by automatically resetting the slide number to 1 whenever the page is loaded, and changes the current slide image in the top frame to correspond.

Another method, if your page uses frames, is to include a text box field in one of the frames. You can make that frame invisible by enlarging the others to take up all available space, or you can push the text box out of the way and make the frame unscrollable and nonresizable. With this approach, the user never sees the text box. You then use JavaScript to write a value to the text box. The value remains even if the document is reloaded or resized. See Chapter 15, "Using JavaScript and Frames," for more details on this technique.

Yet another method is to use something called a "cookie," which is a semipermanent data storage file provided by Netscape. Cookies allow a safe and secure method to

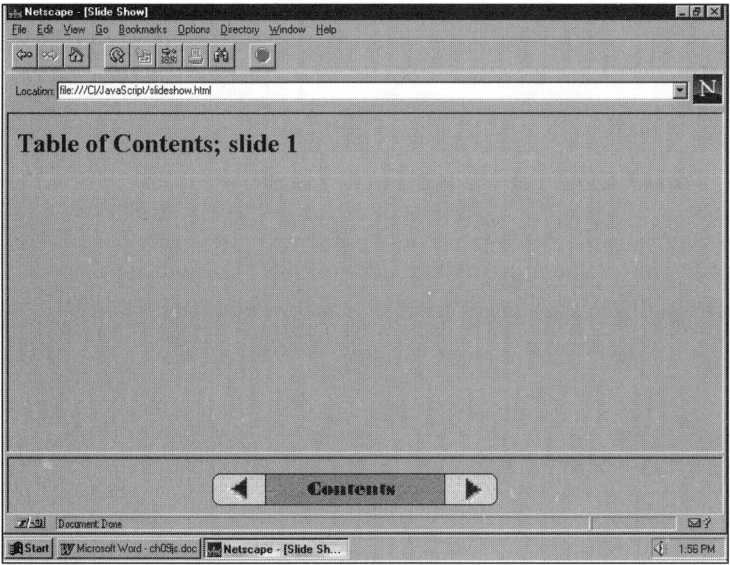

▬▬▬▬ **Figure 9.1** The slide show presenter is designed to re-initialize itself when the window is resized or reloaded.

store data that you want to use later. With a cookie you can store items from the current session of Netscape, or even between sessions. The current session is sufficient for the task of remembering a variable so it will last after a resize or a reload. See Chapter 12, "How Do I," for more details on using cookies to store persistent data.

Using Variable Shortcuts, Tips, and Tricks

A book could be written on useful and interesting shortcuts and tips about JavaScript variables. This section focuses just on some of the more useful ones here.

Declaring Multiple Variables at Once

You can declare several variables at the same time, all on one line, using commas to separate them. Instead of doing this:

```
var MyVar,
var YourVar;
var TheirVar;
```

you can do this:

```
var MyVar, YourVar, TheirVar;
```

Assigning Multiple Variables at Once

If you want to assign the same value to more than one variable at a time, a shortcut method is to use the multiple assignment trick. The following assigns 1 to all of the variables:

```
var MyVar = YourVar = TheirVar = 1;
```

Checking if a Variable Exists

Ordinarily, JavaScript displays an error if you try to reference a variable that doesn't exist. The error reads "xxx is not defined," where *xxx* is the name of the variable. You can get around this error by referencing the variable as a property of the current window or frame. For a single document script (no frames or other windows), the syntax is:

parent.*varname*

with *varname* the name of the variable. The following lines check if the variable exists. The example works with all types of variables, regardless of the data they contain (numbers, strings, boolean, or objects).

```
checkvar = "" + parent.testvar;
if (parent.checkvar == "<undefined>")
        alert ("variable does not exist");
else
        alert ("variable exists");
```

If you're checking for the existence of a string variable, you can use this slightly simpler method:

```
if (parent.testvar == null)
        alert ("variable does not exist");
else
        alert ("variable exists");
```

If you need to check if a variable in another window or frame exists, provide all the necessary object.property names for that window or frame, instead of the parent object. For example, to check if a variable exists in a frame named frame2, use this line:

```
parent.frame2.testvar ...
```

Netscape 3.0 offers a built-in mechanism for testing if a variable exists. See Chapter 22 for more details.

Deleting a Variable from Memory

JavaScript normally deletes any variables when the page that created them is unloaded. However, you can force "early retirement" of variables with this simple technique:

```
varname = null;
```

This clears the memory the variable was using although the variable will still exist. You might use this technique, for example, if you've created a large variable and want to now clear it from memory, to avoid any possible out-of-memory problems.

Converting between Number and String Variables

These topics are covered in Chapter 7, "Expressions," but a brief recap here is in order. To convert a number to a string, add a set of empty quotation marks in front of it, like this:

```
myVar = ""+= MyVar;
```

To convert a string to a number, use the parseInt or parseFloat functions, depending on the number type (parseInt is used for integers; parseFloat is used for numbers with decimal values):

```
MyVar = parseInt(MyInt);
MyVar = parseFloat(MyInt);
```

Understanding Arrays

JavaScript supports *arrays* of variables. For the uninitiated, a variable array is one variable, but with many "compartments." Each compartment stores a different value, such as that shown in Figure 9.2. The compartments in a variable array are called *elements*. The benefit of the variable array is that it allows you to store many values, but you can access these values using a common name.

To be accurate, JavaScript doesn't really support true variable arrays. Rather, it creates arrays of storage elements using an object. To build an array, you create a new object or use the built-in array object JavaScript provides. Then you add information to the object. While JavaScript uses objects rather than variables for arrays, the general process of creating and using the array is virtually identical to the method used in other programming languages. For the sake of simplicity, therefore, arrays are referred to as "variable" arrays here, even though the term is not strictly accurate.

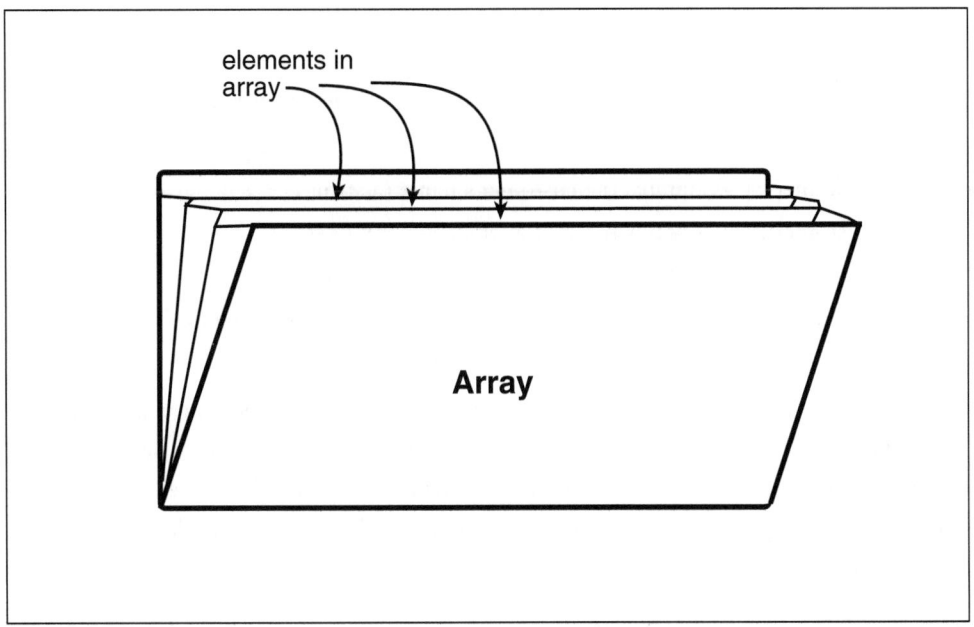

Figure 9.2 Arrays are a single variable, but with multiple "pockets"; each pocket can store a separate piece of information.

How Arrays Work

Each element of the array is referenced by number. This number is called the *subscript* or *index*. The index is separated from the rest of the variable name by enclosing it in brackets, as in *MyVar[1]*. The [1] identifies a particular element of the variable MyVar. Additional elements of the MyVar variable have different index numbers:

```
MyVar[1] // Element number 1
MyVar[2] // Element number 2
MyVar[3] // Element number 3
//... and so forth
```

Note that variable arrays in JavaScript can contain a mix of data types. You are not limited to restricting a particular array to a certain type of data, such as only numbers or only strings. Further, if the array contains strings, the strings can all be of different lengths. This freedom is unusual: many programming languages strictly limit the kinds of information that can be stored in any particular array.

Variable arrays are most often used when you want to store values that go together. For example, you might use the variable Customer to store five different pieces of information: the customer's name, company, address, phone number, and age. These five array elements might be used:

- Customer[1]—Contains the customer's name (a string)
- Customer[2]—Contains the customer's company (a string)
- Customer[3]—Contains the customer's address (a string)
- Customer[4]—Contains the customer's phone number (a numerical string)
- Customer[5]—Contains the customer's age (a number)

Arrays are also useful when you don't know the number of variables you may need to contain the information collected from the user, or from JavaScript itself. You merely create the array, and go about stuffing data into it. You don't even need to consider making the array "large enough" to hold all the data, as you do in many other programming languages. The size of the array can be dynamically increased.

Creating an Array

To create an array, you must first create an object for it. How you do this depends on whether you want to use JavaScript's built-in array object or create an array object yourself (both have similar capabilities, so it's your choice which method you use).

Creating an Array with the JavaScript Array Object

The most straightforward method of creating an array is to build one using the built-in JavaScript array object. The syntax is simple:

ArrayName = new Array(*elements*)

ArrayName is the name you want to give to the array, and *elements* is the number of elements in the array.

Note the new statement. This tells JavaScript to create a new *instance* of the array object. You specify the number of elements you want the array to contain. JavaScript lets you add more elements as you need them, so don't be overly concerned if your original estimate is a little low.

> In fact, you don't need to specify the number of elements for the array.
> JavaScript is perfectly happy with the following syntax:
>
> ```
> MyArray = new Array();
> ```
>
> This creates an array object with no elements. But you can add elements "on the
> fly," merely by assigning values to each of the elements you wish to use.

Each element of the new array is empty (actually, they are all assigned null values).
Your next task is to assign values to each of the elements, using the standard variable assignment technique detailed earlier in the chapter. JavaScript starts with 0
as the first element, but you can use 0 or 1. One option is to start with 1 as the
first index, thus leaving index 0 open to store the number of elements in the array,
as shown here:

```
NumElements = 4;
MyArray   = new Array(NumElements);
MyArray[0] = NumElements;
MyArray[1] = "This is element one.";
MyArray[2] = "This is element two.";
MyArray[3] = "This is element three.";
MyArray[4] = "This is element four.";
alert (MyArray[0]) // displays 4
```

If you prefer to use a named property for the length of the array, you can assign it as
shown in the following code. Both this and the previous example have the same effect.

```
NumElements = 4;
MyArray   = new Array(NumElements);
MyArray.length = NumElements; // place this assignment first
MyArray[1] = "This is element one.";
MyArray[2] = "This is element two.";
MyArray[3] = "This is element three.";
MyArray[4] = "This is element four.";
alert (MyArray.length) // displays 4
```

The array object works differently depending on the version of Netscape you are using. In 2.0 the array object does not provide a length property of its own, so the above code is the recommended procedure. Starting in Netscape 3.0, the array object returns a length property, so it is no longer necessary to set the number of elements. The object itself takes care of this. The following is acceptable in 3.0 and later:

```
NumElements = 4;
MyArray  = new Array(NumElements);
MyArray[1] = "This is element one.";
MyArray[2] = "This is element two.";
MyArray[3] = "This is element three.";
MyArray[4] = "This is element four.";
alert (MyArray.length)  //displays 4
```

Or if you prefer:

```
NumElements = 4;
MyArray  = new Array(NumElements);
MyArray[0] = "This is element one.";
MyArray[1] = "This is element two.";
MyArray[2] = "This is element three.";
MyArray[3] = "This is element four.";
alert (MyArray.length)  //displays 4
```

■■■■■■

Creating an Array with a Custom Array Object

Instead of using the built-in array object, you can create arrays in JavaScript by defining your own array object. You do this by building a function to create the object, and then adding an instruction elsewhere in the script that calls this function. Here is an example of a "constructor" function for building an array:

```
function makeArray (NumElements)  {
        this.length = NumElements;
```

```
     for (Count = 1; Count <= NumElements; Count++)  {
            this[Count] = 0;
     }
     return (this);
}
```

Here's how it works: The function name in this example is called makeArray. The function accepts one parameter, which is the number of elements you want in your array. That number can be as small as 0 (though this choice is obviously not very useful), up to the limits of memory in your computer. Most of the time you'll create arrays with fewer than 50 elements.

This property is used to indicate the current object. The current object is makeArray, which has the same name as the function. The length of the object is defined in the line:

```
this.length = NumElements;
```

which assigns the number of elements you want to the object. For example, if NumElements contains the value 10, then the length of the object is set to 10. By assigning values to higher index numbers, you can add more elements than 10 to the array, but the value 10 is assigned to the length property.

The for loop is used to define initial values for each of the elements in the array objects. The loop counts from 1 to the total number of elements. The line:

```
this[Count] = 0;
```

assigns the value 0 to each of the elements. You can use another value if you wish to assign something different to each element. When the for loop is done, the function returns the just-made makeArray object.

The makeArray function is only half of the story. The other half is the instruction that calls this function and actually creates the array. Here's an example:

```
MyArray = new makeArray(10);
```

This example creates a new array object called MyArray, using the makeArray function described above. JavaScript understands you want to build a new object because of the new statement. Without the new statement, none of this works. In this example, MyArray is created with 10 elements.

Once the array is built, you can fill its elements, just as you would do if you were working with JavaScript's built-in array object. Because the makeArray function creates elements starting with 1, that's the first element used when assigning values to the array.

```
MyArray[1] = 1;
MyArray[2] = "Josie";
MyArray[3] = "Maloy";
MyArray[4] = "555-1212";
```

and so forth. Note that the MyArray[0] (zero) element contains the total number of elements in MyArray (this information is also stored in the length property of the MyArray object; element 0 and the length property are synonymous). You should not assign a new value to the zero element or the length property, unless you have a very good reason for doing so. You can use the value whenever you need to check the total number of elements in the array.

As with the built-in Array object, you can assign values to more array elements than you originally specified when you created the array object. However, for consistency and readability of code, it's better to define the actual number of elements you intend to use when the array is created.

Note that you can make the constructor function for creating the array as simple or as complex as you want. Both of the following examples create a fully functional user-defined array object:

```
function makeArray(){return(this)}
```

Conversely, you can add sophistication to the array-making process by assigning specific values to specific elements. For instance, suppose you want to pre-fill the elements of all new arrays you create. Here's one example.

```
function makeArray() {
```

```
        this[0] = 4 // contains four elements
        this[1] = "Your Name Here"
        this[2] = "Your Address Here"
        this[3] = "City, State, Zip"
        this[4] = "555-1212"
        return (this);
    }
```

This object creates a standardized array of four elements, not counting element 0, which holds the number of elements in the array. Each element is preloaded with text_for example, text boxes in a fill-in form. The text remains in the array until you change it.

Referencing Values in an Array

When you want to reference (use) the variable—regardless of the method you used to create it—you likewise use each array element as if it were a regular variable. Include the subscript number to indicate the element you wish to use:

```
    document.write (MyArray[1]);
    document.write (MyArray[2]);
    document.write (MyArray[3]);
    document.write (MyArray[4]);
    // And so forth
```

Of course, you are not limited to referencing array elements with just the document.write method. For example, you can use alert to display the array element, you can use value method with a text box to place the contents of the array element, and so forth.

Associative Arrays: A Third Way to Create Arrays

JavaScript supports what's known as associative arrays. In an associative array, you use descriptive text to specify elements instead of numbers in brackets. For example, suppose you want to create an array for holding customer information. You use a regular array with numeric elements. The array holds the name, company, and e-mail address for the customer and might go something like this:

```
Customer[1] = "Wally Gator";
Customer[2] = "Florida Everglades";
Customer[3] = "wally@gator.com";
```

With an associative array, you can do away with the hard-to-remember numbers and use plain text instead.

```
Customer.name = "Wally Gator";
Customer.company = "Florida Everglades";
Customer.email = "wally@gator.com";
```

To create such an associative array, you merely build a constructor function, very similar to the one used to make a new regular array:

```
function assocArray(NumElements)   {
        this.length = NumElements;
        return (this);
}
```

Then all you need is to create the new array whenever you want to use it.

```
Customer = new assocArray(3);
```

Customer is the name of the associative array object for this example. Three properties are going to be appended to this array object, so the value 3 is passed to the assocArray function. Once the array object is created, you need to assign properties to it.

The names for the properties are up to you. The idea is to correlate the property name with the contents you plan to store there.

Similarly, to access the contents of the array, you provide the array name and the property you want, as in this line of code:

```
alert ("Hello, " + Customer.name);
```

10

EVENTS

JavaScript events are things that happen to which JavaScript can respond. Most of these events are human-actuated—that is, when you do something on a page, JavaScript reacts in some predefined way. That predefined way is up to you, and this latitude is what gives JavaScript programs an extra edge of usefulness. For example, you can set up a script whereby a message appears when the user clicks a button. This message is in response to an event, caused when the user clicked the button.

This chapter discusses JavaScript's *event handlers*. They are called handlers because they "handle" events. Actually, "react to events" might a more accurate term, but it doesn't sound as technical. In any case, we'll stick to event handler. There are nine event handlers in Netscape 2.0 (additional events are provided in Netscape 3.0; see Chapter 22 for more information). They are:

- onBlur
- onChange
- onClick
- onFocus

- onLoad
- onMouseOver
- onSelect
- onSubmit
- onUnload

Discission of these event handlers is organized in alphabetical order in this chapter. The chapter begins with a quick overview on how the event handlers are used and the JavaScript objects with which they are used.

■■■■■■■ **NOTE**

> Later chapters provide additional detail on using event handlers for special applications. For example, the onClick event handler is covered extensively in Chapter 16, "Using JavaScript with Forms." If you don't find what you're looking for in this chapter, check the index for additional references to a specific event handler.

■■■■■■

How Event Handlers Are Used

All event handlers are designed to be attributes to HTML tags. The syntax, as shown here, is constant regardless of the event handler:

<TAG ATTRIBUTE="blah" *onEvent="doSomething()"*>

- TAG is the name of the tag, such as <BODY>, <FORM>, or <INPUT>.
- ATTRIBUTE is one or more regular HTML attributes used with the tag.
- *onEvent* is the name of the event handler, such as onClick or onLoad. Note that when used in a tag (by far the most common application), capitalization doesn't matter.
- *"doSomething()"* is a JavaScript or user-defined instruction. For example, you can display a message with "alert ('Hello there!')". Note the use of single quotation marks within the double quotation marks.

According to standard practice, the event handler is placed as the last attribute; however, as with all other HTML attributes, the order of the event handler in the tag makes no difference. Neither does capitalization, unless you use the name of the event handler in JavaScript. In that case, the name *must* be spelled in all lowercase.

The bulk of the event handlers are designed to work with form objects, and specifically with certain kinds of form objects. You can't, for example, use the onBlur event with a pushbutton.

Event Handlers for Forms

Handler	Works with These Objects
onBlur	select, text, textarea
onChange	select, text, textarea
onClick	buttons (push, reset, submit radio, checkbox)
onFocus	select, text, textarea
onSelect	select, text, textarea
onSubmit	form

Event Handlers for Links

Handler	Works with These Objects
onClick	links (A HREF=...)
onMouseOver	links (A HREF=...)

Event Handlers for Windows

Handler	Works with These Objects
onLoad	window, frame
onUnload	window, frame

onBlur Event Handler

"Blur" is JavaScript's term for when a select, text, or text area form control loses focus ("focus" is the control that receives input when you press a key on the keyboard). So, an onBlur event occurs when one of these controls is about to lose focus.

Application

The event handler applies to select, text, and textarea control.

Example

The following onBlur event displays an alert box when you click on another control in the form:

```
<INPUT TYPE="text" NAME="textbox" VALUE="" onBlur="alert ('blur')">
<INPUT TYPE="button" VALUE="Click On Me" onClick="alert ('OK')">
```

Purpose

One practical use of onBlur is to ensure that users have provided valid text before they are allowed to proceed with the form. If a user tries to click outside the control, and the text is invalid, you can warn them to provide the correct data. Here's an example:

```
<HTML><HEAD>
<TITLE>Event Handler Test</TITLE>
<SCRIPT LANGUAGE="JavaScript">
function dataCheck(form) {
        if (form.textbox.value == "")
                alert ("The box is empty")
}
</SCRIPT>
<BODY>
<FORM NAME="myform">
<INPUT TYPE="text" NAME="textbox" VALUE="" onBlur="dataCheck(this.form)">
<INPUT TYPE="button" VALUE="Click On Me" onClick="alert ('OK')">
</FORM>
</BODY></HTML>
```

See/Also onChange, onFocus, onSelect.

onChange Event Handler

The onChange event is triggered if you've made a change in a select, text, or text area control and have clicked outside of the control to signal that you're done with it. In this way, this event handler is like the onBlur handler, but it also checks to see if the setting of the control has changed from its previous state.

■■■■ **NOTE**

The onChange handler is buggy in Netscape 2.0 for all platforms. Avoid using it.

■■■■

Application

The event handler applies to select, text, or a textarea control.

Example

The following onChange event displays an alert box when you change the contents of the text box and click on another control in the form:

```
<INPUT TYPE="text" NAME="textbox" VALUE="" onChange="alert ('change')">
<INPUT TYPE="button" VALUE="Click On Me" onClick="alert ('OK')">
```

Purpose

You can use onChange as you would onBlur, but with the added benefit of ignoring the control if its content has not changed. See onBlur for an example.

onClick Event Handler

Of all the event handlers, onClick is used the most. It can be used with both form buttons and links. An onClick event occurs when a button in a form or link is pressed.

Application

This event handler applies to links, button, radio control, checkbox, submit, and reset.

Example

The following onClick event displays an alert box when you click on the form button:

```
<INPUT TYPE="button" VALUE="Click On Me" onClick="alert ('OK')">
```

Purpose

Use onClick whenever you want to trigger JavaScript code with a button or a link. For example, you can can use onClick with any form button, thereby turning the button into a control panel widget.

The onClick handler also works with links, but you must exercise care in how you use it. Even with an onClick handler added to the link, Netscape still jumps to whatever link is specified in the HREF of the <A> tag (and you must include the HREF attribute, or the tag won't be treated as a link). One workaround is as follows:

```
<A HREF="#1" NAME=1" onClick="alert ('Hello')">Click me</A>
```

This "circular reference" treats the tag as both an anchor and a link. See Chapter 12, "How Do I?" for more ideas on using onClick with links.

onFocus Event Handler

"Focus" is JavaScript's term for when you click in a select, text, or text area form control (the control will receive input when you press a key on the keyboard). So, an onFocus event occurs when one of these controls gets the focus.

Application

This event handler applies to a select, text, or textarea control.

Example

The following onFocus event inserts text in the box when you click in it:

```
<INPUT TYPE="text" NAME="textbox" VALUE="" onFocus="this.value='test'">
```

Purpose

One use of onFocus is to provide context-sensitive help. When the user clicks in a box, the text in the status bar provides a reminder of what to do:

onfocus.html

CD-ROM

```
<HTML><HEAD>
<TITLE>Event Handler Test</TITLE>
<SCRIPT LANGUAGE="JavaScript">
function statusText(form, box) {
        if (box.name == "textbox1")
                window.defaultStatus = "Enter your name here"
        if (box.name == "textbox2")
```

```
                    window.defaultStatus = "Enter your age here"


    }
    </SCRIPT>
    <BODY>
    <FORM NAME="myform">
    Name: <INPUT TYPE="text" NAME="textbox1" VALUE=""
            onFocus="statusText(this.form, this)">
    Age: <INPUT TYPE="text" NAME="textbox2" VALUE="" onFocus="
            statusText(this.form, this)">
    </FORM>
    </BODY></HTML>
```

■■■■■■ **CAUTION**

> Do not use an alert, confirm, or prompt box with the onFocus handler.
> Otherwise, Netscape will get caught in an endless loop.

■■■■■

See also onBlur, onChange, onSelect.

onLoad Event Handler

The onLoad event handler triggers when a window finishes loading. It's useful as a timing device, to ensure that some piece of JavaScript code doesn't execute until all of the document has been retrieved. You use the onLoad event handler in the <BODY> tag for individual documents loaded into windows, and in the <FRAMESET> tag for the parent (or top-level) document for documents loaded into frames.

■■■■■■ **NOTE**

> A load event also occurs if the document is resized or reloaded with the
> Reload button (or View, Reload command).

■■■■■

Application

This event handler applies to windows object.

Example

onLoad triggers an event when a document is finished loading. You can use this handler to display a welcome message:

```
<BODY onLoad="alert('Welcome to my page!')">
```

If you are using frames, you can put the onLoad event handler in the first <FRAMESET> tag of the parent document. In this way, the onLoad event is not triggered until all of the frame documents have loaded:

```
<FRAMESET onLoad="alert('Welcome to my frame!')">
```

Purpose

Use onLoad whenever you wish to defer running some JavaScript function until after the document has completely loaded. In the following example, a message appears after the document has loaded and provides instructions. When the user clicks OK, the insertion point is placed in the text box. By delaying this action, you are ensured that the function will not be called until the document has completely loaded (which is useful, for example, if there are a lot of graphics on the page, and you don't want anything to start happening until all the graphics appear).

onload.html

CD-ROM

```
<HTML><HEAD>
<TITLE>Event Handler Test</TITLE>
<SCRIPT LANGUAGE="JavaScript">
function activate() {
        alert ("Please provide your name")
        document.myform.textbox.focus();
        document.myform.textbox.select();
}
</SCRIPT>
<BODY onLoad="activate()">
<FORM NAME="myform">
Name: <INPUT TYPE="text" NAME="textbox" VALUE="">
<INPUT TYPE="button" VALUE="Click On Me" onClick="alert ('OK')">
```

```
</FORM>
</BODY></HTML>
```

▬▬▬▬ **NOTE**

The onLoad event is particularly important when using JavaScript with frames. Be sure to read Chapter 15, "Using JavaScript with Frames," for additional information on this topic.

▬▬▬▬

See also onUnload

onMouseOver Event Handler

The onMouseOver event handler triggers when you move the mouse over a link and is typically used to change the URL text in the status bar. Ordinarily when you move the mouse over a link, the URL for that link appears. With onMouseOver and the window.defaultStatus property, you can change the text in the status bar to whatever you want.

Application

This event handler applies to links.

Example

This example dynamically changes the text of the link (as shown in the status bar) when you pass the mouse over it. Of course, the URL itself is not affected. Note the addition of the "; return true" statement after the alert box. This addition is required; if the return true statement is missing, the onMouseOver event has no effect.

```
<A HREF="test2.html" onMouseOver="alert('hello'); return true">
Click Me </A>
```

Purpose

The onMouseOver event can be used to change status bar text, to pop up windows, and more. Note that, except for status bar changes, using this handler can easily be perceived as intrusive and unexpected. Furthermore, you must exercise care when using the handler to change the status bar text because this text remains until you or Netscape changes it.

The following example shows how to change the status bar text and set up a timer to clear the text after a two-second wait.

CD-ROM

mouseover.html

```
<HTML><HEAD>
<TITLE>Event Handler Test</TITLE>
<SCRIPT LANGUAGE="JavaScript">
function changeStatus() {
        window.status = "Hello there"
        setTimeout ("window.status=''", 2000)
}
</SCRIPT>
<BODY>
<A HREF="test2.html" onMouseOver="changeStatus(); return true">
Click Me</A><P>
</BODY></HTML>
```

onSelect Event Handler

The onSelect event handler triggers an event when you select text in a text or text area field.

 NOTE

The onSelect handler is buggy in Netscape 2.0 for all platforms. Avoid using it.

Application

This handler applies to text and textarea controls.

Example

The following example displays an alert box when you select text in the text box.

```
<INPUT TYPE="text" NAME="textbox" VALUE="Hello"
onSelect="alert('don\'t change this text!')">
```

onSubmit Event Handler

The onSubmit event handler is triggered when a form is submitted, usually in response to pressing the Submit button on the form. You can cancel submission of a form if you return *false* to the onSubmit event handler. Returning *true* submits the form.

Application

The handler is applicable to the form object.

Example

The following example displays an alert box when the form is submitted:

```
<FORM NAME="myform" onSubmit="alert('Form submitted')">
```

Purpose

Use the onSubmit handler whenever you want to exercise control over the form sub-mission process (you can also use the form.submit method for many of the applica-tions used for onSubmit). In the following example, JavaScript checks the entry box for an entry. If the box is empty, an alert message is displayed and the form submis-sion is canceled. If the box is not empty, the form submission is carried out.

onsub.html

CD-ROM

```
<HTML><HEAD>
<TITLE>Event Handler Test</TITLE>
<SCRIPT LANGUAGE="JavaScript">
function dataCheck(form) {
        if (form.textbox.value == "") {
                alert ("The box is empty")
                return (false);
        else
                return (true);
}
```

```
</SCRIPT>
<BODY>
<FORM NAME="myform" onSubmit="return dataCheck(this)">
<INPUT TYPE="text" NAME="textbox" VALUE="">
<INPUT TYPE="Submit">
</FORM>
</BODY></HTML>
```

onUnload Event Handler

The onUnload event handler triggers when a window is about to be unloaded. It's useful as a cleanup device: if you want to remove any windows you've added to delete variables, the onUnload event gives you the opportunity to do so before the window is destroyed. You use the onUnload event handler in the <BODY> tag for individual documents loaded into windows, and in the <FRAMESET> tag for the parent (or top-level) document for documents loaded into frames.

■■■■■ **NOTE**

An unload event also occurs if the document is resized, or reloaded with the Reload button (or View, Reload command).

■■■■■

Application

The event handler applies to window object.

Example

onUnload triggers an event when a document is about to be unloaded. You can use this handler to display a goodbye message:

```
<BODY onUnload="alert('goodby')">
```

If you are using frames, you can put the onUnload event handler in the first <FRAMESET> tag of the parent document. As a result, the onUnload event is not triggered until all of the frame documents have loaded.

```
<FRAMESET onUnload="alert('Bye, bye')">
```

Purpose

Use onUnload whenever you wish to include cleanup code or display a farewell message. JavaScript does a pretty good job of cleaning up after itself, but you may wish to perform manual cleanup as well. In the following example, a new, small window is created when the document is first opened. The small window is automatically closed when the main document is unloaded.

CD-ROM

onunload.html

```
<HTML><HEAD>
<TITLE>Event Handler Test</TITLE>
<SCRIPT LANGUAGE="JavaScript">
var win;
function makeWindow() {
        win = window.open ("", "NewWin",
                "toolbar=0,location=0,directories=0,status=0,menubar=0," +
                "scrollbars=0,resizable=0,width=200,height=100")
}
function killWindow() {
        win.close();
}

</SCRIPT>
<BODY onLoad="makeWindow()"; onUnload="killWindow()">
<FORM>
<INPUT TYPE="button" VALUE="Close" onClick="window.close()">
</FORM>
</BODY></HTML>
```

See also onLoad

JAVASCRIPT IN THE

REAL WORLD

11

DEFINING FUNCTIONS, OBJECTS, AND METHODS

The power of any programming language is the extent to which you can modify it for your own needs. The more you are limited to using just the built-in commands and processes, the more you are limited in what you can do with that language. And the harder it is to write sophisticated programs.

As a modern programming language, JavaScript endorses full extensibility by letting you define your own functions. This flexibility allows you to create routines you can use over and over again. You save time in re-using common "components"; by designing your own functions, you can extend JavaScript's base language to suit your needs. Think of it as "personalized JavaScript."

Being a language based on objects, a JavaScript function can easily be turned into an object, and a method for that object. So, not only can you create user-defined objects to do your bidding, you can create your own objects that behave in exactly the way you want. And you can create methods that act upon those objects. While this capability sounds powerful—and it is—the process of creating functions, objects, and methods is very easy in JavaScript. You only have to learn how to do one of these tasks in order to do all three.

This chapter describes how to create your own user-defined functions and provides plenty of examples. Other topics covered include how to apply functions to make new objects and how to add methods to interact with those objects.

Introducing Functions

You use the *function* statement to create your own JavaScript function. The syntax is:

```
function name (params) {
...function stuff...
}
```

- *name* is the unique name of the function. All functions names in a script must be unique.
- *params* is one or more parameter variables you pass to the function.
- *function stuff* is the instructions carried out by the function.

The { and } brace characters define the function block, and they are absolutely necessary. The braces tell JavaScript where a function begins and where it ends. The parentheses around the parameters are also required. Include the parentheses even if the function doesn't use parameters (and many don't). Here is an example:

```
function noParamsFunction () {
        //blah, blah
}
```

Naming the Function

Names for your user-defined functions are up to you, just as long as you use only alphanumeric characters (the underscore _ character is also permitted). Function names must start with a letter character, but they can include numbers elsewhere in the name.

This book uses the JavaScript style of function name capitalization—that is, initial lowercase, then uppercase characters if the function name is composed of composite words, as in myFuncName, yourFuncName, or theirFuncName. Function names are *case-sensitive*, so be sure to use the same capitalization when you use the function elsewhere in the script. JavaScript considers myFunc different from myfunc.

■■■■■■■ **NOTE**

> To differentiate between functions and variables, you should consider giving your variables initial uppercase characters, such as MyStuff. This immediately differentiates it from a function, which would be named myStuff.

■■■■■■■

Defining and Using a Function

The best way to become acquainted with functions is to watch a simple one in action. Here's a basic function that displays "Hello, JavaScripters!":

```
function basicFunction () {
        alert ("Hello JavaScripters!");
}
```

These lines define the function, but you still have to *call* the function in order to use it. Calling a user-defined function is the same task as calling a JavaScript function. You include the name of the function you want to process. When JavaScript encounters the function name in the script, it completes whatever instructions are in the function. When the instructions have all been performed, JavaScript comes back and processes the remainder of the script, as shown in Figure 11.1.

To call the function in the previous example, just include the text basicFunction()— note the empty parentheses, as they are required. Following is a full working example. Note that the order in which the function and function call appear in the script does not matter.

```
<HTML>
<HEAD>
<TITLE>Basic Function Example</TITLE>
<SCRIPT LANGUAGE="JavaScript">
function basicFunction () {
        alert ("Hello JavaScripters!");
}
```

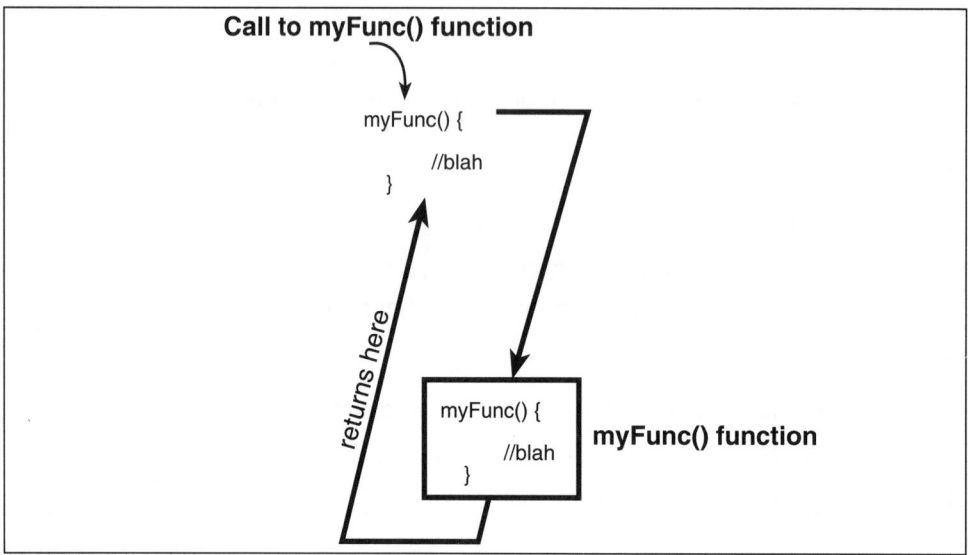

Figure 11.1 When JavaScript encounters the function call, it branches off to the function, executes it, then returns.

```
basicFunction();

</SCRIPT>
</HEAD>
<BODY>
Page has loaded.
</BODY>
</HTML>
```

The browser processes the contents of the <SCRIPT> tag as the document is loading. When it encounters the basicFunction() function call, it pauses momentarily to process the function, and an alert box appears. Click OK and the remainder of the page finishes loading.

Calling a Function with an Event Handler

A common way to call functions is to include a reference to them in a form button or hypertext link. Processing a user-defined function when the user clicks a form button is perhaps the easiest of all. You use the onClick event handler to tell JavaScript to process the specified function when the user clicks on the button. Following is a revised version of the previous example, showing how basicFunction is called when the form button is clicked.

CD-ROM

call_function.html

```
<HTML>
<HEAD>
<TITLE>Basic Function Example</TITLE>
<SCRIPT LANGUAGE="JavaScript">
function basicFunction () {
        alert ("Hello JavaScripters!");
}

</SCRIPT>
</HEAD>
<BODY>
Click to call function.
<FORM>
<INPUT TYPE="button" VALUE="Click" onClick="basicFunction()">
</FORM>
</BODY>
</HTML>
```

Notice the onClick syntax in the <INPUT> tag. The event you want to process on a click is a call to basicFunction. This event is included in double-quotation marks.

Passing a Value to a Function

Functions become more useful when you pass values to them, so they can use these values for processing. For instance, instead of having the alert box say "Hello JavaScripters!" whenever you call it, you can have it say anything you like. The text to display can be passed as a parameter to the function.

To pass a parameter to a function, provide a variable name as the parameter in the function definition. You then use that variable name elsewhere in the function. Here is an example:

```
function basicExample (Text) {
        alert (Text);
}
```

The variable name is Text, which is defined as the parameter for the function. That variable is then used as the text to display in the alert box. When calling the function, you can provide the text you want to show as a parameter of the function call:

```
basicExample ("This says anything I want");
```

NOTE

You can include the actual value of the parameter in the function call, or you can provide the name of a variable that contains the value. The following lines of code have the same effect as the previous example:

```
TextToDisplay = "This says anything I want";
basicExample (TextToDisplay);
```

Passing Multiple Parameters

You can pass multiple parameters to a function. As with built-in JavaScript functions and methods, separate the parameters with commas, as shown here:

```
multipleParams ("one", "two");
...
function multipleParams (Param1, Param2) {
        ...
```

When you define functions with multiple parameters, be sure that the parameters are listed in the same order they are in the function call. Otherwise, your JavaScript code may apply the parameters to the wrong variables, and your function won't work right.

Following is a working example of a function with multiple parameters. It takes two parameters: an input string and a number value. The number value indicates how many characters on the left of the string you want to display in the alert box. When you run the following script, the alert box displays "This is," the first seven characters of the input string.

```
lefty ("This is a test", 7);


function lefty (InString, Num) {
        var OutString=InString.substring (InString, Num);
        alert (OutString);
}
```

Returning a Value from a Function

The functions described so far don't return a value; that is, they do whatever magic you want them to do and then end. No "output" value is provided by the function. In some other languages, this type of function is called a subroutine. However, in JavaScript (as in C and C++), "functions are functions" whether or not they return a value.

It's easy to return a value from a function: use the return statement, along with the value you wish to return. This capability is handy when you want your function to churn through some data and return the processed result. Take the "lefty" function from above. Instead of displaying the chopped-off string, you can return it to the calling function and use the return value in any way you want.

```
var Ret = lefty ("This is a test", 7);
alert (Ret);


function lefty (InString, Num) {
        var  OutString=InString.substring (InString, Num);
        return (OutString);
}
```

This script does essentially the same task as the previous example; but instead of always displaying the chopped-off text, the function merely returns the processed value. The return value is captured in a variable—assigned in the typical JavaScript way—and you are free to use that variable in any way you wish. The above example shows the Ret variable used with an alert box, but you can use it in other ways, too. For example, you can write the contents of the Ret variable using the document.write method:

```
document.write (Ret);
```

My preference is to include parentheses around the value used with the return statement, as in:

```
return (OutString);
```

The parentheses are optional in JavaScript, but I tend to use them out of force of habit from the C programming language. I also think the script is easier to read and understand when the parentheses are included. You are free to use or drop the paranentheses as you wish.

Returning from a Function Prematurally

Under normal circumstances, functions proceed from start to finish. When they finish, JavaScript returns execution to the calling function statement, and the rest of the program is processed. There are times, however, when you want a function to terminate early, and not proceed from start to end. Again, you can use the return statement, with or without a return value. Here's an example without a return value:

```
var Ret = prompt ("Type your name");
displayName (Ret);

function displayName (Name) {
        if ((Name == "" || Name == "<undefined>" || Name == null))
                return;          // don't proceed any further
        alert (Name);
}
```

This script displays the name typed at the prompt box, but only if the value returned from the prompt box was not blank or "<undefined>."

The return statement can be used with a value. In this way, you can return one value for one condition, or other value for another condition. When using one return statement with a value, make sure all other return statements in the function also return a value, even if the value is an empty string, null, or zero value.

```javascript
var Ret = prompt ("Type your name");
var Show = displayName (Ret);
alert (Show);


function displayName (Name) {
        if ((Name == "" || Name == "<undefined>" || Name == null))
                return ("You didn't provide any text")
        else
                return (Name);
}
```

▬▬▬ **NOTE**

Here's another, shorter way of calling the displayName function and displaying the result. It uses displayName as an "in-line" function—it is called in-line with another function or method, in this case, JavaScript's alert method.

```javascript
alert (displayName (Ret));
```

▬▬▬

Defining Local Variables

By default all JavaScript variables are declared global for the document that created them (different documents don't share variables, even global ones, as detailed in Chapter 9, "Variables"). That means when you define a variable in a function, it is also "visible" to any other portion of the script on that document. For example, in the following example, the variable test is visible to the showVar function, even though the variable is defined in the loadVar function.

CD-ROM

global_var.html

```
<HTML>
<HEAD>
<TITLE>Global Variable Example</TITLE>
<SCRIPT LANGUAGE="JavaScript">

function showVar () {
        alert (test)
}

function loadVar () {
        test = "6"
}

loadVar();      // loads variable

</SCRIPT>
</HEAD>
<BODY>
Click to call function.
<FORM>
<INPUT TYPE="button" Value="Click" onClick="showVar()">
</FORM>
</BODY>
</HTML>
```

Sometimes making variables global isn't what you want to do. Instead, you want variables that are local to the function. These variables exist only as long as JavaScript is processing the function. When it exits the function, the variables are lost. In addition, a local variable of a given name is treated as a separate entity from a global variable of the same name. As a result, you don't have to worry about reuse of variable names. The local variable in the function won't have any effect on the global variable used elsewhere in the script.

To declare a local variable, add the var keyword to the beginning of the variable name in the function. This tells JavaScript you want to make the variable local to that function. As a test, change the loadVar function above as shown in the following lines, and re-load the script. When you click the button, JavaScript tells you the variable doesn't exist. This is because test is local only to the loadVar function and does not exist outside the function.

```
function loadVar () {
        var test = "6"
}
```

Calling One Function from Another Function

Code inside a function behaves just like code anywhere else. This means you can call one function from inside another function. As a result, you can "nest" functions: you can create separate functions to perform specific tasks and then run them together as a complete process, one after the other. Following is a function that calls three other mythical functions, each one returning a string of text that has been altered in some way.

```
function run () {
        Ret = changeText ("Change me");
        alert (Ret);
        document.write (Ret);
}
function changeText (Text) {
        Text = makeBold (Text);
        Text = makeItalics (Text);
        Text = makeBig (Text);
        return (Text);
}
function makeBold (InString) {
        return (InString.bold());
}
```

```
function makeItalics (InString) {
        return (InString.italics());
}
function makeBig (InString) {
        return (InString.big());
}
```

Creating Objects with User-Defined Functions

As you know, JavaScript is based on objects: the window is an object, links are objects, forms are objects, even Netscape itself (or another browser) is an object. Using objects can help make programming easier and more streamlined. You can extend the use of objects in JavaScript by making your own. The process uses functions in a slightly modified way. In fact, you'll be surprised how easy it is to make your own JavaScript objects.

Making a Basic Object

Making a new object requires two steps:

1. *Define the object* in a user-defined function.

2. *Use the new keyword* to create (or *instantiate*) the object with a call to the object function.

Here's an example of the world's simplest JavaScript object:

```
// this part creates a new object
ret = new makeSimpleObject();

// this part defines the object
function makeSimpleObject() {
        return (this);
// this is optional
}
```

The new object has been called "ret"; you can use any valid variable name for the new object (lowercase letters have been used for variables that contain objects, as a means of quickly identifying these variables).

You can use the same object function to create any number of new objects. For instance, these lines create four new and separate objects: eenie, meenie, minie, and moe:

```
eenie = new makeSimpleObject();
meenie = new makeSimpleObject();
minie = new makeSimpleObject();
moe = new makeSimpleObject();
```

■■■■■■ **NOTE**

Actually, there is even a shortcut to the above "world's simplest JavaScript object." You don't need to define an object function to make a barebones object. JavaScript supports a generic Object() object, which you can use to make new objects. The following line has the same effect as the previous example, without using an explicit object function:

```
eenie = new Object();
```

■■■■■■

Attaching Properties to User-Defined Objects

With objects created, you can assign values to them. But instead of just assigning a value to the object itself, you should define a new property for the object and assign a value to the property. To create a new property and assign a value to it, simply write a variable expression such as the one here:

myobject.property = *value*;

- *myobject* is the name of the user-defined object
- *property* is the name of the property you want to create
- *value* is the value you want to assign

Suppose you create an object called customer, and you want to define three properties to it: name, address, and phone. Here's one way to do it:

```
customer = new makeSimpleObject();
customer.name = "Fred";
customer.address = "123 Main Street";
customer.phone = "555-1212";
```

```
function makeSimpleObject() {
        return (this);
}
```

You can verify that you've indeed created a new object and assigned properties to the object by adding an alert method to display one of the properties. For example, you could put this after the customer.phone line. When you run the script, the alert box says "Fred":

```
alert (customer.name);
```

Defining Properties When You Create an Object

Another method of defining properties for objects is to include the property names in the object function. You can use this technique to create a new object and define the property values at the same time. You need only a few more lines of code in the object function:

```
customer = new makeCustomer("Fred", "123 Main Street", "555-1212");
alert (customer.name);

function makeCustomer(Name, Address, Phone) {
        this.name = Name;
        this.address = Address;
        this.phone = Phone;
}
```

Note the series of "this" statements. Each this statement assigns a property to the current object, which is the one being created in the makeCustomer object function. Three parameters are passed to the object statement—the customer's name, address, and phone number—and these parameters are used to define the contents of the three properties, which are name, address, and phone.

JavaScript imposes no limitations on the number of properties you can assign to an object. Include as many this statements as you wish in the object function. And, you can assign additional properties to the object later, after it has been created. For instance, if you want to add a salutation property to the customer object, just do this:

```
customer = new makeCustomer("Fred", "123 Main Street", "555-1212");
customer.salutation = "Mr.";
```

Note that other objects you create with the makeCustomer object function will have just the three base properties, but this object for Fred will have an additional property for the salutation. Properties added later do not affect other objects created with the same object function.

Using Index Numbers Instead of Property Names

JavaScript uses what's called "associative arrays" to create objects. This means that an object is an array variable, using names to denote the elements of the array (arrays are more fully discussed in Chapter 8, "Variables"). In most programming languages, each element of the array is numbered, as shown here:

array[0]

array[1]

array[2]

With an associative array, names can be used instead of numbers. Following this approach, you don't have to remember array[1] of the array is for an address, array[2] is for the phone, and so forth. You can just use array.address and array.phone instead.

Go back to the example in the previous section, in which a new customer object is made using the makeCustomer object function. Replace the line:

```
alert (customer.name);
```

with the line:

```
alert (customer[0]);
```

Surprise! Both code segments display "Fred" in the alert box. This is because customer.name is the same as customer[0]. The custom object (which is really an array of values) is equivalent to the following lines of code. As you can see, the index numbering for the array starts at 0.

```
customer[0] = "Fred"
```

```
customer[1] = "123 Main Street"
customer[2] = "555-1212"
```

Which should you use—numbers or names? Associative names are much easier to remember and use. Numbers can come in handy, though, if you want to step through each property of an object using a for loop, as shown in the lines here. Values for the three properties appear in the alert box.

```
Temp = "";
for (Count = 0; Count < 3; Count++)
        Temp += customer[Count] + "\n";
alert (customer[Count]);
```

Creating User-Defined Methods

A user-defined method is yet another way of using functions in JavaScript. Methods act upon objects—either objects built into JavaScript or objects that you've created. A method can either change an object in some way or display a property of an object.

For instance, suppose you want to insert the various contents of the customer object: name, address, and phone number. The "regular method" is to write the code to insert the object contents, then stuff the code in a function. Call the function, using the customer object as a parameter, as shown here:

```
customer = new makeCustomer("Fred", "123 Main Street", "555-1212");
displayCustomer (customer);

function displayCustomer (cust_obj) {
        Temp = "Name: " + cust_obj.name + "\n";
        Temp += "Address: " + cust_obj.address + "\n";
        Temp += "Phone: " + cust_obj.phone + "\n";
        document.write (Temp + "<BR>");
}
```

The lines of code following make up a fully functioning script. To try this out, load the script and click the button. JavaScript outputs the three lines of customer data. Reload the document if you want to run it again.

customer_array1.html

```
<HTML>
<HEAD>
<TITLE>Object Method Example</TITLE>
<SCRIPT LANGUAGE="JavaScript">

function run () {
        customer = new makeCustomer("Fred", "123 Main Street", "555-1212");
displayCustomer (customer);
}

function displayCustomer (cust_obj) {
        Temp = "Name: " + cust_obj.name + "<BR>";
        Temp += "Address: " + cust_obj.address + "<BR>";
        Temp += "Phone: " + cust_obj.phone + "<BR>";
        document.write (Temp + "<P>");
}

function makeCustomer(Name, Address, Phone) {
        this.name = Name;
        this.address = Address;
        this.phone = Phone;
}

</SCRIPT>
</HEAD>
<BODY>
Click to call function.
<FORM>
<INPUT TYPE="button" Value="Click" onClick="run()">
</FORM>
</BODY>
</HTML>
```

The other method is to create a method for the customer object. With this approach, you call the method as part of the object. This helps in defining special method functions that are designed for—and only for—certain kinds of objects. This process forms one of the foundations of object-oriented programming, whereby objects contain their own unique methods of operation. The same script as above is now repeated, but it has been modified so that the customer object contains the displayCustomer method.

customer_array2.html

```
<HTML>
<HEAD>
<TITLE>Object Method Example</TITLE>
<SCRIPT LANGUAGE="JavaScript">

function run () {
        customer = new makeCustomer("Fred", "123 Main Street", "555-1212");
        customer.displayCustomer();

}


function displayCustomer () {
        Temp = "Name: " + this.name + "<BR>";
        Temp += "Address: " + this.address + "<BR>";
        Temp += "Phone: " + this.phone + "<BR>";
        document.write (Temp + "<P>");
}


function makeCustomer(Name, Address, Phone) {
        this.name = Name;
        this.address = Address;
        this.phone = Phone;
        this.displayCustomer = displayCustomer;
}
```

```
</SCRIPT>
</HEAD>
<BODY>
Click to call function.
<FORM>
<INPUT TYPE="button" Value="Click" onClick="run()">
</FORM>
</BODY>
</HTML>
```

As you can see, to display the customer data, you call the displayCustomer method, as shown here:

```
customer.displayCustomer();
```

Notice a few other changes in this version:

- The call to the displayCustomer function no longer uses a parameter.
- The displayCustomer() function no longer uses a parameter.
- The displayCustomer() uses the this keyword to refers to the current object.

When you write your own methods for objects, you'll follow the same pattern as used in the displayCustomer() lines of code. There's no need to pass parameters to the function unless necessary. Refer to properties using the this keyword. And, add the name of the method function in the function that creates the object (in this case, it's the makeCustomer object function).

Extending Built-in Objects

Though it's not common practice, you can "extend" some of JavaScript's built-in objects by giving them additional properties. You might do this, for example, if you want to associate a value with a given object in a document, rather than create variables or a new object to hold the values. Not all JavaScript objects are assignable in Netscape 2.0, however. Here are the objects that generally allow extending:

- navigator

- forms
- form controls (buttons, text boxes, and so forth)
- Math

You assign new properties to these objects by appending a new property to the object name and specifying a value. For example, to specify a new property for a form called "myform," write:

```
document.myform.newprop = "This is a new property";
```

Or, to specify a new property for the navigator object, write:

```
navigator.newprop = "This is also a new property";
```

NOTE

JavaScript specifically rejects assigning new properties to the built-in window and frame objects, displaying an error message in response. In addition, several other object types (such as document, anchor, Date, and link) silently reject new property assignments. However, you can assign new properties to variables that contain copies of these objects.

For example, you use this technique to keep track of the object name of the parent window when spawning a new window. The technique involves assigning a new property to the variable that contains the object reference of the new window. This new property is the object name of the main (top-level) window.

```
win = window.open("second.html", "secwin");
win.creator = self;
```

In this newly opened window (containing the document second.html), you can reference a function or variable in the main window by using this syntax:

```
creator.functionname        // refers to function in the parent window

creator.variable        // refers to a variable in the parent window
```

Understanding and Using Array Objects

Arrays are a very handy form of variable. Arrays let you create one variable and then store a multitude of different pieces of data inside it. Each piece of data is kept separate from the others, so you can easily extract it later on.

■■■■■■■ **NOTE**

> Arrays were first discussed in Chapter 8, "Variables." If the subject of arrays is new to you, be sure to read the arrays section in this chapter.

■■■■■■■

In review, JavaScript supports an Array object for creating new arrays, and you can build your own arrays using the object function methods described earlier in this chapter. The typical self-made JavaScript array uses a function such as the following:

```
function makeArray (NumElements)  {
        this.length = NumElements;
        for (Count = 1; Count <= NumElements; Count++)  {
                this[Count] = 0;
        }
        return (this);          //optional
}
```

To create a new array object, you merely call this object function, using the new keyword. The following creates a new array with 10 elements predefined to have an initial value of 0.

```
MyNewArray = new makeArray (10);
```

Extending the Array Object Function

You can get as fancy as you want with the array object function. Following is a version that lets you define the initial value of each element in the array. To call it, you specify the number of elements and the fill value. For example, here's how to create an array with 20 elements, each filled with the text "hiya."

```
MyArray = new makeArray (20, "hiya")
```

```
function makeArray (NumElements, Fill)  {
        this.length = NumElements;
        for (Count = 1; Count <= NumElements; Count++)  {
                this[Count] = Fill;
        }
        return (this);
}
```

Note the this.length instruction in both this and the previous makeArray function. This line associates the number of elements (NumElements) with a length property. You can use this length property to check how many elements are in the array. This approach is useful in for loops; for example, this short script displays a separate alert box for every element specified in the array. The for loop is controlled by the value in the MyArray.length property.

```
for (Count = 1; Count <= MyArray.length; Count++)
        alert (MyArray[Count]);
```

Making Implicit Arrays

In the arrays above, you must first define the new array object and then fill each element with the proper value (this initial fill value is usually considered temporary; it is replaced with the data you want the array to hold). For example, you might define a Customer array with four elements. After defining the array variable, you then populate the elements with the data you want to store:

```
Customer = new makeArray (4);
Customer[1] = "Fred";
Customer[2] = "123 Main Street";
Customer[3] = "555-1212";
```

You can save yourself the time and space of separately defining each element of the array with an "implicit" array object function. The function that follows lets you create arrays with any number of elements. Just provide the contents of each element as a parameter for the function and separate the elements with commas. The function determines how many parameters have been passed to it and creates that number of elements in the array. It also assigns each parameter to an element.

```
Customer = new makeArrayImplic ("Fred", "123 Main Street", "555-1212")
function makeArrayImplicit () {
        var Count;
        this.length=makeArrayImplicit.arguments.length;
        for (Count = 1; Count < makeArrayImplicit.arguments.length+1; Count ++)
        this[Count]=makeArrayImplicit.arguments[Count-1];
        return (this);
}
```

The "secret" of the implicit array object function is the arguments.length property. This is a special-case property that can be used in functions only. It returns the number of parameters passed to the function. The arguments object, in turn, contains the value of each property passed to the function. In this way, the first parameter is assigned to the first array element; the second parameter is assigned to the second array element, and so forth. Note that the arguments array is "zero-based," which means its contents start from 0, not 1. Element 0 for the new array object is reserved to hold the number of elements of the new object (three, in the case of the above example). So, the function fills in the parameters starting with element 1. The line:

```
this[Count]=makeArrayIbmplicit.arguments[Count-1];
```

ensures that the correct parameter goes into the right element.

Creating Multidimensional Arrays

All of the arrays above have just one dimension. You reference the elements in the array using a single sequence of numbers: 1, 2, 3, 4, and so forth. In a multidimensional array, you reference elements using a more complex hierarchy. Two-dimensional arrays are by far the most common. A two-dimensional array is functionally identical in use and construction as the rows and columns in an electronic spreadsheet program. Think of the rows as one dimension, and the columns as the other dimension, as shown in Figure 11.2. To reference some specific piece of data, you provide both the column and row.

To create a two-dimensional array in JavaScript, you can create two object functions. One defines the array in the first dimensions, and the other creates the contents of the second dimension. Here's an example of the functions you can use to create two-dimensional arrays:

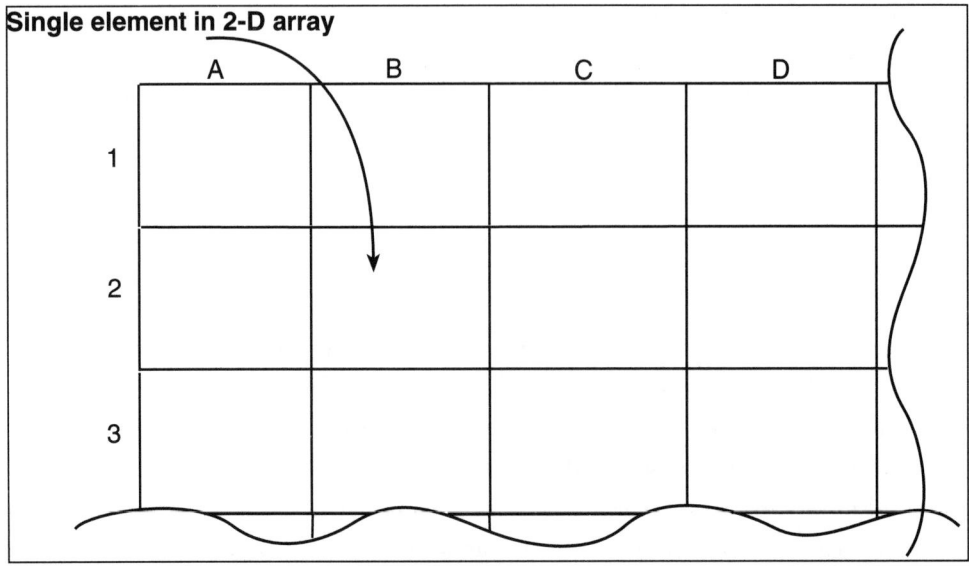

Figure 11.2 A two-dimensional array is similar to the row/column format of an electronic spreadsheet. To access data in an array or spreadsheet, you provide an "address" using coordinates.

```
function makeArray2 (X, Y) {
        var Count;
        this.length = X;
        for (var Count= 1; Count <= X; Count++)
                this[Count] = new makeArray(Y);
}


function makeArray (NumElements) {
        var Count;
        this.length = NumElements;
        for (Count = 1; Count <= NumElements; Count++)
                this[Count]=0;
        return (this);
}
```

To create the two-dimensional array, make a call to the makeArray2 function, specifying the number of main elements as well as the number of subelements in each main element. For instance, to create a two-dimensional array with four main elements, with each main element divided into two subelements, write:

```
var TwoArr = new makeArray2 (4, 2);
```

The TwoArr variable holds the newly created two-dimensional array. You now have to fill it. One way to perform that task is to define each element separately, as shown here:

```
TwoArr[1][1] = "this is sub-element 1 of element 1";
TwoArr[1][2] = "this is sub-element 2 of element 1";
...
TwoArr[2][1] = "this is sub-element 1 of element 2";
TwoArr[2][2] = "this is sub-element 2 of element 2";
```

and so forth. Or, you can use a loop to fill the elements and/or subelements. The following example fills each element of the array with a set of numbers showing the element and subelement number, such as "3, 1" for the third element, first subelement.

```
function run () {
        var TwoArr = new makeArray2 (4, 2);
        for (Count =1; Count <= TwoArr.length; Count ++ ) {
                for (Countx = 1; Countx <= TwoArr[Count].length; Countx++)
                        TwoArr[Count][Countx]=Count + ", " + Countx;
        }
        for (Count =1; Count <= TwoArr.length; Count ++ ) {
                for (Countx = 1; Countx <= TwoArr[Count].length; Countx++)
                        alert (TwoArr[Count][Countx]);
        }
}
```

Creating n-Dimension Arrays

Arrays with more than two dimensions can be created using a number of methods. One method involves creating a main object, then subobjects under that object. You reference the array elements using numbers. For example, suppose you want to create a four-dimensional array of magazine articles. Here's how the dimensions are used:

- Dimension 1: The title of the magazine
- Dimension 2: The issue date of the magazine, by month and year

- Dimension 3: The name of an article of interest in the magazine

Dimension 1 just contains magazine titles. For each specific title, another dimension contains all the issue dates you have recorded. And for each issue date there is one or more article names.

The following code shows one way to create this three-dimensional array. Start by defining the first dimension, which contains the titles of the magazines you want to index. The example uses the makeArrayImplicit function from earlier in this chapter to define this array. Remember that this will be a one-dimensional array:

```
magazine = new makeArrayImplicit ("Pop Science", "Pop Mechanics");
magazine[1] = new makeArrayImplicit ("January", "February");
magazine[2] = new makeArrayImplicit ("January", "February");
magazine[1][1] = new makeArrayImplicit ("PS/1 Jan", "PS/2 Jan");
magazine[1][2] = new makeArrayImplicit ("PS/1 Feb", "PS/2 Feb");
magazine[2][1] = new makeArrayImplicit ("PM/1 Jan", "PM/2 Jan");
magazine[2][2] = new makeArrayImplicit ("PM/1 Feb", "PM/2 Feb");
alert (magazine[2][2][1]);
```

This script displays PM/1 Feb in an alert box. Here's how the [2][2][1] breaks down:

- [?][?][1]—The first dimension contains the magazine, in this case 2, or *Popular Mechanics*.
- [2][2][1]—The second dimension contains the issue, in this case 2, or February.
- [2][2][1]—The third dimension contains the article, in this case 1, or "PM/1 Feb".

In an actual application, you'd use a for loop or other automated system to apply the values to the array indices.

There are yet other ways to build multidimensional arrays, as shown here.

```
magazine = new Object();
Magazine = Issue = Article = 1;
magazine[Magazine + "," + Issue + "," + Article] = "PS/1 Jan "
magazine[Magazine + "," + Issue + "," + (Article+1)] = "PS/2 Jan"
magazine[Magazine + "," + (Issue+1) + "," + Article] = "PS/1 Feb"
magazine[Magazine + "," + (Issue+1) + "," + (Article+1)] = "PS/2 Feb"
```

```
Magazine = 2;
magazine[Magazine + "," + Issue + "," + Article] = "PM/1 Jan "
magazine[Magazine + "," + Issue + "," + (Article+1)] = "PM/2 Jan"
magazine[Magazine + "," + (Issue+1) + "," + Article] = "PM/1 Feb"
magazine[Magazine + "," + (Issue+1) + "," + (Article+1)] = "PM/2 Feb"

Magazine = 1, Issue = 2, Article = 1;
alert (magazine[Magazine + "," + Issue + "," + Article]) // displays PS/1 Feb
```

This approach uses a generic Object object, and each dimension is assigned individually. The array is built associatively, using commas between the dimension indexes. To JavaScript, it sees the array indices as:

magazine[1,1,1]

magazine[1,1,2]

magazine[1,2,1]

and so forth.

12

HOW DO I?

Writing a JavaScript program is akin to taking a hike in the middle of nowhere. You go east, thinking you're heading north. Suddenly you find yourself in Wisconsin, surrounded by cows who are much smarter than you (and they're more useful). If only you had a compass to get you going in the right direction in the first place. If only...

Most JavaScripters have the wits and creativity to write almost any program they can imagine—maybe not as well as the average Holstain, but they can manage quite nicely just the same. A common problem of many JavaScript writers is that they see where they want to go, but they just don't know how to get there. They need a compass to point them in the right direction.

This chapter is your compass for trips with JavaScript. It contains answers to several dozen of the most common questions JavaScript programmers have, such as:

- How do I dynamically reset the Href of a link when it's clicked?
- How do I reload the previous document in the history list?
- How do I play a sound file?

• How do I mail a form using JavaScript?

These topics are referenced in the table of contents for easy perusal. If you ever get stuck in Wisconsin, be sure to bring this chapter along.

Short Takes

Topic	Page
Change the URL of the window	300
Change the URL of a frame	300, 450–452
Play a sound	300, 592–595
Convert a string to a number	301
Convert a number to a string	301
Create a new object	301
Make an array	301

Working with Windows and Frames

Topic	Page
Determine the name of a window	301–302
Create a floating toolbar	302–305
Trigger a function in another window	306–307
Open a document into a window using Macintosh or X-Windows of Netscape	308–309
Check that a new window has been successfully opened with window.open	309
Write <SCRIPT> tags to a new window or frame	309–310

Working with Functions

Topic	Page
Pass a different number of parameters to one function	310–312
Play a script when starting Netscape	312

Working with Forms

Topic	Page
Stop the form from being submitted when I press Enter in a text box	312–314
Mail a form using JavaScript	314–316
Submit a form using a link	317

Short Takes

Change the URL of the window

```
location = URL;
```

URL is the URL you want to use, as in:

```
location = "index.html"
```

Change the URL of a frame

```
parent.framename.location = URL;
```

URL is the fully qualified URL you want to use, as in:

```
parent.frame_a.location = "http://mydomain.com/javascript/index.html"
```

Play a sound

```
location = sound;
```

sound is the sound file you want to use, as in:

```
location = meow.au;
```

Convert a number to a string

```
VarName = "" + Num
```

VarName is the name of the variable that will contain the converted value; *Num* is the number, as in:

```
Val = "" + 54;
```

Convert a string to a number

```
VarName = parseInt(InString);
```

or

```
VarName = parseFloat(InString);
```

VarName is the name of the variable that will contain the converted value; *InString* is the string containing the number (such as "12345" but not "$12345"). Here is an example:

```
Val = parseInt ("12345");
```

Quickly create a new object

```
object_name = new Object();
```

object_name is the name of the new object you wish to create, as in:

```
myObject = new Object();
```

Make an array

```
ArrayName = new Array();
```

or

```
ArrayName = new Object();
```

ArrayName is the name of the array, as in:

```
MyArray = new Object();
```

Working with Windows and Frames

Determine the Name of a Window

The window.name property returns the name of a window. For example, this line returns the name of the current window and places the name in the WinName variable:

```
WinName = window.name;
```

This method works for any window that is not the top-level browser window—in other words, the main browser window. Using the window.open method, you can have JavaScript open additional windows, and these windows are named. But the main top-level window has no name and cannot be given a name.

Following is an example of how to open a new window, and then display its name. The name is "WindowName" (note that no spaces are allowed in a window name).

```
win = window.open ("", "WindowName");
    // repeat the above command if you're using Macintosh or X-Windows
alert (win.name);
```

The window name is handy if you want to refer to the window elsewhere in your script. If you must refer to the main top-level browser window, use the technique described in "Create a floating toolbar," next in this chapter.

Create a floating toolbar

With Netscape's multiwindow personality, and a little bit of JavaScript, you can easily open windows to use as floating toolbars. The toolbar is a small window that "floats" over the main window; it's designed to change the content of the main window in some way, such as change the URL or update some text. The toolbar can stay open, or it can close to get out of the way.

A floating toolbar contains one or more buttons, or it can contain a list of links. First, start with the main window document. An example is shown below:

```
win = window.open ("toolbar.htm","toolbar", "height=250,width=95");
win.creator = self;
```

This script "spawns" a new, small window using some fairly simple code and can be placed anywhere in the document (when the document opens, in an onLoad event, in response to clicking a button, and so forth). For example, placing the code in-line in a function called with onLoad causes the toolbar to open when the main document finishes loading.

float.html

CD-ROM

```
<HTML><HEAD>
<TITLE>Floating Toolbar</TITLE>
<SCRIPT>
function openToolbar() {
        win = window.open ("test.htm","newwin", "height=250,width=95");
        win.creator = self;
}
</SCRIPT>
</HEAD>
<BODY onLoad="openToolbar()">
<H2>This page will change when you click an item in the floating toolbar</H2>
</BODY></HTML>
```

The toolbar document consists of a series of buttons or links, as shown in Figure 12.1. Here's a version that uses buttons centered down the window. Clicking on a button opens the specified document in the main window. In this version, the toolbar stays open.

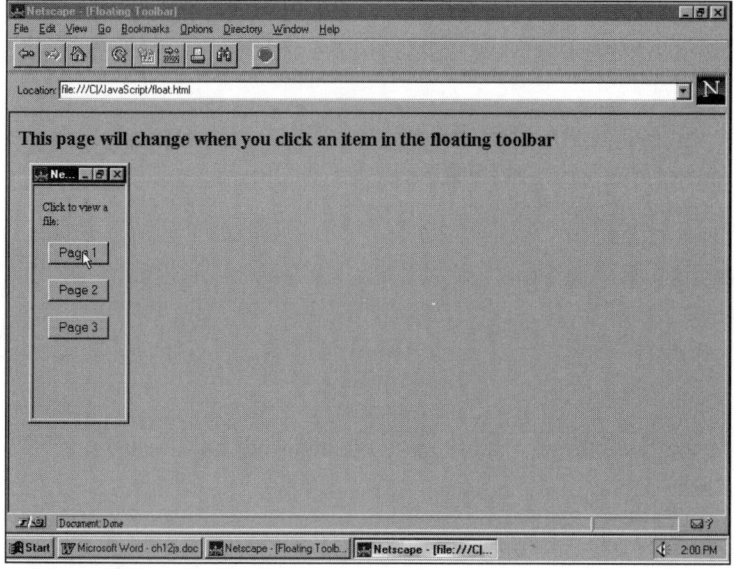

Figure 12.1 The floating toolbar can be used as a navigation aid.

spawnwin.html

```
<HTML>
<SCRIPT>
function changePage(loc) {
        window.close();
        creator.location = loc;
}
</SCRIPT>
<BODY>
<FONT SIZE=-1>Click to view a file:</FONT SIZE><P>
<CENTER>
<FORM>
<INPUT TYPE="button" VALUE="Page 1" onClick="changePage('page1.htm')"><P>
<INPUT TYPE="button" VALUE="Page 2" onClick="changePage('page2.htm')"><P>
<INPUT TYPE="button" VALUE="Page 3" onClick="changePage('page3.htm')"><P>
</FORM>
</CENTER>
</BODY>
</HTML>
```

If you prefer that the toolbar closes after changing the URL (or whatever your script is designed to do) of the main window, revise the changePage function as shown here:

```
function changePage(loc) {
        window.close();
        creator.location = loc;
}
```

You're not limited to using just buttons. Here's the toolbar opener document using links rather than form buttons.

```
<HTML>
<SCRIPT>
function changePage(loc) {
```

```
        //window.close();                  // add if desired
        creator.location = loc;
    }
</SCRIPT>
<BODY>
<FONT SIZE=-1>Click to view a file:</FONT SIZE><P>
<CENTER>
<A HREF="JavaScript:changePage('page1.htm')">Page 1</A><P>
<A HREF="JavaScript:changePage('page2.htm')">Page 2</A><P>
<A HREF="JavaScript:changePage('page3.htm')">Page 3</A><P>
</CENTER>
</BODY>
</HTML>
```

What else can you do with this toolbar idea? You can use any control device in the toolbar window. For example, you can place a series of images as the "click text" for links. Click on an image to activate the script. Or, you can use a client-side image map, where the image is divided into zones, and clicking on a zone activates a different link.

In the code above, the "secret sauce" is the line:

```
win.creator = self;
```

in the main window, and the line:

```
creator.location = loc;
```

in the toolbar window. The win.creator instruction creates a new property for the *win* window object, which is opened with the window.open method. This property is assigned the value of the main window using the self property. In the toolbar window, the creator property is used to tell JavaScript which window you wish to change.

This workaround is necessary because top-level windows (those not opened with window.open) in JavaScript are not named. As a result, referring to the window from another window is impossible, unless you employ a technique such as the above.

Trigger a function in another window

Suppose your JavaScript opens another document in a new window (now you've got two windows opened). In the second window you want to call a function that's in the first window. The technique is simple—when you know "the secret."

You start first with the usual instruction to open the window. It looks like this:

```
win = window.open ("openme.html");
```

(If you are using the Macintosh and Netscape 2.0, you will need to call this line twice, as a workaround for a bug.)

This instruction "spawns" a new window, and the reference to that window is placed in a variable named win. Add to this a second line that creates a new property for the spawned window. You can name it anything you like; "creator" is a good one. You assign the current window object to this creator property, as shown here:

```
win.creator = self;
```

In the second (just opened) window you can refer to functions in the first window using the syntax *creator.func_name* where *func_name* is the name of the function. For example, if the function name is windowTrigger, the instruction line is:

```
creator.windowTrigger();
```

Here is a simple working example. The first document, named *winxfer1.html*, contains the code to open a document in a new window. That document is *winxfer2.html*. JavaScript code in the second window calls the alertMe() function in the first window, then closes the second window.

winxfer1.html

CD-ROM

```
<HTML>
<HEAD>
<TITLE>Window Function Call, Doc 1</TITLE>
<SCRIPT LANGUAGE="JavaScript">
function set () {
```

```
        win = window.open ("winxfer2.html")
        win.creator = self
}


function alertMe() {
        alert ("This is the alertMe function from the first window!")
}
</SCRIPT>
</HEAD>
<BODY>
<FORM>
<INPUT TYPE="button" NAME="button1" VALUE="Click Me!" onClick="set ()">
</FORM>
</BODY>
</HTML>
```

CD-ROM

winxfer2.html

```
<HTML>
<HEAD>
<TITLE>Window Function Call, Doc 2</TITLE>
<SCRIPT LANGUAGE="JavaScript">
function callFunc() {
        creator.alertMe();
        window.close();
}
</SCRIPT>
</HEAD>
<BODY>
<FORM NAME="test">
<INPUT TYPE="button" NAME="button1" VALUE="Now Click Me!" onClick="callFunc()">
</FORM>
</BODY>
</HTML>
```

Open a Document into a Window Using Macintosh or X-Windows

A bug in Netscape 2.0 prevents JavaScript from opening a new window—using the window.open method—and placing a specified document in it. The new window opens, but no document ever appears there. This problem has been fixed in Netscape 3.0, but it continues to bedevil Macintosh and X-Windows Netscape 2.0 users (the bug does not exist on the Windows platforms or in Internet Explorer 3.0).

There are several ways to work around this bug. One is simply to call the window.open method twice in succession. Only one window will open, regardless of platform or version:

```
win = window.open ("mydoc.htm", "MyDoc");
win = window.open ("mydoc.htm", "MyDoc");
```

If you'd like to streamline this code, you can use a for statement:

```
for (i=0; i<2; i++) {win = window.open ("test2.html", "MyDoc")}
```

You can also open the window, then set the URL of the window with the location object.

```
win = window.open ("mydoc.htm", "MyDoc");
win.location = "mydoc.htm"
```

Or, if your JavaScript regularly opens documents you can develop a self-contained function that takes care of the problem for you, and be assured that any workaround is guaranteed to work with all versions.

```
var win = openWindow ("test2.html", "MyNewDoc")


function openWindow (Url, Title) {
        Rep = 1;
        if (navigator.appVersion.substring (0, 1) == "2") {
                Platform = navigator.appVersion;
                if ((Platform.indexOf ("X11") != -1) || (Platform.indexOf
                    ("Mac") != -1))
                        Rep = 2;
        }
```

```
for (Count = 0; Count < Rep; Count ++) {
        var win = window.open (Url, Title)
}
return (win)
```

}

Check the Successful Opening of a New Window with window.open

Occasionally Netscape does not comply with your request to open a window when you use the window.open method. The most likely cause of this failure is insufficient memory. A good script should check for this failure before proceeding with any code that assumes the window was successfully opened. For example, JavaScript reports a syntax error for line 2 if the window is not opened:

```
win = window.open ("mydoc.html", "MyDoc");
win.creator = self;
```

You can avoid crashing scripts by checking if the return value of the window.open method is not null. If it is not null, the window was successfully spawned. If it is null, you know a problem occurred, and your script can handle it accordingly.

```
win = window.open ("mydoc.html", "MyDoc");
if (win != null) win.creator = self;
```

Write <SCRIPT> Tags to a New Window or Frame

You can use JavaScript to create even more JavaScript. Just use the document.write method to insert the JavaScript code of your choice into a new window or a frame (you must do this from another window or frame, or else writing the next script will overwrite the old script).

However, if you try this you'll find that JavaScript invokes an error when it encounters a document.write instruction with the word </SCRIPT> in it. JavaScript sees the </SCRIPT> tag and assumes it means its own script is over.

Fortunately, there's an easy workaround: just add a backslash character before the </SCRIPT> tag, as in \ /SCRIPT. This forces JavaScript to not treat the </SCRIPT>

tag in the document.write instruction as a terminator for its own script. Here is an example:

```
document.write ("<SCRIPT>alert ('hello')<\/SCRIPT>");
```

Working with Functions

Pass a Different Number of Parameters to One Function

Typically, functions are "formally" declared to accept a certain number of parameters, and standard programming practice requires you to always call a function with the right number of parameters. For example, the following script uses a showMessage function that is formally declared to accept two parameters: Message1 and Message2. These parameters are used as messages in an alert box.

```
showMessage ("Hello", "There");

function showMessage (Message1, Message2) {
        alert (Message1);
        alert (Message2);
}
```

But JavaScript is more flexible than this. You can define a function with no formal list of parameters and call it using any number of parameters—or no parameters, if you wish. JavaScript supports a special *arguments* object that is created inside a function. This object is an array; in addition to a length array that specifies the number of arguments passed to the function, each element of the array is a separate parameter passed to the function from the original "caller." For example, if you pass the revised showMessage function two parameters, the arguments object contains these values:

arguments.length = 2

arguments[0] = "Hello"

arguments[1] = "There"

Code inside your function can determine how many arguments to process, and then go through the arguments array one element at a time and pick out the arguments that were passed to the function. Here's the revised version of the showMessage function, this time capable of accepting any number of parameters:

```
showMessage ("Hello", "There");
showMessage ("Hello", "There", "Again!");


function showMessage () {
        for (var Count = 0; Count < showMessage.arguments.length; Count++) {
                alert (showMessage.arguments[Count]);
        }
}
```

■■■■■■ **NOTE**

JavaScript also supports a caller property of the arguments object. This property contains the object string of the function that called this function! You can use the caller property to determine the name of the "calling" function, and that name to determine what course of action to take. You might have your function do one thing if *X* function calls it, and do something else if *Y* function calls it. Here's a short demonstration of the caller property, along with some code to extract just the name of the calling function. This name is displayed in an alert box.

```
<SCRIPT>
function processMessage () {
showMessage ("Hello", "There");
}


function showMessage () {
        var Temp = showMessage.arguments.caller.toString()
        Ret = Temp.substring (Temp.indexOf (" "), Temp.indexOf ("("))
        alert (Ret)
}

</SCRIPT>
```

```
<FORM>
<INPUT TYPE="button" VALUE="Click" onClick="processMessage()">
<INPUT TYPE="button" VALUE="Click" onClick="showMessage()">
</FORM>
```

Play a Script When Starting Netscape

You can play a script when starting Netscape. For example, the following script displays a welcome message when the local home page is loaded:

```
<HTML><HEAD>
<TITLE>Local Home Page</TITLE>
</HEAD>
<SCRIPT>
function greetings() {
        alert ("Howdy!")
}
</SCRIPT>
<BODY onLoad="greetings()">
More body stuff here...
</BODY></HTML>
```

To set the local home page, in Netscape choose Options, General Preferences. Click on the Appearance tab, and choose Home Page Location for the Start With option. Fill in the path and name of the local home page you want. For example, on a PC you'd use the syntax:

```
file:///c|/javascript/homepage.htm
```

Working with Forms

Stop the Form from Being Submitted When Enter Is Pressed

Netscape and many other browsers are designed to automatically submit a form when the user presses the Enter key while in a form with just one text box. This can be a useful feature; for example, it can save the user from having to click on a separate Submit button.

But there are times when you specifically want to avoid submitting a form when the user presses Enter. You can handle this situation with the onSubmit event, placed in the <FORM> tag. Consider the following:

```
<FORM NAME="myform" onSubmit="return false;">
Please type your name, and click OK<BR>
<INPUT TYPE="text" NAME="key1" VALUE = "hello there"><P>
<INPUT TYPE="button" NAME="button" VALUE="OK"
onClick="submitNow(this.form)"><P>
</FORM>
```

The form (named "myform") includes the onSubmit event handler in the <FORM> tag. The handler specifies that when a submit event occurs, JavaScript should return a value of *false*, thereby stopping the submission. The onSubmit event handler takes care of submitting the form when the user presses the Enter key after typing text in the text box.

You will still want a means to submit the form (when the user is ready), and this can be handled by a button. The button uses an onClick event handler to call a function named submitNow. The current form object is passed to this function as this.form. The submitNow function is relatively simple:

```
function submitNow(form) {
        form.submit();
}
```

Notice that the submit method is used with the form object, passed to the submitNow function. This ensures that the proper form is submitted, should you have more than one form in the document. Here's a more complete working example, showing two forms in the document.

If you open this example as a local file on your hard drive, you will see the submit results in the Location URL box. Note that you see the results in URL encoded form, such as

```
file:///c|/javascript/example.htm?myname=Gordon
```

When you click the first OK button, the URL reflects the myname value because this is the form that is submitted; when you click the second OK button, the URL reflects the myaddress value because this is the form that is submitted.

two_form.html

```
<HTML>
<HEAD>
<SCRIPT LANGUAGE="JavaScript">
function submitNow(form) {
        form.submit();
}
</SCRIPT>
</HEAD>
<BODY>
<FORM NAME="form1" onSubmit="return false;">
Please type your name ane click OK<BR>
<INPUT TYPE="text" NAME="myname"><P>
<INPUT TYPE="button" NAME="button" VALUE="OK"
onClick="submitNow(this.form)"><P>
</FORM>
<P>
<FORM NAME="form2" onSubmit="return false;">
Please type your address and click OK<BR>
<INPUT TYPE="text" NAME="myaddress"><P>
<INPUT TYPE="button" NAME="button" VALUE="OK"
onClick="submitNow(this.form)"><P>
</FORM>
</BODY>
</HTML>
```

Mail a Form Using JavaScript

Netscape lets you mail the contents of form fields to yourself or any other valid e-mail address. You can use this feature to process a form, without having to invest time and energy (and maybe money) in a "formmail" CGI program that runs on a server. There are limitations regarding the mailing of forms, however, and some security issues involved. Depending on what you want to do, you may be thrilled or disappointed by what Netscape and JavaScript offer.

Basic <FORM> Tag Syntax for Mailing

The basic HTML syntax for mailing a form is quite simple and does not require JavaScript. You merely add the mailto: protocol, along with the e-mail address, as the ACTION attribute of the <FORM> tag. It looks like this:

```
<FORM ACTION="mailto:jowbloe@domain.com" METHOD=get>
```

Following this tag are one or more form object tags, such as text boxes or radio buttons. You also provide a submit button tag to submit the form. Here's a working form with one text field and a submit button:

```
<FORM ACTION="mailto:jowbloe@domain.com" METHOD=post>
<INPUT TYPE="text" NAME="box1" VALUE="">
<INPUT TYPE="submit">
```

To use this, fill out the text box and click the Submit button (because there's only one text box in this form, pressing Enter while the insertion point is flashing in the box also acts to submit the form).

Because the form uses the post METHOD for sending the form, Netscape's mail message window does not appear. The contents of the form are sent to the address after the mailto: protocol. The contents are URL encoded. Each control of the form is indicated by its name; the value for that control is shown on the other side of the equals sign.

You need to separate the encoded text you receive in your mail box by hand or by using some type of parsing software. You can even use a macro in a word processing program, such as Microsoft Word or WordPerfect, to perform the parsing for you.

▬▬▬▬ **NOTE**

Currently only Netscape and a few other browsers support the mailto: protocol in the ACTION attribute. Therefore, if you use the above technique you should ensure that users have a compatible browser.

▬▬▬▬

Displaying the Mail Window

By leaving off the METHOD=post attribute or changing it to METHOD=get, you force Netscape to bring up the mail window when the form is submitted. This can be advantageous because now the mailed form is received in standard e-mail format and is not URL encoded, as above. You can "prefill" text in most of the mail window entry blanks, saving the user from doing that. You do this by constructing a URL "query string" and assigning standard mail window names and text values.

In the following example, clicking the Submit button displays the mail window, with the mail fields already filled out. The user then writes a message and sends the message when done.

```
<FORM ACTION="mailto:joe@domain.com?subject=Suggestions&cc=fred@domain.com">
```

- The mail to box is prefilled with joe@domain.com.
- The text "Suggestions" is provided as default text for the subject line.
- The text fred@domain.com is provided as default text for the cc line.
- The sender's e-mail address is automatically provided by Netscape.

"Silently" Sending a Form

In the first release of Netscape 2.0, you could "silently" send a form without the user's knowledge. The technique simply used the form.submit method to submit a form. This was deemed a security risk and/or invasion of privacy because it's possible to silently return the e-mail address of anyone who visits a Web site. This capability has been removed in Netscape 2.01 and beyond.

There are perfectly legitimate (in other words, non-hacking) reasons for silently submitting a form. If you're sure your users have the original 2.0, the following method works. Construct the script as follows:

```
<FORM NAME="silentsubmit" ACTION="mailto:me@domain.com" METHOD=post>
<FORM TYPE="hidden" VALUE="silent submission">
</FORM>
<SCRIPT>
document.silentsubmit.submit();
</SCRIPT>
```

Submit a Form Using a Link

If you're tired of boring buttons for submitting forms, you might try a link instead. With the proper formatting of the JavaScript code, you can use a link—as text or as an image—to submit the form.

Here's the basic approach: set up a function (such as submitForm) to handle the actual form submission. Use the JavaScript: protocol for the HREF of the form and call the submitForm function.

```
<SCRIPT>
function submitForm()  {
        document.forms[0].submit();
}

</SCRIPT>
<A HREF="JavaScript:submitForm()">Click to submit</A>

<FORM>
<INPUT TYPE="text" NAME="text1">
<INPUT TYPE="text" NAME="text1">
</FORM>
```

You can use an image instead of text for the link. Just replace the "click text" with the <IMG> tag specifying the image you want to use. For best results, remember to include HEIGHT and WIDTH attributes for the image.

```
<A HREF="JavaScript:submitForm()"><IMG SRC="image.gif"
HEIGHT=40 WIDTH=20>submit</A>
```

The example form submits to itself, which isn't too helpful. You'll probably want to submit the form to some CGI program somewhere, in which case you define the URL for the CGI program in the ACTION= attribute for the <FORM> tag. For instance, to submit the form to a CGI program called former.cgi at domain.com, use:

```
<FORM ACTION="http://domain.com/former.cgi">
```

Submit a Form in a Different Frame

If you're using frames, you may organize the form so that the form content is in one frame, but the controls for submitting the form are in another. You'll need to tell JavaScript what form in what frame you want to submit. The syntax is:

```
parent.framename.document.formname.submit();
```

- *framename* is the name of the frame that contains the form, and
- *formname* is the name of the frame.

Here is an example. Suppose the frame that contains the form is named *formframe* and that the form is named *submitit*. The instruction to submit that form—from any other frame in the frameset—is:

```
parent.formframe.document.submitit.submit();
```

Return a Form Submission to a Frame

Once submitted to a CGI, the CGI program usually does one of three things:

- It reloads the form.
- It sends back dynamically generated text, such as "Thanks for submitting your form."
- It loads another URL into the browser window.

If you are using frames for your form, you may wish to have the CGI script send the output to a specific frame. This is done using the TARGET attribute in the <FORM> tag. Provide the name of the frame as the TARGET, and Netscape will direct the CGI output to that frame. For example, if the frame is called myframe, add the following to the <FORM> tag:

```
<FORM TARGET="myframe">
```

You can, of course, provide other attributes you want to use in the <FORM> tag.

Submit a Form Using a Graphic Button

HTML offers perfectly good buttons for forms. But if you want to get fancy and provide a custom button, you have to use the ol' button-as-a-hypertext-anchor trick, which goes like this:

```
<A HREF="mypage.htm"><IMG SRC="button.gif" ALT="Submit"></A>
```

NOTE

Netscape places a border around the image when it's a hypertext link. If you want to hide the border around the button, add BORDER=0 to the <IMG> tag.

The user sees a graphic button for the button instead of the standard textual link. But the only problem is that HTML doesn't really provide a way to use a graphic button like this to submit a form. Fortunately, JavaScript lets you do an end-run and gives you this capability.

To submit a form using a button, use the onClick event handler and call a JavaScript function as shown in the following script:

```
<SCRIPT>
function formsubmit() {
        document.testform.submit();
}
</SCRIPT>
...
<A HREF onClick="this.href='JavaScript:formsubmit()'">
<IMG SRC="button.gif" ALT="Submit"></A>
<FORM NAME="testform" ACTION="mypage.cgi" METHOD=post>
<INPUT TYPE="text" NAME="text1">
<INPUT TYPE="text" NAME="text2">
</FORM>
```

NOTE

You may also construct the link like this:

```
<A HREF="JavaScript:formsubmit()">
```

The method above offers a little more flexibility overall, especially if you wish to dynamically set the HREF of the link depending on previous user

> input, or if you wish to provide one HREF for non-JavaScript browsers and
> another for JavaScript browsers.

■■■■■■

Before submitting a form using the graphic button technique above, you may wish to verify that all the inputs are valid. Or you may wish to ask the user if he or she is ready to submit the form. This can be done by placing additional code in the submission function—in the above example, this function is called formsubmit.

For instance, the following code displays an OK/Cancel confirmation box before the form is submitted. If the user clicks OK, the form is submitted. If the user clicks Cancel, the form is not submitted.

```
function formsubmit() {
        if (confirm("Do you want to submit this form?"))
        document.testform.submit();
}
```

Submit Multiple Forms with One Click

Some applications call for filling out multiple forms and submitting them one after the other in response to a single Submit action (by clicking a button or link). While this can be done in JavaScript, it is not advisable without some assistance from the CGI program accepting the submission. The reason is timing. The Web can be mercurial. It might take 5 seconds to submit a form—find the server, link to it, and process the form—or it might take 30 or 60 seconds.

As a result, a better approach is to provide a "sentinel" where the CGI response from the first form is used to trigger the submission of the second form. This requires writing or rewriting your CGI script to accommodate the sentinel, but it does guarantee that multiple-form submissions will always be synchronized. Here's one way to do it.

Suppose you have two forms, each in separate frames. These frames are named frame_a and frame_b, and the forms in the them are named form_a and form_b. Clicking a button submits form_a, using the syntax:

```
parent.frame_a.document.form_a.submit();
```

The CGI script returns the following script as part of its response, as a means to trigger the submission of the second form:

```
<SCRIPT>
parent.frame_b.document.form_b.submit();
</SCRIPT>
```

This script is sent to frame_a, using the TARGET attribute detailed in "Return a form submission to a frame," above. When JavaScript receives this script, it automatically fires off the second form. You can repeat this process for as many forms as you need submitted.

Working with Links and Anchors

Programmatically Link to a New URL (Without Using an Hypertext Link)

Though it isn't obvious, JavaScript makes it very easy to link to another document. You use the location property of the document object (note: the location method is different from the location object). Assign a URL to the location property, and JavaScript automatically loads that page. For example, this instruction immediately links the user to the White House home page:

```
location = "http://www.whitehouse.gov";
```

▬▬▬▬▬ **NOTE**

You can use the location property to link to a non-HTML file. The type of file determines how Netscape behaves. For example, if you link to an au or aiff sound file, Netscape automatically loads the NPLAYER audio helper application and plays the sound. If you link to a GIF or JPEG, Netscape displays the image. If you link to some other file type, Netscape handles the file as determined by the Helpers section of the Options, General Preferences dialog box.

▬▬▬▬▬

Dynamically Set the HREF of a Hypertext Link

In normal HTML, you set the HREF (hyperlink reference) of a link using the following syntax, where *document.html* is the name of the document to which you want to link:

```
<A HREF="document.html">Click here</A>
```

Whenever you click on the link, you are transported to document.html. You can also "progammatically" set or change the HREF of a hypertext link using JavaScript. In this way you can change the destination of the link depending on some variable, such as the user's version of Netscape or the day of the week. For example, suppose you want to determine if they are using the Macintosh version of Netscape. If they are, you want the anchor to link to a special Macintosh page. If they aren't using the Mac version of Netscape, they are sent to a normal page.

CD-ROM

set_href.html

```
<HTML>
<HEAD>
<SCRIPT LANGUAGE="JavaScript">

function loadme () {
        var Platform = navigator.appVersion;
        if (Platform.indexOf ("Macintosh") != -1)
                document.links[0].href = "macpage.html";
}

</SCRIPT>
</HEAD>
<BODY onLoad = "loadme()">
This link changes if the user has a Macintosh.
<A HREF="regpage.html">Click here</A>
</FORM>
</BODY>
</HTML>
```

Here's how it works. The anchor is initially set with an HREF of "regpage.html." When the document finishes loading, JavaScript calls the loadme function. In this function, JavaScript compares the platform of Navigator, using the appVersion property of the navigator object. If the appVersion property contains the text "Macintosh", the script changes the HREF of the anchor to "macpage.html".

If you don't have a Macintosh but want to try the script, change the text comparison to the version of browser you are using. For example, if you are using the Windows 95 version, change the if expression to read:

```
if (Platform.indexOf("Win95") != -1)
```

Here's another example of programmatically setting the HREF of an anchor. In this script, the HREF is changed to a document for each day of the week. The loadme function uses the getDay() method of the Date object to return the day of the week (0 is Sunday, 1 is Monday, and so forth). A series of if tests determines which day of the week it is and sets the HREF accordingly.

Notice that the anchor tag itself is specified with an HREF of noday.html. This is a safety precaution should the page be accessed by a non-JavaScript-enabled browser. The link will take the JavaScript-challenged user to some safe page, where you can explain that a browser with JavaScript is required to properly use your site.

day_sound.html

CD-ROM

```
<HTML>
<HEAD>
<SCRIPT LANGUAGE="JavaScript">

function loadme () {
        dateObj = new Date();
        var CurrentDay = dateObj.getDay();
        if (CurrentDay == 0) document.links[0].href ="sunday.html"
        if (CurrentDay == 1) document.links[0].href ="monday.html"
        if (CurrentDay == 2) document.links[0].href ="tuesday.html"
        if (CurrentDay == 3) document.links[0].href ="wednesday.html"
        if (CurrentDay == 4) document.links[0].href ="thursday.html"
```

```
        if (CurrentDay == 5) document.links[0].href ="friday.html"
        if (CurrentDay == 6) document.links[0].href ="saturday.html"
}

</SCRIPT>
</HEAD>
<BODY onLoad = "loadme()">
This link changes depending on the day of the week.<P>
<A HREF="noday.html">Click here</A>
</FORM>
</BODY>
</HTML>
```

Another approach that is handy if you also want to specify the "click text" that appears with the link is shown below. In this case, JavaScript is used to generate the link when the document is loaded. The example uses the link method (a method of the string object) to define a link anchor. The syntax:

```
document.write ("Sunday".link("sunday.html"));
```

is functionally identical to the following HTML markup:

```
<A HREF="sunday.html">Sunday</A>
```

To fully test this script, change the clock in the computer to different days, and reload the page each time. You'll see the text changes to reflect the day. Passing the mouse over the link reveals the appropriate HREF in the status bar.

day_link.html

CD-ROM

```
<HTML>
<HEAD>
<SCRIPT LANGUAGE="JavaScript">
</SCRIPT>
<BODY>
This link changes depending on the day of the week.<P>
<SCRIPT>
```

```
        dateObj = new Date();

        var CurrentDay = dateObj.getDay();

        if (CurrentDay == 0)
                document.write  ("Sunday".link("sunday.html"));

        if (CurrentDay == 1)
                document.write  ("Monday".link("monday.html"));

        if (CurrentDay == 2)
                document.write  ("Tuesday".link("tuesday.html"));

        if (CurrentDay == 3)
                document.write  ("Wednesday".link("wednesday.html"));

        if (CurrentDay == 4)
                document.write  ("Thursday".link("thursday.html"));

        if (CurrentDay == 5)
                document.write  ("Friday".link("friday.html"));

        if (CurrentDay == 6)
                document.write  ("Saturday".link("saturday.html"));

</SCRIPT>

</FORM>

</BODY>

</HTML>
```

Dynamically Reset the HREF of a Clicked Link

Using JavaScript and a little bit of ingenuity, you can dynamically change the URL for a link at the time you click on that link. You can use this technique in a number of different ways. For example, you might use JavaScript to decide which of three different pages to jump to, depending on the Netscape platform the user has. The technique shown below dynamically changes the link when you click on it (the link is initially empty).

click_href.html

CD-ROM

```
<HTML>

<HEAD>

<TITLE>Dynamic Link Change</TITLE>

<SCRIPT LANGUAGE="JavaScript">

function set (changelink) {
```

```
        Version = navigator.appVersion;
        if (Version.indexOf ("Win") != -1) location="js1.htm";
        if (Version.indexOf ("Mac") != -1) location.href="js2.htm";
        if (Version.indexOf ("X11") != -1) location.href="js3.htm";
}
</SCRIPT>
</HEAD>
<BODY>
<A HREF="" onClick="this.href='JavaScript:set()'">Click</A>
</BODY>
</HTML>
```

Of course, you don't need to get this fancy. If you just want to change the HREF of the link to some other page, you can just do this instead (it changes the HREF to "newpage.html"):

```
<A HREF="" onClick="this.href='newpage.html'">Click</A>
```

Stop a Link from Completing

You can use JavaScript to stop a link from completing. Use this generic function to control the link.

```
function event(filename) {
        if (confirm ("Are you sure you want to link to "+filename+"?"))
                location = filename
}
```

Now format the link as follows, using numbers to identify the HREF and NAME of the link as the same element (use different numbers for each link). This allows the anchor to link back to itself. As a result, if the user chooses Cancel, the browser keeps that person in the same area (the document is not reloaded).

```
<A HREF="#1" NAME="1" onClick = "event('another.html')" >
Jump to another page</A>
```

Link to Different Pages for JavaScript and non-JavaScript browsers

A variation on the above theme is to provide a single link that directs JavaScript browsers one way, and non-JavaScript browsers the other way. This is easy to accomplish: simply provide the non-JavaScript link in the HREF= attribute of the link, the change to the new URL for the onClick event handler.

The following example links to the "nojs.htm" page for non-JavaScript browsers and "yesjs.htm" for JavaScript browsers:

```
<A HREF="nojs.htm" onClick="this.href='yesjs.htm'">Click</A>
```

Process a Link Before Loading a New Document

The *process_first.html* example shown here allows you to process a link before loading a new document. The technique uses the JavaScript: protocol as the HREF of the link to call a JavaScript function. In this case, the function is processLink, and the HREF appears as:

```
<A HREF="JavaScript:processLink()">
```

The processLink function contains an alert box that represents whatever processing you want to do before linking to a new URL. In the next line, the code sets the location property to the URL to which you want to go.

process_first.html

CD-ROM

```
<HTML>
<HEAD>
<TITLE>Process Link First</TITLE>
<SCRIPT LANGUAGE="JavaScript">
function processLink (form)  {
       alert ("Process steps here");
       location = "http://someplace.com/";
}
</SCRIPT>
```

```
</HEAD>
<BODY>
<A HREF="JavaScript:processLink()">Click here</A>
</BODY>
</HTML>
```

Note that when you place the mouse over the link, the status bar displays the HREF, which says "JavaScript:processLink()."

One practical application of this approach is to ask the users if they really want to link to a new page or to display a large graphic or sound. The processLink function would then contain:

```
function processLink (form)   {
        if (confirm("Do you want to link to the sound file (145K)?"));
                location = "http://mydomain.com/somesound.au/";
}
```

The confirm box displays a question with Yes and No buttons. If the answer is yes, the sound is loaded. If the answer is no, the location instruction is skipped and the sound is not loaded.

Another method for "preprocessing" a link uses links that are defined with the same HREF and NAME. This allows the anchor to link to itself. The advantage of this method is that you can avoid displaying the JavaScript URL.

```
<A HREF="#1" NAME="1" onClick="processLink()">
```

Display a Link Only for JavaScript Users

By putting the text for a link in JavaScript code, you can display a link for only those with JavaScript. The technique works like this:

```
<SCRIPT>
<!-- hide from other browsers
document.write ('<A HREF="myurl.html">Click here, JavaScripters!</A>')
//-->
</SCRIPT>
```

Only those browsers with JavaScript render the hypertext link. In this way you can custom-design your pages so that those without JavaScript aren't even aware of the JavaScript-only features of your page.

Working with Window Histories

Get URLs from the User's History List

JavaScript's history object is supposed to provide a list of URLs the user has recently visited. The idea of this feature of the history object was to allow JavaScript to sort through the URLs and transport the user back to a specific page. But the original concept was flawed: it's not unusual for the user's history list to contain sensitive information, including passwords and search criteria. Someone with an evil mind could write a JavaScript program that reads the history list and sends it off in a form to a CGI program running on some server. Sooner or later that person would amass quite an inventory of sensitive information!

Before Netscape 2.0 was publicly released, the history list feature of the history object was removed, for security reasons. The history object still supports the go property, which lets you move forward or backward in a person's URL list, but there's no way to know what pages those are ahead of time.

At some future date, the history object should once again return the list of visited URLs, but this will be done only after JavaScript and Netscape provide a protection mechanism—called data tainting—that can check for and mask sensitive information.

Reload the Current Document

The basic syntax for reloading the current document in the browser has one of two forms:

```
history.go(0);
window.history.go(0);
```

You can extend the procedure to reload documents in other windows or frames. Suppose the document you want to reload is in a frame called "second_frame." The instruction would then be:

```
parent.second_frame.history.go(0);
```

If the document is in another window you've opened with the window.open method, you need to use the return object reference obtained when you opened the window as the first element in the instruction:

```
        win = window.open ("mydoc.html", "MyDoc");
 ...
win.history.go(0);
```

Reload the Previous Document in the History List

The basic syntax for reloading the previous document in the history list has one of two forms:

```
history.go(-1);
window.history.go(-1);
```

This is the same as clicking the back button in the browser. Note that this instruction has no effect if there is no previous document in the history list. You can extend the procedure to load documents in other windows or frames using the syntax in the previous section:

```
parent.second_frame.history.go(-1);
```

and

```
win = window.open ("mydoc.html", "MyDoc");
 ...
win.history.go(-1);
```

Use string Methods with the window.location Object

The window.location object returns the URL of the document in the current window. For example, if the window displays the document at http://mydomain.com/index.html, then that's what window.location returns. (Note: window.location is the same as just plain location, assuming you mean the current window; that's exactly what is assumed for the remainder of this section.) You can see this URL string with some simple code:

```
Ret = location;
alert (Ret);
```

There are times when you want to manipulate the string you get with the location object. But if you try something like this:

```
Ret = location;
LastFour = Ret.substring (Ret.length-4, Ret.length);
alert (LastFour);
```

you get an error ("length is not a member"). You get different errors depending on what string methods you try to use. The reason is that location is an object, even though it seems to return a string value—in fact, a value you can readily see using the alert box. You need to convert it to a real string before you can manipulate it with string methods.

One way is to append the toString function to the end of the location object. Then the above script will work.

```
Ret = location.toString();
LastFour = Ret.substring (Ret.length-4, Ret.length);
alert (LastFour);
```

Another method is to use the HREF property of the location object, as here:

```
Ret = location.href;
```

And still another method is to use the location property of the document object, which (depending on circumstances) returns the same URL. The syntax is:

```
Ret = document.location
```

Working with Dates

Display a Clock on a Page

A fairly common application for JavaScript is displaying a clock on the page. It's easy to do, and mildly useful. There are a number of different ways you can implement a clock. One method, using digital number GIF images, is described in Chapter 20, "Using JavaScript for Sound, Animation, and Graphics." Another method for creating a "digital" clock using XBM graphics is detailed in Chapter 17, "Using JavaScript with Advanced HTML."

But those approaches are fairly complex. There is a simpler way to display the current time, using a form text box to keep the time updated. The following script has been written so it would be fairly easy to modify. For example, you can readily alter it so it returns 24-hour time rather than 12-hour time, and you can change the period of updating from once every 30 seconds to a longer or shorter interval.

CD-ROM

basic_clock.html

```
<HTML>
<HEAD>
<TITLE>Clock Set</TITLE>
<SCRIPT LANGUAGE="JavaScript">
function setClock() {
        now = new Date();
        var CurHour = now.getHours();
        var CurMinute = now.getMinutes();
        now = null;
        if (CurHour >= 12) {
                CurHour = CurHour - 12;
                Ampm = "pm";
        } else
                Ampm = "am";
        if (CurHour == 0)
                CurHour = "12"
        CurHour = ""+CurHour;
        Time= CurHour + ":" + CurMinute + Ampm
        document.clocktext.clock.value = Time
        setTimeout ("setClock()", 1000 * 30)
}
</SCRIPT>
</HEAD>
<BODY onLoad = "setClock()">
<FORM NAME="clocktext">
<INPUT TYPE="text" NAME="clock" VALUE="" SIZE=8>
</FORM>
```

```
</BODY>
</HTML>
```

To change the period of updating, modify the last value in the setTimeout function. It's set now for 30 seconds. To change to 15-second intervals, have it read:

```
setTimeout ("setClock()", 1000 * 15)
```

The clock above displays only the hour and minutes. You can display seconds, too, using the sample script below. This script was originally authored by Brendan Eich (the developer of the JavaScript language) of Netscape. Because of its format and use of conditional expressions, it's a little harder to follow and change, but it's more compact than the ones above. You can chose which one you like better and implement it on your pages:

brendans_clock.html

CD-ROM

```
<HTML>
<HEAD>
<TITLE>Clock Set</TITLE>
<SCRIPT LANGUAGE="JavaScript">
function setClock() {
        var now = new Date();
        var Hours = now.getHours();
        var Minutes = now.getMinutes();
        var Seconds = now.getSeconds();
        var Value = "" + ((Hours >12) ? Hours - 12 : Hours)
        Value += ((Minutes < 10) ? ":0" : ":") + Minutes
        Value += ((Seconds < 10) ? ":0" : ":") + Seconds
        Value += (Hours >=12) ? " pm" : " am";
        document.clocktext.clock.value = Value;
        setTimeout ("setClock()", 1000);
}
</SCRIPT>
</HEAD>
<BODY onLoad = "setClock()">
<FORM NAME="clocktext">
<INPUT TYPE="text" NAME="clock" VALUE="" SIZE=11>
```

```
</FORM>
</BODY>
</HTML>
```

Display Elapsed Time

JavaScript's setTimeout function (described in the previous section) can be used to create clocks and timers. One application of the setTimeout function is to monitor how long something takes—akin to a stop watch. The script below displays the current time in hours, minutes, and seconds. Click the Start button and the timer starts—the clock begins ticking. Click the Stop button and the clock stops ticking. In addition, JavaScript calculates the time between the Start and Stop button clicks, and displays the result.

Note that this script uses clearTimeout, which is a companion function to setTimeout. The clearTimeout function erases the timer from the computer's memory. Because you can have more than one timer running at the same time, clearTimeout needs to be told which timer to erase. Therefore, when setTimeout is called, it's "ID" value is saved in a variable.

```
TimerId = setTimeout("showTime()",1000);
```

This variable—TimerId—is then used to extinguish the timer (using clearTimeout) when you click the Stop button.

CD-ROM

elapsed.html

```
<HTML>
<HEAD>
<TITLE>Elapsed Timer</TITLE>
<SCRIPT LANGUAGE="JavaScript">
var TimerId=null;
var TimerOk=false;
var StartTimeSeconds=0;
var EndTimeSeconds=0;
var ShowElapsed=false;

function buttonStart()  {
```

```
        ShowElapsed=true;

        startClock();

        getStartTime();

        return;

}


function buttonStop()  {

        stopClock();

        getEndTime();

        if (ShowElapsed) {

                alert (Math.round((EndTimeSeconds-StartTimeSeconds) / 1000)+
                                " seconds elapsed.")

                ShowElapsed=false;

        }

        else

                alert ("The clock is not running!")

        return;

}


function startClock(){

        stopClock();

        showTime();

        return;

}


function showTime() {

        now = new Date ();

        var now = new Date();

        var Hours = now.getHours();

        var Minutes = now.getMinutes();

        var Seconds = now.getSeconds();

        var Value = "" + ((Hours >12) ? Hours - 12 : Hours)

        Value += ((Minutes < 10) ? ":0" : ":") + Minutes

        Value += ((Seconds < 10) ? ":0" : ":") + Seconds

        document.clock.face.value = Value;
```

```
            TimerId = setTimeout("showTime()",1000);
            TimerOk = true;
            now = null;
            return;
    }

    function stopClock(){
            if(TimerOk) {
                    clearTimeout(TimerId);
                    TimerOk = false;
            }
            return;
    }

    function getStartTime()   {
            Now = new Date();
            StartTimeSeconds=(Now.getTime())
            return;
    }

    function getEndTime ()   {
            Now = new Date();
            EndTimeSeconds=(Now.getTime())
            return;
    }

    function resetClock()   {
            startClock();
            stopClock();
    }

</SCRIPT>
</HEAD>
<BODY>
```

```
<FORM NAME="clock">
<INPUT TYPE="text" name="face" size=8 value=""><P>
<INPUT TYPE="button" name="start" VALUE="Start" onClick="buttonStart()">
<INPUT TYPE="button" name="stop" VALUE="Stop" onClick="buttonStop()">
</FORM>
</BODY>
</HTML>
```

Calculate the Number of Days Until a Given Date

Suppose your Web site is the electronic lobby for a department store. And you're planning a "blowout sale" starting today, and going until next Friday. Each day you want your page to read "Only xxx days left on our HUGE summer blowout sale!," or words to that effect. But you don't want to update the page every day.

One method is to use the daysTil function shown below. It returns the number of days between today and some day in the future. You specify that date by indicating the year, month, and day. You can then use the resulting value any way you like. Here's the basic script, which returns the number of days from "today" until June 15, 1997. Note that the month is 0 based: January is 0, February is 1, and so forth.

```
Ret = daysTil (97, 5, 15)
alert (Ret)


function daysTil(Year, Month, Day)  {
        now = new Date();
        Hour = now.getHours();
        Minute = now.getMinutes();
        Second = now.getSeconds();
        elapse = Date.parse(new Date (Year, Month, Day, Hour, Minute, Second))
              - Date.parse (new Date());
        elapse = Math.round (elapse / (24 * 60 * 60 * 1000));
        return (elapse);
}
```

To use this function in a working page, you might do the following:

CD-ROM

days_til.html

```
<SCRIPT>
function daysTil(Year, Month, Day)  {
        now = new Date();
        Hour = now.getHours();
        Minute = now.getMinutes();
        Second = now.getSeconds();
        elapse = Date.parse(new Date (Year, Month, Day, Hour, Minute, Second))
                - Date.parse (new Date());
        elapse = Math.round (elapse / (24 * 60 * 60 * 1000));
        return (elapse);
}


Ret = daysTil (97, 5, 15);
if (Ret > 1)
        document.write ("Only " + Ret + " days left of our sale!");
else if (Ret == 1)
        document.write ("Hurry, just one day left of our sale!");
else if (Ret -- 0)
        document.write ("Today is the last day of our sale");
else
        document.write ("Sorry! Our sale is over!");
</SCRIPT>
```

Working with Netscape (Or Another Browser)

Display a Local Directory of Files

When working with HTML files in a local directory, you will want to review all the available files in the browser window, rather than search for the one you want in the File Open dialog box. The browser displays an entire directory if you enter a path-only URL—that is, a URL that lacks a filename.

The following JavaScript program gives you a choice of viewing several regularly used local directories (Two are hard-coded; change these directories to suit your needs). You can easily access this program if you add it to your bookmark list.

CD-ROM

directory.html

```
<HTML>
<HEAD>
<TITLE>View local directory</TITLE>
<SCRIPT LANGUAGE="JavaScript">
function openDir (form) {
        if (form.directory.selectedIndex == 0) path = "file://
/c|/javascript/"
        if (form.directory.selectedIndex == 1) path = "file:///
c|/nav20/"
location = path;
}
</SCRIPT>
<BODY>
<FORM NAME="myform">
<SELECT NAME="directory">
<OPTION SELECTED>JavaScript
<OPTION>Navigator 2.0
</SELECT>
<INPUT TYPE="button" NAME="button" VALUE="Open Directory"onClick
="openDir(this.form)">
</FORM>
</BODY>
</HTML>
```

▬▬▬▬ **NOTE**

This JavaScript program can also be used to display a directory of files on a Web server, as long as the following conditions are met:

- The directory does not have an "index" document assigned to it. The index document is the document that is automatically shown when you provide

> just the path for the URL, as in http://mysite.com/. Common names for index documents are index.html and homepage.html.
>
> • The server does not have directory access set as "forbidden."
>
> If you do not want users to view the directory, be sure to either mark directory access as "forbidden" or create an index document for the directory.

■■■■■■

Display the Document Source and Document Info Windows

The View, Document Source and View, Document Info commands are handy features of Netscape.

- • View, Document Source displays the source of the current document in a new window. Close the window when you're done viewing the source (see Figure 12.2).

- • View, Document Info displays a window with two frames; on the top frame is a listing of all file components of the document. These include the frameset document and subframes if you're using frames, as well as

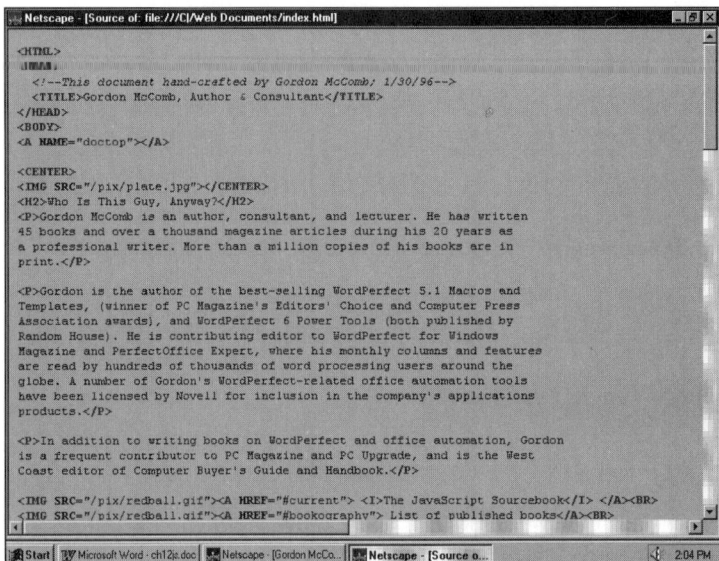

■■■■■■ **Figure 12.2** The Document Source window displays the contents of the current document.

all images. The bottom frame displays information about each file as you click on one in the top frame.

> You can directly save any file with the View, Document Info window by right-clicking on it in the top window—remember, right-click! If you're using a Macintosh, press and hold the mouse button. Choose Save File As to save the file to your hard drive.

You can use a mixture of standard HTML and JavaScript to duplicate these View commands as links in your document. Following is a basic script that performs this task. Load the script and click the "document info" link. You'll see the same window that View, Document Info displays. Close that window and click the "document source" link. Up comes the same window that View, Document Source displays.

```
<HTML>
<HEAD>
<SCRIPT>
function openWin() {
        location = "view-source:" + window.location
}
</SCRIPT>
</HEAD>
<BODY>
<A HREF="about:document">Click me to see document info</A><P>
<A HREF="#" onClick="openWin()">Click me to see document source</A><P>
</BODY>
</HTML>
```

Notice the openWin() function. This function opens the view-source: location of the current document (the current document HREF is returned with window.location). There's no reason to display the current document if that's not your aim. You can provide any fully qualified URL (including protocol and host), and Netscape will open the source for that document.

■■■■■ **NOTE**

> As a security measure, Netscape 2.0 prevents you from using any "about:" protocol in JavaScript code. Therefore you must access about: URLs directly using the HREF= attribute of a link.

■■■■

Determine the Netscape Platform

Netscape is currently available for the Windows 3.1, Windows 95/NT, Macintosh, and Unix X-Windows platforms. There are some differences in the implementation of JavaScript (and Java, for that matter) between these platforms in certain versions. For example, the eval function is badly broken in the initial release of Netscape 2.0 for the Macintosh. Most scripts that use the eval function will crash when run on the Macintosh version of Netscape.

Because of these cross-platform incompatibilities, it is often helpful to determine which version a user has before processing the rest of the script. If your script contains code that is known to be disruptive on one version, you can warn the user about it ahead of time, stop the remainder of the script, or change to a completely different script that doesn't exhibit the problem.

Use the appVersion property of the navigator object to determine the Netscape platform. This property actually contains a number of useful pieces of information, including the version number of Netscape, and whether it is the international or domestic version (this domestic version offers better encryption security; however, as the X-Windows platform does not currently return a value specifying international or domestic, you should not use this information for any mission-critical work).

The string contained in the appVersion property looks like this:

```
2.0 (Win95; I)
```

2.0 is the version, *Win95* is the platform, and *I* denotes International. Here are some variations:

- 2.01 indicates a maintenance release.
- 2.0NOV indicates an OEM (Original Equipment Manufacturer) version of Netscape (in this case, to Novell).
- Win3.1 indicates Windows 3.1 platform.

- Macintosh indicates Mac platform.
- X-* indicates an X-Windows platform

Because the length of the string and its contents can change, depending on versions and platforms, you should use the indexOf string method to look for the unique text of the platform in which you are interested. To test for the Win95 version, for example, write the if test as follows:

```
TempString = navigator.appVersion;
if (TempString.indexOf ("Win95") >= 0)
        alert ("Win95 version");
else
        alert ("Some other version version");
```

If you want to test for any of the four possible platforms, you can use the series of if tests, as shown in this complete, working example:

version.html

CD-ROM

```
<HTML>
<HEAD>
<TITLE>What Version Am I?</TITLE>
<SCRIPT LANGUAGE="JavaScript">
function viewAppVersion (form) {
        TempString = navigator.appVersion;
        if (TempString.indexOf ("Win95") >= 0) {
                alert ("Windows 95/NT version")
        } else if (TempString.indexOf ("Win16") >= 0) {
                alert ("Windows 3.1 version")
        } else if (TempString.indexOf ("Macintosh") >= 0) {
                alert ("Macintosh version")
        } else if (TempString.indexOf ("(X") >= 0) {
                alert ("X-Windows version")
        } else
                alert ("Some other version")
}
```

```
</SCRIPT>
<BODY>
<FORM NAME="myform">
<INPUT TYPE="button" NAME="button" VALUE="Check Version"
       onClick="viewAppVersion(this.form)">
</FORM>
</BODY>
</HTML>
```

■■■■■■■ **NOTE**

Microsoft may continue to number versions of Windows by year (Windows 96, Windows 97, and so forth). If you are merely interested in whether the version of Netscape is for the Windows 32-bit platform NT, Windows 95, or whatever, construct the if test as:

```
if (TempString.indexOf ("Win9") >= 0)
```

This should work until the year 2000, or whenever Microsoft changes their naming scheme for updates to Windows 95. So far there isn't an NT-specific version of Netscape.

■■■■■

Link to a Different Page for non-JavaScript Browsers

Not all browsers support JavaScript. Until and if they do, requiring JavaScript conformance for your home page is probably not a good idea. If possible, design your home page so that its most important features will run on any modern browser. From your home page, you can link to specific JavaScript-enabled pages.

You may ask, how do I prevent users of non-JavaScript-enabled browsers from using those links? The answer is simple: dynamically change the HREF of the link, as described in "Dynamically set the HREF of an hypertext link," elsewhere in this chapter. Here's the basic approach: for those links that require a JavaScript browser, provide an HREF in the HTML markup that links to a standard "sorry" page. The wording of this page might be similar to "Sorry, but you need JavaScript to use this page."

Name this page sorry.html, or something similar. Provide this name as a HREF standard for links to JavaScript pages. Here's an example:

```
<A HREF="sorry.html">Click here</A>
```

To dynamically change the HREF of the links, add the following code in a short function that is called when the document is loaded:

```
function loadFunction () {
        document.links[0].href = "another.html"
        //... and so forth
}
```

When the page is loaded by a non-JavaScript-enabled browser, the JavaScript code is of course ignored, and the sorry.html links remain in place. If the browser does support JavaScript, then the links are changed. Here's a short example using three links, two of which are dynamically changed—the third links to a nojava.html document, which does not need to be re-linked because it does not contain any JavaScript code. The links are identified by index value and correspond to the links in the order they appear in the HTML source.

```
<HTML>
<HEAD>
<TITLE>Re-link if no JavaScript</TITLE>
<SCRIPT LANGUAGE="JavaScript">
<!--
function loadFunction () {
        document.links[0].href = "another1.html"
        document.links[2].href = "another2.html"
}
//-->
</SCRIPT>
<BODY onLoad = "loadFunction()">
<A HREF="sorry.html">Click here 1</A><BR>
<A HREF="nojava.html">Click here 2</A><BR>
<A HREF="sorry.html">Click here 3</A><BR>
</BODY>
```

```
<SCRIPT></SCRIPT>
</HTML>
```

■■■■■■ **NOTE**

> As much as possible, try to limit the amount of JavaScript code in your home page. Some browsers, particular older ones, will not completely hide all the JavaScript code contained in a comment, as they have a limit on the size of commented text.

■■■■■■

Play a Sound with JavaScript

Netscape 2.0 comes with a sound-playing "helper" program called NPLAYER that plays sounds in several sound formats. These are au, snd, aif, aiff, and aifc. Sound files in these formats automatically play when Netscape encounters them. JavaScript makes it very easy to play these sounds through the NPLAYER helper. All it takes is the location method, which is a method of the object property (and is not the same thing as the location object).

■■■■■■ **NOTE**

> You may also use sounds in other formats, such as Windows WAV files, but helpers for these file types may not be available on all Netscape platforms. Whenever possible, use one of the above file types, which are directly supported by the NPLAYER application.

■■■■■■

The basic syntax for playing a sound file in Netscape 2.0 is:

```
location = soundfile;
```

where *soundfile* is the relative or absolute URL of the sound file. For example, the following line plays a sound file named train.au, located in the current path:

```
location = "train.au";
```

How you call this command line is up to you. The following short example shows how to play a sound both when loading a document (with the onLoad event handler in the <BODY> tag), and how to play a sound in response to a button click event (the onClick event handler in the form, <INPUT> tag). In both cases, the name of the sound file to play is passed as a parameter to the playSound function.

CD-ROM

play_sound.html

```
<HTML>
<HEAD>
<TITLE>Play a Sound</TITLE>
<SCRIPT LANGUAGE="JavaScript">
function playSound (soundfile) {
        location = soundfile;
}
</SCRIPT>
<BODY onLoad = "playSound('train.au')">
<FORM>
<INPUT TYPE="button" NAME="button1" VALUE="Click"
onClick="playSound('train.au')">
</FORM>
</BODY>
</HTML>
```

Netscape 3.0 uses a different method to play sounds; see Chapter 22 for more details.

Generate a Random Number

The Math.random method is inactive in all but the X-Windows platform of Netscape 2.0. As a surrogate you can use the following random number generating code, which is adapted from Park-Miller random number generator algorithm (credit for the code goes to David Smith; thanks, David!). Though the code takes up two functions, it is one of the better implementations of random number generator (RNG) and seldom gives two numbers even close to one another. The random number generator code is provided in the *lib.htm* file, included on the CD-ROM with this book, and it is shown in full in the example below.

To use the random number generator, you first create a new randomNumberGenerator object. You then fetch a random number from the object you created using the next property. You can continue fetching more random numbers using the next property two or more times. Here's a basic example of fetching and displaying just one number. In the example the new randomNumberGenerator object is RandNum.

```
RandNum = new randomNumberGenerator();
alert (RandNum.next());
```

Subsequent calls to RandNum.num produce different random numbers each time.

```
RandNum = new randomNumberGenerator();
document.open();
for (Count = 1; Count <=20; Count++) {
        document.write (RandNum.next() + "<BR>")
}
document.close();
```

Note that you get a number in the format of 0.xxxxxxxxxxxxxx (with 16-18 random digits to the right of the decimal point). Only the first 15 to the right of the decimal point are considered significant. You can lop off as many digits as you want by first converting the number to a string, and then using the substring method to return *x* number of digits. The following script picks up the first five characters to the right of the decimal point:

```
RandNum = new randomNumberGenerator();
Num = RandNum.next();
Num = "" + Num; // now a string
Num = Num.substring (2, 7) // returns five characters
alert (Num);
```

Here's a complete random number generator script you can try:

random.html

CD-ROM

```
<HTML>
<HEAD>
<TITLE>Random Number Generator</TITLE>
<SCRIPT LANGUAGE="JavaScript">
function set () {
```

```
RandNum = new randomNumberGenerator();
Num = RandNum.next();
Num = "" + Num; // now a string
Num = Num.substring (2, 7) // returns five characters
alert (Num);
}

function nextRandomNumber ()  {
        var Hi = this.seed / this.Q;
        var Lo = this.seed % this.Q;
        var Test = this.A * Lo - this.R * Hi;
        if (Test > 0)
                this.seed = Test
        else
                this.seed = Test + this.M;
        return (this.seed * this.oneOverM);
}

function randomNumberGenerator() {
        var D = new Date();
        this.seed = 2345678901 +
                (D.getSeconds() * 0xFFFFFF) +
                (D.getMinutes() * 0xFFFF);
        this.A = 48271;
        this.M = 2147483647;
        this.Q = this.M / this.A;
        this.R = this.M % this.A;
        this.oneOverM = 1.0 / this.M;
        this.next = nextRandomNumber;
}
</SCRIPT>
</HEAD>
<BODY>
<FORM>
```

```
<INPUT TYPE="button" NAME="button1" VALUE="Click Me!" onClick="set ()">
</FORM>
</BODY>
</HTML>
```

If you are using Netscape 3.0 or Netscape 2.0 running under X-Windows, you can use Math.random to create a random number. Using it is simple:

```
Num = Math.random();
```

The Num variable contains a random number from 0 to 1, in the form of 0.xxxxxxxxxxxxxx. You can lop off as many digits as you want from the return number using the substring technique shown above.

Round Off Those Incredibly Long Numbers

On some platforms, JavaScript loses accuracy in its calculation of so-called floating-point values—values that have numbers to the right of the decimal point. This is because of the different approaches to floating-point arithmetic on different kinds of computers. So, you often get a number like 17.5399999999999999 for a formula such as

18.73 – 1.19.

Almost any $3.98 calculator will tell you that the answer is 17.54! You can fix the number so that it is accurate on any Netscape platform with this short routine. Pass the floating-point value, as well as the number of digits you want to the right of the decimal point (0 to 15 yields valid results). The number is rounded off to the nearest decimal value. For example, the call:

```
Formula = 18.73 - 1.19;
Ret = floatFix (Formula, 2);
```

results in 17.54, as it should.

float_fix.html

CD-ROM

```
function floatFix (Val, Places) {
        var Res = "" + Math.round(Val * Math.pow(10, Places));
        var Dec = Res.length - Places;
        if (Places != 0)
```

```
      OutString = Res.substring(0, Dec) + "." + Res.substring(Dec, Res.length);
  else
  OutString = Res;
      return (OutString);
  }
```

Write Multiline JavaScript Test Code

You can test JavaScript code line-by-line by typing JavaScript: (don't forget the colon) in the Location box. Follow JavaScript: with the code you want to test. For example, to test an alert box message, type:

```
JavaScript:alert ("Hello!")
```

and press Enter.

The code below is a derivation of this technique, through which you can write multiple lines of test code (see Figure 12.3), and then "submit" it to JavaScript to see what kind of results you get.

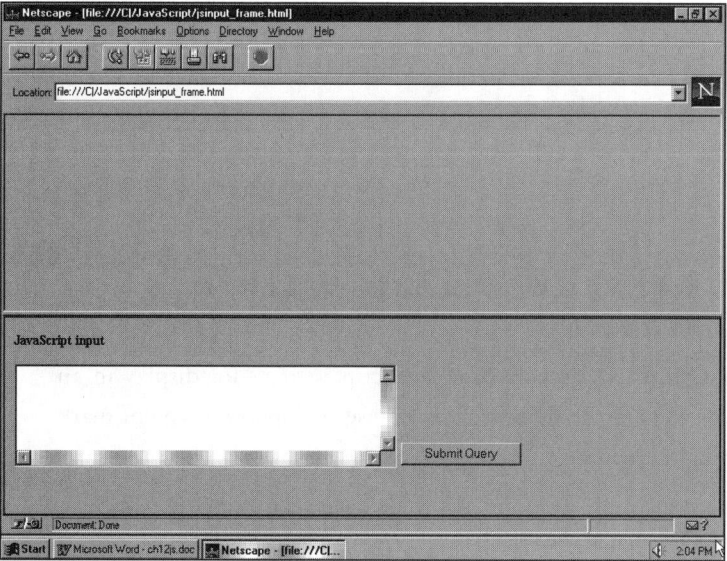

Figure 12.3 The *jsinput_frame.html* and *jsinput.html* documents are used to create a multiline JavaScript tester.

Create the frameset document as follows:

CD-ROM

```
jsinput_frame.html


<frameset rows="50%%,50%%">
<frame name=MochaOutput src=about:blank>
<frame name=MochaInput src="jsinput.html">
</frameset>
```

Create the jsinput.html document as follows:

CD-ROM

```
jsinput.html


<b>JavaScript input</b>
<form action=JavaScript: target=MochaOutput>
<textarea name="isindex" rows=5 cols=50>
</textarea>
<input type="submit">
</form>
```

Here's some sample test code you can try. Enter this in the text area, and then click the Submit button to see the result.

```
temp=""
for (i in document)
temp += i + ": " + document[i] + "\n"
alert (temp)
```

Include Quotation Marks Within Quotation Marks

You can include quotation marks as part of a JavaScript string—for display in an alert box, for example—as long as you remember to use the opposite type of mark that you have delineating the string.

- If you are using double quotation marks to delineate the string, use single quotation marks for inside the string.
- If you are using single quotation marks to delineate the string, use double quotation marks for inside the string.

Here are some examples:

```
Ret = "Hello, my name is 'Mudd'";
Ret = "Come here,' she said."

Ret = 'Hello, my name is "Mudd"';
Ret = '"Come here," she said.';
```

You can also use the \ "escape" character to insert quotation marks. The \ character is especially handy if you just want to include one mark or an apostrophe, as here:

```
Ret = 'Don\'t you think this is nice?';
```

Wait for a Period of Time Before Executing JavaScript Code

JavaScript's setTimer function lets you create a delay of almost any imaginable time period. As long as your page is still loaded, when the delay is up, the action you specify with the setTimer function bounces into action. You can even set up multiple setTimer functions so they all fire at different times. One might trigger a second later, another 10 seconds later, and a third a full minute later.

The time resolution for the setTimeout delay is a minimum of one millisecond (one thousandths of a second), though in actual practice JavaScript is accurate to only about a third of a second.

Here's the basic syntax of the setTimeout function:

```
setTimeout (action, delay);
```

where *action* is a user-defined function or a JavaScript function or method, and *delay* is the time delay, in milliseconds. For example, if you want an alert to appear three and a half seconds after JavaScript processes the setTimeout function, you'd write it this way:

```
setTimeout ("alert('hello')", 3500);
```

You're not limited to using just JavaScript functions and methods for the setTimeout action. Feel free to use your own user-defined functions. Here's a script that displays a message and replaces the current document with another one after waiting 10 seconds.

CD-ROM

time_limit.html

```
<HTML>
<HEAD>
<TITLE>setTimeout Example</TITLE>
<SCRIPT LANGUAGE="JavaScript">
var win;
function setTimer() {
        setTimeout ("killDoc()", 10000);
}


function killDoc() {
        alert ("Sorry, time is up!");
        location = "index.html";
}


</SCRIPT>
</HEAD>
<BODY onLoad = "setTimer()">
Read this document. You have ten seconds.
</BODY>
</HTML>
```

Store Persistent Data with "Cookies"

Netscape supports something called "cookies" for storing semi-permanent data (no, the word "cookies" doesn't mean anything special). The cookies feature can store data in any of two ways:

- The data in a *session-only* cookie lasts only until you quit Netscape. Session-only cookies are retained in Netscape's memory.

- The data in a *dated* cookie lasts until the expiration date of the cookie. Dated cookies are stored in a cookies file, normally named *cookies.txt*.

You might use cookies to store data about your page, such as the current user settings, or a score. Or, you might use cookies to record the date the user last visited your site. You can use that date to tell the user of new additions to your page.

Understanding Cookies

You use the document.cookie property to set and read cookies. In Netscape 2.0, the document.cookie property stores a single string, and it's up to you to manage the string and store and extract values you want. To make matters a little worse, the value portion of the cookie must be in URL-encoded form—characters such as a space must be converted to their encoded counterparts, such as %20 for a space. Fortunately, this can be easily done using the JavaScript escape function (the JavaScript unescape function converts encoded strings back to normal).

The basic method of storing a session-only cookie is:

```
document.cookie = "value";
```

where *value* is a string. Session-only cookies need not be URL-encoded, so plain text is fine. Here's an example:

```
document.cookie = "this text is saved for this page until you exit Netscape"
```

If you want to store a dated cookie, you must provide the expiration date in accepted GMT time format. You can use the Date object for this, and specify the date you want the cookie to expire. For example:

```
Expire = new Date(97, 0, 1); //expire January 1, 1997
CookieName = "mycookie";
ValueString = escape("This is a test");
document.cookie = CookieName + "=" + ValueString + "; expires=" +
        Expire.toGMTString();
```

To read the cookie, you use

```
Ret = document.cookie;
```

The Ret variable contains the cookie, in the form cookiename=value. The example above returns:

```
mycookie=This%20is%20a%20test
```

Using the unescape function, you can make the cookie value easier to read:

```
Ret = unescape(document.cookie);
alert (Ret);
```

Cookie Options

You can set a number of options for cookies by providing the appropriate "switches" after the cookie name. In addition to the expires switch, which you've seen, there are:

- path=—Indicates the path for which the cookie is valid. If omitted, Netscape uses the path of the calling document. The value is a string.
- domain=—Indicates the domain for which the cookie is valid. If omitted, Netscape uses the domain of the calling document. The value is a string.
- secure=—Indicates whether cookie transmission requires a secure channel (a password or credit card number, for example). The value is a Boolean *true* or *false*.

Reading Cookie Values

There can be more than one cookie in the cookie string. This is particularly true if you have not set the path and/or domain. To read back a given cookie, you must find it in the entire returned string, and then grab just the section that you want. All this mess cries out for a set of handy functions to work with cookies; fortunately, someone has already done the grunt work for you. The *cookie functions*, written by Bill Dortch of hIdaho Design, can be freely implemented in any JavaScript program. You can set cookies, get cookies, and delete cookies, all using easy-to-call functions.

The cookie functions are included on the CD-ROM as *cookies.txt*. A working trial version is stored as *cookies.html*. The functions in the files are self-documented.

Cookie Limits

Netscape imposes the following limitations on cookies:

- The *cookies.txt* file can contain more than 300 cookies.
- Each cookie must be 4K or less in size.
- There can be no more than 20 cookies per domain.

See the document http://home.netscape.com/newsref/std/cookies_spec.html for a technical discussion of the implementation of cookies.

Another Way to Store Temporary Data

JavaScript has a tendency to be forgetful. Variables are lost when a page is reloaded or the window is resized. Some pages require setting variables that are used throughout the course of the script. Should the document be reloaded or resized, those variables are lost.

Cookies are an ideal way to store data that is retained through a resizing or reloading. But in Netscape 2.0, using the document.cookie property leaves something to be desired. Another, undocumented approach is to assign unique cookie names to the document.cookie property. These cookies are session-only, but they are retained even during a page reload or resizing.

The basic syntax is:

```
document.cookie.name = "value"
```

where *name* is the unique name you want to give this cookie, and *value* is the value you wish to store. For example, you might want to store the time the user first came to your page as document.cookie.time, as follows:

```
now = new Date();
document.cookie.time = now.toLocaleString();
```

To read back the value stored, use:

```
Ret = document.cookie.time;
```

You can store as many cookies as you wish this way. But remember, the cookies are lost when you exit Netscape. Furthermore, all cookies assigned in this manner are local to the document that created them. This approach does not create "global" cookies.

"PLUG-AND-PLAY"

ROUTINES

Most JavaScript programs are constructed using common building blocks called *routines*. This chapter presents dozens of routines you can use in your scripts. The routines are "encapsulated" into user-defined functions so you can easily incorporate them into your JavaScript programs. Because the routines are user-defined functions, they can be used much like JavaScript functions. Each plug-and-play routine is described, complete with a working example.

Using the Routines

To use any plug-and-play routine described in the chapter, copy the routine from the *library.txt* source file and paste it inside a <SCRIPT> tag in your document. You can then use the routine in your script by typing its name, along with any required parameters.

How Plug-and-Play Routines Are Like JavaScript Functions

The plug-and-play routines are user-defined functions, and most of them return a value of some type. As such, they behave very much like JavaScript functions, such as eval, parseInt, or escape. Take the JavaScript parseInt function as an example. It takes a string and "parses" it to a numeric value. The parseInt function has many uses and syntaxes, but the most common is as follows:

```
var Ret = parseInt ("12345");
```

As shown here the parseInt function takes one parameter, which is a number string value. When JavaScript executes this function it converts the string value to a number—"12345" becomes 12345. In this way the value can be used in mathematical expressions. The returned value is stored in a variable named Ret.

■■■■■■ NOTE

As with built-in JavaScript functions that return a variable, you can often use user-defined functions in complex expressions. For example, JavaScript allows you to use the parseInt function in the following manner because it forms a complex expression using an if statement:

```
StringValue = "12";
if (parseInt(StringValue) < 10)
```

The parseInt function returns the numeric value of the StringValue variable ("12"), and this is used in an if expression. The expression tests if the numeric value 12 is less than the number 10. (In this case, the test proves false).

Now consider a user-defined function, say one that returns the length of a string (this is a good example because it's quick and easy to demonstrate, not because it's particularly useful). The function is defined as:

```
function stringLength(InString) {
        var Temp = InString.length;
        return (Temp);
}
```

To use this function, you provide an instruction elsewhere in your JavaScript program that refers to the function by name and provides the required parameter. For example, this script displays "14" in an alert box. This number is the length, in characters, of the string "This is a test".

```
var Ret;
var MyString = "This is a test";
Ret = stringLength(MyString);
alert(Ret);
```

Copying and Pasting Routines to Your Program

Most of the plug-and-play routines, especially those in the *library.txt* file, are fairly small, so you can readily copy them to your own scripts. To copy a routine, open the plug-and-play routine file, copy the routine you want, and paste it between any <SCRIPT> tags in your document.

Let's take as an example the leftTrim plug-and-play routine, which is located in the *library.txt* file. The leftTrim routine trims any extra spaces that might be on the left side of a string. You give the leftTrim routine the string you want to process, and it gives you back a trimmed version, as shown here:

String going in: " this is a test"

String coming out: "this is a test"

To use the leftTrim routine in your script, open the *library.txt* file, which is included on the CD-ROM that accompanies this book. Use the search feature of your word processor or text editor to locate the text "function leftTrim." Your program will locate the leftTrim routine within the file. Copy to the clipboard all the text between the opening and closing braces of the function.

Close the *library.txt* file (or you can leave it open if you are copying many routines at once). Finally, paste the previously copied text in your JavaScript program. You must place all of your user-defined functions between <SCRIPT> tags, or they will not be recognized by JavaScript as program code (and even worse, the code will appear in your document when it is viewed in Netscape!).

After copying the routine, you use it by "calling" it from anywhere else in your script. As detailed later in this chapter, the leftTrim routine uses one parameter (the string going in) and returns a value—the compressed ("trimmed") string going out. Here's an example of the script line:

```
var Ret = leftTrim("this is a test");
```

As the program is running, JavaScript passes the " this is a test" string through the leftTrim routine. The result that comes back, and is stored in the Ret variable, is the processed string "this is a test" (with the extra spaces removed from the left of the string).

Following is a complete, working script using the leftTrim routine. Though the routine itself may look like a lot of gibberish, remember that you don't have to know how it works to use it. Load this page and type some text into the input box, adding a number of spaces to the beginning. Click the Click button. You'll find that no matter how many spaces you add, they are stripped off and displayed in the alert box (the : colon character is used at the beginning and end of the string, so that you can more easily see the effect of the trimming).

CD-ROM

ltrim_test.html

```
<HTML>
<HEAD>
<TITLE>leftTrim Function Test</TITLE>
<SCRIPT LANGUAGE="JavaScript">
function test (form){
        var Ret = leftTrim(form.inputbox.value);
        alert (":" + Ret + ":");
}

function leftTrim (InString)  {
        var OutString=InString;
        for (Count=0; Count < InString.length; Count++)  {
                var TempChar = InString.substring (Count, Count+1);
                if (TempChar != " ") {
                        OutString=InString.substring (Count, InString.length)
                        break;
                }
```

```
        }
        return (OutString);
}
</SCRIPT>
</HEAD>
<BODY>
<FORM NAME="testform">
Type something with extra spaces at the beginning:
<INPUT TYPE="text" NAME="inputbox" VALUE="">
<INPUT TYPE="button" NAME="button" Value="Click" onClick="test(this.form)"><BR>
</FORM>
</BODY>
</HTML>
```

Passing Parameters

Almost all of the routines described in this chapter use parameters. Parameters work the same way with the plug-and-play routines as they do with JavaScript functions and object methods. In most cases all the specified parameters are required. Be sure to provide all the parameters specified, and in the appropriate order, or an error will result. Providing the parameters for the routine to use is called *passing parameters*. The parameters are contained within parentheses and follow the name of the routine. If more than one parameter is used with a routine, the parameters are separated by a comma, which is JavaScript's syntactical standard.

In almost all cases, you can include the value of the parameter you want the routine to use, as in:

```
var Ret = leftTrim("   This is a test");
```

Alternatively, you can assign the value you want to use for the parameter to a variable, and stick the variable name inside the parentheses, as shown here:

```
var StrVar = "   This is a test";
var Ret = leftTrim(StrVar);
```

As with JavaScript functions and object methods, the user-defined functions in this chapter expect certain kinds of values at each parameter. One parameter may be a string value, another a number, a third an array, and a fourth an object. Be sure to always use the right kind of data or an error is likely to result.

The Plug-and-Play Library Files

This book comes with several plug-and-play routine files. One of the files contains general-purpose routines; the others contain routines for special applications. All of the files are documented here.

File	Contents
library.txt	General-purpose routines
datefunc.txt	Routines for date and calendar functions
n2func.txt	Routines for converting numbers to spelled out word amounts (e.g., "one hundred one" for 101)

The *library.txt* Functions

CD-ROM

The following functions are included in the *library.txt* plug-and-play file. They are listed here in alphabetical order.

Function/Procedure	What It Does
allowBrowser	Check for allowed browsers
allowInString	Check for characters allowed in string
allowNotInString	Check for characters not allowed in string
daysTil	Days until a certain date
filenameOnly	Return filename from URL
formatCommas	Format number with commas
formatDollar	Format number as dollar amount
getMaxList	Return largest value in list
getMinList	Return smallest value in list
ifExists	Check if variable exists
ifExistsString	Check if string variable exists
initUpper	Format string with initial uppercase

Function/Procedure	What It Does
initUpperQualify	Format string with uppercase, qualify words to capitalize
initUpperQualifyWords	List of qualified words for initUpperQualify
isAlphabeticChar	Check if character is alphabetic
isAlphabeticString	Check if string is only alphabetic
isBlank	Check if string is blank
isNotBlank	Check if string is not blank
isNumberChar	Check if character is numeric
isNumberString	Check if string is only numeric
isPunc	Check if character is punctuation
isStringLower	Check if string is lowercase only
isStringUpper	Check if string is uppercase only
isUSZip	Check for valid U.S. Zip code
isWithinRange	Check if number is within a range
leftString	Return left characters from string
leftTrim	Remove spaces from start of string
makeArray	Create array
makeArray2	Create two-dimensional array
makeArrayImplicit	Create array implicitly
makeArraySimple	Create simple array
mask	Verify string matches mask pattern
padTextPrefix	Pad prefix of string to length
padTextSuffix	Pad suffix of string to length
parser	Parse string
pathOnly	Return path only from URL
rightString	Return right characters from string
rightTrim	Remove spaces from end of string
roundDollar	Round number with two digits to the right of the decimal
sortArray	Sort array
spaceTrim	Trim extra spaces from string

Function/Procedure	What It Does
stripChar	Remove character from string
stripCharString	Remove any of *x* characters from string
stripSpaces	Remove all spaces from string
testForLength	Test for string length

allowBrowser Function

The allowBrowser function lets you quickly and easily determine if the user's version of Netscape is allowed for your application. This is handy if you need to prevent a user from accessing parts of your page that may cause problems with a particular Netscape platform. You identify which browsers you want to "allow" by using a letter. You can use the letters singly or in combination, if you wish to allow multiple browsers.

Letter Symbol	Netscape Platform
W	Windows 9*x* (such as Windows 95)
w	Windows 3.1
N	Windows NT
M	Mac PPC
m	Mac 68K
X	X-Windows

Syntax

```
var Ret = allowBrowser (AllowString);
```

AllowString is one or more characters representing the browsers you want to allow.

Return Value

The function returns Boolean *true* if the user's browser is among those listed in *AllowString*, and *false* if not.

Notes and Example

The following example displays *true* if you are using the Windows 9x version of Netscape 2.0, and *false* for any other string.

```
var Ret = allowBrowser("W");
alert (Ret);
```

Feel free to mix-and-match browsers if you want to allow a variety of them. Here are some examples:

Sample function call	Allows
allowBrowser("WwMm")	Windows 3.1, Windows 9x, Mac PPC, Mac 68K
allowBrowser("XWN")	X-Windows, Windows 9x, Windows NT
allowBrowser("wX")	Windows 3.1, X-Windows

A primary purpose of the allowBrowser function is to check the user's browser so that you can avoid any platform-specific bugs. But you can use it for other applications, too. For example, you can check for the Windows versions ("WwN") and display a "Welcome Windows Users" message at the top of your page.

allowInString Function

The allowInString function tests every character in a string against a set of "allowed" characters. If the function finds a character that is not allowed, it returns *false*; otherwise, it returns *true*. A primary use of the allowInString function is with form or input validation.

Syntax

```
var ret = allowInString (InString, RefString);
```

InString is the string you want to test. *RefString* is the list of acceptable characters.

Return Value

The routine returns *true* if InString does not contain any invalid characters, and *false* otherwise.

Notes and Example

The following example displays *false* because the input string contains invalid characters (the dollar sign is not allowed):

```
var TestThisString = "$1,987,239.28";
var ValidString = "01234567890.,";
var Ret = allowInString (TestThisString, ValidString);
alert (Ret);
```

See also allowNotInString.

allowNotInString Function

The allowNotInString function is the logical inverse of the allowInString function. It tests every character in a string against a set of "disallowed" characters. If the function finds any character contained in the disallowed list, it returns *false*. A primary use of the allowNotInString function is with form or input validation.

Syntax

```
var ret = allowNotInString (InString, RefString);
```

InString is the string you want to test. *RefString* is the list of *un*acceptable characters.

Return Value

The function returns *true* if *InString* does not contain any invalid characters, and *false* otherwise.

Notes and Example

The following example displays *true* because the input string does not contain any invalid characters. It tests whether a CompuServe ID number contains 8, 9, or a comma, which is not allowed (the comma is allowed in a CompuServe address, but not when specifying that address through the Internet).

```
var TestThisString = "81333,1776";      // Bad input
var ValidString = "89,";
var Ret = allowNotInString (TestThisString, ValidString);
alert (Ret);
```

See also allowInString.

DaysTill Function

<do>

filenameOnly Function

The filenameOnly function returns just the filename (minus the path) of a fully qualified URL.

Syntax

```
var Ret = filenameOnly(InString);
```

InString is the fully qualified URL you want to use, such as:

```
http://mydomain.com/dir/homepage.html
```

the filenameOnly function returns "homepage.html." If you wish to return the file-name of the current document, use location.href for *InString*.

Return Value

The function returns the filename of the fully qualified URL.

Notes and Example

The following example returns the filename of the current document:

```
var Ret = filenameOnly(location.href);
alert(Ret);
```

See also pathOnly.

formatComma Function

The formatComma function converts a numbers-only string or numeric value to a formatted comma-separated string, in the style of *x,xxx.xx*. The function automati-cally appends trailing zeros to the right of the decimal point if the value lacks them. Commas are added every third digit going to the left.

Syntax

```
var Ret = formatComma (InString)
```

InString is the value you wish to convert. The value can be a string (containing num-bers only) or a numeric value.

Return Value

The function returns the formatted string.

Notes and Example

If you want to include decimal values, you should format the number as a string, not as a floating-point numeric value. Otherwise, rounding errors can occur as JavaScript processes the value.

This example displays 1,234,567.89:

```
var Ret = formatComma ("12345678.90");
```

formatDollar Function

The formatDollar function converts a numbers-only string or numeric value to a formatted dollar string, in the style of $*x,xxx.xx*. The function automatically appends trailing zeros to the right of the decimal point if the value lacks them; otherwise, the "cents" portion of the value is retained. Commas are added every third digit going to the left. The dollar sign can be appended to the beginning of the string.

Syntax

```
var Ret = formatDollar (InString, DollarSign)
```

InString is the value you wish you convert. The value can be a string (containing numbers only) or a numeric value. *DollarSign* indicates if you want to include the dollar sign in the output; use *true* if yes and *false* if no.

Return Value

The function returns a formatted dollar string.

Notes and Example

If you want to include decimal values, you should format the number as a string, not as a floating-point numeric value. Otherwise, rounding errors can occur as JavaScript processes the value.

This example displays $1,234,567.89:

```
var Ret = formatDollar ("12345678.90", true);
```

getMaxList Function

The GetMaxList function returns the greatest value from a list of values.

Syntax

```
var Ret = getMaxList (Number1, Number2, ...)
```

Number1, Number2, and so forth are the values you want to check. You can provide as many numbers as you'd like.

Return Value

The function returns the numeric value of the largest value in the list.

Notes and Examples

The following tests four numbers—75, 100, 150, and 200—and returns 200 because it is the largest:

```
var Ret = getMaxList(75, 100, 150, 200);
alert(Ret);
```

See also getMinList as well as the max and min JavaScript Math object methods.

getMinList Function

The GetMinList function returns the least value in a list values.

Syntax

```
var Ret = getMinList (Number1, Number2, ...)
```

Number1, Number2, and so forth are the values you want to check. You can provide as many numbers as you'd like.

Return Value

The function returns the numeric value of the smallest value in the list.

Notes and Examples

The following lines test four numbers—75, 100, 150, and 200—and return 75 because that number is the smallest:

```
var Ret = getMinList(75, 100, 150, 200);
alert(Ret);
```

See also getMaxList. See also the max and min JavaScript Math object methods.

ifExists Function

The ifExists function determines whether a variable type (such as string, numeric, Boolean, or object) variable exists. You use this function first before referencing a variable that may not exist. To use the function, you must reference the window object that contains the variable, such as *parent.var* or *window.var*.

Syntax

```
var Ret = ifExists (win_obj.VarName)
```

win_obj is the window object that you think contains the variable; *VarName* is the name of the variable you want to check.

Return Value

The function returns *true* if the variable exists and *false* if it does not.

Notes and Example

The following example returns *false* because the variable Test doesn't exist in the parent window (though the variable Text does exist).

```
var Test = 1;
var Ret = ifExists(window.Text);
alert (Ret);
```

See also ifExistsString.

ifExistsString Function

The ifExistsString function determines whether a string variable exists. Use this function first before referencing a variable that may not exist. To use the function, you must reference the window object that contains the variable, such as *parent.var* or *window.var*.

Syntax

```
var Ret = ifExistsString (win_obj.VarName)
```

win_obj is the window object that you think contains the variable; *VarName* is the name of the variable you want to check.

Return Value

The function returns *true* if the variable exists and *false* if it does not.

Notes and Example

The following example returns *false* because the variable Test doesn't exist in the parent window.

```
var Test = "1";
var Ret = ifExistsString(window.Text);
alert (Ret);
```

See also ifExists.

initUpper Function

Use initUpper to capitalize the first character of every word in a string. For instance, if you give the function the string "netscape navigator for windows," the routine returns "Netscape Navigator For Windows."

Syntax

```
var Ret = initUpper(InString)
```

InString is the string you want to convert.

Return Value

The function returns a string value: the converted string.

Notes and Example

The following example capitalizes the first letter of each word in the test string. Note that characters that are already capitalized (if any) are left alone, as are non-alphabetic characters.

```
var TestString = "this is a test";
var Ret = initUpper(TestString)
alert (Ret)
```

initUpperQualify Function

Use initUpperQualify to capitalize the first character of every word in a string, using a list of "qualified" words that should not be capitalized (such as adverbs). For instance, if you give the function the string "netscape navigator for windows," the routine returns "Netscape Navigator for Windows."

You can edit the function to add or remove qualified words. As written, the function does not capitalize the following words: a, an, the, of, at, for, by. These words are defined in the companion initUpperQualifyWords function.

Syntax

```
var Ret = initUpperQualify(InString)
```

InString is the string you want to convert.

Return Value

The function returns a string value, which is the converted string.

Notes and Example

The following example capitalizes the first letter of each word in the test string. Note that characters that are already capitalized (if any) are left alone, as are non-alphabetic characters.

```
var TestString = "this is a test";
var Ret = initUpper(TestString)
alert (Ret)
```

If you use the initUpperQualify function, be sure to also include the initUpperQualify word list.

isAlphabeticChar Function

The isAlphabeticChar routine determines whether a test character is an alphabetic character (A-Z or a-z).

Syntax

```
var Ret = isAlphabeticChar(InString)
```

InString is the test character.

Return Value

The function returns one of two numeric values: 1 if the test character is an alphabetic character and 0 otherwise.

Notes and Example

The following example determines if the test character is an alphabetic character:

```
var Ret = prompt ("Type a single character");
if (isAlphabeticChar(Ret))
        alert ("Is alphabetic");
else
        alert ("Is not alphabetic");
```

isAlphabeticString Function

The isAlphabeticString function determines whether all the characters in a string are alphabetic characters (not numbers or punctuation).

Syntax

```
var Ret = isAlphabeticString (TestString)
```

TestString is the string you want to test.

Return Value

The function returns one of two numeric values: 1 if the string is entirely alphabetic and 0 if it is not.

Notes and Example

The following example displays a 0 because the test string is not composed entirely of alphabetic characters:

```
var Ret = prompt ("Type some characters ");
if (isAlphabeticString(Ret))
        alert ("All characters were alphabetic");
else
        alert ("At least one character was not alphabetic");
```

isBlank Function

The isBlank function tests whether a string is empty or null. Use this function to test if the user has provided a response to a prompt box or a form text box.

Syntax

```
var Ret = isBlank (InString);
```

InString is the string you want to test.

Return Value

The function returns *true* if the string is empty or null; otherwise, it returns *false*.

Notes and Example

The following example tests the string typed in response to a prompt box:

```
var Ret = isBlank(prompt ("Type something", ""));
if (Ret)
        alert ("The box is blank");
```

```
else
        alert ("The box is not blank");
```

See also isNotBlank.

isNotBlank Function

The isNotBlank function tests whether a string is empty or null. Use this function to test if the user has provided a response to a prompt box or a form text box.

Syntax

```
var Ret = isNotBlank (InString);
```

InString is the string you want to test.

Return Value

The function returns *true* if the string is not empty or null; otherwise, it returns *false*.

Notes and Example

The following example tests the string typed in response to a prompt box:

```
var Ret = isNotBlank(prompt ("Type something", ""));
if (Ret)
        alert ("The box is not blank");
else
        alert ("The box is blank");
```

See also isBlank.

isNumberChar Function

The isNumberChar function determines whether a test character is a number (0–9).

Syntax

```
var Ret = isNumberChar(InString);
```

InString is the test character.

Return Value

The function returns one of two numeric values: 1 if the test character is a number and 0 otherwise.

Notes and Example

The following example determines if the test character is a number:

```
var Ret = prompt ("Type a number");
if (isNumberChar(Ret))
        alert ("Is number");
else
        alert ("Is not number");
```

isNumberString Function

The isNumberString function determines whether all the characters in a string are numbers.

Syntax

```
var Ret = isNumberString (TestString);
```

TestString is the string you want to test.

Return Value

The function returns one of two numeric values: 1 if the string is all numbers; 0 if it is not.

Notes and Example

The following example displays a 1 because the test string is composed entirely of numbers.

```
var Ret = prompt ("Type some numbers");
if (isChar(Ret))
        alert ("All characters are numbers ");
else
        alert ("At least one character is not a number");
```

isPunc Function

The isPunc function determines whether a test character is a punctuation character.

Syntax

```
var Ret = isPunc(InString);
```

InString is the test character.

Return Value

The function returns one of two numeric values: 1 if the test character is a punctuation character and 0 otherwise.

Notes and Example

The following example determines whether the test character is punctuation, in other words, one of the following characters: ? ' ! $ ( ) - _ ; : , . < > { } ~:

```
var Ret = prompt ("Type a character");
if (isPunc(Ret))
        alert ("Is a punctuation character");
else
        alert ("Is not a punctuation character");
```

isStringLower Function

The isStringLower function determines whether all the characters in a string are lowercase alphabetic characters.

Syntax

```
var Ret = isStringLower (TestString)
```

TestString is the string you want to test.

Return Value

The function returns one of two numeric values: 1 if the string is composed entirely of lowercase alphabetic characters and 0 if it is not.

Notes and Example

The following example returns 1 because the test string is contains only lowercase alphabetic characters:

```
var Ret = prompt ("Type some characters");
if (isStringLower(Ret))
        alert ("All characters are lowercase");
else
```

```
alert ("At least one character is not lowercase");
```

See also isStringUpper.

isStringUpper Function

The isStringUpper function determines whether a string is composed entirely of uppercase alphabetic characters (A–Z).

Syntax

```
var Ret = isStringUpper(InString)
```

InString is the test string.

Return Value

The function returns one of two numeric values: 1 if the test string is composed of uppercase alphabetic characters, and 0 otherwise.

Notes and Example

The following example determines if a test character is an uppercase alphabetic character:

```
var Ret = prompt ("Type a character");
if (isStringUpper(Ret))
        alert ("Is uppercase");
else
        alert ("Is not uppercase");
```

See also isStringLower.

isUSZip Function

The isUSZip function determines whether a test string is a valid format for a 5-, 9-, or 11-digit U.S. Zip code. (Note: The routine does *not* test whether the Zip code is valid.)

Syntax

```
var Ret = isUSZip(InString);
```

InString is the test string.

Return Value

The function returns one of two numeric values: 1 if the test string is a valid U.S. Zip code and 0 if not.

Notes and Example

The following example determines if the test string is a valid U.S. Zip code:

```
var TestString = "90000-1234";
if (isUSZip(TestString))
        alert("Good Zip Code")
else
        alert("Bad Zip Code")
```

isWithinRange Function

The isWithinRange function tests whether a string numeric value is within a certain range. The function uses a string input because this is the likely data type that a user would enter, for example, in a form text boxes or in a prompt box. You can specify the lower and the upper allowed range.

Syntax

```
var Ret = isWithinRange(InString, RangeMin, RangeMax);
```

- *InString* is the string you want to test.
- *RangeMin* is the minimum value to accept.
- *RangeMax* is the maximum value to accept.

Return Value

The function returns *true* if the value falls within the range specified, and otherwise *false*.

Notes and Example

The following example re-displays the prompt box until the user clicks Cancel or enters a value within the specified range. (Note: this example doesn't test for non-numeric values. You should use the isNumberString function for this.)

```
var Ret;
var CtrlLoop = false;
```

```
while (!CtrlLoop) {
        Ret = prompt ("Type a number between 1 and 10", "");
        CtrlLoop = isWithinRange (Ret, 1, 10);
}
```

leftString Function

The leftString function returns the specified number of characters of a string, starting from the left side. For instance, if you take the string "Netscape Navigator 2.0" and tell the function to lop off all but the first seven characters, the function returns "Netscap."

The leftString routine is the equivalent of the Basic LEFT$ command.

Syntax

```
var Ret = leftString(InString;Chars);
```

InString is the string you want to process. *Chars* is the number of characters you want returned.

Return Value

The function returns a string value, which is the converted string.

Notes and Example

The following example returns just the first 10 characters of the test string:

```
var TestString = "This is a test";
var Chars=10
Var Ret = leftString(TestString, Chars);
alert (Ret);
```

See also rightString.

leftTrim Function

Use leftTrim to trim leading spaces from the beginning of a string. Example:

"This is a string"// Original string.

"This is a string"// Return string

The leftTrim routine is equivalent to the BASIC LTrim$ command.

Syntax

```
var Ret = leftTrim(InString);
```

InString is the string you want to process.

Return Value

The function returns a string value, which is the converted string.

Notes and Example

The following script trims the leading spaces to the left of the test string.

```
var TestString = "    This is a test"';
var Ret = leftTrim(TestString);
alert (ret);
```

See also rightTrim.

makeArray Function

The makeArray function is an object constructor that creates a one-dimensional array, with any number of elements. The first element (element 0) of the returned array contains the number of elements in the array. You can use this value in your script for such chores as looping through all the array elements using a for statement.

Syntax

```
MyArray = new Array(NumElements, FillString)
```

NumElements is the number of elements you wish to create for the new array object. *FillString* is the string you are going to use to fill each new element. This can be an empty string ("”), null, 0, or anything else.

Note the use of the new constructor statement. This must be included to create the new array.

Return Value

The function returns a created array. Element 0 (for example, MyArray[0]) contains the length of the array. This value is also contained in the length property—in this example, MyArray.length.

Notes and Example

This example creates a new array with 10 elements and fills each element with the value of null:

```
MyNullArray = new makeArray (10, null);
```

This example creates a new array with 100 elements, filling each element with the value of 0:

```
MyZeroArray = new makeArray (100, 0);
```

The NumElements parameter is optional. You can make a new array with 0 elements, and JavaScript allows you to add more elements to it later. However, by specifying NumElements, you can "preload" a value into each element you anticipate using.

You can also use two (currently) undocumented objects (array and object) to create arrays in JavaScript. See Chapter 4, "Objects," for more information on this and these two additional plug-and-play functions in the *library.txt* file:

- makeArray2—Makes a two-dimensional array
- makeArrayImplicit—Makes an array implicitly using any number of parameter values

Mask Function

The mask function checks a string against an "input mask." The input mask is used to determine which types of characters are permitted for any part of the string. You can use the mask routine, for example, to ensure that users enter a telephone number in the format *(xxx) xxx-xxxx*, where the *x*'s are numbers, and the parentheses, space, and hyphen are required.

Syntax

```
var Ret = mask (InString, Mask);
```

InString is the string you want to test. *Mask* is the mask string. The *Mask* string uses special symbols to determine the characters to use.

Mask Character	Meaning
#	Character at this position must be a number
?	Character at this position must be an alphabetic character

Mask Character	Meaning
!	Character at this position must be number or alphabetic character
*	Character at this position can be anything

Following are some examples:

Mask	Matching string
###	123
#?#	1A2
#!?	12A

Return Value

This function returns one of two numeric values: 1 if the input string matches the mask and 0 otherwise.

Notes and Example

If you import the mask routine to your own script, be sure to also import the following routines from the *library.txt* library file:

- isNumberChar
- isNumOrChar
- isAlphabeticChar

The following example tests a phone number in the form of (*xxx*) *xxx-xxxx* against a predefined mask:

```
var Ret = Mask ("(800) 555-1212", "(###) ###-####");
alert (Ret);
```

padTextPrefix Function

The padTextPrefix function is the same as padTextSuffix, except that it adds padding character(s) before the input string. For example, suppose the input string is NAV, and the string is padded out with 0s to make a total length of 5. The result is 00NAV. The padTextPrefix function is ideal for making counters, such as 00015.

Syntax

```
padTextPrefix (InString, PadChar, PadLength);
```

InString is the string to convert, *PadChar* is the padding character to use (such as 0, X, or _), and *PadLength* is the total length of the returned string, with padding (if necessary).

Return Value

The function returns a converted (padded) string.

Notes and Example

The following example pads the input value of 1 with four leading 0s, so that the total length of the returned string is five characters. The result is the number 00001.

```
var Ret = PadTextPrefix ("1", "0", 5);
alert(Ret);
```

See also padTextSuffix.

padTextSuffix Function

The padTextSuffix function "pads out" a text string with a specified character so that the string is a given length. For example, suppose the input string is NAV, and the string is padded out with 0s to make a total length of five characters. The result is NAV00.

Syntax

```
var Ret = padTextSuffix(InString, PadChar, PadLength);
```

- *InString* is the string to convert.
- *PadChar* is the padding character to use (such as 0, X, or —).
- *PadLength* is the total length of the returned string, with padding (if necessary).

Return Value

The function returns a converted (padded) string.

Notes and Example

The following example pads the input value of 1 with four trailing 0s, so that the total length of the returned string is five characters. The result is 10000.

```
var Ret = PadTextSuffix("1", "0", 5);
alert (Ret);
```

See also padTextPrefix.

parser Function

The parser function "parses" (breaks apart) a string into its component parts. The component parts are marked by a special parsing character, which can be user-defined (common parsing characters are ~ and ;). The parsed string is returned in a variable array; each element of the array contains a segment of the parsed string.

For example, suppose the input string is "One;Two;Three;Four." After being processed, the variable array contains the following separate elements: One, Two, Three, and Four. The parser routine is helpful whenever you want to break up a large string.

Syntax

```
var Ret = parser(ParseStr, Sep)
```

ParseStr is the string you want to parse (the original string). *Sep* is the parsing character, such as "~" or ";". (The parsing separator can be any single character, but it obviously should not be a character that is found in the string itself.)

Return Value

The filled-out array. Use the element 0 to determine the number of elements in the array, such as Ret[0].

Notes and Example

The following example parses the test string into five elements, then prints out the elements on separate lines:

```
var ParseStr = "one;two;three;four;five"
var Sep=";";
var MyArray = parser(ParseStr, Sep)
var Temp = "";
for (Count=1; Count <=MyArray.length; Count++) {
        Temp += MyArray[Count] + "\n";
}
alert(Temp);
```

pathOnly Function

The pathOnly function returns just the path (minus the filename) of a fully qualified URL. A good use of pathOnly is when you need to determine the path of the current document.

Syntax

```
var Ret = pathOnly(InString);
```

InString is the fully qualified URL you want to use, such as

```
http://mydomain.com/dir/homepage.html.
```

The pathOnly function returns http://mydomain.com/dir/. If you wish to return the path of the current document, use location.href for *InString*.

Return Value

This functions returns the path only (including host, port, domain, and so forth) of the fully qualified URL.

Notes and Example

The following example returns the path of the current document:

```
var Ret = pathOnly(location.href);
alert(Ret);
```

See also filenameOnly.

rightString Function

The rightString function returns the specified number of characters, starting from the right side, of a string. For instance, if you apply the function to the string "Netscape Navigator 2.0" and tell it to lop off all but the last 11 characters, the function returns "vigator 2.0."

The rightString function is the equivalent of the Basic RIGHT$ command.

Syntax

```
var ret = rightString(InString;Chars)
```

InString is the string you want to process. *Chars* is the number of characters you want returned.

Return Value

The function returns a string value, which is the converted string.

Notes and Example

The following example returns just the last 10 characters of the test string:

```
var TestString = "This is a test";
var Chars=10;
var Ret = rightString(TestString, Chars);
alert(Ret);
```

rightTrim Function

Use rightTrim to trim trailing spaces from the end of a string. If you apply the function to "This is a string ", it returns "This is a string."

The rightTrim routine is equivalent to the BASIC RTrim$ command.

Syntax

```
var Ret = rightTrim(InString);
```

InString is the string to process.

Return Value

The function returns a string value, which is the converted string.

Notes and Example

The following example trims the extra spaces from the right of the test string:

```
var TestString = "This is a test    ";
var Ret = rightTrim(TestString);
alert(Ret);
```

See also leftTrim.

roundDollar Function

The roundDollar function "corrects" for JavaScript's occasional overcompensation when using floating-point values. For example, on many platforms a numeric value such as 8.87 becomes something like 8.8699999999999992. This is caused by miscompensation in the floating-point number calculation. The effects vary depending on the platform, as each computer type uses a different method of calculating and storing floating-point values.

The roundDollar function lops off the extra digits and corrects the value, if necessary. The value 8.87 is reconverted back to 8.87. The function can be used for any value with two digits to the right of the decimal point.

Note that during rounding the value becomes a string, so you can no longer perform math calculations on it. In other words, if the value is 8.87 and you add 1 to it, the result is 8.871, not 9.87. You should perform all math calculations before using the roundDollar function.

Syntax

```
var Ret = roundDollar (Val);
```

Val is the floating-point number you want to round. Only the two left fractional digits are returned; therefore, 8.876 comes back rounded as 8.88.

Return Value

The function returns the rounded value, in string form.

Notes and Example

The following example returns the correctly rounded string "8.91"—even though on many platforms, JavaScript overcompensates and stores the value as 8.9100000000000001.

```
Ret = roundDollar (8.91);
alert (Ret);
```

sortArray Function

The sortArray function sorts a series of strings in an array. You might want to sort a list of strings, for example, if you obtain data from the user in a form file and want to store or present it in alphabetical order. The function expects the text strings to be in a 1-based array (the first element starting at index 1). Note that the sortArray function works with string values only; it does not work with number values. If you want to sort a series of numbers, turn them into strings first with the syntax:

```
"" + num;
```

where *num* is the number you want to convert.

Syntax

```
sortArray (Sort);
```

Sort is the array containing the string you want to sort.

Return Value

None.

Notes and Example

The following example creates an array of 10 strings (numbers 1-10 spelled out) and then passes the array to the sortArray function. The array is sorted "in-place," meaning that the array you pass to the function is the one that is sorted. You access the values in the same array you passed to the function. The new order is shown after sorting.

```
var OrigArray = new Array(10);
OrigArray.length = 10;
OrigArray[1] = "one";
OrigArray[2] = "two";
OrigArray[3] = "three";
OrigArray[4] = "four";
OrigArray[5] = "five";
OrigArray[6] = "six";
OrigArray[7] = "seven";
OrigArray[8] = "eight";
OrigArray[9] = "nine";
OrigArray[10] = "ten";

sortArray (OrigArray)
var Temp = "", Count;
for (Count=1; Count<=OrigArray.length; Count++) {
        Temp+=OrigArray[Count] + "\n";
}
alert (Temp)
```

The sort is case sensitive, according to ascending ASCII values, which means that sorting starts with numbers, proceeds to uppercase letters, and then lowercase letters.

Therefore, the word "Zoo" is sorted before the word "aardvark," and the string "1" comes before both of them. To sort the strings in full alphabetical order, you should convert the strings to all lower- or uppercase. Consult an ASCII table for complete information on the order of characters.

The sortArray function correctly sorts strings in proper ascending order—for example, "teen" comes before "ten."

■■■■■■■ **NOTE**

> The sortArray function uses the "exchange sort" method of sorting strings. While it is only modestly efficient, it's one of the easiest sorting algorithms to write and revise.

■■■■■■■

spaceTrim Function

Use the spaceTrim function to remove unwanted extra spaces in a string. The function also removes any extra spaces before or after the string. For example, when processed by spaceTrim, the string " this is a test " becomes a neat and tidy "this is a test".

An ideal use of the spaceTrim function is to clean up a user's response to a prompt box or form text input box.

Syntax

```
var Ret = stripSpaces(InString)
```

InString is the string you wish to process.

Return Value

The function returns the processed string.

Notes and Example

The following example processes the string through the stripSpaces function and displays the cleaned-up version in an alert box. Colon (:) characters are used as a visual reference to demonstrate how the function also removes any leading and trailing spaces in the string.

```
var Ret = stripSpaces("  Netscape  Navigator  2.0  with    JavaScript!!   ");
alert (Ret);
```

stripChar Function

The stripChar function removes any occurrence of the specified character from a string. For example, if you want to strip all lowercase t's from a string, the string

```
"This is a test"
```

becomes

```
"This is a es".
```

To strip more than one character from a string, use the stripCharString function instead of this one. The stripChar function is preferred (for speed reasons) if you have only one character to strip.

Syntax

```
var Ret = stripChar(InString, Char);
```

InString is the string you want to process. *Char* is the character you want to strip.

Return Value

The function returns a string value, which is the stripped string.

Notes and Example

The following example strips the lowercase o's from the test string:

```
var TestString = "The JavaScript Sourcebook, by Gordon McComb";
alert(stripChar(TestString, "o"));
```

See also stripCharString, stripSpaces.

stripCharString Function

The stripCharString function is used to strip two or more characters from a string. Its primary use is to format strings such as "$1,234.56" to plain digits—123456. However, you can use it for any chore for which you need to remove a series of unwanted characters from a string.

Syntax

```
var Ret = stripCharString(InString, CharString)
```

InString is the string you want to process. *CharString* includes the characters you want to strip.

Return Value

The function returns a string value, which is the stripped string.

Notes and Example

The following example strips the string " $1,2460.90 " (note the spaces) and displays the result:

```
Ret = stripCharString (" $1,2560.90 ", "$,. ");
alert (Ret);
```

stripSpaces Function

The stripSpaces function removes all spaces from a string. For example, the string

```
"This is a test"
```

becomes

```
"Thisisatest".
```

Syntax

```
var Ret = stripSpaces(InString);
```

InString is the string you want to process.

Return Value

This function returns a string value, which is the stripped string.

Notes and Example

The following example strips the spaces from the test string:

```
var TestString = "The JavaScript Sourcebook, by Gordon McComb";
alert(stripSpaces(TestString));
```

See also stripChar, stripCharString.

testForLength Function

Use the testForLength function to test for various string length conditions. You can test if a string is equal to a given length, less than or equal to a given length, and greater than or equal to a given length. A primary use of the function is validating input provided in a text box or prompt box.

Syntax

var Ret = testForLength (InString, EqualLength, LTELength, GTELength)

- *InString* is the string to test.
- *EqualLength* is the absolute length for the string (or -1 if using another parameter).
- *LTELength* stands for less than or equal to and represents the maximum length allowed for the string (or -1 if using another parameter).
- *GTELength* stands for greater than or equal to and represents the minimum length allowed for the string (or -1 if using another parameter).

Return Value

The function returns *true* if the test string matches the length criteria, and otherwise *false*.

Notes and Example

The following example tests that the input string (via a prompt box) is exactly 10 characters long:

```
var TestString = prompt ("Type ten characters only", "")
if (TestString != null) {var Ret = testForLength (TestString, 10, -1, -1);
alert (Ret);
}
```

Use the GTELength or LTELength parameters to test for greater than/equal to, and lesser than/equal to:

Example	Tests For
testForLength (TestString (-1, 5, -1)	Maximum string length is 5
testForLength (TestString (-1, -1, 7)	Minimum string length is 7

The *datefunc.txt* Functions

CD-ROM

The following functions are included in the *datefunc.txt* plug-and-play file. All the routines in this library file are designed to aid in date and calendar calculations. They are listed here in alphabetical order.

Function/Procedure	What It Does
calendar	Calculates start day and number of days for any month/year
dateConv	Converts date text
dayOfWeek	Returns day of week
dayOrd	Adds st, nd, rd, th suffix to the day
dayText	Returns the day spelled out
getDateArray	Specifies date returned in array
GetTimeArray	Returns current time in array
leapYear	Determines if year is leap year
monthText	Returns month (numeric) as month string
monthTextAbbr	Returns month (numeric) as abbreviated month string
yearAbbr	Returns last two digits of year
yearComplete	Returns whole (four-digit) year from xx or xxx Date() value
yearText	Returns spelled out year

calendar Function

The calendar function determines the number of days in a given month, as well as the starting day (Sunday through Saturday) of the month. The routine works for any month of any year. The calendar routine is primarily intended for use in those scripts that create calendars.

Syntax

```
var Ret = calendar(Month,Year)
```

Month is the numerical value, minus 1, of the month of the year for the calendar. 0 is January, 1 is February, and so on. *Year* is the year of the calendar.

Return Value

Values returned by the calendar routine are contained in an array.

Array element	Contains
1	Starting position for day of the month
2	The number of days in the month

Array element	Contains
3	The month
4	The year

Notes and Example

If you copy the calendar routine to your script, make sure to copy the following functions from the *datefunc.txt* file:

- leapYear
- makeArrayImplicit
- getDaysofYear

The following example returns the calendar array for October 1997 and displays the starting day:

```
Ret = var calendar (9, 1997);
alert (Ret[1]);
```

dateConv Function

The dateConv function extracts the day, month, and year from various text date formats. For example, if you provide the routine with the string "September 30, 1980", it returns with an array variable filled with three values: 9, 30, and 1980.

The routine is quite flexible in accepting a wide variety of date formats. For example, all of the following are converted to the same [9, 30, 1980] values:

September 30 1980

September 30, 1980

Sep 30 1980

Sep 30, 1980

Sep. 30, 1980

9/30/1980

9-30-1980

Syntax

```
var Ret = dateConv (InString)
```

InString is the date string to convert.

Return Value

The function returns an array variable that contains three elements when the routine is finished.

Array element	Contains
1	The month
2	The day
3	The year

Notes and Example

If you import the dateConv routine into your own script, be sure to also import the following routines:

- leftTrim (in *datefunc.txt* or *library.txt*)
- month (in *datefunc.txt*)
- numOnly (in *datefunc.txt*)

The function returns an empty array with its length property set to 0 if there was an error in conversion. An error occurs if you enter a format that is not supported, such as 10 Sept 1998 or Sep 32, 1998.

The following example prompts for a date and displays the month, day, and year (1, 14, and 1999) in an alert box:

```
var Ret = dateConv ("January 14, 1999");
var Temp = "";
if (Ret.length != 0) {
for (Count = 1; Count < 4; Count++)
      Temp +=;
      alert (Temp);
} else
      alert ("An error occurred in converting the date");
```

dayOfWeek Function

The dayOfWeek function determines the day of the week (Sunday=1, Monday=2, and so on) for a particular date. The dayOfWeek routine is primarily intended to be used in conjunction with the calendar routine, detailed above.

Syntax

```
var Ret = dayOfWeek (DateString);
```

DateString is a fully qualified date, suitable for the JavaScript Date() object, such as "January 14, 1999".

Return Value

The function returns an array variable that contains three elements, as detailed in the following table.

Array element	Contains
1	The day of the week (0=Sunday; 1= Monday, and so on)
2	The day of the week spelled out
3	Three-letter abbreviation for the day of the week

Notes and Example

The following example determines the day of the week, spelled out in abbreviated form, for January 14, 1998. (The result is "Wed".)

```
WeekDay = dayOfWeek ("January 15, 1998");
alert (WeekDay[3]);
```

This example returns the day of the week, spelled out in full form, for the current date:

```
var now = new Date();
var Ret = dayOfWeek(now.toString())
alert (Ret[2])
```

■■■■■■ **CAUTION**

Netscape can crash if you use an invalid date. Be sure the date is on or after January 1, 1970, and that the date is valid (for example, do not use February 30, 1990).

■■■■

dayOrd Function

The dayOrd function returns the specified date with an ordinal suffix, as in 1st, 2nd, 3rd, or 4th.

Syntax

```
var Ret = dayOrd(InString);
```

InString is the number of the day you want to use, such as 1 for 1st or 10 for 10th. You can also use a numeric value for this parameter.

Return Value

The function returns a string with the ordinal suffix attached.

Notes and Example

The following example displays "31st":

```
var Ret = dayOrd ("31");
alert (Ret);
```

See also dayText, monthText, monthAbbr, yearText, and yearAbbr.

dayText Function

The dayText function transforms a number from 1 to 31 to a corresponding spelled-out ordinal word. For example, the string "1" (or the numeric value 1) is returned as "first"; the string "14" is returned as "fourteenth," and so forth.

Syntax

```
var Ret = dayText (InString);
```

InString is the number of the day you want to use, such as 1 for first or 10 for tenth. You can also use a numeric value for this parameter.

Return Value

This function returns a spelled-out ordinal string for the date.

Notes and Example

The following example displays "twenty-third":

```
var Ret = dayText ("23");
alert (Ret);
```

See also dayOrd, monthText, monthAbbr, yearText, and yearAbbr.

getDateArray Function

The getDateArray routine returns the current date in a variable array. You can then access the elements of the array to obtain the parts of the date (day, month, year) that you want. The current date is set by your computer's clock.

Syntax

```
var Ret = dateDateArray(DateString);
```

DateString is a fully qualified date, suitable for the JavaScript Date() object, such as "January 14, 1999".

Return Value

This function returns a variable array containing values returned by the getDateArray routine.

Array element	Contains
1	Month (January=1)
2	Day
3	Year

Notes and Example

The following example displays the current date in mm/dd/yy format:

```
var now = new Date();
var Ret = getDateArray(now.toString())
var Temp = Ret[1] + "/" + Ret[2] + "/" + Ret[3]
alert (Temp)
```

This example displays the specified date in mm/dd/yy format:

```
var Ret = getDateArray("January 1, 1970")
var Temp = Ret[1] + "/" + Ret[2] + "/" + Ret[3]
alert (Temp)
```

■■■■■■ **CAUTION**

Netscape can crash if you use an invalid date. Be sure the date is on or after January 1, 1970, and that the date is valid (for example, do not use February 30, 1990).

■■■■■■

getDaysofYear Function

The getDaysofYear function is primarily for use with the calendar function, described earlier in this chapter. The function fills in an array with the number of days for each month of the year. The function must be used with the leapYear and makeArrayImplicit functions, which are included in the *datefunc.htm* file.

Syntax

```
var Ret = getDaysofYear(Year);
```

Year is the year you want to use for the array (the February element differs if it's a leap year).

Return Value

The function returns an array containing 12 elements; each element contains the number of days for the year. February contains 28 or 29 days, depending on whether it's a leap year.

Notes and Example

The following example displays 31 for the number of days in December (any year):

```
var Ret = getDaysofYear (1996);
alert (Ret[12]);
```

getTimeArray Function

The getTimeArray routine returns the current time in a variable array. You can then access the elements of the array to obtain the parts of the time (hour, minute, second, hundredth of a second) that you want. The current time is determined by your computer's clock. The hour is in 24-hour format. The minutes and second values are padded with leading zeros when necessary.

Syntax

```
var Ret = getTimeArray();
```

Return Value

The function returns a variable array containing values returned by the getTimeArray routine.

Array element	Contains
1	Hour
2	Minute
3	Second

Notes and Example

The following example types the time in hh:mm format:

```
var Ret = getTimeArray()
var Temp = Ret[1] + ":" + Ret[2] + ":" + Ret[3]
alert (Temp)
```

leapYear Function

Use the leapYear function to determine if any given year is a leap year.

Syntax

```
var Ret = leapYear(Year);
```

Year is the year to check.

Return Value

The function returns one of two numeric values. 1 if the year specified in *Year* is a leap year or 0 if it is not.

Notes and Example

The following example tests whether 2000 is a leap year (the answer is 1):

```
var Ret = leapYear(2000);
alert (Ret);
```

monthText Function

The monthText function converts the month as a number to the month as a string. For instance, month 2 is converted to "February".

Syntax

```
var Ret = monthText (Month);
```

Month is the month value (1 to 12).

Return Value

The function returns the month as a string.

Notes and Example

The following example returns May:

```
var Ret = monthText(5);
alert(Ret);
```

■■■■■■ **NOTE**

> Use monthTextAbbr if you want the month returned in short form, such as "Jan" for January.

■■■■■

monthTextAbbr Function

The monthTextAbbr function converts the month as a number to the month as an abbreviated string. For instance, month 2 is converted to "Feb."

Syntax

```
var Ret = monthTextAbbr (Month);
```

Month is the month value (1 to 12).

Return Value

The function returns the month as a string.

Notes and Example

The following example returns Oct:

```
var Ret = monthTextAbbr(10);
alert(Ret);
```

■■■■■■ **NOTE**

> Use monthText if you want the month returned in long form, such as "January" for January.

■■■■■

yearAbbr Function

The yearAbbr function returns the last two digits of a four-digit year string. For example, the year 1999 is returned as 99.

Syntax

```
var Ret = yearAbbr (Year);
```

Year is the year you want converted.

Return Value

The function returns the year with just the last two digits.

Notes and Example

The following example returns 98 for the year 1998.

```
var Ret = yearAbbr (1998);
alert(Ret);
```

See also dayOrd, dayText, monthText, monthAbbr, yearText, yearComplete.

yearComplete Function

The yearComplete function returns the complete four-digit year given the form 0–99 for the 1900s, and 100 and greater for the 2000s. This function is most useful in conjunction with JavaScript's Date() object, which does not return the first two digits for the year. Instead, "96" is 1996, "99" is 1999, and "105" is 2005.

Syntax

```
var Ret = yearComplete (Year);
```

Year is the year you want converted.

Return Value

The function returns the complete year.

Notes and Example

The following example returns the year 2010:

```
var Ret = yearComplete (110);
```

```
alert(Ret);
```

See also dayOrd, dayText, monthText, monthAbbr, yearAbbr, and yearText.

yearText Function

The yearText function returns the specified year, spelled out. In other words, 1997 would be returned as "nineteen hundred and ninety-seven".

Syntax

```
var Ret = yearText (Year);
```

Year is the year you want converted. Valid years lie between 1995 and 2010.

Return Value

The function returns the year, spelled out.

Notes and Example

The following example returns the year 1999, spelled out:

```
var Ret = yearText (1999);
alert(Ret);
```

See also dayOrd, dayText, monthText, monthAbbr, and yearAbbr.

Number-to-Word Functions (n2wrds.txt)

CD-ROM

The *n2wrds.txt* (number-to-words) file, included on the CD-ROM accompanying this book, contains numerous functions for processing a numeric string value up to 9,999,999 and returning a spelled-out version. For example, the number 2763 is returned as "two thousand seven hundred sixty-three". You can use the number-to-words functions to represent a numeric value as a spelled-out string, such as a hit counter. For example, instead of showing your hit counter as "You are visitor 12875," you can display it as "You are visitor twelve thousand eight hundred seventy-five."

In most cases you will use all of the functions in the *n2dfunc.htm* file to process numbers. However, the functions are "compartmentalized" to make it easier to lop off those you do not need for your application. Here are the functions in the *n2dfunc.htm* file, with a note indicating whether it's required or not. The assumption is made that you at least want to count to 999.

Function	Required	Purpose
toWords	Yes	Main number-to-words function
convertOnes	Yes	Converts "ones" values
convertTens	Yes	Converts "tens" values
convertHundreds	Yes	Converts "hundreds" values
convertThousands	No	Converts "thousands" values
convertTenThousands	No	Converts "ten thousands" values
convertHundredThousands	No	Converts "hundred thousands" values
convertMillions	No	Converts "millions" values
stripOutChars	No	Strips out any non-numeric character
spaceTrim	No*	Strips out spaces in the resulting number word text

*While optional, it is highly recommended because there can be extra spaces in the spelled-out number text.

If you wish to remove the stripOutChars and/or spaceTrim functions, you must modify the toWords function:

- Remove the line *InString = stripOutChars (InString)*, to remove the stripOutChars function.
- Remove the line *OutString = spaceTrim(OutString)*, to remove the spaceTrim function.

If you remove any of the conversion functions (thousands to millions, for example), you should also revise this line to prevent the script from attempting to call those functions that are no longer available:

```
if (InString.length > 7) return (InString);
```

Change the number value to the maximum length of the number you wish to process. For example, if you only wish to process numbers up to 999, change the line to read:

CD-ROM

```
if (InString.length > 3) return (InString);
n2wrds.htm
```

A working example of the number-to-words script is provided in the file *n2wrds.htm*.

■■■■■ NOTE

> If you wish to spell out the current date, such as converting 12/25/98 to "December twenty-five, nineteen hundred and ninety-eight, use the appropriate date functions detailed earlier in this chapter. These functions work a bit differently and are tailored for converting date values to string text. Note, for instance, that the year is spelled out in the mostly customary "hundreds" rather than "thousands."

■■■■■

14

FIXING BROKEN

JAVASCRIPT

PROGRAMS

"Errors in my script? Impossible!"

Well, it's not really impossible. Everyone makes mistakes writing JavaScript programs. Errors don't know experts from novices, so the next time you get an error message while trying to play a macro you've written, don't feel bad. JavaScript provides error messages as a means to help you spot mistakes in your macros. Read the message; then take the appropriate steps to fix the error.

When something doesn't work right in computer programs, it is called a bug. Understandably enough, ridding your scripts of bugs is called "debugging." This topic is important enough to any serious JavaScript writer to devote an entire chapter to it. If you are experiencing problems with your scripts, read through this chapter first before pulling out your hair. In this chapter, you'll learn what errors are, what they mean, and how to fix them. And you will discover the most common error messages you will encounter when writing JavaScript programs.

Isolating the Problem

Mistakes during script writing or editing are common, so you should always double-check your work at the first sign of a problem.

There are three general types of errors that can occur when playing a JavaScript program:

- Load-time errors
- Run-time errors
- Logic errors

Understanding Load-Time Errors

Load-time errors are those that are caught by JavaScript as the browser program loads the script. These errors are the major boo-boos that prevent the script from functioning, even before it has a chance to start. It is during the loading process that JavaScript spots any serious errors that will cause your script to fail right off the bat. The script cannot be run until it has been successfully loaded.

Load-time errors are perhaps the most common errors and are generally caused by problems in syntax. For example, you made a spelling error or forgot a punctuation character like one of those pesky braces! To help you identify the problem, JavaScript displays a warning box (see Figure 14.1) when a load-time error occurs. The warning box tells you the problem and, most of the time, shows you the actual text of the problem.

Bear in mind that the warning box doesn't always indicate the actual error. Depending on the problem, the error may be located at a different part of the line, or

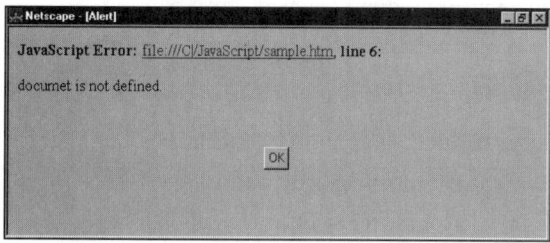

Figure 14.1 A load-time error message, such as this one, appears if JavaScript has a problem with your script when the page is loaded into the browser.

even on another line. This is because of the way JavaScript "parses" the script into its individual components.

To close the error box, click OK. Multiple error messages can appear if your script contains many errors. You must click OK to dismiss each error message.

Understanding Run-time Errors

Even if your script loads without a peep, there is no guarantee that it will run smoothly. *Run-time* errors are those that occur when the script is actually playing. As with load-time errors, run-time errors are displayed in an alert box. The nature of the error is specified, along with a line number so you can hunt down the error in the document.

Where load-time errors are generally caused by mistakes in syntax, run-time errors are most often the fault of improper use of commands. For instance, you will receive a run-time error if you reference a variable that hasn't been defined. A common cause of this problem is misspelling variables when defining them (note the different spelling of the word Message).

```
Messsage = "This is a test";
document.write(Message);
```

Another type of run-time error occurs when you misapply one of JavaScripts objects. For example, the following code fragment results in an error because you cannot assign a value directly to the document object. (The exact error message is "document cannot be set by assignment.")

```
document="test";
```

Understanding Logic Errors

A *logic error* occurs when your script does something other than what is suggested by "logic." The error isn't because of a misplaced parenthesis or misapplied statement, but rather a blooper in the way you've constructed the script.

You cannot anticipate every possible event or combination of events, but you should build logic error protection into your scripts as much as possible, or at least warn readers of potential problems so they can avoid the errors.

Another type of logic error results when a script just isn't written properly and does the wrong things. Let's say you want a script that displays a form, asking the user for a name and address. You've identified the two text boxes in the form as "username" and "address," but you've switched them. You have the textbox "username" identifying the address text box and "address" identifying the name text box. Obviously, when you fetch the data typed into these boxes, the information will be reversed.

Common Problems

You'll find that most of the errors that beset your scripts are caused by the same, rather simple, mistakes. Watch out for the following:

- *Proper variable names.* Keep a sharp eye out for the variables you use and their names. Avoid giving two variables similar names, such as *MyVar* and *MyVal*. Avoid one-character differences in variable names, such as *Name* and *Names*. Be sure that the variables you use are spelled properly throughout the macro. And remember: JavaScript variables are case sensitive. MyVar is not the same as myvar.

- *Proper function names.* Be sure function names are spelled correctly and that they don't have any extraneous characters or spaces.

- *Unique function names.* Function names can be used only once in a script (of course you can call a function any number of times). Review all functions to make sure that you haven't duplicated them.

- *Commas for arguments.* With the exception of the for statement, JavaScript uses the comma as the separator character for arguments (the for command uses semicolons, following the standard in C, C++, and Java). Leaving out a needed comma causes the script to fail.

- *Proper placement of braces.* This one is a real bug-a-boo. JavaScript uses the { and } brace characters to define a *block* of statements. A typical block includes all the statements in a function.

- *Quotation marks around strings.* All strings should have quotation marks around them. Be especially careful putting marks around strings used with the document.write method. This line causes an error:

```
document.write("This is a test:);
```

This is a surprisingly common mistake. Likewise, be sure to include quotation marks around string variable assignments, as in MyString="Quotation marks on both sides." Failure to add the proper number of quotation marks can lead to all sorts of red herring errors, as JavaScript tries to figure out what your program is supposed to do.

- *Proper script code.* Check to make sure that you are using the proper statements, methods, functions, and objects (collectively called entities). Review the script carefully and watch for misplaced entities. For best results, format your script with hard returns and tabs to show the relationship of all entities, as shown in Figure 14.2. This helps you follow the action of the script more easily.

- *Proper script sequence.* You can easily enter a statement into a script at the wrong place while editing it, especially if you're using time-saving cut-and-paste techniques. Double check.

- *Wrong object names.* Be sure that names for objects are spelled *exactly*, and with the proper capitalization. Remember that the Date and Math objects have initial caps; all others in JavaScript start with lowercase.

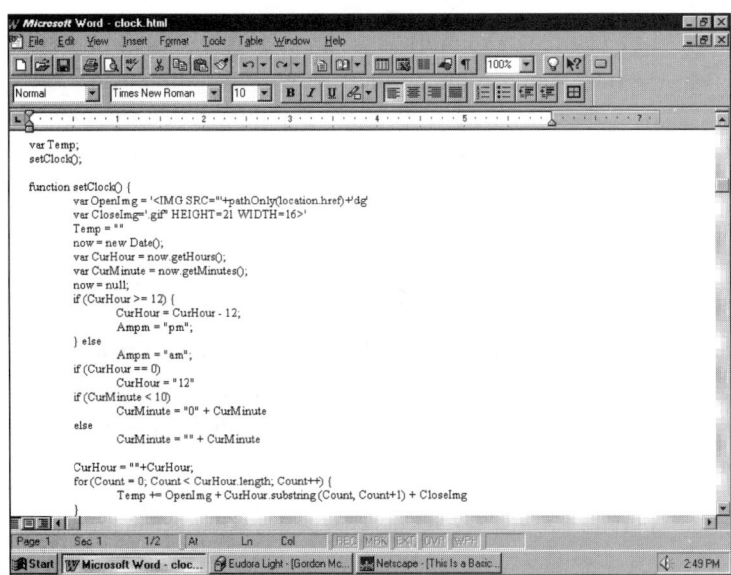

Figure 14.2 Using consistent and clear formatting for your JavaScript programs can make them easier to debug.

Develop a consistent naming convention for your variables, objects, and functions. One approach is to use initial caps for variables and initial lowercase for objects and functions.

Determining the Source of a Problem

An important step in repairing a broken script is isolating its various functions and routines, and analyzing it on a piece-by-piece basis. Does this part work? If the answer is "Yes," then go on to the next part. Does this part work? And so forth.

If the script is longer than two or three windows of material, you will probably have an idea of the approximate location of the difficulty. If the script isn't able to access data from a form, for instance, you know to look in the routine that processes the form input.

Setting Watchpoints: The Low-Tech Approach to Checking Variables

Many logic errors are caused by incorrect values in variables. One way to help you spot these logic errors is to set watchpoints at one or more spots in the script. These *watchpoints* are alert boxes that display the contents of the variables. You can also use alert boxes to determine if your code is reaching a certain point in the program (for example, *alert("to here")* to verify the code is working). Remove the alert watchpoints after the script has been debugged.

Making Paper Copies of Scripts

JavaScript programs are composed of text embedded in HTML documents. Therefore, you can use any text editing program that has a print capability to make paper copies of your scripts. The paper copies can help you find errors that are otherwise hidden in lines of code displayed on your monitor.

You will probably use the same text editor for printing your JavaScript programs that you use for writing them. Note that Word or WordPerfect both provide a line-numbering feature that is handy in cross-referencing mistakes (JavaScript displays most error messages with a line number, though the number does not accurately indicate the source of the problem):

- In WordPerfect for Windows 6.1 and later, choose Format, Line, Numbering, and choose the option in the dialog box that appears to turn on line numbering.
- In Word 6.0 and later, choose File, Page Setup, Choose Layout, then choose Line Numbers. Use the option in the dialog box that appears to turn on line numbering.

Printing JavaScript programs in a monospaced font, such as Courier, can help you spot mistakes such as a string that is empty but should contain a space. Because the monospace font takes up more space on a line, you should use a smaller font size, such as 9 or 10 point. This technique requires that you have a printer that supports scaleable fonts or that has a variety of font sizes available.

The 11 Most Common Mistakes

We're only human, after all, and making misteaks is part of our nature. We also tend to make the same kind of misteaks; some of us even tend to make the same misteakes over and over, never learning from them. Here are the more common goofs macro writers make. Knowing about them probably won't keep you from making them yourself, but being aware of the kinds of misteaks (enough already!) that can happen might help you track down the bugs in your scripts.

1. Missing Quotation Marks for Strings

Remember to provide quotation marks (either single or double) for all strings. The obvious use—and most common site of abuse—is the document.write command. This line:

```
document.write(<H1>This is a heading</H1>);
```

causes a load-time error. JavaScript doesn't know quite what's wrong here; it just tells you there's a syntax error and leaves it to you to figure out what's wrong (see Figure 14.3). To fix this common problem, edit the script in one or the other of these ways:

```
document.write("<H1>This is a heading</H1>");
document.write('<H1>This is a heading</H1>');
```

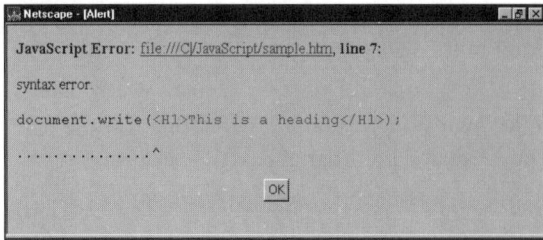

■■■■■■■■■ **Figure 14.3** The ubiquitous "syntax error" can be the hardest to solve,

2. Mismatched Quotation Mark Types

JavaScript lets you use the single quotation mark (') or the double quotation mark (") to delineate strings. However, you must be careful to stick with the same type, or else JavaScript displays an error message. The following line is not allowed because the quotation marks are mismatched:

```
document.write("<H1>This is a heading</H1>');
```

Do note that JavaScript lets you "embed" quoted strings within another string. In this case, you will be using both quotation mark types. However, keep in mind that for every type of quotation mark that starts the string, you must have a matching end mark. Here's an example. Notice that the entire string is enclosed in single quotation marks, and the "internal" string is enclosed in double quotation marks. The result is a heading that appears as *Ways to "Improve" Your JavaScript Programs*.

```
document.write("<H1>Ways to "Improve" Your JavaScript Programs</H1>');
```

3. Missing Quotation Marks for String Comparisons

Quotation marks must be used when you are comparing strings in expressions. Typically, you'll compare the value of a variable with a literal string, such as:

```
if (MyVar == "*")
```

Be sure to enclose the string in quotation marks, or JavaScript assumes you're comparing one variable against another.

4. Single Equals Instead of Double Equals in Comparison Expressions

This mistake is so common (unless you're a dyed-in-the-wool C programmer) that you're bound to make it at least once. JavaScript expects to see two equals signs in a comparison expression, not one. This is a mistake:

```
if(MyVar = "xyz")
```

Like C, C++, and Java, JavaScript insists you place two equals signs in the expression:

```
if(MyVar == "xyz")
```

5. Improperly Nested if Statements

Many scripts use lots of if expressions. To provide greater flexibility, these if statements are sometimes *nested* inside one another. The intent is to perform additional tests should the first test return *true* or *false*. Here is an example:

```
if (Var1 == 1) {
        if (Var2 == 1)
                // do this if Var1=1 and Var2=2;
        // do this if only Var1=1;
} else
        // do this if Var1<>1;
```

Eagle eyes will see that if Var1 does not equal 1, the inside test (Var2 == 1) is never performed. Be sure this is what you want. If it isn't, this logic error is hard to spot.

6. Sending Output to the Script Document

The document.write method writes over any text you have in your document, including text created using HTML markup. The following lines produce an error ("test is not defined") because JavaScript writes over the form before it has a chance to set a value in it:

```
<SCRIPT>
document.write ("Hello<P>");
document.test.box.value = "Hello again";
</SCRIPT>
```

```
<FORM NAME="test">
< INPUT TYPE="text" NAME="box">
</FORM>
```

You should avoid using the document.write method to write into a document that contains HTML you want to keep.

7. Forms Belong to the Document, Not the Window

A common problem is referring to a form as a property of a window. This results in a confusing error—*"formname* has no properties" (*formname* is the name of the form). For example, the following JavaScript says "test has no properties," yet it's obvious the test form has a perfectly valid input property:

```
<SCRIPT>
window.test.box.value = "Hello ";
</SCRIPT>
<FORM NAME="test">
<INPUT TYPE="text" NAME="box">
</FORM>
```

The fix is to reference the form as a document property. This rule also applies to frames. Mistakes such as those in the line below are common (the frame used is named framename):

```
parent.framename.test.box.value = "Hello";
```

Instead, the code should read:

```
parent.framename.document.test.box.value = "Hello";
```

8. Using String Methods with the Wrong Objects

Some of JavaScript's objects return values that look like strings, but they are not true strings. For instance, the following line displays the name of the current document URL. Although the "string" looks like a string, it is not (JavaScript internally converts it before displaying the value):

```
alert (location);
```

An error is displayed if you use string methods—such as indexOf or substring—with an object that returns one of these pseudostrings. Because the object isn't a string, it lacks the string methods. Instead, you need to convert the return value to a true string and work with that. The toString function offers a general approach:

```
Ret = location.toString();
alert (Ret.toUpperCase());
```

9. Endless Loops Lock Up Netscape

An endless loop is a for or while loop that does not break out. This causes JavaScript to execute the loop over and over again. Here's an example of an endless loop (there's no expression in the second argument for terminating the loop):

```
for (Count = 0; Count; Count++) {
    ....
```

JavaScript prevents a complete runaway train by limiting the number of loops to a million (it takes about 30–90 seconds for the loops to be processed, depending on the processor speed of the computer). At that point, JavaScript displays the message box in Figure 14.4. Click Cancel to stop the looping.

10. Poor or Missing Placement of { and } Block Character

You must exercise caution that you provide the proper { and } characters to define the blocks of the if statements. Otherwise, your script is bound to behave in truly strange ways!

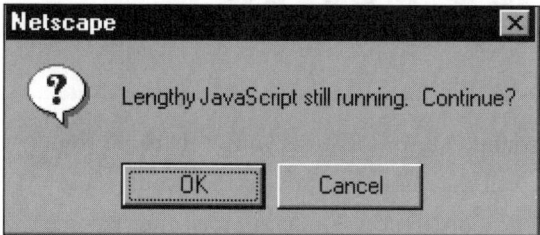

Figure 14.4 JavaScript won't allow runaway scripts; instead, it displays this message if the script has processed a million instructions.

Take the next example. Suppose you forget to use the { and } characters to block out the (Var1 == 1) if expression. What happens? JavaScript assumes that after the first line, all the following code should be executed whether or not the Var1 == 1 expression evaluates as *true*. The user sees the "Congratulations!" message either way.

```
Var1 = 2;
if (Var1 == 1)
        alert ("var1 = 1");
        alert ("Congratulations!");
```

The script should read:

```
Var1 = 2;
if (Var1 == 1) {
        alert ("var1 = 1");
        alert ("Congratulations!");
}
```

11. Missing return Statement

The return statement at the end of a function tells JavaScript to exit the function and return to the calling statement—the command line that called the function in the first place. If return is missing, JavaScript proceeds to the end of the function and returns anyway. There's nothing wrong here, assuming the function does not return a value. But if the function returns a value, JavaScript automatically returns a *null*, which is a "blank" result. That could cause other parts of your script to malfunction.

Common (and Some Not So Common) JavaScript Error Messages

This section contains a list of the more common error messages you are likely to run into when working with JavaScript, as well as a brief mention of their causes and cures. The messages are listed in alphabetical order, in two sections: load-time errors (errors that occur when a script is loaded into the browser) and run-time errors (errors that occur when you play a script).

Load-Time Error Messages

These error messages typically appear when an HTML document containing JavaScript is first loaded. The messages are displayed even before the JavaScript code has a chance to run because the JavaScript interpreter in the browser encountered a problem.

break used outside a loop and

continue used outside a loop

JavaScript found a break or continue command outside of a loop (such as for, for/in, or while). These statements can only be used inside a loop.

function defined inside a function

JavaScript does not support "nested functions," that is, placing one function in another, as here:

```
function firstFunction() {
        function secondFunction() {
  ...
```

You must rewrite the code so that each function is separate.

function does not always return a value

JavaScript found one or more return statements in a function that returned a value, and at least one return statement that didn't return anything. For example, the following lines result in an error:

```
function myBadFunction (val)  {
        if (val==0)
                return;
  else
                return ("some text")
  }
```

To fix this error, make sure all of the return statements are the same. All should return either something or nothing.

identifier is a reserved word

You tried to name a variable or object with a word that is reserved by JavaScript. Some words are reserved because they are used by JavaScript as names for statements, functions, methods, or objects. And some words are reserved for future use by JavaScript, even though they are not currently in use.

For example, the name *int* is reserved for future use (as of Netscape 2.0). Using int as the name of a variable results in the "identifier is a reserved word" error:

```
int = "this is a test";
```

Note that misuse of many of JavaScript's currently used statements and other keywords can result in other errors. For example, the following line:

```
for = "this is a test";
```

results in the error "missing (after for." Therefore, you cannot count on a single error message to let you know if you've used a reserved word for a variable or object.

missing (after for

missing (before condition

missing (before formal parameters

missing) after argument list

missing) after condition

missing) after constructor argument list

missing) after for-loop control

missing) after formal parameters

missing) in parenthetical

These errors occur when you've forgotten to add the appropriate opening or closing parenthesis in your JavaScript code. For example, the "missing) after for-loop control" error occurs with the following:

```
for (Count=1; Count<100; Count++ {
```

missing : in conditional expression

You've used the ? shorthand conditional expression but forgot the colon (:) to separate the true and false results, both of which are mandatory. The following code works:

```
color="blue";
        (color=="blue") ? alert ("is blue") : alert ("is not blue");
```

But this code results in an error:

```
color="blue";
(color=="blue") ? alert ("is blue");
```

missing ; after for-loop condition and

missing ; after for-loop initializer

The for statement is missing one or more semicolons (;) to separate its arguments. This error typically occurs when you've used commas instead of semicolons—a typical mistake because JavaScript uses commas as an argument separator for everything but the for loop (the syntax of the JavaScript for loop comes from C). As an example, this results in an error:

```
for (Count, Count<10, Count++) {
```

missing] in index expression

You see this error if you've forgotten to add the closing bracket when referring to an index of an array:

```
myArray = new Array (10);
        myArray[1] = "test";
        myArray[2 = "another test";
```

missing { before function body

missing } after function body

missing } in compound statement

These errors occur when you forget to add the requisite brace either for a function or as part of a compound statement (with, if, for, for/in, while). For instance, in the following you need a } to close out the for loop.

```
for (Count=1; Count<10; Count++) {
                varOne=1;
                varTwo=2;
```

missing exponent

missing formal parameter

missing function name

missing operand in expression

missing operator in expression

missing semicolon before statement

missing variable name

JavaScript has determined that you are missing a critical portion of code. The missing portion is noted in the error message. However, note that JavaScript may misinterpret the code, telling you something is missing when in fact it's really there. This occurs when there are other syntax errors in the code, and JavaScript cannot properly parse the program.

To fix the error, either provide the missing piece (it might be a line above or below the actual error), or repair the syntax error so that JavaScript can properly parse your program.

nested comment

JavaScript doesn't like you to nest /* multiline comments. The following results in an error. To fix the error remove the second /*.

```
/* this is a test /* of a nested comment*/
```

out of memory

In practical terms, this is a rare error message that says JavaScript is out of memory and cannot perform any more actions. But it can happen in certain types of scripts that create lots of string objects. A typical example is the scrolling "marquee" used to move a train of characters across the screen or status bar. The better-written marquees do not exhibit a serious "out of memory" problem; but because of code-cleanup bugs in JavaScript, continued use of the script will eventually lead to a memory failure.

return used outside a function

The return statement is limited to use inside a function. The following lines result in an error:

```
function myFunction () {

        ...

}
return;
```

*stack overflow in **xyz***

A stack overflow is typically caused when you've repeatedly called the same function from within an "infinite loop" function, as here:

```
function test () {
        test();
}
```

JavaScript loops through about 400–500 times before it runs out of "stack space" and returns the error.

syntax error

This is JavaScript's generic error message. It appears if JavaScript detects a syntax problem with the script but cannot determine precisely what it is, usually because the code leaves JavaScript in an unknown state. The error message also appears where there is no specific message for the error. For example, an incomplete assignment such as the following triggers the "syntax error" message:

```
ThisResultsInAnError=;
```

test for equality (==) mistyped as assignment (=)? Assuming equality test

JavaScript uses double equals signs when testing for equality, such as in an if or while expression. This error occurs if you use only one equals sign:

```
if (color="blue")
```

Fix the problem by adding a second equals sign. You can expect to make this error frequently if you are used to Basic or a similar programming language that uses single equals signs for equality expressions.

this used outside a function

The this statement is limited to use inside a function. The following lines result in an error:

```
function myFunction () {

                ...

}
test.propery = property;
```

unterminated comment

JavaScript likes to see a */ pair for every /* pair when defining comments. This results in an error:

```
/*this is an unterminated comment
```

To fix the problem, add a */ to complete the comment. Note that the // form of comment automatically terminates at the end of the line (marked by a hard return in the JavaScript code).

unterminated string literal

This is a common problem, caused when you forget to append a " or ' character to end a string literal, as here:

```
NameOfMyCat="Santana
```

Fix the error by adding a " (or ', as needed) quotation mark to complete the string literal.

This error also occurs if the string you've defined in your script in Netscape 2.x is too long (over 254 characters). To fix this error, you'll need to break up the string into smaller chunks and assemble it in this manner:

```
MyString = "first part ";
MyString += "second part ";
MyString += "third part";
```

Each separate string assignment should be 254 or fewer characters long. There is virtually no limit to the overall length of the string you define in this way.

Run-Time Error Messages

In the following error messages, *xyz* denotes variable text that JavaScript provides, such as a function or variable name. These errors typically occur only at run-time, that is, after the script has been loaded and code is executed.

▇▇▇▇▇ **NOTE**

Because of a quirk in JavaScript, the "xyz" identifier does not always appear in the error message. For example, instead of saying "myObject cannot be indexed as an array," the error message simply says, "cannot be indexed as an array." These error messages are not very useful, because determining the fault in the script can be hard. Fortunately, JavaScript does provide the number of the approximate line that contains the error, which can help in tracking down the source of a problem.

▇▇▇▇▇

xyz cannot be incremented or

xyz cannot be decremented

This error is generally caused when you try to increment or decrement a non-number value.

xyz cannot be deleted

This message appears when you attempt to delete an object (using the undocumented delete function) that is either a string or does not exist.

xyz cannot be indexed as an array

Only objects can be indexed as an array, and this error typically occurs when you attempt to use a non-object as an array (the error also occurs if you attempt to use an array not supported by a given object, such as *document.elements[0]*). The following results in an error because window.length is a "single-ended" property, and not an object (it has no properties dependent on it).

```
alert (window.length[0]);
```

However, the following does work because a number of properties are contained in the document object, and the array index values access each of the available properties:

```
alert (document[0]);
```

xyz cannot be set by assignment

The value of most of the built-in objects (built-in as opposed to ones you create) cannot be set by assignment. For instance, the following is a no-no:

```
document="test";
```

xyz cannot be used in a with statement

This error indicates you've attempted to use an object with the with statement, and the with statement is not supported for that object. Typically this occurs when you've misspelled the name of an object and JavaScript can't find it. For instance, the following script results in an error because the name of the text box is "textbox1," not "textbox."

```
<HTML><HEAD>
<TITLE>This is a test</TITLE>
<SCRIPT LANGUAGE="JavaScript">
function test () {
        with (document.forms[0].textbox) {
                alert (value);
        }
}
</SCRIPT>
</HEAD>
<BODY>
<FORM NAME="testform">
<INPUT TYPE="button" NAME="button1" VALUE="Start" onClick="test(this.form)"><P>
<INPUT TYPE="text" NAME="textbox1"><P>
</FORM>
</BODY></HTML>
```

xyz has no properties

The object you've referenced has no properties. This is a common error and usually the result of misusing objects. This error would be displayed, for example, if you wrote the line:

```
alert (parent.frame1.form.textbox.value);
```

Forms are a property of documents, and the document object is missing from the object/property hierarchy. The correct syntax is:

```
alert (parent.frame1.document.form.textbox.value);
```

xyz is not a constructor

You see this error message if you try to use the new keyword with an object that you can't "instantiate" (create a new instance, or copy, of). For example, the error message appears in the following because you cannot use the new statement to create a new window object:

```
test = new window;
```

xyz is not a function

You typically see this error when you try to use a JavaScript object, method, or property as a function. Note that there is some inconsistency in the terminology used by JavaScript. JavaScript supports a number of statements called functions: these include eval, parseInt, and parseFloat. These are functions because they are not connected to any object (if they were, they'd be called methods).

However, JavaScript also considers many methods to be functions because they alter an object in some way and return the change to the object. This error message is most common when you attempt to use a method for an object that does not support that method.

For example, the click() method is used with several form objects, notably push buttons, checkboxes, and radio buttons. The following line results in a "is not a function" error message because the click() method cannot be used with a string:

```
"my string".click();
```

xyz is not a numeric literal

This error occurs when you attempt to use a non-numeric value as a number. For example, JavaScript cannot complete the expression on the third line because it cannot multiply a number by a text string.

```
var1 = 1;
var2="gordon";
newvar = var1 * var2;
```

xyz is not defined

This error occurs when your JavaScript code references a variable or object that does not exist. For example, you would see the error if you wrote the following two lines of code. Note that the assigned variable is Test, whereas the variable used with the alert method is Text.

```
Test="This is a test;
alert (Text);
```

Another common mistake is to use the wrong capitalization when referring to variables and objects. This code results in an error, even though the variable name is spelled correctly:

```
Test="This is a test;
alert (test);
```

15

USING JAVASCRIPT IN

FRAMES

Netscape 2.0 ushered in a bevy of new concepts to World Wide Web browsers. These include JavaScript, Java, plug-ins, and a feature called frames. Frames let you divide a window into sections–like frames in a window–and view different documents in each frame. Frames offer far-reaching potential. With frames you can:

- Display a table of contents and the body text both at the same time
- Allow users to navigate your pages while the position of the "control panel" remains static on the screen
- Show "before" and "after" documents, allowing users to scroll through each one independently for comparison
- Provide a list of links and have those links appear in another frame
- Continuously display a company name, logo, Java applet, plug-in, or other special element

Frames appear simple, but are actually quite complex, even to the point of being dumbfounding. To learn more about frames than is covered in this book, you should read the relevant documentation at the Netscape Web site, work through the various tutorials on frames located throughout the Web, or find an advanced book on Netscape.

This chapter is dedicated to using JavaScript in concert with frames. JavaScript reserves a special relationship with frames, and proper integration of the two takes patience and a little bit of know-how.

Overview of the Frameset Document Structure

Frames begin with a frameset document. This is the document that defines the layout of the frames and specifies which documents go into which frames. Unless you use an obtuse method (described later in this chapter), Netscape does not allow you to create a frameset *and* populate the frames with content all in the same document. Though you can define a frameset document with just one frame, most of the time you'll create documents with two or more frames.

Netscape has a practical limit of no more than about two dozen frames in any one window–memory gets tight after that. However, from the user's standpoint, a window should not contain more than six to eight frames, or the content becomes too crowded.

Here is a basic frameset document. The frames are defined within <FRAMESET> tags; content between <NOFRAME> tags is ignored by Netscape and other frame-capable browsers (such as Microsoft Internet Explorer 3.0), but is picked up by the others. This document creates the frame output seen in Figure 15.1.

```
<HTML>
<TITLE>Frame Example</TITLE>

<FRAMESET COLS="20%, *">
  <FRAME SRC="frame1.htm" NAME="frame1">
  <FRAME SRC="frame2.htm" NAME="frame2">
</FRAMESET>

<NOFRAME>
```

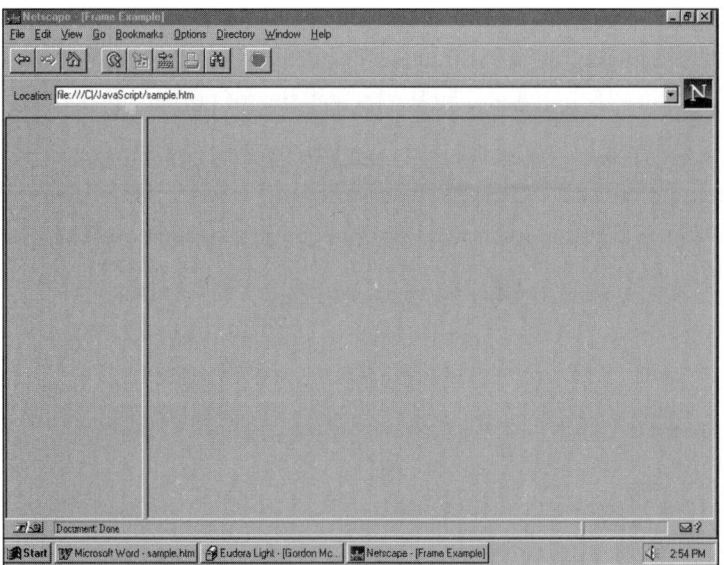

Figure 15.1 Frames allow you to subdivide the window into two or more components. Each frame is a "porthole" that can display a different document.

If you see this text, you're not using a browser with frames:

```
</NOFRAME>
</HTML>
```

Notice the <FRAME> tags. These specify the source (SRC=) of the documents you want to display in the frames, as well as provide unique names for each frame. Names are necessary when you are using frames with JavaScript. Valid frame names contain only alphanumeric characters and the underscore (_), but nothing else (including spaces).

Understanding the Frameset Window Hierarchy

Each frame is considered a separate window. These frame windows are considered subordinate to the main window, which contains the frameset. You can't directly see the content of the frameset document, but it's there nonetheless. For maximum flexibility, JavaScript uses a hierarchy to define these windows. It begins with the frameset window, which is called the *parent*. The individual frame windows are *child* windows, and they are called by the names given in the frameset document—such as "frame1" and "frame2." Refer to Figure 15.2 for a graphical representation of the parent-child frame relationship.

Keep this hierarchy in mind because you need it when writing JavaScript that refers to the frameset (parent, also called top-level) window or another frame window. The syntax is fairly straightforward:

```
parent.framename
```

where *framename* is the name of the frame window. Here are some examples:

```
parent.frame1    // refers to the frame1 window
parent.frame2    // refers to the frame2 window
parent // refers to the frameset (parent) window
```

You still use the *window* or *self* object names when writing JavaScript that refers to the current window. The current window is considered to be the same as the window that contains the JavaScript code currently running. That is, if the JavaScript code is

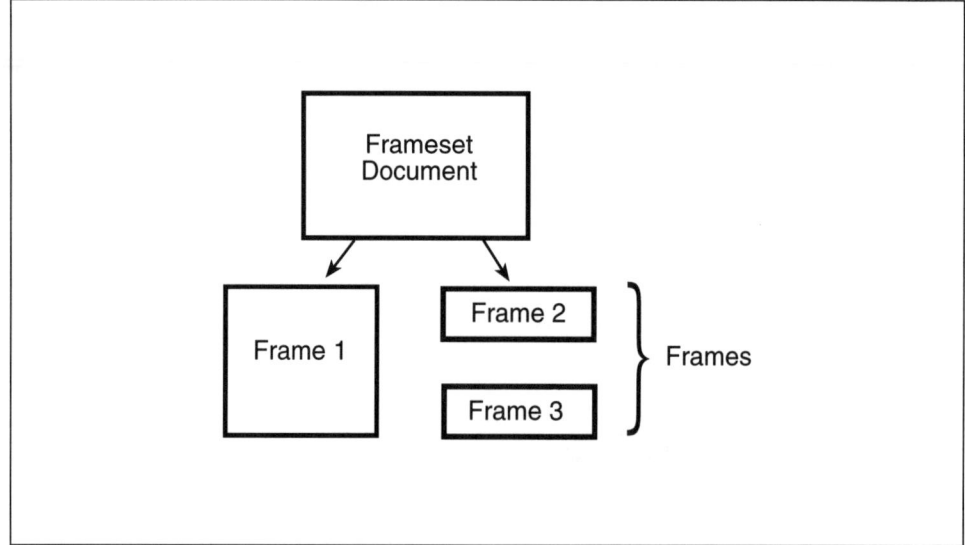

■■■■■ **Figure 15.2** All frames require a parent document and one or more child documents. The child documents each fill a different frame in Netscape's window.

in frame1 and it does something in frame1, then there's no reason to use the parent.framex approach. Simply refer to the window in the usual manner, as in:

```
window.location = "newURL";
```

or simply:

```
location = "newURL"      // current window implied
```

■■■■■■■ **NOTE**

> Using nested frames, you can have "grandchild" windows subordinate to child frame windows. That is, the hierarchy is:
>
> parent.child.grandchild
>
> - *child* is the name of a child frame window under the frameset (parent) window.
> - *grandchild* is the name of a subordinate child frame window under the child frame window.
>
> While both Netscape and JavaScript support nested frames, they can be difficult. Consider avoiding nested frames as much as possible, and try to devise a layout of frames using a single "generation" of parent and kids.

■■■■■■■

Other Supported Frame Reference Styles

JavaScript supports other variations of frame references, such as using the frames[] array and following this syntax:

```
parent.frames['framename'];
```

where *framename* is the name of a frame.

Another alternative is:

```
parent.frames[x];
```

where *x* refers to a frame specified in the frameset document. Counting starts at 0, so the first frame defined is frames[0], the second is frames[1], and so forth.

Note that these types of references are provided for your information; this book uses the frame reference described in the previous section.

Practicing with Frames and JavaScript

There's no better way to learn the basics of frames and JavaScript than to practice with them. Below are two documents: a frameset document and a control document. The frameset defines a window divided into four frames. The control document is loaded into the upper-left frame and is used to experiment with different ways of frame referencing. The other three frames are filled with an empty document called *dummy.htm*.

Note that each of the frames in the frameset document is currently named: frame1, frame2, frame3, and frame4. You can use any names you like, as long as the names conform to the requirements described earlier in the chapter. Providing names that describe the function of the frame, such as "control" or "output," is a good idea.

Here is the frameset document:

CD-ROM

practice_frameset.html

```
<HTML>
<HEAD>
<TITLE>Framer</TITLE>
</HEAD>
<FRAMESET ROWS="*, 20%">
<FRAMESET COLS="20%, *">
<FRAME NAME="frame1" SRC="practice.htm">
<FRAME NAME="frame2" SRC="dummy.htm">
</FRAMESET>
<FRAMESET COLS="30%, *">
<FRAME NAME="frame3" SRC="dummy.htm">
<FRAME NAME="frame4" SRC="dummy.htm">
</FRAMESET>
</FRAMESET>
```

```
</HTML>
```

Here is the control document:

practice.htm

```
<SCRIPT>
function checkFrame (FrameNum) {
        if (FrameNum == 1) alert (parent.frame1.name); else
        if (FrameNum == 2) alert (parent.frame2.name); else
        if (FrameNum == 3) alert (parent.frame3.name); else
        if (FrameNum == 4) alert (parent.frame4.name)
}


function writeFrame (FrameNum) {
        if (FrameNum == 2) parent.frame2.document.write
        ("This is frame 2<BR>"); else
        if (FrameNum == 3) parent.frame3.document.write
        ("This is frame 3<BR>"); else
        if (FrameNum == 4) parent.frame4.document.write
        ("This is frame 4<BR>")
}


function clearFrames() {
        for (Count = 1; Count <4; Count++) {
                parent.frames[Count].document.close();
                parent.frames[Count].document.open();
                parent.frames[Count].document.writeln("");
        }
}


</SCRIPT>

<FORM>
Check Name:<BR>
<INPUT TYPE="button" VALUE="Frame1" onClick="checkFrame(1)"><BR>
```

```
<INPUT TYPE="button" VALUE="Frame2" onClick="checkFrame(2)"><BR>
<INPUT TYPE="button" VALUE="Frame3" onClick="checkFrame(3)"><BR>
<INPUT TYPE="button" VALUE="Frame4" onClick="checkFrame(4)"><P>

Write to frame: <BR>
<INPUT TYPE="button" VALUE="Frame2" onClick="writeFrame(2)"><BR>
<INPUT TYPE="button" VALUE="Frame3" onClick="writeFrame(3)"><BR>
<INPUT TYPE="button" VALUE="Frame4" onClick="writeFrame(4)"><P>

<INPUT TYPE="button" VALUE="Clear All" onClick="clearFrames()"><P>
</FORM>
```

Load the frameset document into Netscape; your window should look like the one in Figure 15.3. Click each of the four buttons under Check Name. Each button displays the name of a frame. This name is not hardcoded into the script; rather, it is retrieved using the syntax:

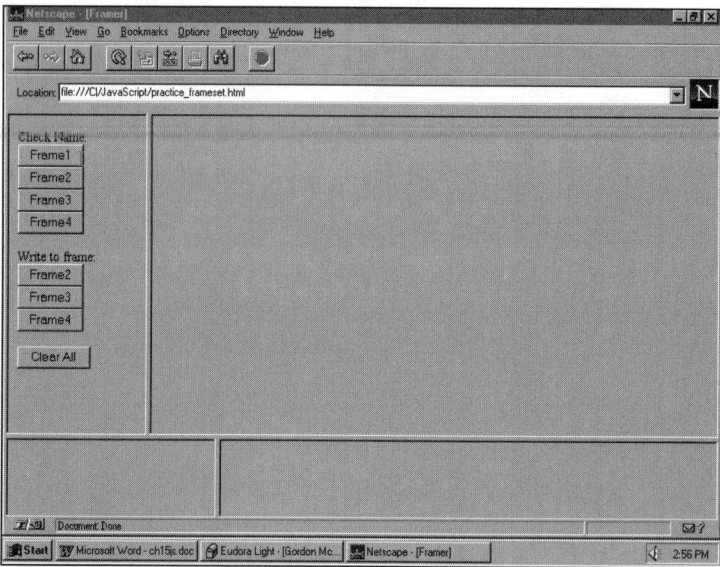

■■■■■■ **Figure 15.3** The frame demonstrator helps you experiment with using JavaScript and frames. Buttons allow you to retrieve values from frames and write content to frames.

```
alert (parent.framex.name)
```

where *x* is one of the frame numbers (1 through 4).

- *parent* is the frameset document.
- *framex* is the frame window being referenced.
- *name* is the name property for that window.

Now click one of the three buttons under Write to a frame (a button for frame1 is not provided, as writing to this frame would erase the buttons!). A line of text is inserted into each frame. This task is performed with the instruction:

```
parent.framex.document.write ("This is frame x<BR>")
```

where *x* is one of the frame numbers (1 through 4). This demonstrates passing data (in this case, text) to frames.

- *parent* is the frameset document.
- *framex* is the frame window being referenced.
- *document* is the document property for that window.
- *write* is the method used to insert text into the frame.

You can clear the text in all three frames by clicking the Clear All button. This executes the following bit of code. Note that a frames array is used rather than separate frame names.

```
function clearFrames() {
        for (Count = 1; Count <4; Count++) {
                parent.frames[Count].document.close();
                parent.frames[Count].document.open();
                parent.frames[Count].document.writeln("");
        }
}
```

This code demonstrates how to manipulate frames with document methods and how to reference frames using the frames[] array.

- *parent* is the frameset document.
- *frames[]* is the frames array.
- *document* is the document property for that window.

- *close*, *open*, and *writeln* are methods for the frame window document, and act to clear the window.

Each element of the frames[] array contains one frame. Counting starts at 0 for the first frame, then goes to 1 for the second frame, and so forth. In order not to clear the control frame, counting in this example started at 1 (the control frame is 0), and continued to 3. The script clears the specified frame with each loop.

Another Example of Frames and JavaScript

The calendar.htm frameset is a more practical example of using framesets and frames: this project is a perpetual calendar created using frames, tables, and JavaScript. This frameset creates two frames: a smaller control frame on the left and a larger output frame on the right. As in the previous example, the output frame is just a blank document created with the *dummy.htm* file.

Here is the *calendar.htm* frameset document:

CD-ROM

```
calendar.htm
```

```
<HTML>
<TITLE>Calendar</TITLE>

<FRAMESET COLS="150, *">
<FRAME SRC="cal_ctrl.htm" NAME="cal_ctrl" MARGINWIDTH=1 NORESIZE NOSCROLL>
<FRAME SRC="cal_res.htm" NAME="cal_res" NORESIZE MARGINWIDTH=1>
</FRAMESET>
</FRAMESET>


<NOFRAME>
This calendar requires Netscape 2.0 or better.
</NOFRAME>
<HEAD>
</HEAD>
</HTML>
```

In this example, extra frameset options were used to make the frames non-resizable and the margin width was reduced to 1, the smallest allowable. The margin width removes the extra space Netscape automatically places inside the frame; that means the content can be placed right to the borders of the frame. An example of the calendar is shown in Figure 15.4.

Here is the *cal_ctrl.htm* document:

CD-ROM

cal_ctrl.htm

```
<HTML>
<HEAD>
<SCRIPT LANGUAGE="JavaScript">

function selectCurrent () {
        var now = new Date();
        var Year = now. getYear() - 95;
        var Month = now.getMonth();
```

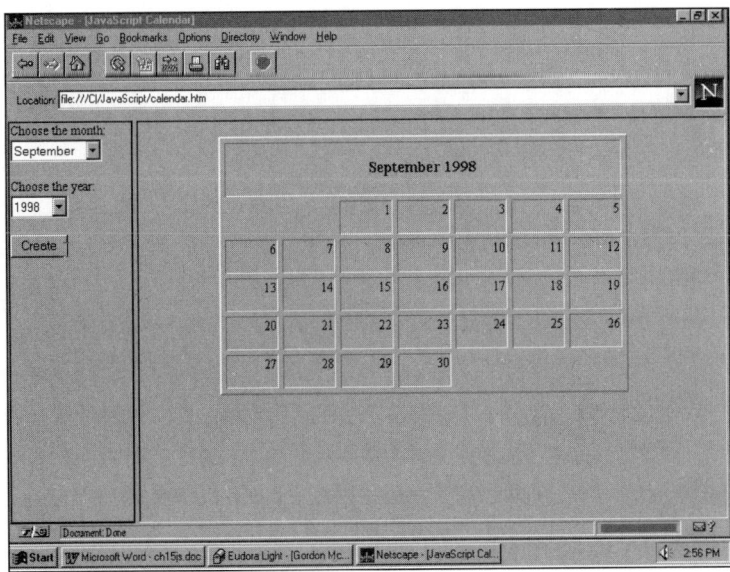

Figure 15.4 *Calendar.htm* produces a framed document displaying a perpetual calendar. Choose the month and the year, and the calendar is created for you.

```
            document.calendar_control.month.selectedIndex = Month;

            document.calendar_control.year.selectedIndex = Year;

            doCal (document.calendar_control);

    }


    function doCal (form) {

            var ret=calendar (form.month.selectedIndex, form.year.selectedIndex);

            var doc = parent.frames.cal_res.document;

            doc.close ();

            doc.open ("text/html");

            var result=fetchText (ret)

            doc.write (result)

            doc.close();

    }


    function calendar (SelMonth, SelYear) {

            var Month=SelMonth+1

            var Year=SelYear+1995

            var ret=getDaysofYear(Year);

            var Days=ret[Month];

            var firstOfMonth = new Date (Year, Month-1, 1);

            var StartingPos=firstOfMonth.getDay();

            var retVal= new Object();

            retVal[1]=StartingPos;

            retVal[2]=Days;

            retVal[3]=Month;

            retVal[4]=Year;

            return  (retVal);

    }


    function leapYear (Year) {

            if (((Year % 4)==0) && ((Year % 100)!=0) || ((Year % 400)==0))

                    return (1);

            else
```

```
                return (0);
}


function getDaysofYear (Year)   {
        if (leapYear (Year)==1)
                Leap=29;
        else
                Leap=28;
        var daysOfYear = new Object();
        daysOfYear[1] = 31; daysOfYear[2] = Leap; daysOfYear[3] = 31;
        daysOfYear[4] = 30;
        daysOfYear[5] = 31; daysOfYear[6] = 30; daysOfYear[7] = 31;
        daysOfYear[8] = 31;
        daysOfYear[9] = 30; daysOfYear[10] = 31; daysOfYear[11] = 30;
        daysOfYear[12] = 31;
        return (daysOfYear);
}


function fetchText (InArray)   {
        var Month;
        var Year=""+InArray[4];
        if (InArray[3]==1) Month="January";
        if (InArray[3]==2) Month="February";
        if (InArray[3]==3) Month="March";
        if (InArray[3]==4) Month="April";
        if (InArray[3]==5) Month="May";
        if (InArray[3]==6) Month="June";
        if (InArray[3]==7) Month="July";
        if (InArray[3]==8) Month="August";
        if (InArray[3]==9) Month="September";
        if (InArray[3]==10) Month="October";
        if (InArray[3]==11) Month="November";
        if (InArray[3]==12) Month="December";
        var result='<HTML><HEAD><TITLE>Calendar</TITLE></HEAD>'
        result+='<BODY>'
```

```
        result+='<BR><CENTER>'
        result+='<TABLE BORDER=2 CELLSPACING=5>'
        result+='<TH COLSPAN="7" VALIGN="center"><BR><BIG>'+Month+'    '+Year
        result+='</BIG><P></TH>'
        var CellKeeper=0
        var Digit=1
        var CountRow;
        for (CountRow = 1; CountRow <=6; CountRow++)   {
                result+='<TR ALIGN="right" VALIGN="top">'
                for (CountColumn = 1; CountColumn <=7; CountColumn++)   {
                        if (CellKeeper<InArray[1])
                                result+='<TD></TD>'
                        else   {
                                result+='<TD><DD>' + Digit + '<P></TD>'
                                Digit++
                        }
                        if (Digit<=InArray[2])
                                CellKeeper++
                        else
                                break;
                }
                result+='</TR>'
                if (Digit>InArray[2])
                        break;
        }
        result+='</TABLE><CENTER>'
        result+='</BODY></HTML>'
        return (result);
}

</SCRIPT>
</HEAD>
<BODY onLoad="selectCurrent()">
<FORM NAME="calendar_control">
```

```
Choose the month:<BR>
<SELECT NAME="month">
<OPTION>January
<OPTION>February
<OPTION>March
<OPTION>April
<OPTION>May
<OPTION>June
<OPTION>July
<OPTION>August
<OPTION>September
<OPTION>October
<OPTION>November
<OPTION>December
</SELECT><P>
Choose the year: <BR>
<SELECT NAME="year">
<OPTION>1995
<OPTION>1996
<OPTION>1997
<OPTION>1998
<OPTION>1999
<OPTION>2000
</SELECT><P>
<INPUT TYPE="button" NAME="button1" VALUE="Create" onClick="doCal(this.form)">
</FORM>
</BODY>
</HTML>
```

The HTML portion of this document creates a form with a button and two lists. One list displays the months of the year; the other list displays the years 1995 to 2000. A series of JavaScript functions go about creating the calendar:

- The *selectCurrent* function selects the current month and year in the list boxes. This function is called in the document's onLoad event handler. The calendar for the current month is initially displayed when the document is loaded.

- The *doCal* function is called to generate a new calendar. It is called when the document is first loaded and when the user clicks the form button.

- The *calendar*, *leapYear*, *getDaysofYear*, and *fetchText* functions create the actual calendar.

The entire contents of the output window are written by the control script. This process involves creating the table and filling it with numbers; each number is placed in the correct table cell for the given month.

Running Script in Another Frame

Including JavaScript in two or more of the documents loaded into frame windows is not uncommon. For example, you might have an overall control frame with JavaScript contained in it, and use another frame for navigation chores. The scripts in each frame sometimes need to communicate with one another, which is possible in JavaScript.

Here's the scenario. You have code in frame2 that you want to access from code in frame1. You can't simply call the function, as JavaScript won't see it–the "scope" of the function is outside the current window. In order to use the function in the other frame, you must provide the required parent.frame hierarchy.

Suppose the function name is doIt, and the frame name is frame2. In frame1 you call the function with:

```
parent.frame1.doIt();
```

The process is similar if you want to access a function in the frameset (parent) window (such scripts should be included *before* the frameset tags). The syntax for accessing the doIt function in the parent is simply:

```
parent.doIt();
```

Accessing a Variable in Another Frame

Akin to accessing a function in another frame is accessing a variable defined in another frame (or more accurately, in a document loaded into that frame).

To retrieve the value of a variable defined in another frame, use the syntax:

```
Ret = parent.framename.varname;
```

- *Ret* is the return variable you want to use in the local (current) frame.
- *framename* is the name of the frame.
- *varname* is the name of the variable. The variable can contain a numeric, a string, a Boolean, or an object.

To retrieve the value of a variable defined in the parent frameset, use the syntax:

```
Ret = parent.varname;
```

Setting Variables Across Frames

To set the value of a variable originally defined in another frame, use the syntax:

```
parent.frameneme.varname = new_value;
```

new_value can be a string, a numeric, a Boolean, or an object.

To set the value of a variable originally defined in the parent frameset, use the syntax:

```
parent.varname = new_value;
```

Overcoming a Nasty Cross-Frame JavaScript Bug

Bill Dortch, of hIdaho Design, is one of the early pioneers of using JavaScript with frames. He encountered–and overcame–a number of bugs in Netscape 2.0 related to the combination. His solution to a problem caused by sharing a string variable between frames is outlined here.

In this situation, if the framed document that has set a variable in the parent frameset or another frame is unloaded, the value in that variable can become corrupted. A document is unloaded for a variety of reasons, including loading a new document in that frame or reloading the same document in the frame because the frame has been resized.

For example, suppose you have a frameset with two frames, frame1 and frame2. In frame1 is the following function, which is intended to set a string variable in the document for that frame:

```
var myVariable;
```

```
function setVar (value) {
        myVariable = value;
}
```

Then in frame2, you have:

```
parent.frame1.setVar ("This var is set from frame2");
```

If the document in frame2 is unloaded, the value in myVariable can become cor-rupted. The workaround is to change the setVar function to explicitly recast the value to a string, thus creating a whole new string object variable:

```
var myVariable;
function setVar (value) {
        myVariable = "" + value;
}
```

■■■■■■ **NOTE**

This technique is not required when you are setting numeric or Boolean vari-able types because the bug does not affect these variable types. For vari-ables that contain objects, your best bet is to avoid resetting the content of an object variable from another frame.

■■■■■■

"Lost" Variables on Reloads

Netscape 2.0 loses all JavaScript variables when a window is reloaded. This applies to standalone windows and any window in a frameset. The problem is particularly troublesome when using frames because only one frame may reload, while the others remain the same. This can be a problem if the reloaded frame contains variables that are needed in your script.

The following events cause a reload of one or more frames:

- Clicking the reload buttons (frameset and all frames reloaded)
- Choosing View, Reload (frameset and all frames reloaded)
- Retyping the URL of the frameset in the Location box (frameset and all frames reloaded)

- Resizing the overall window (frameset and all frames reloaded)
- Changing the size of a frame border with the mouse (surrounding frames reloaded)

The last item can be "fixed" by disallowing frame resizing. In the frameset document, specify NORESIZE to prevent the user from changing the size of the frame with the mouse. If you take this approach, be sure the frame is large enough–for all resolutions of the screen–to accommodate its contents.

The remaining items can't be prevented, as these are standard Netscape command options. Rather, you have to develop your JavaScript code to handle reload events. Here are some techniques you can use:

- If you don't need to retain the values of variables, start the script all over again by adding an onLoad event to either the frameset document or the "control" frame document (see "Adding onLoad and onUnload Events to Frames," later in this chapter, for more details).

- If you need to retain the values of variables, you can place the values in a document cookie; a cookie is a file maintained by Netscape for semiperma-nent data storage. Cookies are addressed in Chapter 12, "How Do I?".

- Another method for storage of data is to use "hidden" form text fields. These fields retain their content even if the frameset and frames are loaded. By using hidden fields, you can place the text boxes in a frame you don't show. Or you can "push" the box out of view in a small frame that has been specified as NORESIZE and NOSCROLL. The text box(es) will be out of view. Note that "hidden" form text fields are not the same thing as the hidden type of text fields. Text fields are the regular "visible" kind; they are merely placed out of view of the user. Unfortunately, hidden text fields lose their content when a window is reloaded.

Here's a short example of using the hidden text field approach. The frameset document specifies three documents, one of which is given no space at the bottom of the window. This frame is therefore effectively hidden.

```
<HTML>
<TITLE>Frame Test</TITLE>

<FRAMESET COLS="50%, 50%, *">
   <FRAME SRC="frame1.htm" NAME="frame1">
   <FRAME SRC="frame2.htm" NAME="frame2">
```

```
    <FRAME SRC="frame3.htm" NAME="frame3">
</FRAMESET>

<NOFRAME>
You need a frames-capable browser to view this document.
</NOFRAME>
</HTML>
```

The *frame3.htm* file contains the text box for storing the data. You can use multiple text boxes if you wish.

```
<FORM NAME="storage">
<FORM TYPE="text" NAME="store">
</FORM>
```

Using JavaScript from one of the other frames, you can write to the "store" box with the following:

```
parent.frame3.document.storage.store = "hello";
```

And you can read back the contents, even after a reload event, with:

```
Ret = parent.frame3.document.storage.store;
```

Changing the URL of a Frame

Recall from earlier in the chapter that frames are really windows. The content of a frame is a document, just as the content of the Netscape browser window is a document. Therefore, anything you can do with a document in a "regular" window you can do with frames. This includes changing the document URL of the frame so it shows a different document.

The syntax for changing the URL of a frame is:

```
parent.framename.location = URL;
```

- *framename* is the name of the frame you want to change.
- *URL* is the new URL you want to use. The URL should be *absolute and fully qualified*.

For example, suppose the URL you want to use for the frame is http://mydomain.com/newpage.html and that the name of the frame is "myframe." The instruction is:

```
parent.myframe.location = "http://mydomain.com/newpage.html";
```

You can use the same technique to change the URLs of multiple frames. Just put the parent...location instruction in a function and call the function. For instance, the following code is a "control" script that changes the URL of two other frames in the frameset. These frames are named frame1 and frame2. The function can be called using a link or a button. Both methods are shown. In both cases, the full path for the file is obtained using a pathOnly function; this function chops off the filename of the current document and returns just the path information. The path is used to complete the URL for each file. Alternatively, you can hardcode the complete URL.

Using a form button:

chframe_form.html

CD-ROM

```
<HTML><HEAD>
<SCRIPT LANGUAGE="JavaScript">
function changeFrameUrls() {
        parent.frame1.location = pathOnly(location.href) + "newloc1.html";
        parent.frame2.location = pathOnly(location.href) + "newloc2.html";
}

function pathOnly (InString)   {
        LastSlash=InString.lastIndexOf ('/', InString.length-1)
        OutString=InString.substring  (0, LastSlash+1)
        return (OutString);
}

</SCRIPT>
</HEAD>
<BODY>
<FORM>
```

```
<INPUT TYPE="button" VALUE="Click" onclick="changeFrameUrls()">
</FORM>
</BODY></HTML>
```

Using a link, the code is as follows:

chframe_link.html

```
<HTML><HEAD>
<SCRIPT LANGUAGE="JavaScript">
function changeFrameUrls() {
        parent.frame1.location = pathOnly(location.href) + "newloc1.html";
        parent.frame2.location = pathOnly(location.href) + "newloc2.html";
}

function pathOnly (InString)  {
        LastSlash=InString.lastIndexOf ('/', InString.length-1)
        OutString=InString.substring  (0, LastSlash+1)
        return (OutString);
}

</SCRIPT>
</HEAD>
<BODY>
<A HREF="#" oncClick="changeFrameUrls()">Click Me</A>
</BODY></HTML>
```

Moving Through the History List of a Frame

As each frame is a separate window to Netscape, each frame has a separate history list. The history list contains the URLs of pages you've visited in the current session. As with a regular window, you can use the properties of the history object to go back or forward through the history list for a given frame. This allows you to control the URL for one frame, while not changing the others.

The syntax for using the history list with a frame is:

```
parent.framename.history.go(x)
```

- *framename* is the name of the frame.
- *x* is the number of the URL in the history list with respect to the current URL.

For example, to go back one URL in the history list, use:

```
parent.frame2.history.go (-1);
// or use parent.frame2.history,.back();
```

To go forward, you use:

```
parent.frame2.history.go (1)
// or use parent.frame2.history.forward();
```

To reload the same document in the frame, you use:

```
parent.frame2.history.go (0);
```

▮▮▮▮▮▮▮ **NOTE**

Netscape does nothing if the history list contains no URLs. Only if the history *for that frame* contains a list will the history methods work.

▮▮▮▮

Dynamically Creating a Frameset Document

As JavaScript can generate HTML markup on the fly, you can readily use it to define the frameset of your frames. Because JavaScript is creating the HTML markup as it goes along, you can make the frameset structure as simple or as complex as you wish. The main requirement is that JavaScript must create the entire <FRAMESET> tag structure, not just a portion of it.

The code below is an example of how to create a four-window frameset "on-the-fly," selecting the content of the main frame (frame2) according to the day of the week. Three of the frames (frame1, frame3, and frame4) are filled with the blank *dummy.htm* document. In a working script, you'd exchange these filenames with others. The day-of-the-week files are named *day0.html* through *day6.html*, for Sunday though Saturday. If you load the page on a Wednesday, for example, Netscape uses the file *day3.html* for the main frame.

CD-ROM

dynamic_frameset.html

```
<HTML>
<HEAD>
<TITLE>Dynamic Framer</TITLE>
</HEAD>
<SCRIPT>
<!-
function frameToday() {
        now = new Date();
        Day = now.getDay();
        return ("day" + Day + ".html")
}


Temp = '<FRAMESET ROWS="*,60">'
Temp += '<FRAMESET COLS="135, *">'
Temp += '<FRAME NAME="frame1" SRC="dummy.htm">'
Temp += '<FRAME NAME="frame2" SRC="' + frameToday () + '">'
Temp += '</FRAMESET>'
Temp += '<FRAMESET COLS="44, *">'
Temp += '<FRAME NAME="frame3" SRC="dummy.htm">'
Temp += '<FRAME NAME="frame4" SRC="dummy.htm">'
Temp += '</FRAMESET>'
Temp += '</FRAMESET>'
document.write (Temp)
//-->
</SCRIPT>
<NOFRAMES>
Sorry, you need a frames-compatible browser to view this page.
</NOFRAMES>
</HTML>
```

Loading the "Referring Page" into a Frame

The Web keeps track of which user came from where. When you click on a link in a page, the receiving page is told the URL of where you came from. This is called the document *referrer*. Ordinarily, this is information only a server would use. But JavaScript makes it available to you as well, as a property of the document.referrer property.

By consulting the document.referrer property, you can ascertain where a visitor has come from and display content accordingly (do note that the referrer information must be supplied by the server; if it is not, document.referrer is empty). For example, if the visitor has come from the http://home.netscape.com server, you print a greeting such as "Thanks for clicking on my link from Netscape's home page!"

This technique is marginally practical, though admittedly "cool." A more practical technique is to display the referring page in one of the frames of a frameset. That is, the user can click on a link to your page, and the previous page remains in view. You can use the referrer-frame technique for your own pages as well; the frameset is generic and will work with any of your documents. Here's the code:

CD-ROM

frame_referrer.html

```
<HTML>
<HEAD>
<TITLE>Dynamic Framer</TITLE>
</HEAD>
<SCRIPT>
<!-
function framesReferrer() {
        if (document.referrer == "")
                parent.frame2.location = pathOnly(location.href) +
                "stuff.html"
        else
                parent.frame2.location = document.referrer;
}


function pathOnly (InString)  {
```

```
      LastSlash=InString.lastIndexOf ('/', InString.length-1)

      OutString=InString.substring  (0, LastSlash+1)

      return (OutString);

}


//-->

</SCRIPT>

<FRAMESET ROWS="*,60" onLoad="framesReferrer()">

<FRAMESET COLS="135, *">

<FRAME NAME="frame1" SRC="stuff1.htm">

<FRAME NAME="frame2" SRC="stuff2.htm">

</FRAMESET>

<FRAMESET COLS="44, *">

<FRAME NAME="frame3" SRC="stuff3.">

<FRAME NAME="frame4" SRC="stuff4.htm">

</FRAMESET>

</FRAMESET>


<NOFRAMES>

Sorry, you need a frames-compatible browser to view this page.

</NOFRAMES>

</HTML>
```

Note the framesReferrer function. This function determines if the document.referrer property is blank–which is the case if the user types your URL from the Location box. If it is, then the URL for frame2 (the main frame) is set to "*stuff.htm*", which contains a default page. If the document.referrer property is not blank, JavaScript loads in the referring page, and it's shown in the main frame.

Creating Double-Purpose Frame/No-Frame Pages

If the code in your frame pages references other frames or the parent frameset, you'll probably see a JavaScript error if you try to load these pages by themselves (that is, outside of the frameset). If needed, and if your application supports it, you can create a "double-purpose" document that can be used both with and without frames.

Add the following function to your frame document to determine if it is loaded as part of a frameset or as a standalone document:

```
function usingFrames() {
        return (window.frames.length);
}
```

The function returns 0 if the document is loaded standalone, and some positive value (usually 2 or more) if the document is loaded as part of the frameset. The function returns the number of items in the frames[] array, which is a property of the window object. The length property of this array is 0 if the document does not belong to a frameset, and some other value if it does.

Here's a basic example of using the function:

```
if (usingFrames()) {
        // run this code if the document is in a frame
} else {
        // run this code if the document is not in a frame
}
```

Adding onLoad and onUnload Events to Frames

The onLoad and onUnload events let you execute JavaScript code when a document finishes loading into a window and when it is about to be unloaded, respectively. You can use onLoad and onUnload with frames, as they are really windows. But you must do so with some care–at least for the onLoad event handler, which is the more commonly used. The reason is that, except for the parent frameset document, you can never be sure of the order of frame loading. Suppose your frameset defines three frames. Sometimes they may load in 1, 2, 3 order, but other times they may load in some other order—3, 2, 1 or 2, 1, 3, for example.

This inexact loading sequence becomes a problem if script in one frame depends on the existence of another frame. That frame may not be loaded when the script runs, and you could find yourself staring at an ugly message box. Worse, the error can occur at some times, but not others!

The moral of this story is to use an onLoad event in a frame document only if the script in that document does not depend on another frame document.

But what can you do if your JavaScript code *must* interact with other frames—or even the frameset itself—upon loading? There are a number of ways around this problem. The best may be to simply place an onLoad even handler in the frameset document that starts the process rolling. The frameset is guaranteed to finish loading only after all its sibling frames have been loaded. Therefore, an onLoad event in the frameset occurs only after all documents of the frame have been safely loaded.

Here's an example:

```
<HTML>
<TITLE>Frame Test</TITLE>

<FRAMESET COLS="20%, *" onLoad="alert('I\'m loaded!')">
   <FRAME SRC="frame1.htm" NAME="frame1">
   <FRAME SRC="frame2.htm" NAME="frame2">
</FRAMESET>

<NOFRAME>
You need a frames-capable browser to view this page.
</NOFRAME>
</HTML>
```

Note that the onLoad event is placed in the <FRAMESET> tag, whereas the onLoad event is normally placed in the <BODY> tags of "normal" documents. The <FRAMESET> tag is used for the onLoad handler because the tag replaces the traditional <BODY> tags (in fact, if you put <BODY> tags in a frameset, Netscape ignores the <FRAMESET> tags!).

To trigger an action in another frame, just call it from the frameset. Remember the hierarchy: parent.framename.functionname. The following example calls the initialize function in frame2 after complete loading of the frameset:

```
<HTML>
<TITLE>Frame Test</TITLE>

<FRAMESET COLS="20%, *" onLoad="parent.frame2.initialize()">
  <FRAME SRC="frame1.htm" NAME="frame1">
  <FRAME SRC="frame2.htm" NAME="frame2">
</FRAMESET>

<NOFRAME>
You need a frames-capable browser to view this page.
</NOFRAME>
</HTML>
```

See the following files from the CD-ROM for other examples of using onLoad with frames:

- *animate_frame.html*
- *plugin3_frame.html*
- *slideshow.html*
- *banner_start.html*

The same general rule applies to the onUnload event. This event is triggered when a window is about to be unloaded. As with the onLoad event, there is no rhyme-or-reason to the order of unloading by the child windows. And as with the onLoad event, the parent frameset is unloaded last.

Putting the onUnload handler in the frameset document probably won't help you if you need to process code in one or more of the child frame windows. By the time the onUnload event occurs in the frameset, the child frames have been unloaded and JavaScript is reporting an error. Therefore, avoid code in any frame or frameset document that relies on that document being around when an onUnload event occurs. If necessary, each document can contain its own onUnload event handler in its <BODY> tag to "clean up" for the unloading sequence.

Using the "hIdaho Frameset"

Bill Dortch of hIdaho Design came up with something he called "the hIdaho Frameset," a series of functions to make it easier to work with complex frames, especially nested frames. The set of functions is provided on the CD-ROM as the file *frameset.txt*. Basic documentation for the use of the functions is provided in the file. The frameset functions also allow for more elaborate load-event sequences, if your application requires it (though, in reality, few do).

Bill reworks the frameset functions from time to time. Try the following URL to make sure you have the latest version: http://www.hidaho.com/frameset/.

USING JAVASCRIPT

AND FORMS

JavaScript wears many hats. You can use it to create special effects. You can use it to make your HTML pages "smarter" by using its decision-making capabilities. And you can use it to enhance HTML forms. This last application is of particular importance and merit. Of all the hats JavaScript can wear, its form-processing features are among the most sought and used.

Without JavaScript, forms are pretty much the domain of CGI programs and scripts. You use HTML to create the form, but the form itself is accepted and processed by some program running on the computer. With JavaScript, you can process simple forms without invoking the server. And when submitting the form to a CGI program is necessary, you can have JavaScript take care of all the preliminary requirements, such as validating input.

Using JavaScript with forms is of such importance that there are two chapters on this topic: this chapter and Chapter 18, "Using CGI with JavaScript." This chapter details how to interface a form created with standard HTML tags with

JavaScript, and how to perform tasks such as input validation. Chapter 18 is devoted to the CGI side of things, linking a JavaScript-enhanced form to a CGI program or script that runs on the server.

Creating the Form

There are few differences between a straight HTML form and a JavaScript-enhanced form. The main difference is that a JavaScript form relies on one or more "on..." event handlers. These invoke a JavaScript action when the user does something in the form, such as clicking a button. The "on..." event handlers, which are placed with the rest of the attributes in the <FORM> tags, are invisible to a browser that doesn't support JavaScript. As a result, you can often use one form for both JavaScript and non-JavaScript browsers (though from a support standpoint, creating two different forms is generally a better idea).

Typical form objects include the following (this book calls them "objects" rather than the oft-used "widgets," because that's how JavaScript treats them):

- Text box for entering a line of text
- Push button for selecting an action
- Radio buttons for making one selection among a group of options
- Checkboxes for selecting or deselecting a single, independent option

This chapter does not cover the attributes of these elements or how to use them in HTML. Almost any reference on HTML provides these details.

For use with JavaScript, you should always remember to provide a name for the form itself, and each element (object) you use. The names allow you to reference the objects in your JavaScript program.

Code for a typical form looks like the following example. Notice that NAME= attributes have been provided for all form objects, including the form itself (which is also treated as a JavaScript object):

```
<FORM NAME="myform" ACTION="" METHOD="GET">
Enter something in the box:<BR>
<INPUT TYPE="text" NAME="inputbox" VALUE=""><P>
```

```
<INPUT TYPE="button" NAME="button" Value="Click"
onClick="testResults(this.form)">
</FORM>
```

- *FORM NAME="myform"* defines and names the form. Elsewhere in the JavaScript, you can reference this form by the name *myform*. The name you give your form is up to you, but it should comply with JavaScript's standard variable/function naming rules (no spaces, no weird characters except the underscore, and so on).

- *ACTION=" "* defines how you want the browser to handle the form when it is submitted to a CGI program running on the server. As this form is not designed to submit anything, the typical URL for the CGI program is omitted.

- METHOD="GET" defines that the method data is passed to the server when the form is submitted. As this form is not going to submit anything, in this case the attribute is actually wasted puffery. It's shown here for example purposes.

- *INPUT TYPE="text"* defines the text box object. This is standard HTML markup here.

- *INPUT TYPE="button"* defines the button object. This is standard HTML markup except for the onClick handler.

- *onClick="testResults(this.form)"* is called an event handler—it handles an event, in this case clicking the button. When the button is clicked, JavaScript executes the expression within the quotes. The expression says to call the testResults function elsewhere in the script, and pass to it the current form object (accomplished with the this.form parameter).

Getting a Value from a Form Object

Here's the full script you can try as you experiment obtaining values from form objects. Load the page, then type something into the text box. Click the button, and what you typed is shown in the alert box. The output of this script is shown in Figure 16.1.

testform.html

CD-ROM

```
<HTML>
<HEAD>
```

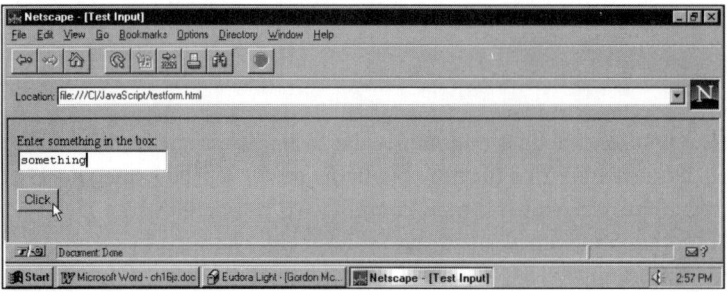

Figure 16.1 The form test input script.

```
<TITLE>Test Input </TITLE>
<SCRIPT LANGUAGE="JavaScript">
function testResults (form) {
        var TestVar = form.inputbox.value;
        alert ("You typed: " + TestVar);
}
</SCRIPT>
</HEAD>
<BODY>
<FORM NAME="myform" ACTION="" METHOD="GET">
Enter something in the box:<BR>
<INPUT TYPE="text" NAME="inputbox" VALUE=""><P>
<INPUT TYPE="button"NAME="button"Value="Click"onClick="testResults(this.form)">
</FORM>
</BODY>
</HTML>
```

Here's how it works. When you click the button, JavaScript calls the testResults function, which is passed the form object. This object has been given the name *form* inside the testResult function, but you can name this object anything you like.

This concept bears repeating in slightly different terms. The onClick="testResults (this.form)" passes the current form to the testResults function. In the testResults function this object goes by the name *form*. You do not use "this.form" within the testResults function because JavaScript won't know what the "this" belongs to.

The function is simple— it merely copies the contents of the text box to a variable named TestVar. Notice how the text box contents were referenced. A form object was defined (called *form*), as well as an object within the form (called *inputbox*), and a property of that object (the *value* property).

```
var TestVar = form.inputbox.value;
```

■■■■■■ **NOTE**

Strictly speaking, you don't have to pass the form object to a function in order to use that object within the function. Because the form is named, you can reference it explicitly as a member of the document object. The following expression has the same effect as the one above:

```
var TestVar = document.myform.inputbox.value;
```

Here's how it breaks down, going from right to left:

- *value* is a property of the inputbox form control.
- *inputbox* is a member of the myform form object.
- *myform* is a member of the current *document*.

■■■■■■

Setting a Value in a Form Object

The value property of the input box, shown in the previous example, is both readable and "writable." That is, you can read whatever somebody types into the box, and you can write data back into it. The process of setting the value in a form object is just the reverse of reading it. Following is a short example to demonstrate. It is similar to the previous example, except that this time there are two buttons, and the buttons have been relabeled. Click the "Read" button and the script reads what you typed into the text box. Click the "Write" button and the script writes a particularly lurid phrase into the text box.

CD-ROM

set-formval.html

```
<HTML>
<HEAD>
```

```
<TITLE>Test Input </TITLE>
<SCRIPT LANGUAGE="JavaScript">
function readText (form) {
        TestVar =form.inputbox.value;
        alert ("You typed: " + TestVar);
}


function writeText (form) {
        form.inputbox.value = "Have a nice day!"
}
</SCRIPT>
</HEAD>
<BODY>
<FORM NAME="myform" ACTION="" METHOD="GET">
Enter something in the box:<BR>
<INPUT TYPE="text" NAME="inputbox" VALUE=""><P>
<INPUT TYPE="button" NAME="button1" Value="Read" onClick="readText(this.form)">
<INPUT TYPE="button" NAME="button2"Value="Write" onClick="writeText(this.form)">
</FORM>
</BODY>
</HTML>
```

- When you click the Read button, JavaScript calls the readText function, which reads and displays the value you entered into the text box.
- When you click the Write button, JavaScript calls the writeText function, which writes (yuk) "Have a nice day!" in the text box.

Reading Other Form Object Values

The text box is perhaps the most common form object you'll read (or write) using JavaScript. However, you can use JavaScript to read and write values these form objects as well :

- Hidden text box (TYPE="hidden")
- Radio button (TYPE="radio")

- Check box (TYPE="checkbox")
- Text area (<TEXT AREA>)
- Lists (<SELECT>)

■■■■■■■ **NOTE**

In Netscape 2.0, JavaScript cannot be used to read or write data using the password style of text box.

■■■■■■

Using Hidden Text Boxes

From a JavaScript standpoint, hidden text boxes behave just like regular text boxes, sharing the same properties and methods. From a user standpoint, hidden text boxes "don't exist" because they do not appear in the form. Rather, hidden text boxes are the means by which special information can be passed between server and client. They can also be used to hold temporary data that you might want to use later.

For server/client communications, the server can send data to the client, storing a special value in a hidden field that the user doesn't see. For example, the value might be the number of times the user has submitted a form in the same session. If it's more than say, five times, the server knows not to accept any more entries from that user. The submission count is stored in a hidden field.

Hidden fields are particularly handy for storing temporary data that your JavaScript program may need. Store the data in a hidden field, and it stays as long as the document remains loaded. (However, note that the contents of hidden fields are lost when a document or frame is reloaded or resized.)

Using Radio Buttons

Radio buttons are used to allow the user to select one, *and only one*, item from a group of options. Radio buttons are always used in multiples; there is no logical sense in having just one radio button on a form. After you click on it, you can't unclick it. If you want a simple click/unclick choice, use a checkbox instead.

To define radio buttons for JavaScript, provide each object with the same name. JavaScript creates an array of buttons out of them; you then reference the buttons using the array indexes. The first button in the series is numbered 0, the second is numbered 1, and so forth. Note that the VALUE attribute is optional for JavaScript-only forms. You'll want to provide a value if you submit the form to a CGI program running on the server, however.

```
<INPUT TYPE="radio" NAME="rad" VALUE="radio-button1" onClick=0>
<INPUT TYPE="radio" NAME="rad" VALUE="radio-button2" onClick=0>
<INPUT TYPE="radio" NAME="rad" VALUE="radio-button3" onClick=0>
<INPUT TYPE="radio" NAME="rad" VALUE="radio-button4" onClick=0>
```

■■■■■ NOTE

The onClick event handler in this markup acts as a work-around for a bug in Netscape 2.0. Without the onClick event handler, JavaScript returns the buttons in reverse order: 3, 2, 1, 0—instead of the proper 0, 1, 2, 3. The onClick handler does nothing, as its value is set to 0.

■■■■■

Following is an example of testing which button is selected. The for loop in the testButton function cycles through all of the buttons in the "rad" group. When it finds the button that's selected, it breaks out of the loop and displays the button number (remember: starting from 0).

CD-ROM

form-radio.html

```
<HTML>
<HEAD>
<TITLE>Radio Button Test</TITLE>
<SCRIPT LANGUAGE="JavaScript">
function testButton (form){
        for (Count = 0; Count < 3; Count++) {
                if (form.rad[Count].checked)
                        break;
        }
```

```
            alert ("Button " + Count + " is selected");
   }
</SCRIPT>
</BODY>
<FORM NAME="testform">
<INPUTTYPE="button "NAME="button" Value="Click"onClick="testButton(this.form)"><BR>
<INPUT TYPE="radio" NAME="rad" Value="rad—button1" onClick=0><BR>
<INPUT TYPE="radio" NAME="rad" Value="rad—button2" onClick=0><BR>
<INPUT TYPE="radio" NAME="rad" Value="rad—button3" onClick=0><BR>
</FORM>
</HTML>
```

> If you want to have more than one set of radio buttons in your form, just
> give them different names. For example, the first group of buttons might
> be named "rad1" and the second "rad2." The browser lets you select a
> button from each group.

Setting a radio button selection is even easier. If you want the form to initially appear
with a given radio button selected, just add the CHECKED attribute to the HTML
markup for that button:

```
<INPUT TYPE="radio" NAME="rad" Value="rad—button1" CHECKED onClick=0><BR>
```

You can also set the button selection programmatically with JavaScript, using the
checked property (there is also a selected property, but it is not properly functioning
on all platforms supported by Netscape 2.0). Just specify the index of the radio button array you want to select.

```
form.rad[0].checked = true;   // sets to first button in the rad group
```

Using Checkboxes

Checkboxes are standalone elements; that is, they don't interact with neighboring elements as radio buttons do. Therefore they are a bit easier to use. Using JavaScript,

you can test if a check box is checked or not using the checked property. Likewise, you can set the checked property to add or remove the checkmark from a checkbox.

form—check.html

```
<HTML>
<HEAD>
<TITLE>Checkbox Test</TITLE>
<SCRIPT LANGUAGE="JavaScript">
function testButton (form){
        alert (form.check1.checked);
}
</SCRIPT>
</BODY>
<FORM NAME="testform">
<INPUT TYPE="button"NAME="button"Value="Click"onClick="testButton(this.form)"><BR>
<INPUT TYPE="checkbox" NAME="check1" Value="Check1">Checkbox 1<BR>
<INPUT TYPE="checkbox" NAME="check2" Value="Check2">Checkbox 2<BR>
<INPUT TYPE="checkbox" NAME="check3" Value="Check3">Checkbox 3<BR>
</FORM>
</HTML>
```

As with the radio button object, add a CHECKED attribute to the HTML markup for that checkbox if you want to set a checkbox when the form first appears.

```
<INPUT TYPE="checkbox" NAME="check1" Value="0" CHECKED>Checkbox 1<BR>
```

You can also set the button selection programmatically with JavaScript, using the checked property. Just specify the name of the checkbox you want to check. Remember that you can check multiple checkboxes.

```
form.check1.checked = true;
```

Using Text Areas

Text areas are used for multiple-line text entry. The default size of the text box is 1 row by 20 characters. You can change the size using the COLS and ROWS attributes. Here's a typical example of a text area with a text box 40 characters wide by 7 rows:

```
<TEXTAREA NAME="myarea" COLS="40" ROWS="7">
</TEXTAREA>
```

You can use JavaScript to read the contents of the text area box. This is done with the value property. Here is an example:

CD-ROM

form—textarea.html

```
<HTML>
<HEAD>
<TITLE>Text Area Test</TITLE>
<SCRIPT LANGUAGE="JavaScript">
function seeTextArea (form) {
        alert (form.myarea.value);

}
</SCRIPT>
</HEAD>
<BODY>
<FORM NAME="myform">
<INPUT TYPE="button" NAME="button3" Value="Test" onClick=
        "seeTextArea(this.form)">
<TEXTAREA NAME="myarea" COLS="40" ROWS="5">
</TEXTAREA>
</FORM>
</BODY>
</HTML>
```

You can preload text into the text area in either of two ways. You can enclose the text between the <TEXTAREA> and </TEXTAREA> tags, as shown in Figure 16.2. This method is useful if you want to include hard returns, as these are retained in the text area box. Or, you can set it programmatically with JavaScript (but in this case you cannot add hard returns). Here's an example of the first method:

```
<TEXTAREA NAME="myarea" COLS="40" ROWS="7">
Initial text displayed here
</TEXTAREA>
```

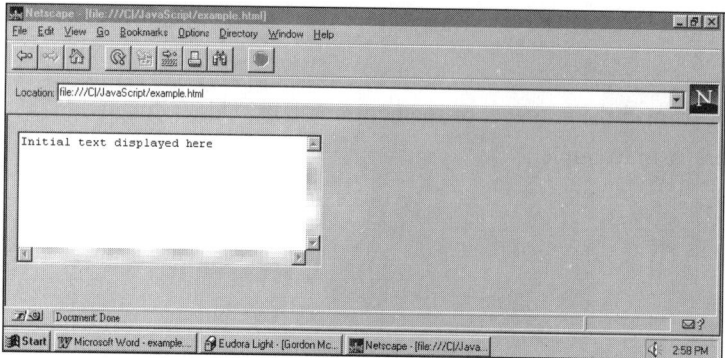

Figure 16.2 Default text can be placed between <TEXTAREA> tags.

Using JavaScript, you set the text area value:

```
formname.textarea.value = "Text goes here";
```

formname is the name of the form, *textarea* is the name of the textarea, *"Text goes here"* is the text you want to display.

■■■■■■■ **NOTE**

Text you write to the text area is treated as "unformatted." Any markup tags you use—such as <P> or <BR> for line breaks—appear as-is in the text area box.

■■■■■

Using Selection Lists

List boxes let you pick the item you want out of a multiple-choice box. The listbox itself is created with the <SELECT> tag, and the items inside it are created by one or more <OPTION> tags. You can have any number of <OPTION> tags in a list. The list is terminated with a </SELECT> tag.

The list can appear with many items showing at once, or it can appear in a drop-down box—normally you see one item at a time, but click to see more. The markup for the two styles is identical, except for the optional SIZE attribute. Leave off SIZE to make a drop-down box; use SIZE to make a list box of the size you wish.

Here is an example of a drop-down list (displays only one item unless you click on the list):

```
<SELECT NAME="list">
<OPTION>This is item 1
<OPTION>This is item 2
<OPTION>This is item 3
<OPTION>This is item 4
</SELECT>
```

Here is an example of a drop-down list (displays all four items):

```
<SELECT NAME="list" SIZE="4">
<OPTION>This is item 1
<OPTION>This is item 2
<OPTION>This is item 3
<OPTION>This is item 4
</SELECT>
```

Use the selectedIndex property to test which option item is selected in the list. The item is returned as an index value, with 0 being the first option, 1 being the second, and so forth (if no item is selected, the value is -1). Here's a working example:

form—select.html

CD-ROM

```
<HTML>
<HEAD>
<TITLE>List Box Test</TITLE>
<SCRIPT LANGUAGE="JavaScript">
function testSelect(form) {
        alert (form.list.selectedIndex);
}
</SCRIPT>
</HEAD>
<BODY>
<FORM NAME="myform" ACTION="" METHOD="GET">
<INPUT TYPE="button" NAME="button" Value="Test" onClick="testSelect(this.form)">
```

```
<SELECT NAME="list" SIZE="3">
<OPTION>This is item 1
<OPTION>This is item 2
<OPTION>This is item 3
</SELECT>
</FORM>
</BODY>
</HTML>
```

If you want the text of the selected list item instead of the index, use this in the testSelect function:

```
function testSelect (form) {
        Item = form.list.selectedIndex;
        Result = form.list.options[Item].text;
        alert (Result);
}
```

Other Capabilities of <SELECT> Objects

The <SELECT> object causes a lot of confusion to many JavaScript programmers. This section in intended as a rundown of what you can do with the list boxes created with the <SELECT> object. In all of the examples in this section, *formname* is the unique name of the form and *selectname* is the unique name of the select object you want to test.

- Determine the index of the selected option:
  ```
  Result = formname.selectname.option[index];
  ```
  index is the index value of the option that is selected (numbering starts at 0)

- Set the selected option:
  ```
  formname.selectname.selectedIndex = [index];
  ```
  index is the index value of the option you want selected (numbering starts at 0)

- Determine the text of the selected item:
  ```
  Item = formname.selectname.selectedIndex;
  Result = formname.selectname.options[Item].text;
  ```

- Determine how many items are in the <SELECT> object:
  ```
  Result = formname.selectname.length
  ```

- Set the text of a select option, as long as you also tell JavaScript to reload the page:

```
formname.selectname.options[index].text = "Text";
history.go(0);
```

index is the index of the option that you want to change, and *"Text"* is the text to which you want to change.

Testing for Multiple Selections with the Selected Property

You can allow for multiple selections in a list by using the MULTIPLE attribute in the <SELECT> tag. The JavaScript code necessary to process this is a bit more involved because you need to test each item of the list to see if it's selected. A perfect way to perform this task is to use a for counter that enumerates through all the <OPTION> tags in a <SELECT> object (you control the number of iterations of the for loop by using the length property of the select object).

For example, say you have a list with five items on it, and the user selects the first and fourth item. The box in the JavaScript program below displays:

Option 0 is selected

Option 3 is selected

in the alert box. Once again, note that the option items are numbered starting from zero. The first option is 0, the second is 1, and so forth.

form—multiple.html

CD-ROM

```
<HTML>
<HEAD>
<TITLE>Multiple Selection Test </TITLE>
<SCRIPT LANGUAGE="JavaScript">
function selectedItem (form) {
        var Temp = "";
        for (Count = 0; Count < form.list.length; Count++) {
                if (form.list[Count].selected)
                        Temp += "Option " + Count + " is selected\n";
        }
```

```
        alert (Temp);
    }
</SCRIPT>
</HEAD>
<BODY>
<FORM NAME="myform">
<INPUT TYPE="button" NAME="button3" Value="Test"
        onClick="selectedItem(this.form)">
<SELECT NAME="list" SIZE="5" MULTIPLE>
<OPTION>This is item 1
<OPTION>This is item 2
<OPTION>This is item 3
<OPTION>This is item 4
<OPTION>This is item 5
</SELECT>
</FORM>
</BODY>
</HTML>
```

Other Events You Can Trigger within a Form

The onClick event handler has been used in all of the examples in this chapter because you are most likely to deal with this handler in your forms. Yet JavaScript supports a number of other event handlers as well. Use these as the need arises, and the mood fits. The event handlers used with form object are:

- *onFocus*—an event is triggered when a form object gets input focus (the insertion point is clicked there).

- *onBlur*—an event is triggered when a form object loses input focus (the insertion point is clicked away from there).

- *onChange*—an event is triggered when a new item is selected in a list box. This event is also triggered when a text or text area box loses focus and the contents of the box have changed.

- *onSelect*—an event is triggered when text in a text or text area box is selected.
- *onSubmit*—an event is triggered when the form is submitted to the server (more about this important handler later in the chapter).

▪▪▪▪▪▪ NOTE

In Netscape 2.0 the onChange and onSelect event handlers do not work properly on all platforms, and therefore they should not be used if these browsers can access your page. For a list box, the onChange event is triggered only when clicking in the box or when choosing an item in the list and manually moving the focus outside of the list. The onChange event is not triggered when using the cursor keys to move up and down the list. And onSelect appears to be generally out-of-order for any control.

▪▪▪▪▪▪

▪▪▪▪▪▪ CAUTION

Be careful with onFocus! Don't use onFocus with an alert, prompt, or confirmation box. If you do, you could wind up with an endless loop, and you'll have to forcibly terminate Netscape to get out of it. When the dialog box appears, focus is temporarily removed from the text box. When you click OK to dismiss the dialog box, focus returns to the text box, which fires the onFocus event handler. The vicious cycle repeats itself until you're old and gray, or hit the reset button, whichever comes first.

▪▪▪▪▪▪

Submitting the Form to the Server

In all of the previous examples, the action of the form has been limited to within JavaScript only. Many forms are designed to send data back to the server. This is called "submitting" the form, and it is accomplished using either of two JavaScript instructions: the onSubmit event handler or the submit method. In most instances, you use one or the other, *not both*!

- Place the *onSubmit* event hander in the <FORM> tag. This tells JavaScript what it should do when the user clicks the Submit button (this is a button defined as TYPE="submit").

- Place the *submit* instruction anywhere in your JavaScript. It can be activated by any action, such as clicking a form button that has been defined with the onClick event handler.

Using onSubmit

Here's an example of using the onSubmit event handler to send mail. The onSubmit event handler tells JavaScript what to do when the user clicks the Submit button: it should call the mailMe() function, where the fields are appended to a mailto: URL. Netscape automatically opens a new mail window with the fields filled in. Write the body of the message, and send the mail off to the recipient.

CD-ROM

onsubmit.html

```
<HTML>
<HEAD>
<TITLE>onSubmit Test</TITLE>
<SCRIPT LANGUAGE="JavaScript">
function mailMe(form){
        Subject=document.testform.inputbox1.value;
        CC= document.testform.inputbox2.value;
        BCC= document.testform.inputbox3.value;
        location="mailto:gmccomb@gmccomb.com?subject="+Subject+"&Bcc="+BCC+"
            &cc="+CC;
        return true;
}
</SCRIPT>
</HEAD>
<BODY>
<FORM NAME="testform" onSubmit="return mailMe(this.form)">
Subject of message: <BR>
<INPUT TYPE="text" NAME="inputbox1" VALUE="This is such a great form!"
SIZE=50><P>
Send cc to: <BR>
```

```
<INPUT TYPE="text" NAME="inputbox2" VALUE="" SIZE=50><P>
Send blind cc to: <BR>
<INPUT TYPE="text" NAME="inputbox3" VALUE="" SIZE=50><P>
<INPUT TYPE="submit"><BR>
</FORM>
</BODY>
</HTML>
```

Using the submit Method

In the next example, the submit method is used. The script is little changed from the previous example, except that the onSubmit handler is removed and an onClick handler for a renamed form button is added in its place. The submit() method replaces the return true statement in the previous example. Personally, I prefer the submit method because it provides a little more flexibility. But either one will work.

CD-ROM

submit.html

```
<HTML>
<HEAD>
<TITLE>test</TITLE>
<SCRIPT LANGUAGE="JavaScript">
function mailMe(form){
        Subject=document.testform.inputbox1.value
        CC= document.testform.inputbox2.value
        BCC= document.testform.inputbox3.value
        location = "mailto:gmccomb@gmccomb.com?subject="+Subject+
                "&Bcc="+BCC+"&cc="+CC
        document.testform.submit();
}
</SCRIPT>
</HEAD>
<BODY>
<FORM NAME="testform">
Subject of message: <BR>
<INPUT TYPE="text" NAME="inputbox1" VALUE="This is such a great form!"
```

```
 SIZE=50><P>
Send cc to: <BR>
<INPUT TYPE="text" NAME="inputbox2" VALUE="" SIZE=50><P>
Send blind cc to: <BR>
<INPUT TYPE="text" NAME="inputbox3" VALUE="" SIZE=50><P>
<INPUT TYPE="button" VALUE="Send Mail" onClick="mailMe()"><BR>
</FORM>
</BODY>
</HTML>
```

Remaining details on using the onSubmit and submit instructions are included in
Chapter 18, "Using CGI with JavaScript."

■■■■■■■ **NOTE**

At first blush, it looks like you can use the mailto: URL as the ACTION string
for the form. This should have the effect of automatically sending the contents of the text boxes straight to the recipient's mail box. The syntax looks
like this:

```
<FORM NAME="testform" ACTION="mailto:someone@domain.com">
```

In fact, this method does work with the initial release of Netscape 2.0. But
because it is possible to submit a form without the user knowing (using the
submit method), Netscape has removed this functionality in subsequent
releases. This is a minor security issue where e-mail addresses can be
picked up and mailed back to someone. These e-mail addresses could then
be used for advertising or marketing purposes.

■■■■■

Validating Form Data Using JavaScript

The World Wide Web "grew up" when the ability to display forms was added. In the
days before forms, the Web was only mildly interactive, with just hypertext links to take
readers from location to location. Forms allow users to truly interact with the Web. For
example, readers can specify search queries using a simple one-line text box.

As you've read earlier in the chapter, forms on the Web consist of two parts: the form itself, which is rendered in the browser, and a CGI script or program located on the server. This script processes the user's input. While it's not exactly rocket science, a stumbling block in creating great Web forms is writing the CGI program. In most cases, these programs are written in Perl or C, and they can be a bother to implement and debug. A primary job of the CGI program is to validate that the reader has provided correct data, and this can requires pages of code.

JavaScript changes that. With JavaScript you can check the data provided by the reader before it's ever sent to the CGI program. In this way the CGI program can be kept to a bare minimum. And, because the data is sent only after it has been validated, the server need not be bothered until the form entry is known to be good. This saves valuable server resources.

Input Validation Routines

Most form validation chores revolve around basic data checking: did the user remember to fill in a box? Is the string the right length? Does it contain valid characters? With most forms, you can readily answer these questions with a small handful of validation routines. You can write them yourself or use any of the two dozen or so validation routines included with this book.

One typical validation routine determines if an input box contains only numeric digits. If the entry contains non-numeric characters, you can ask the user to enter the correct data. A ready-made routine for this is the isNumberString function, which returns the value 1 if the string contains only numbers, and 0 if it contains any non-numeric characters. To use it, provide the data string as the parameter. The value returned by the function tells you if the data is valid. Here's an example:

CD-ROM

valid–simple.html

```
<HTML>
<HEAD>
<TITLE>Test Input Validation</TITLE>
<SCRIPT LANGUAGE="JavaScript">
```

```
function testResults (form) {

        TestVar = isNumberString (form.inputbox.value)

        if (TestVar == 1)

                alert ("Congratulations! You entered only numbers");

        else

                alert ("Boo! You entered a string with non-numbers
                        characters");

}


function isNumberString (InString)  {

        if(InString.length==0) return (false);

        var RefString="1234567890";

        for (Count=0; Count < InString.length; Count++)  {

                TempChar= InString.substring (Count, Count+1);

                if (RefString.indexOf (TempChar, 0)==-1)

                        return (false);

        }

        return (true);

}
</SCRIPT>
</HEAD>
<BODY>
<FORM NAME="myform">
Enter a string with numbers only:
<INPUT TYPE="text" NAME="inputbox" VALUE="">
<INPUT TYPE="button" NAME="button" Value="Click"
onClick="testResults(this.form)">
</FORM>
</BODY>
</HTML>
```

Note that the isNumberString function is also smart enough to check for an empty input box. It treats an empty box as an invalid entry, returning a 0. If this test were not provided, a blank entry would be treated as valid input.

Overview of Validation Routines

This section contains a rundown on some of the other input validation routines provided on the CD-ROM included with this book. These—and other—routines are more completely documented in Chapter 13, "Plug-and-Play Routines." Also included here are various string-processing routines that are helpful when working with forms.

Data Validation Routines

Routine	What It Does
allowInString	Allow specified characters in string
allowNotInString	Don't allow specified characters in string
isAlphabeticChar	Checks whether string (one character) is an alphabetic
isAlphabeticString	Checks whether string (multiple characters) is an alphabetic
isNumberChar	Checks whether string (one character) is a number
isNumberString	Checks whether string (multiple characters) is a number
isCharUpper	Checks whether string (multiple characters) is uppercase
isCharLower	Checks whether string (multiple characters) is lowercase
isPunc	Checks whether string (one character) is punctuation
isUSZip	Checks whether string is a valid 5- or 9-digit US Zip code
isWithinRange	Checks whether number value is within a specified range
isBlank	Check whether entry is blank
isNotBlank	Check whether entry is not blank
Mask	Validate entry against pre-defined input mask

Input Processing Routines

Routine	What It Does
allowInString	Allow special characters in string
allowNotInString	Do not allow special characters in string
formatDollar	Converts number value into dollar format

Routine	What It Does
leftTrim	Trims extra spaces on left of string
rightTrim	Trims extra spaces on right of string
leftString	Returns only X characters from left of string
rightString	Returns only X characters from right of string
stripSpaces	Strips all spaces from string
stripChar	Strips all occurrences of X character in string
stripCharString	Strips all occurrences of specified characters in string
padTextSuffix	Pads end of string to length with X character
padTextPrefix	Pads beginning of string to length with X character
initUpper	Capitalizes first letter in each word
initUpperQualify	Capitalizes first letter in each word following lexical rules
parser	Parses string into component parts
testStringLength	Determines if string matches length requirements

Practical Examples of Input Validation

This section contains two examples of how to use JavaScript for form input validation. Four text boxes are provided; beside each one is a button. Enter text into one of the boxes, and click the button beside it. If you have not entered valid data, you are asked to re-enter it. Figure 16.3 shows the *valid.htm* document displayed in Netscape.

- Box 1 tests for a valid e-mail address. In the example, the test is limited to looking for a @ symbol.
- Box 2 tests for input of exactly five characters.
- Box 3 tests for input of three or more characters.
- Box 4 tests for non-blank input.

CD-ROM

valid.htm

```
<HTML>
<HEAD>
<TITLE> Verifying Form Input with JavaScript</TITLE>
<SCRIPT LANGUAGE="JavaScript">
```

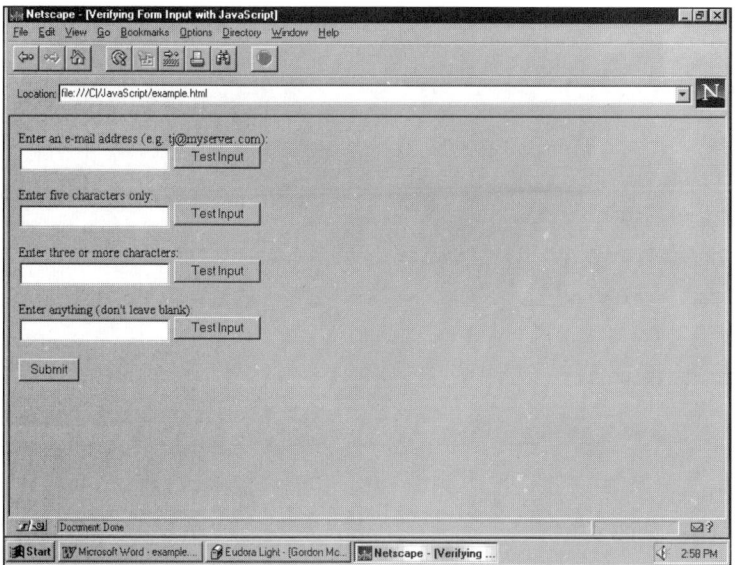

▬▬▬▬ **Figure 16.3** The *valid.htm* document, ready for text input.

```
function runTest(form, button)   {
        Ret = false;
        if (button.name == "1") Ret = testBox1(form);
        if (button.name == "2") Ret = testBox2(form);
        if (button.name == "3") Ret = testBox3(form);
        if (button.name == "4") Ret = testBox4(form);
        if (Ret)
                alert ("Successful input!");
}

function testBox1(form) {
        Ctrl = form.inputbox1;
        if (Ctrl.value == "" || Ctrl.value.indexOf ('@', 0) == -1) {
                validatePrompt (Ctrl, "Enter a valid email address")
                return (false);
        } else
```

```
                            return (true);
        }

        function testBox2(form) {
                Ctrl = form.inputbox2;
                if (Ctrl.value.length != 5) {
                        validatePrompt (Ctrl, "Provide five characters")
                        return (false);
                } else
                        return (true);
        }


        function testBox3(form) {
                Ctrl = form.inputbox3;
                if (Ctrl.value.length < 3) {
                        validatePrompt (Ctrl, "Provide at least three characters")
                        return (false);
                } else
                        return (true);
        }


        function testBox4(form) {
                Ctrl = form.inputbox4;
                if (Ctrl.value == "") {
                        validatePrompt (Ctrl, "Provide a value for this box")
                        return (false);
                } else
                        return (true);
        }

        function runSubmit (form, button)  {
                if (!testBox1(form)) return;
                if (!testBox2(form)) return;
                if (!testBox3(form)) return;
```

```
        if (!testBox4(form)) return;

        alert ("All entries verified OK!");

        //document.test.submit();        // un-comment to submit form

        return;

}


function validatePrompt (Ctrl, PromptStr) {

        alert (PromptStr)

        Ctrl.focus();

        return;

}
</SCRIPT>
</HEAD>
<BODY>
<FORM NAME="test" ACTION="http://domain.com/cgi-bin/val.cgi"
METHOD=GET>
Enter an e-mail address (e.g. tj@myserver.com): <BR>
<INPUT TYPE="text" NAME="inputbox1">
<INPUT TYPE="button" NAME="1" VALUE="Test Input"
        onClick="runTest(this.form, this)"><P>
Enter five characters only: <BR>
<INPUT TYPE="text" NAME="inputbox2">
<INPUT TYPE="button" NAME="2" VALUE="Test Input"
        onClick="runTest(this.form, this)"><P>
Enter three or more characters: <BR>
<INPUT TYPE="text" NAME="inputbox3">
<INPUT TYPE="button" NAME="3" VALUE="Test Input"
        onClick="runTest(this.form, this)"><P>
Enter anything (don't leave blank): <BR>
<INPUT TYPE="text" NAME="inputbox4">
<INPUT TYPE="button" NAME="4" VALUE="Test Input"
        onClick="runTest(this.form, this)"><P><P>
<INPUT TYPE="button" NAME="Submit" VALUE="Submit"
        onClick="runSubmit(this.form, this)"><P>
</FORM>
</BODY>
</HTML>
```

Experiment with the *valid.htm* to see how the various validation routines work. The example actually double-checks each input, then checks again when you click the Submit button. When you use it, you need test only once, typically when the Submit button is pressed. When all the blanks have been entered correctly, the script announces, "All entries verified OK!"

■■■■■■ **NOTE**

> The focus method is used in the above example to set focus in a text box to prompt the user that the input for that box is incorrect. Under some plat-forms (such as Windows), the focus method doesn't always display a flash-ing bar when the insertion point is placed in a text box.
>
> Focus is properly set in the desired box, but there may not be visual confir-mation of it. Therefore, don't assume the user is aware that focus has been returned to the box. If your form contains many input boxes, specify the box that needs correct input by name.

■■■■■■

Validating Non-Text Controls

The text control is the natural candidate for form validation (hidden text controls need no user validation; and in Netscape 2.0, the value of the password text control cannot be read). In the previous examples you've seen how to validate the content of text controls. Here's how to validate other commonly used controls and control structures in HTML forms. In all of the following, the form name is *myform*, and the control name is *control*. Here is a typical example:

```
<SCRIPT LANGUAGE="JavaScript">
function testform() {
        alert (document.myform.control.value)
}
</SCRIPT>
<FORM NAME="myform">
<TEXTAREA NAME="control" COLS=40 ROWS=5>
```

```
</TEXTAREA>
<INPUT TYPE="button" VALUE="Click" onClick="testform()">
</FORM>
```

Validating Text Areas

As with text boxes, use the value property to test the content of text areas. Here are some examples:

```
Ret = document.myform.control.value;            // assigns content
                                                // to Ret

Ret = document.myform.control.value.length;     // assigns length of
                                                // content to Ret

Ret = document.myform.control.value.indexOf ("\n")   // value 0 or above
                                                     // indicates hard return
```

Validating Checkboxes

The checkbox controls are either on or off. Use the checked property of the control to validate if a checkbox is checked or not checked. Here are some examples:

```
Ret = document.myform.control.checked;        // true if checked;
                                              //false if not checked
```

Validating Radio Buttons

Only one radio button in a group can be selected at one time. You can check which one is selected using a loop like the following (this is described earlier in the chapter; it checks three buttons in the *rad* group):

```
for (Count = 0; Count < 3; Count++) {
        if (form.rad[Count].checked)
                break;
}
```

You can use this loop to determine if any of the radio buttons are selected. This step may be necessary if you must initially display all of the radio buttons in a group as unselected, but require one of them to be selected.

```
Selected = false;
for (Count = 0; Count < 3; Count++) {
        if (form.rad[Count].checked) {
```

```
                        Selected = true;

                        break;

                }

        }

        if (Selected)

                // a radio button is selected

        else

                // no radio button is selected
```

Validating Selection Lists

You can validate that at least one option in a selection list is selected with the following for loop:

```
Selected = false;

for (Count = 0; Count < document.myform.control.length; Count++) {

        if (form.list[Count].selected)

                Selected = true;

}

if (Selected)

        // an option is selected

else

        // no option is selected
```

When using multiple-choice selection lists, you can verify that at least a certain number of options are selected with the following (this assumes at least three options in the list must be selected to pass verification):

```
Selected = 0;

for (Count = 0; Count < document.myform.control.length; Count++) {

        if (form.list[Count].selected)

                Selected++;

}

if (Selected < 3)

        // fewer than 3 selected

else

        // 3 or more selected
```

You can use opposite logic to verify that no more than a certain number of options are selected:

```
Selected = 0;
for (Count = 0; Count < document.myform.control.length; Count++) {
        if (form.list[Count].selected)
                Selected++;
}
if (Selected > 3)
        // more than three selected
else
        // 3 or less selected
```

Using Forms to Provide Password Protection of Files

Suppose you have some documents on your Web site that are not meant to be viewed by the general public. One solution is to have your Web server provide some sort of password access to the page, or perhaps even password-protect an entire directory. This is the ideal method if security is vital. Only a password authentication program running on a server can provide the kind of secure access you need for sensitive information.

On the other hand, most of us don't work with truly sensitive stuff. We merely want to provide a barrier to restrict casual access by the general public. One low-tech approach is to merely remove any external links to your sensitive page. That way, users must explicitly type the path and name of the document. This method works best if the document is in a directory that contains an "index" or main home page. That way, if a user specifies just the path, they get the index document, and not the directory of files in that path.

The problem with this method is that once you give out the filename, people can continue to access it. You may wish to limit the accesses to your restricted pages in some way—for example, allow access on one day but not on another. For this application, JavaScript can help. With JavaScript, you can create a basic, no-frills enciphering program that converts a plain-text filename to an enciphered filename.

A numeric key can be used to increase the variability of the enciphering. The key has 63 possible values. Each of the keys results in a different enciphered filename from the same "plain-text" filename. You might use values 1 through 31, for example, as keys for each day of the month. This allows you to restrict access to your pages on specific days.

The encoding system used in the examples in this section is extremely simple and can be broken in a matter of minutes by a trained cryptographer. However, to the average user the encoding scheme is not immediately obvious; there are no "secret words" or numbers stored in the script that a user can view.

◼◼◼◼ **NOTE**

> For the inquisitive, the script uses a simple cipher technique known as XORing, in which the numeric value of each character of the plain-text password is mixed with a numeric key value. The result is similar to the old-fashioned "decoder ring" that used to be given away in cereal boxes, which substituted each letter with another. The benefit is that it's easy to change the key against which the letter values are matched.

◼◼◼

A reverse process can be used to decode the cipher back to its plain-text filename. In fact, the exact same JavaScript program is used as both the encoder and as the decoder. Use the cipher text as the password, and provide the same key value used for encoding (remember: the encrypted text alone isn't enough—you need the key value!).

Enciphering the Filename

Cipher.html can be used to determine the enciphered filename using whatever plain-text word or filename you wish. It's also a good demonstrator for the whole process. Use View, Document Source to look at the file, and you'll see that the code is actually quite simple. If you know a little about encryption systems, feel free to enhance and modify this basic script.

CD-ROM

```
cipher.html
```

```
<HTML>
```

```
<HEAD>
<TITLE>Password Encyphering test</TITLE>
<SCRIPT LANGUAGE="JavaScript">
function testEncode(form) {
        var Ret = encode (form.inputbox1.value, form.inputbox2.value)
        form.inputbox3.value = Ret
}



function encode (OrigString, CipherVal) {
        Ref="0123456789abcdefghijklmnopqrstuvwxyz.—~ABCDEFGHIJKLMNOPQRSTUVWXYZ"
        CipherVal = parseInt(CipherVal)
        var Temp=""
        for (Count=0; Count < OrigString.length; Count++) {
                var TempChar = OrigString.substring (Count, Count+1)
                var Conv = cton(TempChar)
                var Cipher=Conv^CipherVal
                Cipher=ntoc(Cipher)
                Temp += Cipher
        }
        return (Temp)
}

function cton (Char) {
        return (Ref.indexOf(Char));
}

function ntoc (Val) {
        return (Ref.substring(Val, Val+1))
}
</SCRIPT>
</HEAD>
<BODY>
<FORM NAME="testform">
```

```
Plain text: <BR>
<INPUT TYPE="text" NAME="inputbox1" VALUE=""><P>
Key value:<BR>
<INPUT TYPE="text" NAME="inputbox2" VALUE=""><P>
Cipher:<BR>
<INPUT TYPE="text" NAME="inputbox3" VALUE=""><P>
<INPUT TYPE="button"NAME="button"Value="Encode"
        onClick="testEncode(this.form)"><BR>
</FORM>
</BODY>
</HTML>
```

To use the script, enter a word to encrypt. The script is set up to use only lowercase values, underscores, and periods (like Web filenames). Avoid using uppercase letters, and do not use any characters not allowed in Web filenames. You must also enter a key value, from 1 to 63. Leaving this entry blank or using a 0 results in the same cipher text as the plain text.

Click the Encode button to view the enciphered result. For example, suppose you specify *the_beatles* as the plain-text and *4* as the key. The resulting cipher text is *plaxfaephao*. Therefore, the filename you will use with this combination is *plaxfaephao*. It's up to you to add an *htm* or *html* extension (some servers are picky when it comes to files without extensions).

If your server limits filenames to eight characters, the plain-text filename should likewise be limited to eight characters. If you specify *beatles* as the plain-text, for example, and *12* as the key, you get *726hp2g*. Figure 16.4 shows a sample result.

Asking Users for a Password to Access a Page

Use *cipher.html*, from the previous section, to determine the ciphered filename, based on the password you want to use and a key value from 1 to 63. Once you've obtained the ciphered filename, you can create and store the restricted access page on your server using that name.

The *password.html* file demonstrates a JavaScript program showing the basic principle of allowing access to the restricted page. The program allows the user to enter a password.

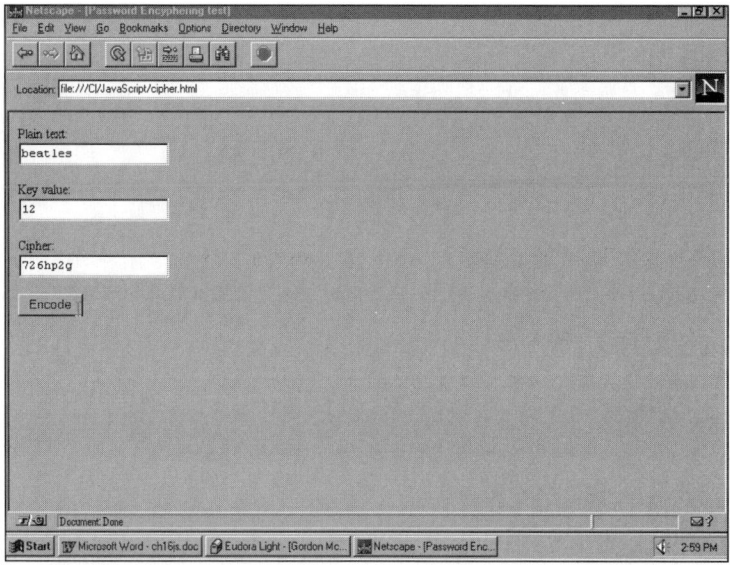

Figure 16.4 Use the *cipher.html* file to determine enciphered words.

Clicking the Submit button decodes the password and links to that page. Note that if the user selects the wrong password, an incorrect decipher string is generated, and Netscape attempts to link to a file that does not exist. An error message results.

The key value gives you many more password combinations. The *password.html* file uses the current day of the month as the key value. This allows the user to access the page for one day only. The next day the key value changes, and therefore the same password yields a different enciphered result. This system is particularly useful if you cannot update the restricted files on a regular basis. The files "self-expire" according to the current date.

CD-ROM

password.html

```
<HTML>
<HEAD>
<TITLE>JavaScript Password File</TITLE>
<SCRIPT LANGUAGE="JavaScript">
function testEncode(form) {
        var dater = new Date();
```

```
                Day = dater.getDate();

                dater = null;

                var Ret = encode (form.inputbox1.value, Day)

                location = Ret + ".html"

        }


function encode (OrigString, CipherVal) {

                Ref="0123456789abcdefghijklmnopqrstuvwxyz.—ABCDEFGHIJKLMNOPQRSTUVWXYZ"

                CipherVal = parseInt(CipherVal)

                var Temp=""

                for (Count=0; Count < OrigString.length; Count++) {

                        var TempChar = OrigString.substring (Count, Count+1)

                        var Conv = cton(TempChar)

                        var Cipher=Conv^CipherVal

                        Cipher=ntoc(Cipher)

                        Temp += Cipher

                }

                return (Temp)

        }


function cton (Char) {

        return (Ref.indexOf(Char));

}


function ntoc (Val) {return (Ref.substring(Val, Val+1))

}
</SCRIPT>
</HEAD>
<BODY>
<FORM NAME="testform" onSubmit=false;>
Please enter your password: <BR>
<INPUT TYPE="text" NAME="inputbox1" VALUE=""><P>
<INPUT TYPE="button" NAME="button" Value="Submit"
        onClick="testEncode(this.form)"><BR>
```

```
<INPUT TYPE="hidden" NAME="hidden" VALUE=""><P>
</FORM>
</BODY>
</HTML>
```

Creating a "Secret Message" Game Page

Passwords aren't just for restricting access to pages on the Web. You can use the basic XOR enciphering technique for a number of projects, including games. If you're into cryptography, you can devise even more elaborate encoding and decoding schemes using JavaScript.

This section contains the script for a sample page that uses JavaScript to present a "secret message." The game asks a riddle, the answer to which is the plain-text password used to unlock the message. The riddle game uses a slightly modified reference string to allow spaces and punctuation characters (which are not allowed in a resulting Internet filename, so they are not used in the previous examples). A short routine has also been added to arrive at the key value. This routine adds up the numeric value of each character in the "password," then divides that value by the number of characters in the string. Of course, any word with the same value average will unlock the message, but in practice the likelihood of typing a response that results in the proper value isn't as high as you'd think.

The answer to the riddle has intentionally been kept fairly simple. As you can see, the same encoding routine is also used for decoding—a benefit of the XOR enciphering technique. (The answer, of course, is what you're reading now!)

To change the secret code message, type it into the "Encoded text" box. Pick a password, and press the Decode button. The result, in the "Decoded text" box, is the enciphered text. Modify the VALUE= attribute for the first textbox in the *riddle.html* file to display your new enciphered text. Reload the *ridddle.html* file, type the password, and clock the Decode button. Your original coded message should appear in the "Decoded text" box. Figure 16.5 shows the *riddle.html* document in Netscape.

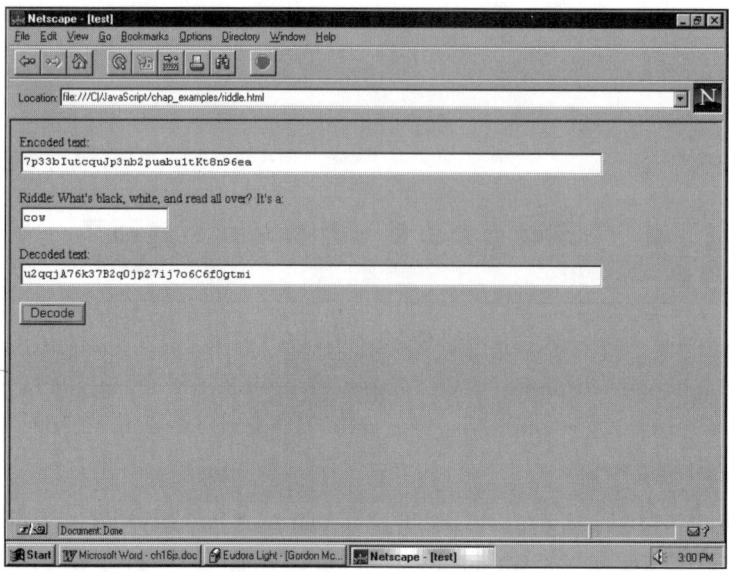

■■■■■■■ **Figure 16.5** Answer the riddle and a secret message appears.

CD-ROM

riddle.html

```
<HTML>

<HEAD>

<TITLE>test</TITLE>

<SCRIPT LANGUAGE="JavaScript">


function testEncode(form) {

        Ref="0123456789 abcdefghijklmnopqrstuvwxyz.,!?~" +"ABCDFGHIJK
        LMNOPQRSTUVWXYZ"

        var Ret = encode (form.inputbox1.value, avgWord(form.
        inputbox2.value))

        form.inputbox3.value = Ret
}


function avgWord (InString) {

        var Temp = 0
```

```
        for (Count=0; Count < InString.length; Count++)
                Temp = Temp + parseInt(cton(InString.substring(Count,
Count+1)))
        return (Math.round(Temp/InString.length))
}


function encode (OrigString, CipherVal) {
        CipherVal = parseInt(CipherVal)
        var Temp=""
        for (Count=0; Count < OrigString.length; Count++) {
                var TempChar = OrigString.substring (Count, Count+1)
                var Conv = cton(TempChar)
                var Cipher=Conv^CipherVal
                Cipher=ntoc(Cipher)
                Temp += Cipher
        }
        return (Temp)
}


function cton (Char) {
        return (Ref.indexOf(Char));
}


function ntoc (Val) {
        return (Ref.substring(Val, Val+1))
}


</SCRIPT>
</HEAD>
<BODY>
<FORM NAME="testform">
Encoded text: <BR>
<INPUT TYPE="text" NAME="inputbox1"
        VALUE="4500aFrodnrI505mac5r8ar2oLo7m 1b8S" SIZE=80><P>
```

```
Riddle: What's black, white, and read all over?  It's a:<BR>

<INPUT TYPE="text" NAME="inputbox2" VALUE=""><P>

Decoded text:<BR>

<INPUT TYPE="text" NAME="inputbox3" VALUE="" SIZE=80><P>

<INPUT TYPE="button"NAME="button"Value="Decode"
        onClick="testEncode(this.form)"><BR>

</FORM>

</BODY>

</HTML>
```

EXTENDING

JAVASCRIPT

USING JAVASCRIPT

WITH ADVANCED

HTML

JavaScript is a great tool for extending HTML. With a bit of ingenuity, there's almost no limit to the ways JavaScript can be used to manipulate HTML elements. This chapter presents a number of advanced applications in JavaScript and is suited for those familiar with both JavaScript and HTML. JavaScript inspires new ideas; consider the projects in this chapter as springboards for your own efforts.

The following list outlines the topics covered in this chapter. Except for the topics under the "More JavaScript Projects" heading, all of the topics include full documentation on their inner workings.

- Creating a digital clock with JavaScript
- Using arrays for form input
- Augmenting counters with JavaScript
- Using JavaScript with client-side image maps
- Creating a slideshow control bar
- Using "client pull" with JavaScript
- Using setTimeout for a self-running presenter

- Using the image form control with JavaScript
- Using JavaScript to build a small database
- More JavaScript Projects

Creating a Digital Clock with JavaScript

The *clock.html* project uses JavaScript to display the current time. Unlike many other JavaScript clocks you may have seen, this one does not just display the time in a text box. Rather, this clock shows the time in big green LED digits. The digits are formed using individual GIFs; the images are strung together to form the face of a digital clock.

The digit GIFs were provided by Russ Walsh. You can use any digits you wish for your clock, as long as you provide a separate GIF file for each numeral and separate files each for the colon and A.M./P.M. indicators. Change the *clock.html* code to reference the digit files you wish to use. Figure 17.1 shows an example of a couple of clock faces using different GIF file sets.

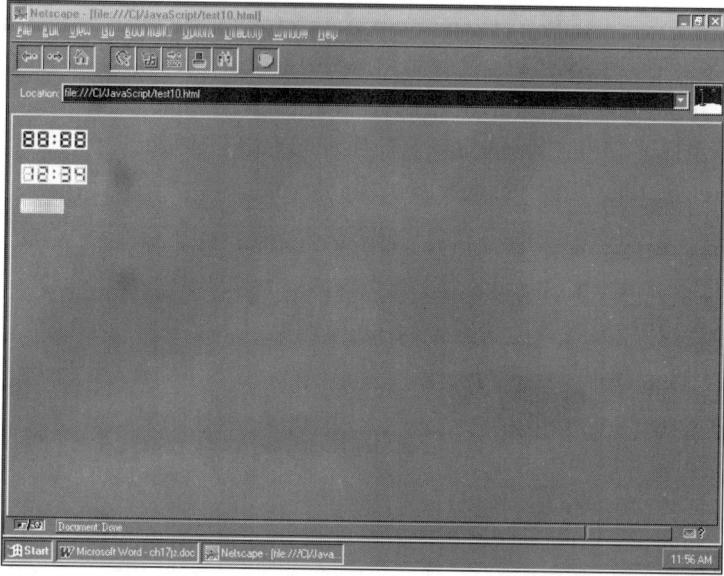

■■■■■■ **Figure 17.1** You may use any digit GIFs with the JavaScript clock.

The heart of the JavaScript digital clock is the following short routine, which not only determines the current time—as set by the user's computer—but assembles the series of <IMG> tags to create the clock face. The function, setClock, begins with the following lines, which define local variables for the basic <IMG> tag structure. To create a digit, all that's needed is the OpenImg variable, the unique digit value for the image wanted, the CloseImg variable.

```
var OpenImg = '<IMG SRC="'+pathOnly(location.href)+'dg'
var CloseImg='.gif">'
```

The routine then extracts the current time using a new instance of the Date object. You're interested in the hours and minutes, so variables are defined that separately hold the current hour and the current minutes.

```
now = new Date();
var CurHour = now.getHours();
var CurMinute = now.getMinutes();
now = null;
```

The time returned by the getHours method is in 24-hour format. The next lines of code determine if it's A.M. or P.M.:

```
if (CurHour >- 12) {
        CurHour = CurHour - 12;
        Ampm = "pm";
} else
        Ampm = "am";
if (CurHour == 0)
        CurHour = "12"
```

The value returned by the getMinutes method can contain one or two digits—one digit if the minutes value is between 0 and 9, and two digits otherwise. This code pads a 0 to the beginning of the minutes if the value is between 0 and 9:

```
if (CurMinute < 10)
        CurMinute = "0" + CurMinute
else
        CurMinute = "" + CurMinute
```

A for loop is used to build the hours portion of the display. There may be one or two digits for the hours, and the for loop repeats either one or two times, respectively. The script then adds the colon to separate the hours and minutes, then appends the minutes, followed by the A.M. or P.M. indicator. Finally, the whole thing is written to the document using the document.write method.

```
for (Count = 0; Count < CurHour.length; Count++) {
        Temp += OpenImg + CurHour.substring (Count, Count+1) + CloseImg
        }
Temp += OpenImg + "c" + CloseImg
for (Count = 0; Count < CurMinute.length; Count++) {
        Temp += OpenImg + CurMinute.substring (Count, Count+1) + CloseImg
}
Temp += OpenImg + Ampm + CloseImg
document.write(Temp)
```

Here is the entire *clock.html* file, including a call to setClock within <SCRIPT> tags after the text "The current time is:" The output is shown in Figure 17.2.

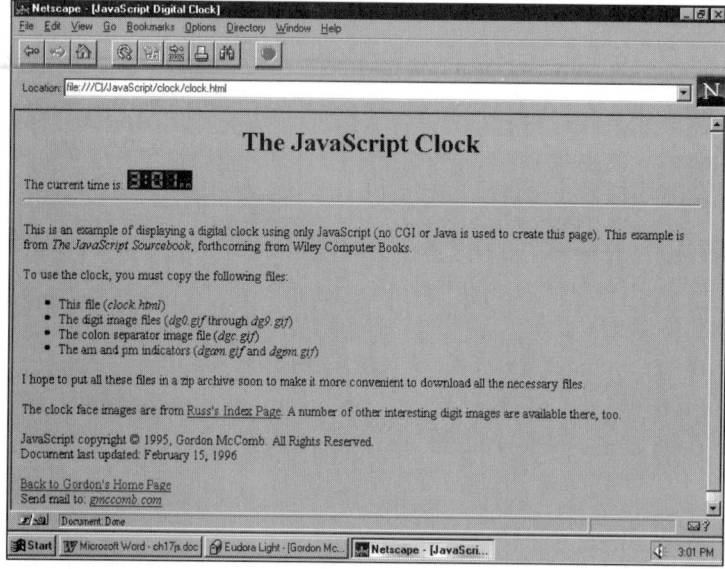

Figure 17.2 The output of *clock.html*, showing the current time.

CD-ROM

clock.html

```
<HTML>
<HEAD>
<TITLE>JavaScript Digital Clock</TITLE>
<SCRIPT LANGUAGE="JavaScript">
<!--
function setClock() {
        OpenImg = '<IMG SRC="'+pathOnly(location.href)+'dg'
        CloseImg='.gif">'
        Temp = ""
        now = new Date();
        CurHour = now.getHours();
        CurMinute = now.getMinutes();
        now = null;
        if (CurHour >= 12) {
                CurHour = CurHour - 12;
                Ampm = "pm";
        } else
                Ampm = "am";
        if (CurHour == 0)
                CurHour = "12"
        if (CurMinute < 10)
                CurMinute = "0" + CurMinute
        else
                CurMinute = "" + CurMinute

        CurHour = ""+CurHour;
        for (Count = 0; Count < CurHour.length; Count++) {
                Temp += OpenImg + CurHour.substring (Count, Count+1)
                  + CloseImg
        }
        Temp += OpenImg + "c" + CloseImg
```

```
          for (Count = 0; Count < CurMinute.length; Count++) {
                  Temp += OpenImg + CurMinute.substring (Count, Count+1)
                  + CloseImg
          }
          Temp += OpenImg + Ampm + CloseImg
          document.write(Temp)
  }


  function pathOnly (InString)   {
          LastSlash=InString.lastIndexOf ('/', InString.length-1)
          OutString=InString.substring   (0, LastSlash+1)
          return (OutString);
  }


  //-->
  </SCRIPT>
  <BODY>
  <H1 ALIGN=CENTER>The JavaScript Clock</H1>
  The current time is:
  <SCRIPT>setClock()</SCRIPT>
  <HR>
  </BODY>
  <SCRIPT></SCRIPT>
  </HTML>
```

Using Arrays for Form Input

Text boxes in forms traditionally have different names so that JavaScript or a
CGI program (running on the server) can differentiate the different boxes on the
form. For example, one box may be called *inputbox1*, another *inputbox2*, and
so forth. The box name is defined with the NAME attribute in the <INPUT> tag,
as follows:

```
  <INPUT TYPE="text" NAME="box_name" VALUE="">
```

This creates a box called *box_name*, with a null (empty) value.

If you don't plan on passing the form to a CGI script running on the server, you can use a little-known JavaScript trick to create an array of same-name boxes. This lets you refer to the boxes with the same root name. Just change the array index value for each box.

For instance, instead of referring to the boxes with explicit names such as inputbox1 and inputbox2, you refer to them as inputbox[1], inputbox[2], and so forth. One advantage of this method is that you can use a counter or some other mechanism to quickly and easily access or set the contents of each box.

In the following example, the text boxes are all named "box." As a result, JavaScript creates an array in order to identify them. Each text box is identified by number, starting from 0. Because there are three boxes, the array JavaScript creates is:

box[0]—the first box

box[1]—the second box

box[3]—the third box

The getBoxContents function is used for testing purposes. It shows how to access the contents of each box, using a numeric variable for the array index. When you run this example, type text into each of the three boxes, then click the button. The contents of the boxes are shown in an alert box.

box_array.html

CD-ROM

```
<HTML>
<HEAD>
<TITLE>Box Array</TITLE>
<SCRIPT LANGUAGE="JavaScript">
function getBoxContents (form){
        Temp="";
        for (Count = 0; Count < 3; Count++) {
                Temp += form.box[Count].value + "\n"
        }
```

```
        alert (Temp)
    }
</SCRIPT>
<FORM NAME="testform">
<INPUT TYPE="button" NAME="button" Value="Click"
onClick="getBoxContents(this.form)"><BR>
<INPUT TYPE="text" NAME="box" Value="" onClick=0><BR>
<INPUT TYPE="text" NAME="box" Value="" onClick=0><BR>
<INPUT TYPE="text" NAME="box" Value="" onClick=0><BR>
</FORM>
</BODY>
</HTML>
```

■■■■■ **NOTE**

While the array technique is useful for scripts that are confined to
JavaScript only, it is not as useful when the form is eventually sent to a CGI
script running on the server. When the form is submitted, the browser
sends just the root name of the text box, rather than the root name and
array index. Therefore, the CGI script will not know which box is which
because they all share the same name.

■■■■■

By the way, notice the *onClick=0* event handler at the end of each text box tag. This
handler doesn't actively do anything; rather it is there to get around a bug in Netscape
2.0 whereby an array of text objects is returned in reverse order. Without the onClick
event handler, when you click the button JavaScript receives the array of text boxes
last to first, instead of the usual first to last (this same bug afflicts radio buttons, and
the fix for them is to add an onClick handler, too). The onClick workaround corrects
for this mistake and ensures that the script will continue to work in future versions of
Netscape, when this bug has been eradicated.

Of course, you are not limited to using this array technique for text boxes only. You
can use the technique, as needed, with checkboxes and buttons, too (the array technique is already used with radio buttons).

Augmenting Counters with JavaScript

A favorite pastime of many Web developers is counting the "hits" to their home pages. There are a number of methods for accomplishing this, including running a "statistics" programs on a server and paying an outside service to monitor the accesses to your page.

Yet another method is to use a visual counter. Such visual counters display the number of visitors either since the counting was established or since the counter was last updated. The count is displayed either as text or, more often, as an image, such as an odometer (see Figure 17.3).

A visual counter requires some type of program running on the server, typically a program written using the CGI standard. The server maintains a database of the number of times visitors have accessed a given page and increments the counter with each visit. If you have access to the CGI directory on the server that houses your pages,

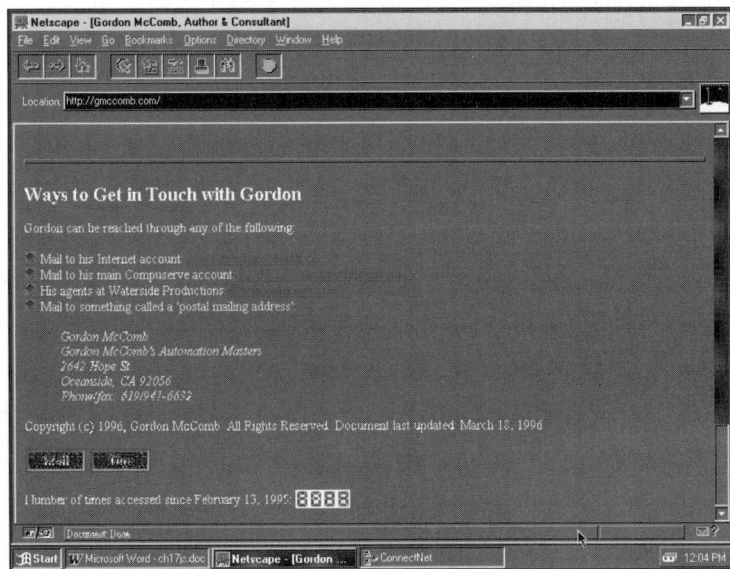

Figure 17.3 A typical Web page "hit" counter image provided by a counter service.

you can set up a counter directly within that server. There are many public domain, shareware, and commercial counter programs available, each one with different features. You'll want to consult with your Web administrator about setting up counter access for your pages.

You do not need a counter program on your server to enjoy a counter on your page. A number of companies provide free and paid counters for use on almost any Web server. These are called public counters, for the lack of a better term. One of the most popular counters is available through Net Digits, at http://www.digits.com. They offer free counters for low-volume users (less than about 50 hits per day) and paid counters for heavier users and users requiring extra features.

As with counter CGI programs that can be used on your own server, the counter (paid and free) at Net Digits is user-configurable. You can change a number of visual aspects of the counter (including the number of "padding zero" digits shown, such as 000025 or 025, or just 25), the color of the digits, the color of the background, and whether the digits appear with a border. These configuration options are available at run-time; that is, they are part of the URL that is used to access the counter. The counter, in turn, provides a single GIF image using the configuration options you've specified.

Ordinarily you merely hardcode the configuration options you want. Here's a sample URL for a standard white-on-black odometer counter. Note that the URL is part of an <IMG> tag (it's broken into two lines here because of its long length);

```
<IMG SRC="http://counter.digits.com/wc?-d&6&my_counter_name" ALIGN=absmiddle
WIDTH=90 HEIGHT=20 BORDER=0>
```

This configuration references a counter named "my_counter_name" at Net Digits (their ULR is http://counter.digits.com).

- *-d&6* specifies the number of digits.
- *&my_counter_name* establishes the name of the counter in the Net Digits database.

The remainder of the <IMG> is standard HTML. The ALIGN attributes set the alignment, the WIDTH and HEIGHT attributes specify the width and height of the odometer image, and the BORDER attributes remove the border around the image.

As specified in the documentation available from Net Digits, you can specify other configuration options as well. One of them is the style of the counter. The "space-age" LED digits are a nice option, and this option has been added to the SRC URL:

```
&-c&4
```

This line tells the Net Digits counter program to display a counter using "character set 4," which is described in the Net Digits documentation. Other configuration options include changing the colors or adding or removing zero padding.

As you have probably surmised by now, you can use JavaScript to programmatically change the configuration of the counter, rather than include the configuration options as part of the HTML markup. For example, you might display one style of counter for the daylight hours and another for the nighttime hours.

▬▬▬▬ **NOTE**

Not everyone visiting your site will have a JavaScript-enabled browser. Be sure to take this into consideration when setting the dynamic configuration of your counter. Avoid using JavaScript to define the entire <IMG> tag. If you do, non-JavaScript-enabled browsers will skip the counter, and the counting will be off. This is actually harder than it sounds, especially if you want to maintain strict adherence to HTML rules.

▬▬▬▬

The technique detailed here uses some roundabout methods of "hiding" the hard-coded <IMG> tag from JavaScript, but allowing it to be passed through on non JavaScript-enabled browsers. Likewise, the JavaScript code is visible on JavaScript-enabled browsers.

Use comments in the <SCRIPT> tag to hide the text and code you don't want the JavaScript and non-JavaScript browsers to see.

- To provide HTML markup that JavaScript will ignore but that will be read by most non-JavaScript browsers, start the <SCRIPT> tag and include the <!-- --> comment pair. If the text is too long to fit the line, make sure that you don't press Enter to wrap the line. Let the line be long, or allow your text editor to auto-wrap the line. Otherwise JavaScript reports an error.

- To provide JavaScript code that JavaScript will read, but that will be ignored by most non-JavaScript browsers, place the JavaScript code between the traditional <!-- and //--> characters.

The following example uses different counter styles to show that the two <IMG> tags are rendered differently, depending on whether a JavaScript or non-JavaScript browser is used. The <IMG> tag in the regular HTML markup is displayed using character 8 of the Net Digits character set (using the *&-c&8* style), and the <IMG> tag in the JavaScript code uses character number 4, and sets the foreground color to solid green (with the *&-f&a00ff00* style).

```
<SCRIPT>
<!-- --> <IMG SRC=""http://counter.digits.com/wc?-d&6&my_counter&-c&8"
ALIGN=absmiddle WIDTH=90 HEIGHT=20 BORDER=0><BR>
<!--
document.write ('<IMG SRC=""http://counter.digits.com/wc?-' +
'd&6&my_counter&-c&4&-f&a00ff00" ALIGN=absmiddle '+
'WIDTH=90 HEIGHT=20 BORDER=0>')
//-->
</SCRIPT>
```

You may, if you wish, include additional JavaScript code to provide additional flexibility over the style of the counter. For instance, change between light blue for the day and deep purple for the night:

```
now = new Date();
CurHour = now.getHours();
if ((CurHour > 5) && (CurHour <18))
        Color = "&-f&affff00";
else
        Color = "&-f&a00ff00";
document.write ('<IMG SRC="http://counter.digits.com/wc?-' +
'd&6&my_counter&-c&4' + Color + '" ALIGN=absmiddle '+
        'WIDTH=90 HEIGHT=20 BORDER=0>')
```

▬▬▬▬ **NOTE**

For additional projects with counters, see Chapter 18, "Using CGI with JavaScript."

▬▬▬

Using JavaScript with Client-Side Image Maps

If you're lucky enough to have control over the server that contains your published Web pages, you've probably dabbled with server-side image maps. These are images that have been "dissected" into smaller chunks; as the user clicks on each chunk, the server responds to a different action. For example, you might have a graphic of a city map. The map is divided into quadrants; clicking on a quadrant displays a new page of real estate information for that area of the city.

The downside to server-side image maps is that you need a CGI program running on the server to handle the click requests. Not everyone has this ability, and even when they do, much extra effort can be involved in getting the whole system to work. Generic image map CGI programs exist for all of the major server platforms (such as Unix, Windows, Netscape), but many still require hand-tweaking.

Client-side image maps change that. The "intelligence" for dissecting the image and directing the user to the proper link—based on the area of the image that was clicked—is built into the browser, or "client." Netscape 2.0 and above is one of many browsers to support this new standard. Microsoft Internet Explorer and NCSA Mosaic 2.1 and above also support client-side image maps.

Netscape takes the process a step further, however, in letting you integrate client-side image maps with JavaScript. In an ordinary client-side image map, you are limited to linking to another page. That's something, but not enough for some users. You can "link" to a JavaScript function, thereby giving your image maps even more intelligence. For instance, you might create a control panel that lets users successfully click on an image button only if some piece of information—say, a user name—has been provided.

An Introduction to Client-Side Image Maps

Netscape, Microsoft, and NCSA provide detailed information on creating client-side image maps, but the fundamentals are quickly reviewed here. You'll want to locate more complete information from these and other sources.

Two new HTML tags are used to create client-side image maps. They are the <MAP> tag, which defines the map structure, and one or more <AREA> tags, which define the clickable areas within the image. Client-side image maps are currently limited to providing rectangular areas; free-form polygon shapes (possible with server-side image maps) will probably come in future releases of Netscape and other browsers.

To create the image map, define a <MAP> tag and give the mapping a name. The syntax is:

```
<MAP NAME="mapname">
```

You can use almost any name for the map, but it should contain only alphabetic and numeric characters. The exception is the underscore, but avoid using an underscore for the first character. You will use the name later in the HTML markup, so remember it!

Next you define one more <AREA> tag to define the areas of your image. The tag takes the syntax:

```
<AREA SHAPE="rect" COORDS="x1,y1,x2,yx" HREF="url">
```

- *SHAPE* is the shape of the area. You can specify *rect* (rectangular), *circ* (circular), or *poly* (polygon).
- *COORDS* is the bounding area of the shape. The first two values are for the upper-left corner (x and y); the second two values are for the lower-right corner.
- *HREF* is the URL you want to link to when the user clicks on the area. This can be any valid URL.

After the last <AREA> tag, use the </MAP> tag to denote the end of the mapping.

The last item is the image you want to use, with a reference to the area map you've previously defined. Use the standard <IMG> tag, with a new USEMAP attribute. For the USEMAP attribute, provide the name of the map. Here's a full example:

```
<MAP NAME="control">
<AREA SHAPE=RECT COORDS="0,0,57,31" HREF="/index.html">
<AREA SHAPE=RECT COORDS="58,0,255,31" HREF="toc.html">
<AREA SHAPE=RECT COORDS="256,0,313,31" HREF="backpage.html">
</MAP>
<IMG SRC="control.gif" USEMAP="#control" BORDER=0 HEIGHT=34 WIDTH=314>
```

This map uses an image named *control.gif*. The <IMG> tag references the map name, which is control (note the hash before the name). Other attributes provided with the <IMG> tag are no border (BORDER=0), and the width and height of the image. See Figure 17.4 for an example of how the image looks when rendered in Netscape.

When a user clicks on the back arrow (which is the first area defined), the index.html page opens. Conversely, if a user clicks on the contents "button" (the second area defined), a page called toc.html opens. And if the forward arrow is clicked, a page called backpage.html opens.

Adding JavaScript

To add flexibility to standard client-side image maps, provide the name of a JavaScript function for the HREF in the <AREA> tag. Instead of a jump to some page, your JavaScript code is executed, and you can use that script to perform anything you want. The trick is to use the JavaScript "protocol" for the URL and follow it with the name of the function you wish to use.

For example, suppose you want to go back one page in the history list if the user clicks the back arrow. You can use the window.history.go(-1) method to jump back

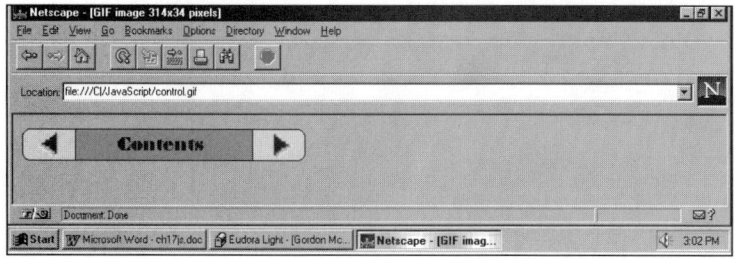

▬▬▬▬▬ **Figure 17.4** Use client-side image maps to create clickable regions in any graphic.

one page in the user's history list. You can either provide this entire function after the JavaScript: protocol or call a user-defined function that contains this instruction. Here are both methods:

```
<AREA SHAPE=RECT COORDS="0,0,57,31" HREF="JavaScript:window.history.go(-1) ">
```

```
<AREA SHAPE=RECT COORDS="0,0,57,31" HREF="goBack()">
```

and elsewhere in the document:

```
<SCRIPT>
function goBack() {
        window.history(-1)
}
```

The second of these methods is preferable if you need to provide a number of JavaScript functions to perform.

Following is a working example of how to use client-side image maps with JavaScript. The buttons display an alert box to show you that the JavaScript: URL is indeed working. And the forward and back buttons work—assuming you have pages forward and backward in your history list. If you don't, then the current page remains.

CD-ROM

imagemap_control.html

```
<HTML>
<HEAD>
<SCRIPT LANGUAGE="JavaScript">
function goBack() {
        alert ("Back");
        window.history.go (-1)
}

function goForward() {
        alert ("Forward");
        window.history.go (1)
}
```

```
function toc() {
        alert ("Table of contents")
}

</SCRIPT>
</HEAD>
<BODY>
<CENTER>
<MAP NAME="control">
<AREA SHAPE=RECT COORDS="0,0,57,31" HREF="JavaScript:goBack()">
<AREA SHAPE=RECT COORDS="58,0,255,31" HREF="JavaScript:toc()">
<AREA SHAPE=RECT COORDS="256,0,313,31" HREF="JavaScript:goForward()">
</MAP>
<IMG SRC="control.gif" USEMAP="#control" BORDER=0 HEIGHT=34 WIDTH=314>
</BODY>
</HTML>
```

Creating a Slideshow Control Bar

A terrific use of JavaScript and client-side image maps is a control panel placed in a frame. The smaller control panel stays, but the content in the larger frame changes. You can, of course, use standard client-side image maps techniques for this as well, but JavaScript gives you an edge in providing extra features.

Figure 17.5 shows a control panel (the same one we've used earlier) placed in the bottom frame. This frame is static and does not change. The large frame above is used to hold the content, which is a slide show. The user can click the forward and back arrow buttons to move through the slides, or click the Contents button to view the table of contents. JavaScript is used to keep track of the current page so that the user can step forward and back through each slide. When you look at the script, you can see that it's laughably simple; yet the effect can be quite compelling and useful.

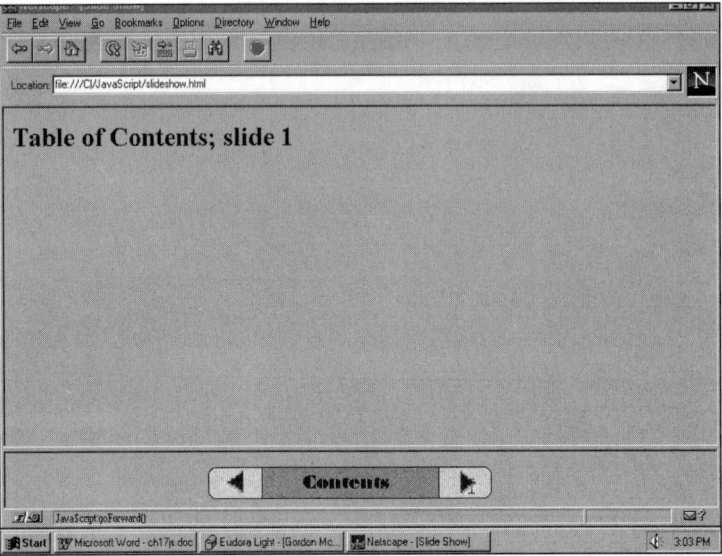

The Frameset Document

slideshow.html is the frameset document for the slide show. It contains a frameset definition for two frames, positioned as rows. The frames are named frame1 and frame2. Frame1 (the top frame) contains the slide show content; frame2 contains the image map. Frame1 initially uses a "dummy" (blank) document; it is filled in with page 1 later.

Note the loadVars function and onLoad event handler, which ensure that page 1 (the contents page) is redisplayed if the user resizes or reloads the document. The onLoad event handler is placed in the frameset document because it is always guaranteed to be the last document completely loaded. That is, the child frames (frame1 and frame2) are always loaded before the frameset finishes loading.

The MaxPages variable is used to indicate the maximum number of pages in the slide show. In this example it is set at five, but it can be any number. There must be a slide show document for each slide, or Netscape displays an error.

CD-ROM

slideshow.html

```
<HTML>
<TITLE>Slide Show</TITLE>
<HEAD>
<SCRIPT LANGUAGE="JavaScript">
<!--
var CurrentPage, MaxPages, sCurPage;
function loadVars() {
        CurrentPage = 1;
        MaxPages = 5;
        sCurPage = CurrentPage;
        frame1.location = "slide"+sCurPage+".html"
}
//-->
</SCRIPT>
</HEAD>
<FRAMESET ROWS="85%, *" onLoad="loadVars()">
  <FRAME SRC="dummy.htm" NAME="frame1">
  <FRAME SRC="slidemap.htm" NAME="frame2" MARGINWIDTH=1>
</FRAMESET>

<NOFRAME>
This demo requires Netscape.
</NOFRAME>

</HTML>
```

The Control Document

slidemap.htm is the slide show control document, which also contains the Back/Contents/Forward image. The document uses variables—CurrentPage and MaxPages—set in the frameset document. As a result, the variable names include the "parent" identifier. This forces JavaScript to look into the parent (frameset) document for the variables.

slidemap.htm

CD-ROM

```
<HTML>
<HEAD>
<SCRIPT LANGUAGE="JavaScript">

function goBack() {
        if (parent.CurrentPage!=1) {
                sCurPage = --parent.CurrentPage;
                parent.frame1.location = "slide"+sCurPage+".html"
        }
}

function goForward() {
        if (parent.CurrentPage < parent.MaxPages) {
                sCurPage = ++parent.CurrentPage;
                parent.frame1.location = "slide"+sCurPage+".html"
        }
}

function toc() {
        sCurPage = parent.CurrentPage = 1;
        parent.frame1.location = "slide"+sCurPage+".html"
}

</SCRIPT>
</HEAD>
<BODY>
<BR>
<CENTER>
<MAP NAME="control">
<AREA SHAPE=RECT COORDS=0,0,57,31 HREF="JavaScript:goBack()">
<AREA SHAPE=RECT COORDS=58,0,255,31 HREF="JavaScript:toc()">
<AREA SHAPE=RECT COORDS=256,0,313,31 HREF="JavaScript:goForward()">
</MAP>
```

```
<IMG SRC="control.gif" USEMAP="#control" BORDER=0 HEIGHT=34 WIDTH=314>
</BODY>
</HTML>
```

The Slide Documents

slidex.html are the slide documents. The first slide is *slide1.html*, the second *slide2.html*, and so forth. To show how the system works, just five basic slide documents have been provided in this example. In a real slide show, you'd put a table of contents or "welcome" screen in slide1.html.

Recall the MaxPages variable. You should have a slide document for all slides up to the number specified for this variable. If you have 10 slides, for instance, MaxPages is set to 10 in the frameset document. You must therefore have documents slide1.html through slide10.html.

■■■■■■■ **NOTE**

For best results, avoid using pages for the slide documents that are themselves frameset documents. Frames can be nested, so a slide document that also displays frames will appear inside the top frame of the slide show window. This can yield unexpected results and can make navigation more difficult.

■■■■■■■

Modifying the Slide Show

There are many ways you can modify the slide show, such as:

- Replace the lame image map provided for the control panel. If you do so, you will need to revise the <AREA> tags in the *slidemap.html* document. You'll also need a graphics program that displays the coordinates of the image.

- Design a columns-based slide show, in which the image is on the right or left (left is more common).

- Use local links instead of external links to other pages. Instead of linking to a page named slide3.html, for example, revise the script so that it links to #slide3. You can do this by adding a hash symbol to the "slide" text and lopping off the .html extension. The location command in the goBack, goForward, and toc functions in the slidemap.html document would then look like this: parent.frame1.location = "slide#"+sCurPage;.

Be sure to design your slide page so that it has anchors identifying each linked-to spot, such as:

```
<A NAME="slide3"> </A><H1>Slide 3</H1>
```

Using "Client Pull" with JavaScript

Netscape 2.0 and above supports a technique called "client pull," which—among other tasks—allows the browser to fetch another page. Client pull is often used in animation (see Chapter 20, "Graphics, Sound, and Animation") because it can repeatedly load a series of pages. Client pull can also be used for repeating sound playback. You can load a page into a frame and have just that page "pulled in." This approach avoids having the entire page reloaded for each pull.

Client pull—and it's more complex cousin, server push—is detailed on Netscape's home page at http://home.netscape.com. This section concentrates on some handy techniques for combining JavaScript with client pull, to give this great feature even more flexibility.

A Brief Overview of Client Pull

To add client pull to your page, you insert a <META> tag into the head of the document, as shown here:

```
<META HTTP-EQUIV="Refresh" CONTENT="5">
```

This tag tells Netscape to refresh (reload) the document after a five-second wait. You can alternatively load a different page rather than the same page by specifying an URL:

```
<META HTTP-EQUIV="Refresh" CONTENT="5; URL=http://mydomain.com/page.html">
```

Here are some points to keep in mind.

- You must provide a fully qualified path in the URL. Relative paths aren't enough.
- Notice the quoting scheme. The quote starts after CONTENT= and ends after the URL.
- Don't forget the semicolon after the CONTENT=x attribute, or you'll wind up reloading the same page instead of the new page.

- You can specify any time delay you want, including 0. With 0, Netscape fetches the page (either the same page or a new URL) as soon as the current one has finished loading.

Writing the <META> Tag with JavaScript

You can use JavaScript to write the <META> tag, thereby dynamically specifying the delay and/or URL. Use the standard document.write method to output the <META> tag in the head of the document. The following example loads the first page, waits 10 seconds, then loads a second page. Note the pathOnly function; it returns just the current path, and it is used to give the second page an absolute URL.

CD-ROM

clientpull.html

```
<HTML>
<HEAD>
<TITLE>Client Pull Example</TITLE>
<SCRIPT LANGUAGE="JavaScript">

Text = "<META HTTP-EQUIV='Refresh' CONTENT='10; URL="+
pathOnly (location.href) + "second.html'>"
document.write (Text)

function pathOnly (InString)  {
        LastSlash=InString.lastIndexOf ('/', InString.length-1)
        OutString=InString.substring  (0, LastSlash+1)
        return (OutString);
}

</SCRIPT>
</HEAD>
<BODY>
</BODY>
</HTML>
```

A Practical Use of JavaScript for Client Pull

The previous example has the same effect as a hardcoded <META> tag; instead, its purpose is to demonstrate how to write the <META> tag using JavaScript. Because JavaScript writes the tag, you can use variables for either the time delay (the CONTENT attribute), the URL, or both.

For example, suppose you've set up a single home page that has different destination pages for Netscape 2.0 and 3.0. Using the navigator.appVersion property, you can determine which version your user has and take your users to that page. Now you want to provide a time delay before you display the new page. This is an ideal task for the client pull technique. The following script extracts the first character returned from the navigator. appVersion property (a 2 or a 3 is expected). That number is then used to form the page to go to after the time delay. The two pages are named *nsversion2.html* and *nsversion3.html*.

```
Version = navigator.appVersion.substring(0, 1)
Text = "<META HTTP-EQUIV='Refresh' CONTENT='10; URL="+
        pathOnly (location.href) + "nsversion_" + Version + ".html'>"
document.write (Text)


function pathOnly (InString)  {
        LastSlash=InString.lastIndexOf ('/', InString.length-1)
        OutString=InString.substring  (0, LastSlash+1)
        return (OutString);
}
```

Using setTimeout for a Self-Running Presenter

The setTimeout function is perfect for almost any application in which you want to wait a certain period of time. You can set the timed interval for seconds, minutes, even hours, then trigger any event you wish. One practical application of setTimeout is creating a self-running demonstration. The demonstration displays a series of pages, pausing between each one. Optional controls allow the user to start and stop the show, or start over.

Such an application is shown in the documents below. It uses frames to display each "slide" of the show, along with a control panel on the bottom. The first document is a parent frameset, and it contains almost all of the intelligence for the slideshow. The other document is used to provide control over the show: the user can start and stop the automatic slide changes, and he can start the show over.

In addition, the slide show system uses individual slide pages. These are standard HTML documents, with the exception of a JavaScript onLoad event handler placed in their <BODY> tags.

The frameset document creates the two frames (organized into rows, with the control buttons on the bottom, as shown in Figure 17.6). The setTimeout function is called whenever a slide page finishes loading. The setTimeout function sets the next page change to five seconds (as specified for the Delay variable; the delay is specified in milliseconds, 5000 is five seconds).

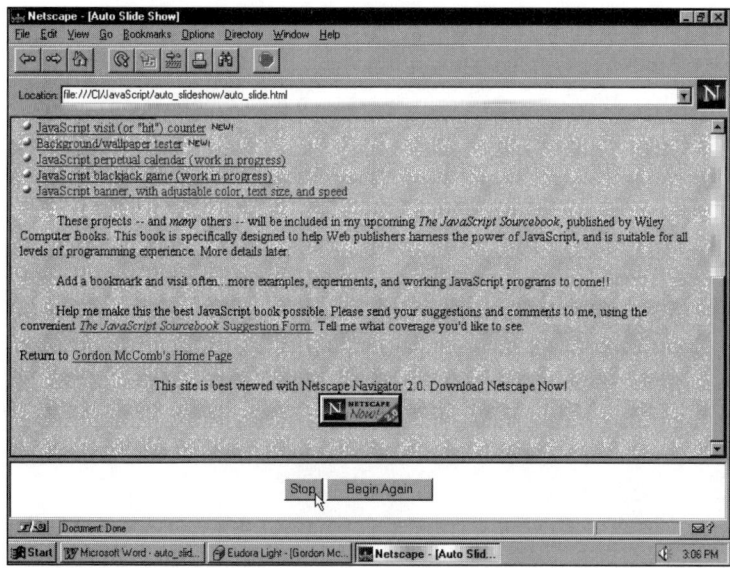

Figure 17.6 The auto-slide presenter changes slides at pre-defined intervals.

auto_slide.html

```
<HTML>
<TITLE>Auto Slide Show </TITLE>
<HEAD>
<SCRIPT>
var CurrentPage = 0
var MaxPages = 3
Delay = 5000;
var ShowFlag = true;
TimerID = 0;
Loop = false;
ShowRunning = true;

function reload() {
        CurrentPage = 0
        ShowFlag = true;
        ShowRunning = true;
        parent.frame1.location = "timedshow.htm";
        if (TimerID)
                clearTimeout (TimerID)
}

function runShow() {
        if (CurrentPage < MaxPages) {
        CurrentPage++;
                NextPage = "page_" + CurrentPage + ".html";
        parent.frame2.location = NextPage;
        } else
        if (Loop) {
                CurrentPage = 1;
                NextPage = "page_" + CurrentPage + ".html";
                parent.frame2.location = NextPage;
        } else
                ShowRunning = false;
```

```
}


function triggerTimer() {
        if (ShowFlag)
                TimerID = setTimeout ("runShow()", Delay);
        else
                clearTimeout (TimerID);
}


function setShowFlag () {
        ShowFlag = !ShowFlag;
        if (!ShowFlag)
                clearTimeout (TimerID);
        else
                TimerID = setTimeout ("runShow()", 500);
        if (ShowRunning)
                parent.frame1.location = "timedshow.html";
}


</SCRIPT>
</HEAD>

<FRAMESET ROWS="85%, 15%" onLoad="reload(); runShow()">
<FRAME SRC="dummy.htm" NAME="frame2">
<FRAME SRC="timedshow.html" NAME="frame1" NOSCROLL MARGINWIDTH=2>
</FRAMESET>

<NOFRAME>
This demo requires Netscape.
</NOFRAME>
</HTML>
```

The control panel document contains a form with two buttons. One of the buttons is set dynamically, based on the value of the ShowFlag variable, which is set in the parent (this variable is set before the frame documents are loaded, to ensure that the variable exists by the time this code is run). If ShowFlag is set to true, the Stop button appears. If ShowFlag is set to false, the Start button appears. Pushing the Stop/Start button executes the run function, which in turn executes the setShowFlag function in the parent frameset (this function toggles the ShowFlag variable).

The Begin Again button is a standard HTML button and remains the same. Pushing it runs the reload and runShow functions in the parent frameset document.

CD-ROM

timedshow.htm

```
<HTML>
<HEAD>
<TITLE>Control</TITLE>
<SCRIPT LANGUAGE="JavaScript">

function run () {
        parent.setShowFlag();
}

</SCRIPT>
</HEAD>
<BODY BGCOLOR="white" TEXT="black">
<BR>
<CENTER>
<FORM>
<SCRIPT>
if (parent.ShowFlag)
        document.write ('<INPUT TYPE="button" Value="Stop" onClick="run()">');
else
        document.write ('<INPUT TYPE="button" Value="Start" onClick="run()">');
</SCRIPT>
<INPUT TYPE="button" name="button" Value="Begin Again"
        onClick="parent.reload(); parent.runShow()">
```

```
</FORM>
</CENTER>
</BODY>
</HTML>
```

Additional files used by the auto slide show script are *dummy.htm*, which is a blank document, and the individual slide show documents, numbered *page_x.html*, where *x* is a number from 1 to the number of slides in the show. Three slide files have been provided with the example, named *page_1.html*, *page_2.html*, and *page_3.html*. Each slide page you use must contain the following onLoad event in the <BODY> tag:

```
<BODY onLoad="parent.triggerTimer()">
```

There are a number of ways to modify the auto slide show script:

- Change *MaxPages* in the parent frameset document to the total number of slide pages in your show.
- Change *Delay* in the parent frameset document to the desired delay between frames. This is the delay after the page has been loaded. This takes into account server speed, large graphics, sounds, and other media that affect access.
- Change the "root" name of the slide pages in the frameset document if you don't want to use *page*.

▆▆▆▆▆ **NOTE**

Under Netscape 2.0, animated GIFs (using the GIF89a file format) will not function when a setTimeout timer is used. Only the first "frame" of the animation appears. This limitation applies to any use of setTimeout in conjunction with an animated GIF.

▆▆▆▆▆

Does the setTimeout function create a recursive loop?

The nature of the setTimeout function is a subject of confusion among JavaScript developers. Most applications of setTimeout construct a repeating loop, as follows:

```
function repeatLoop () {
        // do something here
```

```
        setTimeout ("repeatLoop(); 1000)
}
```

This function is repeated once every second. On the surface, this appears to be a recursive loop. A recursive loop is one that calls itself repeatedly. Ordinarily, such repeated calls can cause stack overflow problems (the stack is used to store the state of JavaScript at any given time). Following is an example of a true recursive loop. If you run it, JavaScript quickly runs out of stack space and displays an error:

```
function stackOverflow() {
        stackOverflow();
}
```

Loops created with setTimeout are actually not recursive. When you set a timer, it's a one-shot, and it sets a "hook" in the operating system. This hook tells the operating system to do something at a certain time. After the setTimeout hook has been planted, JavaScript completely exits the function. Because the function is exited, the loop is not recursive. When the timer alarm rings, the operating system informs JavaScript, and JavaScript in turn calls whatever function is indicated in the setTimeout instruction.

Some uses of setTimeout have caused JavaScript problems. After a certain number of loops, JavaScript breaks down and signals an out-of-memory error. This condition is not due to recursive calls to the same function, but rather to the JavaScript memory cleanup system. JavaScript does not always flush objects away as it should—especially string objects. Depending on how they are written, JavaScript programs such as repeating marquees can eventually overflow JavaScript's memory. The memory error occurs when new string objects are created, leaving the old ones still in place. Sooner or later, JavaScript runs out of memory.

You can test the effects of the setTimeout function and recursive loops with the sample script below. Load it into Netscape, then push the Stack Test button. In a very short period of time, JavaScript signals a stack overflow message. Click OK to dismiss the error and the text box shows the number of loops JavaScript was able to perform before the error occurred (about 500 loops). Now click on the setTimeout Test button. JavaScript should continually loop through, updating the number at each pass. Theoretically JavaScript should never end with an error message with this kind of loop. The script has been tested with an excess of 15,000 iterations with no problems.

stacktest.html

```
<HTML>
<HEAD>
<TITLE>Gordon's McComb's Funky Stack/setTimeout Test</TITLE>
<SCRIPT LANGUAGE="JavaScript">
var Count = 0;

function doSomething1() {
        document.myform.textbox1.value = Count++;
        setTimeout ("doSomething1()", 1);
}

function doSomething2() {
        document.myform.textbox2.value = Count++;
        doSomething2();
}

</SCRIPT>
<BODY>
<FORM NAME="myform">
setTimeout iterations: <INPUT TYPE="text" NAME="textbox1" Value="0">
<INPUT TYPE="button" VALUE="setTimeout Test" onClick="Count = 0;
        doSomething1()"><P>
JavaScript blew its stack at: <INPUT TYPE="text" NAME="textbox2" Value="0">
<INPUT TYPE="button" VALUE="Stack Test" onClick="Count = 0;
        doSomething2()"><BR>
</FORM>
</BODY>
</HTML>
</Note>
```

Using the TYPE="image" Form Control

Netscape supports a little-known "secret" form control called an image. This image acts like an image map: click on the image and Netscape returns the X and Y position of the mouse as it submits the form. It's an unusual form control, and with client-side Netscape's image map capability, it isn't relied upon as much as it might otherwise be.

Still, the control offers some interesting possibilities, especially if you can upload CGI programs to your server, and it is a good alternative to server-side image maps. The form image control submits a form using the standard GET or POST method, so you don't need image map software to determine where on the image the mouse was clicked. When used with the GET submission method, clicking on the image produces an encoded URL that loops like this:

```
http://mydomain.com/form_image.html?button.x=296&button.y=25
```

- *http://mydomain.com/form_image.html* is the path and name of the current document.
- *?* separates the path and name from the URL encoded string provided by the form image control.
- *button.x=296* is the X position of the mouse when it clicked on the control (it's named button in this example).
- *button.y=25* is the Y position of the mouse when it clicked on the control. An & character separates the X and Y positions.

Figure 17.7 shows an example of an image containing several regions (it's the same image used in the client-side image map examples earlier in the chapter). The page was constructed with the following script:

```
<HTML>
<HEAD>
<TITLE>Image Form Control</TITLE>
</HEAD>
<BODY>
<CENTER>
```

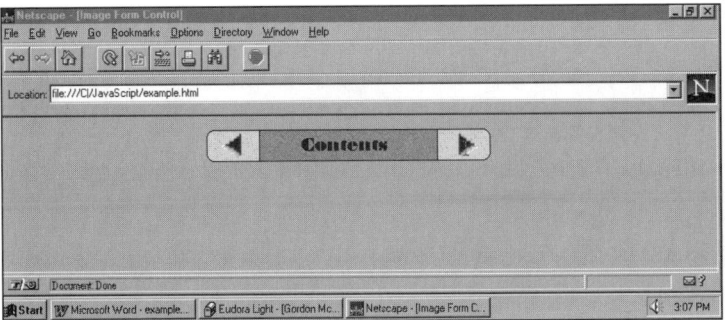

■■■■■■■■ **Figure 17.7** You can use an image form control as a means to produce client-side image maps.

```
<FORM ACTION="image_target.html" METHOD=get>
<INPUT TYPE="image" SRC="control.gif" name="button" BORDER=0>
</FORM>
</CENTER>
</BODY>
</HTML>
```

Notice the "image" <INPUT> type. This type uses an SRC attribute to specify the source. The standard BORDER=0 attribute has also been included to remove the border from the image. Also notice the filename given for the ACTION attribute in the <FORM> tag. This is the file that will be called when the image is clicked.

Normally, this would be a CGI program that would read the coordinates passed in the URL (or as an environment variable when using the POST submission method). But for your purposes, you can demonstrate the image form control using JavaScript. The *image_target.html* file is shown below. The document is designed so that it will not attempt to process the URL string if the "referring" document— the document that contains the form image control—is not *form_image.html*, the name of the file for the previous script. Assuming the "referring" document is *form_image.html*, this script determines where in the image the mouse was clicked and prints the result in the document.

CD-ROM

image_target.html

```
<HTML>

<HEAD>

<TITLE>Form Image Target Example</TITLE>

<SCRIPT LANGUAGE="JavaScript">


if (document.referrer.indexOf ("form_image.html") != -1) {

        Loc = location.href;

        XPos = Loc.substring (Loc.indexOf ("button.x=")+9, Loc.indexOf
        ("&button.y="))

        if ((XPos >= 0) && (XPos <=60)) document.write ("back")

        if ((XPos > 60) && (XPos <=255)) document.write ("contents")

        if ((XPos >= 256) && (XPos < 315)) document.write ("forward")

}


</SCRIPT>

</HEAD>

<BODY>

</BODY>

</HTML>
```

▆▆▆▆▆▆▆ **NOTE**

In this example the X/Y decoding is fairly straightforward because the image is composed of just "buttons" aligned horizontally. The Y position is inferred. If your image contains clickable regions at different X and Y positions, you'll need to add extra if tests to determine the exact zone where the mouse was clicked.

▆▆▆▆▆▆

Unfortunately, you cannot currently prevent the form image control from submitting the form, as it doesn't respond to either the onClick or the onSubmit event handlers. This means you can't intercept the URL—and its X/Y position data. The form is always submitted. But, as you can see in the previous example, it is possible to provide the name of another HTML document, and use JavaScript to pick apart the resulting encoded URL.

Using JavaScript to Build a Small Database

A common request of JavaScript is to build a database, using just JavaScript to look up and present data. This is an ideal use of JavaScript, as long as the database is relatively small. Databases like Yahoo! and Alta Vista require large storage of data, and that data stays on the server machine. JavaScript can't readily access specific data on a server (at least not with help for CGI programs), which means all the data in the database must be part of the page that is loaded into the user's machine.

Obviously, a user on a dial-up Internet connection will not want to wait several minutes for a large database of information to be downloaded. Too, JavaScript cannot currently handle code blocks larger than about 40K, which is another limitation to using it as a database retrieval system.

Still, for simple database tasks JavaScript can be used to process user input, match that input against variables, and display the appropriate data. The design of your page will greatly influence the complexity of the JavaScript code you must write to support the underlying database. If you allow users to enter freeform text (that is, type any text) rather than select from option menus, your JavaScript code needs to be far more robust. The reason is that you need to "parse out" the user's entry into a form compatible with your database.

There are many ways to implement data storage in a database. One method is presented here using paired array objects, but you can modify or augment this method as you see fit. Alternatively, chose a different approach altogether.

Creating the Database Array Objects

The basic idea behind a database is that you store data in a way that can be easily searched, using an index, like an index of a book. The data itself can be stored elsewhere in the database. You look up what you want in the index, note the location, and go there to retrieve the data.

This method can readily be applied in JavaScript using arrays. You need only two arrays for simple data storage: one array contains the index of the items in the database, and the other array contains the actual items.

The *color_database.html* file shows an example. Two arrays are created using the generic Object object. The arrays are named *Idx* and *Data*, for index and data, respectively. These arrays are used to store the first 10 named colors used by Netscape for color choices (the entire list can be found in Chapter 21, "All About HTML"). A sample of *color_database.html* is shown in Figure 17.8.

CD-ROM

```
color_database.html


<HTML>
<HEAD>
<TITLE>Color Database</TITLE>
<SCRIPT LANGUAGE="JavaScript">
Idx = new Object();
Data = new Object();

Idx[0]=10
Idx[1]="aliceblue"
```

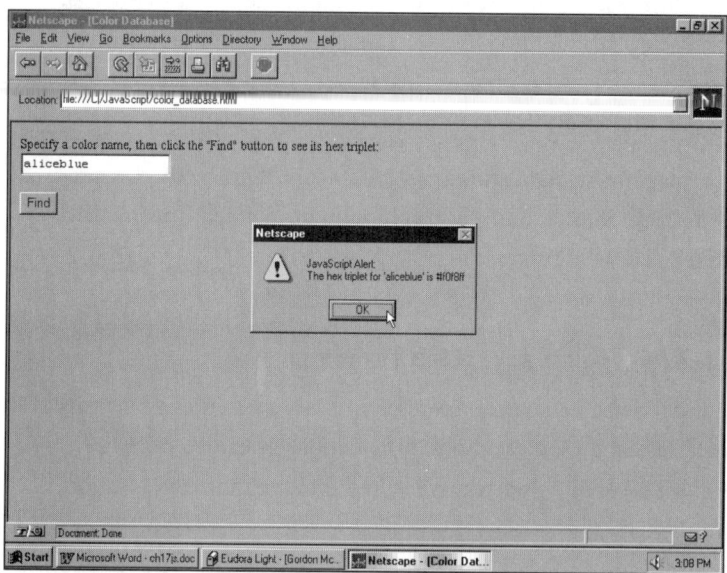

Figure 17.8 Enter a color in the text box, click Find, and JavaScript consults its database of colors to find the matching hex triplet value.

```
Idx[2]="antiquewhite"

Idx[3]="aqua"

Idx[4]="aquamarine"

Idx[5]="azure"

Idx[6]="beige"

Idx[7]="bisque"

Idx[8]="black"

Idx[9]="blanchedalmond"

Idx[10]="blue"


Data[1]="f0f8ff"

Data[2]="faebd7"

Data[3]="00ffff"

Data[4]="7fffd4"

Data[5]="f0ffff"

Data[6]="f5f5dc"

Data[7]="ffe4c4"

Data[8]="000000"

Data[9]="ffebcd"

Data[10]="0000ff"


function checkDatabase() {
        var Found = false;
        var Item = document.testform.color.value.toLowerCase();
        for (Count = 1; Count <= Idx[0]; Count++) {
                if (Item == Idx[Count]) {
                        Found = true;
                        alert ("The hex triplet for '" + Item + "' is #" +
                                Data[Count]);
                        break;
                }
        }
        if (! Found)
                alert ("Sorry, the color '" + Item +"' is not listed in the
```

```
                              database.");

    }
    </SCRIPT>
    <FORM NAME="testform" onSubmit="checkDatabase()">
    Specify a color name, then click the "Find" button to see its hex triplet:<BR>
    <INPUT TYPE="text" NAME="color" Value="" onClick=0> <P>
    <INPUT TYPE="button" NAME="button" Value="Find" onClick="checkDatabase()">
    </FORM>
    </BODY></HTML>
```

After loading of the *color_database.html* file, JavaScript creates the two arrays and fills them with the necessary data. These arrays are global, and they are "visible" to any script in the document. The user enters a color in the text box and then clicks the Find button. This actuates the checkDatabase function, which attempts to match the entry of the text box with its list of color names. A for loop iterates through all of the indexed items in the Idx array. If there's a match, the hex triplet is displayed in an alert box. If the for loop finishes without making a match, another alert box appears telling the user the search failed.

Note the toLowerCase method used in the searchDatabase function. This method forces the user's entry to all lowercase. This is desirable because this database works by comparing strings. String comparisons are case-sensitive; the toLowerCase method ensures that the input string is all lowercase, in order to match the entries in the Idx array.

You will want to provide additional string checking and management if you want to disallow other extraneous input, like spaces, nonalphabetic characters, or symbols. Many of the plug-and-play functions detailed in Chapter 13, "Plug-and-Play Routines," help you manage strings for exactly this purpose. For example, the leftTrim and rightTrim functions remove extra spaces at the beginning and ending of a string.

Also note the break statement in the for loop. This breaks JavaScript out of the loop should it find a match. The break statement is not mandatory, but it reduces the work JavaScript must perform. Without the break, JavaScript continues to search through the Idx array even after it's found a match.

Storing Field of Data

You can use the technique in *color_database.html* for almost any application, including databases in which the data is composed of separate fields. For this application, the data can be stored in a single array or multiple arrays (or multdimensional arrays). Storing the data in a single string in a one-dimensional array is a good option. Separate fields—such as a name, address, and phone number—can be marked off with special characters. Code in the script can be used to separate the single string into individual fields.

In the *names_database.html* example that follows, the database stores names of clients. The last name of the client is used as the index. The data itself is stored in a separate array; the name, address, and phone number are separated by the | (pipe) character. A generalized parser function (borrowed by Chapter 13, "Plug-and-Play Routines") separates the fields into individual elements of a new array. The resulting data is displayed in an alert box; in an actual application, you'll probably want to do more than just display the data as a message, but this gives you an idea of how the system works. Figure 17.9 shows an example of *names_database.html* in action.

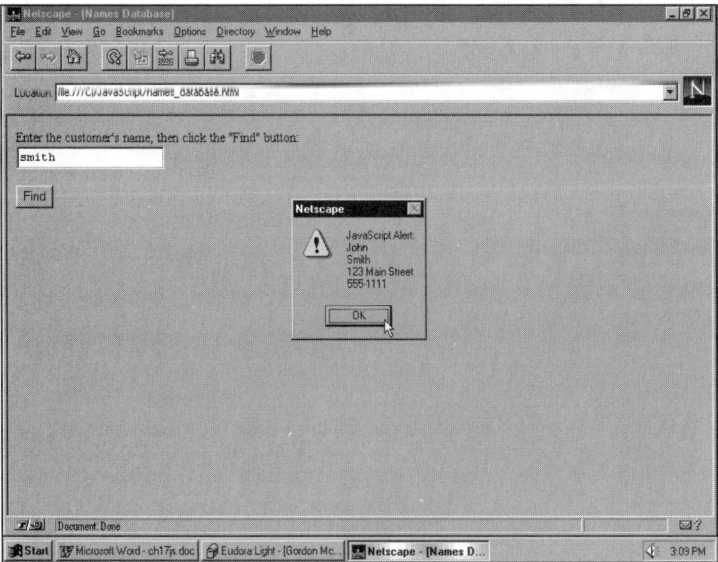

▬▬▬▬▬ **Figure 17.9** When a name is found, an alert message displays all four pieces of information about the customer.

CD-ROM

names_database.html

```
<HTML>
<HEAD>
<TITLE>Names Database</TITLE>
<SCRIPT LANGUAGE="JavaScript">
Idx = new Object();
Data = new Object();

Idx[0]=10
Idx[1]="smith"
Idx[2]="jones"
Idx[3]="michaels"
Idx[4]="avery"
Idx[5]="baldwin"

Data[1]="John|Smith|123 Main Street|555-1111"
Data[2]="Fred|Jones|PO Box 5|555-2222"
Data[3]="Gabby|Michaels|555 Maplewood|555-3333"
Data[4]="Alice|Avery|1006 Pike Place|555-4444"
Data[5]="Steven|Baldwin|5 Covey Ave|555-5555"

function checkDatabase() {
        var Found = false;
        var Item = document.testform.customer.value.toLowerCase();
        for (Count = 1; Count <= Idx[0]; Count++) {
                if (Item == Idx[Count]) {
                        Found = true;
                        var Ret = parser (Data[Count], "|");
                        var Temp = "";
                        for (i = 1; i <= Ret[0]; i++) {
                                Temp += Ret[i] + "\n";
                        }
```

```
                            alert (Temp);

                            break;

                    }

            }

        if (! Found)

                alert ("Sorry, the name '" + Item +"' is not listed in the
database.")


}


function parser (InString, Sep)   {

        NumSeps=1;

        for (Count=1; Count < InString.length; Count++)   {

                if (InString.charAt(Count)==Sep)

                        NumSeps++;

        }

        parse = new Object();

        Start=0; Count=1; ParseMark=0;

        LoopCtrl=1;

        while (LoopCtrl==1)   {

                ParseMark = InString.indexOf(Sep, ParseMark);

                TestMark=ParseMark+0;

                if ((TestMark==0) || (TestMark==-1)){

                        parse[Count]= InString.substring (Start,
                                InString.length);

                        LoopCtrl=0;

                        break;

                }

                parse[Count] = InString.substring (Start, ParseMark);

                Start=ParseMark+1;

                ParseMark=Start;

                Count++;

        }

        parse[0]=Count;
```

```
        return (parse);
}


</SCRIPT>
<FORM NAME="testform" onSubmit="checkDatabase()">
Enter the customer's name, then click the "Find" button:<BR>
<INPUT TYPE="text" NAME="customer" Value="" onClick=0> <P>
<INPUT TYPE="button" NAME="button" Value="Find" onClick="checkDatabase()">
</FORM>
</BODY></HTML>
```

More JavaScript Projects

The following JavaScript examples are included on the CD-ROM accompanying this book. The examples are commented within the file so that you can adapt the example to your needs.

Building an Outline Manager

JavaScript experimenter Stefan Raab was the first to think of this great application: use JavaScript to display and manage a collapsible outline. Click on an item in the outline to expand or condense it. The effect is similar to the file management interface used with Windows and the newsgroups listings in Netscape's News window.

Both the e2_outline.html and outline manager are designed to be fairly easy to modify with your own contents. As such, both limit you to a top level and a single "child" level. Check the author's site at http://gmccomb.com/sourcebook/ for additional outline managers you might want to use.

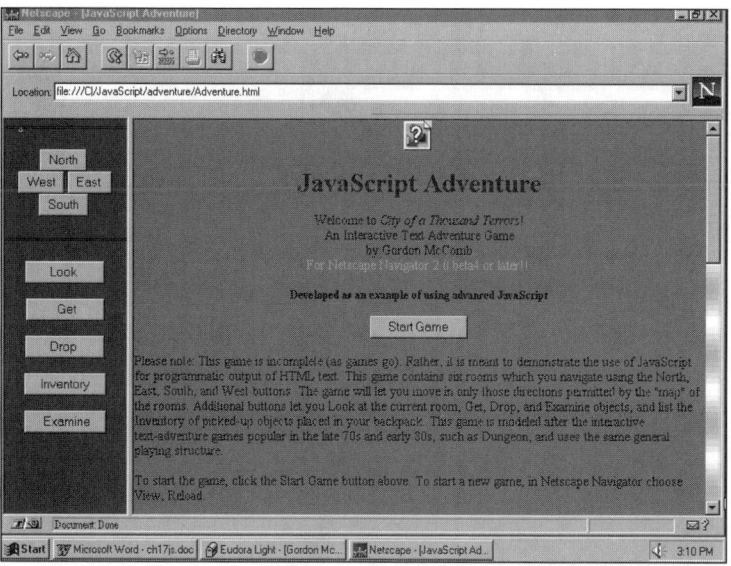

▰▰▰▰▰▰ **Figure 17.10** The adventure game lets you write your own text adventures. You can even add sound effects and graphics, if you prefer a multimedia presentation.

JavaScript Adventure Game

JavaScript isn't just for business; you can use it for games as well. The *adventure.html* file (and associated files) creates a limited adventure game, in the spirit of the old text-based adventure games popular in the late 1970s and early 1980s (see Figure 17.10). This one has only a half-dozen rooms and doesn't keep score. But you can use the ideas behind it—including object creation and management—for a more elaborate game of your own devising.

The design goal of *adventure.html* is that the game contents can be changed, without having to write any JavaScript code to control the game. You use the same "guts" for each game and change the text and object behaviors (weapons, creatures, and so forth) in a data document.

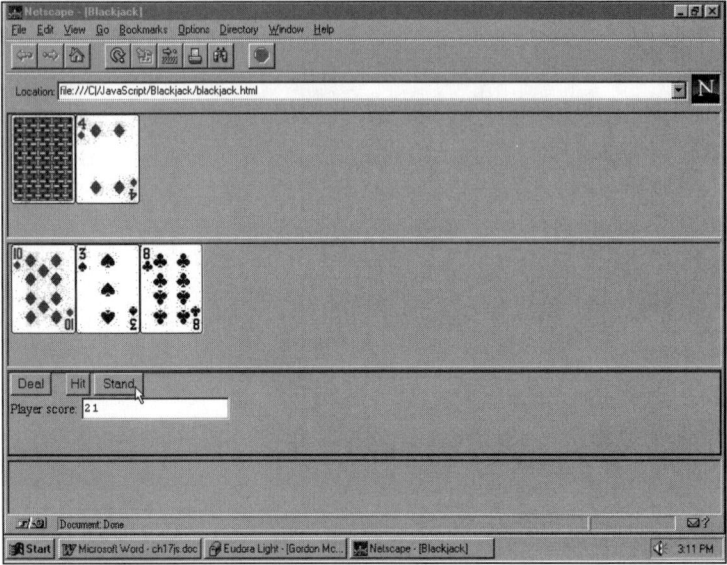

Figure 17.11 JavaScript blackjack lets you bet against your computer.

JavaScript Blackjack

Blackjack.html demonstrates how to use JavaScript as a card hustler. The game deals a standard hand of Blackjack, as shown in Figure 17.11. You're given the option to hit or stand. The game uses GIFs for each card of a deck, so it's best played on a local computer. JavaScript (the dealer) follows standard Las Vegas rules: hit to 16, stand on 17 and over. For simplicity, this game doesn't provide extras such as insurance or double-down.

18

USING CGI WITH

JAVASCRIPT

Nothing strikes more fear in the heart of a Web publisher than these three letters: C-G-I. CGI stands for *common gateway interface*, a mechanism for safely transporting data from a client (a browser like Netscape) to a server. CGI requires a program or script (like a batch file) running on the server to accept data from the client and process it. While most all of us work with programs on our local computer—running them, feeding them data, and so forth—for some reason CGI programs seem more troublesome and ornery.

While CGI can be scary stuff, it's also awe-inspiring in light of what it can do. CGI can process forms, for example, display "hit" counters, as well as search databases and return a result.

JavaScript is one of several client-based programming tools designed to reduce the reliance on CGI for advanced Web work. In the past, for example, if you wanted to ensure that the user filled in all the entry blanks of a form, you'd have to spend hours—if not days—writing and debugging a CGI program. A large part of this time-consuming task was in uploading and testing new versions, which is a typical problem for those of us who don't have direct access to our server except through relatively slow phone lines. JavaScript eases this burden by allowing you to verify the form before you send the data to the server. You still need a CGI program to accept and process the data; but because it has already been validated, the CGI portion can be much simpler.

Chapter 16, "Using JavaScript with Forms," details the many aspects of designing HTML forms for use with JavaScript. In all likelihood, many of the forms that you create with JavaScript will be standalone and will not require CGI processing. But for those forms that do, this chapter provides the other half of the forms equation: submitting the data to the form and processing it. This chapter also discusses several other uses of CGI as it relates to JavaScript, including creating a JavaScript-based visit counter.

The subject of CGI is vast. If you need additional assistance, or want to learn specifics, you should check out the latest books on CGI at the bookstore. Also consult the Web for CGI documentation, tutorials, and examples.

A Non-Technical Introduction to CGI

The HTTP protocol used by the Web is mostly a one-way street: from server to client. The vast bulk of data on the Web travels down this one-way street, and this includes all the text, graphics, sound effects, VRML movies, and other data you see in a browser. But there's also a narrow back alley that allows traffic in the other direction, as shown in Figure 18.1. This is the "requester path," where the browser can ask the server to display this or that file.

There is actually quite a bit of data that flows in this requester path, including your identification (at least your domain), your "user agent" (the kind of browser you have), and other variables such as a list of file types that your browser can render. When the server gets this data, it can decide what kind of data to send to you, based on the information it has received. And of course, it also receives a URL of the page you want to view.

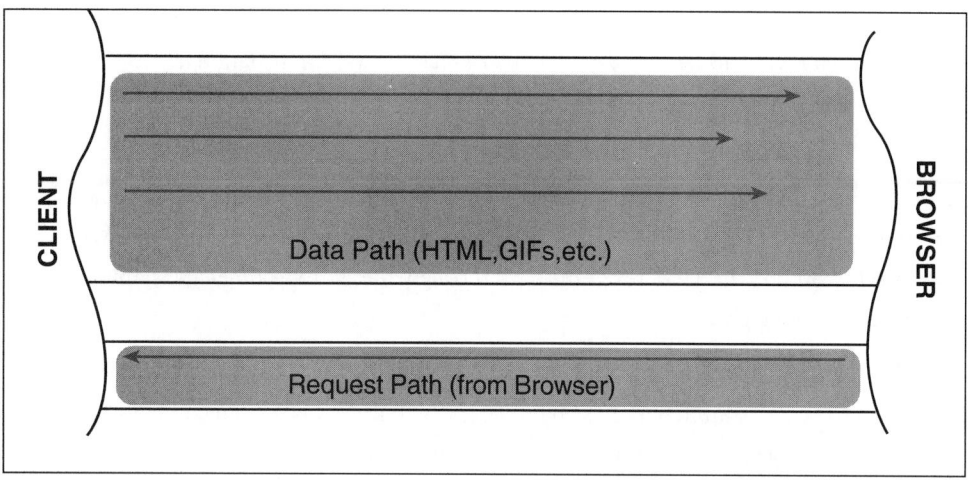

Figure 18.1 The two-way street of the Web is more like a main highway for the data you receive, and a little back alley for the data sent to the server.

It is in this requester path that CGI also functions. CGI has two means of passing data from the client to the server: one is URL-based and you can readily see it; the other is hidden away, like everything else the browser passes back to the server.

First, let's look at the URL approach, which is more accurately called the *GET* method. You've probably seen it at work if you've ever seen an URL like this one:

```
http://mydomain.com/cgi-bin/program.cgi?subject=JavaScript
```

The text beyond the ? question mark character is data sent to the server, ostensibly to be used with a CGI program. The program itself is the basic URL:

```
http://mydomain.com/cgi-bin/program.cgi
```

and the rest is treated like a "command-line option" (similar to those used in DOS, Windows, and Unix). The CGI program fetches the command-line option as the data and processes it so it knows what information to return. The GET method is also sometimes referred to as URL encoding because the CGI portion of the string is part of the URL. It is also encoded to contain only valid URL characters—that is, no spaces, or most other types of punctuation. These characters are encoded using %nn number sets—for example, a space is encoded as %20.

The other method used by CGI is called *POST*. It leaves the URL alone and instead passes its data via hidden *environment variables*. The CGI program is activated merely by specifying it in an URL:

```
http://mydomain.com/cgi-bin/program.cgi
```

This line passes a series of data structures, including one or more hidden environment variables, from the browser to the client through the back-alley requester path. With the POST method, the CGI program sifts through these environment variables in order to collect the data.

Which is better? CGI programs that use the GET method are generally the easier to write, but the URL is limited to 256 characters, which is the maximum command line length imposed by most operating systems, including Unix. The POST method is ideal when lots of data has to be provided by the client. The data can be any length—hundreds of kilobytes or more, if necessary.

Programming CGI

Because CGI is just a program, any programming language that runs on the server can be used to create it. On Unix servers—still the most common on the Web—it's not unusual to find CGI programs written using a shell language, which is similar to a DOS batch file. Such CGI programs are more accurately called *scripts* or *shell scripts* because they are not self-running programs on their own; rather, they require another program on the computer to operate. But we'll refer to them all as "CGI programs" just to avoid being wordy.

Another popular CGI programming language for Unix is Perl. Perl is not a simple language, but it isn't a difficult one, either. It is often favored by CGI programmers because it offers extensive string-handling functions. Like a shell script, Perl does not build standalone programs. It needs an external *Perl interpreter* program to run.

And of course, Unix supports CGI scripts written in the C language. C is favored in some circles because it offers a great deal of speed, power, and flexibility, and it is reasonably portable. A C program written for a Unix computer has a fair chance of running under DOS or Windows.

While Unix remains the most common operating system for the Internet and the World Wide Web, it is by no means the only one. Other operating systems include SunOS (from Sun Microsystems, developer of Java and co-developer of JavaScript), Windows 3.1, Windows 95, Windows NT, MacOS, and even DOS. Each of these operating systems offers its own variations for writing CGI programs. SunOS is Unix-like and therefore uses a lot of Unix programs. The Windows platforms can run a variation of the Unix Perl language, as well as programs written in Visual Basic or C, and the MacOS generally uses AppleScript. DOS can run CGI programs of just about any flavor, including those written with old-fashioned DOS batch files and Basic!

An Example of CGI

Here's an example of a CGI program written in Perl for the typical Unix server. It's a public domain, generic "use-it-anywhere" form mail processor. The filename is *formmail.cgi*. It collects data filled into an HTML form and then mails the data—nicely formatted—off to your e-mail address.

For the most part, the *formmail.cgi* program does not need customization. You tell it the e-mail address to which you want to send mail, and the rest is done for you. However, you may need to alter the script a bit to suit the requirements of your server. For example, the script assumes the Perl interpreter program is found on a root directory of the server named /usr/local/bin/perl (this is by far the most common location). However, if the Perl interpreter is in another directory on your server, you will need to modify this line. The *formmail.cgi* program also assumes your server uses the (fairly) standard sendmail program. You'll need to modify the script if your server uses something different.

```
#! /usr/local/bin/perl
######################
# General Mail Form To Work With Any Fields
# Created 6/9/95              Last Modified 6/11/95
# Version 1.0
# http://mydomain.com/cgi-bin/formmail.cgi?http://mydomain.com/mypage.html
# Define Variables
```

```
$mailprog = '/usr/lib/sendmail';
$date = `date`; chop ($date);


#####################
# Necessary Fields in HTML Form:    (Read the README file for more info)
# recipient = specifies who mail is sent to
# username = specifies the remote users email address for replies
# realname = specifies the remote users real identity
# subject = specifies what you want the subject of your mail to be


# Print the Initial Output Heading
print "Location: ";
print  $ENV{'QUERY-STRING'};
print "\n\n";


# Get the input
read(STDIN, $buffer, $ENV{'CONTENT-LENGTH'});


# Split the name-value pairs
@pairs - split(/&/, $buffer);


foreach $pair (@pairs)
{
    ($name, $value) = split(/=/, $pair);

    # Un-Webify plus signs and %-encoding
    $value =~ tr/+/ /;
    $value =~ s/%([a-fA-F0-9][a-fA-F0-9])/pack("C", hex($1))/eg;
    $name =~ tr/+/ /;
    $name =~ s/%([a-fA-F0-9][a-fA-F0-9])/pack("C", hex($1))/eg;

    # Stop people from using subshells to execute commands
    # Not a big deal when using sendmail, but very important
    # when using UCB mail (aka mailx).
```

```perl
    # $value =~ s/~!/ ~!/g;


    # Uncomment for debugging purposes
    # print "Setting $name to $value<P>";


    $FORM{$name} = $value;
}


# Print Return HTML
#print "<html><head><title>Thanks You</title></head>\n";
#print "<body><h1>Thank You For Filling Out This Form</h1>\n";
#print "Thank you for taking the time to fill out our feedback form.";
#print $ENV{'QUERY—STRING'};


# Open The Mail
open (MAIL, "|$mailprog $FORM{'recipient'}") || die "Can't open $mailprog!\n";
print MAIL "From: $FORM{'username'} ($FORM{'realname'})\n";
print MAIL "Reply-To: $FORM{'username'} ($FORM{'realname'})\n";
print MAIL "To: $FORM{'recipient'}\n";
print MAIL "Subject: $FORM{'subject'}\n\n",
print MAIL "Below is the result of your feedback form. It was submitted by
$FORM{'realname'} $FORM{'username'} on $date\n";
print MAIL "-----------------------------\n";
foreach $pair (@pairs)
{
    ($name, $value) = split(/=/, $pair);


    # Un-Webify plus signs and %-encoding
    $value =~ tr/+/ /;
    $value =~ s/%([a-fA-F0-9][a-fA-F0-9])/pack("C", hex($1))/eg;
    $name =~ tr/+/ /;
    $name =~ s/%([a-fA-F0-9][a-fA-F0-9])/pack("C", hex($1))/eg;


    # Stop people from using subshells to execute commands
```

```
        # Not a big deal when using sendmail, but very important
        # when using UCB mail (aka mailx).
        # $value =~ s/~!/ ~!/g;

        # Uncomment for debugging purposes
        # print "Setting $name to $value<P>";

        $FORM{$name} = $value;

   # Print the MAIL for each name value pair
      print MAIL "$name:   $value\n";
      print MAIL "————————————————————————————————\n\n";

   # Print the Return HTML for each name value pair.
   #   print "$name = $value<hr>\n";
   }
   close (MAIL);
   #print "</body></html>";
```

To call the script, you submit a form created with standard HTML markup. Here's a basic form (using no JavaScript). It asks for the user's name and e-mail address and has form controls for a checkbox and a text area. Clicking the Submit Form button submits the form.

```
<FORM METHOD=POST ACTION="/cgi-bin/formmail.cgi?http://mydomain.com">
<INPUT TYPE="hidden" NAME="recipient" VALUE="me@mydomain.com">
<INPUT TYPE="hidden" NAME="subject" VALUE="Stuff">
Name: <INPUT TYPE="text" NAME="realname" SIZE=40><BR>
E-Mail: <INPUT TYPE="text" NAME="username" SIZE=40><P>
Do you like us?
<INPUT TYPE="checkbox" NAME="include" CHECKED><P>
Please write your comments here.<BR>
<TEXTAREA NAME="comments" ROWS=10 COLS=60>
</TEXTAREA><P><INPUT TYPE="subit" VALUE="Submit Form">
<INPUT TYPE="reset" VALUE=" Erase Form">
</FORM>
```

- The form is sent to the URL specified in the ACTION parameter. This includes the path and name of the CGI program (in this case *cgi-bin/for-mmail.cgi*).

- The *formmail.cgi* script takes one URL parameter: the URL you want to return to when the form has been submitted. This can be a home page or a "form successfully submitted page."

- The NAME="recipient" hidden field stores the e-mail address to send the completed form.

- The NAME="subject" hidden field stores the subject of the e-mail message (which is useful if you use the *formmail.cgi* script for other forms on your pages).

The remainder of the form is standard HTML form markup, including text fields, a checkbox, a text area box, a reset button, and a submit button. Figure 18.2 shows an example of an e-mail processed and send using the formmail.cgi script.

Adding JavaScript to the Mix

Basic form tasks don't need JavaScript. The HTML markup does all the work necessary to submit the form. However, JavaScript can be a useful component depending

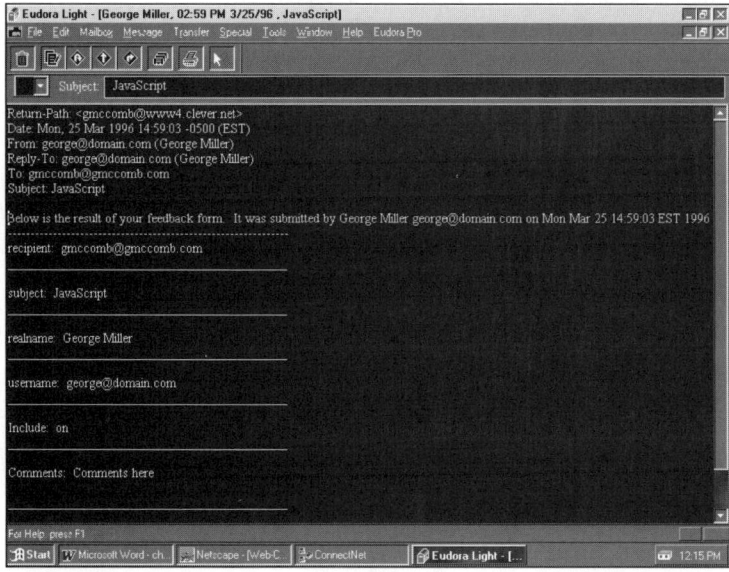

■■■■■■■■■ **Figure 18.2** E-mail received from the generic form mailer.

on the level of control you want to provide and the kinds of fail-safe mechanisms you want to include. The most common—and practical—application of JavaScript with forms is validating user input. Chapter 16, "Using JavaScript with Forms," spends much time on this topic. If you haven't yet read that chapter, you'll probably want to now before proceeding any further with this one.

One of the greatest strengths of JavaScript is that it can be used to delay or even cancel a form submission. In delaying a form submission, you can use JavaScript code to validate input or ask the user whether to continue or cancel the submission. Canceling a submission is helpful if your JavaScript has detected a problem in one or more of the input fields. You can cancel the submission of the form to the CGI program and ask the user to re-enter the data.

There are two ways to control form submission with JavaScript: using the *onSubmit event handler* and using the *submit() method*.

Using the onSubmit Event Handler

The onSubmit event handler is the obvious choice for dealing with form submission—though, in fact, it isn't always the best choice. JavaScript, however, is nothing if not a language of choice, so you can pick the approach you want to use.

The onSubmit event handler is placed in the <FORM> tag, as follows:

```
<FORM METHOD=get ACTION="http://domain.com/page.cgi" onSubmit="return
doSomething()">
```

Ordinarily, the browser would submit the form to the URL specified in the ACTION attribute. With the onSubmit event handler, the browser first hands off the submission request to JavaScript—in this case, a function elsewhere in the script called doSomething. The innards of this function are irrelevant at this time, except for one item: the function should return a value of some type. If it returns *true*, the submission is carried out. If it returns *false*, the browser assumes you want to deny submitting the form, and the form submission is canceled. While the return value is supposedly optional, you should include it in all cases, as JavaScript can behave erratically otherwise.

Here's a working example:

```
<HTML>
```

```
<HEAD>

<TITLE>Form Submission Example</TITLE>

<SCRIPT LANGUAGE="JavaScript">

function doSomething () {

        if (confirm ("Submit form?"))

                return true;

        else

                return false;

}

</SCRIPT>

<BODY>

Below is a form

<FORM NAME="test" METHOD=get ACTION="onsubmit.htm" onSubmit="return
doSomething()">

<INPUT TYPE="text" NAME="textbox1" Value=""><BR>

<INPUT TYPE="text" NAME="textbox2" Value=""><BR>

<INPUT TYPE="submit">

</FORM>

</BODY>

</HTML>
```

The onSubmit event handler reads:

```
onSubmit="return doSomething()"
```

The return causes the value returned from the doSomething function to be sent back to the onSubmit handler. If this value is *true*, the form is submitted; if it's *false*, it's not submitted. The confirm box asks if you wish to submit the form. Answering No returns *false*, and answering Yes returns *true*.

When you try this script, you can see the results of your response. Type some text into the two text boxes, and then click the Submit Query button. If you respond Yes, you see the URL encoding for the form after the path and filename (you can use the same name for the ACTION attribute as for the name of the file, which is *onsubmit.htm*). Completely reload the document—make sure the URL in the Location box is cleared of all the URL encoding mess—and try submitting again, only this time respond with No in the confirm box. The URL encoding is not placed there, showing you that the form was not submitted.

Using the submit Method

The submit method is the preferred choice if your form doesn't have a Submit Query button. The submit method merely tells JavaScript to submit the specified form. You can identify the form by name, if the form has a name, or identify the form using the forms[] array index. Here's the way to submit a form using the form object (named *form* in the example), passed to the doSomething function.

```
<HTML>
<HEAD>
<TITLE>Form Submission Example</TITLE>
<SCRIPT LANGUAGE="JavaScript">
function doSomething (form) {
        if (confirm ("Submit form?"))
                form.submit();
}
</SCRIPT>
<BODY>
Below is a form
<FORM NAME="test" METHOD=get ACTION="test1.htm">
<INPUT TYPE="text" NAME="textbox1" Value=""><BR>
<INPUT TYPE="text" NAME="textbox2" Value=""><BR>
<INPUT TYPE="button" VALUE="Submit Me Now!"
onClick="doSomething(this.form)">
</FORM>
</BODY>
</HTML>
```

- To refer to the form with the forms[] array, use *document.forms[x].submit()*, where *x* is the index of the form object you want (this is usually 0, as there is typically just one form in a document).

- To refer to the form by name, use *document.formname.submit()*, where *formname* is the unique name of the form.

- To refer to a form in another frame, provide the full hierarchy for the frame and its contents: *parent.framename.document.formname.submit()*. Here, *framename* is the unique name of the frame, and *formname* is the unique name of the form. (You may also use the frames[] array to specify the frame and the forms[] array to specify the form.)

- To refer to a form in another window, provide the full hierarchy for the window and its contents: *windowname.document.formname.submit()*. Here, *windowname* is the unique name of the window (as named using window.open), and *formname* is the unique name of the form (you may also uses the forms[] array).

Verifying Input and Submitting the Form

One of the primary purposes of using JavaScript with forms is to provide user input validation. The validation can be simple—"is this entry box blank?"—or it can be complex. See Chapter 16, "Using JavaScript with Forms," for a more complete rundown of validation techniques. For this discussion, let's set up a simple validation process to check if one input box has at least some data (is not blank), and that another contains only numbers.

verity.html

CD-ROM

```
<HTML>
<HEAD>
<TITLE>Form Submission Example</TITLE>
<SCRIPT LANGUAGE="JavaScript">
function doSomething (form) {
        SubmitMe=true;
        if (form.textbox1.value =="")
                SubmitMe = false;
        if (isNumberString(form.textbox2.value) == false)
                SubmitMe = false;
        if (SubmitMe == true)
                form.submit();
```

```
            else
                    alert ("One of the entry blanks is invalid")
    }


    function isNumberString (InString)  {
            if(InString.length==0)
                    return (false);
            for (Count=0; Count < InString.length; Count++)  {
                    TempChar= InString.substring (Count, Count+1);
                    if ("1234567890".indexOf (TempChar, 0)==-1)
                            return (false);
            }
            return (true);
    }


    </SCRIPT>
    <BODY>
    Below is a form
    <FORM NAME="test" METHOD=get ACTION="test1.htm">
    <INPUT TYPE="text" NAME="textbox1" Value=""> <BR>
    <INPUT TYPE="text" NAME="textbox2" Value=""><BR>
    <INPUT TYPE="button" VALUE="Click Me" onClick="doSomething(this.form)">
    </FORM>
    </BODY>
    </HTML>
```

- The form is submitted if, and only if, there is text in textbox1 and at least one number in textbox2.

- The statement *if (form.textbox1.value ==""")* tests if textbox1 is empty. If the statement is *true*, the SubmitMe variable is set to *false*, and form submission is canceled.

- The statement *if (isNumberString(form.textbox2.value) == false)* tests if textbox2 is empty or contains non-numeric characters. If the statement is *true*, the SubmitMe variable is set to *false*, and form submission is canceled. The isNumberString function, provided later in the script, performs the number validation check.

Resetting the Form

When a form is successfully submitted, the server has the job of replacing the page with another (such as, "Thanks for submitting the form") for redisplaying the old form page. The latter causes the values of the form to be reset to their default state. Because most controls have no default (text boxes are blank, checkboxes and radio buttons are unchecked), resetting effectively clears the form. Of course, if you don't want to clear the form completely, be sure to provide default values for the controls. For example, to provide a default in a text box, use the VALUE= attribute. Or to set a button as checked, use the CHECKED attribute:

```
<INPUT TYPE="text" NAME="textbox1" VALUE="Default Text">
<INPUT TYPE="checkbox" NAME="checkbox1" CHECKED>
```

There are times when you wish to force a reset of the form, without submitting it. The TYPE="reset" attribute for the <INPUT> tag acts to reset the form. Resetting is handy when you want to allow the user to start all over again from scratch. The syntax of the reset button is:

```
<INPUT TYPE="reset" VALUE="Reset Me">
```

Note that the VALUE of the reset button is optional. If you omit this attribute, the browser defaults to "Reset" as the label for the button.

Using CGI to Build a "Hit" Counter with JavaScript

No doubt you've seen—and perhaps used—a "hit counter" on one or more pages at your Web site. The counter increments with each "hit," or visitor, to your page. Many people like hit counters because they provide instant feedback on the popularity of a site. With the global nature of the Web, it is not unusual for even a highly specialized page to receive hundreds of hits over the course of a year.

There are several ways you can implement a counter on your Web page. The easiest method is to use a free or commercial counter service, such as Net Digits. These services allow you to "borrow" their server, which stores and provides the count information. You can use these counters with or without JavaScript. If you want to embellish a page counter with JavaScript, see Chapter 17, "Using JavaScript with Advanced HTML," for more information.

Here's how the basic hit counter works: Your Web page contains an <IMG> tag that references a program available on the server. When a visitor comes to your page, the browser encounters the <IMG> tag, and it links to the CGI counter program on the designated server. The program, in turn, looks up the number of visits previously to your site, adds one more, then dynamically creates an image that depicts the number of hits to your page. This image—which is usually in the form of an odometer—is used as the graphic for the <IMG> tag. This odometer is what the visitor sees when the page loads. See Figure 18.3 for an example.

By their nature, all counters use CGI or some other program running on the server to display the number of hits. A server program is necessary because the number of visits must be recorded in a file on the server. The design of the Web allows only authorized write-access to the server, so the user's browser program cannot update the counter file. Not all counters use straight CGI. Some use a technique called server-side includes (SSI) that is somewhat similar to CGI. While CGI is supported on most

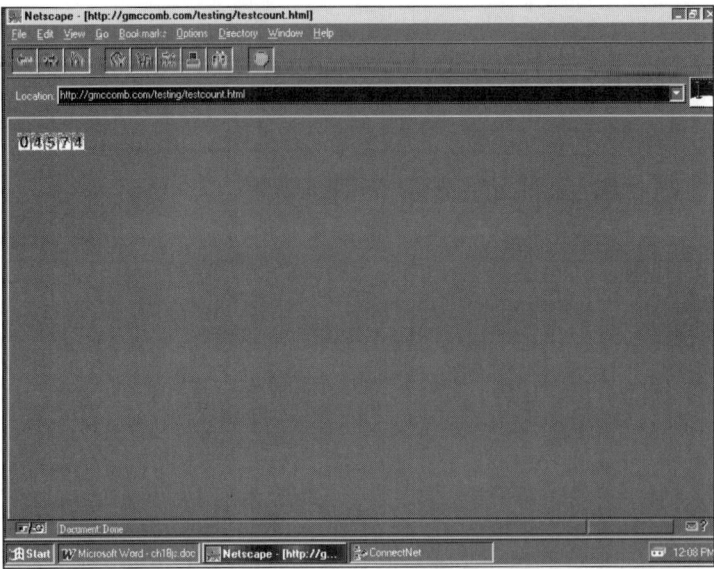

Figure 18.3 An example of the ubiquitous Web page hit counter.

servers, server-side includes are not. You'll want to keep this in mind because the JavaScript counter technique detailed in this chapter requires the server support SSI. Contact your server administrator if you're not sure what your server supports.

Understanding Counters and JavaScript

There are numerous counter programs available on the Web. Most are free, although the authors often ask for an acknowledgment link to their site. Others are shareware (most under $20), while a few are full-blown commercially supported programs. Bear in mind that like any program, the counter program you choose must be compatible with the server you are using. Not only must you match up the operating system (Unix, NT, or Windows, for example), but also the type of server software and the availability of program interpreters such as Perl.

Finding a counter for your kind of server is relatively easy—once you determine what your server offers, and what it doesn't. The tough part is installing and setting up the program on your server. For that, this can't help you much. The good news, however, is that some of the counter programs available are specifically designed for easy installation, with clear and concise documentation.

■■■■■■ NOTE

> There are many CGI scripts for hit counters available. Check with the Web search sites, such as Alta Vista and Yahoo, using *CGI* and *counter* as the search terms.

■■■■■■

Why use JavaScript to make a hit counter? Doesn't the counter program do all the work? Yes and no. While some counter programs create fancy counter images in all sorts of colors and sizes, most programs available for free or shareware on the Web—and that are easy to install on a server—return plain and boring text. JavaScript is ideal for these kinds of programs because you can use JavaScript to retrieve the count value and display it in another form. For instance, you can use fancy "LED" digits, such as those shown in Figure 18.4. You can use any set of digits you like, such as the ones included on the CD-ROM accompanying this book, or you can design your own.

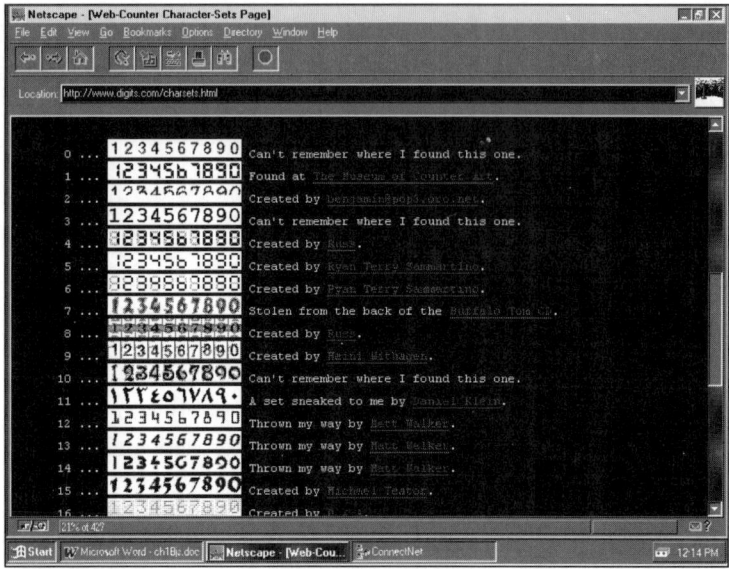

Figure 18.4 You can endow your JavaScript hit counter with any kind of digit graphics.

Or you can convert the number and display the value as spelled-out text. Instead of a counter that reads "345" for the number of visits, yours can read "three hundred forty-five."

Preparing the Counter Program

For the JavaScript-enhanced hit counter, Counter 4.0 was used. This is a freeware counter program written by George Burgyan and available at *http://www. webtools.org/counter/* (for your convenience, the program is also included on the CD-ROM). This counter is written in the Perl language, which is an interpreted language similar to Basic. Perl is a favorite among CGI programmers because it is fairly robust and is portable across a number of platforms. As written, Counter 4.0 is designed for Unix-based servers. The only requirement is that your server have a Perl interpreter installed on it. This interpreter is a program that reads Perl programs and executes them.

To install the Counter 4.0 program, follow the directions provided at the Counter 4.0 Web site (or in the readme file included with the program on the CD-ROM).

You will need to copy or FTP the program file to your CGI directory on your server. You will also need to use Telnet to install and test the software, or some other file access programs (Telnet is relatively easy to use, especially if you're familiar with Unix or MS-DOS).

"Out of the box" the Counter 4.0 program is not designed to interface with JavaScript. The program ordinarily displays the count information as plain text, surrounded by a hypertext link to the George's site. The link is not compatible with most JavaScript integration techniques, so it needs to be removed. The script supports an option to suppress the link, but depending on the server you are using, editing the program may be easier.

To make the Counter 4.0 program completely "JavaScript-enabled," you can make the following simple changes after the counter program is installed on your server (and after you are sure it works). The relevant text is located under "Stage 10" of the counter script (the script is commented for easy reading).

```
Add comments (# characters) as shown to the indicated lines:
# print "<a href=\"$nLink\">" if $nLink;
print $count;
# print "</a>" if $nLink;
```

Save your changes, make sure to set the file permissions to read and execute (on Unix use Telnet and issue the command *chmod a+rw counter.cgi*). Installation and modification of the counter program is now complete.

Constructing the Counter Page

With the counter program installed and ready to go, it's time now to turn to the HTML and JavaScript page you'll use to access the counter. Following is a bare-bones file for testing the counter. It accesses the counter program (using server-side includes) and displays the value.

■■■■■■■ **NOTE**

If you get a server error when you load this page, double-check your work with the script. The Counter 4.0 program provides context-sensitive help for the most common mistakes.

■■■■■■■

CD-ROM

counter–test.shtml

```
<HTML>
<HEAD>
<TITLE>JavaScript Visit Counter</TITLE>
<SCRIPT LANGUAGE="JavaScript">
</SCRIPT>
<BODY>
You are visitor:
<SCRIPT>
        Count = "<!–#exec cgi="/cgi-bin/counter.cgi" –>"
        document.write(Count);
</SCRIPT>
<P>Text goes here.
</BODY>
</HTML>
```

■■■■■■ **NOTE**

You may need to edit the line *<!–#exec cgi="/cgi-bin/counter.cgi" –>*, to point to the path that contains the *counter.cgi* program file on your server. Otherwise you will get an error when you attempt to run this script.

■■■■■

Give this script the name *test_count.shtml*—the *s* in front of the standard *html* extension denotes that it's a server-side include file, and that your server should process it specially (the server does this by "parsing through" the file, looking for <!-- #> server-side include instructions). If you're using Windows 3.1, name the file *test_co.sht*. You'll probably want to rename it later—once you've uploaded it to your server—if the server does not understand the "sht" extension as a server-side file. (You might want to check with the server administrator to see what file extensions are recognized for server-side includes.)

To test this script, upload it to your site, and then load it into the browser. If all is working properly, you'll get the current count value (it will start out at 1). If you see the text:

```
<!--#exec cgi="/cgi-bin/counter.cgi" -->
```

it means the file wasn't correctly processed (most likely the server failed to recognize the file as having a server-side include instruction in it, or the server does not support server-side includes).

How the Counter Script Works

When the *test_count.html* document is requested, the server fetches it and parses through it for server-side include statements. The text:

```
<!--#exec cgi="/cgi-bin/counter.cgi" -->
```

is one such statement. It tells the server to execute the *counter.cgi* program, which is in the cgi-bin directory. In response, the counter program inserts a new form with a hidden text field; the text field contains the count value. JavaScript picks up the count field and inserts it with the document.write method.

Displaying Graphics for Count Value

Plain old text gets pretty boring. You can use JavaScript to substitute the number placed into the hidden form field with graphics. For best results, use counter digits with standardized names, such as *digit0.gif*, *digit1.gif*, and so forth. That makes it easier to convert the number values to GIF images.

The following script uses digit files named *xfdb.gif*, where *x* is a number from 0 to 9. Additional digit characters provide the A.M./P.M. indicator, and the colon:

- *afdb.gif* displays A.M.
- *pfdb.gif* displays P.M.
- *cfdb.gif* displays the colon.

These digit GIFs are included on the CD-ROM accompanying the book, along with many others. They were provided by Russ Walsh. Change the filename prefix or suffix as needed to modify the script to work with other digits. Figure 18.5 shows an example of the visit counter script in action.

CD-ROM

```
visit-count.shtml

<HTML>
<HEAD>
<TITLE>JavaScript Visit Counter</TITLE>
```

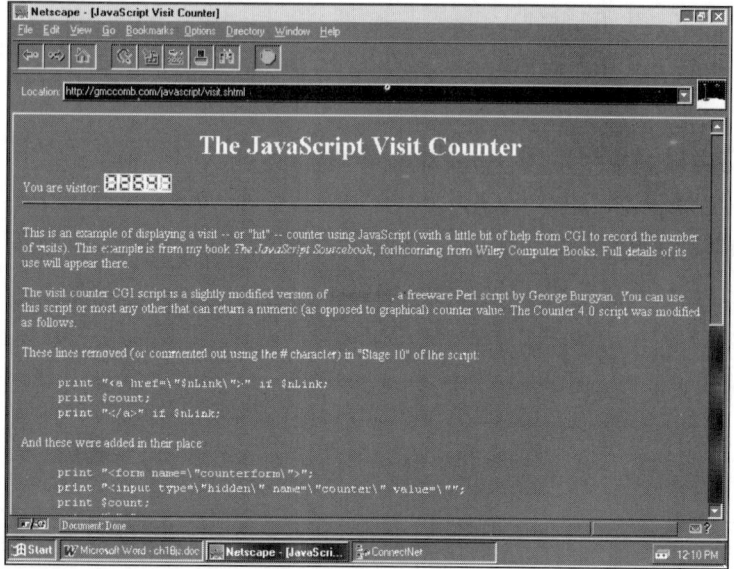

■■■■■■ **Figure 18.5** The JavaScript hit counter, in action.

```
<SCRIPT LANGUAGE="JavaScript">

function getCount() {
var CounterValue = "<!-#exec cgi="/cgi-bin/counter.cgi" ->"
if (CounterValue == "")
        return ("");
        var OpenImg = '<IMG SRC="'+pathOnly(location.href)
        var CloseImg='fdb.gif" HEIGHT=20 WIDTH=15>'    //change filename as
needed
        CounterValue = padTextPrefix (CounterValue, "0", 5)
        var Temp = ""
        for (Count = 0; Count < CounterValue.length; Count++) {
                Temp += OpenImg + CounterValue.substring (Count, Count+1) +
CloseImg
        }
        return (Temp);
}
```

```
function padTextPrefix (InString, PadChar, DefLength)  {
        if (InString.length>=DefLength)
                return (InString);
        OutString=InString
        for (Count=InString.length; Count<DefLength; Count++)  {
                OutString=PadChar+OutString;
        }
        return (OutString);
}


function pathOnly (InString)  {
        LastSlash=InString.lastIndexOf ('/', InString.length-1)
        OutString=InString.substring  (0, LastSlash+1)
        return (OutString);
}


</SCRIPT>
<BODY>
<H1 ALIGN=CENTER>The JavaScript Visit Counter</H1>
You are visitor:
<SCRIPT>
        Temp = getCount();
        document.write(Temp);
</SCRIPT>
<HR>
<P>This is an example of displaying a visit—or "hit"—counter using JavaScript
(with a little bit of help from CGI to record the number of visits). This
example is from my book <I>The JavaScript Sourcebook</I>, published by John
Wiley & Sons, Inc.
</BODY>
</HTML>
```

The script is simple. It takes the counter number stored in the CounterValue variable and, character by character, assigns the value as a matching digit GIF filename. For example, if the number stored in the hidden text field is 528, then the script converts the numbers to reference these GIF files, and in this order:

- *5fdb.gif*
- *2fdb.gif*
- *8fdb.gif*

The pathOnly function is provided to return the current path so JavaScript can locate the image files. If the files are located elsewhere, you can hardcode the location instead of using the pathOnly function.

Note the pathTextPrefix function. This function is used to pad zeros so that the count is always the same number of displayed digits. You can add as many zeros as you want or skip this function altogether (show only the digits for the current count, with no padding). To change the number of padding digits, specify a new value as the third parameter in the line:

```
padTextPrefix (CounterValue, "0", 5);
```

For example, to make the count always contain seven digits, change the last value to 7. Examples include 0000001, 0000123, 0123456, and 1234567.

Displaying Spelled-Out Text

Another variation on the hit counter is displaying spelled-out text rather than graphical digits. The *count_words.html* file, included on the CD-ROM, does this. The file uses a set of number-to-words functions that count up to 9,999,999. The counter script is mostly identical to the previous version, except the getCount routine is simply:

```
function getCount() {
var CounterValue = "<!--#exec cgi="/cgi-bin/counter.cgi" -->"
        CounterValue = padTextPrefix (CounterValue, "0", 5)
        return (toWords (CounterValue))
}
```

The remainder of the functions process the value and turn the text into numbers. See Chapter 13, "Plug-and-Play Routines," for more information on using the number-to-word functions.

WORKING WITH JAVA

AND NETSCAPE

PLUGS-INS

One of the benefits of Netscape is its extensibility—various hooks and gateways into the browser that allow other programs to integrate with it. JavaScript is an integral part of Netscape's extensibility; other important features of extensibility are Java and plug-ins.

Java is a robust applications development language from Internet leader Sun Microsystems that creates machine-independent program. *Machine-independent* means that a Java program can run on any computer (assuming that the computer is outfitted with the minimum files needed to interpret a Java program).

Netscape 2.0 and later uses Java and plug-ins to extend its own features—hence the concept of extensibility. For example, Netscape 2.0 doesn't come out of the box with background audio playback capability, but this is readily accomplished by using one of many Java programs—called "applets"—or plug-ins that are available. Some are even free.

Other books and documentation are available that provide detailed information on writing Java applets and plug-in programs. This chapter focuses on how to integrate JavaScript with both Java and plug-ins. Several Java applets and plug-in programs are included in the CD-ROM packaged with this book. This chapter uses these as examples to demonstrate how to connect JavaScript with Java and plug-ins; of course, you can use this information to integrate JavaScript with other Java applets or plug-ins you already have. The process is actually rather simple and straightforward, though there are some "gotchas!" along the way.

What Is a Java Applet?

A Java applet is very much like any other program you run on your computer. But in the context of Netscape, this program has the specific task of augmenting the browser's innate capabilities. The applet is transmitted to the user's computer along with the rest of an HTML page (text, graphics, sound, and so forth).

A typical Java applet displays some moving text or an animated screen. These features aren't part of Netscape's ordinary feature set. The applet is designed to run under a browser and cannot be used—without modification—by itself as a full-blown application.

Java applets are created by writing a program using C/C++ syntax. The syntax is similar to JavaScript, but there are many more statements and other commands. Like the C++ language, JavaScript is built around the object-oriented paradigm of programming, meaning that a program is built from individual objects that work independently of one another. Though JavaScript also uses objects, they are not quite the same as the ones found in Java. Java's objects offer a rich array of features and capabilities; because of this, Java is a much more difficult language to learn and use than JavaScript.

After a Java applet has been written, it must be compiled. Unlike JavaScript, which is merely embedded in the same document with the rest of the HTML markup tags, Java applets are self-contained entities and are processed so that the applet itself is in a compressed form more fitting for reading by a computer than by a human. If you were to look at a Java applet (which traditionally has a file extension of *.class*) in a text editor, you'd see mostly gibberish rather than programming commands.

Using an Applet in an HTML Document

To use the Java applet in an HTML document, you reference it using a special <APPLET> tag. Browsers that don't run Java applications ignore the <APPLET> tag and therefore the Java applet never runs.

Included in the typical <APPLET> tag are one or more parameters. These are values sent to the Java applet to tell it how to behave. Parameters aren't strictly required, but most Java applets use them. If you find a Java applet you'd like to use in your HTML page, not only do you need the actual *.class* file for the applet (and sometimes there are many of these for a single applet), but you need the parameter list to know how to communicate with the applet.

Here is an example of a simple applet that creates jumping or "nervous" text. In fact, that's the name of this applet, which is one of the first Java applications to be demonstrated when the language was just starting to take the Internet by storm. The applet creates text like that shown in Figure 19.1. The <APPLET> tag used to "call" this applet and activate it for the page is:

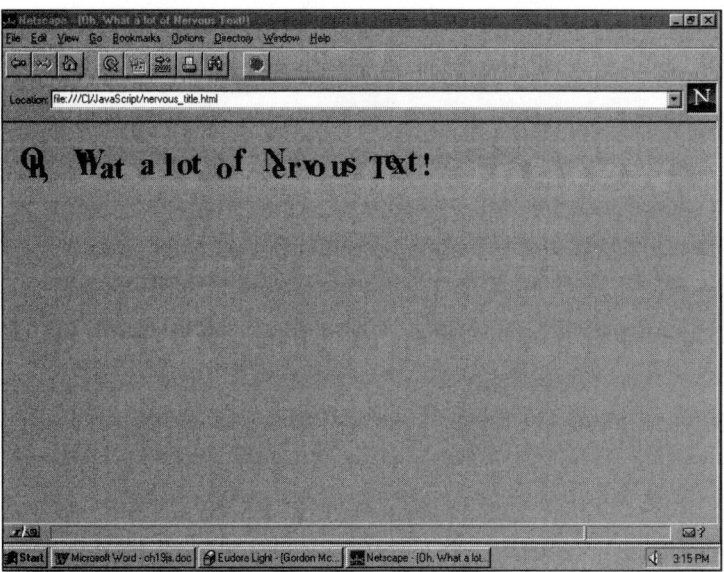

■■■■■■ **Figure 19.1** The now-infamous "nervous text" by Daniel Wyszynski; its sole purpose is to make jumping-bean text.

```
<APPLET CODE="NervousText.class" WIDTH=200 HEIGHT=50>
<PARAM NAME=text VALUE="Hello There!!">
</APPLET>
```

- The *<APPLET>* tag contains three attributes: CODE names the applet class name ("NerverText.class). WIDTH and HEIGHT set the width and height of the applet, respectively. In many ways applets are treated in Netscape as a kind of graphical image (even if the applet just displays text). The <APPLET> tag supports more attributes, but these three are the minimum you should always use.

- The *<PARAM>* tag contains two attributes. These vary depending on the needs of the applet. Of primary importance is the VALUE parameter, as it defines the text you want to display.

Integrating the Applet with JavaScript

Now comes the fun part: making JavaScript and the applet talk to one another. Sadly, Netscape 2.0 lacks many features for direct communication between JavaScript and Java, but you can nevertheless modify the behavior of the applet using the intelligence built into JavaScript. The technique involves dynamically creating the <APPLET> tag at run-time, rather than hardcoding the tag in the HTML document. As you create the text of the tag, you can decide what parameters to pass to the applet.

Let's go back to the nervous text example. Here's Java code that dynamically creates the <APPLET> tag with JavaScript using the same parameters as before:

```
<SCRIPT>
Text = "";
Text += '<APPLET CODE="NervousText.class" WIDTH=200 HEIGHT=50>';
Text += '<PARAM NAME=text VALUE="Hello There!!">';
Text +- '</APPLET>';
document.write (Text);
</SCRIPT>
```

Of course, this example doesn't give you anything you don't have with the hardcode method. But as you've probably guessed, you can replace the hardcoded parameters with JavaScript variables. Here's an example that asks the user what text to display:

```
<TITLE>Nervous Text</TITLE>
```

```
<SCRIPT>
DisplayText = prompt ("Nervous text", "Hello There!!");
Text = "";
Text +='<APPLET CODE="NervousText.class" WIDTH=200 HEIGHT=50>';
Text +='<PARAM NAME=text VALUE="' + DisplayText + '">';
Text +='</APPLET>';
document.write (Text);
</SCRIPT>
</BODY>
</HTML>
```

■■■■ **NOTE**

Most Java applets do not reset when you reload the page (click Reload, or choose View, Reload). Instead, if you are accessing the page from a local hard drive, you must choose File, Open, and re-open the file. If you are accessing the page on the Internet, click on Netscape's Back button, then the Forward button. This usually reloads the page and resets the applet.

■■■■

Setting Parameters Based on Browser Variables

It's not uncommon to set applet parameters based on one or more Netscape variables, such as the background color or the local time. You can use these variables as needed as values for the applet. Here's the nervous text applet displaying the title of the document, using the document.title value. This example also shows how to dynamically set the parameter for width. This value is defined as the number of characters to display times 16. This allows for enough space to adequately display all the characters. The Width variable takes the place of the hardcoded WIDTH= attribute, used in the example above.

nervous—title.html

CD-ROM

```
<HTML>
<HEAD>
<TITLE>Oh, What a lot of Nervous Text!</TITLE>
```

```
<SCRIPT>
DisplayText = document.title;
Width = DisplayText.length * 16;
Text = "";
Text +='<APPLET CODE="NervousText.class" WIDTH=' +
Width + ' HEIGHT=50>';
Text +='<PARAM NAME=text VALUE="' + DisplayText + '">';
Text +='</APPLET>';
document.write (Text);
</SCRIPT>
</BODY>
</HTML>
```

A Scrolling Marquee Using Java

Another example of using JavaScript to dynamically set the parameters of a Java applet is shown below. This script displays a scrolling marquee. The Marquee.class applet lets you set the text to display, the speed of the scroll, the foreground and background colors, the font, and the font size.

This example uses variables you set yourself in the script, as well as variables obtained by Netscape when the page is loaded. Of particular interest is the background color. The script decodes the red, green, and blue components of the current background color for the page and applies that to the background of the marquee. In this way, you don't have to worry about setting the background color, as it will always be the same as the background shown in the browser. You can test this by changing the BGCOLOR attribute in the <BODY> tag or by over-riding the background color setting in Netscape and choosing your own default. Figure 19.2 shows the result of the demonstration script.

java—marquee.html

CD-ROM

```
<BODY BGCOLOR="white">
<CENTER>
```

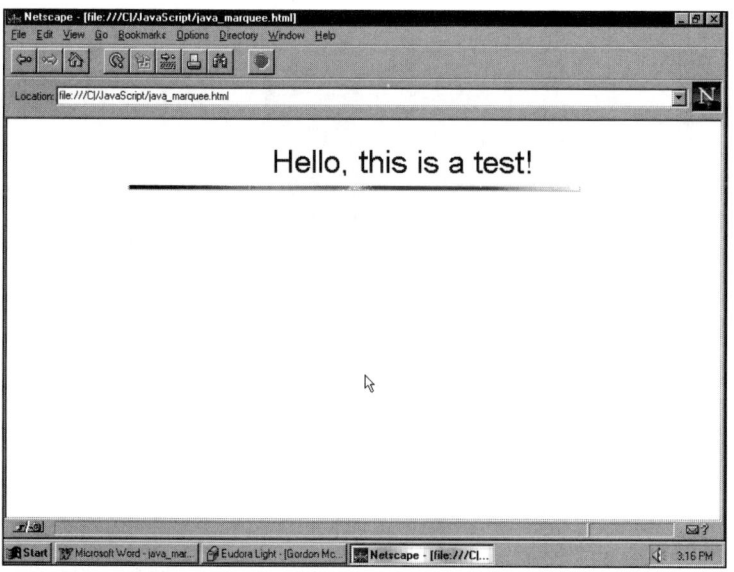

▬▬▬▬ **Figure 19.2** Use a Java-based marquee to create crawling text.

```
<SCRIPT>
        var Text = "Hello, this is a test!";
        var Width = 500
        var Height = 45
        var ForeColor = "#0000ff";
        var FontSize = "35";
        var Speed = "1";

        var FgColorRed = parseInt (ForeColor.substring (1, 3), 16);
        var FgColorGreen = parseInt (ForeColor.substring (3, 5), 16);
        var FgColorBlue = parseInt (ForeColor.substring (5, 7), 16);
        var BgColorRed = parseInt (document.bgColor.substring (1, 3), 16);
        var BgColorGreen = parseInt (document.bgColor.substring (3, 5), 16);
        var BgColorBlue = parseInt (document.bgColor.substring (5, 7), 16);
        result = ''
        result += '<applet code="Marquee.class" width='+Width +
' height=' + Height + '>\n'
```

```
          result += '<param name=label value="' + Text + '">\n'
          result += '<param name=font value="TimesRoman">\n'
          result += '<param name=ptsize value="' + FontSize + '">\n'
          result += '<param name=step value="' + Speed + '">\n'
          result += '<param name=fred value="' + FgColorRed + '">\n'
          result += '<param name=fgreen value="' + FgColorGreen + '">\n'
          result += '<param name=fblue value="' + FgColorBlue + '">\n'
          result += '<param name=bred value="' + BgColorRed + '">\n'
          result += '<param name=bgreen value="' + BgColorGreen + '">\n'
          result += '<param name=bblue value="' + BgColorBlue + '">\n'
          result += '</applet>'
          document.write (result)
  </SCRIPT>
  <BR>
  <IMG SRC="bar4.gif" WIDTH=500 HEIGHT=5>
  </CENTER>
  </BODY>
```

To customize this script, change the variables as follows:

- *var Text* = The text to display in the marquee
- *var Width* = The width of the marquee (text does not scroll outside this)
- *var Height* = The height of the marquee, which should be large enough to display all of the text
- *var ForeColor* = The color of the text, which is assigned in the same way as the BGCOLOR and TEXT attributes of the <BODY> tag
- *var FontSize* = The size of the font (a size of 25 to 55 is ideal)
- *var Speed* = The speed of the scroll (for best results, leave at 1 or 2)

Playing Java in a Frame

There are a few bugs related to Java and Netscape 2.0 (some of the bugs may be repaired in future releases of Netscape and/or Java). Simply put, Java doesn't like Netscape frames very much. The usual problem is that the applet loads into the frame but never starts running.

Fortunately, there are a few workarounds you can use to enable Java in frames, and JavaScript is just the tool for it! The limitation is that the JavaScript that dynamically inserts the applet code must be in the same frame in which the applet appears. This means you can't yet use one frame to control another frame that contains the applet.

When constructing the frames, place the Java-making code in the document for the frame where you want the applet to appear. The following example uses three documents:

- *banner_frameset.html* is the frameset document.
- *banner_framea.html* is the upper frame and is where the regular HTML tags go.
- *banner_frameb.html* is the lower frame and contains the banner.

The *banner_frameset.html* file defines the frameset, creating two rows.

CD-ROM

```
banner_frameset.html
```

```
<HTML>
<TITLE>Banner in a Frame</TITLE>
<HEAD>
<SCRIPT LANGUAGE="JavaScript">
</SCRIPT>
</HEAD>


<FRAMESET ROWS="75%, *">
<FRAME SRC="applet3.html " NAME="frame2">
<FRAME SRC="applet3a.html" NAME="frame1">
</FRAMESET>


<NOFRAME>
This demo requires Netscape.
</NOFRAME>
</HTML>
```

The *banner_framea.html* file is whatever you want to make it. A document is shown here with a sample heading.

banner_framea.html

```
<HTML>
<HEAD>
<TITLE>Banner in a Frame</TITLE>
<BODY>
<H2>Other document goes here.</H2>
</BODY>
</HTML>
```

The *banner_frameb.html* file contains the JavaScript for running the Java applet. It is essentially the same as the previous examples using the banner applet.

banner_frameb.html

```
<HTML>
<HEAD>
<TITLE>Banner in a Frame</TITLE>
<BODY>
<SCRIPT>
    Text = "Hello and Welcome to the Java/JavaScript Page!"
    var Width = 500
    var Height = 50
    var ForeColor = "#0000ff";
    var FontSize = "35";
    var Speed = "1";

    var FgColorRed = parseInt (ForeColor.substring (1, 3), 16);
    var FgColorGreen = parseInt (ForeColor.substring (3, 5), 16);
    var FgColorBlue = parseInt (ForeColor.substring (5, 7), 16);
    var BgColorRed = parseInt (document.bgColor.substring (1, 3), 16);
    var BgColorGreen = parseInt (document.bgColor.substring (3, 5), 16);
    var BgColorBlue = parseInt (document.bgColor.substring (5, 7), 16);
    result = '<CENTER>'
    result += '<APPLET CODE="Marquee.class" WIDTH='+
```

```
Width + ' HEIGHT=' + Height + '>\n'
        result += '<PARAM NAME=label VALUE="' + Text + '">\n'
        result += '<PARAM NAME=font VALUE="TimesRoman">\n'
        result += '<PARAM NAME=ptsize VALUE="' + FontSize + '">\n'
        result += '<PARAM NAME=step VALUE="' + Speed + '">\n'
        result += '<PARAM NAME=fred VALUE="' + FgColorRed + '">\n'
        result += '<PARAM NAME=fgreen VALUE="' + FgColorGreen + '">\n'
        result += '<PARAM NAME=fblue VALUE="' + FgColorBlue + '">\n'
        result += '<PARAM NAME=bred VALUE="' + BgColorRed + '">\n'
        result += '<PARAM NAME=bgreen VALUE="' + BgColorGreen + '">\n'
        result += '<PARAM NAME=bblue VALUE="' + BgColorBlue + '">\n'
        result += '</APPLET>'
        result += '</CENTER>'
        document.write (result);
    </SCRIPT>
    </BODY>
    </HTML>
```

Figure 19.3 shows the result of loading these files into Netscape.

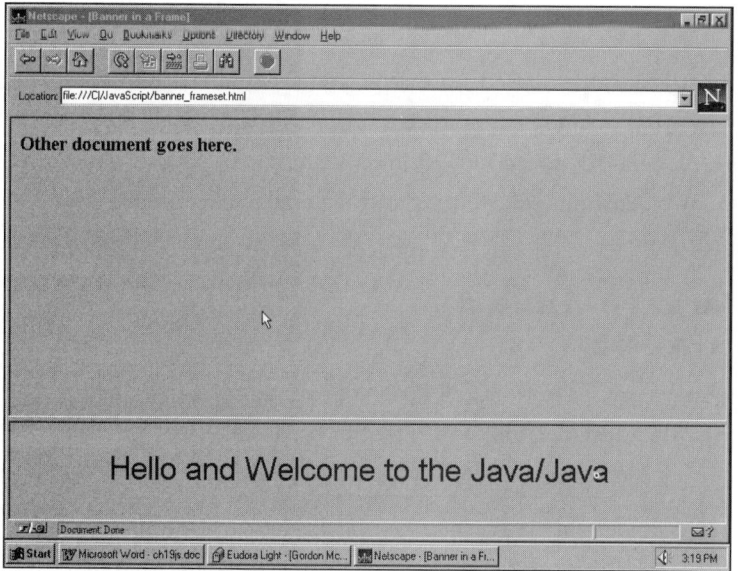

▰▰▰▰▰ **Figure 19.3** Using the Java marquee applet in a frame.

Getting Java to Trigger a JavaScript Function

If you are a Java applet programmer, you can use a simple technique to activate a JavaScript function from within JavaScript. The syntax is:

```
getAppletContext().showDocument(new URL("javascript:/**/function(param)"));
```

- *function* is the name of the JavaScript function you want to call.
- *param* is one or more parameters you want to pass to the function.

As of Netscape 2.0, the function you call needs to be in the same document that contains the applet; otherwise, Java won't be able to locate the function you want to use. Note the /**/ characters. These empty comment characters prevent JavaScript from appending a / character at the front of the function name.

What Is a Plug-In?

A plug-in is similar to a Java applet, but it uses a different mechanism to interact with Netscape. Plug-ins tend to be larger and more complex than Java applets, and they are designed to the installed into Netscape by the user. They are not downloaded as part of the HTML page.

By their nature, plug-ins are machine-dependent; that is, you install a version of the plug-in specifically for the kind of computer system you have. Because of their popularity, there are more plug-ins for Windows 95 and Windows 3.1 than for the Macintosh and X-Windows platforms. However, the real popular plug-ins tend to support all Netscape platforms.

Using a Plug-In in an HTML Document

Before you can use a plug-in, you have to install it on your computer. Most plug-in packages come with their own installer program. Just run the installer, identify the Netscape Plugin directory (if the installer can't find it), and you're done.

The most common source of plug-ins is the Internet itself. Netscape's home page (http://home.netscape.com) lists many of the plug-ins you can download. Many are "trial versions" of shareware or commercial plug-in programs. You can test the plug-in before you spend money on it.

This book also comes with a number of plug-ins. One of the most useful is ToolVox, which plays a highly compressed sound file through your computer's audio system (if you have a PC, you need a sound card to hear the sounds). Because of the high compression ToolVox uses, it is not suitable for music or sound effects. But most voice recordings, especially those made with a quality microphone, are quite intelligible.

Netscape interacts with plug-ins through the <EMBED> tag. The <EMBED> tag includes SRC attributes to tell Netscape the name of the file to use. The file includes a header that identifies the data contained within it. This tells Netscape which plug-in to use with the file. Also included with the <EMBED> tag is any other information that the plug in requires, such as height, width, play modes, and so forth. Different plug-ins use different attributes in the <EMBED> tag.

Here's an example of an <EMBED> tag that plays a sound file with the ToolVox plug-in. The name of the sound file is called *meow.vox*.

```
<EMBED SRC="meow.vox" PLAYMODE="auto" VISUALMODE="embed"
HEIGHT=82 WIDTH=160>
```

Notice the PLAYMODE and VISUALMODE attributes, which are specific to the ToolVox plug in. Here are the valid parameters for these attributes (check the documentation that comes with the ToolVox player for the complete run-down).

The PLAYMODE attribute is covered in the following table.

Value	What It Does
User	To begin playing sound, the user must click either the ToolVox icon or the player window's Start button on the Web page.
Auto	The sound begins to play automatically when the Web page is displayed in the browser.
Cache	The user downloads the entire file (without playing it) and stores it for playing later.

The VISUALMODE attribute is covered in the following table.

Value	What It Does
Icon	The Voxware face icon appears on the Web page. While the sound is playing the icon is red.
Background	There is no user interface on the page—and no way to stop the sound from playing.
Embed	The sound player window appears on the Web page.
Float	The sound player appears as a floating window that you can minimize or close.

Also included are HEIGHT and WIDTH attributes. These attributes set the size of the ToolVox player console (when using the Embed or Float values for the VISUALMODE attribute) or the ToolVox "face icon" (when using the Icon value). An example of the ToolVox player is shown in Figure 19.4.

Integrating the Plug-In with JavaScript

As with Java applets, you can use JavaScript to dynamically define the <EMBED> tag or a plug-in. This lets you change the characteristics of the plug-in. You can even divide to skip the creation of the <EMBED> tag in response to a query to the user.

Here's the basic approach, using the ToolVox plug-in as a model:

```
<HTML>
<HEAD>
<TITLE>Plug-in Test</TITLE>
<BODY>
```

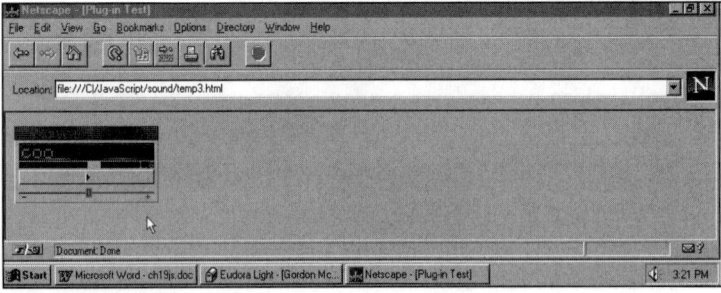

■■■■ **Figure 19.4** The ToolVox player can be displayed or hidden for sound playback.

```
<SCRIPT>
Text=""
Text += '<EMBED SRC="coo.vox" PLAYMODE="auto"'
Text += ' VISUALMODE="embed" height=82 width=160>'
document.write (Text)
</SCRIPT>
</BODY>
</HTML>
```

You can replace the hardcoded attributes with variables for easier programming. This example uses a variable to change the name of the sound file:

```
<HTML>
<HEAD>
<TITLE>Plug-in Test</TITLE>
<BODY>
<SCRIPT>
Soundfile = "coo.vox"
Text=""
Text += '<EMBED SRC="' + Soundfile + ' " PLAYMODE="auto"'
Text += ' VISUALMODE="embed" height=82 width-160>'
document.write (Text)
</SCRIPT>
</BODY>
</HTML>
```

Using JavaScript to Play a Different Sound for Every Day of the Week

One practical example of this type of script is a "custom" greeting based on the day of the week. Suppose you record seven sound files, each with a 10-second spiel that announces the special features at your site for that particular day. Monday's message might say one thing, Tuesday's might say another, and so forth. With the help of JavaScript, you can easily rotate those sounds so the user gets the right sound for each day.

The script for this is pretty simple. You use the getDay property of the Date object to determine the day of the week (Sunday is 0, Monday is 1, and so forth). You then apply the proper sound file accordingly. In this example, the sound files are named *sunday.vox*, *monday.vox*, and so forth.

CD-ROM

day—sound—vox.html

```
<HTML>
<HEAD>
<TITLE>A Different Sound Each Day!</TITLE>
<BODY>
<SCRIPT>
now = new Date();
Today = now.getDay();
if (Today == 0) Soundfile = "sunday.vox";
if (Today == 1) Soundfile = "monday.vox";
if (Today == 2) Soundfile = "tuesday.vox";
if (Today == 3) Soundfile = "wednesday.vox";
if (Today == 4) Soundfile = "thursday.vox";
if (Today == 5) Soundfile = "friday.vox";
if (Today == 6) Soundfile = "saturday.vox";
Text=""
Text += '<EMBED SRC="' + Soundfile + ' " PLAYMODE="auto"'
Text += ' VISUALMODE="embed" height=82 width=160>'
document.write (Text);
</SCRIPT>
</BODY>
</HTML>
```

ToolVox doesn't load its play console or icon if the sound file doesn't exist. If you try the above example, nothing appears to happen unless you have the days-of-the-week sound files. If you don't have them, you can use the ToolVox encoder to record and compress your sounds. As with the ToolVox player, the ToolVox encoder is included on the CD-ROM that accompanies this book. It is also available from ToolVox via its URL.

Running a Plug-In in a Frame

Plug-ins are perfectly happy running in a single window or within a frame. The same considerations that apply to any use of JavaScript and frames applies to plug-ins. Merely use document.write to insert the plug-in definition in the desired frame instead of the main document window.

For the most part, the plug-in is treated like an image. Because of requirements of JavaScript, this requires you to provide the path to the file used with the plug-in as well as the name. Assuming the plug-in file is in the same directory as the JavaScript file you are using, you can obtain the path using location.href and removing the file-name from the returned string. You do not need to hardcode the path information, though you certainly can.

In the example below are two HTML documents (frameset and "control") that demonstrate using a plug-in with frames. The plug-in for the demonstration is ToolVox, which plays highly compressed audio files.

When you load the frameset document, the Netscape window is divided into two parts: the left side provides a prompt and the right side provides a series of buttons for different sound files (these sound files are provided on the CD-ROM included with this book). Click a button and the ToolVox plug-in is loaded into the left frame, where it plays the desired sound.

To use this example, be sure to copy the sound files to the same path that contains the frameset and control HTML files. Otherwise, the ToolVox plug-in will not be able to locate the audio file you picked, and nothing will happen.

The frameset document includes a loadTime function, which is triggered by the onLoad event of the frameset. This event does not occur until all of the child frames in the frameset have finished loading. It's a good place to put JavaScript code that is executed upon loading.

CD-ROM

picksound-frameset.html

```
<HTML>
<TITLE>Pick a Sound</TITLE>
<HEAD>
<SCRIPT LANGUAGE="JavaScript">
var Soundfile;
function loadTime ()   {
        DisplayText = "<H3>Click a button to play a sound here!</H3>";
        self.frames[0].document.write(DisplayText);
        self.frames[0].document.close ();
}
</SCRIPT>
</HEAD>

<FRAMESET COLS="30%, *" onLoad = "loadTime()">
  <FRAME SRC="about:blank" NAME="frame1">
  <FRAME SRC="picksnd.htm" NAME="frame2">
</FRAMESET>

<NOFRAME>
This demo requires Netscape.
</NOFRAME>
</HTML>
```

The control document includes the form with the four push buttons, as well as the general logic for playing the sounds. Notice that each button calls the playSound function using the onClick event. Each button passes a different sound filename to the function.

Also notice that the document.write and document.close methods refer to the other frame (it's frame 0 because it's the first frame specified in the frameset document). If you do not specify a particular frame, JavaScript assumes it's the current frame (the frame that contains the script code). This results in the plug-in appearing in the frame on the right, which also deletes the control buttons!

The current path is returned using the pathOnly function. This function takes the entire URL of the current document (using location.href), and strips off the filename part, leaving just the path.

CD-ROM

picksnd.htm

```
<HTML>
<HEAD>
<TITLE>Pick a Sound</TITLE>
<BODY>
<SCRIPT>
function PlaySound (Soundfile) {
        Soundfile = pathOnly (location.href) + Soundfile;
        Text=""
        Text += '<EMBED SRC="' + Soundfile + ' " PLAYMODE="auto"';
        Text += ' VISUALMODE="embed" HEIGHT=82 WIDTH=160 ' ;
        Text += ' VSPACE=10 HSPACE=10>';
        parent.frames[0].document.write (Text);
        parent.frames[0].document.close();
        return;
}

function pathOnly (InString)  {
        LastSlash=InString.lastIndexOf ('/', InString.length-1)
        OutString=InString.substring  (0, LastSlash+1)
        return (OutString);
}

</SCRIPT>
<FORM>
<INPUT TYPE="button" NAME="button" VALUE="Coo "
onClick="PlaySound('coo.vox')"><P>
<INPUT TYPE="button" NAME="button" VALUE="JFK "
onClick="PlaySound('jfk8.vox')"><P>
```

```
<INPUT TYPE="button" NAME="button" VALUE="Intro"
onClick="PlaySound('intro.vox')"><P>
<INPUT TYPE="button" NAME="button" VALUE="Hitch"
onClick="PlaySound('hitch.vox')"><P>
</FORM>
</BODY>
</HTML>
```

Interested in sound applications using JavaScript? See Chapter 20, "Using JavaScript for Sound, Animation, and Graphics" for additional ideas, including how to use repeating sounds, "synchronizing" sound and pictures, and more.

20

USING JAVASCRIPT FOR SOUND, ANIMATION, AND GRAPHICS

Everybody likes a good show. Loud noises, bright colors, and constant movement have always captivated us. We are drawn to dynamic sight and sound.

The World Wide Web was first developed as a medium to distribute text-intensive technical documents. Graphics, when used, were intended only for illustrative purposes. When the Internet was turned over for public and commercial use, it quickly became a vehicle for multimedia presentations. In its current state, limitations in *bandwidth*—the amount of data that can be funneled through a connection, such as a phone line—prevent it from becoming a true multimedia system, but those days are probably coming.

In the mean time, Web developers are busy creating pseudo-multimedia pages for their sites. Some rely on plug-ins, such as Shockwave, specifically designed to crunch the sound, graphics, and animation popular in multimedia products into a small package for delivery over the Internet. In fact, helper applications like Shockwave remain the best way to distribute multimedia content over the Web.

Other Web developers, conscious that not everyone has plug ins like Shockwave, use regular HTML markup tags, with perhaps a little help from JavaScript to do the job. The results aren't always as spectacular as what you can do with a dedicated plug-in like Shockwave, but the end result is attractive just the same.

This chapter describes how to use JavaScript to endow your pages with sound, animation, and graphics. For example, you'll learn how to:

- Play sounds with nothing more than Netscape
- Integrate a third-party plug-in like ToolVox to play sounds
- Create animated effects with graphics
- Produce fades in documents and frames
- Build images on-the-fly in JavaScript
- Create unusual graphic effects with small images

■■■■■■ **NOTE**

Many of the sound related techniques described in this chapter are best used with Netscape 2.X only. Netscape 3.0 and later espouses the concept of plug-ins for playing sound. See chapter 22 for more informaton on the changes in Netscape 3.0.

■■■■■■

Playing a Sound

Netscape for Windows comes ready to play sounds. The NPLAYER helper application included with Netscape understands several popular sound formats commonly used on the Web, including au, snd, and aif. Sound files in au sounds are particularly plentiful on the Web because they are commonly used with Java applets.

There are no specific HTML tags for this purpose, but playing sounds can easily be accomplished with JavaScript. You can play a sound while the page is loading, after it has loaded, or in response to some user action. Following are several methods for playing sounds in Netscape. (Internet Explorer provides a BGSOUND option, and many of the techniques covered in this chapter are not needed.)

Playing a Sound While a Page Is Loading

To play a sound while a page is loading, insert a *location = soundURL* instruction at the head of the document. When JavaScript encounters the instruction, and assuming the sound file is in a format compatible with the NPLAYER helper program, Netscape "spawns" the NPLAYER application, and the sound plays, even as the rest of the document loads. As the sound plays, you will see a control panel, where you can control playback, if desired.

```
<HTML>
<HEAD>
<SCRIPT>
location = "sound.au"
</SCRIPT>
</HEAD>
<BODY>
<H2>Sound playback</H2>
</BODY>
</HTML>
```

Playing a Sound After a Page Has Loaded

Use the onLoad event handler to play a sound after the page has loaded. This prevents the sound from playing until all elements of the page have been inserted. Here are two versions: the first version directly loads the sound file with the onLoad event; the other calls a function that does the job.

```
<HTML>
<HEAD>
</HEAD>
<BODY onLoad="location = 'sound.au'">
<H2>Sound playback</H2>
</BODY>
</HTML>
```

```
<HTML>
<HEAD>
<SCRIPT>
function runAtLoad () {
        location = "sound.au"
}
</SCRIPT>
</HEAD>
<BODY onLoad="runAtLoad()">
<H2>Sound playback</H2>
</BODY>
</HTML>
```

Playing a Sound in Response to a User Action

You can use standard HTML or JavaScript to play a sound in response to action from the user. The basic method is the <A> link anchor. Instead of linking to another page, link to the sound file. When the user clicks the link, the sound is played.

```
<HTML>
<HEAD>
</HEAD>
<BODY>
<H2>Sound playback</H2>

<A HREF="sound.au">Play a sound</A>
</BODY>
</HTML>
```

The other method uses a form button. Click the button and the sound is played, using the onClick event handler. As with using the onLoad event handler, you can play the sound directly by using the location instruction for onClick, or you can call a function. The function method is covered here:

```
<HTML>
<HEAD>
```

```
<SCRIPT LANGUAGE="JavaScript">
function playSound() {
        location = "sound.au"
}
</SCRIPT>
</HEAD>
<BODY>
<H2>Sound playback</H2>
<FORM>
<INPUT TYPE="button" NAME="button" VALUE="Play Sound"
onClick="playSound()">
</BODY>
</HTML>
```

Playing a Sound with a Plug-In

A number of Netscape plug-ins support sound playback. A popular and common sound plug-in is ToolVox. It uses highly compressed files so that even several minutes of speech take up only 10 or 15K. Because of the high compression ratios, the ToolVox plug-in is best suited for voice; it has a hard time reproducing sound effects and music.

Because ToolVox is a plug-in, you use the <EMBED> tags to place the sound playback information in your HTML page. You can hardcode the tags in the HTML or use JavaScript to "dynamically" write the <EMBED> tags into the document. The technique of dynamically writing an <EMBED> tag is covered in more detail in Chapter 19. If you're new to this concept, you may wish to read that chapter first. Several basic sound-oriented examples are provided in that chapter, as well.

Repeating a Plug-In Sound

Background sound can be achieved by repeating the same sound over and over again. You can use a sound playback plug-in and have it "regenerated" at desired intervals to create the necessary repeat. For example, you can repeat a welcome greeting or repeat a reminder for the user. A popular plug-in like ToolVox is ideal for this application because many Netscape users already have it. Plus, its sound files are highly compressed and, therefore, small. Using JavaScript you can time the repeat to as short as about a third of a second, to several seconds, minutes, and even hours! Repeats of every 10 to 30 seconds are the most common.

JavaScript can control a single-play sound plug-in, such as ToolVox, by dynamically writing a plug-in <EMBED> tag to a document or frame. The time delay is accomplished using the setTimeout method; this method "fires" the plug-in at almost any interval you desire.

Because the <EMBED> tag for the plug-in is continually rewritten, you must use frames for repeating sound with ToolVox. One frame contains all the necessary logic to play the sound; an "invisible" frame is used as the target for the JavaScript-generated <EMBED> tag. And of course, a frameset document pulls it all together.

Following is the frameset document for the repeating sound example. Notice that the frames are divided into two rows, with the first frame taking up 100 percent of the space. The second frame is effectively hidden.

This particular example continually plays the voice of famed movie director Alfred Hitchcock proclaiming, "Good eeeeevening, ladies and gentlemen!" (This sound clip is provided as *hitch.vox* on the CD-ROM that accompanies this book.)

Here is the sound clip frameset document:

CD-ROM

plugin-4_frame.html

```
<HTML>
<TITLE>Repeat a Sound</TITLE>
<HEAD>
<SCRIPT LANGUAGE="JavaScript">
function loadTime () {
        self.frames[0].setSound ('hitch.vox')
        self.frames[1].document.close ();
}
</SCRIPT>
</HEAD>
```

```
<FRAMESET ROWS="100%, *" onLoad = "loadTime()">
  <FRAME SRC="sounder.htm" NAME="frame1">
  <FRAME SRC="dummy.htm" NAME="frame2">
</FRAMESET>

<NOFRAME>
This demo requires Netscape.
</NOFRAME>
</HTML>
```

And here is the sound clip control document:

CD-ROM

sounder.htm

```
<HTML>
<HEAD>
<TITLE>Repeat a Sound</TITLE>
<BODY>
<SCRIPT>

var SoundVal = true;

function toggleSound () {
        SoundVal = !SoundVal;
        playSound();
        return;
}

function setSound(Soundfile) {
        document.myform.soundfile.value = Soundfile
        playSound ();
}

function playSound () {
```

```
        if (!SoundVal) return;
        Soundfile = document.myform.soundfile.value
        Soundfile = pathOnly (location.href) + Soundfile;
        Text=""
        Text += '<EMBED SRC="' + Soundfile + ' " PLAYMODE="auto"';
        Text += ' VISUALMODE="embed" HEIGHT=82 WIDTH=160 ' ;
        Text += ' VSPACE=10 HSPACE=10>';
        parent.frames[1].document.write (Text);
        parent.frames[1].document.close();
        ret = setTimeout ("playSound ()", 5000);
        return;
    }


function pathOnly (InString)   {
        LastSlash=InString.lastIndexOf ('/', InString.length-1)
        OutString=InString.substring   (0, LastSlash+1)
        return (OutString);
    }


</SCRIPT>
<BODY>
<FORM NAME="myform">
<INPUT TYPE="hidden" NAME="soundfile">
<INPUT TYPE="button" NAME="button" VALUE="Stop/Start Sound"
onClick = "toggleSound()">
</FORM>
</BODY>
</HTML>
```

The *sounder.htm* document contains all the necessary code for repeating the sound. The sound repeat delay is set for five seconds, which is defined in the setTimeout method as 5000 (5000 milliseconds; there are 1000 milliseconds to a second). Do note that the time delay of the setTime method is not 100% accurate. It may trigger before or after five seconds, depending on other tasks being performed by your computer. However, the time delay is generally close enough for applications such as this. If you use a longer sound, be sure to extend the time delay, or else the sound will get cut off as it starts another iteration.

Also note the addition of a Stop/Start button. This push button controls the repeat of the sound. When the document loads, the sound repeat value (SoundVal) is initially set to *true*, so the sound repeats. When you press the button, it reverses the state of the SoundVal variable; *true* becomes *false*, and the sound stops (and if you press the button again, *false* becomes *true*, and the sound starts again).

Using "Client Pull" for Repeating Sounds

Another method you can use with Netscape browsers is the "client pull" technique, which repeatedly reloads the desired page. By placing the <EMBED> tag in a hidden frame and reloading that frame, you can achieve repeating sound with very little effort. Here's the basic frameset that doesn't even use JavaScript. It shows two frames; the top frame contains the text and graphics and other elements you want your users to see (the generic *dummy.htm* document has been moved here); the bottom frame is invisible and is the one that is pulled in at regular intervals. This document is named *basic_clientpull.html*.

CD-ROM

```
basic_clientpull.html
```

```
<HTML>
<TITLE>Basic Client Pull Sound Example</TITLE>
<HEAD>
</HEAD>

<FRAMESET ROWS="100%, *">
<FRAME SRC="dummy.htm" NAME="frame1">
<FRAME SRC="bas_pull.htm" NAME="frame2">
</FRAMESET>
```

```
<NOFRAME>
This demo requires Netscape.
</NOFRAME>
</HTML>
```

The *bas_pull.htm* document is equally simple. Notice the <META> tag. This is the "secret" behind the client pull technique.

- The HTTP-EQUIV="Refresh" attribute tells Netscape you want to refresh the document.
- The CONTENT=5 attribute tells Netscape you want to refresh the document in five-second intervals (give or take a little).

CD-ROM

bas_pull.htm

```
<HTML>
<HEAD>
<META HTTP-EQUIV="Refresh" CONTENT=5>
</HEAD>
<BODY>
<EMBED SRC="hitch.vox" PLAYMODE="auto" VISUALMODE="embed"
        WIDTH="2" HEIGHT="2">
</BODY>
</HTML>
```

The example below adds some bells and whistles for the sake of consistent performance. For best results you should be sure of the loading sequence of the parent (frameset) document and child frame document, or else the sound may start playing at unplanned moments. This can be a particular nuisance if your site is complex, with lots of text and graphics. In this next example, the frameset document includes an onLoad event handler that sets a "flag" variable. As long as this flag variable is false, sound play does not begin.

The *better_clientpull.html* frameset document:

CD-ROM

better_clientpull.html

```
<HTML>
```

```
<TITLE>Better Client Pull Sound Example</TITLE>
<HEAD>
<SCRIPT>
var runSound = false;
</SCRIPT>
</HEAD>

<FRAMESET ROWS="100%, *" onLoad="runSound=true;">
<FRAME SRC="dummy.htm" NAME="frame2">
<FRAME SRC="bet_pull.htm" NAME="frame1">
</FRAMESET>

<NOFRAME>
This demo requires Netscape.
</NOFRAME>
</HTML>
```

The *bet_pull.htm* document:

CD-ROM

bet_pull.htm

```
<HTML>
<HEAD>
<META HTTP-EQUIV="Refresh" CONTENT=5>
</HEAD>
<BODY>
<SCRIPT>

function testFlag () {
        if (!parent.runSound)
                ret = setTimeout ("testFlag()", 1000)
        else
                playSound()
}
```

```
function playSound() {
        Voicefile = pathOnly (location.href) + "hitch.vox"
        Result = '<EMBED SRC="' +Voicefile+ '" PLAYMODE="auto"
                VISUALMODE="embed"'
        Result += 'WIDTH="2" HEIGHT="2">'
        document.write (Result+"<P>")
}


function pathOnly (InString)  {
        LastSlash=InString.lastIndexOf ('/', InString.length-1)
        OutString=InString.substring  (0, LastSlash+1)
        return (OutString);
}


testFlag()
</SCRIPT>
</BODY>
</HTML>
```

You can also use the same technique to repeat a sound played through the NPLAYER sound helper application that comes with Netscape. The following script repeats the sound every 10 seconds. (Note: a bug in Netscape 2.0 may prevent the sound from continually playing.)

```
<HTML>
<HEAD>
<META HTTP-EQUIV="Refresh" CONTENT=10>
<SCRIPT>
location = "sound.au"
</SCRIPT>
</HEAD>
<BODY>
<H2>Sound playback</H2>
</BODY>
</HTML>
</Note>
```

JavaScript for Animation

Image animation—making pictures move—is in the top-ten list of "hot" projects for beginning JavaScript developers. On the surface, JavaScript seems well adapted to controlling the content of pages, which means it should be ideal for animation. While JavaScript is an acceptable animation tool, it is actually no better than other methods that do not require JavaScript coding. The chief problem is that JavaScript cannot update an image "in place"; that is, if you want to create an animated banner at the top of your page, JavaScript has to redraw the whole page just to make the picture move.

Still, JavaScript has its place as an animation tool, and with careful planning and the use of other Netscape features, you can use JavaScript as a powerful "animation controller."

Before getting into using JavaScript for animation, let's review some of the other options available to anyone using Netscape 2.0 or later.

- *Java applet.* Unlike JavaScript, a Java applet can update an image in place. Pros: Java animations are fast, and you can precisely control the speed and size of the image. Cons: You need considerable programming experience to write a Java applet. In addition, the first release of Netscape 2.0 for Macintosh and Windows 3.1 lacked Java support.
- *Client pull.* The client pull method "pulls" an image from the computer at a preselected interval. By changing the URL of the image that is received, you can build a progressive moving picture. Pros: It's relatively easy to do, and the speed is reasonable. Cons: You have to reload the entire page (which contains the image as an <IMG> tag). You can't just reload the image.
- *Server push.* If you have access to the CGI-BIN of your server, you can write a fairly simple CGI program that "force feeds" a progression of images to the user. Pros: The image is updated in place; the rest of the document need not be redrawn. Cons: You need access to the CGI-BIN of your server, and you must write a CGI script to control the process.
- *GIF 89a image format.* A little-known feature of the GIF 89a image format is that it can actually contain many "frames" of an image.
- *In place image replacement.* Available only with Netscape 3.0 and later, this feature lets you replace images without rewriting the whole page. See Chapter 22 for more information.

The methods of animating solely with JavaScript involve loading a progression of images. The timing of the images is most often limited by the speed at which they can be downloaded from the server. When viewed on a local machine, JavaScript animations appear sprightly and energetic. Published on the Web and accessed with a dial-up connection, your cute little Disneyque cartoon merely grinds along.

Because good animation depends on the steady inflow of images, you should consider various techniques to speed things up. As one option, you can pre-load all the images in a hidden frame before you start the movie. The user won't see the images, but they will be in Netscape's local cache when you're ready to "start the show." This is the approach taken in the animation technique outlined later in this section.

Animating Within a Frame

The basic animation technique with JavaScript is displaying an image in the entire document. Recall, however, that JavaScript cannot (as yet anyway) update just the image; it must update the entire page. Obviously, this isn't a good technique if there's a lot of other stuff on your page.

Another disadvantage of animating in a whole window is that when you rewrite the document window, the JavaScript code in that document is removed as well. That means you can't readily write one script and have it control the animation process: the script is deleted the first time the picture changes. Because of this limitation, using frames to create animation systems in JavaScript is a far better approach. One frame (which can be displayed or hidden) controls the animation; the other is for the output.

At the heart of any JavaScript animation system is the "frame cycler," that part that goes from one frame to the next. The best cycler uses the setTimeout method; using a for loop that makes JavaScript count to some large number before proceeding merely chews up processor time, and that processor time is needed to accept the images as they are downloaded.

■■■■■ NOTE

JavaScript animation often looks best when all the files are on a local computer, or when you're connected to the Internet via ISDN or another fast method. Even when you cache images, you can "lose" them in a JavaScript animation sequence. The reason is that the animation can get ahead of the loading of the images, even when the images have been saved in the cache. The browser always checks the Internet host first for the image, and then compares that file with the one in the cache. If they match, the browser uses the cache file. This approach still takes time because it requires a re-connection to the server. If the server is slow to respond, the animation effect will not be very good.

If your JavaScript animations are limited to a local computer, or an "intranet" in your company, you should have no problems. But if you plan on creating JavaScript animation for distribution on the public Web, make sure the images are small and simple, and that the "frame rate" for the images is no less than about a second apart. If your server is slow, you may even need to set a slower frame rate.

▬▬▬▬

The Frameset Document

You need a frameset document with at least three frames:

- Frame 1 is the "control" frame, which includes the JavaScript code for running the animation. You can also put other HTML markup in this frame, such as a welcome screen, graphics, and so forth.

- Frame 2 is the "output" frame, where the animation takes place. This is the frame that will be redrawn completely for each step of the animation.

- Frame 3 is the hidden "cache" frame, where the images are first placed before the animation begins. This helps improve the animation.

Here is a basic frameset document for animating. The screen is divided into two rows; the top row is further divided into two columns. The bottom row is actually hidden when the frameset is loaded, so you'll only see the two columns, as shown in Figure 20.1. (For your reference, a version of the frameset in which the rows are split 80/20 is shown in Figure 20.2. This gives you an idea of how the frameset is constructed.)

frame_animate1.html

CD-ROM

```
<HTML>
<HEAD>
<TITLE>Frame Animation</TITLE><HEAD>
<SCRIPT LANGUAGE="JavaScript">
```

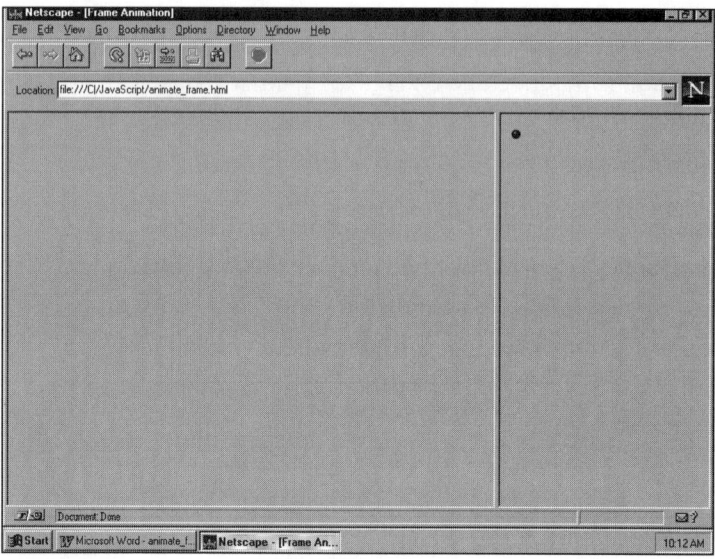

Figure 20.1 The basic animation-in-frame design displays the animation in one frame (usually a small one), while the other frame contains text and the JavaScript control program.

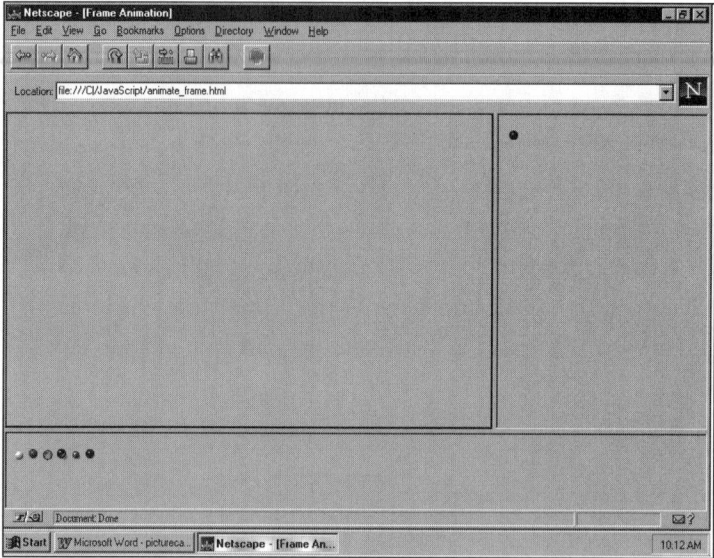

Figure 20.2 The animation-in-frame approach uses a hidden frame to "preload" the images to cache, which helps improve the speed of the animation.

```
function loadTime ()   {
        self.frames["control"].animate();
}
</SCRIPT>
</HEAD>


<FRAMESET ROWS="80%, *" onLoad = "loadTime()">
<FRAMESET COLS="70%, *" >
      <FRAME SRC="animate.htm" NAME="control" >
      <FRAME SRC="dummy.htm" NAME="output">
</FRAMESET>
<FRAMESET COLS="100%">
<FRAME SRC="picturecache.html" NAME="cache" >
    </FRAMESET>
</FRAMESET>


<NOFRAME>
This demo requires Netscape.
</NOFRAME>
</HTML>
```

The Animation Document

The animation document (*animate1.htm*) controls the animation. The images to display are shown in the pictureShow = new cells command line. You can use any number of images you like.

CD-ROM

animate1.htm

```
<HTML>
<HEAD>
<TITLE>Frame Animation</TITLE>
<SCRIPT>
pictureShow = new cels ("ball1.gif", "ball8.gif", "ball3.gif","ball11.gif",
"ball5.gif", "ball7.gif")
```

```
function animate () {
        if (pictureShow.currentitem < pictureShow.length) {
                parent.frames["output"].document.open();
                Temp = '<IMG SRC="' + pathOnly (location.href) +
                        pictureShow[pictureShow.currentitem] + '">'
                parent.frames["output"].document.write (Temp)
                parent.frames["output"].document.close ()
                pictureShow.currentitem++
                ret = setTimeout ("animate()", 800)
        }
}


function cels () {
        for (Count = 0; Count < cels.arguments.length; Count++) {
                this[Count] = cels.arguments[Count];
        }
        this.length = cels.arguments.length;
        this.currentitem = 0
        return (this);
}


function pathOnly (InString)  {
        LastSlash=InString.lastIndexOf ('/', InString.length-1)
        OutString=InString.substring  (0, LastSlash+1)
        return (OutString);
}



</SCRIPT>
</HEAD>
</HTML>
```

Finally, the picture cache file is just a series of <IMG> tags. You should provide a tag
for each image you use in the animation.

```
<IMG SRC="BALL1.GIF">
<IMG SRC="BALL8.GIF">
<IMG SRC="BALL3.GIF">
<IMG SRC="BALL11.GIF">
<IMG SRC="BALL5.GIF">
<IMG SRC="BALL7.GIF">
```

Customizing the JavaScript Animator

You may customize the JavaScript animator by re-arranging the frames in the frame-set document. You may add extra frames, but be sure the frameset has at least the three frames shown. The frames are referred to by their names, so you can change their order in the frameset and the script will still work.

You can also change the images you use for the animation. The example uses simple bullet GIFs for the animation, but you can use anything. The images should be fairly small—thumbnails are best. Larger images take far too long to download, even at 14.4K or 28.8K bps, and users may not be willing to twiddle their thumbs as 25 full-color, full-size frames of your animation load over a period of a couple of minutes.

You can use as many—or as few—images as you like. The user-defined cels object can accommodate any number of images. The instruction to create a new cels object uses the syntax:

```
pictureShow = new cels ("ball1.gif", "ball8.gif", ...)
```

- *pictureShow* is the new cels object you create.
- *"ball1.gif, "ball8.gif"*, and so forth are the images you want to use. Enclose the names of the image files in quotes, and separate them with a comma. All the images are assumed to be in the same directory as the animation control and frameset documents.

Setting Width and Heights for the Images

Ideally, all of the images you use in your animation should have the same width and height. The animation control script, shown above, does not insert the width and height attributes when it builds the animation. Including the width and height attributes is strongly recommended, however, because of a number of bugs related to this issue.

If all of the images have the same width and height, you can simply modify the document.write line to include the dimensions. Change this instruction in the animate function:

```
Temp = '<IMG SRC="' + pathOnly (location.href) +
        pictureShow[pictureShow.currentitem] +
' WIDTH=10 HEIGHT=20">'
```

Your job is tougher if your images are different sizes, and you want to show them in their respective sizes. In that case, you should provide the width and height parameters for each image. (Use a graphics program to determine the width and height, or open the image in Netscape and choose View, Document Info).

You can use two more objects to define the width and height of the images. While you can create a single object to hold all of this information, it's not necessarily easier to use; so let's keep the system basically as is, and add the two additional objects to separately hold the height and width.

Creating a "Fade In" and "Fade Out" Look

Movies and TV shows have us accustomed to the "fade in" and "fade out." These effects are similar in function to the theatrical technique of starting and stopping a scene because they help cue the audience that action is about to begin and that it has ended (and it's time to applaud!).

You can use the same technique with JavaScript to create fades for entire document windows or individual frames. You can fade from black to white, or white to black, giving the effect of a movie fade-in or fade-out, respectively. You can even fade to a specific color, though the black-to-white and white-to-black transition is often the most distinctive.

The technique used in JavaScript is to set the bgColor property of the document object. By looping through a sequence of shades, you can readily create a fade of just about any duration you want. The following example fades from black to white, pauses for a moment, then fades from white to black. The script contains two primary functions:

- *fadeIn* fades through the background colors you've specified in the order that you specified
- *fadeOut* fades through the background colors in reverse order that you specified.

■■■■■■ **NOTE**

The full effect of the fading scripts in this section requires the Windows versions of Netscape.

■■■■■■

The script also contains a colorArray function that creates a user-defined object. This object is essentially an array that holds the color values you want to fade through. A timerDelay function acts to pause between color changes. The method used is a "crow bar" technique of chewing up processor time with a for loop. The method is used rather than setTimeout because the lowest time resolution is about a third of a second. This is too long for most fades. The for loop method produces faster fades, but because it is dependent on the speed of the CPU, the actual speed of the fade will vary from computer to computer.

The script starts with a black background color, set using the BGCOLOR attribute in the <BODY> tag. The fadeIn function is called first when the document is loaded. After a short delay (20,000 "units"), the fadeOut function is called.

fade_demo.html

CD-ROM

```
<HTML>
<HEAD>
<TITLE>Fade In Demo</TITLE>
<SCRIPT LANGUAGE="JavaScript">

function fadeOut () {
        timerDelay (20000) // delay between fade in and fade out
        var Count;
```

```
        for (Count = Colors.length; Count >= 0; Count-) {
                BGColor = Colors[Count]+Colors[Count]+ Colors[Count]
                document.bgColor=BGColor;
                timerDelay (500);   // change this alter delay
        }
}


function fadeIn () {
        var Count;
        for (Count = 0; Count < Colors.length; Count++) {
                BGColor = Colors[Count]+Colors[Count]+ Colors[Count]
                document.bgColor=BGColor;
                timerDelay (500); // change this alter delay
        }
}


function colorArray () {
        for (Count = 0; Count < colorArray.arguments.length; Count++) {
                this[Count] = colorArray.arguments[Count];
        }
        this.length = colorArray.arguments.length;
        this.currentitem = 0
        return (this);
}


function timerDelay(Delay) {
        var Count;
        for (Count=0 ; Count < Delay; Count++){}
        return;
}



Colors = new colorArray (
."11", "22", "33", "44", "55", "66",
```

```
"77","88", "99", "aa", "bb",
"cc", "dd", "ee", "ff"
)


</SCRIPT>
</HEAD>
<BODY bgColor="#000000" onLoad="fadeIn();fadeOut()">
<H1 ALIGN=CENTER>Hello there!</H1>
<P>Fade in, and fade out.</P>
</BODY>
</HTML>
```

You can alter the script by setting new delays, and also new colors in the Colors = new colorArray command line. Only one hex value is provided for each color value you want to step through. This value is duplicated for all three colors of the RGB triplet. As shown here, the fade progresses through even shades of gray from black through white.

Not all shades will appear as distinct, however, depending on the screen settings on the computer. For example, you will not see all the shades if you use Windows 95 set at 256 colors; you need to use the High Color or True Color setting to see the full array of colors. You can usually skip every other value—22, 44, 66, and so forth—and still achieve the same overall look. However, the more steps you have, the smoother the transitions of the fading.

Fading into a Color

If you want to fade through colors instead of gray, use the following script instead. This one fades from black to bright green. Only the fade-in process is shown.

fade_color.html

CD-ROM

```
<HTML>
<HEAD>
<TITLE>Fade In Demo</TITLE>
<SCRIPT LANGUAGE="JavaScript">
```

```
function doFade () {
        for (Count = 0; Count < Colors.length; Count++) {
                document.bgColor=Colors[Count];
                timerDelay (500);
        }
}


function colorArray () {
        for (Count = 0; Count < colorArray.arguments.length; Count++) {
                this[Count] = colorArray.arguments[Count];
        }
        this.length = colorArray.arguments.length;
        this.currentitem = 0
        return (this);
}


function timerDelay(Delay) {
        var Count;
        for (Count=0 ; Count < Delay; Count++){}
        return;
}


Colors = new colorArray (
        "001100","001100","003300","004400","005500","006600",
"007700","008800","009900","00aa00","00bb00","00cc00",
"00dd00","00ee00","00ff00"
)

</SCRIPT>
</HEAD>
<BODY bgColor=#000000 onLoad="doFade()">
<H1 ALIGN=CENTER>Hello there!</H1>
<P>Fade from black</P>
</BODY>
```

████████ **NOTE**

> If you prefer to use the setTimeout method, here's a routine you can use instead of the timerDelay function. Replace the code in the doFade function with this:
>
> ```
> document.bgColor = Colors[Colors.currentitem]
> if (Colors.currentitem < Colors.length-1) {
>         ret = setTimeout ("doFade()", 50)
>         Colors.currentitem++
> }
> ```

████████

Fading in a Frame

The scripts above fade an entire document window. But you can use the same technique to fade just one frame of a multiframe document. Just add the frame name to the beginning of the document.bgcolor method to tell JavaScript which frame you want to fade. The script below is an example of the revised doFade function. The frame to fade is identified by the frames[1] array index. You can use a frame name if you prefer. To fade a different frame, change the array index value or frame name.

```
function doFade () {

        var Count;
        for (Count = 0; Count < Colors.length; Count++) {
                parent.frames[1].document.bgColor=Colors[Count];
                timerDelay (500);
        }

}
```

Fading Multiple Frames

You have the option to fade in other frames in your frameset, either at the same time or one after the other. If you want to fade the frames at the same time, create multiple Colors objects (name them Colors1, Colors2, etc.). And provide a separate document.bgColor statement for each one. For best results, and to make the coding easier, all the frames should have the same number of steps.

Here's the revised Colors*x* objects. It cycles to green in one frame, to yellow in the other.

```
Colors1 = new colorArray (
        "0011000","002200","003300","004400","005500","006600","007700",
        "008800","009900","00aa00","00bb00","00cc00","00dd00","00ee00",
"00ff00"
)
Colors2 = new colorArray (
        "111111","222200","333300","444400","555500","666600","777700",
"888800","999900","aaaa00","bbbb00","cccc00","dddd00","eeee00",  "ffff00"
)
```

Here's the revised doFade routine:

```
function doFade () {
        var Count;
        for (Count = 0; Count < Colors1.length; Count++) {
                parent.frames[0].document.bgColor=Colors1[Count];
                parent.frames[1].document.bgColor=Colors2[Count];
                timerDelay (500);
        }
}
```

Using XBM Graphics with JavaScript

If you're not an X Window user, you probably haven't heard of the XBM graphics format. This format is supported by Netscape and many other browsers. It's a simple format that offers only black-and-white rendition and is intended to be used in X Window applications for basic icons. It's occasionally used in Web pages to produce icons, hit counter digits, and various other graphic images.

What makes the XBM format particularly interesting to JavaScripters is that you can create the XBM image in JavaScript and display it in Netscape. This capability allows you to create and manipulate simple images in real time, with nothing more than JavaScript. The images are limited to black-and-white only (actually gray-and-black, when using Netscape 2.X); if you need to display color, you should use standard GIF or JPEG images.

This section introduces several projects involving XBM images in JavaScript. Each image is prepared on-the-fly, assigning the value to a variable. The variable is then used with the document.write method to insert the image into the document.

Understanding the XBM Format

The XBM format is really a C-language variable assignment. The XBM file format begins with two define statements that indicate the width and height, in pixels, of the image. The width is usually, but not always, stated in multiples of eight. The height can be any value.

Next comes the bit representation of the image. This consists of one or more values, specified in hexadecimal format. Each value defines an area of up to eight pixels wide by one pixel in height. For instance, the following XBM file produces a small 8x1 pixel line:

```
#define text_width 8
#define text_height 1
static unsigned char text_bits[] = {0xff};
```

Note that you can make the line shorter by specifying a smaller width. But you cannot make a line longer without adding more hex values. You can do this by separating each value with a comma, like this:

```
#define text_width 16
#define text_height 1
static unsigned char text_bits[] = {0xff,0xff};
```

This defines a 16x1 pixel line. Each 0xff value is used for eight pixels of the line.

Of course, an XBM graphic of just a very short line isn't too useful. Most of the time you will want to add height to the image. This is also done by increasing the height value and by adding more hex values in the list. Netscape reads the image going from left to right, top to bottom. You can better visualize the arrangement of the values if you put them in "spreadsheet" column/row format. Each column represents eight bits of width; each row represents one bit of height.

The following produces a 16x8 bar. Notice the formatting of the 0xff values. This is purely for human readability. It helps you visualize the two 8-pixel columns (for a total of 16 pixels), and 8 rows. That makes for the 16x8 image.

```
#define text_width 16
#define text_height 8
static unsigned char text_bits[] = {
        0xff,0xff,
        0xff,0xff,
        0xff,0xff,
        0xff,0xff,
        0xff,0xff,
        0xff,0xff,
        0xff,0xff,
        0xff,0xff};
```

In all of the above examples, the graphic is composed of all-black line segments. You can use other hex values to produce line segments with black and white bits. White (actually, the absence of black) is represented as a 0 bit; black is represented by a 1 bit. Put eight bits together and you get a value from 0 to 255. The hex value 0xff is decimal 255, or binary 11111111. All those 1s create the all-black line. Conversely, 0x00 makes an all-white line because it's decimal 0, or 00000000.

To make an image, different number values are used to represent the bit pattern desired. The pattern 1000001, which is decimal 128 (or hex 0x81), produces a line with only one bit turned on at each end. The middle is white. The bits of the digit are organized right to left (not the traditional left to right) with respect to how the bits appear on the screen. Remember this when calculating the bits to make a picture.

With this in mind, here's an XBM graphic that produces a set of concentric boxes. It also shows a "fix" to a bug in Netscape 2.0 that lops off the first row of pixels in a multipixel image. The image is therefore defined as 17 pixels high, even though only rows 1 through 16 are shown (row 0, the first one, is lopped off).

```
#define text_width 16
#define text_height 17
static unsigned char test_bits[] = {
```

```
0xff,0xff,
0xff,0xff,
0x01,0x80,
0xfd,0xbf,
0x05,0xa0,
0xf5,0xaf,
0x15,0xa8,
0xd5,0xab,
0x55,0xaa,
0x55,0xaa,
0xd5,0xab,
0x15,0xa8,
0xf5,0xaf,
0x05,0xa0,
0xfd,0xbf,
0x01,0x80,
0xff,0xff};
```

████████ **NOTE**

Most people can't think in terms of converting binary digits to hex values. You can use a binary to hex calculator, which is included in Windows 3.1 and 95 and is available as freebie software for most other computers. (The Windows calculator is switchable between standard and scientific; you want the scientific mode.) To determine the hex value to use, type in the binary string you want (remember: no more than eight bits), and then press the Hex button to convert it to hexadecimal format.

████████

Simple XBM images such as lines and bars can be designed by mentally envisioning the bit pattern for the lines and converting the pattern to hex. But for more elaborate images, you really need a graphics conversion program that can do the job for you. Sadly, there aren't many. See sources.htm on the CD-ROM.

Producing Separator Bars Using XBM Images

Because XBM images are merely a collection of hex values strung together in width-by-height order, it's fairly easy to string along a bunch of eight-bit-wide lines to construct bars of different lengths and patterns. The *xbm_graphics.html* example that follows demonstrates how to do this.

xbm_graphics.html

CD-ROM

The script is composed of two working parts: the createBar function and setHead function. The setHead function creates a bar segment of a given height and width. It's best to keep the width and height a reasonable size—say, no more than about 96 pixels wide by 32 pixels high. For best results, specify the width in multiples of eight. Otherwise, Netscape could choke as it processes the string that comprises the image. The createBar function is also told what binary sequence to use to render the bar. The sequence "ff" creates an all-black bar, whereas the sequence "0c" (just as an example) creates a dashed bar.

The createBar function prints the bar, any number of times. Duplicating the bar several times to make it longer is better than specifying a long bar in the setHead function. So, as shown in the example, the 32-pixel-wide bar is repeated 10 times, to make a 320-pixel-wide line.

```
function doBar() {
        MakeBar = setHead (32, 11, "ff");
        createBar (MakeBar, 10);
}


function createBar (MakeBar, Len) {
        for (Count = 1; Count <= Len; Count++)
                document.write ("<IMG SRC='JavaScript:MakeBar'
                        ALIGN='baseline'>")
}


function setHead (Width, Height, Pattern) {
        var Count, Countx;
        var Head = "#define count_width "+Width+"\n#define count_height
```

```
"+Height+
                "\nstatic char count_bits[] = {"
        var Bar = Head;
        for (Count = 1; Count <= Height; Count++) {
                for (Countx = 1; Countx <= Math.ceil(Width/8); Countx++)
                        Bar +="0x"+Pattern+","
        }
        Bar +="};"
        return (Bar)
}
```

Figure 20.3 shows some other line samples. They were created using the values in the following table. Notice that line 4 produces an uneven "bar code" look because the setHead width is not in a multiple of 8. This technique can be used for special effects, when you want them.

Line Number	setHead Width	setHead Height	Pattern	Repeat
1	32	7	"0c"	10
2	32	3	"fc"	10
3	32	2	"83"	10

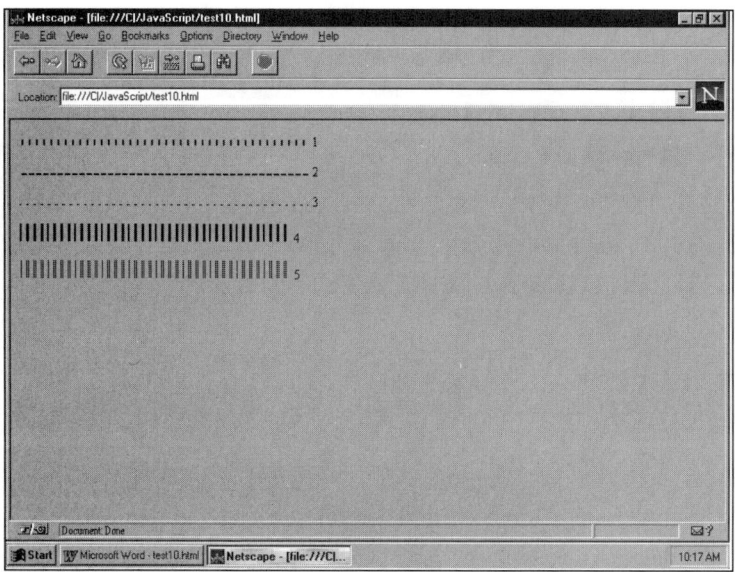

▰▰▰▰ **Figure 20.3** Use XBM images to create interesting bar patterns.

Line Number	setHead Width	setHead Height	Pattern	Repeat
4	30	20	"83"	10
5	30	20	"82"	10

Creating Bar Charts with XBM Graphics

With the routines in the previous example, you can readily create bar charts in your Web pages. The length of the bar is determined by the setHead width and/or the number of repeats. For example, the following script creates three bars of differing lengths, all using the same basic all-black XBM line segment of 16-by-11 pixels. The length of the line is changed by altering its repeat. Following each line is a caption for the bar. You can test a working example of this script in *xbm_barchart.html*.

CD-ROM

xbm_barchart.html

```
function doBar() {
        MakeBar = setHead (16, 11, "ff");
        createBar (MakeBar, 20); document.write("  dogs<BR>")
        createBar (MakeBar, 10); document.write("  cats<BR>")
        createBar (MakeBar, 4); document.write("  cockroaches<BR>")

}
```

Creating a Digital Clock Using XBM Graphics

Numbers in an 8-wide-by-16-high block can be easily represented using XBM bitmaps. The *xbm_clock.html* example shows how this is done. Here, the unique values for each digit are assigned to an array variable. The 0 digit, for example, is assigned as:

```
Digit[0]=Head+"0xff,0xff,0xff,0xc3,0x99,0x99,0x99,0x99,0x99,0x99,"+
"0x99,0xc3,0xff,0xff,0xff};"
```
xbm_clock.html

CD-ROM

To display the digital clock, the Date object is used to determine the current hour and minutes. These values are then used to pick the right XBM bit digits. The digits are written to the document in order, to produce the digital readout. Figure 20.4 shows the output of the digital clock. You can insert the clock anywhere in your page by calling the setClock function. The *xbm_clock.html* file uses this in the body of the document:

```
<BODY>
The time is now:
<SCRIPT>
setClock();
</SCRIPT>
</BODY>
```

Creating a Hit Counter Using XBM Graphics

Yet another good use of XBM graphics is displaying a hit counter (to determine the number of people who visited the site). You can apply the same digit bitmaps used in the XBM clock.

By itself, JavaScript is not capable of storing the number of times someone visits your Web site. This requires a CGI program; such a program is described in more detail in

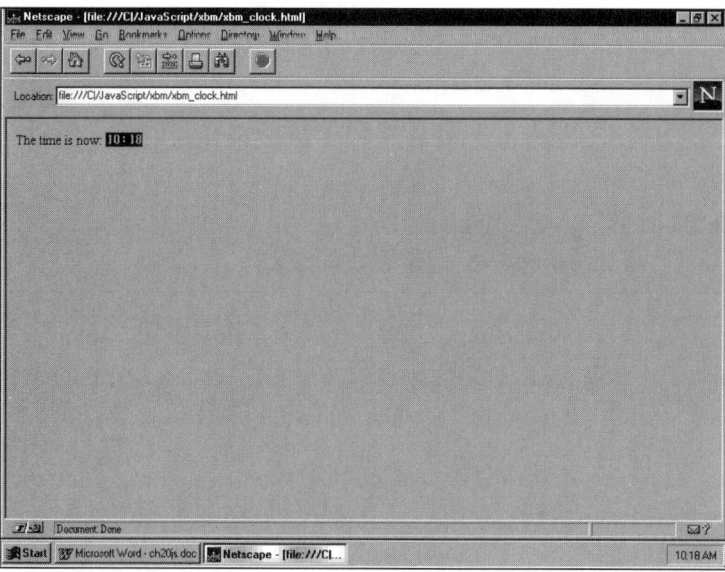

▬▬▬▬▬ **Figure 20.4** The JavaScript clock, using XBM graphics.

Chapter 18, "Using CGI with JavaScript." The following example, however, creates a "fake" hit counter that can be used instead. This hit counter makes up an absurdly large number and displays that as the number of people who have visited the page. It's intended to serve as comic relief; of course, you should not represent the number as valid because some people take "hit counters" pretty seriously.

The random hit counter script, *xbm_hitcount.html*, is similar to the clock script, except that it includes routines for returning a random number. Specific routines are used instead of JavaScript's Math.random property because in Netscape 2.0 the random property functions only when on the Unix platform. The random number generator used in *xbm_hitcount.html* is the same one used in the blackjack game, described in Chapter 17, "Using JavaScript with Advanced HTML."

xbm_hitcount.html

The random number itself is obtained with the following three lines of code. The number is converted to a string—by prepending the empty quotes to the returned value—and characters 2 through 12 are extracted from the number (the random number begins with "0," which you don't want in the output).

```
RandNum = new randomNumberGenerator();
val = RandNum.next() + ""
val = val.substring (2, 12)
```

Figure 20.5 shows an example of how the "faux hit counter" looks in Netscape.

Using JavaScript for "On-the-Fly" Image Sizing

JavaScript and Netscape make a wonderful pair. Netscape lets you size a graphic to any dimension you want. And JavaScript lets you define graphics and graphic attributes on the fly. Put these two features together, and what do you have: on-the-fly sizing of graphics.

If you've been using Netscape to write HTML pages, you've probably already used the sizing trick. One common application is using a small GIF image for any sized bar on the screen. Suppose the GIF is 16-by-16 pixels. An <IMG> tag like the following "stretches" it to 16 by 200 pixels:

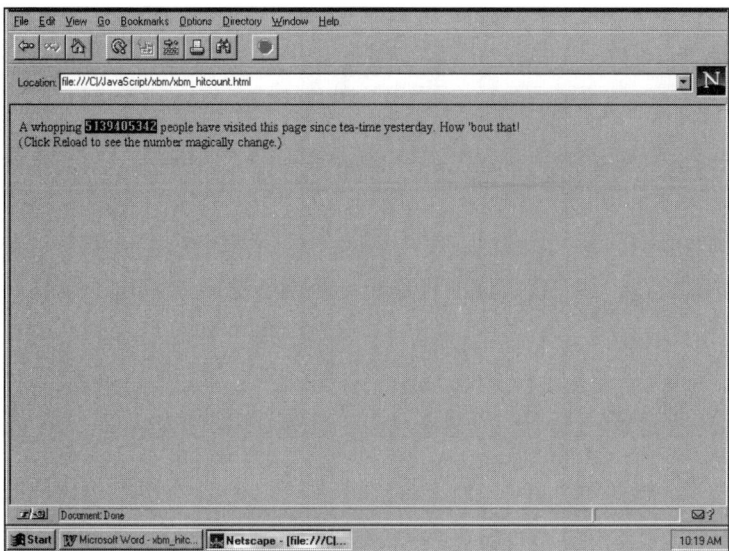

■■■■■■■■ **Figure 20.5** The "faux counter," using CBM graphics. The digits are created by JavaScript on-the-fly.

```
<IMG SRC="small_box.gif" HEIGHT=16 WIDHT=26>
```

As long as the image is a solid color, it will not degrade when you resize it. The image
can even contain stripes of other colors, but the colors must be horizontal. The stripes
stretch with the rest of the image, and it looks like one long bar.

Creating Bar Charts with JavaScript

Instead of hardcoding the width and/or height of an image, you can have JavaScript
do it for you. You can use this technique to create horizontal bar charts or to design
special effects for your page. The following script provides an example of using
JavaScript to make a bar chart. The function stretches a small solid GIF image (the
actual size is unimportant; the smaller the better for transmission speed) to the width
specified. Figure 20.6 shows the result.

size_graphic.html

CD-ROM

```
document.open ("text/html");
makeBar ("250", "Cat");
```

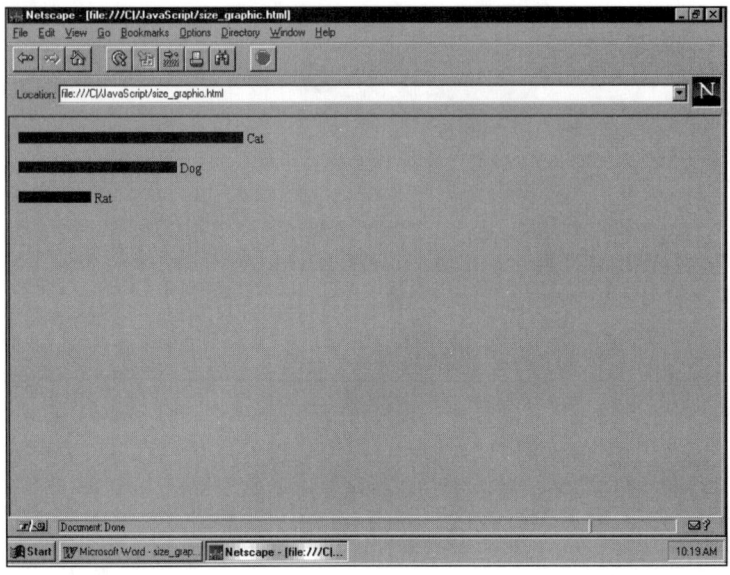

▄▄▄▄▄▄▄▄ **Figure 20.6** Use JavaScript to stretch or shrink a GIF to any size you wish.

```
makeBar ("175", "Dog");
makeBar ("80", "Rat");

function makeBar (Width, Text) {
        var GifName = pathOnly (location.href) + "blu.gif";
        var Height = 12;
        var Temp = "<IMG SRC='" + GifName + "' HEIGHT='" + Height + "' WIDTH=" +
                Width + "' ALIGN=baseline> " + Text + "<P>";
        document.write (Temp);
}

function pathOnly (InString)  {
        LastSlash=InString.lastIndexOf ('/', InString.length-1);
        OutString=InString.substring  (0, LastSlash+1);
        return (OutString);
}
```

You can readily modify the script to use a different GIF image and to increase or decrease the height of the bars. In the example, the bars are set at 12 pixels high, which is a good balance between too fat and too skinny.

Creating Separator Bars

Of course, there's no reason to limit the horizontal bars to bar charts only. You can use the technique to create divider bars rather than rely on the tried-and-true <HR> tag. You can customize each divider bar, so that one small GIF file can create a variety of shapes and sizes. One bar may be long and thin, another short and fat.

Because the GIF file is small, load time for your images is cut drastically, especially if you use just one or two GIFs for all your separator bars. Figure 20.7 gives some examples. Notice that a few of the bars contain horizontal striping. You can include color and pattern change in the bar, as long as it is in the X (horizontal) axis.

Creating Vertical Bars

Another use of "expandable GIFs" is creating vertical bars at the right or left margin. By using just one small GIF file, you can create vertical bars of just about any length. Netscape lets you place the bar on the left or right margin, with text sitting beside it. Look at Figure 20.8 for an example. The bar was created using a small 16-by-16 pixel GIF file. The bar was stretched to a length of 175 pixels. The text is aligned to the right

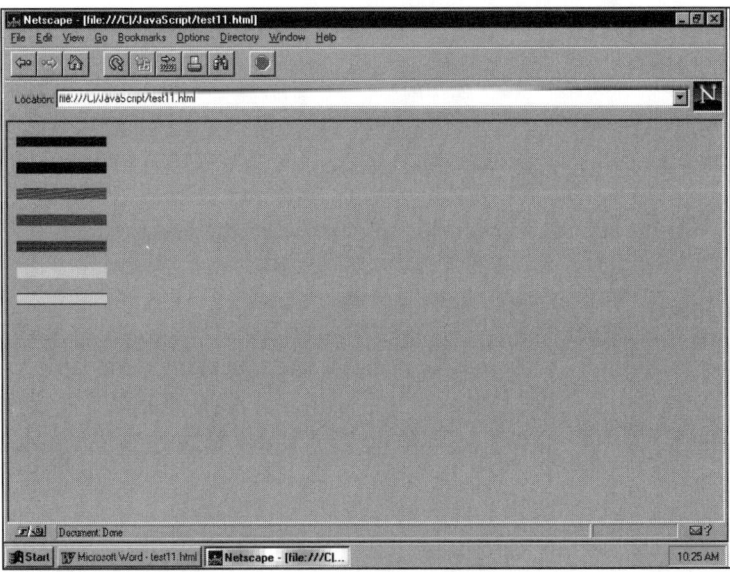

▰▰▰▰▰ **Figure 20.7** Experiment with colors and stripes to make interesting separator bars.

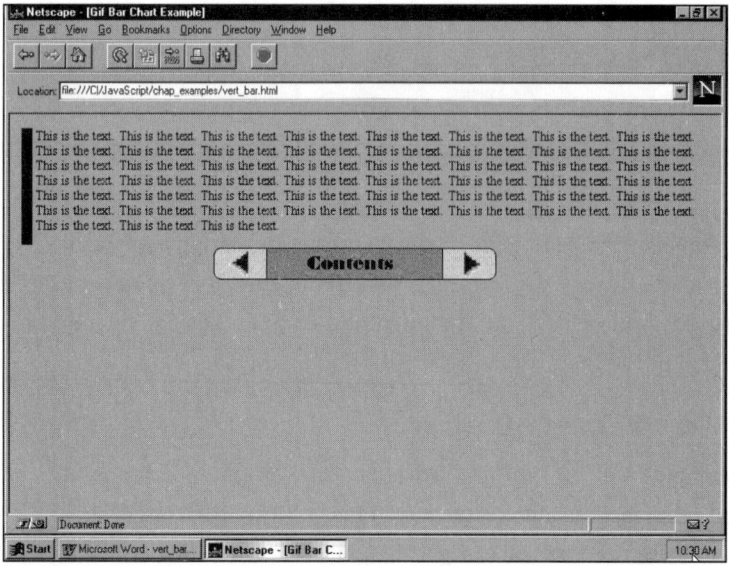

■■■■■■■■ **Figure 20.8** Vertical bars can be used to accentuate text. The length of the
bar can be controlled by JavaScript.

using the Netscape ALIGN=left attribute in the <IMG> tag. (The alignment attribute
is relative to the line, not the text.)

The basic HTML tag for a left-aligned vertical line is:

```
<IMG SRC="blu.html WIDTH=16 HEIGHT=200 ALIGN=left>
```

This line is 16 pixels wide by 200 pixels high. If you don't want the left (or right)
alignment, you can remove the ALIGN attribute or replace it with one of the other
attributes Netscape supports.

This next script demonstrates how to use JavaScript to create a bar down the left
margin and how to place text to the right. The text wraps around the line. If the line
is shorter than the depth of the text, the text rewraps to the full margin as soon as it's
clear of the line.

CD-ROM

margin_bar.html

```
<HTML>
<HEAD>
<TITLE>Gif Margin Chart Example</TITLE>
```

```
<SCRIPT LANGUAGE="JavaScript">

function makeBarVert (Height, Align) {
        var GifName = pathOnly (location.href) + "blu.gif"
        var Width = 12;
        var Temp = "<IMG SRC=" + GifName + " HEIGHT=" + Height + "  WIDTH=" +
                Width + " ALIGN="+ Align + "><P>"
        document.write (Temp)
}


function pathOnly (InString)  {
        LastSlash=InString.lastIndexOf ('/', InString.length-1)
        OutString=InString.substring  (0, LastSlash+1)
        return (OutString);
}


</SCRIPT>
</HEAD>
<BODY>
<SCRIPT>makeBarVert ("125", "right")</SCRIPT>
```

Now here's where JavaScript comes in. Instead of hardcoding the width and/or height of the image, have JavaScript do it for you. You can use this technique to create horizontal bar charts or to design special effects for your page. Here's an example of using JavaScript to make a bar chart. The function stretches a small solid GIF image (the actual size is unimportant; the smaller the better for transmission speed) to the width specified.

```
</BODY>
</HTML>
```

Shortcuts with Graphics and Text

With JavaScript, there's no need to create your Web pages one HTML tag after another. If your pages have a healthy mixture of text, graphics, and special formatting—perhaps centering, font color changes, and various headings—you know that keeping all the tags straight can be a big job.

Things aren't always simple if you use a *wysiwyg* HTML editor to create your pages. Most such editors limit the HTML tags you can use, and even the most elaborate ones won't often let you combine HTML tags unless it's a sequence the editor allows. As a result, you have to format your Web pages according to someone else's idea of how HTML tags should go together. As long as you produce valid HTML markup, you should be allowed to combine the tags in any way you see fit.

Thanks to JavaScript, you can greatly reduce the effort involved in hand-coding an elaborate HTML document. Actually, the document need not be elaborate to make good use of JavaScript as a formatting tool. With JavaScript producing the special formatting, you can more easily design pages that follow a style guide. The style is in the routines you use to produce the output you want.

Most of the examples in this chapter are for inspirational purposes. Feel free to use the JavaScript code as-is or modify it to suit your tastes.

The Pros and Cons of Using JavaScript for Output

If you publish your pages on the public Web, remember that not everyone has a JavaScript-compatible browser. If you use JavaScript to generate text and graphics, you should also prepare a non-JavaScript version. This version can be plain text, or it can contain the graphic embellishments as well.

If you have to re-create the page for non-JavaScript browsers, why even bother with the JavaScript version? First, you may be creating pages for a "closed" environment, like a company intranet, where you are assured all the users have a JavaScript-endowed browser. And second, JavaScript makes it easier to modify the document later on. For example, you can quite easily change the entire look and layout of a document just by changing a few lines of JavaScript code. This means you can usually update and revise the JavaScript much more quickly.

Another critical issue is the following. Under Netscape, text and images rendered on the screen by JavaScript cannot be saved or printed. This may or may not be a limitation for you. If you expect your users to save or print the page, you should avoid using JavaScript to output the page contents, or even parts of it. However, if you plan on creating pages for viewing only, then the JavaScript methods outlined below are perfectly acceptable.

Furthermore, you can also use this feature to good advantage to create two versions of your documents. You can create a visually rich version that the user sees and a simpler version that the user saves or prints.

Enhancing Headings

Web documents stand out when they are divided into headings. The standard <Hx> headings are perfectly fine for most documents; but if you want something extra, consider adding such formatting features as centering and coloring. And you can dress up even plain black, flush-left headings by adding graphic widgets to the front and/or end of the text. See Figure 20.9 for a bevy of different heading styles. These are created using JavaScript routines that apply various formatting to text you provide.

A sample heading style routine is shown here. The routine is designed to produce a flush-left or centered heading, with an image—such as a bullet—to the left of the

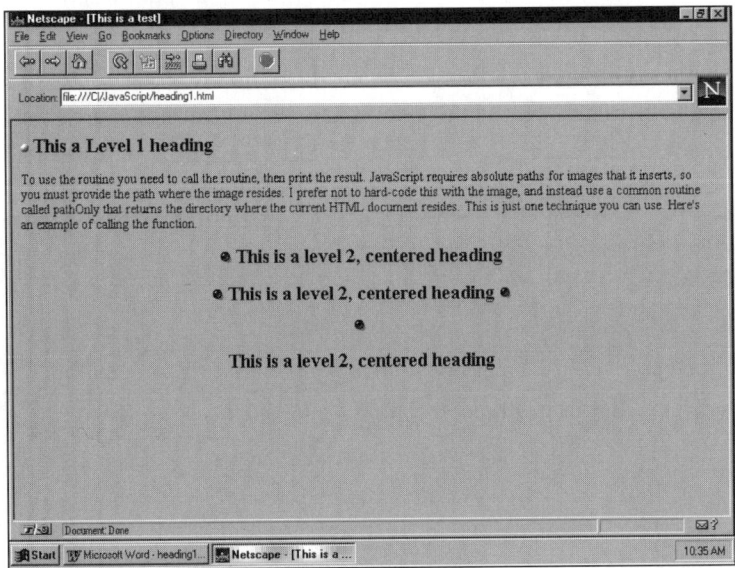

▬▬▬▬ **Figure 20.9** An assortment of some of the heading styles you can quickly create using JavaScript.

heading. You choose the name, height, and width of the image, the heading level, the text, and whether you want it centered.

```
function headingStyleA (Gif, Height, Width, Level, Text, Center) {
        Output = ""
        if (Center)
                Output += '<CENTER>'
        Output += '<H' + Level + '>';
        Output += '<IMG SRC="' + Gif + '" HEIGHT=' +Height+
' WIDTH=' +Width+ '> ';
        Output += Text;
        Output += '</H' + Level + '>';
        if (Center)
                Output += '</CENTER>'
        return (Output);
}
```

To use the routine, you need to call the routine and then print the result. JavaScript requires absolute paths for images that it inserts, so you must provide the path where the image resides. One option is to choose not to hardcode this with the image. Instead, you use a common routine called pathOnly that returns the directory where the current HTML document resides. This is just one technique you can use. Here's an example of calling the function.

```
UrlPath=pathOnly (location.href);
Ret=headingStyleA (UrlPath+"ball1.gif", 9, 9, "2",
"This is a sample heading", false)
document.write (Ret);
```

Putting all of this in perspective, try creating a document with text (manually inserted) and several headings. In this example, the text is kept short to save space.

CD-ROM

gr_enhance.html

```
<HTML>
<HEAD>
<TITLE>This is a test</TITLE>
```

```
<SCRIPT LANGUAGE="JavaScript">
UrlPath=pathOnly (location.href);
function headingStyleA (Gif, Height, Width, Level, Text, Center) {
        Output = ""
        if (Center)
                Output += '<CENTER>'
        Output += '<H' + Level + '>';
        Output += '<IMG SRC="' + Gif + '" HEIGHT=' +Height+
' WIDTH=' +Width+ '> ';
        Output += Text;
        Output += '</H' + Level + '>';
        if (Center)
                Output += '</CENTER>'
        return (Output);
}
function pathOnly (InString)  {
        LastSlash=InString.lastIndexOf ('/', InString.length-1)
        OutString=InString.substring  (0, LastSlash+1)
        return (OutString);
}
</SCRIPT>
</HEAD>
<BODY>
<SCRIPT>
Ret=headingStyleA (UrlPath+"ball1.gif", 9, 9, "2",
"This a Level 1 heading", false)
document.write (Ret);
</SCRIPT>
<P>To use the routine, you need to call the routine, and then print the
result. JavaScript requires absolute paths for images that it inserts, so you
must provide the path where the image resides. I prefer not to hard-code this
with the image, and instead use a common routine called pathOnly that returns
the directory where the current HTML document resides. This is just one tech-
nique you can use. Here's an example of calling the function.
</P>
<SCRIPT>
```

```
Ret=headingStyleA (UrlPath+"ball11.gif", 13, 13, "2",
"This is a level 2, centered heading", true)
document.write (Ret);
</SCRIPT>
</BODY>
</HTML>
```

The benefit of this approach is that you needn't bother with HTML tags to make changes, and the changes can be made quickly. If you always use the same heading level and GIF, you can simplify the routine even more, to save you additional time and trouble. Create custom versions of the heading style routine as shown here:

```
function headingStyleACustom (Text) {
        Gif = pathOnly (location.href) + "ball1.gif"
        Height = 9
        Width = 9
        Level = "2"
        Center = false
        Output = ""
        if (Center)
                Output += '<CENTER>'
        Output += '<H' + Level + '>';
        Output += '<IMG SRC="' + Gif + '" HEIGHT=' +Height+
                ' WIDTH=' +Width+ '> ';
        Output += Text;
        Output += '</H' + Level + '>';
        if (Center)
                Output += '</CENTER>'
document.write (Output);
}
```

You call the routine anywhere in the page, as shown here:

```
<SCRIPT>
headingStyleACustom ("This a Level 2 heading")
</SCRIPT
```

CD-ROM

heading_styles.html

A number of these heading styles have been created and saved in *heading_styles.html* for your convenience.

Setting Colors and Sizes

Along similar lines of using JavaScript to enhance headings, you can use JavaScript format text with unusual effects. This is especially handy when a number of formats are applied to the text—for example, a font size change, a font color change, and centering. You can use a similar approach to that of creating custom headings. Here's just one example.

CD-ROM

settext_color.html

```
<HTML>
<HEAD>
<TITLE>Set Text Color</TITLE>
<SCRIPT LANGUAGE="JavaScript">
function textStyle (Text, FontSize, FontColor, Bold) {
        Output = Text.fontsize(FontSize)
        Output = Output.fontcolor (FontColor)
        if (Bold)
                Output = Output.bold()
document.write (Output);
}
</SCRIPT>
</HEAD>
<BODY BGCOLOR="white">
<P>This is text before</P>
<SCRIPT>
textStyle ("This is a test", "+3", "cadetblue", true)
</SCRIPT>
<P>This is text after</P>
</BODY>
</HTML>
```

The textStyle function takes the following parameters:

- *Text* is the text you want to write to the document.
- *FontSize* is the size of the font, such as "3" or "+2."
- *FontColor* is the color of the font, expressed as a hex triplet or a color name, such as "cadetblue."
- Bold is a *true* or *false* value and indicates if you want the text in bold.

ALL ABOUT HTML

Need a reminder of how to use an HTML tag? Found a tag that's new to you? This chapter reviews the most commonly used HTML tags as they are applied in Netscape 2.0 and above. This is not an exhaustive list of HTML tags by any means, but the following represents about 95 percent of the tags you'll use in your pages.

The chapter is divided into these major sections:

- Typical HTML document
- Anchor element
- Block elements
- Inline elements
- Image element
- List elements
- Form elements
- Frameset elements
- Table elements

Typical HTML Document

While there is really no such thing as a "typical" HTML document, there is a typical structure for one. This structure follows, and it is referred to as an example throughout the chapter. The structure is shown with indenting, though such indenting is completely optional.

```
<HTML>
        <HEAD>
                <TITLE>This is the title</TITLE>
        </HEAD>
        <BODY>
                The body of the document goes here.
        </BODY>
</HTML>
```

HTML Anchor Element

The anchor element comes in two general forms: a NAME tag that indicates a named anchor (or target) in a document and a HREF (HREF stands for *hypertext reference*) tag that indicates a link to some other document or a location elsewhere in the same document.

Because of the dual nature of the anchor element, it is sometimes referred to as an "anchor" or a "link." It's an *anchor* when used with NAME and a *link* when used with HREF.

The "anchor" form of the anchor element is:

```
<A NAME="link_to_this_spot">...optional text here...</A>
```

This element creates a target anchor—a link point to this anchor. You can include optional text between the <A> and </A> tags. The text appears in standard body format and does not take on the customary appearance—color and underline—of a link anchor. This type of anchor is similar to a bookmark in a word processor. It marks a spot in the document to which to jump.

The "link" form of the anchor element is:

```
<A HREF="link_to_another_spot ">...optional text here...</A>
```

This element creates an anchor meant to reference another document or an anchor in the same document (it can even reference another document and an anchor within that document).

The optional text is the "click text" or label text—the text that you click on to activate the link. Though the text is shown here as optional, you must include something between the <A> and </A> tags so you can click on the link to activate it. An image, or a combination of an image and text, can be enclosed between the <A> and </A> tags. If an image is used, the image becomes "hot," that is, clicking on the image activates the link.

Though not often used, an anchor can be both a link and a target destination, simply by using both NAME and HREF in the same anchor:

```
<A NAME="link_to_this_spot" HREF="link_to_another_spot">Click here</A>
```

Acceptable HREF Entries

When using the anchor element as a hypertext link, you must specify a valid URL or anchor name after the HREF attribute. Enclose the text in quotes. A typical URL is:

```
http://www.anywhere.com/mypage.html
```

When you click on an anchor that contains this line for the HREF attribute, the browser program links to the *mypage.html* document at the location http://www.anywhere.com. Other valid URLs include ftp (file download) sites, local files on your own computer's hard disk drive, newsgroups, telnet, and target (named) anchors. When using the last of these, prefix the anchor name with a # symbol, as in:

```
HREF="#anchor_name"
```

This links to a bookmark anchor elsewhere in the document. You can also combine a URL to another document and an anchor within that document with the following technique:

```
HREF="http://www.anywhere.com/mypage.html/#bookmark_name"
```

Acceptable NAME Entries

With the exception of the # (hash) character, there is virtually no limitation to the text you can use for the NAME attribute in an anchor. However, it's best to keep the name short. To maintain consistency, avoid spaces and capitalized characters (however, much of this is personal taste). Here are some examples:

Good	Not so good
anchorname	#anchorname
contents	Contents
tableofcontents	Table of Contents
my_references	MyReferences

Examples of Actual Anchor Tags

Here are some examples of anchor tags as used in working HTML pages.

Bookmark anchor to a table of contents:

```
<A NAME="contents"><H2>Table of Contents</H2></A>
```

Link anchor to the table of contents of a document:

```
See the <A HREF="#contents">Table of Contents</A> for more information.
```

Link anchor to another document on the Web:

```
Visit <A HREF="http://www.anywhere.com/ugly.html">the ugliest page on the
Web</A> to see some bad examples of HTML page design.
```

Link anchor to a specific bookmark in another document on the Web:

```
See the <A HREF="http://www.anywhere.com/ugly.html/#contents">table of contents
for the ugliest page</A> on the Web.
```

Remember that images can be used in place of, and in addition to, the text used between the <A> and </A> tags. See the entry for the <IMG> element elsewhere in this reference for more information.

HTML Block Elements

Block elements literally "block" text in an HTML document, for the purpose of rendering in a special format. They are called block elements because they work with blocks of text and often cannot contain other block elements or are restricted in the type of other block elements that can be included.

<ADDRESS>

The address element defines text in a document that you want to display as a mailing or Internet address. Most browsers render this text in italics or some other special way. The address element serves to provide a visual cue that the text within it should be given special consideration.

Address is an HTML block element and therefore contains paired tags: <ADDRESS> and </ADDRESS>. The syntax of the address element looks like this:

```
<ADDRESS>address goes in here</ADDRESS>
```

Quite often you want to include a mailing address, complete with the usual line breaks between the name, address, city, and so forth. This is accomplished within the address block with the use of
 (line break) tags. Following is a typical example of the address element.

```
<ADDRESS>
John Doe & Associates<BR>
John Doe, President<BR>
123 Main Street<BR>
Anytown, US 12345<BR>
</ADDRESS>
```

<BODY>

The body element encloses all of the text and tags that are meant to be displayed in the document. In reality, most Web browsers display text outside the body element, but they may not always behave this way in the future. It's a good idea to include the body element in all your Web documents, if nothing else for consistency.

Body is a block element and therefore consists of a start tag, <BODY>, and an end tag, </BODY>. Between these tags go all the other formatting and tags you want displayed in your document. See the "Typical HTML Document" example earlier in this chapter to see how the body element is used.

The <BODY> tag accepts a number of attributes. These attributes are used to control the overall appearance of the background and text of the document (though the user has the option to ignore these attributes and stay with default choices). These attributes include:

- Background color
- Text color
- Link color
- Visited link color
- Active link color
- Wallpaper

These attributes can be used alone or in conjunction with any of the others.

Specifying a Background Color

The background color can be set for a Web page with the BGCOLOR attribute. The color is specified using an "RBG triplet" (see "Deciphering RGB Triplet Values," later in this chapter). The value for an all-black background is #000000; the value for an all-white background is #ffffff. The default medium gray is specified as #0c0c0c. The following example creates a red background:

```
<BODY BGCOLOR="#ff0000">
```

Specifying a Foreground Color

The foreground color sets the color of text. Normally the text is black, but it can be changed to any other color. As with the background, the foreground color is specified using an RBG triplet (see "Deciphering RGB Triplet Values," later in this chapter). Use the TEXT attribute to change the foreground color. The following example creates green text:

```
<BODY TEXT="#00ff00">
```

Specifying Link Colors

You can choose colors for the three kinds of links: new (never-before-visited), visited, and active. The color for each is specified as an RBG triplet or as a valid color name, such as "white," "black," or "cadetblue" (see "Deciphering RGB Triplet Values," later in this chapter). The attributes are:

Link Type	Attribute
New link	LINK= #nnnnnn
Visited link	VLINK=#nnnnnn
Active link	ALINK=#nnnnnn

Here are some examples:

```
<BODY LINK="#ff1494">   (makes pink)
<BODY VLINK="#ffd700">  (makes yellow)
```

Specifying a Wallpaper Graphic

If you're not satisfied with a solid color background, you can cover the background with "wallpaper," a small graphic that is repeated as needed to fill the entire background area. Most wallpaper images are small 1-by-1 pixel GIF or JPG graphics files—the smaller the better, so they don't take a long time to transmit to the user's computer.

To specify a wallpaper image, use the BACKGROUND attribute, along with the name of the graphic file you wish to use. This can be the filename alone if the file is included in the same directory as the HTML document currently viewed, or it can be in a different directory or even on a different server. The following example specifies a background file called BG.GIF:

```
<BODY BACKGROUND="bg.gif">
```

If you wish to use a graphic not contained in the same directory as the current HTML file, include a URL path. Use an absolute or relative URL, as needed. Here's an example using an absolute URL:

```
<BODY BACKGROUND="http://anywhere.com/mypages/bg.gif.">
```

Specifying Multiple Background Options

Feel free to combine background attributes as desired. For example, to specify a white background and blue text, use the following:

```
<BODY BGCOLOR="#ffffff" TEXT="#0000ff">
```

Ordinarily, if you specify a wallpaper image your background color setting is ignored. This is true if the wallpaper graphic is not transparent. The background color will show through if the image is transparent (it can be made transparent using the transparency option in many advanced graphics programs).

■■■■■■ **NOTE**

If you specify one <BODY> tag element, such as foreground color or text color, you should specify them all. Otherwise, your unique color setting may conflict with default settings made by the user.

■■■■■■

< B L O C K Q U O T E >

The blockquote element defines text in a document that you want to display as a large segment of "quoted" text, such as from a book or magazine article. Most browsers render this text in a special way, usually as standard text with indenting. The blockquote element serves to provide a visual cue that the text within it should be given special consideration.

Blockquote is an HTML block element and therefore contains two paired tags: <BLOCKQUOTE> and </BLOCKQUOTE>. The syntax of the blockquote element looks like this:

```
<BLOCKQUOTE>Text goes in here</BLOCKQUOTE>
```

Most often, blockquoted text is rendered with indenting on the right and left, as shown in Figure 21.1. The effect of the blockquote is most obvious with lots of text.

You can use blockquote to create some indented special effects. For example, suppose you are writing a Hollywood screenplay and want to use the standard script format, in which character names are centered and dialog appears indented from the left and right margins. The text for "action" descriptions spans from margin to margin. You can accomplish this by nesting several blockquote elements within one another. Nesting four blockquote elements looks like this:

```
<BLOCKQUOTE><BLOCKQUOTE><BLOCKQUOTE><BLOCKQUOTE>
Text goes here
</BLOCKQUOTE></BLOCKQUOTE></BLOCKQUOTE></BLOCKQUOTE>
```

Character names are formatted with the <CENTER> tag to center them.

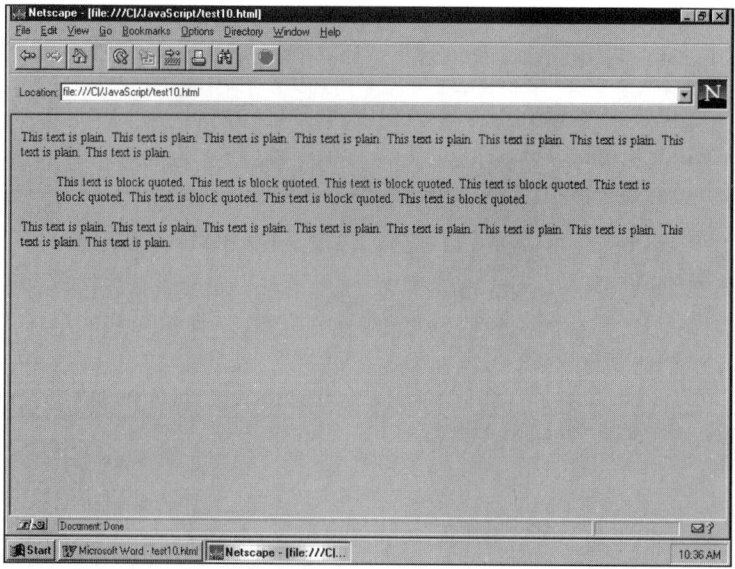

■■■■■■■■ **Figure 21.1** Blockquoted text appears indented from, and on some browsers, in a different font from, the body text.

<CENTER>

The center element centers text and images between the visible window margins of the browser. It is used entirely for cosmetic purposes and goes a long way to improving the looks of Web pages.

Center is an HTML block element and therefore contains two paired tags: <CENTER> and </CENTER>. The syntax of the center element looks like this:

```
<CENTER>Centered text goes in here</CENTER>
```

Once you turn centering on, it remains on until you turn it off with the </CENTER> tag, so be sure to switch it off when you're done using it. Remember that centering affects all text and images, as well as tables and forms.

 (Line Break)

The line break element starts text or graphics on a new line. It acts like a hard return in a word processor, where pressing Enter begins another line. To insert a line break, use <BR>. The <BR> tag is used by itself and has no end-tag.

Note that the <BR> tag inserts a line break without extra spacing before or after the line. If you want to add extra spacing between text, use the <P> tag instead.

Netscape understands a small assortment of attributes for the <BR> tag. These attributes relate to how text wraps around images. Use the CLEAR attribute in the <BR> tag to indicate how you want the text to flow around the image:

- Use CLEAR="left" to break the line and move down vertically until the left margin is clear of the image.
- Use CLEAR="right" to break the line and move down vertically until the right margin is clear of the image.
- Use CLEAR="all" to break the line and move down vertically until the left and right margins are clear of the image.

<FONT>

The font element lets you change the color and size of individual text (it has no effect on the size of the font used in headings, form buttons, and other elements). The font element is not supported by all browsers, but is supported by most of the modern ones, such as Netscape. The text appears normally when viewed on a browser that does not understand the font element.

The attributes for the <FONT> tag are:

Attribute	What it does
SIZE	Sets the size of the text that follows
COLOR	Sets the color of the text that follows

Font is an HTML block element and is normally used with paired tags: <FONT> and </FONT>. The syntax of the FONT element looks like this:

```
<FONT SIZE=value>Text go here</FONT SIZE>
```

Substitute value with size of the font you want to display, with 1 being the smallest and 7 being the largest. The default is 3. For example, to set the font size to 5 (two steps larger than the default), use:

```
<FONT SIZE="5">Text go here</FONT SIZE>
```

When the browser reaches the </FONT> tag, it reverts to the default font size.

Note that the user can select the default size for body text as a setting in the browser. The values used with the font element are relative; as a result, even if the user has selected a large font already, specifying a larger font in a font element produces even larger text. You should take this into account when changing the size of font to any great extent, especially when making fonts very small. For example, it's possible for the user to choose an 8-point font for regular text. If you reduce the font size to 1 with the font element, that text will be impossibly small when viewed in the browser. Therefore, you should avoid using font size values smaller than 1 and greater than 5.

You can also assign a relative size value, which helps to ensure that the font size actually displayed is not overly large or small. To specify a relative size, place a + or - symbol before the font value, as in:

```
<FONT SIZE="+2">Text go here</FONT SIZE>
```

This example increases the size of the body font by two steps. Conversely, you can specify a smaller font by using a negative number, as in:

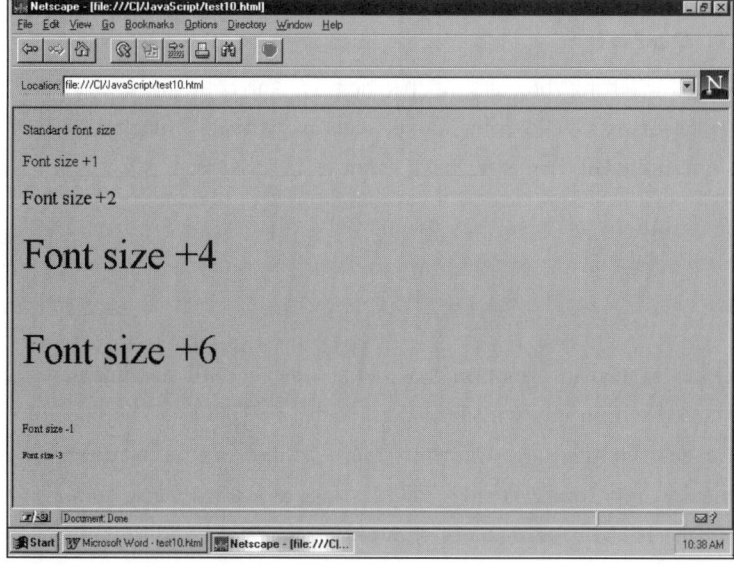

Figure 21.2 The <FONT> tag can be used with the ASIZE attribute to specify an absolute or relative size for text.

```
<FONT SIZE="-1">Text go here</FONT SIZE>
```

This decreases the size of the body font by one step. See Figure 21.2 for an example of an assortment of font sizes.

Setting the Overall Font Size

While the font element is designed to be used with paired tags, you can leave off the </FONT> end-tag if there is no need to revert to the standard font size. For instance, this sets the font size value to 4 for the remainder of the document:

```
<FONT SIZE="4">Text follows, with no end-tag...
```

Setting a Base Font

The open-ended method of setting a font size is not the preferred method to use. Rather, if you wish to set a default body text font size for the entire document, use the <BASEFONT> tag, as follows:

```
<BASEFONT SIZE=value>
```

As with the <FONT> tag, use a value from 1 to 7 for the basefont font size.

Setting Font Color

Also use the <FONT> tag for setting the color of specific text. The color for each is specified as an RBG triplet or as a valid color name, such as "white," "black," or "cadetblue" (see "Deciphering RGB Triplet Values," later in this chapter).

```
<FONT COLOR="#ff1494">This is pink text!</FONT COLOR>
<FONT COLOR="pink">This is also pink text!</FONT COLOR>
```

<HEAD>

The head element encloses special information that defines the HTML document. This information is enclosed within its own set of tags, such as <TITLE>. The tags within the head element describe the data. Currently there are few tags used in the head element. Of particular importance is the <TITLE> tag, along with any comments that are stored in the HTML file, but not shown in the viewer. Additionally, the head contains the tag that identifies JavaScript as an embedded language used in the HTML document.

Head is an HTML block element and therefore contains two paired tags: <HEAD> and </HEAD>. The syntax of the head element looks like this:

```
<HEAD>Additional tags go here</HEAD>
```

As the head element is almost always used to enclose the <TITLE> tag, which defines the title of the document (the title usually appears in the caption for the browser window). A typical example is:

```
<HEAD><TITLE>This is the title of the document</TITLE></HEAD>
```

An HTML document that contains JavaScript uses the <SCRIPT> tag, also contained within the head element. Here's a barebones example, formatted onto separate lines for easy reading:

```
<HEAD>
        <TITLE>HTML document with JavaScript</TITLE>
        <SCRIPT LANGUAGE="JavaScript"></SCRIPT>
</HEAD>
```

Comments regarding the construction of the document are also typically included in the head element, using <!- -> comment tags. Though the head is the usual place for comments, they can be placed anywhere in the document. The text contained in the comment tag is ignored by the browser.

```
<HEAD>
        <!–This is a document that contains JavaScript–>
        <TITLE>HTML document with JavaScript</TITLE>
        <SCRIPT LANGUAGE="JavaScript"></SCRIPT>
</HEAD>
```

▰▰▰▰▰ **NOTE**

Many older browsers use a simplified technique for terminating a comment. The comment is terminated as soon as the browser encounters the first > character. This means that a comment such as:

```
<!--This is a comment for the <HEAD> tag -->
```

inserts the text tag –> into the browser.

<H1> through <H6> (Headings)

HTML supports headings to separate the text of a document. These headings are numbered 1 through 6, with heading 1 being a top-level heading for main sections of a document, and heading 6 being a subheading for minor sections. Few HTML documents use more than the first two or three headings.

The basic syntax for all six heading levels is the same, except for the number that defines the level. As headings are block elements, they consist of a starting tag, <Hx>, and an ending tag, </Hx>. The x is a number from 1 to 6. Here's an example of a top-level (level 1) heading:

```
<H1>This is a main heading</H1>
```

By definition, a heading appears on a line by itself, so any text that follows it will begin on a new line. All browsers add extra spacing to the top and bottom of the heading to make it sound out in the text. Figure 21.3 shows an example of how all six heading levels look in Netscape. Each heading level is rendered in a slightly different format.

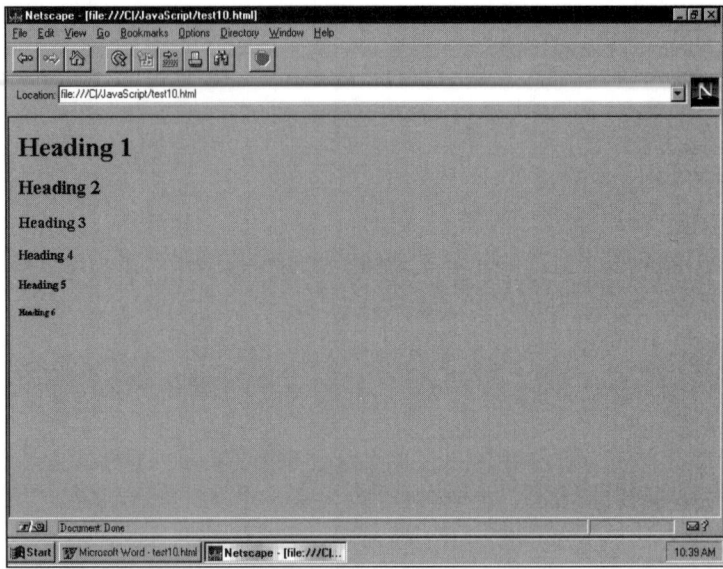

■■■■■■ **Figure 21.3** The six levels of headings.

How to Effectively Use Headings

One of the bug-a-boos of Web page design is proper use of headings. Lots has been written on this subject, and almost any book or reference describing good print lay-out design is also applicable to Web page design.

Of most importance is that the headings should convey a hierarchy. Avoid using a level 1 heading and following it with a level 3 heading. Readers are accustomed to using the relative size of headings to help convey the structure of a text—main head-ings, subheadings, sub-subheadings, and so forth.

Though not a rule, headings are typically applied so that there are at least two at any given level in a section. For example, if you have one level 2 heading in a section, you should have at least one more. Again, this helps denote structure to the reader. Here is an example of a good heading structure:

- Main heading 1
  - Subheading 1
  - Subheading 2
- Main heading 2
  - Subheading 1
  - Subheading 2
  - Subheading 3

This heading structure, however, is not ideal:

- Main heading 1
  - Sub heading 1
- Main heading 2
  - ...

When possible, avoid inserting a subhead immediately following the next higher level. Insert at least one sentence of plain text to separate them.

Finally, many Web pages use the first level head, <H1>, for the main title or banner at the start of the document (often, but not always, the same as the document title, which is defined using the <TITLE> element). Level 2 headings are then used as the main headings within the document.

Using Other Elements with Headings

By design, heading elements are meant to stand alone and cannot often mix other HTML elements with a heading. There are notable exceptions.

- You may use all or part of the heading text as the "click text" of an anchor. Here is an example: <H1><A HREF="url">This is a heading</A></H1>

- You may add italics and other character attributes to the text of a heading. Here is an example: <H1>This is a <I>heading</I></H1>.

- Most browsers add extra space for formatting following the </Hx> end tag. To add a horizontal line with only a small space between it and a preceding heading, include the <HR> tag within the heading definition. Here is an example: <H1>This is a heading<HR></H1>.

- Conversely, if you want more space between the heading and the horizontal line, place the <HR> tag outside of the header definition. Here is an example: <H1>This is a heading</H1><HR>.

- The same technique mentioned in the above two items can also be applied to horizontal lines added before the heading. Here are examples: <H1><HR>This is a heading</H1> and <HR><H1>This is a heading</H1>. Figure 21.4 shows some examples.

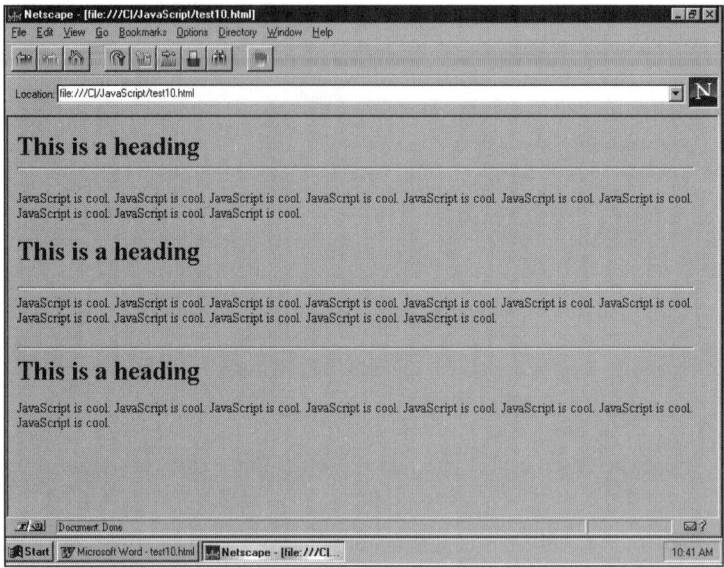

■■■■■■■ **Figure 21.4** Creative placement of the <HR> tag within the <Hx> heading tags yields various spacings.

<HR> (Horizontal Rule)

The horizontal rule element inserts a margin-to-margin line across the page and is used to optically separate areas of the page (no, there is no built-in vertical rule element, though this would be a good idea). The horizontal rule element is a simple standalone tag (there is no end-tag). To insert a horizontal tag, use <HR>. The actual appearance of the rule depends on the browser. Navigator renders the rule with a 3D appearance, but some other browsers use a simple black line.

Navigator also adds a number of options to the <HR> tag. These options set the width and size of the rule, as well as its shading.

- Use the *SIZE* attribute to set the thickness of the rule. The default is roughly 2 pixels.
- Use the *WIDTH* attribute to set the width of the rule. You can either use pixels or percentage. Because browsers are used at different screen resolutions, it's almost always better to rely on the percentage measurement.
- Use the *NOSHADE* attribute to tell Navigator that you do not want the rule to be rendered in 3D.
- Use the *ALIGN* attribute to align the line to the left, center, or right. Valid parameters are "left," "right," and "center."

The following table displays some examples:

Example	Definition
<HR SIZE=5 WIDTH=50%>	Size of 5 pixels, 50 percent width
<HR SIZE=10 WIDTH=100%>	Size of 10 pixels, 100 percent width
<HR SIZE=3 WIDTH=300>	Size of 10 pixels, 300 pixels width
<HR SIZE=1 WIDTH=33%>	Size of 1 pixels, 33 percent width
<HR SIZE=2 NOSHADE>	Size of 2 pixels, no shading
<HR SIZE=2 ALIGN=1"center" WIDTH=33%>	Size of 2 pixels, no shading

Note that Navigator renders a one-pixel rule as a simple black line, whether or not you use the NOSHADE attribute.

By default, all browsers add a new line after each horizontal rule. You cannot remove this line break, but you can increase the distance between rules if you are inserting more than one. Use either a <P> or <BR> tag after the <HR> tag to increase the spacing. Here is an example:

```
<HR><BR>
<HR>
```

<HTML>

The HTML element defines the text and tags within it as conforming to the HTML specification. While the HTML element is wholly optional, it is highly recommended because future Web pages may contain formatting for a number of browser technologies. All the text and formatting is included in separate sections of the same document.

HTML is a block element and therefore contains two paired tags: <HTML> and </HTML>. The syntax of the HTML element looks like this:

```
<HTML>
...everything else goes in here
</HTML>
```

See the "Typical HTML Document" example earlier in this chapter to see how the body element is used.

<META>

The <META> tag provides "extra" information—called metainformation—for the server. A common use for the <META> tag is providing keywords for cataloging the document. A "search robot" (a program that roams the Web looking for pages to catalog) reads the content of the <META> tag and stores it.

The <META> tag—which is placed in the <HEAD> structure—is traditionally used with three attributes—though, because the tag has no specific application, additional attributes may be added. These attributes are:

- NAME—Provides the name for a keyword.
- HTTP-EQUIV—Provides an equivalent HTTPd (Web server) header. The most commonly used application of HTTP-EQUIV is for "client-pull," where the browser automatically fetches a URL.
- CONTENT—Provides the content for a named keyword or HTTP-EQUIV action.

The following example provides two keywords for cataloging the document:

```
<META NAME="Author" CONTENT="Gordon McComb">
```

```
<META NAME="Subject" CONTENT="JavaScript">
```

The following uses the "client pull" method to fetch another URL 10 seconds after the current document has been loaded:

```
<META HTTP-EQUIV="Refresh" CONTENT="10; http://mydomain.com/home.htm">
```

<NOBR> (No Break)

The no break element tells the browser to render the body text without wrapping each line at the right margin. You would not normally do this without a good reason, except for certain special effects, and when you don't want a stream of characters broken up. The no break element is not provided in all browsers (but is in Netscape Navigator), so use it with caution.

No break is a block element and therefore contains two paired tags: <NOBR> and </NOBR>. The syntax of the no break element looks like this:

```
<NOBR>text you don't want broken up</NOBR>
```

See also the <WBR> word break element for an associated tag you can use with no break.

<P> (Paragraph)

The paragraph element ends the current body text and starts a new line. It also adds extra spacing at the start of the new paragraph, to help set it off from the rest of the text. To insert a new paragraph, use <P>.

Note that the <P> tag inserts a new paragraph and line break with extra spacing. If you want the line break but without the extra spacing, use a line break (<BR>) instead.

Often, the <P> tag is used by itself, though HTML does specify an end-tag, </P>. The following structure is perfectly acceptable to most browsers, where each <P> tag starts a new paragraph:

```
This is a line of text<P>
This is another line<P>
And yet another line
```

But Web browsers are getting more picky, and one day may require (or at least prefer) the following structure. So you should start using it now. This example is rendered exactly the same as the previous example.

```
<P>This is a line of text</P>
<P>This is another line</P>
<P>And yet another line</P>
```

Netscape supports several <P> tag attributes, all of which are part of the HTML 3.0 specification:

- ALIGN=center—aligns the paragraph in the center
- ALIGN=right—aligns the paragraph to the right
- ALIGN=left—aligns the paragraph to the left (default)

Here is an example:

```
<P ALIGN=center>
```

<PRE> (Preformatted Text)

Web browsers try to be as conservative as possible, and they remove any extra spaces, tabs, and hard returns contained in the source HTML document. That means you can't normally use spaces, tabs, and hard returns to format your text. However, if strict formatting is absolutely required, you can usually obtain it with the preformatted text element. When a browser encounters this element, it respects most of the formatting found inside.

Preformatted text is an HTML block element and therefore contains two paired tags: <PRE> and </PRE>. The syntax of the preformatted element looks like this:

```
<PRE>text and formatting goes here</PRE>
```

You're free to include extra spaces and hard returns in a preformatted text element; however, some Web browsers, particularly older ones, continue to ignore some formatting (such as extra hard returns). As Figure 21.5 shows, the formatting is carried through and is displayed, rather than ignored, which is the usual behavior for Web browsers.

Note that some browsers use a different font for the text inside a preformatted text element. The font is usually monospaced and is used to indicate that the text is of a special nature.

<SCRIPT>

The <SCRIPT> tag is used to enclose runnable script, such as JavaScript. The <SCRIPT> tag is used with an end tag, </SCRIPT>. In a JavaScript-compatible

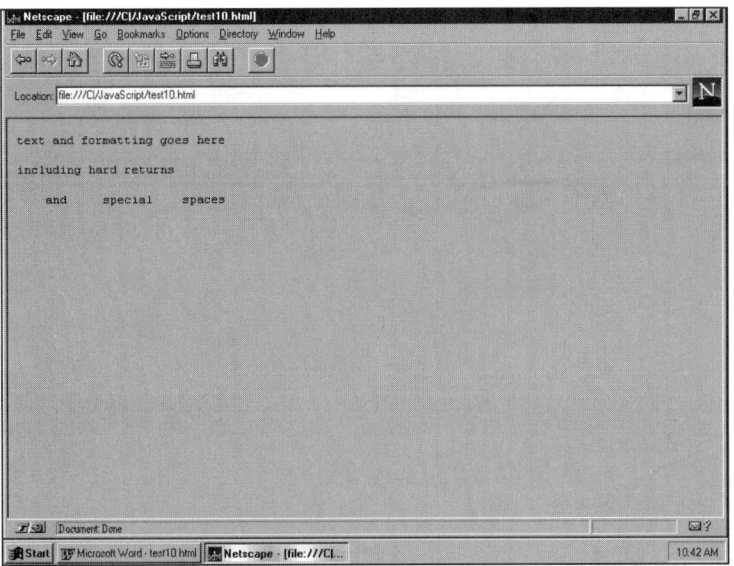

text and formatting goes here

including hard returns

    and   special   spaces

Figure 21.5 Formatting is preserved for text in a <PRE> tag.

browser, text between these tags is interpreted as executable code, rather than document content. In a non-JavaScript browser, the <SCRIPT> tag is ignored, and the
script text is rendered in the browser. For this reason, it is advisable to place HTML
comments at the beginning and end of the script code to help prevent this text from
appearing in the browser.

As used with Netscape 2.0, the <SCRIPT> tag accepts a LANGUAGE attribute. For
JavaScript, this attribute is set to LANGUAGE="JavaScript."

Here is an example:

```
<SCRIPT LANGUAGE="JavaScript">
<!- Hide script text from most non-JavaScript browsers
document.write ("Hello JavaScripters!");
//->
</SCRIPT>
```

<TITLE>

The title element defines the title of the document file. This title typically appears in
the browser's window caption. Additionally, if you save the page as a bookmark (so

you can easily return to it at a later date), most browsers use the title—rather than the actual URL of the page—to identify it.

The title element is actually optional. If you don't include a title, either nothing appears in the browser's window caption or the name of the browser is placed there instead.

Title is an HTML block element and therefore contains two paired tags: <TITLE> and </TITLE>. The syntax of the title element looks like this:

```
<TITLE>This is the title of the document</TITLE>
```

While the <TITLE> tag can actually go anywhere in the document (most browsers accept this), the <TITLE> tag is really designed to be placed in the <HEAD> element. See "Head" for more information.

<WBR> (Word Break)

The word break element tells the browser that it is acceptable to break a body of text formatted with the <NOBR> (no break) element, so that the text can be more naturally formatted if needed. The word break element is not provided in all browsers (but is in Netscape), so use it with caution.

Word break uses just one tag; there is no end-tag. Place the tag at the spot where you want to allow the browser to break the line.

```
<NOBR>text you don't want broken up<WBR>except where permitted</NOBR>
```

See also the <NOBR> no break element.

HTML Inline Elements

Inline elements modify the appearance of text, typically body text. For example, the bold element adds bolding to characters, whereas the underline element adds underlining. In most cases—and assuming a modern browser such as Netscape 2.0—inline elements can also be used in conjunction with other inline elements (bolding and italics, for example), and within many block elements, such as headings. Note that you don't always see a visible difference. You won't notice anything if you add the bolding element to heading text because heading text is already bolded.

For example, this works with most browsers:

```
<H2><I>This is italicized</I></H2>
```

All inline elements have paired tags: the first tag turns on the character attribute and the second tag turns it off. Be sure to include the end-tag for all inline elements start tags, or else your Web documents will not be rendered properly.

There are two forms of inline elements: *physical* and *logical*.

- The physical inline elements are bold, underline, and italics. They are called physical elements because they are designed to do have the same effect in all browsers, no matter what personalization settings the user has adopted.

- The logical inline elements include emphasis, strong, and citation (there are others as well). They are called logical elements because their effect is determined by browser settings. Depending on the features of the browser, users can turn off formatting for logical elements or change the default formatting.

Which do you use, physical elements or logical elements? It depends. If you absolutely want to convey text using a particular format, such as bold, use a physical element. But if you merely want to set off text in some special way, without worrying about what that format actually is, use a logical element.

Element	Start tag	End tag	Type
Bold	<B>	</B>	Physical
Citation	<CITE>	</CITE>	Logical
Code	<CODE>	</CODE>	Logical
Emphasis	<EM>	</EM>	Logical
Italics	<I>	</I>	Physical
Keyboard	<KBD>	</KBD>	Logical
Sample	<SAMP>	</SAMP>	Logical
Strong emphasis	<STRONG>	</STRONG>	Logical
Typewriter	<TT>	</TT>	Logical
Underlined	<U>	</U>	Physical
Variable	<VAR>	</VAR>	Logical

- Bold renders the text in boldface.
- Citation specifies a citation (like a bibliographic entry) and is typically rendered as italics.

- Code specifies a code segment (like programming code) and is typically rendered as monospaced.

- Emphasis specifies emphasized text and is typically rendered in italics.

- Italics renders the text in italics.

- Keyboard specifies a series of keyboard steps and is typically rendered as monospaced.

- Sample specifies a sequence of literal characters (such as information you're supposed to type in response to a prompt) and is typically rendered as monospaced.

- Strong emphasis specifies strongly emphasized text and is typically rendered in boldface.

- Typewriter specifies a sequence of literal characters (like text you see displayed by the computer or printed on a page) and is typically rendered as monospaced.

- Underlined renders the text underlined.

- Variable specifies a variable name (like a variable in a program) and is typically rendered as italics.

Remember that the rendering of logical elements is completely up to the browser and the user's settings within the browser.

HTML Image Element

Despite consisting of nothing more than text, HTML documents can still display full color graphics. This bit of magic is actually sleight of hand: the graphic (called an image in Web parlance) is not actually a part of the HTML document. Rather, the HTML document merely "points to" a binary image file, stored elsewhere on the computer. In truth, the image doesn't even have to be in the same computer as the HTML document. The image can be located on a different computer, half way around the world.

The HTML specification supports one element for images, and this is the <IMG> tag. This one element does quite a bit of work. It not only defines the filename of the image to use, but it can specify text to use if the browser does not display graphics. It can also specify the alignment of the image relative to other images or text and the desired size of the image.

The syntax of the basic <IMG> is:

```
<IMG SRC="url">
```

where "url" is a properly constructed URL for the image file. The URL can be absolute or relative. This is an example of <IMG> that uses an absolute URL:

```
<IMG SRC="http://www.anywhere.com/myfiles/myimage.gif">
```

These examples show how to use an <IMG> tag with a relative URL:

```
<IMG SRC="myimage.gif">
<IMG SRC="./myimage.gif">
<IMG SRC="myfiles/myimage.gif">
<IMG SRC="../myimage.gif">
```

Note that the URL is relative to the HTML document that contains the <IMG> tag. If the image is located in another directory (or another computer altogether), you should provide enough information so that the browser can locate it.

Specifying Alternate Text

Not all browsers are equipped to display graphics. And while most modern browsers are graphics-aware, some users intentionally turn graphics display off. This substantially reduces the time it takes to load a page when using a dial-up Internet connection and slow modem. Therefore, it's advisable to include "alternate text" with the image for those who are image-challenged. This alternate text is encoded with the <IMG> tag, so that it always stays with the image.

Use the ALT attribute inside the <IMG> tag to specify alternate text. Here's an example:

```
<IMG SRC="../myimage.gif" ALT="This is the myimage.gif graphic">
```

Note that the alternate text does not appear unless the browser does not display the image. The alternate text is not used as a caption for the image.

Specifying Alignment

Images are considered "inline" because they are treated just like text characters. That means you can intersperse images with text, and the browser will take care of making sure everything flows properly. This technique is handy when you want to add small icons to the text, such as a little button or a miniature graphic that says "New."

Most images are taller than the text that surround them, however. The normal behavior of most browsers is to place the bottoms of the image flush with the bottom of the text that surrounds it. But you can change this behavior if you want a different alignment. The most common alignment choices, understood by all browsers that display images, are:

- bottom—Aligns the text to the bottom of the image. This is the default.
- middle—Aligns the text to the middle of the image.
- top—Aligns the text to the top of the image.

Figure 21.6 shows examples of all three kinds of alignment types. Notice that the middle and top alignments place only one line of text beside the image. While it's ugly and probably not what you wanted, this is the way it was designed to work.

Netscape provides additional alignment choices:

- *left*—Aligns the text to the *right* of the image. If there is more than one line of text, the additional lines are also aligned to the right until the text clears the image.

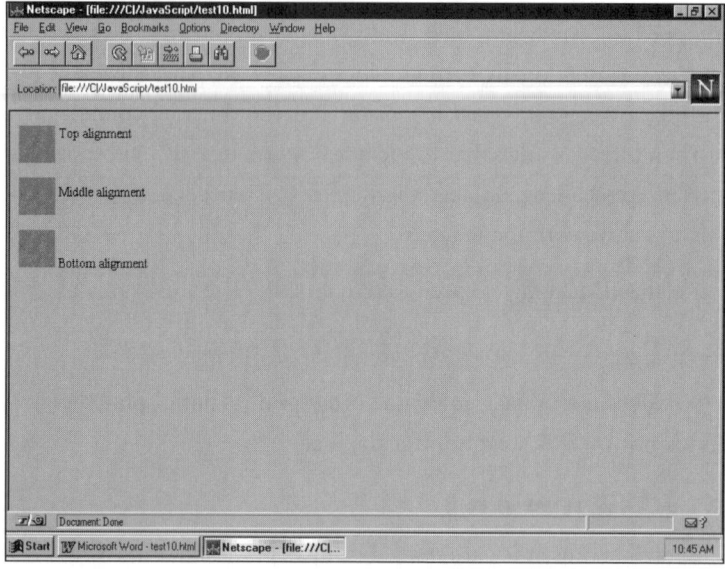

■■■■■■■ **Figure 21.6** Use the ALIGN attribute in the <IMG> tag to align text to the top, middle, or bottom of an adjacent image.

- *right*—Same as left, but the text is placed on the *left* side of the image.
- *texttop*—Same as top, except that the text is aligned to the tallest characters in the line.
- *absmiddle*—Same as middle, but more accurately places the middle of the line of text to the middle of the image.
- *absbottom*—Same as bottom, but more accurately places the bottom of the line of text to the bottom of the image.
- *baseline*—Same as bottom.

You can use only one alignment at a time. The syntax is:

```
<IMG SRC="myimage.gif" ALIGN="alignment">
```

Replace "alignment" (keep the quotes) with any of the alignment options specified above. For example, to use the left alignment and alternate text, use:

```
<IMG SRC="myimage.gif" ALT="Alternate text1" ALIGN="left">
```

Sizing the Image

Browsers ordinarily display images in their "natural size." If an image is 100 pixels by 100 pixels, for example, that's how big it is when rendered on the browser's screen. But you can change the size of the image if you want it smaller or larger by using the WIDTH and HEIGHT attributes. These attributes are also useful because the browser creates an empty box for the image, then fills the box with the image as the entire page loads. This cues users of your page and lets them know how long they'll have to wait as the image loads.

You can use the WIDTH and HEIGHT attributes separately or together. Follow the attributes with the dimensions of the image, in pixels (Netscape tells you the size of the image—look at the title bar in the window—if you load the graphic into the browser).

- Specifying just the width *or* height changes the size of the image in proportion. For example, specifying WIDTH="100" sizes a square image to a height and width of 100 pixels. If the original image is not square, it is sized in relative proportion. For instance, if the original image is 400 pixels wide by 100 pixels high, changing the width to 100 pixels reduces the image to 25 pixels high.

- Specifying the width *and* height lets you change the proportion of the image in any way you like. For example, you can transform that 400 by 100 pixel image to 200 by 200, 500 by 150, or anything else.

Here's an example of the WIDTH and HEIGHT attributes:

```
<IMG SRC="myimage.gif" ALT="Alternate text1" HEIGHT="100" WIDTH="100">
```

■■■■■■■■ **NOTE**

Using the HEIGHT and WIDTH attributes is a good idea, even if you don't want to intentionally make an image larger or smaller. Providing these attributes allows Netscape to load all the text of the page, leaving just the right amount of space for the images. To the user, your pages will appear to load faster.

When using JavaScript, you should always provide the HEIGHT and WIDTH attributes. Otherwise, you may get inconsistent results or crash.

■■■■■■■

Adding and Removing Image Borders

Images you display in your Web pages don't normally have borders (unless they are included inside an anchor element, as detailed below). You can add a border by using the BORDER attribute. The value used with the BORDER attribute is the size of the border, in pixels. The following example places a border of about five-pixels around the image:

```
<IMG SRC="myimage.gif" ALT="Alternate text1" BORDER=5>
```

Images placed inside hypertext elements normally have a colored border of two to three pixels, so the user can distinguish it as a hypertext link. If desired, you can remove this border, but remember that if you do, your users may not be aware that the image serves as a link. To remove the border, use 0 as the BORDER value:

```
<IMG SRC="myimage.gif" ALT="Alternate text1" BORDER=0>
```

Controlling the Spacing Around Images

Most browsers insert spacing around images so that the surrounding text maintains a comfortable distance. The VSPACE and HSPACE attributes can be used to control the spacing around the image. As their names imply, VSPACE controls the spacing above and below the image, whereas HSPACE controls the spacing to the left and right of the image. Values are in pixels, where 0 butts the text against the image or very close to it. The default is a spacing of approximately two to three pixels. Following is an example of wide spacing:

```
<IMG SRC="myimage.gif" ALT="Alternate text1" HSPACE="10" VSPACE="10">
```

Embedding an Image Inside a Hypertext Link

You don't need to stick with words for the "click text" in a hypertext link (the "click text" is the text that appears colored and underlined, and which you click to activate the link). You can alternately use an image for the click text, or both an image and text. Merely place the <IMG> tag between the <A> and </A> hypertext link tags, as follows:

```
<A HREF="another.html"><IMG SRC="another.gif"></A>
```

If you'd like text to appear with the image, include it before or after the <IMG> tag:

```
<A HREF="another.html">Click here!<IMG SRC="another.gif"></A>
```

Figure 21.7 shows some examples of images used in hypertext links. Notice the example where the "Click here!" text is centered beneath the image. This formatting was accomplished using tables, described under "HTML Table Element," in this chapter.

ISMAP Attribute

Some Web pages use a single image as a way to convey a number of hypertext links. A given link is activated depending on where on the image you click. The image is dissected like a "map"; the attribute to activate this feature is therefore logically called ISMAP.

Be aware that you can't use this feature without a program running on the server, along with your pages. This program typically conforms to the CGI (Common Gateway Interface) standard and requires a script that you write. Simply adding the ISMAP attribute to a graphic does not automatically endow that graphic with multiple hyperlinking capability.

That said, Netscape supports "client-side" image-maps, whereby the intelligence of the multiple links for one image is built into the HTML page. See Chapter 17, "Using

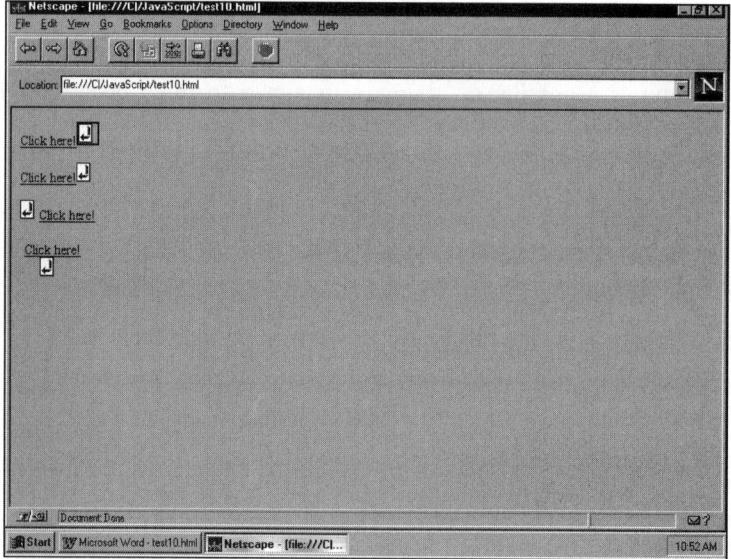

Figure 21.7 Use images with hypertext links to create active buttons and other objects on your page.

JavaScript with Advanced HTML," for more information on using the client-side image-mapping capability, as found in Netscape Navigator.

The ISMAP attribute is not used with a parameter. To use the image as an image map (assuming you've taken care of the CGI script on the server), merely add the ISMAP attribute to the <IMG> tag:

```
<IMG SRC="myimage.gif" ALIGN="left" ISMAP>
```

HTML List Elements

HTML supports a wide variety of lists, including numbered and bulleted lists. The numbers and bullets, as well as the overall formatting of the list, are provided by the browser and aren't included in the text of the document. This allows more control over the appearance of the list, and it speeds up the rendering of the page on the browser's screen.

There are three general forms of lists: ordered (numbered), unordered (bulleted), and definition. The HTML specification also supports something called menu lists and directory lists, but these are functionally the same as unordered (bulleted) lists. See Figure 21.8 for an example of the three types of HTML lists.

<DL> (Definition List)

The definition list element creates a "glossary" type of format; the typical use is to render terms and their definitions. The terms appear flush left, and the definitions are indented under the words.

Definition list is an HTML block element and therefore contains two paired tags: <DL> and </DL>. These tags define the start and end of the list, respectively. Inside these tags go additional tags—<DT> for term and <DD> for definition. For each <DT> you should have a corresponding <DD>, but there is no absolute rule that says you must do this. In fact, some interesting formatting is possible when using just the <DD> tags inside a definition list.

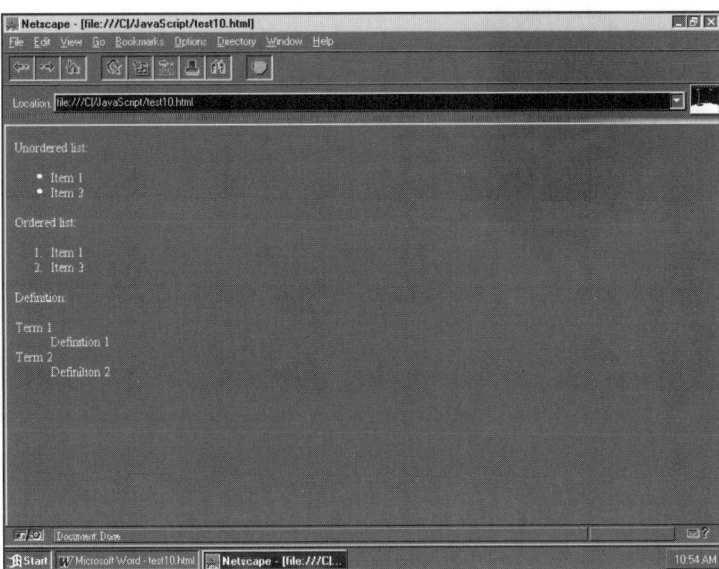

▰▰▰▰▰ **Figure 21.8** The most commonly used HTML lists are ordered, unordered, and definition.

The syntax of the definition list is shown here, with tags for the terms and definitions also added. This example has been formatted for clarity; the formatting is optional.

```
<DT>

        <DT>Term 1
                <DD>Definition 1.
        <DT>Term 2
                <DD>Definition 2.
        <DT>Term 3
                <DD>Definition 3.
<DT>
```

Note that there is no end-tag for the <DT> and <DD> tags. Also note that if the text following <DD> spans more than one line, the extra lines are also indented. This preserves the unique formatting of the definition list.

The <DL> description list element supports a variant called COMPACT that is meant to make the formatting of the list more compact. In reality, however, the COMPACT attribute has little effect in most cases, and you probably never need to use it. If you do, the syntax is:

```
<DL COMPACT>
```

<OL> (Ordered List)

Ordered lists are numbered lists. Each element of the list is preceded by a number. The browser formats the list with numbers automatically. The browser also adds appropriate indentation and tabbing to make the list look nice.

Ordered list is an HTML block element and therefore contains two paired tags: <OL> and </OL>. These tags define the start and end of the list, respectively. Inside these tags go additional tags, specifically <LI> for each list item. The end of the list item can be marked off with an </LI> tag, though this is optional. For consistency, you may want to get in the habit of providing the </LI> tag.

The syntax of the ordered list is shown here, with tags for the list items also added. This example has been formatted for clarity; the formatting is optional.

```
<OL>
        LI>This is the first item.</LI>
        <LI>This is the second item.</LI>
        <LI>This is the third item.</LI>

<OL>
```

You can create multiple-level lists by adding additional <OL> tags (be sure to end each <OL> structure with a matching </OL>). The following example creates a two-level list, as shown in Figure 21.9. You can create lists with up to seven levels.

```
<OL>
        <LI>This is the first item.</LI>
        <LI>This is the second item.</LI>
        <OL>
        <LI>This is an item in the second level</LI>
                <LI>So is this</LI>
</OL>
        <LI>This is the third item.</LI>
</OL>
```

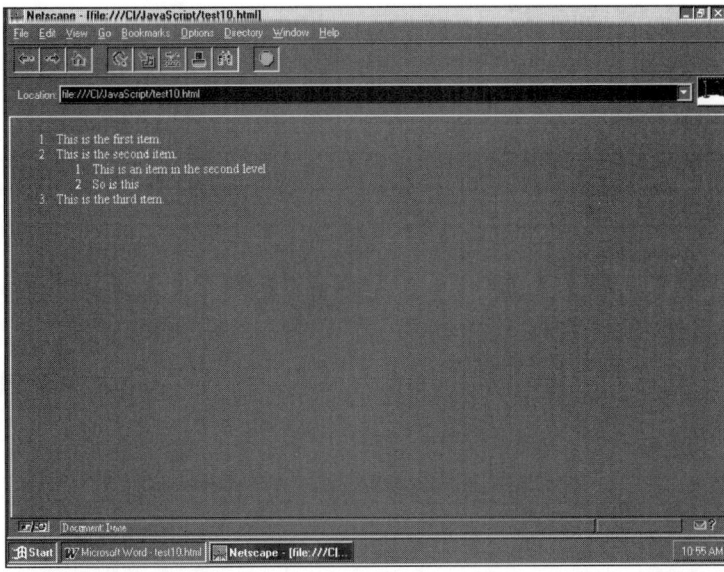

Figure 21.9 You can nest <OL> tags to create multiple level lists.

Netscape lets you specify the type of number to use. This is done with the TYPE attribute, which is specified in the <OL> tag. Five types of numbering are allowed:

- TYPE="1"—The default numbering scheme, in which the list is ordered with Arabic numerals (1, 2, 3,...).
- TYPE="A"—The list is ordered with uppercase alphabetic characters (A-Z).
- TYPE="a"—The list is ordered with lowercase alphabetic characters (a-z).
- TYPE="I"—The list is ordered with uppercase Roman numerals (I, II, III...).
- TYPE="i"—The list is ordered with lowercase Roman numerals (i, ii, iii...).

<UL> (Unordered List)

Unordered lists are bulleted lists. Each element of the list is preceded by a bullet. The browser formats the list with the bullet automatically. The browser also adds appropriate indentation and tabbing to make the list look nice.

Unordered list is an HTML block element and therefore uses paired tags: <UL> and </UL>. These tags define the start and end of the list, respectively. Inside these tags go additional tags, specifically <LI> for each list item. The end of the list item can be marked off with an </LI> tag, though this is optional. For consistency you may want to get in the habit of providing the </LI> tag.

The syntax of the ordered list is shown here, with tags for the list items also added. This example has been formatted for clarity; the formatting is optional.

```
<UL>
        <LI>This is the first item.</LI>
        <LI>This is the second item.</LI>
        <LI>This is the third item.</LI>
</UL>
```

You can create multiple-level lists by adding additional <UL> tags (be sure to end each <UL> structure with a matching </UL>). The following example creates a two-level list. You can create lists with up to seven levels.

```
<UL>
        <LI>This is the first item.</LI>
        <LI>This is the second item.</LI>
        <UL>
```

```
        <LI>This is an item in the second level</LI>
                <LI>So is this</LI>
  </UL>
        <LI>This is the third item.</LI>
  </UL>
```

Many browsers, such as Netscape Navigator, allow you to specify the type of bullet to use. This is done with the TYPE attribute, which is specified in the <OL> tag. Three types of bulleted are allowed:

- TYPE="disc"—Bullets appear as a round, hollow disc.
- TYPE="circle"—Bullets appear as a circle.
- TYPE="square"—Bullets appear as a square.

Combining List Types

Most Web browsers let you combine the three common list types to produce embedded lists. For example, you can place an unordered list as a second level to an ordered list. Merely add the appropriate start and end tags, furnish the list items, and the browser does the rest. Here's an example (see the result in Figure 21.10):

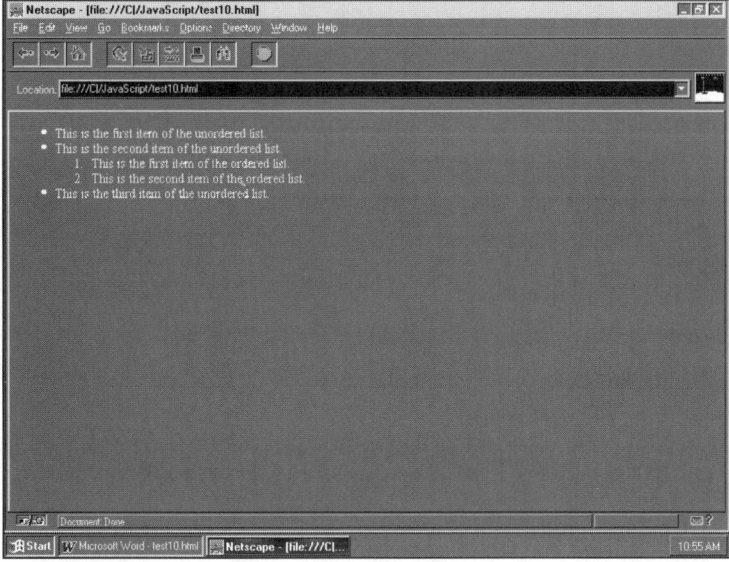

Figure 21.10 List types can be combined. Here, an ordered list is shown nested inside an unordered list.

```
<UL>
        <LI>This is the first item of the unordered list.</LI>
        <LI>This is the second item of the unordered list.</LI>
        <OL>
        <LI>This is the first item of the ordered list.</LI>
                <LI>This is the second item of the ordered list.</LI>
</UL>
        <LI>This is the third item of the unordered list.</LI>
</UL>
```

Formatting for the Other List Types

As mentioned above, the HTML specification defines two other list types: directory and menu. With one exception, most browsers render these the same as unordered lists.

The syntax for the menu list is as follows. The list appears the same as an unordered (bulleted) list.

```
<MENU>
        <LI>This is the first item.</LI>
        <LI>This is the second item.</LI>
        <LI>This is the third item.</LI>
</MENU>
```

The syntax for the directory list is as follows. The list also appears the same as an unordered (bulleted) list. At one time the directory list formatted text in multiple columns, but few modern browsers render the list in this way.

```
<DIR>
        <LI>This is the item 1.</LI>
        <LI>This is the item 2.</LI>
        <LI>This is the item 3.</LI>
</DIR>
```

Interesting Tidbits Regarding Lists

There are some useful tips and techniques you can employ with list tags to create special effects. Do note that not all of these techniques work with all browsers, but they do with Netscape. Examples of the techniques are shown in Figure 21.11.

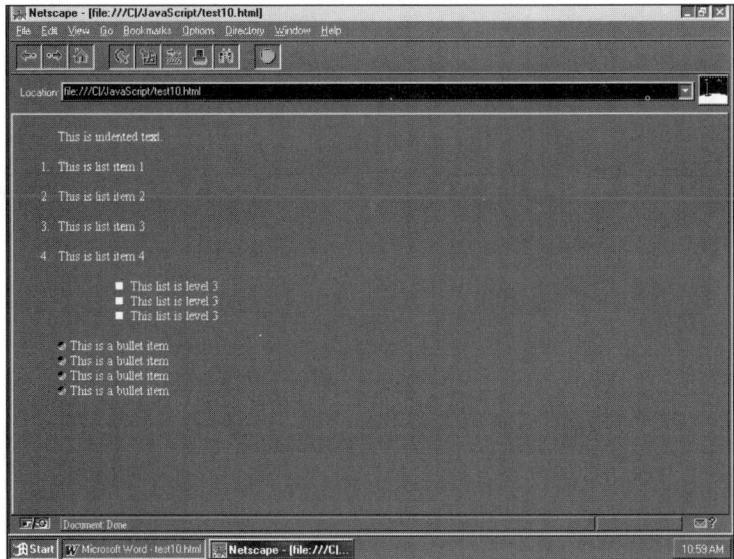

▬▬▬▬▬▬ **Figure 21.11** Combining list tags in creative ways produces special formatting.

Indenting with <DD>

One very useful trick is to use a <DD> tag by itself to insert indented text. Here is an example:

```
<DD>This is indented text.
```

Unfortunately, you cannot add extra <DD> tags to add more indenting.

Adding Extra Space Between List Items

Ordinarily each list item is separated by just a line break. If you want more spacing between the lines, add <P> tags after the list items, or a pair of <BR> tags. Here are some examples:

```
<OL>
        <LI>This is list item 1</LI><P>
        <LI>This is list item 2</LI><P>
        <LI>This is list item 3</LI><BR><BR>
        <LI>This is list item 4</LI><BR><BR>
</OL>
```

Adding More Indenting to Ordered and Unordered Lists

You can easily add more indentation to the beginning of ordered and unordered lists by preceding the <LI> tag with a <DD> tag. Here is an example:

```
<DD><LI>This is an indented list item.</LI>
```

"Nested-in" List

Typically, ordered and unordered lists start at level 1 (using the numbering and bullet choices for that level), with one indent. You can create empty nests that force the browser to choose the number and bullet styles for a lower list. The list is also indented more. To create an empty nest, insert multiple <OL> or <UL> tags to define the list (of course, be sure to counter these tags with an equal number of </OL> and </UL> tags). Here is an example:

```
<UL><UL><UL>
        <LI>This list is level 3</LI>
        <LI>This list is level 3</LI>
        <LI>This list is level 3</LI>
</UL></UL</UL>
```

Making Your Own Bulleted Lists

After a while, the bullet lists the browser makes can get downright boring. Try making your own bulleted lists using small bullet-shaped images. Just about any image will do, as long as it's no taller than the body text. If the image is too big, the text will not wrap around it properly.

To create a bullet list, define a definition list (this part is actually optional), and place <IMG> tags at the start of each line for the bullets. Here's an example. Be sure to add a space between the <IMG> tag and the text.

```
<DL>
        <DD><IMG SRC="ball1.gif"> This is a bullet item
        <DD><IMG SRC="ball1.gif"> This is a bullet item
        <DD><IMG SRC="ball1.gif"> This is a bullet item
        <DD><IMG SRC="ball1.gif"> This is a bullet item
</DL>
```

If you want to add more space between the image and the bullet, use the VSPACE attribute in the <IMG> tag to increase the spacing on the left and right of the image. Here is an example:

```
<DL>
        <DD><IMG SRC="ball1.gif" HSPACE="5"> This is a bullet item
        <DD><IMG SRC="ball1.gif" HSPACE="5"> This is a bullet item
        <DD><IMG SRC="ball1.gif" HSPACE="5"> This is a bullet item
        <DD><IMG SRC="ball1.gif" HSPACE="5"> This is a bullet item
</DL>
```

HTML Form Elements

Forms let your Web documents interact with the user. Forms contain all the familiar trappings of a graphic user interface like Windows, including text entry boxes, push buttons, radio buttons, checkboxes, and list boxes.

In the past, forms were intended to be used with special software on the server that processed the user's input. This is still possible, but new technologies such as JavaScript make it possible to process form input and manipulate the document while on the client computer. No information need be traded between the server and the client.

The following description of the form elements includes just the standard HTML specifications. JavaScript adds a number of additional attributes to the form elements, and these are detailed in the appropriate chapters in this book (specifically, Chapter 16, "Using JavaScript with Forms").

<FORM>

The form element defines the actual form. Inside the form are placed the various "controls," such as push buttons and radio buttons.

Form is an HTML block element and therefore contains two paired tags: <FORM> and </FORM>. The syntax of the form element looks like this:

```
<FORM>Additional tags and text go here</FORM>
```

The <FORM> tag can be used with the following attributes. These attributes tell Netscape how to submit the form to a server.

- NAME—The name of the form
- METHOD—The submission method, either POST or GET
- ACTION—The URL for submitting the form (the form is sent here)
- TARGET—The window or frame name where the form output (from the CGI program) should be placed
- ENCTYPE—The encoding format of the form

Here is an example:

```
<FORM NAME="myform" ACTION="http://mydomain.com/cgibin/form/" METHOD=get>
```

<INPUT>

The input element defines various types of input controls for the form. These controls are:

- *checkbox*—Select or deselect an option
- *button*—Create a push button with any text on it
- *submit*—Create a special Submit button to submit the form to the server
- *reset*—Create a special Reset button to return the controls to their default values
- *text*—Create a text entry box to enter a line of text
- *hidden*—Create a hidden text field that can contain data, but does not appear in the browser
- *password*—Create a text entry box for storing a password; text the user types does not appear in the box
- *image*—Create an "image button" that, when clicked, submits the form and passes the *x,y* coordinates of the mouse to the server.

Except for the reset and submit types, form controls support the optional attributes noted below.

Checkbox and radio buttons:

- NAME—Name of the control
- VALUE—Unique value for control when form is submitted
- CHECKED—Initial checked state

Button:

- NAME—Name of the control
- VALUE—Text of the button

Text, password, and hidden text:

- NAME—Name of the control.
- VALUE—Initial text.
- SIZE—Width of the text box
- MAXLENGTH—Maximum allowable characters

Image:

- NAME—Name of the control
- SRC—Source for image

The following example creates a text box and a Submit button:

```
<INPUT TYPE="text" NAME="textbox" VALUE="">
<INPUT TYPE="submit">
```

<SELECT>

The select element defines a selection list in the form. The list contains one or more options. By sizing the list, you can display it as a drop-down box or as a standard select box. Scrollbars appear on the right of the list if there are more options than can be shown at one time. Selection lists can provide for single or multiple choices. The attributes for a select list are:

- NAME—Name of list
- SIZE—Size of list (number of rows to display)
- MULTIPLE—Specifies multiple choice

One or more <OPTION> tags are placed in a selection list. The <OPTION> tags accept the following attributes:

- SELECTED—Default selection
- VALUE—Value of item when form is submitted

The following example displays a selection list with three items:

```
<SELECT SIZE=3>
<OPTION SELECTED VALUE=1>This is item 1
<OPTION VALUE=2>This is item 2
<OPTION VALUE=3>This is item 3
</SELECT>
```

<TEXTAREA>

The <TEXTAREA> tag creates a multiple-line text box. There are three attributes for the textarea control:

- NAME—Names the control
- ROWS—The height of the control, in lines
- COLS—The width of the control, in characters

The <TEXTAREA> tag is always used with its end tag, which is </TEXTAREA>. Text that you wish to initially appear in the text box can be placed between these tags. Formatting, including new lines, is retained. Here is an example:

```
<TEXTAREA ROWS=4 COLS=40>
This is default text
</TEXTAREA>
```

HTML Table Element

Table elements let you display text and graphics in tabular format. The tables can appear with and without borders, and you can change the width of borders. Various combinations of table elements let you specify an almost unlimited arrangement of columns and rows. See Figure 21.12 for an example of a table you can create with HTML.

<TABLE>

The table definition begins with the <TABLE> tag and ends with the </TABLE> tag. All of the subordinate table tags must appear between this pair. A one-column, one-row table can be created as simply as:

```
<TABLE>
        <TD>This is a simple table</TD>
</TABLE>
```

Optional attributes for the <TABLE> tag are:

- BORDER
- CELLPADDING
- CELLSPACING
- WIDTH

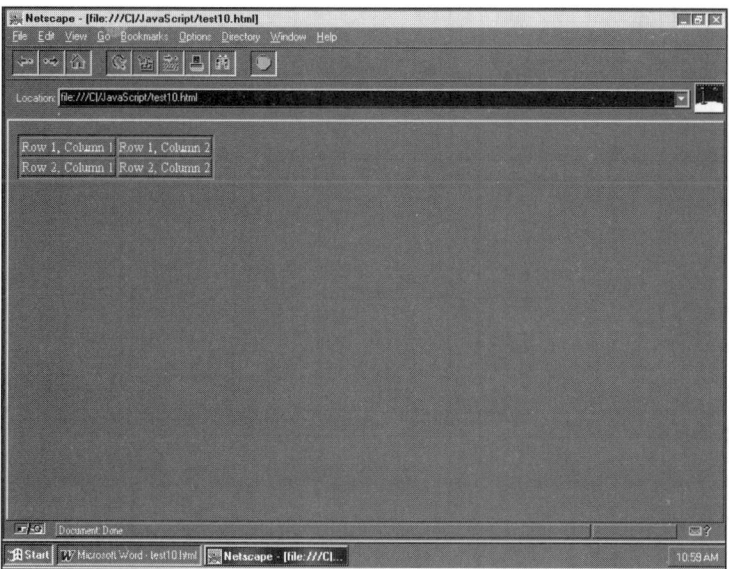

Figure 21.12 One of an almost unlimited number of table designs you can create with the HTML <TABLE> tag.

These attributes can be used alone or in combination.

BORDER Attribute

With the BORDER attribute, you can specify the size of the border, if any. The default value for BORDER is 1. The syntax is:

```
<TABLE BORDER>
<TABLE BORDER=x>
```

- Specify the default border with BORDER (no value).
- Specify no border with BORDER=0.
- Specify a wider border with BORDER=x, where x is a number greater than 1. Avoid very thick table borders.

CELLPADDING Attribute

With the CELLPADDING attribute, you change the margin area within each cell, if any. The syntax is:

```
<TABLE CELLPADDING=x>
```

- Specify CELLPADDING=0 for no cell padding.

- Specify the cellpadding amount with CELLPADDING=x, where x is 1 or higher.

CELLSPACING Attribute

With the CELLSPACE attribute, you can change the spacing between cells. The syntax is:

```
<TABLE CELLSPACING=x>
```

- Specify CELLSPACING=0 for no cell spacing.
- Specify the cellspacing amount with CELLSPACING=x, where x is 1 or higher.

WIDTH Attribute

With the WIDTH attribute, you can change the overall width of the table (normally, the table appears only as wide as it needs to be to display its contents).

```
<TABLE WIDTH=x>
<TABLE WIDTH=x%>
```

- Specify the width of the table in pixels with TABLE=x, where *x* is a positive number.
- Specify the width of the table in a percentage of the total page width TABLE=x%, where *x* is a positive number.

<TR> (Table Row)

The <TR> tag defines a row within a table. Tables can contain any number of rows that you like. Each row should be marked with a <TR> tag to start and a </TR> tag to end.

```
<TABLE BORDER>
        <TR><TD>This is row 1</TD></TR>
        <TR><TD>This is row 2</TD></TR>
</TABLE>
```

<TD> (Table Cell Definition)

The <TD> tag marks the text (or image) within a cell. If you create a table without a <TD> tag pair for a row, the table appears with a "blank" at that spot.

```
<TABLE BORDER>
        <TR><TD>The row below appears blank.</TD></TR>
```

```
        <TR><TD></TD></TR>
</TABLE>
```

Each <TD></TD> tag pair within a row defines a new column. If you want to create a table with more than one column, add more <TD> tags within a row.

```
<TABLE BORDER>
        <TR><TD>Row 1, Column 1</TD><TD>Row 1, Column 2</TD></TR>
        <TR><TD>Row 2, Column 1</TD><TD>Row 2, Column 2</TD></TR>
</TABLE>
```

A number of attributes are supported for the <TD> tag. These are listed in the following table.

Tag	What It Does
<TD ALIGN=val>	Aligns contents in cell as specified; use RIGHT, LEFT, or CENTER for val.
<TD VALIGN=val>	Aligns contents in cell vertically as specified; use TOP, MIDDLE, or BOTTOM for val.
<TD WIDTH=x>	Specifies width of cell, in pixels.
<TD WIDTH=x%>	Specifies width of cell, in percentage of table width.
<TD ROWSPAN=x>	Specifies how many rows cell spans.
<TD COLSPAN=x>	Specifies how many columns cell spans.

Of these attributes, ROWSPAN and COLSPAN are often used to create a wide variety of table formats. With these attributes, you can specify that a given column or row should be wider than the standard 1x1 size. Here are some examples. All sorts of variations are possible.

```
<TABLE BORDER=2 CELLPADDING=5>
        <TR><TD COLSPAN=2>Spanned</TD><TD>Col 2</TD><TD>Col 3</TD></TR>
        <TR><TD>Col 1</TD><TD>Col 2</TD><TD COLSPAN=2>Spanned</TD></TR>
</TABLE>
```

```
<TABLE BORDER=2 CELLPADDING=5>
        <TR><TD ROWSPAN=2>Spanned</TD><TD>Col 2</TD><TD>Col 3</TD></TR>
        <TR><TD>Col 1</TD><TD>Col 2</TD><TD COLSPAN=2>Spanned</TD></TR>
</TABLE>
```

<TH> (Table Header)

Use the <TH> tag to define a heading along the side or top of the table. There are a number of ways to use the <TH> tag (in all cases, the closing tag is /TH>):

Tag	What It Does
<TH>	Creates header in cell on top, bold and centered.
<TH ALIGN=val>	Aligns header in cell as specified; use RIGHT, LEFT, or CENTER for val.
<TH VALIGN=val>	Aligns header vertically in cell as specified; use TOP, MIDDLE, or BOTTOM for val.
<TH WIDTH=x>	Specifies width of header cell, in pixels.
<TH WIDTH=x%>	Specifies width of header cell, in percentage of table width.
<TH ROWSPAN=x>	Specifies how many rows header cell spans.
<TH COLSPAN=x>	Specifies how many columns head cell spans.

```
<TABLE BORDER>
        <TR><TH>Column 1</TH><TH>Column 2</TH></TR>
        <TR><TD>Row 1, Column 1</TD><TD>Row 1, Column 2</TR>
        <TR><TD>Row 2, Column 1</TD><TD>Row 2, Column 2</TR>
</TABLE>
```

<CAPTION>

The <CAPTION> tag lets you specify a caption for the table. The caption appears centered at the top of the table.

```
<TABLE BORDER>
        <CAPTION>This is the caption</CAPTION>
        <TR><TD>Row 1, Column 1</TD><TD>Row 1, Column 2</TR>
        <TR><TD>Row 2, Column 1</TD><TD>Row 2, Column 2</TR>
</TABLE>
```

HTML Frameset Elements

Starting with Netscape 2.0, you can divide the document window into many "frames." Each frame can contain different content because each one can actually be a different HTML document. Frames have a particularly close relationship with JavaScript because the frames are often used for JavaScript output results.

<FRAMESET>

The <FRAMESET> tag defines the frames that you want to appear in the window. This tag appears in the "primary" HTML document that the user loads (that is, the URL to your page that uses frame should point to this document). Within the <FRAMESET> tag, you define how you want the page divided, using the ROWS and COLS attributes.

```
ROWS="row_height_value_list"
COLS="cols_width_list"
```

For rows, you specify the width of each of the frames, either in pixels or in percentage (or both). For columns, you specify the height of each of the frames, also in pixels and/or percentage. Here are some examples:

```
<FRAMESET ROWS="50%, 50%">
       <FRAMESET COLS="50%, 50%">
```

creates a four-panel frameset, with two rows dividing the document window in half vertically. Two columns divide the document window in half horizontally.

```
<FRAMESET ROWS="200, *">
```

creates a two-panel frameset with the document window divided into two rows. The first row is 200 pixels in height. The * tells the browser to use the remaining width for the second row. No COL attribute is provided, so it is assumed the document window is not divided into columns.

The frameset is ended with the </FRAMESET> tag. This tag appears after any <FRAME> tags that are included.

<FRAME>

The <FRAME> tags specify the actual content of the frames, now that the frameset has been defined.

There are a number of attributes for use with the <FRAME> tag, as specified in the following table.

Attribute	What It Does
SRC	The URL of the document you want to place in the frame.
NAME	The name identifier you want to use for the frame.
MARGINWIDTH	The size of the margin on the left and right of the frame.
MARGINHEIGHT	The size of the margin on the top and bottom of the frame.
SCROLLING	Specifies if you wish the frame window to have a scrollbar.
NORESIZE	Specifies if you wish to allow the user to resize the frame.

Following are some examples, shown with the <FRAMESET> tag. See Figures 21.13 through 21.16 to see how these frames turn out. (In all cases, the actual frame contents are shown empty.)

```
<FRAMESET ROWS="200, *">
        <FRAME SRC="dummy.htm" NAME="frame1" MARGINWIDTH=2>
```

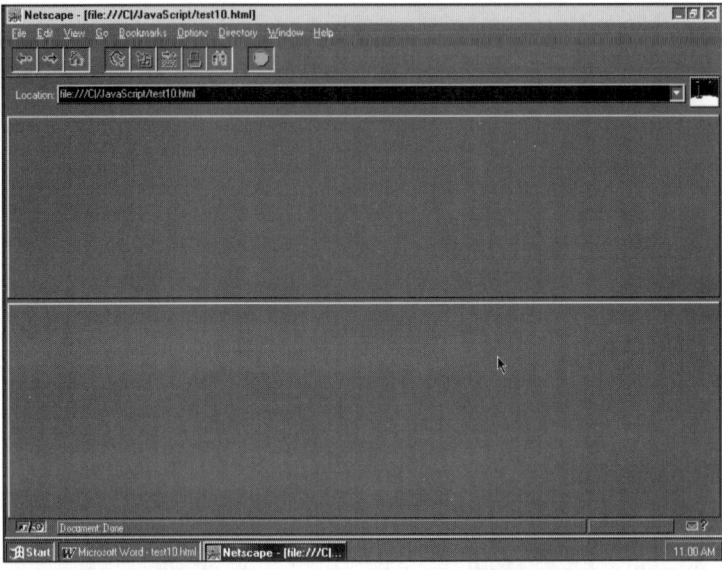

Figure 21.13 Two frames, in two equal rows.

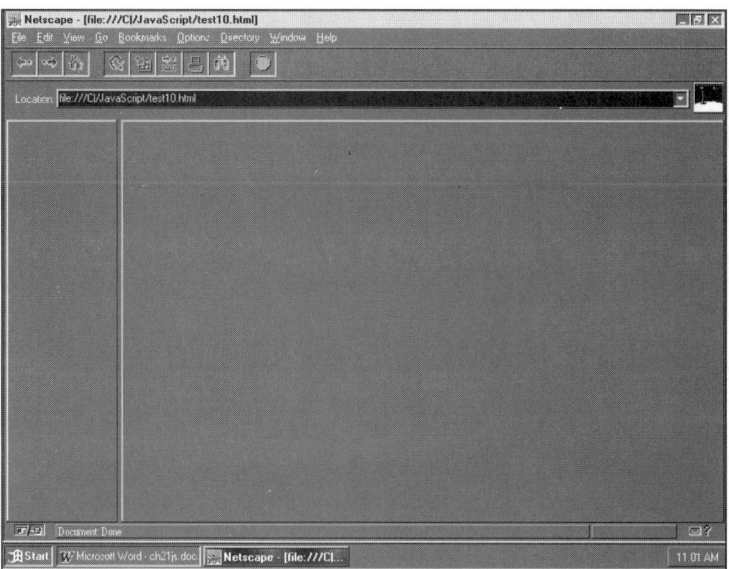

Figure 21.14 Two frames, in columns, with the right column larger.

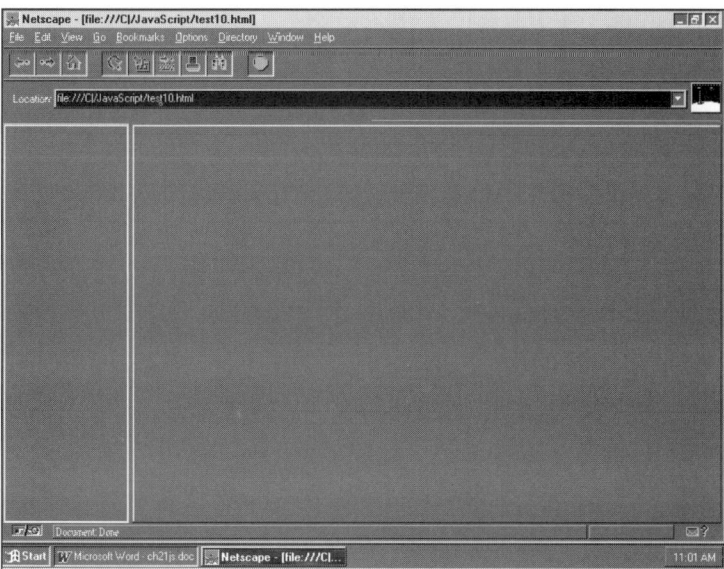

Figure 21.15 Three frames, with the first frame "hidden" (it contains data).

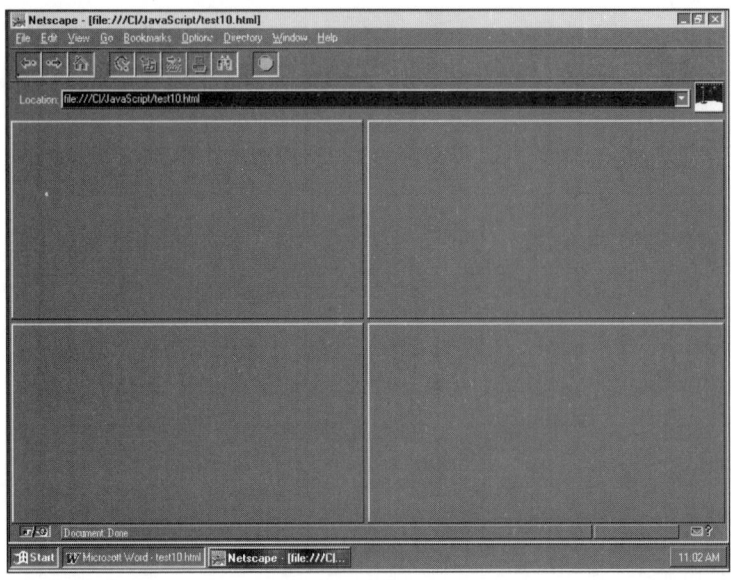

Figure 21.16 Four frames, in window pane fashion.

```
          <FRAME SRC="dummy.htm" NAME="frame2" SCROLLING="no">
</FRAMESET>
<FRAMESET COLS-"130, *">
<FRAME SRC="dummy.htm" NAME="frame1" MARGINWIDTH=1 NORESIZE NOSCROLL>
<FRAME SRC="dummy.htm" NAME="frame2" NORESIZE MARGINWIDTH=0>
</FRAMESET>
<FRAMESET ROWS="*, 100%">
<FRAME SRC="dummy.htm" NAME="text" SCOLLING="no">
  <FRAMESET COLS="150, *">
    <FRAME SRC="dummy.htm" NAME="ctrl" MARGINWIDTH=1 SCROLLING="no">
    <FRAME SRC="dummy.htm" NAME="result" MARGINWIDTH=1>
  </FRAMESET>
</FRAMESET>
<FRAMESET ROWS="50%, 50%">
        <FRAMESET COLS="50%, 50%">
                <FRAME SRC="dummy.htm">
                <FRAME SRC="dummy.htm">
        </FRAMESET>
```

```
<FRAMESET COLS="50%, 50%">
        <FRAME SRC="dummy.htm">
        <FRAME SRC="dummy.htm">
    </FRAMESET>
</FRAMESET>
```

<NOFRAMES>

Use the <NOFRAMES> tag to provide alternative text for those browsers that do not support the frames feature. Place the text and HTML markup you wish to display between the <NOFRAMES> and </NOFRAMES> tags. Often, this text consists only of:

```
<NOFRAMES>You need Netscape 2.0 or later to view this page!</NOFRAMES>
```

If your page does not require other Netscape 2.0-specific features (like JavaScript), consider offering a no-frames alternative for your site. You can place the no-frames version within the <NOFRAMES> tag or simply provide a hyperlink to guide people to a completely separate no-frames page.

```
<NOFRAMES>Since your browser doesn't support frames use the
<A HREF="noframes.html">no frame version<A> </NOFRAMES>
```

Deciphering RGB Triplet Values

Netscape uses three pairs of hexadecimal values to represent the red, green, and blue (RGB) component of colors used for backgrounds and text. Hexadecimal values are base-16 and range from 00 (for 0) to ff (for 255). The typical RGB triplet looks like this:

```
"#00ffoc"
```

The # character is used to prevent leading zeros from being dropped if the value is not enclosed in quotation marks. Here's how the three values work out:

- 00 is the red component. 00 means no intensity.
- ff is the green component. ff means full intensity.
- 0c is the blue component. 0c means about half intensity.

■■■■■ NOTE

A scientific calculator or any decimal-to-hex calculator is helpful if you're not familiar with hexadecimal notation. The calculator that comes with Windows can perform decimal-to-hex conversions.

■■■■■

Netscape also supports many dozens of named colors. The correct appearance of these colors depends on the video settings of your computer. Don't expect all the colors to be rendered properly if your computer displays only 16 or 256 colors.

Color	RGB triplet	Color	RGB triplet
aliceblue	f0f8ff	darkcyan	008b8b
antiquewhite	faebd7	darkgoldenrod	b8860b
aqua	00ffff	darkgray	a9a9a9
aquamarine	7fffd4	darkgreen	006400
azure	f0ffff	darkkhaki	bdb76b
beige	f5f5dc	darkmagenta	8b008b
bisque	ffe4c4	darkolivegreen	556b2f
black	000000	darkorange	ff8c00
blanchedalmond	ffebcd	darkorchid	9932cc
blue	0000ff	darkred	8b0000
blueviolet	8a2be2	darksalmon	e9967a
brown	a52a2a	darkseagreen	8fbc8f
burlywood	deb887	darkslateblue	483d8b
cadetblue	5f9ea0	darkslategray	2f4f4f
chartreuse	7fff00	darkturquoise	00ced1
chocolate	d2691e	darkviolet	9400d3
coral	ff7f50	deeppink	ff1493
cornflowerblue	6495ed	deepskyblue	00bfff
cornsilk	fff8dc	dimgray	696969
crimson	dc143c	dodgerblue	1e90ff
cyan	00ffff	firebrick	b22222
darkblue	00008b	floralwhite	fffaf0

Color	RGB triplet	Color	RGB triplet
forestgreen	228b22	lightyellow	ffffe0
fuchsia	ff00ff	lime	00ff00
gainsboro	dcdcdc	limegreen	32cd32
ghostwhite	f8f8ff	linen	faf0e6
gold	ffd700	magenta	ff00ff
goldenrod	daa520	maroon	800000
gray	808080	mediumaquamarine	66cdaa
green	008000	mediumblue	0000cd
greenyellow	adff2f	mediumorchid	ba55d3
honeydew	f0fff0	mediumpurple	9370db
hotpink	ff69b4	mediumseagreen	3cb371
indianred	cd5c5c	mediumslateblue	7b68ee
indigo	4b0082	mediumspringgreen	00fa9a
ivory	fffff0	mediumturquoise	48d1cc
khaki	f0e68c	mediumvioletred	c71585
lavender	e6e6fa	midnightblue	191970
lavenderblush	fff0f5	mintcream	f5fffa
lawngreen	7cfc00	mistyrose	ffe4e1
lemonchiffon	fffacd	moccasin	ffe4b5
lightblue	add8e6	navajowhite	ffdead
lightcoral	f08080	navy	000080
lightcyan	e0ffff	oldlace	fdf5e6
lightgoldenrodyellow	fafad2	olive	808000
lightgreen	90ee90	olivedrab	6b8e23
lightgrey	d3d3d3	orange	ffa500
lightpink	ffb6c1	orangered	ff4500
lightsalmon	ffa07a	orchid	da70d6
lightseagreen	20b2aa	palegoldenrod	eee8aa
lightskyblue	87cefa	palegreen	98fb98
lightslategray	778899	paleturquoise	afeeee
lightsteelblue	b0c4de	palevioletred	db7093

Color	RGB triplet	Color	RGB triplet
papayawhip	ffefd5	skyblue	87ceeb
peachpuff	ffdab9	slateblue	6a5acd
peru	cd853f	slategray	708090
pink	ffc0cb	snow	fffafa
plum	dda0dd	springgreen	00ff7f
powderblue	b0e0e6	steelblue	4682b4
purple	800080	tan	d2b48c
red	ff0000	teal	008080
rosybrown	bc8f8f	thistle	d8bfd8
royalblue	4169e1	tomato	ff6347
saddlebrown	8b4513	turquoise	40e0d0
salmon	fa8072	violet	ee82ee
sandybrown	f4a460	wheat	f5deb3
seagreen	2e8b57	white	ffffff
seashell	fff5ee	whitesmoke	f5f5f5
sienna	a0522d	yellow	ffff00
silver	c0c0c0	yellowgreen	9acd32

22

JAVASCRIPT ADDITIONS IN NETSCAPE 3.0

The Internet remained relatively unchanged for almost two decades, until it went "commercial" in the early 1990s. From that point on, the Internet has undergone massive, whirlwind changes every year. Software for the Internet is showing the same pattern. Not long after users download new pieces of software, the companies release yet-newer versions. As of this writing, for example, the Netscape Navigator has released five major versions of its browser in little more than 18 months.

Netscape 2.0, which is the base version for this book, is the first version to support JavaScript. While this book was being prepared, Netscape released beta versions of Netscape 3.0 (code-named "Atlas"), with some useful additions to the JavaScript family of objects. In some cases, 3.0 fixed bugs that exist in JavaScript for Netscape 2.0; in other cases, 3.0 added new functionality over what is available in 2.0. And in a few cases, changes to the way Netscape 3.0 works makes JavaScript programs for 2.0 inoperative. Such is the price of rapid change.

This chapter reviews the new JavaScript features of Netscape 3.0 and notes major differences between the way JavaScript objects behave in 2.0 and 3.0. Change is inevitable, and no book can be completely up-to-date with the changes in a fast-moving target like Netscape. Visit the Web support site for this book at http://gmccomb.com/sourcebook/ for the absolute latest on what's new with JavaScript.

Built-in Object Constructors

Netscape 3.0 sports a number of built-in object constructors to make programming easy. Two of them—Date, Array, and Object—are available in Netscape 2.0. Netscape 3.0 adds functionality to the Array constructor and adds new object constructor function you can use. In review, an object constructor is a function that creates an object. For example, you can create an object with the current date with the following:

```
now = new Date();
```

Netscape 3.0 supports the following object constructors. In all cases these constructors are used with the new statement to create new "instances" of objects.

- Array
- Boolean
- Date
- Function
- Number
- Object
- String

The Date and Object constructors have not been changed since Netscape 2.0. The rest of this section describes what's new with the Array, Boolean, Function, Number, and String constructors.

Array Constructor

The Array object constructor was introduced in Netscape 2.0, but it is refined in Netscape 3.0. You use it with a new operator to create a new array. Here's one example that creates an array with 10 elements, numbered 0 through 9:

```
myarray = new Array(10);
```

Elements can be added dynamically to an Array object. For instance, the following creates a basic array variable, and the number of elements contained in the array is set dynamically by assigning values to the upper and lower index ranges:

```
var myarray = new Array();
myarray[0] = "first element";
myarray[99] = "last element";
```

This array has 100 elements numbered 0 though 99. You can test the number of elements in an array by using the length property. This example shows how to display the number of elements of an array using the length property:

```
alert (myarray.length);
```

As a handy shortcut, Netscape 3.0 supports what some programmers call a "dense array," which is an array for which the array is constructed and elements are defined in one step. Another term for this kind of array is "implicit assignment" because the elements are implicitly assigned as the array variable itself is defined. The following example creates an array with three elements numbered 0, 1, and 2:

```
myarray = new Array("element 0", "element 1", "element 2");
```

Netscape 3.0 adds several new methods to string and Array objects. These include sort and split.

- Use split to split a string to make an array (syntax: stringname.split (",");)
- Use sort to sort an array in alphabetical order (syntax: arrayname.sort();)

Boolean Constructor

Use the Boolean constructor to explicitly create a variable with a Boolean value. Here's one quick example; the value of the bool variable is automatically set to false:

```
bool = new Boolean();
```

You can define a logical value either when you define the variable or afterwards. This example defines the value when the new Boolean variable is created:

```
bool = new Boolean(true);
```

Function Constructor

Use the Function constructor to create "anonymous" functions, such as when you are creating functions on the fly. Here's an example:

```
var mul = new Function ("x", "y", "return x * y")
var Result = mul(5,4)
alert (Result)  // displays 20
```

Number Constructor

The Number constructor is used to define a number variable. Here is an example:

```
mynumber = new Number (123.45);
```

A practical use of the Number constructor is to "case" a string as a number. The following line of code turns the string "123.45" into a number:

```
mynumber = new Number ("123.45");
```

String Constructor

The String constructor lets you explicitly define a new string. You can define an empty string object and then fill it with text. Alternatively, you can simultaneously define the string object and assign text to it. Here are examples of both methods:

```
myString = new String ();
myString = "This is a test";
anotherString = new String ("Text goes here");
```

Image Object

Images defined by the <IMG> tag are now reflected in JavaScript. All images in a document are in an array called document.images. The number of images in a document is document.images.length. For example, you can now refer to the first image in a document as document.images[0], the second image as document.images[1], and so on.

Each image object has properties for the IMG attributes, as shown in the following table.

Property	Description
src	SRC attribute: URL of the image. This is the only required attribute.
lowsrc	LOWSRC attribute: URL of the low-resolution image, if any.
height, width	HEIGHT, WIDTH attributes: height and width of image in pixels.
border	BORDER attribute: width of image border in pixels.
vspace, hspace	VSPACE, HSPACE attributes: horizontal and vertical space in pixels.

You can set the src and lowsrc properties with new images and therefore dynamically change the content of graphics. This is the great benefit of the new feature in Netscape 3.0. For example, the following line of code changes the first image in the document with a new file:

```
document.images[0].src = "http://myserver.com/pix/newimage.gif";
```

As shown in the following table, there are three event-handlers for images, although they are not used often.

Event Handler	Description
onLoad	Triggers when image is loaded
onError	Triggers if there is an error loading the image
onAbort	Triggers if user aborts image loading (such as clicking a link or clicking the Stop button)

New Event Handlers

Netscape 3.0 offers some new event handlers and refines the way some of the existing event handlers work. The new handler for the link object is onMouseOut, which defines what should happen when the mouse is moved from a link. onMouseOver, which is provided in Netscape 2.0, defines what should happen when the mouse moves over a link. The onMouseOut event handler is used the same way as you use onMouseOver.

Additionally, onMouseOver and onMouseOut now also work with client-side image maps created with the <AREA> tag. In this way, you can display text in the status bar:

```
<AREA SHAPE=RECT COORDS="3,2,17,16"
HREF="one.html" onMouseOver="window.status='go to one.html'; return true">
```

Netscape 3.0 improves the way onClick works when used with objects that support onClick, but onClick is now particularly handy when used with links. For example, you can now return true or false with onClick to control how JavaScript executes the HREF portion of the link. In the following, clicking the link goes to the gothere.html page. The HREF to gohere.html is completely ignored.

```
<A HREF="gohere.html" onClick="location='gothere.html'; return false">
```

Windows and frames respond to onFocus and onBlur events in Netscape 3.0. You can use these event handlers to determine what happens when focus is set or removed from a given window or frame. These handlers are meant to be added to the <BODY> tag (when used for a window) and <FRAMESET> tag (when used for a frame). For example, suppose you open a new window with the following:

```
win = window.open ("newwin.html", mynewwin)
```

In the newwin.html file you have set an onBlur or onFocus handler as shown here. In this example JavaScript calls the winFocus function when focus is set to the window.

```
<BODY onFocus="winFocus()">
```

Similarly, windows now respond to the focus() and blur() methods in Netscape 3.0. You can set focus to a window by appending these methods to the window object. For example:

```
win = window.open ()
win.focus();          // sets focus (brings to top)
win.blur();           // removes focus (brings another window to top)
```

■■■■■■ **NOTE**

Additional special-purpose event handlers for images are described in the section "Image Object," earlier in the chapter.

■■■■■■

JavaScript Libraries

A long-awaited addition to JavaScript is the ability to define a separate page for the JavaScript program. This is now done in Netscape 3.0 using the SRC attribute of the <SCRIPT> tag. Here's an example:

```
<SCRIPT SRC="library.js">
```

- Files used with the SRC attribute should end with the js file extension.
- When defining a SRC for the <SCRIPT> tag, you do not need to add a </SCRIPT> end tag.
- You can include JavaScript code in the same document with the <SCRIPT> tag, to provide compatibility with Netscape 3.0. Be sure to include the </SCRIPT> tag in these cases.

```
<SCRIPT SRC="library.js">
alert ("This is for Netscape 2.0");
</SCRIPT>
```

Netscape 3.0 also adds a <NOSCRIPT> tag. The contents of this tag are ignored by JavaScript but processed as HTML when JavaScript is disabled or not implemented. Here is an example:

```
<NOSCRIPT>
<H1>No JavaScript</H1>
You see this text if JavaScript is disabled or unimplemented.
</NOSCRIPT>
```

The typeof Operator

Netscape 3.0 provides a new typeof operator, which queries the type of variable given to it. The result is one of the following:

- Undefined (no variable defined of that name)
- Array
- Boolean
- Date

- Function
- Number
- Object
- String

The typeof operator is especially handy if you want to see if a variable has been defined. To use the typeof operator, enclose the name of the variable in parentheses. Here's an example (the answer is String):

```
var Test = "This is a test"
var Result = typeof(Test)
alert (Result)
```

Form Element type Property

In Netscape 3.0 all form elements now have a type property, which represents the type of control ("widget") defined in the form. You can use the type property, for instance, if you need to test the type of control. For example, the following line of code displays the information that follows it:

```
alert (document.formname.elements[0].type)
```

HTML element	Value of type property
INPUT TYPE=text	text
INPUT TYPE=radio	radio
INPUT TYPE=checkbox	checkbox
INPUT TYPE=hidden	hidden
INPUT TYPE=submit	submit
INPUT TYPE=reset	reset
INPUT TYPE=password	password
INPUT TYPE=button	button
SELECT	select-one
SELECT MULTIPLE	select-multiple
TEXTAREA	textarea
INPUT TYPE=image	image
INPUT TYPE=file	file

Connecting with Java

JavaScript now shares a closer relationship to Java. You can write JavaScript that initiates a public variable or method in a Java applet you've loaded, for example, and you can even write some Java code directly in JavaScript!

Each applet in a document is reflected by the new document.appletName property, where *appletName* is the name of the applet, defined by the NAME attribute of the <APPLET> tag. For example, the following HTML includes a simple applet called "mojaApplet":

```
<APPLET CODE=Mojatest.class NAME=mojaApplet WIDTH=60 HEIGHT=30>
<PARAM NAME=label VALUE=Mojatest>
</APPLET>
```

You would then reference it in JavaScript as follows:

```
document.mojaApplet
document.applets["mojaapplet"]
```

You can also reference applets by index, starting with 0 for the first applet in the document, 1 for the next, and so forth. Here is an example:

```
document.applets[0]
```

The value of document.applets.length is the number of applets in the document.

All public variables declared in an applet (as well as its ancestor classes and packages) are available in JavaScript. Static methods and properties declared in an applet are available in JavaScript as methods and properties of the applet object. You can get and set property values, and you can call methods that return string, numeric, and Boolean values. For more information on how values are passed from Java and JavaScript, be sure to consult the JSObject Package documentation, provided by Netscape.

The top level of the Java package name space appears in JavaScript under the name Packages. Aliases are used to provide a convenient method to access pages. You can refer to the Java class java.lang.System as Packages.java.lang.System or just java.lang.System (the latter is the method most often used). Once you have a reference to this class, you can access fields and methods with the same syntax that you would use in Java.

For example, the following code snippet prints a message to the Java console:

```
var System = java.lang.System;
System.err.println("Hello from JavaScript");
```

You can also use Java class constructors in JavaScript. For example, the following is allowed in Netscape 3.0:

```
var mydate = new java.util.Date();
```

■■■■ **NOTE**

Be sure to visit http://gmccomb.com/sourcebook/ for up-to-date information and many more examples of the Java/JavaScript connection.

■■■■

Testing for Plug-Ins

JavaScript now has the ability to test if a user has installed a particular plug-in, such as Shockwave or ToolVox. You can also check if the browser is capable of handling a particular MIME (Multipart Internet Mail Extension) type.

The navigator object has two properties for checking installed plug-ins:

- The mimeTypes object is an array of all MIME types supported by Netscape (either internally, via helper applications, or by plug-ins). Each element of the array is a mimeType object; available properties are provided for type, description, and file extensions.
- The plug-ins object is an array of all plug-ins currently installed. Each element of the array is a plug-in object, which has properties for its name and description as well as an array of mimeType objects for the MIME types supported by that plug-in.

For example, the following code checks to see if the Shockwave plug-in is installed and displays an embedded Shockwave movie if it is:

```
var plugin = navigator.plugins["Shockwave"];
if (plugin)
        document.writeln("<EMBED SRC="Movie.dir" HEIGHT=100 WIDTH=100>")
```

```
else
        document.writeln("You don't have Shockwave installed!")
```

A mimeType object has three predefined properties, as shown in the following table.

Property	Description
name	Name of the MIME type (for example, video/mpeg, audio/x-wav)
description	Description of the type
suffixes	String listing possible file suffixes (also known as filename extensions) for the MIME type

This property is a string consisting of each valid suffix, typically three letters long, separated by commas.

Similarly, the plug-ins object has three basic properties and one array property.

Property	Description
name	Name of the plug-in
filename	Name of the plug-in file on disk
description	Description supplied by the plug-in itself
[...]	Array of mimeType objects, indexed by number or type, that the plug-in can handle
length	Number of elements in the array

For example, the following code assigns shorthand variables for the predefined Shockwave properties:

```
var plugin = navigator.plugins["Shockwave"].name
var pluginFile = navigator.plugins["Shockwave"].filename
var pluginDesc = navigator.plugins["Shockwave"].description
```

The following test demonstrates the use of several Navigator object plug-in properties to determine if the browser supports a given MIME type (in this case, midi sound):

```
Ret = testForPlugin ("audio/midi")
alert (Ret);


function testForPlugin (Plugin) {
```

```
        Plugin = Plugin.toLowerCase();

        var Found = false, i, j;

        for (i = 0; i < navigator.plugins.length; i++) {

                for (j = 0; j < Math.round(navigator.plugins[i].length); j++) {

                        if (navigator.plugins[i][j].type == Plugin) {

                                Found = true;

                                break;

                        }

                if (Found) break;

                }

        }

        return (Found);

}
```

■■■■■■ NOTE

Be sure to visit http://gmccomb.com/sourcebook/ for up-to-date information and many more examples of the Java/JavaScript connection.

■■■■■

Extending Objects

Netscape 3.0 supports an official method for extending objects, using a new property
called prototype. The prototype property lets you associate new properties with an
object, either a built-in JavaScript object or an object you create yourself. For example, the following code adds a new property to the Date object and returns the text
of the current month:

```
function _getMonthStr() {

return (new Array ("Jan", "Feb", "Mar", "Apr", "May", "Jun", "Jul","Aug",
"Sep", "Oct", "Nov", "Dec"))[this.getMonth()];

}


Date.prototype.getMonthStr = _getMonthStr;

alert ((new Date()).getMonthStr())
```

Window opener Property

In Netscape 3.0, windows opened or created by executing the open method have a new property called opener that refers to the window containing the document that called the method. This property remains even if a document is unloaded in the opened window. The benefit of the opener property is that you no longer have to set a "creator" or "owner" property.

For example, suppose you have a script in window A that opens a new window (window B):

```
win = window.open();
```

In the opened window (window B), the following code refers to window A:

```
var winA = win.opener;
```

If you need to remain compatible with Netscape 2.0, the following code creates an opener property if there isn't one.

```
var win = window.open();
if (win.opener == null)
        win.opener = window;
```

Modifiable select Objects

Netscape 3.0 lets you modify the content of selection lists (created with the <SELECT> tag). For example, take the following <SELECT> tag:

```
<SELECT name="changeMe">
<OPTION>Choice 1
<OPTION>Choice 2
<OPTION>Choice 3
</SELECT>
```

You can set the text of the selection option by referring to its value:

```
myform.changeMe.options[0].text = "New Choice 1;
```

Miscellaneous Netscape 3.0 Changes to JavaScript

- You can now get and set the name of a window, even if JavaScript didn't create the window.
  For example: window.name = "my new window"

- The Math.random method works on all platforms, not just Unix.

- The isNaN() function now works on all platforms, not just Unix.

- The navigator.javaEnabled() property returns true or false if Java is enabled.

Appendix A

Using the CD-ROM

This book comes with a CD-ROM. It contains all the example JavaScript files and applications detailed in *The JavaScript Sourcebook*.

The CD-ROM can be used by IBM-style PCs, the Macintosh, and most Unix computers. All of the JavaScript examples can be used by either computer type, but differences in the implementation of JavaScript across platforms may occur. The example JavaScript programs in this book were written using Windows 95 as the primary target platform.

All of the files on the CD-ROM are in uncompressed format. To retrieve a JavaScript file and use it, all you need to do is locate it on the disc, and load it into Netscape. Specific details of opening a file on the CD-ROM are provided later in this appendix.

The CD-ROM is divided into several directories:

Directory	Contents
adventure	JavaScript adventure game
banners	Scrolling banners using JavaScript
bg_select	Background color selector example
Blackjack	JavaScript blackjack game
clock	Digital clock using JavaScript
digits	Additional GIF images for use with JavaScript clocks and counters
examples	Files used as examples in the book
ezoutline	JavaScript outline application
formmail	Support files for CGI formmail
guitar	JavaScript guitar chord application
hidaho	JavaScript function sets from hIdaho Design (cookies, frameset)
img	Selection of XBM format graphics
pix	Selection of GIF and JPG format graphics
shortcuts	Using JavaScript for easier HTML graphics

Hardware and Software Requirements

To use the software on this CD-ROM you need Netscape Navigator 2.0 or later. Note that the Netscape Navigator software is not included on the CD-ROM. This software is available through Netscape at http://home.netscape.com.

The data on the CD-ROM is encoded so that it can be read by IBM PCs and compatibles, Apple Macintosh, Sun workstations, and most machines running the Unix operating system.

Using the Software

The files included on the CD-ROM need not be copied to your computer's hard disk drive before you can use them. You may instead open the files directly using Netscape, using the following steps:

1. Insert the CD-ROM into the CD-ROM drive.
2. In Netscape, choose File, Open.
3. Change to the drive that contains the CD-ROM.
4. Change to the directory that contains the file you want to use.
5. Select the file, and choose OK.

About the sources.htm file

The sources.htm file in the root directory of the CD-ROM contains dozens of links you can use to locate resources of interest on the Web. Links are provided for JavaScript, HTML, CGI, programming topics, and more. To use this file, load it into Netscape, then click on a link.

■■■■ **NOTE**

Remember that links can change quickly on the Web. See

http://gmccomb.com/sourcebook/

for an up-to-date version of the sources.htm file.

▬▬▬

Note to Windows 3.1 Users

The names used for some of the HTML and Java files exceed the "8+3" filename convention used in Windows 3.1 and MS-DOS. For the benefit of Windows 3.1 users, a self-extracting archive of files that conform to the 8+3 filename standard is available at

    http://gmccomb.com/sourcebook

User Assistance and Information

The software accompanying this book is being provided as is without warranty or support of any kind. Should you require basic installation assistance, or if your media is defective, please call our product support number at (212) 850-6194 weekdays between 9 am and 4 pm Eastern Standard Time. Or, we can be reached via e-mail at: wprtusw@jwiley.com.

To place additional orders or to request information about other Wiley products, please call (800) 879-4539.

Additional support for this book is available at the author's Web site, at:

    http://gmccomb.com/sourcebook.

Please note that because of the volume of mail received, the author is not able to provide individual support for examples and/or topics not included in this book, nor is he able to provide assistance in modifying the examples.

Appendix B JavaScript Object Map

window
properties
defaultStatus
frames[]
length
name
parent
self*
status
top
window
*self is a synonym for
the current window

events
onLoad
onUnload

methods
alert("message")
close()
clearTimeout(ID)
confirm("message")
open("url","name","options")
prompt("message","default")
setTimeout("exp",delay)

frame
properties
frames[]
name
length
parent
*self
window
*self is a synonym for
the current frame

events
onLoad
onUnload

methods
clearTimeout(ID)
setTimeout("exp",delay)

history
properties
length

events
<none>

methods
back()
forward()
go(int)

document
properties
alinkColor
anchors[]
bgColor
cookie
fgColor
forms[]
lastModified
linkColor
links[]
location
referrer
title
vlinkColor

events
<none>

methods
clear()
close()
open("mimetype")
write("string")
writeln("string")

location
properties
hash
host
hostname
href
pathname
port
post
protocaol
search
target

events
<none>

methods
<none>

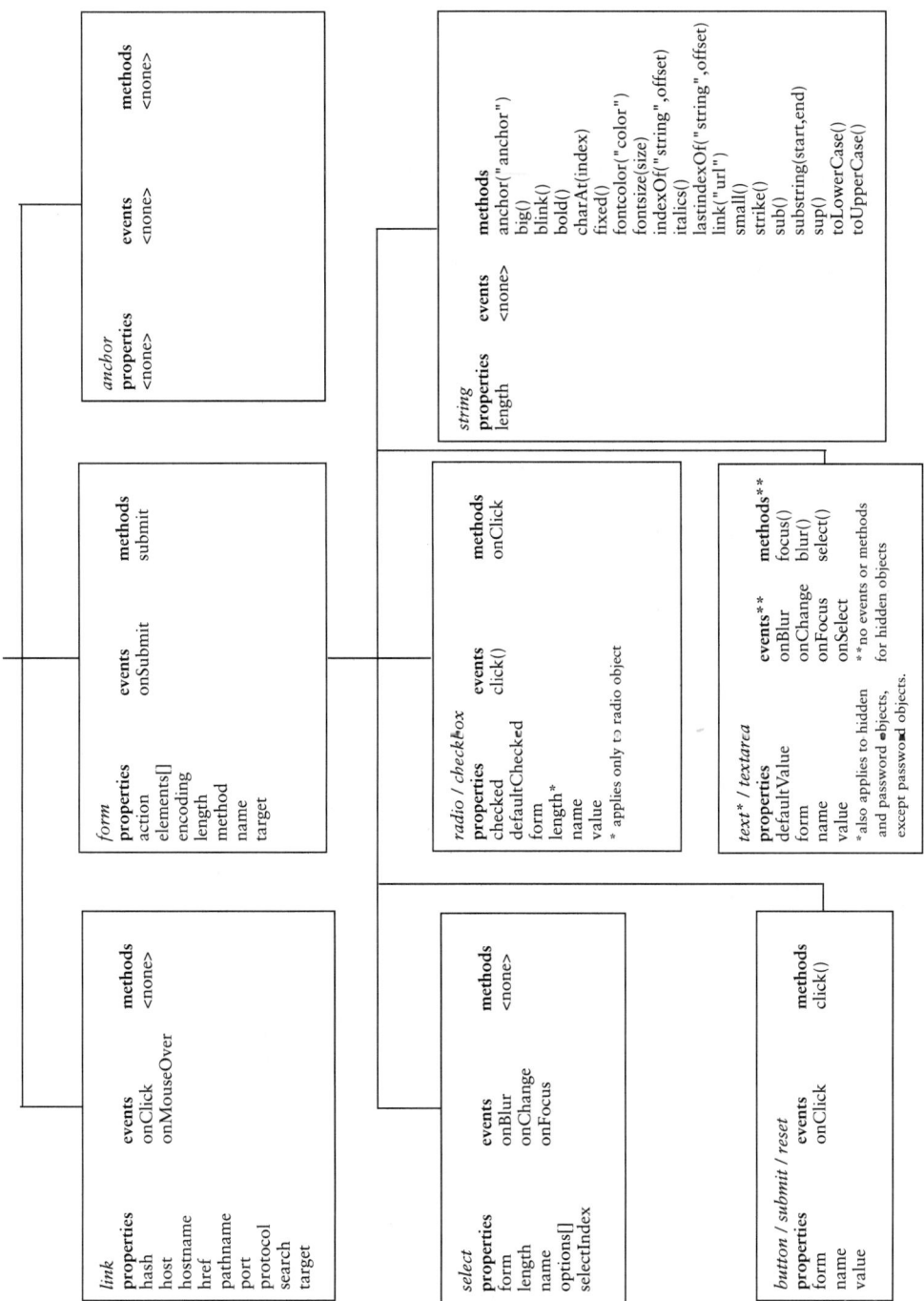

link
properties: hash, host, hostname, href, pathname, port, protocol, search, target
events: onClick, onMouseOver
methods: <none>

form
properties: action, elements[], encoding, length, method, name, target
events: onSubmit
methods: submit

anchor
properties: <none>
events: <none>
methods: <none>

select
properties: form, length, name, options[], selectIndex
events: onBlur, onChange, onFocus
methods: <none>

radio / checkbox
properties: checked, defaultChecked, form, length*, name, value
events: click()
methods: onClick
* applies only to radio object

string
properties: length
events: <none>
methods: anchor("anchor"), big(), blink(), bold(), charAt(index), fixed(), fontcolor("color"), fontsize(size), indexOf("string",offset), italics(), lastindexOf("string",offset), link("url"), small(), strike(), sub(), substring(start,end), sup(), toLowerCase(), toUpperCase()

text* / textarea
properties: defaultValue, form, name, value
events**: onBlur, onChange, onFocus, onSelect
methods**: focus(), blur(), select()
* also applies to hidden and password objects,
** no events or methods for hidden objects, except password objects.

button / submit / reset
properties: form, name, value
events: onClick
methods: click()

Relational Operators

Operator	Function
v1==v2	Test that v1 and v2 are equal.
v1<>v2	Test that v1 and v2 are not equal.
v1>v2	Test that v1 is greater than v2.
v1>=v2	Test that v1 is greater than or equal to v2.
v1<v2	Test that v1 is less than v2.
v1<=v2	Test that v1 is less than or equal to v2.
! value	Evaluates the logical NOT of value.
v1 && v2	Evaluates the logical AND of v1 and v2.
v1 || v2	Evaluates the logical ORof v1 and v2.

Assignment Operators

Operator	Function
=	Assigns value to variable.
+=	Adds value to value already in variable.
−=	Subtracts value to value already in variable.
*=	Multiplies value with value already in variable.
/=	Divides value with value already in variable.
%=	Divides value with value already in variable; returns remainder.

Math Operators

Operator	Function
− value	Treats the value as a negative number.
v1 + v2	Adds values v1 and v2 together, adds strings together.
v1 − v2	Subtracts value v2 from v1.
v1 * v2	Multiplies value v1 and v2.
v1 / v2	Divides value v1 by v2.
v1 % v2	Divides value v1 by v2; returns floating-point remainder.
v1++	Adds 1 to v1.
v1−−	Subtracts 1 from v1.

string
properties	methods
length	anchor("anchor")
	big()
	blink()
	bold()
	charAt(index)
	fixed()
	fontcolor("color")
	fontsize(size)
	indexOf("string",offset)
	italics()
	lastindexOf("string",offset)
	link("url")
	small()
	strike()
	sub()
	substring(start,end)
	sup()
	toLowerCase()
	toUpperCase()

Date
properties	methods
<none>	get/setDate()
	get/setDay()
	get/setHours()
	get/setMinutes()
	get/setMonth()
	get/setSeconds()
	get/setTime()
	get/setYear()
	getTimezoneOffset()
	parse("date")
	toGMTString()
	toLocaleString()
	toString()*
	UTC(date)

*toString is a generic method that can be used with several object types

navigator
properties
appName
appVersion
appCodeName
userAgent

Math
properties	methods
E	abs(val)
LN2	acos(val)
LN10	asin(val)
LOG2E	atan(val)
LOG10E	ceil(val)
PI	ceil(val)
SQRT1_2	cos(val)
SQRT2	exp(val)
	floor(val)
	log(val)
	max(val1,val2)
	min(val1,val2)
	pow(val,power)
	random()
	round(val)
	sin(val)
	sqrt(val)
	tan(val)

Properties of Object Arrays
anchors
  length
elements
  length
forms
  length
frames
  length
links
  length
options
  options[].defaultSelected
  options[].index
  options[].length
  options[].name
  options[].selected
  options[].selectedIndex
  options[].text
  options[].value

INDEX

CUSTOMER NOTE: